GUINNESS
BOOK OF
WORLD RECORDS

LONGEST TIGHTROPE WALK: Karl Wallenda, age 65, took this 821-foot-long walk in 616 steps over the 750-foot-deep Tallulah Gorge in Georgia in July, 1970. The whole walk took only 20 minutes, and on the way he made two headstands.

NORRIS and ROSS Mc WHIRTER

GUINNESS
BOOK OF
WORLD RECORDS

★ ★ ★ ★ ★

STERLING
PUBLISHING CO., INC. NEW YORK

Eleventh Edition

Revised American Edition © 1972, 1971, 1970, 1969,
1968, 1966, 1965, 1964, 1963, 1962
by Sterling Publishing Co., Inc.
419 Park Avenue South, New York, N.Y. 10016
© 1960 by Guinness Superlatives Ltd., London
Manufactured in the United States of America
All rights reserved
Library of Congress Catalog Card No.: 65–24391
ISBN 0–8069–0004–0
8069–0005–9

CONTENTS

... Basketball ... Bicycling ... Billiards ... Bobsledding ...
Bowling ... Boxing ... Bridge (Contract) ... Bull Fighting
... Canoeing ... Cave Exploration ... Chess ... Curling ...
Equestrian Sports ... Fencing ... Field Hockey ... Fishing
... Football ... Gliding ... Golf ... Greyhound Racing ...
Gymnastics ... Handball ... Harness Racing ... Hockey
... Horse Racing ... Ice Skating ... Ice Yachting ... Jai-Alai
Judo ... Karate ... Lacrosse ... Motorcycling ...
Mountaineering ... Olympic Games ... Pentathlon, Modern
... Pigeon Racing ... Polo ... Powerboat Racing ... Rodeo
... Roller Skating ... Rowing ... Shooting ... Skiing ...
Snowmobiling...Soccer... Squash ... Surfing ... Swimming
... Table Tennis ... Tennis ...Tiddleywinks... Track and
Field ... Trampolining ... Volleyball ... Walking ... Water
Polo ... Water Skiing ... Weightlifting ... Wrestling ...
Yachting

FOREWORD

By the Right Honourable the Earl of Iveagh

When we first brought out this book some sixteen years ago, we did so in the hope of providing a means for the peaceful settling of arguments about extremes and record performances in this record-breaking world in which we live. We realize, of course, that much joy lies in the argument, but how exasperating it can be if there is no final means of finding the answer.

In the event, we found that the interest aroused by this book has exceeded our wildest expectations. This is the eleventh edition in the United States and translations into Czech, Danish, Dutch, French, Finnish, German, Italian, Japanese, Norwegian, Spanish and Swedish have shown the universality of its appeal. In total we have had produced almost 7,000,000 copies.

Whether the discussion concerns the smallest fish ever caught, the most expensive wine, the greatest weight lifted by a man or a woman, the world's longest horse race, or—an old bone of contention —the longest river in the world. I can but quote the words used in introducing the first edition. "How much heat these innocent questions can raise: Guinness, in producing this book, hopes that it may assist in resolving many such disputes, and may we hope turn heat into light."

[BENJAMIN GUINNESS]
EARL OF IVEAGH, Chairman
Arthur Guinness, Son & Co., Ltd.,
August, 1972   St. James's Gate Brewery, Dublin, Ireland.

PREFACE

This eleventh U.S. edition has been brought up to date and provided with additional illustrations. We wish to thank correspondents from most of the countries of the world for raising and settling various editorial points. Strenuous efforts have been made to improve the value of the material presented and this policy will be continued in future editions.

NORRIS D. MCWHIRTER   *Compilers*
A. ROSS MCWHIRTER

Main Editorial Office,
2 Cecil Court,
London Road, Enfield,
Middlesex, England.

TALLEST MAN: Robert Wadlow reached the height of 8 feet 11.1 inches when he was 22.4 years old. At the time, he weighed 439 lbs., after having weighed 491 lbs.

Chapter One

THE HUMAN BEING

1. Dimensions

Tallest Giants

The height of human giants is a subject in which accurate information is frequently obscured by exaggeration and commercial dishonesty. The only admissible evidence on the true height of giants is that collected in recent years under impartial medical supervision.

The Biblical claim that Og, the Amorite king of Bashan and Gilead in *c.* 1450 B.C., stood 9 Hebrew cubits (13 feet 2½ inches) is based solely on the length of his basalt sarcophagus or "iron bedstead." The assertion that Goliath of Gath (*c.* 1060 B.C.) stood 6 cubits and a span (9 feet 6½ inches) suggests a confusion of units or some over-enthusiastic exaggeration by the Hebrew chroniclers. The Hebrew historian Flavius Josephus (born in 37 or 38 A.D., died after 93 A.D.) and some of the manuscripts of the Septuagint (the earliest Greek translation of the Old Testament) attribute to Goliath the more credible height of 4 Greek cubits and a span (6 feet 10 inches).

Extreme medieval data, taken from bone measurements, invariably refer to specimens of extinct whale, giant cave bear, giant ape, mastodon, woolly rhinoceros or other prehistoric non-human remains.

Paul Topinard (1830–1911), a French anthropometrist, stated that the tallest man who ever lived was Daniel Mynheer Cajanus (1714–49) of Finland, standing 9 feet 3.4 inches. In 1872 his right femur, now in the Leyden Museum, in the Netherlands, was measured by Prof. Carl Langer of Germany and indicated a height of 7 feet 3.4 inches. Pierre Lemolt, a member of the French Academy, reported in 1847 that Ivan Stepanovich Lushkin (1811–44), a drum major in the Russian Imperial Regiment of Guards at Preobrazhenskiy, measured 3 arshin 9¼ vershok (8 feet 3¾ inches) and was "the tallest man that has ever lived in modern days." However, his left femur and tibia, which are now in the Museum of the Academy of Sciences in Leningrad, U.S.S.R., indicate a height of 7 feet 10¼ inches.

An extreme case of exaggeration concerned Siah Khan ibn Kashmir Khan (born 1913) of Bushehr (Bushire), Iran, Prof. D. H. Fuchs showed photographs of him at a meeting of the Society of Physicians in Vienna, Austria, in January, 1935, claiming that he was 10 feet 6 inches tall. Later, when Siah Khan entered the Imperial Hospital in Teheran for an operation, it was revealed that his actual height was 7 feet 2.6 inches.

Modern opinion is that the tallest recorded man of whom there is irrefutable evidence was Robert Pershing Wadlow, born in Alton, Illinois, on February 22, 1918. Weighing 8½ lbs. at birth, his abnormal growth began almost immediately. His height progressed as follows:

Age in Years	Height ft.	ins.	Weight in lbs.	Age in Years	Height ft.	ins.	Weight in lbs.
5	5	4	105	15	7	8	355
8	6	0	169	16	7	10½	374
9	6	2½	180	17	8	0½	315*
10	6	5	210	18	8	3¾	—
11	6	7	—	19	8	5½	480
12	6	10¼	—	20	8	6¾	—
13	7	1¾	255	21	8	8¼	491
14	7	5	301	22.4†	8	11.1	439

* Following severe influenza and infection of the foot.
† He was still growing during his terminal illness.

Dr. C. M. Charles, Associate Professor of Anatomy at Washington University School of Medicine, in St. Louis, measured him at 8 feet 11.1 inches, on June 27, 1940. He died 18 days later, on July 15, 1940, in Manistee, Michigan, as a result of cellulitis of the feet aggravated by a poorly fitted brace. He was buried in Oakwood Cemetery, Alton, Illinois, in a coffin measuring 10 feet 9 inches in length, 32 inches in width, and 30 inches in depth.

His greatest recorded weight was 491 lbs., on his 21st birthday. He weighed 439 lbs. at the time of his death. His shoes were size 37AA (18½ inches long) and his hands measured 12¾ inches from the wrist to the tip of the middle finger.

The tallest recorded "true" (non-pathological) giant was Angus MacAskill (1825–63), born on the island of Berneray, in the Sound of Harris, in the Outer Hebrides, Scotland. He stood 7 feet 9 inches and died in St. Ann's, on Cape Breton Island, Nova Scotia, Canada.

The only other men for whom heights of 8 feet or more have been reliably reported are the seven listed next. In each case gigantism was followed by acromegaly, a disease which causes an enlargement of the nose, lips, tongue, lower jaw, hands and feet, due to renewed activity by the already swollen pituitary gland, which is located at the base of the brain.

		ft.	in.
John F. Carroll (1932–69) of Buffalo, New York	(a)	8	7¾
John William Rogan (1871–1905), a Negro of Gallatin, Tennessee	(b)	8	6
Don Koehler (1929–fl. 1972) of Denton, Montana (see photo)	(c)	8	2
Väinö Myllyrinne (1909–63) of Helsinki, Finland	(d)	(8	1.2)
Gabriel Estavo Monjane (born 1944) of Monjacaze, Mozambique	(f)	8	1.0
Constantine (1872–1902) of Reutlingen, West Germany	(e)	(8	0.8)
Sulaiman 'Ali Nashnush (born 1943) of Tripoli, Libya	(g)	(8	0.4)

(a) Carroll was a victim of severe kypho-scoliosis (two-dimensional spinal curvature). The figure represents his height with assumed normal spinal curvature, calculated from a standing height of 8 feet 0 inches, measured on October 14, 1959. His standing height was 7 feet 8¼ inches shortly before his death.

(b) Measured in a sitting position. Unable to stand owing to ankylosis (stiffening of the joints through the formation of adhesions) of the knees and hips.

(c) He has a twin sister who is 5 feet 9 inches tall.

(d) Stood 7 feet 3½ inches at the age of 21 years. Experienced a second phase of growth in his late thirties and may have stood 8 feet 3 inches at one time.

(e) Height estimated, as both legs were amputated after they turned gangrenous. He claimed a height of 8 feet 6 inches.

(f) Abnormal growth started at the age of 10, following a head injury. He is still growing. Unconfirmed and exaggerated reports in July, 1969, suggested that he had by then attained 8 feet 6 inches.

(g) Operation to correct abnormal growth in Rome in 1960 was successful.

TALLEST LIVING MAN: Don Koehler, born in Denton, Montana, was pictured recently in Detroit, standing 8 feet 2 inches high. His twin sister is only 5 feet 9 inches.

Circus giants and others who are exhibited are normally under contract not to be measured and are, almost traditionally, billed by their promoters at heights up to 18 inches in excess of their true heights. The acromegalic giant Eddie Carmel (b. Tel Aviv, Israel, 1938), formerly the "Tallest Man on Earth" of Ringling Bros. & Barnum & Bailey's Circus, is allegedly 9 feet $0\frac{5}{8}$ inches tall (weight 535 lbs.), but photographic evidence suggests that his height is *c.* 7 feet 6 inches.

Other notable examples of such exaggeration are given below:

Name	*Dates*	*Country*	*Claimed Height* ft.	in.	*Actual Height* ft.	in.
Gerrit Bastiaansz	1620–68	Netherlands	8	3	7	1
Cornelius Magrath	1736–60	Ireland	8	6	7	$2\frac{1}{4}$
Bernardo Gigli	1736–62	Italy	8	0	7	$6\frac{1}{2}$
Patrick Cotter O'Brian	1760–1806	Ireland	8	$7\frac{3}{4}$	7	10.86
Charles Byrne	1761–83	Ireland	8	4	7	7
Sam McDonald	1762–1802	Scotland	8	0	6	10
"Lolly"	1783–1816	Russia	8	$4\frac{1}{2}$	7	3
James Toller	1795–1819	England	8	6	7	6
Arthur Caley	1829–53	Isle of Man	8	4	7	6
Patrick Murphy	1834–62	Ireland	8	10	7	3.4
Martin van Buren Bates	1845–1919	U.S.	7	$11\frac{1}{2}$	7	$2\frac{1}{2}$
Chang Wu-gow	1846–93	China	9	2	7	$8\frac{3}{4}$
Joseph Drazel	1847–86	Germany	8	$3\frac{1}{2}$	7	6.5
Paul Henoch	1852–76	Germany	8	3	7	2
Franz Winkelmeier	1867–89	Austria	8	9	7	5.7
Lewis Wilkins	1873–1902	U.S.	8	2	7	$4\frac{1}{2}$
John Turner	1876–1911	U.S.	8	3	7	3
Baptiste Hugo	1879–1916	France	8	10	7	6.5
Fyodor Machnov	1880–1905	Russia	9	$3\frac{1}{2}$	7	9.7
Frederick Kempster	1889–1918	England	8	$4\frac{1}{2}$	7	$8\frac{1}{2}$
Johnny Aasen	1890–1937	U.S.	8	0	7	0
Bernard Coyne	1897–1921	U.S.	8	2	7	8
Albert Johann Kramer	b. 1897	Netherlands	9	$3\frac{1}{2}$	7	$8\frac{1}{4}$
Clifford Thompson	b. 1904	U.S.	8	8	7	5
Jacob Ehrlich, *alias* Jack Earle	1906–52	U.S.	8	7	7	$7\frac{1}{2}$
Aurelio Tomaini	1912–62	U.S.	8	$4\frac{1}{2}$	7	4
Henry Mullens, *alias* Henry Hite	b. 1915	U.S.	8	2	7	$6\frac{3}{4}$
Rigardus Riynhout	b. 1922	Netherlands	9	$1\frac{1}{2}$	7	8.1
William Camper	1924–42	U.S.	8	6	7	2
Edward Evans	1924–58	England	9	3	7	$8\frac{1}{2}$
Poolad Gurd	b. 1927	Iran	8	2	7	3
Max Palmer	b. 1928	U.S.	8	$0\frac{1}{2}$	7	7

NOTE: The heights of John Turner, Frederick Kempster, Clifford Thompson and Max Palmer are estimated from photographs. Each of the other heights given in the last column above was obtained by an independent medical authority, the first from evidence of his leg bones.

The claim that Sa'id Muhammad Ghazi (born 1909) of Alexandria, Egypt (now the United Arab Republic) attained a height of 8 feet 10 inches in February, 1941, is now considered unreliable. Photographic evidence suggests his height was more nearly 7 feet $10\frac{1}{2}$ inches, though he may have reached 8 feet at the time of his death.

Tallest Giantesses

Giantesses are rarer than giants but their heights are still spectacular. The tallest woman in medical history was the acromegalic giantess Jane ("Ginny") Bunford, born on July 26, 1895, at Bartley Green, Northfield, Birmingham, England. Her abnormal growth started at the age of 11 following a head injury, and on her 13th

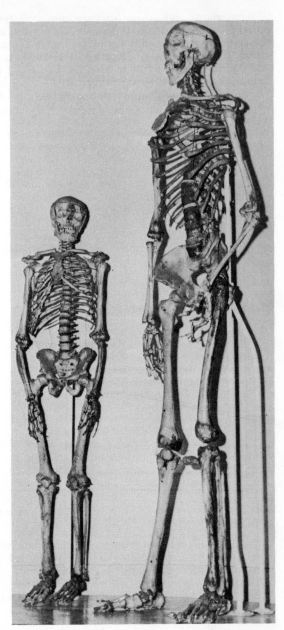

TALLEST WOMAN'S SKELETON: Jane Bunford of England probably stood 7 feet 7 inches.

birthday she measured 6 feet 6 inches. Shortly before her death on April 1, 1922, she stood 7 feet 7 inches tall, but she had a severe curvature of the spine and would have measured about 7 feet 11 inches with assumed normal curvature. Her skeleton, now preserved in the Anatomical Museum in the Medical School at Birmingham University, has a mounted height of 7 feet 4 inches.

Archeologists announced on February 10, 1972, the discovery of the remains of a medieval giantess reputedly 8 feet 3 inches in the Laga Mountains near Abruzzi, Italy. Anna Hanen Swan (1846–88) of Nova Scotia, Canada, was billed at 8 feet 1 inch but actually measured 7 feet 5½ inches. In London, on June 17, 1871, she married Martin van Buren Bates (1845–1919), of Whitesburg, Letcher County, Kentucky, who stood 7 feet 2½ inches. Ella Ewing (1875–1913) of Goring, Missouri, was billed at 8 feet 2 inches and reputedly measured 6 feet 9 inches at the age of 10 (*cf.* 6 feet 5 inches for Robert Wadlow at this age). She measured 7 feet 4½ inches at the age of 23 and may have attained 7 feet 6 inches before her death.

Living. The tallest living woman is believed to be a eunuchoidal giantess named Tiliya (b. 1947) who lives in the village of Saidpur in Bihar State, northeastern India. She stands 7 feet 5 inches tall. In November, 1971, a height of 7 feet 2¼ inches was reported for Mildred Tshakayi (b. 1946), a Rhodesian bush dweller. The tallest woman recently living was believed to be Dolores Ann Johnson, *née* Pullard (b. August 13, 1946), a Negress from De Quincy, Louisiana. She measured 6 feet 10 inches in March, 1961, and grew to 7 feet 5 inches by October, 1964. She reportedly wore size 52 dresses and size 23 shoes and weighed 435 lbs. At the time of her death in Houston, Texas, on May 19, 1971, she was credited with a height of 8 feet 2 inches, but her true stature was 7 feet 5½ inches.

Shortest Dwarfs

The strictures which apply to giants apply equally to dwarfs, except that exaggeration gives way to understatement. In the same way 9 feet may be regarded as the limit toward which the tallest giants tend, so 23 inches must be regarded as the limit toward which the shortest mature dwarfs tend (*cf.* the average length of new-born babies is 18 to 20 inches). In the case of child dwarfs the age is often enhanced by their agents or managers.

The shortest type of dwarf is an ateliotic dwarf, known as a midget. In this form of dwarfism the skeleton tends to remain in its infantile state. Midgets seldom grow to more than 40 inches tall. The most famous midget in history was Charles Sherwood Stratton, *alias* "General Tom Thumb," born in Bridgeport, Connecticut, on January 11, 1832. He measured 25 inches at the age of 5 months and grew to only 27.6 inches by the age of 13½. He was 30½ inches tall at the age of 18 and 35 inches at 30. He stood 40 inches tall at the time of his death on July 15, 1883.

Another celebrated midget was Józef ("Count") Boruwlaski (born November, 1739) of Poland. He measured only 8 inches long at birth, growing to 14 inches at the age of one year. He stood 17 inches at 6 years, 21 inches at 10, 25 inches at 15, 35 inches at 25 and 39 inches at 30. He died near Durham, England, on September 5, 1837, aged 97.

The shortest mature human of whom there is independent evidence was Pauline Musters ("Princess Pauline"), a Dutch midget. She was born at Ossendrecht on February 26, 1876, and measured 12 inches at birth. At the age of 4 she was only 15 inches tall. At the age of 9 she was 21.65 inches tall and weighed only 3 lbs. 5 oz. She died, at the age of 19, of pneumonia, with meningitis, in New York City on

SHORTEST ADULT: Only 23.2 inches tall at age 19, this Dutch midget called "Princess Pauline" weighed 9 lbs. at her heaviest in 1895.

March 1, 1895. Although she was billed at 19 inches, she was measured shortly before her death and was found to be 23.2 inches tall. A *post mortem* examination showed her to be exactly 24 inches (her body was slightly elongated after death). Her mature weight varied from 7½ lbs. to 9 lbs. and her "vital statistics" were 18½–19–17.

The Italian girl Caroline Crachami, born in Palermo, Sicily, in 1815, was only 20.2 inches tall when she died in London, England, in 1824, aged 9. At birth she measured 7 inches long and weighed 1 lb. Her skeleton, measuring 19.8 inches, is now part of the Hunterian collection in the Museum of the Royal College of Surgeons, London.

Male. The shortest recorded adult male dwarf was Calvin Phillips, born in Bridgewater, Massachusetts, on January 14, 1791. He weighed 2 lbs. at birth and stopped growing at the age of 5. When he was 19 he measured 26½ inches tall and weighed 12 lbs. with his clothes on. He died two years later, in April, 1812, from progeria, a rare disorder characterized by dwarfism and premature senility.

William E. Jackson, *alias* "Major Mite," born on October 2, 1864, in Dunedin, New Zealand, measured 9 inches long and weighed 12 oz. at birth. In November, 1880, he stood 21 inches and weighed 9 lbs. He died in New York City, on December 9, 1900, when he measured 27 inches.

Another notable case was Max Taborsky, *alias* "Prince Kolibri," born in Vienna, Austria, in January, 1863. He measured 13.8 inches at birth and stopped growing at the age of 9. When he died, aged 25, in 1888, he stood 27.2 inches tall and weighed 11 lbs.

Adam Rainer, born in 1899 in Graz, Austria, measured 3 feet 10.45 inches at the age of 21. But then he suddenly started growing upwards at a rapid rate, and by 1931 he had reached 7 feet 1¾ inches. He became so weak as a result that he was bedridden for the rest of his life. He died on March 4, 1950, aged 51.

Most Variable Stature. By constant practice in muscular manipulation of the vertebrae, the circus performer Clarence E. Willard (1882–1962) of the U.S. was, at his prime, able to increase his apparent stature from 5 feet 10 inches to 6 feet 4 inches at will.

Races

Tallest. The tallest race in the world is the Tutsi (also called Batutsi, Watutsi, or Watussi), Nilotic herdsmen of Rwanda and Burundi, Central Africa, whose males average 6 feet 1 inch, with a maximum of 7 feet 6 inches. A tribe with an average height of more than 6 feet was discovered in the inland region of Passis Manua of New Britain in December, 1956. In May, 1965, it was reported that the Crahiacoro Indians in the border district of the States of Mato Grosso and Pará, in Brazil, are exceptionally tall—certainly with an average of more than 6 feet. A report in May, 1966, specifically attributed great stature to the Kran-hacacore Indians of the Xingu region of the Mato Grosso. In December, 1967, the inhabitants of Barbuda, Leeward Islands, were reported to have an average height in excess of 6 feet.

The Tehuelches of Patagonia, long regarded as of gigantic stature (*i.e.* 7 to 8 feet), have in fact an average height (males) of 5 feet 10 inches with a maximum of just over 6 feet 6¾ inches.

Shortest. The world's smallest known race is the Negrito Onge tribe, of whom only 12 men and 10 women survived on Little Andaman Island in the Indian Ocean by May, 1956. Few exceeded 4 feet. The smallest pygmies are the Mbuti, with an average height of 4 feet 6 inches for men and 4 feet 5 inches for women, with some groups averaging only 4 feet 4 inches for men and 4 feet 1 inch for women. They live in the forests near the river Ituri in the Congo (Kinshasa), Africa. In June, 1936, there was a report, not subsequently substantiated, that there was a village of dwarfs numbering about 800 in the Hu bei (Hupeh) province of Central China between Wu han and Lishan in which the men were all less than 4 feet tall and the women slightly taller.

In October, 1970, a tribe of pygmies, reportedly measuring only 3 feet 3.4 inches tall, was discovered in the border area of Bolivia, Brazil and Peru.

Weight

Lightest Humans. The lightest recorded adult was Lucia (or Zuchia) Zarate (1863–89), an emaciated Mexican midget of 26½ inches who weighed 4.7 lbs. at the age of 17. She "fattened up" to 13 lbs. by her 20th birthday. At birth she weighed 2½ lbs.

The thinnest recorded adults of normal height are those suffering from Simmonds' disease (Hypophyseal cachexia). Losses up to 65 per cent of the original body weight have been recorded in females, with a "low" of 45 lbs. In cases of anorexia nervosa, weights of under 70 lbs. have been reported.

It was recorded that the American exhibitionist Rosa Lee Plemons (born 1873) weighed 27 lbs. at the age of 18. Edward C. Hagner

LIGHTEST HUMAN ADULT: Lucia Zarate of Mexico weighed 4.7 lbs. at the age of 17 and stood 26½ inches tall.

(1892–1962), *alias* Eddie Masher, is alleged to have weighed only 48 lbs. at a height of 5 feet 7 inches. He was also known as "the Skeleton Dude." In August, 1825, the biceps measurement of Claude-Ambroise Seurat (born April 10, 1797, died April 6, 1826), of Troyes, France, was 4 inches and the distance between his back and his chest was less than 3 inches. He stood 5 feet 7½ inches and weighed 78 lbs., but in another account was described as 5 feet 4 inches and only 36 lbs.

Heaviest Man. The heaviest medically weighed human was the 6-foot-0½-inch tall Robert Earl Hughes (born 1926) of Monticello, Illinois. An 11¼-lb. baby, he weighed 203 lbs. at 6 years, 378 lbs. at 10, 546 lbs. at 13, 693 lbs. at 18, 896 lbs. at 25, and 945 lbs. at 27. His greatest recorded weight was 1,069 lbs. in February, 1958, and he weighed 1,041 lbs. at the time of his death. His claimed waist of 122 inches, his chest of 124 inches and his upper arm of 40 inches were the greatest on record. Hughes died of uremia (condition caused by retention of urinary matter in the blood) in a trailer at Bremen, Indiana, on July 10, 1958, aged 32, and was buried in Benville Cemetery, near Mount Sterling, Illinois. His coffin, as large as a piano case measuring 7 feet by 4 feet 4 inches and weighing nearly 1,100 lbs., had to be lowered by crane. It was once claimed by a commercial interest that Hughes had weighed 1,500 lbs.—a 40 per cent exaggeration.

Johnny Alee (1853–87) of Carbon (now known as Carbonton), North Carolina, is reputed to have weighed 1,132 lbs. when he fell through the flooring of his log cabin to die of a heart attack as he was suspended by his armpits. The accuracy of this story has not yet been substantiated.

The only other men for whom weights of 800 lbs. or more have been *reliably* reported are the seven listed below:

Mills Darden (1798–1857) U.S. (7 ft. 6 in.)	1,020 lbs.
John Hanson Craig (1856–94) U.S. (6 ft. 5 in.)	907 (c)
Arthur Knorr (1914–60) U.S. (6 ft. 1 in.)	900 (a)
Toubi (b. 1946) Cameroon	857½
T. A. Valenzuela (1895–1937) Mexico (5 ft. 11 in.)	850
David Maguire (1904–*fl.* 1935) U.S. (5 ft. 10 in.)	810
William J. Cobb (b. 1926) U.S. (6 ft. 0 in.)	802 (b)

(a) Gained 300 lbs. in the last 6 months of his life.
(b) Reduced to 232 lbs. by July, 1965.
(c) Won $1,000 in a "Bonny Baby" contest in New York City in 1858.

Michael Walker (b. 1934) was treated for obesity and drug-induced bulimia (morbid desire to overeat) in a caravan outside the Ben Taub Hospital, Houston, Texas in December, 1971. Reports on his weight varying between 800 lbs. and 900 lbs. were received. A business partner in the company which exhibited him claimed that in the summer of 1971 he had reached a peak of 1,100 lbs.

Heaviest Twins. The heaviest are Bill and Ben, the McCreary twins (born 1948), farmers of Henderson County, North Carolina, who, in March, 1970, weighed 660 lbs. and 640 lbs., respectively.

Heaviest Woman. The heaviest woman ever recorded was a Negress whose name was not recorded. She died in Baltimore, Maryland, on September 4, 1888. Her weight was stated to be 850 lbs. A more reliable and better documented case was that of Mrs. Flora Mae (or May) Jackson (*née* King), a 5-foot-9-inch Negress born in 1930 at Shuqualak, Mississippi. She weighed 10 lbs. at birth; 267 lbs. at the age of 11; 621 lbs. at 25; and 840 lbs. shortly before her death in Meridian, Florida, on December 9, 1965. She was known in show business as "Baby Flo."

Slimming

The greatest recorded slimming feat was that of William J. Cobb (born 1926), *alias* "Happy Humphrey," a professional wrestler of Macon, Georgia. It was reported in July, 1965, that he had reduced from 802 lbs. to 232 lbs., a loss of 570 lbs., in 3 years. His waist measurement declined from 101 inches to 44 inches.

The U.S. circus fat lady, Mrs. Celesta Geyer (born 1901, *alias* Dolly Dimples), reduced from 553 lbs. to 152 lbs. in 1950–51, a loss of 401 lbs. in 14 months. Her vital statistics diminished *pari passu* from 79–84–84 to a *svelte* 34–28–36. Her book "How I Lost 400 lbs." was not a best seller. In December, 1967, she was reportedly down to 110 lbs.

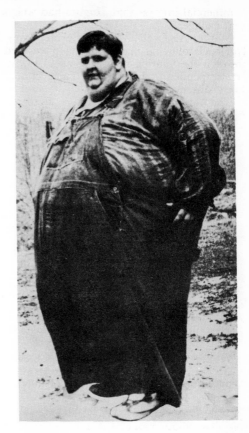

HEAVIEST HUMAN of all time: This is Robert Earl Hughes when he weighed only 700 lbs. He later reached a top weight of 1,069 lbs. He was buried in a coffin the size of a piano case.

HEAVIEST TWINS: The McCreary brothers, Bill and Ben, weighed 660 and 640 lbs., left and right respectively, in 1970.

The speed record for slimming was established by Paul M. Kimelman, 21, of Pittsburgh, Pennsylvania, who from December 25, 1966, to August, 1967, went on a crash diet of 300 to 600 calories per day to reduce from 427 lbs. to 130 lbs. In his prime he wore size 56 trousers into one leg of which he can now step easily.

Weight Gaining

A probable record for gaining weight was set by Arthur Knorr (born May 17, 1914), who died on July 7, 1960, aged 46, in Reseda, California. He gained 300 lbs. in the last 6 months of his life and weighed 900 lbs. when he died. Miss Doris James of San Francisco, is alleged to have gained 325 lbs. in the 12 months before her death in August, 1965, aged 38, at a weight of 675 lbs. She was only 5 feet 2 inches tall.

2. Origins

EARLIEST MAN

The earliest known primates appeared in the Paleocene period of about 70,000,000 years ago. The sub-order of higher primates, called Simiae (or Anthropoidea), evolved from the catarrhine or old-world sect nearly 30,000,000 years later in the Lower Oligocene period. During the Middle and Upper Oligocene the super-family Hominoidea emerged. This contains three accepted families, *viz.* Hominidae (bipedal, ground-dwelling man or near man), Pongidae (brachiating forest apes) and Oreopithecidae, which includes *Apidium* of the Oligocene and *Oreopithecus* of the early Pliocene. Opinion is divided on whether to treat gibbons and their ancestors as a fourth full family (Hylobatidae) or as a sub-family (Hylobatinae) within the Pongidae. Some consider the Proconsulidae should also comprise a family, although others regard the genus *Proconsul*, who lived on the open savannah, as part of another sub-family of the Pongidae.

Earliest Hominid

There is a conflict of evidence on the time during which true but primitive Hominidae were evolving. Fossil evidence indicates some time during the Upper Miocene (about 10,000,000 to 12,000,000 years ago). Evidence published in August, 1969, indicated that *Ramapithecus*, from the northeastern Indian sub-continent, was not less than 10,000,000 years old and *Australopithecus*, from Eastern Africa, possibly 6,000,000 years old.

Earliest Genus Homo

The earliest known true member of the genus *Homo* was found between December 6, 1960 and 1963 by Dr. Louis S. B. Leakey, (b. August 7, 1903), Hon. Director of the Kenya National Museum's Centre for Pre-History and Palaeontology, in Nairobi, and his wife Mary in Bed I in the Olduvai Gorge, Tanganyika (now part of Tanzania). These remains have been determined by stratigraphic, radiometric and fission-track dating to have existed between 1,750,000 and 2,300,000 years ago. They were first designated "*pre-Zinjanthropus*" but in March, 1964, were renamed Handy Man (*Homo*

HOME OF EARLIEST HUMAN: Olduvai Gorge in Tanzania, East Africa, where bones of the "Handy Man," the first man (about 4 feet tall), were found between 1960 and 1963.

habilis), to differentiate them from the more primitive Nutcracker Man (*Zinjanthropus boisei*), an East African australopithecine who was contemporary with Handy Man throughout Bed I and the greater part of Bed II times. Handy Man was about 4 feet tall.

In August, 1965, a fragment of a *humerus* bone from a hominine upper arm was found near Kanapoi, Kenya,, by Professor Bryan Patterson, a vertebrate paleontologist of the Museum of Comparative Zoology, Harvard University. It was announced in January, 1967, that this bone dated from between 2,300,000 and 2,700,000 years ago.

Earliest Homo Sapiens

Man (*Homo sapiens*) is a species in the sub-family Homininae of the family Hominidae of the super-family Hominoidea of the sub-order Simiae (or Anthropoidea) of the order Primates of the infraclass Eutheria of the sub-class Theria of the class Mammalia of the sub-phylum Vertebrata (Craniata) of the phylum Chordata of the sub-kingdom Metazoa of the animal kingdom.

The earliest recorded remains of the species *Homo sapiens*, variously dated from 300,000 to 450,000 years ago, in the middle Pleistocene period, were discovered on August 24, 1965, by Dr. László Vértes in a limestone quarry at Vértesszóllós, about 30 miles west of Budapest, Hungary. The remains, designated *Homo sapiens palaeo-hungaricus*, comprised an almost complete occipital bone, part of a skull with an estimated cranial capacity of nearly 1,400 cubic centimeters (85 cubic inches).

Earliest man in the Americas dates from at least 50,000 B.C. and "more probably 100,000 B.C." according to Dr. Leakey after the examination of some hearth stones found in the Mojave Desert, California, and announced in October, 1970. The earliest human relic is a skull found in the area of Los Angeles, California, dated in December, 1970, to be from 22,000 B.C.

Scale of Time

If the age of the earth-moon system (latest estimate at least 4,700 million years) is likened to a single year, Handy Man appeared on the scene at about 8:35 p.m., on December 31, Britain's earliest known inhabitants arrived at about 11:32 p.m., the Christian era began about 13 seconds before midnight and the life span of a 113-year-old man (see Oldest Centenarian) would be about three-quarters of a second. Present calculations indicate that the sun's increased heat, as it becomes a "red giant," will make life insupportable on earth in about 10,000 million years. Meanwhile there may well be colder epicycles. The period of 1,000 million years is sometimes referred to as an eon.

3. Longevity

Oldest Centenarian

No single subject is more obscured by vanity, deceit, falsehood and deliberate fraud than the extremes of human longevity. Extreme claims are generally made on behalf of the very aged rather than by them.

Many hundreds of claims throughout history have been made for persons living well into their second century and some, insulting to the intelligence, for people living even into their third. The facts are that centenarians surviving beyond their 110th year are of the extremest rarity and the present absolute limit of proven human longevity does not admit of anyone living to celebrate a 114th birthday.

It is highly significant that in Sweden, where alone proper and thorough official investigations follow the death of every allegedly very aged citizen, none has been found to have surpassed 110 years. The most reliably pedigreed large group of people in the world, the British peerage, has, after ten centuries, produced only one peer who reached even his 100th birthday. However, this is possibly not unconnected with the extreme draughtiness of many of their residences.

Scientific research into extreme old age reveals that the correlation between the claimed density of centenarians in a country and its regional illiteracy is 0.83 ±0.03. In late life, very old people often tend to advance their ages at the rate of about 17 years per decade. This was nicely corroborated by an analysis of the 1901 and 1911 censuses of England and Wales. Early claims must necessarily be without the elementary corroboration of birth dates. England was among the earliest of all countries to introduce local registers (1538) and official birth registration (July 1, 1837), which was made fully compulsory only in 1874. Even in the United States, where, in 1971, there were reputed to be 12,642 centenarians, 45 per cent of births occurring between 1890 and 1920 were unregistered.

Several celebrated super-centenarians are believed to have been double lives (father and son, brothers with the same names or successive bearers of a title). The most famous example is 'Christian Jakobsen Drackenberg allegedly born in Stavenger, Norway, on November 18, 1626, and died in Aarhus, Denmark, aged seemingly 145 years 326 days on October 9, 1772. A number of instances have been commercially sponsored, while a fourth category of recent claims are those made for political ends, such as the 100 citizens of the Russian Soviet Federative Socialist Republic (population about 132,000,000 at mid-1967), claimed in March, 1960, to be between 120 and 156. From data on documented centenarians, actuaries have shown that only one 115-year life can be expected in 2,100,000,000 lives (cf. world population was estimated to be 3,730,000,000 at mid-1972).

The height of credulity was reached on May 5, 1933, when a news agency solemnly filed a story from China with a Peking dateline that Li Chung-yun, the "oldest man on earth," born in 1680, had just died aged 256 years (sic). Currently the most extreme case of longevity claimed is 167 years for Shirali Muslimov of Azerbaijan, U.S.S.R., reputedly born on March 26, 1805. It was reported in 1954 that in the Republic of Georgia, U.S.S.R., 2.58 per cent of the population was aged over 90—some 25 times the proportion in the U.S. In 1972 there were an estimated 25,000 centenarians living in the world.

Sylvester Magee died at Marion County General Hospital, Columbia, Mississippi, on October 15, 1971, at a claimed age of 130 years 139 days. Though illiterate, he alleged that a family bible destroyed in a fire in 1966 showed that he was born at a now disappeared village called Carpet, North Carolina, on May 29, 1841. It was claimed on his behalf that, though he fought and was twice wounded at the Civil War siege of Vicksburg in 1863, being an "impressed" slave, the Army kept no records of the service for which he drew veteran's benefits. He flew in a jet plane in February and also was divorced in April, 1971.

Another American, still living, named Emma Spriggs, claims to have been born in Washington, D.C., in 1853, the daughter of a slave, but birth records are not available as proof. Neither can authenticity be given the claim of Charlie Smith of Barton, Florida, that he was born in Africa in 1842.

Mythology often requires immense longevity; for example, Larak the god-King lived according to Sumerian mythology 28,800 years and Dumuzi even longer. The most extreme biblical claim is that for Methuselah at 969 years (Genesis V, verse 27.)

Oldest Authenticated Centenarian

The greatest authenticated age to which a human has ever lived is 113 years 124 days in the case of Pierre Joubert, a French-Canadian bootmaker. He was born in Charlesbourg, Quebec Province, Canada, on July 15, 1701, and died in Quebec on November 16, 1814. His longevity was the subject of an investigation in 1870 by Dr. Tache, Official Statistician to the Canadian Government, and the proofs published are irrefutable. The following national records can be taken as authentic:—

	Years	Days	Born	Died
Canada (a) .	113	124	Pierre Joubert ....July 15, 1701	Nov. 16, 1810
U.S. (b)......	112	305	John B. Salling ....May 15, 1846	Mar. 16, 1959
Morocco ...	112		El Hadj Mohammed el Mokri (Grand Vizier)............... 1844	Sept. 16, 1957
U.K. (c) ...	111	339	Ada Rowe (*née* Giddings) ...Feb. 6, 1858	Jan. 11, 1970
Ireland	111	327	The Hon. Katherine Plunket..Nov. 22, 1820	Oct. 14, 1932
South Africa (d) .	111	151	Johanna Booyson ....Jan. 17, 1857	June 16, 1968
Czechoslovakia...	111	+	Marie Bernatkova...............Oct. 22, 1857	fl. Oct., 1968
Channel Islands ...	110	321	Margaret Ann Neve (*née* Harvey) (See photo).........May 18, 1792	Apr. 4, 1903
Yugoslavia .	110	150+	Demitrius Philipovitch ....Mar. 9, 1818	fl. Aug., 1928
Japan (e) ...	110	114	Yoshigiku Ito.....................Aug. 3, 1856	Nov. 26, 1966
Australia (f)	110	39	Ada Sharp (Mrs.)................Apr. 6, 1861	May 15, 1971
Netherlands	110	5	Baks Karnebeek (Mrs.).........Oct. 2, 1849	Oct. 7, 1959
France	109	309	Marie Philomene Flassayer...June 13, 1844	Apr. 18, 1954
Italy	109	179	Rosalia Spoto.....................Aug. 25, 1847	Feb. 20, 1957
Scotland ...	109	14	Rachel MacArthur (Mrs.)...Nov. 26, 1827	Dec. 10, 1936
Norway......	109	+	Marie Olsen (Mrs.) ....May 1, 1850	fl. May, 1959
Tasmania ...	109	+	Mary Ann Crow (Mrs.)......Feb. 2, 1836	1945
Germany (g)	108	128	Luise Schwarz ....Sept. 27, 1849	Feb. 2, 1958
Portugal ...	108	+	Maria Luisa Jorge...............June 7, 1859	fl. July, 1967
Finland......	107	+	Marie Anderson..................Jan. 3, 1829	1836
Belgium ...	106	267	Marie-Joseph Purnode (Mrs.).Apr. 17, 1843	Nov. 9, 1949
Austria	106	231	Anna Migschitz...................Feb. 3, 1850	Nov. 1, 1956
Sweden	106	98	Emma Gustaffsson (Mrs.)...June 18, 1858	Sept. 14, 1964
Spain (h) ...	106	14	Jose Palido........................Mar. 15, 1866	Mar. 29, 1972
Malaysia ...	106	+	Hassan Bin Yusoff...............Aug. 14, 1865	fl. Jan., 1972
Isle of Man .	105	221	John Kneen ....Nov. 12, 1852	June 9, 1958

(a) Mrs. Ellen Carroll died in North River, Newfoundland, Canada on December 8, 1943, reputedly aged 115 years 49 days.

(b) Mrs. Betsy Baker (*née* Russell) was born August 20, 1842, in Brington, England, and died in Tecumseh, Nebraska, on October 24, 1955, reputedly aged 113 years 65 days.

(c) London-born Miss Isabella Shepherd was allegedly 115 years old when she died at St. Asaph, North Wales, on November 20, 1948, but her official age was believed to have been 109 years 90 days.

(d) Mrs. Susan Johanna Deporter of Port Elizabeth, South Africa, was reputedly 114 years old when she died on August 4, 1954.

(e) A man named Nakamura of Kamaishi, northern Japan, was reported to have died on May 4, 1969, aged 116 years 329 days.

(f) Reginald Beck of Sydney, was allegedly 111 years old when he died on April 13, 1928.

(g) Friedrich Sadowski of Heidelberg reputedly celebrated his 111th birthday on October 31, 1936.

(h) Juana Ortega Villarin, Madrid, Spain, allegedly 112 years in February, 1962.

In the face of the above data the claim published in the April, 1961, issue of the Soviet Union's *Vestnik Statistiki* ("Statistical Herald") that there were 224 male and 368 female Soviet citizens aged in excess of 120 recorded at the census of January 15, 1959, indicates a reliance on hearsay rather than evidence. Official Soviet insistence on the unrivalled longevity of the country's citizenry is curious in view of the fact that the 592 persons in their unique "over 120" category must have spent at least the first 78 years of their prolonged lives under Czarism. It has recently been suggested that the extreme ages claimed by men in Georgia, U.S.S.R., are the result of attempts to avoid military service when younger, by assuming the identities of older men.

4. Reproductivity

MOTHERHOOD

Most Children. The greatest number of children produced by a mother in an independently attested case is 69 by the first wife of Fyodor Vassilet (1816–72) a peasant of the Moscow Jurisdiction, Russia, who in 27 confinements, gave birth to 16 pairs of twins, 7 sets of triplets and 4 sets of quadruplets. Most of the children attained their majority. Mme. Vassilet became so renowned that she was presented at the court of Czar Alexander II.

Currently the highest reliably reported figure is a 32nd child born on November 11, 1970, to Maria Addolorata Casalini (b. 1929) of Brindisi, Italy. She was married at 17 and so far has had, in 23 confinements, two sets of quadruplets, one of triplets, one of twins and 19 single births. Only 15 children survive.

Oldest. Medical literature contains extreme but unauthenticated cases of septuagenarian mothers. The oldest recorded mother of

110-YEAR-OLD WOMAN (left): Mrs. Margaret Neve of the Channel Islands, in a photo from 1903. OLDEST MOTHER (right): At the age of 57 years 129 days, Mrs. Ruth Kistler of California, in 1956, gave birth to daughter Suzan, shown with her.

whom there is certain evidence is Mrs. Ruth Alice Kistler (*née* Taylor), formerly Mrs. Shepard, of Portland, Oregon. She was born at Wakefield, Massachusetts, on June 11, 1899, and gave birth to a daughter, Suzan, in Glendale, California, on October 18, 1956, when her age of 57 years 129 days. (See photo, previous page.)

The incidence of quinquagenarian births varies widely with the highest known rate in Albania (nearly 5,500 per million).

Descendants

In polygamous countries, the number of a person's descendants soon becomes incalculable. The last Sharifian Emperor of Morocco, Moulay Ismail (1672–1727), known as "The Bloodthirsty," was reputed to have fathered a total of 548 sons and 340 daughters.

Capt. Wilson Kettle (born 1860) of Grand Bay, Port Aux Basques, Newfoundland, Canada, died on January 25, 1963, aged 102, leaving 11 children by two wives, 65 grandchildren, 201 great-grandchildren, and 305 great-great grandchildren, a total of 582 living descendants. Mrs. Johanna Booyson (see table, page 24), of Belfast, Transvaal, was estimated to have 600 living descendants in South Africa in January, 1968.

Multiple Great-Grandparents

Theoretically a great-great-great-great-grandparent is a possibility, although, in practice, countries in which young mothers are common generally have a low expectation of life. Mrs. Ella M. Prince of the U.S., who died, aged 91, on May 29, 1970, had three great-great-great-grandchildren among her 60 living descendants, while Hon. General Walter Washington Williams (1855–1959) of Houston, Texas, was reportedly several times a great-great-great-grandfather.

On October 8, 1971, Mrs. Mary Williams (allegedly born March 18, 1856) died at Forest Park, Atlanta, Georgia. She reportedly left, among 192 living descendants, seven great-great-great-great-great-grandchildren. This was most probably a confusion with her leaving five generations, since an age of 115 and seven successive generations producing children at an average interval of 16 years strains all credence.

Multiple Births

It was announced by Dr. Gennaro Montanino of Rome that he had removed the fetuses of ten girls and five boys from the womb of a 35-year-old housewife on July 22, 1971. A fertility drug was responsible for this unique and unsurpassed instance of quindecaplets.

With multiple births, as with giants and centenarians, exaggeration is the rule. Since 1900, two cases of nonuplets, five cases of octuplets, 19 cases of septuplets and at least 23 cases of sextuplets have been reported.

Mrs. Geraldine Broderick, 29, gave birth to five boys (two stillborn) and four girls—the only certain nonuplets—at the Royal Hospital, Sydney, Australia, on June 13, 1971. The last survivor, Richard (12 oz.) died on the sixth day.

Archbishop Etstathios of Salonika, Greece (d. 1150), once alluded to a woman in the Peloponese, named Geyfyra, who produced nine surviving nonuplets. Jamaica has the highest incidence of multiple births (i.e. triplet and upward) at 4 per 1,000.

Octuplets. The only confirmed case of live-born octuplets was the four boys and four girls, totaling 9 lbs. 10 oz., born to Señora María Teresa Lopez de Sepulveda, aged 21, in a nursing home in Mexico City, Mexico, between 7 p.m. and 8 p.m. on March 10, 1967. All the boys were named José and all the girls Josefina. Their weights ranged from 1 lb. 3 oz. to 14 oz. They all died within 14 hours.

There have been four unconfirmed reports of octuplets since 1900: to Señora Enriquita Ruiba at Tampico, Mexico, in 1921; seven boys and one girl to Mrs. Tam Sing at Kwoom Yam Sha, China, in June, 1934; a case near Tientsin, China, on September 29, 1947 (one baby died); and stillborn babies to Señora Celia Gonzalez at Bahía Blanca, Argentina, on May 2, 1955.

Septuplets. There have been six confirmed cases of septuplets since 1900: stillborn babies to Britt Louise Ericsson, aged 34, in Uppsala, Sweden, in August, 1964; five girls and two boys to Mme. Brigitte Verhaeghe-Denayer in Brussels, Belgium, on March 25, 1966 (all the babies died soon afterwards); four girls and three boys to Mrs. Sandra Cwikielnik in Boston, on October 1, 1966 (one was born dead and the others died within minutes); a stillborn set in Sweden in 1966; a case from Addis Ababa, Ethiopia, in March, 1969, of seven babies to Mrs. Verema Jusuf of whom two died immediately; and seven babies to Señora Garcelia Caldeson Avilia of Santiago, Chile, on November 6, 1971.

Sextuplets. Among sextuplet births, the case of Mrs. Philip Speichinger provides the best evidence in the person of a surviving daughter, Marjorie Louise, of Mendon, Missouri, born on August 9, 1936. The other five children were stillborn.

Mrs. Alincia Parker (*née* Bushnell) was always cited as the last survivor of the sextuplets reputedly born on September 15, 1866, to Mrs. James B. Bushnell in Chicago. She died, aged 85, in Warsaw, New York, on March 27, 1952. The birth was registered by Dr.

SIAMESE TWINS (left): Born in 1811 in Siam, the twins Chang and Eng Bunker married sisters at age 32 and fathered 10 and 12 children respectively. SEXTUPLET (right): Marjorie Louise Speichinger, the world's only surviving sextuplet. She was born in Missouri on August 9, 1936.

James Edwards but, for obscure reasons, was unrevealed until about 1912. The other children were identified as Lucy (died at 2 months), Laberto (died at 8 months), Norberto (died in 1934), Alberto (died in Albion, New York, in *c.* 1940) and Mrs. Alice Elizabeth Hughes (*née* Bushnell) who died in Flagstaff, Arizona, on July 2, 1941.

From sextuplets born to Maria Garcia, wife of an Indian farmer in Michoacán State, Mexico, on September 7, 1953, three (one boy and two girls) are reputedly still living. A woman living in a remote village in the Faridpur district of East Pakistan allegedly gave birth to six sons on November 11, 1967.

Mrs. Sheila Ann Thorns (*née* Manning) (b. October 2, 1938) of Birmingham, England, gave birth to sextuplets at the New Birmingham Maternity Hospital on October 2, 1968. In order of birth they were Lynne (2 lbs. 6 oz., died October 22), Ian (2 lbs. 13 oz., died October 13), Julie (3 lbs. 1 oz.), Susan (2 lbs. 11 oz.), Roger (2 lbs. 10 oz.) and a girl (died after one hour). A seventh child did not develop beyond the third month of this pregnancy which had been induced by a fertility drug.

A second set of British sextuplets were delivered, after use of a fertility drug, of Mrs. Rosemary Letts (*née* Egerton) (b. Watford, England, 1946) by Caesarean section at University College Hospital, London, on December 15, 1969. One girl was stillborn but the others Cara Dawn (2 lbs. 13 oz.), Sharon Marie (2 lbs. 9 oz.), Joanne Nadine (2 lbs. 7 oz.), Gary John (1 lb. 11½ oz.) and Tanya Odile (2 lbs. 1 oz.) survived.

Quintuplets. The earliest sets of quintuplets in which all survived were the Dionnes: Èmilie (died August 6, 1954, aged 20), Yvonne (now in a convent), Cecile (now Mrs. Philippe Langlois), Marie (later Mrs. Florian Houle, died February 28, 1970) and Annette (now Mrs. Germain Allard), born in her seventh pregnancy to Mrs. Oliva Dionne, aged 25, near Callander, Ontario, Canada, on May 28, 1934 (aggregate weight 13 lbs. 6 oz. with an average of 2 lbs. 11 oz.).

Heaviest Quints. It was reported that quintuplets weighing 25 lbs. were born on June 7, 1953, to Mrs. Lui Saulien of Chekiang province, China. A weight of 25 lbs. was also reported for quints born to Mrs. Kamalammal in Pondicherry, India, on December 30, 1956. They all died shortly afterwards.

Heaviest Quads. The heaviest quadruplets ever recorded were Brucina Paula (5 lbs. 7 oz.), Clifford (5 lbs. 0 oz.), Stanford (4 lbs. 15 oz.) and Stacey Lynn (4 lbs. 7 oz.), totaling 19 lbs. 13 oz., born by Caesarean section to Mrs. Ruth Becker, aged 28, between 5:15 a.m. and 5:18 a.m. on August 3, 1962, at the Vancouver General Hospital in Vancouver, British Columbia, Canada.

Heaviest Triplets. There is an unconfirmed report of triplets (two boys and a girl) weighing 26 lbs. 6 oz. born to a 21-year-old Iranian woman reported on March 18, 1968. Three boy triplets weighing 23 lbs. 1 oz. were born in the Yarrawonga District Hospital, Victoria, Australia, on August 8, 1946. They weighed 7 lbs. 13 oz., 7 lbs. 12 oz. and 7 lbs. 8 oz.

OLDEST SURVIVING TRIPLETS: The Lutey triplets of England, born in 1891.

Most Triplets. The greatest reported number of sets of triplets born to one woman is 15 (*cf.* 7 to Mme. Vassilet, holder Most Children record, p.25) to Maddalena Granata (1839–*fl.* 1886) of Nocera Superiore, Italy.

Oldest Surviving Triplets. The oldest known surviving triplets in the world are Richard Henry, John James and Catherine Vivian (now Mrs. Ellis) Lutey born in Carfury, Cornwall, England, on April 24, 1891.

Twins

Heaviest. The heaviest twins at birth were two boys, the first weighing 17 lbs. 8 oz. and the second 18 lbs., born in Derbyshire, England. This was reported in a letter in *The Lancet* of December 6, 1884. A more reliable recent case is that of John and Jane Haskin weighing 14 lbs. and 13¾ lbs., born to Mrs. J. P. Haskin on February 20, 1924, in Fort Smith, Arkansas.

Lightest. The lightest recorded birth weight for surviving twins was 2 lbs. 8 oz. in the case of Andrew (19 oz.) and Brian (21 oz.) delivered of Mrs. M. at the Isle of Thanet District Hospital, Margate, Kent, England, on July 16, 1971.

Oldest. The oldest recorded twins were Gulbrand and Bernt Morterud, born at Nord Odal, Norway, on December 20, 1858. Bernt died on August 1, 1960, in Chicago, aged 101, and his brother died at Nord Odal on January 12, 1964, aged 105.
Twin sisters, Mrs. Vassilka Dermendjhieva and Mrs. Vassila

Yapourdjieva of Sofia, Bulgaria, allegedly celebrated their joint 104th birthday on September 27, 1966.

The chances of identical twins both reaching 100 are said to be one in 1,000 million.

"Siamese." Conjoined twins derived this name from the celebrated Chang and Eng Bunker, born at Maklong, Thailand (Siam), on May 11, 1811. They were joined by a cartilaginous band at the chest and married in April, 1843, the Misses Sarah and Adelaide Yates. They fathered ten and twelve children respectively. They died within three hours of each other on January 17, 1874, aged 62. (See page 27 for photo.) There is no genealogical evidence for the existence of the Chalkhurst twins, Mary and Aliza, of Biddenden, England, allegedly born in *c.* 1550. Daisy and Violet Hilton, born in Brighton, England, on February 5, 1908, were joined at the hip. They died in Charlotte, North Carolina, on January 5, 1969, aged 60.

The earliest successful separation of Siamese twins was performed on Prisna and Napit Atkinson (b. May, 1953, in Thailand) by Dr. Dragstedt at the Univerisity of Chicago on March 29, 1955.

BABIES

Largest. The heaviest normal newborn child recorded in modern times was a boy weighing 24 lbs. 4 oz., born on June 3, 1961, to Mrs. Saadet Cor of Ceyhan, southern Turkey.

There is an unconfirmed report of a woman giving birth to a 27-lb. baby in Essonnes, a suburb of Corbeil, central France, in June, 1929. A deformed baby weighing 29¼ lbs. was born in May, 1939, in a hospital at Effingham, Illinois.

Most Bouncing Baby. The most bouncing baby on record is Elias Daou (b. Suniani, Ghana, on October 12, 1969). At the age of 22 months, Elias weighed 61½ lbs. and his circumference was 35¾ inches.

Smallest. The lowest birth weight for a surviving infant, of which there is definite evidence, is 10 oz. in the case of Marion Chapman, born on June 5, 1938, in South Shields, County Durham, England. She was 12¼ inches long. By her first birthday her weight had increased to 13 lbs. 14 oz. She was born unattended, and was nursed by Dr. D. A. Shearer, who fed her hourly through a fountain pen filler. Her weight on her 21st birthday was 106 lbs.

A weight of 8 oz. was reported on March 20, 1938, for a baby born prematurely to Mrs. John Womack, after she had been knocked down by a truck in East St. Louis, Illinois. The baby was taken alive to St. Mary's Hospital, but further information is lacking. On February 23, 1952, it was reported that a 6 oz. baby only 6½ inches in length lived for 12 hours in a hospital in Indianapolis. A twin was stillborn.

Longest Pregnancy. The longest pregnancy reported is one of 389 days for a woman aged 25 in Woking Maternity Hospital, Surrey, England, in 1954. The baby, weighing 7 lbs. 14 oz., was stillborn. (The average pregnancy is 273 days.)

The longest pregnancy for a live-born baby was one of 381 days attributed to Mrs. Christine Houghton, 28, of Walberton, Sussex, England, on May 22, 1971. The baby, Tina, weighed 7 lbs. 7 oz.

5. Physiology and Anatomy

Bones

Longest. The thigh bone or *femur* is the longest of the 206 bones in the human body. It constitutes usually $27\frac{1}{2}$ per cent of a person's stature, and may be expected to be $19\frac{3}{4}$ inches long in a 6-foot-tall man. The longest recorded bone was the *femur* of the German giant Constantine, who died in Mons, Belgium, on March 30, 1902, aged 30. It measured 29.9 inches. The *femur* of Robert Wadlow, the tallest man ever recorded, measured approximately $29\frac{1}{2}$ inches.

Smallest. The *stapes* or stirrup bone, one of the three auditory ossicles in the middle ear, is the smallest human bone, measuring from 2.6 to 3.4 millimeters (0.10 to 0.17 of an inch) in length and weighing from 2.0 to 4.3 milligrams (0.03 to 0.065 of a grain). Sesamoids are not included among human bones.

Muscles

Largest. Muscles normally account for 40 per cent of the body weight and the bulkiest of the 639 muscles in the human body is the *gluteus maximus* or buttock muscle, which extends the thigh.

Smallest. The smallest muscle is the *stapedius*, which controls the *stapes* (see above), an auditory ossicle in the middle ear, and which is less than 1/20th of an inch in length.

Smallest Waists

Queen Catherine de Médici (1519–89) decreed a standard waist measurement of 13 inches for ladies of the French court. This was at a time when females were more diminutive. The smallest recorded waist among women of normal stature in the 20th century is a reputed 13 inches in the case of the French actress Mlle. Polaire (1881–1939) and Mrs. Ethel Granger (born April 12, 1905) of Peterborough, England, who reduced from a natural 22 inches over the period 1929–39. (See photo, next page.)

Largest Chest Measurements

The largest chest measurements are among endomorphs (those with a tendency toward globularity). In the extreme case of Robert Earl Hughes of Monticello, Illinois (the heaviest recorded human), this was reportedly 124 inches, but in the light of his known height and weight a figure of 104 inches would be more supportable. Among muscular subjects (mesomorphs), chest measurements above 56 inches are very rare. The largest such chest measurement ever recorded was that of Angus MacAskill (1825–63) of Berneray, Scotland, who may well have been the strongest man who ever lived. His chest must have measured 65 inches at his top weight of 525 lbs.

Brain

The brain has 1.5×10^{10} cells each containing 10^{10} macromolecules. Each cell has 10^4 interconnections with other cells. At the age of 18 the brain loses some 10^3 cells every day but the macromolecular content of each cell is renewed 10^4 times in a normal life span.

MOST DESCENDANTS (left): When Captain Wilson Kettle of Newfoundland died in 1963, he left 582 descendants (see page 26). SMALLEST WAIST (right): Mrs. Ethel Granger of England, with a 13-inch waist, has the tiniest beltline for a normal-sized person.

Largest. The brain of an average adult male (30–59 years) weighs 2 lbs. 13.21 oz., falling to 2 lbs. 4.33 oz. That of the average young adult female weighs 2 lbs. 12.83 oz. The heaviest brain ever recorded was that of Ivan Sergeyevich Turgenev (1818–83), the Russian author. His brain weighed 4 lbs. 6.96 oz.

Smallest. The brain of Anatole France (1844–1924), the French writer, weighed only 2 lbs. 4 oz. without the membrane, but there was some shrinkage due to old age. His brain probably weighed *c.* 2 lbs. 7.78 oz. at its heaviest.

Brains in extreme cases of microcephaly may weigh as little as 10.6 oz. (*cf.* 20 oz. for the adult male gorilla, and 16–20 oz. for other anthropoid apes).

Longest Necks

The maximum measured extension of the neck by the successive fitting of copper coils, as practiced by the Padaung or Mayan people of Burma, is 15¾ inches. From the male viewpoint the practice serves the dual purpose of enhancing the beauty of the female and ensuring fidelity. The neck muscles become so atrophied that the removal of the support of the rings produces asphyxiation.

Commonest Illness

The commonest illness in the world is coryza (acute nasopharyngitis) or the common cold.

Commonest Disease

The commonest disease in the world is dental caries or tooth decay, known to afflict over 53 per cent of the population of the U.S. During their lifetime few completely escape its effects. Infestation with pinworm (*Enterobius vermicularis*) approaches 100 per cent in some areas of the world.

Rarest Disease

Medical literature periodically records hitherto undescribed diseases. Kuru, or laughing sickness, afflicts only the Fore tribe of eastern New Guinea and is 100 per cent fatal.

The only recorded case of congenital agammaglobulinaemia was reported from Houston, Texas, in February, 1972.

Most and Least Infectious Diseases

The most infectious of all diseases is the pneumonic form of plague, with a mortality rate of 99.99 per cent. Leprosy transmitted by *Mycobacterium leprae* is the least infectious of communicable diseases.

Highest Morbidity

Rabies in humans is uniformly fatal when associated with the hydrophobia symptom. A 25-year-old woman, Candida de Sousa Barbosa of Rio de Janeiro, Brazil, was believed to be the first ever to survive the disease in November, 1968. In 1969, all 515 cases reported were fatal.

Most Notorious Carrier

The most notorious of all typhoid carriers was Mary Mallon, known as Typhoid Mary, of New York City. She was the source of the 1903 outbreak with 1,300 cases. Because of her refusal to leave employment, often under assumed names, involving the handling of food, she was placed under permanent detention from 1915 until her death in 1938.

Most Bee Stings

The greatest number of bee stings sustained by any surviving human subject is 2,443 by Johannes Relleke, at the Gwaii River in the Wankie District of Rhodesia, on January 28, 1962.

Touch Sensitivity

The extreme sensitivity of the fingers is such that a vibration with a movement of 0.02 of a micron can be detected. On January 12, 1963, the Soviet newspaper *Izvestia* reported the case of a totally blind-folded girl, Rosa Kulgeshova, who was able to identify colors by touch alone. Later reports confirmed in 1970 that under rigorous test conditions, this claimed ability totally disappeared.

Most Fingers

Voight records a case of someone with 13 fingers on each hand and 12 toes on each foot.

Longest Finger Nails

The longest recorded finger nails were reported from Shanghai in 1910, in the case of a Chinese priest who took 27 years to achieve nails up to $22\frac{3}{4}$ inches in length. Probably the longest nails now grown are those of Ramesh Sharma of Delhi, India, whose nails on his left hand now aggregate $52\frac{1}{2}$ inches after 10 years of growth,

LONGEST(?) BEARD:
Unless Richard Latter's beard grew after this picture was taken, his claim of 18 feet cannot be regarded as the true record.

with his best at 15 inches. Human nails normally grow from cuticle to cutting length in from 117 to 138 days.

Longest Hair

The longest recorded hair was that of Swami Pandarasannadhi, the head of the Thiruvadu Thurai monastery, India. His hair was reported in 1949 to be 26 feet in length.

Longest Beard

The longest beard preserved was that of Hans Langseth (1846–1927) of Norway, which measured $17\frac{1}{2}$ feet at the time of his death in 1927, after 15 years residence in the U.S. The beard was presented to the Smithsonian Institution, Washington, D.C. in 1967.

Richard Latter (1831–1914) of Tunbridge Wells, England, reputedly had a beard 18 feet long, but contemporary independent corroboration is lacking. Photographic evidence indicates that this figure was exaggerated. (See above.)

The beard of the bearded lady Janice Deveree (born in Bracken County, Kentucky, in 1842) was measured at 14 inches in 1884.

Longest Moustache

The longest moustache on record is that of Masuriya Din (born 1916), a Brahmin of the Partabgarh district in Uttar Pradesh, India. It grew to an extended span of 102 inches between 1949 and 1962, and costs over $30 per year in upkeep. (See photo.)

Largest Vein

In the human body, the largest is the cardiac vein known as the vena cava.

Blood Transfusion

The greatest recorded blood infusion is 2,400 pints, required by a 50-year-old hemophiliac, Warren C. Jyrich, when undergoing open heart surgery at the Michael Reese Hospital, Chicago, in December, 1970.

Champion Blood Donor

Joseph Elmaleh (born 1915) of Marseilles, France, donated on May 22, 1968, his 597th pint of blood making a total of 74 gallons 5 pints since 1931.

Joe Thomas of Detroit was reported in August, 1970, to have the highest known count of Anti-Lewis B, the rare blood antibody. A U.S. biological supply firm pays him $1,500 per quart—an income of $12,000 per annum. The Internal Revenue regard this income as a taxable liquid asset.

Blood Groups

The preponderance of one blood group varies greatly from one locality to another. On a world basis Group O is the most common (46 per cent), but in some areas, for example London and Norway, Group A predominates.

The rarest blood group on the ABO system, one of nine systems, is AB. The rarest type in the world is a type of Bombay blood (sub-type A-h) found so far only in a Czechoslovak nurse in 1961 and in a brother and sister in New Jersey, reported in February, 1968. The brother has started a blood bank for himself.

Longest Coma

Karoline Karlsson (b. Monsteras, Sweden, 1862) survived a coma of 32 years 99 days, from December 25, 1875, to April 3, 1908. She died on April 6, 1950, aged 88.

The longest continuing period of human unconsciousness has been that of Elaine Esposito (born December 3, 1934) of Tarpon Springs, Florida. She has never stirred since an appendectomy on August 5, 1941, when she was six, in Chicago. She was still living in 1969.

MOUSTACHE AT LEAST 102 INCHES LONG: The longest moustache on record belongs to Masuriya Din of India.

Temperature

Highest. Temperatures of up to 107.6°F. are induced and maintained in robust subjects undergoing pyrexial therapy. Sustained body temperatures of much over 109°F. are normally incompatible with life, although recoveries after readings of 111°F. have been noted. Marathon runners in hot weather attain 105.8°F.

In a case reported in the British medical magazine, *Lancet* (October 31, 1970), a woman following halothane anesthesia ran a temperature of 112° F. She recovered after a procainamide infusion.

A temperature of 115°F. was recorded in the case of Christopher Legge in the Hospital for Tropical Diseases, London, England, on February 9, 1934. A subsequent examination of the thermometer disclosed a flaw in the bulb, but it is regarded as certain that the patient sustained a temperature of more than 110°F.

Lowest. The lowest body temperature ever recorded for a living person was 60.8°F. in the case of Vickie Mary Davis (born December 25, 1953) of Milwaukee, Wisconsin, when she was admitted to the Evangelical Hospital, Marshalltown, Iowa, on January 21, 1956. The house in which she had been found unconscious on the floor was unheated and the air temperature had dropped to —24°F. Her temperature returned to normal (98.4°F.) after 12 hours and may have been as low as 59°F. when she was first found.

Heart Stoppage

The longest recorded heart stoppage is 3 hours in the case of a Norwegian boy, Roger Arntzen, in April, 1962. He was rescued, apparently drowned, after 22 minutes under the waters of the River Nideelv, near Trondheim.

The longest recorded interval in a post-mortem birth was one of at least 80 minutes in Magnolia, Mississippi. Dr. Robert E. Drake found Fanella Anderson, aged 25, dead in her home at 11:40 p.m. on October 15, 1966, and he delivered her of a son weighing 6 lbs. 4 oz. by Caesarean operation in the Beacham Memorial Hospital at 1 a.m. on October 16, 1966.

Largest Stone

The largest stone or vesical calculus reported in medical literature was one of 13 lbs. 14 oz., removed from an 80-year-old woman by Dr. Humphrey Arthure at Charing Cross Hospital, London, England, on December 29, 1952.

Earliest Influenza

An epidemic bearing symptoms akin to influenza was first recorded in 412 B.C. by Hippocrates (*c.* 460–*c.* 375 B.C.).

Earliest Duodenal Ulcer

The earliest description in medical literature of a duodenal ulcer was made in 1746 by Georg Erhard Hamberger (1697–1755).

Earliest Slipped Disc

The earliest description of a prolapsed intervertebral cartilage was by George S. Middleton and John H. Teacher of Glasgow, Scotland, in 1911.

Pill Taking

It is recorded that among hypochondriacs Samuel Jessup (born 1752), a wealthy grazier of Heckington, Lincolnshire, England has never had a modern rival. His consumption of pills from 1794 to 1816 was 226,934, with a peak annual total of 51,590 in 1814. He is also recorded as having drunk 40,000 bottles of medicine before death overtook him at the surprisingly advanced age of 65.

Most Tattoos

Vivian "Sailor Joe" Simmons, a Canadian tattoo artist, had 4,831 tattoos on his body. He died in Toronto on December 22, 1965, aged 77.

Hiccoughing

The longest recorded attack of hiccoughs was that afflicting Jack O'Leary of Los Angeles. It was estimated that he "hicked" more than 160,000,000 times in an attack which lasted from June 13, 1948, to June 1, 1956, apart from a week's respite in 1951. His weight fell from 138 lbs. to 74 lbs. People sent 60,000 suggestions for cures, of which only one apparently worked—a prayer to St. Jude, the patron saint of lost causes.

The infirmary at Newcastle upon Tyne, England, is recorded to have admitted a young man from Long Witton, Northumberland, on March 25, 1769, suffering from hiccoughs which could be heard at a range of more than a mile.

Sneezing

The most chronic sneezing fit ever recorded was that of June Clark, aged 17, of Miami, Florida. She started sneezing on January 4, 1966, while recovering from a kidney ailment in the James M. Jackson Memorial Hospital, Miami. The sneezing was stopped by electric "aversion" treatment on June 8, 1966, after 155 days. The highest speed at which expelled particles have been measured to travel is 103.6 m.p.h.

Loudest Snore

Research at the Ear, Nose and Throat Department of St. Mary's Hospital, London, published in November, 1968, shows that a rasping snore can attain a loudness of 69 decibels.

Yawning

In a case reported in 1888, a 15-year-old female patient yawned continuously for a period of five weeks.

Swallowing

The worst known case of compulsive swallowing was reported by the *Journal of the American Medical Association* in December, 1960. The patient, who complained only of swollen ankles, was found to have 258 items in his stomach, including a 3-lb. piece of metal, 26 keys, 3 sets of rosary beads, 16 religious medals, a bracelet, a necklace, 3 pairs of tweezers, 4 nail clippers, 39 nail files, 3 metal chains and 88 assorted coins.

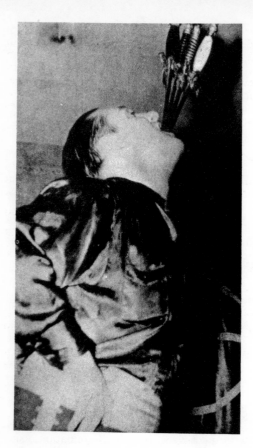

"SWALLOWS" FOUR SWORDS: Alex Linton from Ireland shows how he "swallows" four 27-inch blades at one time.

Coin Swallowing

The most extreme recorded case of coin swallowing was revealed by Sedgefield General Hospital, County Durham, England, on January 5, 1958, when it was reported that 366 halfpennies, 26 sixpences, 17 threepences, 11 pennies, and four shillings (424 coins valued at about $5) and 27 pieces of wire totaling 5 lbs. 1 oz. had been extracted from the stomach of a 54-year-old man.

Sword "Swallowing"

The longest length of sword able to be "swallowed" by a practiced exponent, after a heavy meal, is 27 inches. Perhaps the greatest exponent is Alex Linton, born on October 25, 1904, in Boyle, County Roscommon, Ireland. He stands 5 feet 3 inches tall and has "swallowed" four 27-inch blades at one time. He now lives in Sarasota, Florida. (See photograph, above.)

Fire-Eating

The hardest blowing, most voracious fire-eater is Kjell Swing (Sweden), who can produce a flame 6½ feet long.

Dentition

Earliest. The first deciduous or milk teeth normally appear in infants at five to eight months, these being the mandibular and maxillary first incisors. There are many records of children born with teeth, the most famous example being Prince Louis Dieudonné, later Louis XIV of France, who was born with two teeth on September 5, 1638. Molars usually appear at 24 months, but in 1956 Bellevue Hospital, New York City, reported a molar in a one-month-old baby, Robert R. Clinton.

Most. Cases of the growth in late life of a third set of teeth have been recorded several times. A reference to an extreme case in France of a fourth dentition known as Lison's case was published in 1896. A triple row of teeth was noted in 1680 by Albertus Hellwigius.

Most Dedicated Dentist. Brother Giovanni Battista Orsenigo of the Ospedale Fatebenefratelli, Rome, Italy, a religious dentist, conserved all the teeth he extracted in three enormous boxes during the time he exercised his profession from 1868 to 1904. In 1903, the number was counted and found to be 2,000,744 teeth.

Smallest Visible Object

The resolving power of the human eye is 0.0003 of a radian or an arc of one minute (1/60th of a degree), which corresponds to 100 microns at 10 inches. A micron is a thousandth of a millimeter, hence 100 microns is 0.003937, or less than four thousandths, of an inch. The human eye can, however, detect a bright light source shining through an aperture of only 3 to 4 microns across.

Color Sensitivity

The unaided human eye, under the best possible viewing conditions, comparing large areas of color, in good illumination, using both eyes, can distinguish 10,000,000 different color surfaces. The most accurate photo-electric spectrophotometers possess a precision probably only 40 per cent as good as this.

Color Blindness. The most extreme form of color blindness, monochromatic vision, is very rare. The highest rate of red-green color blindness exists in Czechoslovakia and the lowest rate among Fijians and Brazilian Indians.

Voice

Highest and Lowest. The highest and lowest recorded notes attained by the human voice before this century were a C in *altissimo* (*c'''*) by Lucrezia Agujari (1743–83), noted by the Austrian composer, Wolfgang Amadeus Mozart (1756–91) in Parma, northern Italy, in 1770, and an *A'* (55 cycles per second) by Kaspar Foster (1617–73). Since 1950 singers have achieved high and low notes far beyond the hitherto accepted extremes. Notes, however, at the bass and treble extremities of the register tend to lack harmonics and are of little musical value, while the topmost notes must be regarded as almost purely sinusoidal. Fraulein Marita Günther, trained by Alfred Wolfsohn, has covered the range of the piano from the lowest note A'' to C''''''. Of this range of $7\frac{1}{4}$ octaves, 6 octaves are considered to be of musical value. Mr. Roy Hart, also trained by Wolfsohn, has reached notes below the range of the piano.

The highest being sung by a tenor is G in *alt-altissimo* by Louis Lavelle, coached by Mr. S. Pleeth, in *Lovely Mary Donelly*. The lowest note put into song is D'' by the singer Tom King, of King's Langley, Hertfordshire, England. The highest note called for in singing was an f'''' #, which occurred twice in Zerbinetta's Recitative and Aria in the first (1912) version of the opera *Ariadne auf Naxos* by Richard Strauss (1864–1949). It was transposed down a tone in 1916.

Greatest Range. The normal intelligible outdoor range of the male human voice in still air is 200 yards. The *silbo*, the whistled language of the Spanish-speaking Canary Island of La Gomera, is intelligible across the valleys, under ideal conditions, at 5 miles. There is a recorded case, under freak acoustic conditions, of the human voice being detectable at a distance of $10\frac{1}{2}$ miles across still water at night. It was said that Mills Darden (see Heaviest Man) could be heard 6 miles away when he shouted at the top of his voice.

Lowest Detectable Sound. The intensity of noise or sound is measured in terms of power. The power of the quietest sound that can be detected by a person of normal hearing at the most sensitive frequency of *c.* 2.750 Hz is 1.0×10^{-16} of a watt per square centimeter. One tenth of the logarithm (to the base 10) of the ratio of the power of a noise to this standard provides a unit termed a decibel. Noises above 150 decibels will cause immediate permanent deafness, while a noise of 30 decibels is negligible.

Highest Detectable Pitch. The upper limit of hearing by the human ear has been regarded as 20,000 Hz (cycles per second), although children with asthma can often detect a sound of 30,000 cycles per second. It was announced in February, 1964, that experiments in the U.S.S.R. had conclusively proved that oscillations as high as 200,000 cycles per second can be heard if the oscillator is pressed against the skull.

Operations

Longest. The most protracted operations are those involving brain surgery. Such an operation lasting up to 31 hours was performed on Victor Zazueta, 19, of El Centro at San Diego Hospital, California, by Dr. John F. Alksne and his team on January 17–18, 1972.

Oldest Subject. The greatest recorded age at which a person has been subjected to an operation is 111 years 105 days in the case of James Henry Brett, Jr. (born July 25, 1849, died February 10, 1961) of Houston, Texas. He underwent a hip operation on November 7, 1960.

Youngest Subject. The youngest reported subject in a major operation—on the heart—has been identified only as "Hamish." He underwent such an operation at the Royal Alexandra Hospital, Sydney, Australia, on April 15, 1971, at the age of two days.

Heart Transplants

The first human heart transplant operation was performed on Louis Washkansky, aged 55, at the Groote Schuur Hospital, Cape Town, South Africa, between 1:00 and 6:00 a.m. on December 3, 1967, by a team of 30 headed by Prof. Christiaan N. Barnard (born 1922). The donor was Miss Denise Ann Darvall, aged 25. Washkansky died on December 21, 1967.

The longest-surviving heart transplant patient is Louis B. Russell, Jr., 47, of Indianapolis, Indiana, who, in July, 1972, was within one month of entering the fifth year of his "second life." His operation was on August 24, 1968. He is a teacher of industrial art and entered the list as a Democratic candidate in Indiana politics. By September, 1971, only 27 of the 174 recipients of new hearts were still living.

Longest Survival in Iron Lung

The longest survival in an iron lung is 22 years since 1950 by Mrs. Mary Ann Hough (b. 1923) of Hillsborough, California.

Earliest Appendectomy

The earliest recorded successful appendix operation was performed in 1736 by Claudius Amyand (1680–1740). He was Serjeant Surgeon to King George II (reigned 1727–60) of Great Britain.

Earliest Anesthesia

The earliest recorded operation under general anesthesia was for the removal of a cyst from the neck of James Venable by Dr. Crawford Williamson Long (1815–78), using diethyl ether $((C_2 H_5)_2 O)$, in Jefferson, Georgia, on March 30, 1842.

Fastest Amputation

The shortest time recorded for the amputation of a limb in the pre-anesthetic era was 33 seconds through a patient's thigh by Robert Liston (1794–1847) of Edinburgh, Scotland. This feat caused his assistant the loss of three fingers from his master's saw.

Surgical Instruments

The longest surgical instruments are bronchoscopic forceps which measure up to $23\frac{1}{2}$ inches over-all. Robot-tractors for abdominal surgery made by Abbey Surgical of England weigh 11 lbs. The smallest is Elliot's eye trephine which has a blade 0.078 of an inch in diameter.

Human Memory

Mehmed Ali Halici of Ankara, Turkey, on October 14, 1967, recited 6,666 verses of the Koran from memory in six hours. The recitation was followed by six Koran scholars.

Calculating

Greatest Number of Places of Pi. The greatest number of places to which pi (π) has been memorized is 750 by David Richard Spencer (b. December 10, 1952) of Powell River, British Columbia,

Canada. He desisted in going further on making the disconcerting discovery that two sources disagreed on the 512th place.

Extracting Roots. Herbert B. de Grote of Mexico City, Mexico, has been attested to have extracted the 13th root of a 100-digit number by an algorithm of his own invention in 23 minutes in a test in Chicago, on October 5, 1970. His answer was 46,231,597. No comparable feat has been recorded.

Highest I.Q.

On the Terman index for Intelligence Quotients, 150 represents genius level. The indices are sometimes held to be immeasurable above a level of 200, but a figure of 210 has been attributed to Kim Ung-Yong of Seoul, South Korea (born March 7, 1963). He composed poetry and spoke four languages (Korean, English, German and Japanese), and performed integral calculus at the age of 4 years 8 months on television in Tokyo on "The World Surprise Show" on November 2, 1967. Both his parents are university professors and were both born at 11 a.m. on May 23, 1934. Research into past geniuses at Stanford University, California, has produced a figure of "over 200" for John Stuart Mill (1806–73), who began to learn ancient Greek at the age of three. A similar rating has also been attributed to Johann Wolfgang von Goethe (1749–1832) of Frankfurt am Main, Germany. More than 20 per cent of the 15,000 members of the international Mensa society have an I.Q. of 161 or above on the Cattell index which is equivalent to 142 on the Terman index.

Fastest Talker

Extremely few people are able to speak articulately at a sustained speed above 300 words per minute. The fastest broadcaster has usually been allowed to be Jerry Wilmot, the Canadian ice hockey commentator in the post World War II period. Raymond Glendenning of the British Broadcasting Corporation once spoke 176 words in 30 seconds while commentating on a greyhound race. In public life the highest speed recorded is a 327-words-per-minute burst in a speech made in December, 1961, by John Fitzgerald Kennedy (1917–63), then President of the U.S. In October, 1965, it was reported that Peter Spiegel, aged 62, of Essen, West Germany, achieved 908 syllables in one minute at a rally of shorthand writers.

Dr. Charles Hunter of Rochdale, Lancashire, England in March, 1968, demonstrated an ability to recite the first 262 words of the soliloquy *To Be or Not To Be* from Shakespeare's *Hamlet* (Act III, Scene I) in 41 secs. or at a rate of 383 words per minute. He covered the first 50 words in 7.2 secs. (a rate of 416.6 words per minute).

Fasting

Most humans experience considerable discomfort after an abstinence from food for even 12 hours, but this often passes off after 24–28 hours. Records claimed without unremitting medical surveillance are of little value.

The longest period for which anyone has gone without food is 382 days by Angus Barbieri (born 1940) of Tayport, Fife, Scotland. He lived on tea, coffee, water and soda water from June, 1965, to

HIGHEST I.Q.: This Korean boy, with a 210 quotient, at the age of 4 years 8 months, spoke four languages, composed poetry and performed integral calculus. Here he is shown in a Tokyo television studio.

July, 1966, in Maryfield Hospital, Dundee, Angus, Scotland. His weight declined from 472 lbs. to 178 lbs.

Dr. Stephen Taylor, 43, of Mount Roskill, New Zealand, fasted 40 days with only a glass of water per day in a political protest in 1970.

Hunger Strike

The longest recorded hunger strike was one of 94 days by John and Peter Crowley, Thomas Donovan, Michael Burke, Michael O'Reilly, Christopher Upton, John Power, Joseph Kenny and Sean Hennessy in Cork Prison, Ireland, from August 11 to November 12, 1920. These nine survivors (Joseph Murphy died on the 76th day) owed their lives to expert medical attention.

Sleeplessness

Researches indicate that the peak of efficiency is attained between 8 p.m. and 9 p.m., and the low comes at 4 a.m.

The longest recorded period for which a person has voluntarily gone without sleep, while under medical surveillance, is 282 hours 55 minutes (11 days 18 hours 55 mins.) by Mrs. Bertha Van Der Merwe, aged 52, a housewife of Cape Town, South Africa, ending on December 13, 1968.

It was reported that Toimi Artturinpoika Silvo, a 54-year-old port worker of Hamina, Finland, stayed awake for 32 days 12 hours from March 1 to April 2, 1967. To stay awake he walked 17 miles per day, and lost 33 lbs. during this time.

A man named Eustace Rushworth Burnett (born 1880) of Hose, Leicestershire, England, claimed to have lost all desire to sleep in 1907, and that he never again went to bed. He died 58 years later, aged 85, in January, 1965.

Motionlessness

The longest that a man has voluntarily remained motionless is 4½ hours by Private (1st Class) William A. Fuqua of Fort Worth, Texas. He is a male mannequin or "fashioneer" in civil life earning up to $1,300 per hour for his ability to "freeze." The job is hazardous for it was reported in November, 1967, that he was stabbed in the back by a man "proving" to his wife that Fuqua was only a dummy.

Isolation

The longest recorded period for which any volunteer has been able to withstand total deprivation of all sensory stimulation (sight, hearing and touch) is 92 hours, recorded in 1962 at Lancaster Moor Hospital, England.

Human Salamanders

The highest dry-air temperature endured by naked men in U.S. Air Force experiments in 1960 was 400°F. and for heavily clothed men 500°F. (Steaks require only 325°F.) Temperatures of 284°F. have been found quite bearable in Sauna baths.

Extrasensory Perception

The highest consistent performer in tests to detect powers of extrasensory perception is Pavel Stepánek (Czechoslovakia) known in parapsychological circles as "P.S." His performance in correctly naming hidden white or green cards from May, 1967, to March, 1968, departed from a chance probability yielding a Chi² value

BEST AT EXTRA-SENSORY PERCEPTION: Pavel Stepánek of Czechoslovakia named hidden cards' colors for almost a year, and the results were 100 octillion times better than chance.

UNDERWATER LONGEST: Robert L. Foster of California, while he held his breath for a record 13 minutes 42½ seconds in a swimming pool. Record-breaking of this kind is extremely dangerous.

corresponding to $P < 10^{-50}$ or odds of more than 100 octillion to one against the achievement being one of chance. One of the two appointed referees recommended that the results should not be published.

The highest published scores in any E.S.P. test were those of a 26-year-old female tested by Prof. Bernard F. Reiss of Hunter College, New York City, in 1936. In 74 runs of 25 guesses each, she scored one with 25 all correct, two with 24, and an average of 18.24, as against a random score of 5.00. Such a result would depart from chance probability by a factor $> 10^{700}$.

Underwater

The world record for voluntarily staying under water is 13 minutes 42.5 seconds by Robert Foster, aged 32, an electronics technician of Richmond, California, who stayed under 10 feet of water in the swimming pool of the Bermuda Palms at San Rafael, California, on March 15, 1959. He hyperventilated with oxygen for 30 minutes before his descent. His longest breath-hold without oxygen was 5 mins. 40 secs. It must be stressed that record-breaking of this kind is *extremely* dangerous.

g Forces

The acceleration due to gravity (g) is 32 feet 1.05 inches per second per second at sea level at the Equator. A *sustained* force of 31 g was withstood for 5 seconds by R. Flanagan Gray, aged 39, at

ENDURING GREATEST G FORCE: Eli L. Beeding, Jr., white-lipped, as his water-braked rocket sled creates an 82.6 g force in New Mexico in 1958. He spent the next three days in the hospital.

the U.S. Naval Air Development Center in Johnstown, Pennsylvania, in 1959. This makes the bodyweight of a 185-lb. man seem like 5,700 lbs. The highest force endured in a dry capsule is 25g.

The highest g force endured was 82.6 g for 0.04 of a second on a water-braked rocket sled by Eli L. Beeding, Jr., at Holloman Air Force Base, New Mexico, on May 16, 1958. He was put in the hospital for three days. (See photo.)

A man who fell off a 185-foot cliff has survived a *momentary* g force of 209 in decelerating from 68 m.p.h. to stationary in 0.015 of a second.

Fastest Reflexes

The results of experiments carried out in 1943 have shown that the fastest messages transmitted by the nervous system travel at 265 m.p.h. With advancing age, impulses are carried 15 per cent more slowly.

Most Alcoholic Person

It is recorded that a hard drinker named Vanhorn (1750–1811), born in London, England, averaged more than four bottles of ruby port per day for 23 years prior to his death at 61. He is believed to have emptied 35,688 bottles.

Most Durable "Ghosts"

Ghosts are not immortal and, according to the *Gazetteer of British Ghosts*, seem to deteriorate after 400 years. The most outstanding exception to their normal "half-life" is the ghost of a Roman centurion that still reportedly haunts Strood, Mersea Island, Essex, England, after 15½ centuries. The book's author, Peter Underwood, states that Britain has more reported ghosts per square mile than any other country with Borley Rectory near Long Melford, Suffolk, the site of unrivaled activity between 1863 and its destruction by fire in 1939.

MIGHTIEST MEMBER of the animal kingdom: The blue whale is probably the largest animal that ever lived.

Chapter Two

THE ANIMAL AND PLANT KINGDOMS

ANIMAL KINGDOM (ANIMALIA)

Largest and Heaviest Animal

The largest and heaviest animal in the world, and probably the biggest creature which has *ever* existed, is the blue or sulphur-bottom whale (*Balaenoptera musculus*), also called Sibbald's rorqual. The largest accurately measured specimen on record was a female taken near the South Shetland Islands, off Scotland, in March, 1926, which measured 109 feet 4¼ inches in length. Another female measuring 96¾ feet brought into the shore station at Prince Olaf, South Georgia, Falkland Islands, off Argentina, in *c*. 1931 was calculated to have weighed 183.34 tons, inclusive of blood, judging by the number of cookers that were filled by the animal's blubber, meat and bones. The total weight of the whale was believed to have been 195 tons. On the principle that the weight should vary as the cube of the linear dimensions, a 100-foot blue whale in good condition should weigh about 179 tons, but in the case of pregnant females the weight could be as much as 200 or more tons.

Longest Animal

The longest animal ever recorded is the giant jellyfish (*Cyanea arctica*), which is found in the northwest Atlantic Ocean. One specimen washed up on the coast of Massachusetts, *c*. 1865, had a bell 7½ feet in diameter and tentacles measuring 120 feet, thus giving a theoretical tentacular span of some 245 feet.

Tallest Animal

The tallest living animal is the giraffe (*Giraffa camelopardalis*), which is now found only in the dry savannah and semi-desert areas of Africa south of the Sahara. The tallest ever recorded was a Masai bull (*G. camelopardalis tippelskirchi*) shot in Kenya before 1930 which measured 19 feet 3 inches between pegs (tip of forehoof to tip of "false" horn with neck erect) and must have stood about 19 feet when alive. Less credible heights of up to 23 feet have been claimed.

Longest-Lived Animal

Few creatures live longer than humans. It would appear that tortoises are the longest-lived animals. The greatest authentic age recorded for a tortoise is 152-plus years for a male Marion's tortoise (*Testudo sumeirii*), brought from the Seychelles to Mauritius in 1766 by the Chevalier de Fresne, who presented it to the Port Louis army garrison. This specimen (it went blind in 1908) was accidentally killed in 1918. When the famous Royal Tongan tortoise "Tu'malilia" (believed to be a specimen of *Testudo radiata*) died on May 19, 1966, it was reputed to be over 200 years old, having been presented to the then King of Tonga by Captain James Cook (1728–79) on October 22, 1773, but this record lacks proper documentation.

Smallest Animal

The smallest of all free-living organisms are pleuropneumonia-like organisms (P.P.L.O.) of the *Mycoplasma*. One of these, *Mycoplasma laidlawii*, first discovered in sewage in 1936, has a diameter during its early existence of only 100 millimicrons, or 0.000004 of an inch.

Fastest Animal

The fastest reliably measured speed of any animal is 106.25 m.p.h. for a spine-tailed swift (*Chaetura caudacuta*), reported from the U.S.S.R. in 1942. In 1934, ground speeds ranging from 171.8 to 219.5 m.p.h. were recorded by stop-watch for spine-tailed swifts over a 2-mile course in the Cachar Hills of northeastern India, but scientific tests since have revealed that this species of bird cannot be seen at a distance of 1 mile, even with standard binoculars. This bird is the fastest moving living creature and has a blood temperature of 112.5°F. Speeds even higher than a free-fall maximum of 185 m.p.h. have been ascribed to peregrine falcons (*Falco peregrinus*) in a stoop, but in recent experiments in which miniature air speedometers were fitted, the maximum recorded diving speed was 82 m.p.h.

Rarest Animal

The best claimant to the title of the world's rarest land animal is probably the tenrec, *Dasogale fontoynonti*, which is known only from the type specimen collected in eastern Madagascar and now preserved in the Paris (France) Museum of Natural History.

The pygmy opossum, believed to have been extinct for 20,000 years until a single example was caught in 1966, is no longer the rarest, as three more specimens have been discovered in Australia.

Commonest Animal

It is estimated that man shares the earth with 3×10^{33} (or 3 followed by 33 zeros) other living things. Of these, more than 75 per cent are bacteria, which scientists no longer classify as animals, but as protista.

Fastest Growth

The fastest growth in the animal kingdom is that of the blue whale calf. A barely visible ovum weighing 0.000035 of an ounce grows to a weight of *c.* 29 tons in 22¾ months, made up of 10¾ months gestation and the first 12 months of age. This is equivalent to an increase of 30,000 million fold.

Largest Egg

The largest egg of any living animal is that of the whale-shark (*Rhineodon typus*). One egg case measuring 12 inches by 5.5 inches by 3.5 inches was picked up by the shrimp trawler "Doris" on June 29, 1953, at a depth of 186 feet in the Gulf of Mexico, 130 miles south of Port Isabel, Texas. The egg contained a perfect embryo of a whale-shark 13.78 inches long.

Greatest Size Difference Between Sexes

The largest female deep-sea angler fish of the species *Ceratias holboelki* on record weighed half a million times as much as the smallest known parasitic male. It has been suggested that this fish would make an appropriate emblem for Women's Lib.

Largest Eye

The giant squid *Architeuthis* sp. has the largest eye of any living animal. The ocular diameter may exceed 15 inches, compared to 3.93 to 4.71 inches for the largest blue whale.

1. Mammals *(Mammalia)*

Largest on Land. The largest living land animal is the African bush elephant (*Loxodonta africana africana*). The average adult bull stands 10 feet 6 inches at the shoulder and weighs 6½ tons. The largest specimen ever recorded was a bull shot 48 miles northwest of Macusso, Angola, on November 13, 1955. Lying on its side this elephant measured 13 feet 2 inches in a projected line from the highest point of the shoulder to the base of the forefoot, indicating that its standing height must have been about 12 feet 6 inches. Other measurements included an over-all length of 33 feet 2 inches (tip of extended trunk to tip of extended tail) and a maximum bodily girth of 19 feet 8 inches. The weight was estimated at 24,000 lbs. On March 6, 1959, the mounted specimen was put on display in the rotunda of the Smithsonian Institution in Washington, D.C. (see also Shooting, Chapter 12).

Another outsized bull elephant known as "Zhulamati" (Taller than the Trees), reputed to stand over 12 feet at the shoulder, was shot in southeastern Rhodesia in 1967 in mysterious circumstances.

Largest and Heaviest is the blue whale (see page 48). One whale, a female taken by the *Slava* whaling fleet of the U.S.S.R. in the Antarctic on March 17, 1947, measured 90 feet 8 inches in

LARGEST LAND ANIMAL: This African bull elephant, standing 13 feet 2 inches at the shoulder and weighing 12 tons, was shot in Angola in 1955, and is now preserved in the Smithsonian Institution, Washington, D.C.

length. Its tongue and heart weighed 4.73 tons and 1,540 lbs. respectively.

Blue whales inhabit the colder seas and migrate to warmer waters in winter for breeding. Observations made in the Antarctic in 1947–8 showed that a blue whale can maintain speeds of 20 knots (23 m.p.h.) for 10 minutes when frightened. This means a 90-foot blue whale traveling at 20 knots would develop 520 horsepower. The young measure up to 28.5 feet long at birth and weigh up to 3.1 tons.

It has been estimated that there were about 100,000 blue whales living throughout the oceans in 1930, but that less than 7,500 survived (6,500 of them in the Southern Hemisphere) in 1971.

The greatest recorded depth to which a whale has dived is 620 fathoms (3,720 feet) by a 47-foot bull sperm whale (*Physeter catodon*) found with his jaw entangled with a submarine cable running between Santa Elena, Ecuador, and Chorillos, Peru, on October 14, 1955. At this depth the whale withstood a pressure of 1,680 lbs. per square inch.

On August 25, 1969, a sperm whale was killed 100 miles south of Durban, South Africa, after it had surfaced from a dive lasting 1 hour 52 minutes, and inside its stomach were found two small sharks which had been swallowed about an hour earlier. These were later identified as *Scymnodon sp.*, a species found only on the sea floor. At this point from land the depth of water is in excess of 1,646 fathoms (10,476 feet) for a radius of 30–40 miles, which now suggests that the sperm whale sometimes may descend to a depth of over 10,000 feet when seeking food.

Tallest is the giraffe (see page 49).

Smallest. The smallest recorded mammal is Savi's white-toothed pygmy shrew (*Suncus etruscus*), also called the Etruscan shrew, which is found along the coasts of the northern Mediterranean and southwards to Cape Province, South Africa. Mature specimens have a body length of only 1.32–2.04 inches, a tail length of 0.94–1.14 inches, and weigh between 0.062 and 0.09 oz.

The smallest totally marine mammal is the sea otter (*Enhydra lutris*), which is found in coastal waters off California, western Alaska and islands in the Bering Sea. Adult specimens measure 47.24–61.5 inches in total length, and weigh 55–81.4 lbs.

Fastest. The fastest of all land animals over a short distance (*i.e.* up to 600 yards) is the cheetah or hunting leopard (*Acinonyx jubatus*) of the open plains of East Africa, Iran, Turkmenia and Afghanistan, with a probable maximum speed of 60–63 m.p.h. over suitably level ground. Speeds of 71, 84 and even 90 m.p.h. have been claimed for this animal, but these figures must be considered exaggerated. Tests in London in 1937 showed that· on an oval greyhound track over 345 yards a female cheetah's average speed over three runs was 43.4 m.p.h. (compare with 43.26 m.p.h. for the fastest race horse), but this specimen was not running at its best.

The fastest land animal over a sustained distance (*i.e.* 1,000 yards or more) is the pronghorn antelope (*Antilocapra americana*) of the western United States. Specimens have been observed to travel at 35 m.p.h. for 4 miles, at 42 m.p.h. for 1 mile and 55 m.p.h. for half a mile. On August 14, 1936, at Spanish Lake, Lake County, Oregon, a hard-pressed buck was timed by a car speedometer at 61 m.p.h. over 200 yards.

Slowest. The slowest moving land mammal is the ai or three-toed sloth (*Bradypus tridactylus*) of tropical America. The usual ground speed is 6 to 8 feet a minute (0.068 to 0.098 m.p.h.), but one mother sloth, speeded up by the calls of her infant, was observed to cover 14 feet in one minute (0.155 m.p.h.). In the trees, this speed may be increased to 2 feet a second (1.36 m.p.h.). (Compare these figures with the 0.03 m.p.h. of the common garden snail and the 0.17 m.p.h. of the giant tortoise.)

Rarest Mammal is the tenrec, *Dasogale fontoynonti* (see page 50).

The rarest placental mammal in the world is now probably the Javan rhinoceros (*Rhinoceros sondaicus*). In mid-1970, there were an estimated 28 in the Udjung-Kulon reserve of 117 square miles at the tip of western Java, Indonesia. There may also be a few in the Tenasserim area on the Thai-Burmese border. Among subspecies, there are believed to be only a dozen specimens of the Javan tiger (*Leo tigris sondaica*) left in the wild, all of them in eastern Java.

The rarest marine mammals are the three species which have been recorded only once. These are: Hose's Sarawak dolphin (*Lagenodelphis hosei*), which is known only from the type specimen collected at the mouth of the Lutong River, Barama, Borneo in 1895; the New Zealand beaked whale (*Tasmacetus shepherdi*), which is known only from the type specimen cast up on Ohawe Beach, New Zealand, in 1936; and Longman's beaked whale (*Mesoplodon pacificus*), which is known only from a skull discovered on a Queensland beach in 1926.

Longest-Lived. No mammal can match the extreme proven age of 113 years attained by man (*Homo sapiens*). It is probable that the closest approach is over 90 years by the killer whale (*Orcinus orca*). A bull with distinctive markings, known as "Old Tom," was observed every winter from 1843 to 1930, in Twofold Bay, Eden, New South Wales, Australia.

The longest-lived land mammal, excluding man, is probably the Asiatic elephant (*Elephas maximus*). The greatest age that has been verified with reasonable certainty is an estimated 69 years in the case of a female named "Jessie," who was taken in 1882 to the Taronga Zoological Park in Sydney, Australia, where she had to be destroyed, on September 26, 1939, after developing abscesses on her feet, which eventually made walking impossible. Her age on arrival was probably 12, but may have been as high as 20 years. An elephant's age is indicated by the persistence of its teeth, which generally wear out around the 50–55th year.

Highest Living. The highest-living mammal in the world is probably the yak (*Poephagus grunniens*), the wild ox of Tibet, which has occasionally been found at an altitude of 20,000 feet in the Himalayas.

Largest Herd. The largest herds on record were those of the South African Springbok (*Antidorcas marsupialis*) during migration in the 19th century. In 1849, Sir John Fraser of Bloemfontein reported seeing a herd that took three days to pass through the settlement of Beaufort West, Cape Province. Another herd seen in the same province in 1888 was estimated to contain 100,000,000 head.

Longest and Shortest Gestation Periods. The longest of all mammalian gestation periods is that of the Asiatic elephant (*Elephas maximus*), with an average of 609 days (or just over 20 months) and a maximum of 760 days (2 years and 30 days)—more than $2\frac{1}{2}$ times that of a human.

The shortest gestation period is that of the American opossum (*Didelphis marsupialis*), also called the Virginian opossum, normally 12 to 13 days, but it may be as short as 8 days.

The gestation periods of the rare water opossum or Yapok (*Chironectes minimus*) of central and northern South America (average 12–13 days) and the Eastern native cat (*Dasyurus viverrinus*) of Australia (average 12 days) may also be as short as 8 days.

Largest Litter. The greatest recorded number of young born to a wild mammal at a single birth is 32 (not all of which survived), in the case of the common tenrec (*Centetes ecaudatus*), found in Madagascar and the Comoro Islands. The average litter is 13 to 14.

In March, 1961, a litter of 32 was also reported for a house mouse (*Mus musculus*) at the Roswell Park Memorial Institute in Buffalo, N.Y. (average litter size 13–21). (See also Chapter 7, prolificacy records—pigs.)

Fastest Breeder. The streaked tenrec (*Hemicentetes semispinosus*) of Madagascar is weaned after only 5 days, and females are capable of breeding 3–4 weeks after birth.

Heaviest Brain. The sperm whale (*Physeter catadon*) has the heaviest brain of all living animals. The brain of a 49-foot-long bull processed aboard the Japanese factory ship, *Nissin Maru No. 1* in the Antarctic on December 11, 1949, weighed 9,200 grams (20.24 lbs.), compared to 6,900 grams (15.38 lbs.) for a 90-foot blue whale. The heaviest brain recorded for an elephant is 16.5 lbs. in the case of an Asiatic bull.

Longest Hibernation. The common dormouse (*Glis glis*) spends more time in hibernation than any other mammal. The hibernation

MOST PROLIFIC MAMMAL: The streaked tenrec gives birth after 5 days. Another species of tenrec (see page 50) is the world's rarest mammal.

usually lasts between 5 and 6 months (October to April), but there is a record of an English specimen sleeping for 6 months 23 days without interruption.

Carnivores

Largest. The largest living terrestrial member of the order Carnivora is the Kodiak bear (*Ursus arctos middendorffi*) of Alaska. The average adult male has a nose-to-tail length of 8 feet and weighs 1,050–1,175 lbs. In 1894, a weight of 1,656 lbs. was recorded for a male shot at English Bay, Kodiak Island, whose *stretched* skin measured 13 feet 6 inches overall. This weight was exceeded by a male in the Cheyenne Mountain Zoological Park, Colorado Springs, which scaled 1,670 lbs. at the time of its death on September 22, 1955.

The Peninsular brown bear (*Ursus arctos gyas*), also found in Alaska, is almost as large, adult males measuring $7\frac{3}{4}$ feet nose-to-tail length and weighing about 1,100 lbs. A specimen 10 feet long, with an estimated weight of between 1,600 and 1,700 lbs. was shot near Cold Bay, Alaska, on May 28, 1948.

Weights in excess of 1,600 lbs. have also been reported for the male polar bear (*Ursus maritimus*), which has an average nose-to-tail length of $7\frac{3}{4}$ feet and weighs 850-900 lbs. In 1960, a polar bear allegedly weighing 2,210 lbs. was shot at the polar entrance to Kotzebue Sound, northwest Alaska. In April, 1962, the mounted specimen, measuring 11 feet $1\frac{1}{2}$ inches, was put on display at the Seattle World's Fair. (See photo, page 57.)

The largest toothed mammal ever recorded is the sperm whale (*Physeter catodon*), also called the cachalot. The average adult bull is 47 feet long and weighs about 37 tons. The largest specimen ever to be measured accurately was a bull 67 feet 11 inches long, captured off the Kuril Islands in the northwest Pacific by a U.S.S.R. whaler during the summer of 1950. The whale was not weighed but it must have scaled 87 tons.

A measurement of 68 feet was credited for a bull killed 60 miles west of the Shetland Islands, north of Scotland, on June 25, 1903, and landed at the Norrona whaling station. The measurement, however, was made over the curve of the body and not in a straight line. In the summer of 1948 a bull with an alleged length of 90 feet was killed off the northwestern coast of Vancouver Island, British Columbia, Canada, and brought into Nanaimo. Later, however, the length was amended to 56 feet.

Rarest. The rarest land carnivore is probably the Mexican grizzly bear (*Ursus nilsoni*), of which no more than 20–30 survive in a small patch of territory about 50 miles north of Chihuahua.

Smallest. The smallest living toothed carnivore is the least weasel (*Mustela rixosa*), also called the dwarf weasel, which is circumpolar in distribution. Four races are recognized, the smallest of which is the *M. r. pygmaea* of Siberia. Mature specimens have an overall length (including tail) of 6.96–8.14 inches and weigh between $1\frac{1}{4}$ and $2\frac{1}{2}$ oz.

Largest Feline. The largest member of the cat family (Felidae) is the long-furred Siberian tiger (*Leo tigris altaica*), also known as the Amur or Manchurian tiger. Adult males average 10 feet 4 inches in length (nose to tip of extended tail), stand 39–42 inches at the shoulder, and weigh about 585 lbs. The heaviest specimen on record was one shot by a German hunter near the Amur river in *c.* 1933 which weighed 770 lbs. In 1970, the total wild population, now strictly protected, was estimated at 160–170 animals.

The average adult African lion (*Leo leo*) measures 9 feet overall, stands 36–38 inches at the shoulder, and weighs 400–410 lbs. The heaviest recorded specimen found in the wild was one weighing 690 lbs., shot near Hectorspruit, in the eastern Transvaal, South Africa, in 1936. In 1953, an 18-year-old liger (a lion-tigress hybrid) at the Zoological Gardens, Bloemfontein, South Africa, was weighed at 750 lbs. In July, 1970, a weight of 826 lbs. was reported for an 11-year-old black-maned lion named "Simba" at the Colchester Zoo, Essex, England.

Smallest Feline. The smallest member of the cat family is the rusty-spotted cat (*Felis rubiginosa*) of southern India and Ceylon. The average adult male has an overall length of 25–28 inches (tail 9–10 inches) and weighs about 3 lbs.

Pinnipeds (Seals, Sea Lions and Walruses)

Largest. The largest of the 32 known species of pinnipeds is the southern elephant seal (*Mirounga leonina*) which inhabits the sub-Antarctic islands. Adult bulls average 16½ feet in length (snout to tip of tail), 12 feet in girth and weigh 5,000 lbs. The largest specimen on record was a bull killed in Possession Bay, South Georgia, on February 28, 1913, which measured *c.* 22½ feet in length or 21 feet 4 inches after flensing and weighed at least 9,000 lbs. There are old records of bulls measuring 25, 27 and even 35 feet, but all lack confirmation. A length of 22 feet has been reported in 1870 for the northern elephant seal (*Mirounga angustirostris*), killed on Santa Barbara Island, California, but this measurement may have been made over the curve of the body. Adult bulls average 14 feet in length. The largest elephant seal ever held in captivity is believed to have been "Goliath," a bull of the southern race, received at Carl Hagenbeck's Tierpark, Hamburg-Stellingen, Germany, in 1928 from South Georgia (now the U.S.S.R.), who measured 20½ feet in length and weighed over 6,700 lbs. at the time of his death in 1930.

Smallest. The smallest pinniped is the Baikal seal (*Pusa sibrica*) of Lake Baikal, a large fresh-water lake near Irkutsk in southern Siberia, U.S.S.R. Adult specimens measure about 4 feet 6 inches from nose to tail and weigh about 140 lbs.

Fastest and Deepest. The highest speed measured for a pinniped is 25 m.p.h. for a California sea lion (*Zalophus californianus*). It was reported in March, 1966, that a dive of 1,968 feet had been recorded by a depth gauge attached to a Weddell seal (*Laptonychotes weddelli*) which stayed under water for 43 minutes 20 seconds in McMurdo Sound, Antarctica. The seal withstood a pressure of 875 lbs. per square inch of body area. The harp seal (*Pagophilus groenlandicus*) also called the Greenland seal, may also dive deeper than 1,000 feet.

HEAVIEST POLAR BEAR: This 2,210-lb. specimen, 11 feet 1½ inches tall, was displayed at the Seattle World's Fair.

HEAVIEST OF CAT FAMILY: "Simba," 11-year-old black lion, weighed 826 lbs. in 1970.

Longest-Lived. A female gray seal (*Halichoerus grypus*) shot at Shenni Wick on Shetland Island, Scotland, on April 23, 1969, was believed to be at least 46 years old, based on a count of dental annuli.

Rarest. The Caribbean or West Indies monk seal (*Monachus tropicalis*) was last seen on the beach of Isla Mujeres off the Yucatan Peninsula, Mexico, in 1962, and is now believed to be on the verge of extinction. Of sub-species, the Japanese sea lion (*Zalophus californianus japonicus*), formerly widespread in the Japanese archipelago, probably became extinct in the early 1950's.

Bats

Largest. The only flying mammals are bats (order Chiroptera), of which there are about 1,000 living species. The bat with the greatest wing span is *Pteropus niger*, also called the kalong, a fruit bat found in Indonesia. It has a wing span of up to 5 feet 7 inches and weighs up to 31.7 oz. Some unmeasured specimens of *Pteropus neohibernicus*, another fruit bat, which is found in New Guinea, may possibly reach 6 feet in wing span.

Smallest. The smallest species of bat is *Pipistrellus nanulus*, found in West Africa. It has a wing span of about 6 inches and a length of 2½ inches, of which one inch is tail. Its average weight is about 0.088 of an ounce. It rivals the Etruscan pygmy shrew (*Suneus etruscus*) for the title of *Smallest Living Mammal*.

Fastest. The greatest speed attributed to a bat is 32 m.p.h. in the case of a free-tailed or guano bat (*Tadarida mexicana*) which flew 31 miles in 58 minutes. This speed is closely matched by the noctule bat (*Nyctalus noctula*) and the long-winged bat (*Miniopterus schreibersi*), both of which have been timed at 31 m.p.h.

Longest-Lived. The greatest age reliably reported for a bat is "at least 24 years" for a female little brown bat (*Myotis lucifugus*) found on April 30, 1960, in a cave on Mount Aeolis, East Dorset, Vermont. It had been banded at a summer colony in Mashpee, Massachusetts, on June 22, 1937.

Highest Detectable Pitch. Because of their ultrasonic echolocation bats have the most acute hearing in the animal world. Vampire bats (*Desmodontidae*) and fruit bats (*Pteropodidae*) can hear frequencies as high as 150,000 cycles per second (compare with 15,000 cycles per second for the average adult human).

Primates

Largest. The largest living primate is the eastern lowland gorilla (*Gorilla gorilla graueri*), which inhabits the lowlands of the eastern part of the Upper Congo (Zaïre) and southwestern Uganda. An average adult bull stands 5 feet 8 inches tall, measures 58–60 inches around the chest and weighs 360–400 lbs. The average adult female stands about 4 feet 7 inches and weighs 170–210 lbs. The greatest height (crown to heel) reliably recorded for a gorilla is 6 feet 2 inches for a bull of the mountain race (*Gorilla g. beringei*) shot in the eastern Congo in c. 1921. The heaviest gorilla ever kept in captivity was a bull of the mountain race named "Mbongo,"

LARGEST MONKEY:
The mandrill of West Africa weighs up to 119 lbs. and may grow to 3 feet in height.

who died in San Diego Zoological Gardens, on March 15, 1942. During an attempt to weigh him shortly before his death, the platform scales "fluctuated from 645 pounds to nearly 670." This specimen measured 5 feet 7½ inches in height and 69 inches around the chest.

Smallest. The smallest known primate is the lesser mouse lemur (*Microcebus murinus*) of Madagascar. Adult specimens have a head and body length of 4.9–5.9 inches and a tail of about the same length. The weight varies from 1.58 to 2.99 oz.

Longest-Lived. The greatest irrefutable age reported for a primate (excluding humans) is 50 years 3 months for a male chimpanzee (*Pan troglodytes*) named "Heine" of Lincoln Park Zoological Gardens, Chicago. He arrived there on June 10, 1924, when about 3 years of age, and died on September 10, 1971.

Strength. "Boma," a 165-lb. male chimpanzee at the Bronx Zoo, New York City, in 1924 recorded a right-handed pull (feet braced) of 847 lbs. on a dynamometer (compare with 210 lbs. for a man of the same weight). On another occasion an adult female chimpanzee named "Suzette" (estimated weight 135 lbs.) at the same zoo registered a right-handed pull of 1,260 lbs. while in a rage.

Largest and Smallest Monkeys. The largest monkey is the mandrill (*Mandrillus sphinx*) of equatorial West Africa, weighing up to 119 lbs., with a total length of 36 inches, plus tail of 3 inches. Unconfirmed weights of up to 130 lbs. have been reported.

The smallest monkey is the pygmy marmoset (*Cebuella pygmaea*) of Ecuador, northern Peru and western Brazil. Mature specimens have a maximum total length of 12 inches, half of which is tail, and weigh 1.7 to 2.81 oz. which means it rivals the mouse lemur for the title of *Smallest Living Primate*.

LARGEST INSECT-EATING MAMMAL: The moon rat (left) of Thailand and Malaysia grows to more than 27 inches. SMALLEST ANTELOPE (right) is the Royal Antelope of West Africa, which stands only 10 inches high at the shoulder.

Rarest. The rarest monkey is the hairy-eared mouse lemur (*Cheirogaleus trichotis*) of Madagascar, which was known, until fairly recently, only from a type specimen and two skins. However, in 1966 a live one was found on the east coast near Mananara.

Most and Least Intelligent. Of sub-human primates, chimpanzees appear to have the most superior intelligence. Lemurs have less learning ability than any monkey or ape, and in some tests, are inferior to dogs and even pigeons.

Longest-Lived Monkey. The greatest reliable age reported for a monkey is *c.* 46 years for a male mandrill (*Mandrillus sphinx*) named "George" of London Zoological Gardens, who died on March 4, 1916.

Rodents

Largest. The world's largest rodent is the capybara (*Hydrochoerus hydrocharis*), also called the carpincho or water hog, which is found in tropical South America. Mature specimens have a head and body length of $3\frac{1}{4}$ to $4\frac{1}{2}$ feet and weigh up to 150 lbs.

Smallest. The smallest rodent is the Old World harvest mouse (*Micromys minutus*), of which some forms weigh between 4.2 and 10.2 grams (0.15 to 0.36 of an ounce) and measure up to 5.3 inches long, including the tail. It was announced in June, 1965, that an even smaller rodent had been discovered in the Asian part of the U.S.S.R., probably a more diminutive form of *M. minutus*, but further information is lacking.

Rarest. The rarest rodent in the world is believed to be the James Island rice rat (*Oryzomys swarthi*). Four were collected on this island in the Galápagos group in the eastern Pacific Ocean in 1906. The next trace was a skull of a recently dead specimen found in January, 1966.

Longest-Lived. The greatest reliable age reported for a rodent is 22 years for an Indian crested porcupine (*Hystrix indica*) which died in Trivandrum Zoological Gardens, southwestern India, in 1942.

Insectivores

Largest. The largest insectivore (insect-eating mammal) is the moon rat (*Echinosorex gymnurus*) also known as Raffles gymnure, found in Burma, Thailand, Malaysia, Sumatra and Borneo. Mature specimens have a head and body length of 10.43–17.52 inches, a tail measuring 7.87–8.26 inches, and weigh up to 3.08 lbs.

Smallest. The smallest insectivore is Savi's white-toothed shrew (see *Smallest Mammal*).

Longest-Lived. The greatest reliable age recorded for an insectivore is 6½ years for a Haitian solenodon (*Solenodon paradoxus*) which died in Leipzig Zoological Gardens, Germany, in 1950.

Deer

Largest. The largest deer is the Alaskan moose (*Alces gigas*). A bull standing 7 feet 8 inches at the withers, and weighing 1,800 lbs., was shot in 1897 in the Yukon Territory, Canada. Unconfirmed measurements of up to 8½ feet at the withers and 2,600 lbs. have been claimed. The record antler span is 78½ inches.

Rarest. The rarest deer in the world is Fea's muntjac (*Muntiacus feae*), which is known only from two specimens collected on the borders of Tenasserim (in Burma) and Thailand.

Smallest. The smallest deer, and the smallest known ruminant, is the lesser Malayan chevrotain or mouse deer (*Tragulus javinicus*) of southeastern Asia. Adult specimens measure 8–10 inches at the shoulder and weigh 6–7 lbs.

Antelopes

Largest. The largest of all antelopes is the rare Lord Derby eland (*Taurotragus derbianus*), also called the giant eland, of west and north-central Africa, which surpasses 2,000 lbs. The common eland (*T. oryx*) of east and south Africa has the same shoulder height, of up to 70 inches, but is not quite so massive, although there is one record of a 65-inch bull being shot in Nyasaland (now Malawi) in *c.* 1937 which weighed 2,078 lbs.

Smallest. The smallest known antelope is the Royal antelope (*Neotragus pygmaeus*) of West Africa, measuring only 10 to 12 inches at the shoulder, and weighing only 7 to 8 lbs. The slenderer Swayne's dik-dik (*Madoqua swaynei*) of Somali, East Africa, when adult, stands about 13 inches at the shoulder, weighs only 5 to 6 lbs.

Rarest. The rarest antelope is probably Jentink's duiker (*Cephalopus jentinki*), also known as the black-headed duiker, which is found only in a restricted area of tropical West Africa. Its total population may be only a few dozen, or as many as a few hundred.

Tusks and Horns

Longest. The longest recorded elephant tusks (excluding prehistoric examples) are a pair from the eastern Congo (Zaïre) preserved in the National Collection of Heads and Horns, kept by

LONGEST TUSKS: Weighing 293 lbs. and measuring more than 11 feet, these elephant tusks from the Congo are in the Bronx Zoo.

the New York Zoological Society in Bronx Park, New York City. One measures 11 feet 5½ inches along the outside curve and the other measures 11 feet. Their combined weight is 293 lbs. A single tusk of 11 feet 6 inches has been reported, but details are lacking.

Heaviest. The heaviest recorded tusks are a pair in the British Museum (Natural History), London, England, which were collected from an aged bull shot at the foot of Mt. Kilimanjaro, Kenya, in 1897. They were measured in 1955, when the first was 10 feet 2½ inches long, weighing 226½ lbs., and the second 10 feet 5½ inches long, weighing 214 lbs., giving a combined weight of 440½ lbs. When fresh, these tusks are said to have exceeded their present weight by about 20 lbs.

A single tusk with an alleged weight of 258 lbs., collected in Dahomey, Western Africa, was exhibited at the Paris Exposition of 1900.

Longest Horns. The longest recorded animal horn was one measuring 81¼ inches on the outside curve, with a circumference of 18¼ inches, found on a specimen of domestic Ankole cattle (*Bos taurus*) near Lake Ngami, Botswana (formerly called Bechuanaland).

The longest horns grown by any wild animal are those of the Pamir argali (*Ovis poli*), also called Marco Polo's argali, a wild sheep found in Central Asia. One of these has been measured at 75 inches along the front curve, with a circumference of 16 inches.

The longest recorded anterior horn of a rhinoceros is one of 62¼ inches, found on a female southern race white rhinoceros (*Ceratotherium simum*) shot in South Africa *c.* 1848. The interior horn measured 22¼ inches. An unconfirmed length of 81 inches has also been once reported.

Blood Temperatures

The highest mammalian blood temperature is that of the domestic goat (*Capra hircus*) with an average of 103.8°F., and a normal range of from 101.7° to 105.3°F. The lowest mammalian blood temperature is that of the spiny anteater (*Tachyglossus aculeatus*), a monotreme found in Australia and New Guinea, with a normal range of 72° to 87°F. The blood temperature of the golden hamster (*Mesocricetus auratus*) sometimes falls as low as 38.3°F. during hibernation, and an extreme figure of 29.6°F. has been reported for a myotis bat (family Vespertilionidae) during a deep sleep.

Most Valuable Furs

The highest-priced animal pelts are those of the sea otter (*Enhydra lutris*), also known as the Kamchatka beaver, which fetched up to $2,700 each before their 55-year-long protection started in 1912. The protection ended in 1967, and at the first legal auction of sea otter pelts in Seattle, Washington, on January 31, 1968, Neiman Marcus, the famous Dallas department store, paid $9,200 for four pelts from Alaska. On January 30, 1969, a New York company paid $1,100 for an exceptionally fine pelt from Alaska.

On Feb. 26, 1969, forty selected pelts of the mink-sable crossbreed "Kojah" from the Piampiano Fur Ranch, Zion, Illinois, realized $2,700 in New York City. In May, 1970, a Kojah coat costing $125,000 was sold by Neiman Marcus to Welsh actor Richard Burton for his wife.

Ambergris

The heaviest piece of ambergris on record weighed 1,003 lbs. and was recovered from a sperm whale (*Physeter catadon*) on December 3, 1912, by a Norwegian whaling company in Australian waters. The lump was sold in London for £23,000 (then $111,780).

Marsupials

Largest. The largest of all marsupials is the red kangaroo (*Macropus rufus*) of southern and eastern Australia. Adult males or "boomers" stand 6–7 feet tall, weigh 150–175 lbs. and measure up to 8 feet 11 inches in a straight line from the nose to the tip of the extended tail. The great gray kangaroo (*Macropus giganteus*) of eastern Australia and Tasmania is almost equally large, and there is an authentic record of a boomer measuring 8 feet 8 inches from nose to tail (9 feet 7 inches along the curve of the body) and weighing 200 lbs. The skin of this specimen is preserved in the Australian Museum, Sydney, New South Wales.

Smallest. The smallest known marsupial is the Kimberley planigale (*Planigale subtilissima*), which is found only in the Kimberley district of Western Australia. Adult males have a head and body length of 1.75 inches, a tail length of 2 inches and weigh about 0.141 oz. Females are smaller than males.

Rarest. The rarest marsupial is probably the little-known thylacine or Tasmanian wolf or tiger (*Thylacinus cnyocephalus*), which is now confined to the remoter parts of Tasmania, Australia. The last thylacine kept in captivity was taken in a trapper's snare in the Florentine Valley a few miles west of Mountain Field National Park in 1933, and exhibited at Hobart Zoo, Tasmania. It died a few months later.

On January 2, 1957, it was reported that one had been kept in sight for two minutes and photographed by a helicopter pilot, Capt. J. Ferguson, on Birthday Bay Beach, 35 miles southwest of Queenstown, Tasmania. Experts, who examined the photograph, however, declared that the animal was a dog.

In 1961, a young male was accidentally killed at Sandy Cape on the west coast of Tasmania, and in December, 1966, the traces of a lair in which a female and pups had been living were found by zoologists in the boiler of a wrecked ship near Mawbanna on the west coast. On November 3, 1969, the tracks of a thylacine were positively identified in the Cradle Mountain National Park, and other definite sightings have been made since in the Cardigan River area on the northwest coast and the Tooms Lake region.

Highest and Longest Jump. The greatest measured height cleared by a hunted kangaroo is a pile of timber 10 feet 6 inches high. The longest recorded leap was reported in January, 1951, when, in the course of a chase, a female red kangaroo (*Macropus rufus*) made a series of bounds which included one of 42 feet. There is an unconfirmed report of a great gray kangaroo (*Macropus giganteus*) jumping nearly 44 feet 8½ inches on the flat.

DOMESTICATED ANIMALS

Horses and Ponies

Age. The oldest acceptable age for a horse (*Equus caballus*) is 52 years for a draught breed named "Monty," owned by Mrs. Marjorie Cooper of Albury, New South Wales, Australia, which died on January 25, 1970. His jaw is now preserved in the School of Veterinary Science at Melbourne University. He was foaled in Wodonga, New South Wales in 1917.

On November 30, 1969, a mare named "Nellie" died of a heart attack on a farm near Danville, Missouri, reputedly foaled in March, 1916, and thus aged 53½, but this claim has not yet been fully substantiated.

The greatest reliable age recorded for a pony is 54 years for a stallion owned by a farmer in central France which was still alive in 1919. In June, 1970, a Welsh pony living on a farm near Pebbles Bay, Gower Peninsula, South Wales, was reported to be 66 years old, but this claim lacks proper documentation.

Largest. The heaviest horse ever recorded was "Brooklyn Supreme," a pure-bred Belgian stallion weighing 3,200 lbs. and standing 19½ hands (6 feet 6 inches). He died on September 6, 1948, aged 20, in Callender, Iowa.

The tallest horse ever recorded was "Firpon" which stood 21 hands 1 inch (7 feet 1 inch) and weighed 2,976 lbs. He died on a ranch in Argentina on March 14, 1972.

Smallest. The smallest breed of horse are those bred by Julio

RAREST DOG (left): This is the löwchen or lion dog of which only 52 exist. OLDEST DOG (right): "Adjutant," a black Labrador gun dog, lived 27 years 3 months in England.

Falabella at the El Peludo Ranch, Argentina. Adult specimens range from under 12 inches to 42 inches at the shoulder and weigh up to 150 lbs.

The smallest breed of pony is the Shetland pony, which usually measures 8–10 hands (32–40 inches) and weighs 275–385 lbs. In March, 1969, a measurement of $3\frac{1}{2}$ hands (14 inches) was reported for a "miniature" Shetland pony named "Midnight," owned by Miss Susan Perry of Worths Circus, Melbourne, Australia.

Heaviest Load Haul. The greatest load hauled by a pair of draught horses was 50 logs comprising 36,055 board-feet of lumber (59.2 tons) hauled on the Nester Estate at Ewen, Ontonagon County, Michigan, in 1893.

Dogs

Oldest. Dogs of over 20 are very rare but even 34 years has been accepted by one authority. The oldest reliably reported dog in the world was "Adjutant," a black Labrador gun dog who was whelped on August 14, 1936, and died on November 20, 1963, aged 27 years 3 months, in the care of his lifetime owner, James Hawkes, a game-keeper at the Revesby Estate, near Boston, Lincolnshire, England. (See photo.) Less reliable is a claim of 28 years for an Irish terrier which died in 1951.

Rarest. The rarest dog in the world is the löwchen or lion dog of which only 52 (45 in Britain, 5 in West Germany, and 2 in Majorca) were reported in October, 1971. The breed was a famous lapdog of the nobility of southern Europe during the Renaissance period.

The Chinese crested dog (now extinct in China) is also extremely rare, with world population in 1971 estimated at 55 to 60.

Largest. The heaviest breed of domestic dog (*Canis familiaris*) is the St. Bernard. The heaviest example is "Schwarzwald Hot Duke" owned by Dr. A. M. Bruner of Oconomowoc, Wisconsin. He was whelped on October 8, 1964, and weighed 295 lbs. on May 2, 1969. He died in August, 1969.

Tallest. The world's tallest breed of dog is the Irish wolfhound. The extreme recorded example was "Broadbridge Michael" (born 1926), owned by Mrs. Mary Beynon, then of Sutton-at-Hone, Kent, England. He stood 39½ inches at the shoulders when aged 2 years.

Smallest. The smallest breed of dog is the Chihuahua from Mexico. New-born pups average 3½–4½ oz. and weigh 2–4 lbs. when fully grown, but some "miniature" specimens weigh only 16 oz.

In January, 1971, a full-grown white toy poodle named "Giles," owned by Mrs. Sylvia Wyse of Bucknall, Staffordshire, England, stood 4½ inches at the shoulder and weighed 13 oz. Shortly afterwards he was exported to Canada.

Fastest. The fastest breed of untrained dog is the saluki, also called the Arabian gazelle hound or Persian greyhound. Speeds up to 43 m.p.h. have been claimed, but tests in the Netherlands have shown that it is not as fast as the present day greyhound which has attained a measured speed of 41.7 m.p.h. on a track.

Largest Litter. The largest recorded litter of puppies is one of 23 thrown on February 11, 1945, by "Lena," a foxhound bitch owned by Commander W. N. Ely of Ambler, Pennsylvania.

Most Prolific. The dog who has sired the greatest recorded number of puppies was the greyhound "Low Pressure" whelped in 1957 and owned by Mrs. Bruna Amhurst of Regent's Park, London.

STRONGEST DOG: This Newfoundland named "Newfield's Nelson," pulled 3,260 lbs. 15 feet in under 90 seconds.

Before he died in November, 1969, he had fathered 2,414 registered puppies, with at least 600 others unregistered.

Most Expensive. In January, 1956, Miss Mary de Pledge, of Bracknell, Berkshire, England, turned down an offer of £10,500, then $29,400, from an American dog breeder for her 3½-year-old champion Pekingese "Caversham Ku-Ku of Yam."

The highest price ever paid for a dog is £2,000 (about $10,000 then) by Mrs. A. H. Hempton in December, 1929, for the champion greyhound "Mick the Miller" (whelped in Ireland in June, 1926, and died 1939).

"Top Dog." The greatest altitude attained by any animal is 1,050 miles by the Samoyed husky (Russian, *laika*) bitch fired as a passenger in *Sputnik II* on November 3, 1957. The dog was variously named "Kudryavka"(feminine form of Curly), "Limonchik" (diminutive of lemon), "Malyshka," "Zhuchka" or by the breed name "Laika."

Highest and Longest Jump. It has been claimed that a male Bouvier of Flanders cattle dog weighing 140 lbs. has been trained to scale a 16-foot-high wall at Stormville, New York, in 1971.

Strongest. The greatest load ever shifted by a dog was 3,260 lbs. pulled over 15 feet in under 90 secs. in accordance with international rules by a champion Newfoundland dog named "Newfield's Nelson," owned by Mr. and Mrs. Allen A. Wolman, aged 6½ and weighing 164 lbs. on October 10, 1970, at Bethell, Washington.

In the annual 15-mile dog sled race at Whitehorse, Yukon Territory, Canada, the record time was set by a driver named Charlie in 1967 at 59 min. 33 secs.

Ratting. James Searle's bull terrier bitch "Jenny Lind" killed 500 rats in 1 hour 30 minutes at "The Beehive" in Liverpool, England, in 1853.

Tracking. The greatest tracking feat recorded was performed by the Doberman *Sauer*, trained by Detective-Sergeant Herbert Kruger. In 1925, he tracked a stock thief 100 miles across the Great Karroo, South Africa, by scent alone. In January, 1969, a German shepherd bitch was reported to have followed her master 745 miles from Brindisi to Milan, Italy, in four months. The owner had left her when he went on a visit. A German shepherd's sense of smell is one million times better than man's.

Cats

Heaviest. The heaviest domestic cat (*Felis catus*) reliably recorded was Gigi, which died in Cumberland, England, in 1972, and weighed 42 lbs. in July, 1970. A U.S. report of a 48-lb. cat is unconfirmed.

Oldest. The oldest cat ever recorded was the tabby "Puss," owned by Mrs. T. Holway of Clayhidon, North Devon, England. He was 36 on November 28, 1939. A more recent and better documented case was that of the female tabby "Ma," owned by Mrs. Alice St. George Moore, of Drewsteignton, Devon, England. She was put to sleep on November 5, 1957, aged 34.

According to the American Feline Society, a cat living in Hazleton, Pennsylvania, celebrated its 37th birthday on November 1,

1958, but it was later discovered that two or more cats were involved.

Largest Litter. The largest litter ever recorded was one of 13 kittens born on April 13, 1969, to "Boccaccio Blue Danielle," a one-year-old blue-pointed Siamese cat owned by Mrs. Helen J. Coward of Klemzig, South Australia. The usual litter size is between 5 and 9. On April 30, 1971, a litter of 13 (11 stillborn) was also reported for a 9-month-old black cat named "Spur," owned by Mrs. Grace Sutherland of London, England. In July, 1970, a litter of 19 kittens (four incompletely formed) was reportedly born by Caesarean section to "Tarawood Antigone," a brown Burmese owned by Mrs. Valerie Gane of Oxfordshire, England, but this claim has not yet been fully substantiated. The litter was stated to have been the result of a mismating with a half Siamese.

Most Prolific. A cat named "Dusty," aged 17, living in Bonham, Texas, gave birth to her 420th kitten on June 12, 1952.

Greatest Fall. "Fat Olive" was reported by Mrs. Pat Lazaroff of Toronto, Canada, to have survived a fall on grass from a 160-foot-high penthouse on July 18, 1972. He (a tomcat) only broke two legs.

Most Lives. "Thumper," a 2½-year-old tabby owned by Mrs. Reg Buckett of Westminster, London, was trapped in an elevator shaft without food or water for 52 days from March 29, 1964.

Richest. Dr. William Grier of San Diego, California, died in June, 1963, leaving his entire estate of $415,000 to his two 15-year-old cats, "Hellcat" and "Brownie." When the cats died in 1965 the money went to George Washington University, Washington, D.C.

Most Valuable. In 1967, Miss Elspeth Sellar of Bromley, England, turned down an offer of 2,000 guineas (then $5,880) from an American breeder for her 2-year-old champion white Persian tom, "Coylum Marcus" (born March 28, 1965).

Ratting. A 5-month-old tabby kitten named "Peter" living at Stonehouse railway station, Gloucestershire, England, killed 400 rats during a 4-week period in June–July, 1938. Many of the kitten's victims seemed almost as large as itself. The greatest mouser on record was a tabby named "Mickey," owned by Shepherd & Sons Ltd. of Burscough, Lancashire, England, which killed more than 22,000 mice during 23 years with the firm. He died in November, 1968.

Cat Population. The largest cat population is in the U.S.— 28 million. Of Britain's cat population of 6 million, an estimated 100,000 are "employed" by the civil service.

Rabbits

The largest breed of rabbit (*Oryctolagus cuniculus*) is the Flemish giant, with a weight of 12–14 lbs. This breed measures up to 36 inches long from toe to toe, when fully extended. The heaviest specimen recorded was a male named "Floppy," who weighed 25 lbs. shortly before dying in June, 1963, aged 8. In May, 1971, a weight of 25 lbs. was also reported for a 4-year-old Norfolk Star named

"Chewer," owned by Edward Williams of Attleborough, Norfolk, England.

Oldest. The greatest reliable age recorded for a domestic rabbit is 18 years for a doe which was still alive in 1947.

Most Prolific. The most prolific domestic breed is the Norfolk Star. Females produce 9 to 10 litters a year, each containing about 10 young (compare with 5 litters and 3 to 7 young for the wild rabbit).

For auction prices, milk yield and prolificacy records for cattle, sheep and pigs, see Agriculture, Chapter 7.

2. Birds (Aves)

Largest. Of the 8,600 known living species, by far the largest is the North African ostrich (*Struthio camelus camelus*) which lives south of the Atlas Mountains from Upper Senegal and Niger country across to the Sudan and central Ethiopia. Male examples of this flightless or *ratite* bird reach 345 lbs. in weight and stand 9 feet tall.

The heaviest flying bird, or *carinate*, is the Kori bustard or paauw (*Otis kori*), which has a wing span up to 8 feet 4 inches. Cock birds weighing up to 40 lbs. have been shot in South Africa, and one enormously fat specimen, killed in Transvaal in *c.* 1892, was estimated to weigh 54 lbs. The mute swan (*Cygnus olor*) also exceeds 40 lbs. on occasion, and there is a record from Poland of a cob weighing 49.5 lbs.

The heaviest flying bird of prey is the Andean condor (*Vultur gryphus*). Adult males average 20–25 lbs., but one specimen shot on San Gallan Island off the coast of Peru in 1919 weighed 26½ lbs.

Smallest. The smallest bird in the world is the bee hummingbird (*Mellisuga helenae*), also known as Helena's hummingbird or "the fairy hummer," found in Cuba. An average male adult has a wing span of 1.11 inches and weighs only 2 grams or 1/18th of an ounce (0.070 oz.). This is less than a Sphinx moth. It has an overall length of 2.28 inches, the bill and tail accounting for about 1.6 inches. The adult females are slightly larger. The bee hummingbird (*Acestrura bombus*) of Ecuador is about the same size, but is slightly heavier.

Largest Wing Span. The wandering albatross (*Diomedea exulans*) of the southern oceans has the largest wing span of any bird, adult males averaging 10 feet 2 inches with wings tightly stretched. The largest recorded specimen was a male measuring 11 feet 10 inches caught by banders in Western Australia in *c.* 1957, but some unmeasured birds may exceed 12 feet. This size is closely matched by the Andean condor (*Vultur gryphus*). Adult males commonly have a wing span of 9 feet 3 inches, and some specimens exceed 11 feet. One bird killed in southern Peru in *c.* 1714 was alleged to have had a wing span of 12 feet 3 inches, but this measurement must be regarded as excessive. In extreme cases the wing span of the marabou stork (*Leptoptilus crumeniferus*) may also exceed 10 feet (average span 9 feet), and there is an unconfirmed record of 13 feet 4 inches for

BIRD WITH LARGEST WING SPAN: The marabou stork has a wing span of 9 feet or more—with an unconfirmed record 13 feet 4 inches. This specimen was shot in Central Africa in the 1930's.

a specimen shot in Central Africa in the 1930's. In August, 1939, a wing span of 12 feet was recorded for a mute swan (*Cygnus olor*) named "Guardsman" (died 1945) at the famous swannery at Abbotsbury, Dorset, England. The average span is 8½–9 feet.

Most Abundant. The most abundant of all birds is the chicken, the domesticated form of the wild red jungle fowl (*Gallus gallus*) of southeast Asia. There are believed to be about 3,500,000,000 chickens in the world, or nearly one chicken for every member of the human race.

The most abundant wild bird is believed to be the starling (*Sturnus vulgaris*), with an estimated world population of well over 1,000,000,000. The most abundant and also the smallest of all sea birds is Wilson's petrel (*Oceanites oceanicus*), being only 7 inches long. It is found as far south as Antarctica.

The most abundant species of bird ever recorded was the passenger pigeon (*Ectopistes migratoria*) of North America. It has been estimated that there were between 5,000,000,000 to 9,000,000,000 of this species before *c.* 1840. Thereafter the birds were killed in vast numbers and the last recorded specimen died in the Zoological Gardens in Cincinnati, on September 1, 1914. This bird, a female named "Mertha," aged 12, was mounted and is now on exhibition in the Smithsonian Institution, Washington, D.C.

Rarest. Perhaps the best claimants to this title would be the ten species last seen in the 19th century, but still just possibly extant. They are the New Caledonian lorikeet (*Vini diadema*) (New Caledonia *ante* 1860); the Himalayan mountain quail (*Ophrysia superciliosa*) (eastern Punjab, 1868); the forest spotted owlet (*Athene blewitti*) (Central India, *c.* 1872); the Samoan wood rail (*Pareudiastes pacificus*) (Savaii, Samoa, 1873); the Fiji bar-winged rail (*Rallina poecilopterus*) (Ovalau and Viti Levu, 1890); the Koa "finches"

(*Psittirostrata flaviceps* and *P. palmeri*) (Kona, Hawaii, 1891 and 1896); the Akepa (*Loxops coccinea*) (Oahu, Hawaii, 1893); the Kona "finch" (*Psittirostrata kona*) (Kona, Hawaii, 1894) and the Mamo (*Drepanis pacifica*) (Hawaii, 1898). The ivory-billed woodpecker (*Campephilus principalis*) has been confirmed as surviving since 1963. The Puerto Rican nightjar (*Caprimulgus ruficollis*), believed extinct since 1888, was rediscovered in 1962.

Longest-Lived. The greatest irrefutable age reported for any bird is 68 years in the case of a female European eagle-owl (*Bubo bubo*) living in 1899. Other records which are regarded as probably reliable include 73 years (1818–91) for a greater sulphur-crested cockatoo (*Cacatua galerita*), 72 years (1797–1869) for an African gray parrot (*Psittacus erithacus*), 70 years (1770–1840) for a mute swan (*Cygnus olor*), and 69 years for a raven (*Corvus corax*). An Egyptian vulture (*Neophron percnopterus*) which died in the menagerie at Schonnbrunn, Vienna, Austria, in 1824 was stated to have been 118 years old, but the menagerie was not founded until 1752. On March 22, 1968, an Asiatic white crane (*Megalornis leucogeranus*) died in the National Zoological Gardens, Washington, D.C., after spending 61 years 8 months 25 days in captivity.

Fastest-Flying. The spine-tailed swift (see page 50) is the fastest bird.

The bird which presents the hunter with the greatest difficulty is the spur-wing goose (*Plectropterus gambensis*), with a recorded air speed of 88 m.p.h. in level flight.

Fastest and Slowest Wing Beat. The fastest recorded wing beat of any bird is 90 beats per second by the hummingbird (*Heliactin cornuta*) of tropical South America.

Large vultures (family Vulturidae) can soar for hours without beating their wings, and sometimes exhibit a flapping rate as low as one beat per second.

Fastest Swimmer. Gentoo penguins (*Pygoscelis papua*) have been timed at 22.3 m.p.h. under water, which is a respectable flying speed for some birds.

Longest Flights. The greatest distance covered by a ringed bird during migration is 14,000 miles by an Arctic tern (*Sterna paradisaea*), which was banded as a nestling on July 5, 1955, in the Kandalaksha Sanctuary on the White Sea coast of the U.S.S.R., north of Archangel, and was captured alive by a fisherman 8 miles south of Fremantle, Western Australia, on May 16, 1956.

Highest-Flying. The celebrated example of a skein of 17 Egyptian geese (*Alopochen aegyptiacus*), photographed by an astronomer crossing the sun from Dehra Dun, India, on September 17, 1919, at a height estimated at between 11 and 12 miles (58,080–63,360 feet), has been discredited by experts. The highest acceptable altitude is 26,902 feet by a small group of alpine choughs (*Pyrrhocorax graculus*) which followed the successful British expedition led by Colonel John Hunt up Mount Everest in 1953, but their take-off point may have been as high as 20,000 feet. On three separate occasions in 1959, a radar station in Norfolk, England, picked up flocks of small passerine night migrants flying in from Scandinavia at up to 21,000 feet. They were probably warblers (*Sylviidae*), chats (*Turnidae*) and fly-catchers (*Muscicapidae*).

Most Airborne. The most airborne of all birds is the common swift (*Apus apus*) which remains aloft for at least nine months of the year.

Most Acute Vision. Tests have shown that under favorable conditions the long-eared owl (*Asio otus*) and the barn owl (*Tyto alba*) can swoop on targets from a distance of 6 feet or more in an illumination of only 0.00000073 of a foot candle (equivalent to the light from a standard candle at a distance of 1,170 feet). This acuity is 50–100 times as great as that of human night vision. In good light and against a contrasting background a golden eagle (*Aquila chrysaetos*) can detect an 18-inch-long hare at a range of 2,150 yards (possibly even 2 miles).

Eggs—Largest. Of living birds, the one producing the largest egg is the North African ostrich (*Struthio camelus camelus*). The average egg weighs 3.63 to 3.88 lbs., measures 6 to 8 inches in length, 4 to 6 inches in diameter and requires about 40 minutes for boiling. The shell is 1/16th of an inch thick and can support the weight of a 252-lb. man.

Eggs—Smallest. The smallest egg laid by any bird is the egg of the bee hummingbird (*Mellisuga helenae*), the world's smallest bird. One measuring 0.45 of an inch long and 0.32 of an inch wide is now in the Smithsonian Institution in Washington, D.C. This egg, which weighs 0.176 oz., was collected at Boyate, Santiago de Cuba, on May 8, 1906.

Incubation. The longest incubation period is that of the wandering albatross (*Diomedea exulans*), with a normal range of 75 to 82 days. The shortest incubation period is probably that of the hawfinch (*Coccothraustes coccothraustes*), which is only 9–10 days. The idlest of cock birds are hummingbirds (family Trochilidae), among whom the hen bird does 100 per cent of the incubation, whereas the female common kiwi (*Apteryx australis*) leaves this entirely to the male for 75 to 80 days.

Longest Feathers. The longest feathers known are those of the cock birds of the Japanese long-tailed fowls, or onagadori (a strain of *Gallus gallus*) bred in Kochi in Shikoku, with tail coverts up to 30 feet in length.

Most Feathers. In a series of "feather counts" on various species of bird a whistling swan (*Cygnus columbianus*) was found to have 25,216 feathers. A ruby-throated hummingbird (*Archilochus colubris*) had only 940, although hummingbirds have more feathers per area of body surface than any other living bird.

Domesticated Birds

Largest Turkey. The greatest *live* weight recorded for a turkey (*Meleagris gallopavo*) is 70 lbs., reported in December, 1966, for a white Holland stag named "Tom" owned by a breeder in California.

The heaviest weight recorded for a *clean plucked* turkey is 65 lbs. 4 oz. for a Triple Six stag shown at the International Poultry Show in London, England, on December 14, 1971. It was bred and reared by Hugh Arnold of British United Turkeys, Ltd., and weighed about 68 lbs. when alive.

Most Talkative Bird. The world's most talkative bird is a male African gray parrot (*Psittacus erythacus*) named "Prudle," owned by Mrs. Lyn Logue of Golders Green, London, England, which has won the "best talking parrot-like bird" title at the National Cage and Aviary Bird Show in London for seven years, 1965–71. Prudle was taken from a nest in a tree about to be felled at Jinja, Uganda, in 1958.

Longest-Lived. The budgerigar (parakeet) has an average life span of 6 to 8 years. A specimen named "Pretty Boy" (hatched November, 1948), owned by Mrs. Anne Dolan of Loughton, Essex, England, died on February 25, 1972, aged 23 years 3 months. The largest caged budgerigar (*Melopsittacus undulatus*) population is probably that of the United Kingdom with an estimated $3\frac{1}{2}$–4 million. In 1956, the population was about 7 million.

3. Reptiles *(Reptilia)*

(Crocodiles, snakes, turtles, tortoises and lizards.)

Largest and Heaviest. The largest reptile in the world is the estuarine or salt-water crocodile (*Crocodylus porosus*) of southeast Asia, northern Australia, New Guinea, the Philippines and the Solomon Islands. Adult bulls average 12–14 feet in length and scale about 1,100 lbs. In 1823 a notorious man-eater measuring 27 feet in length and weighing an estimated 4,400 lbs. was shot at Jala Jala on Luzon Island in the Philippines after terrorizing the neighborhood for many years. Its skull, the largest on record (if we exclude fossil remains) is now preserved in the Museum of Comparative Zoology at Harvard University, Cambridge, Massachusetts. Another outsized example with a reputed length of 33 feet and a maximum bodily girth of 13 feet 8 inches was shot in the Bay of Bengal, India, in 1840, but the dimensions of its skull (preserved in the British Museum, Natural History, London) suggest that it must have come from a crocodile measuring about 24 feet. In April, 1966, an estuarine crocodile measuring 20 feet 9 inches in length and weighing more than a ton was shot at Liaga, on the southeast coast of Papua.

Smallest. The smallest species of reptile is believed to be *Sphaerodactylus parthenopion*, a gecko found only on the island of Virgin Gorda, British Virgin Islands in the Caribbean. It is known from 15 specimens, including some gravid females, found between August 10 and 16, 1964. The three largest females measured 0.71 of an inch from snout to vent, with a tail of approximately the same length.

It is possible that another gecko, *Sphaerodactylus elasmorhynchus*, may be even smaller. The only specimen ever discovered was an apparently mature female, with a snout-vent length of 0.67 of an inch and a tail of the same length, found on March 15, 1966, among the roots of a tree in the western part of the Massif de la Hotte in Haiti.

A species of dwarf chameleon, *Evoluticauda tuberculata*, found in Madagascar, and known only from a single specimen, has a snout-vent length of 0.71 inches and a tail length of 0.55 inches. Chameleons, however, are more bulky than geckos, and it is not yet known if this specimen was fully grown.

Fastest. The highest speed measured for any reptile on land is 18 m.p.h. by a six-lined race-runner (*Cnemidophorus sexlineatus*) pursued by a car near McCormick, South Carolina, in 1941. The highest speed claimed for any reptile in water is 22 m.p.h. by a frightened Pacific leatherback turtle (see *Largest Chelonians*).

Largest Lizard. The largest of all lizards is the Komodo monitor or Ora (*Varanus komodoensis*), a dragon-like reptile found on the Indonesian islands of Komodo, Rintja, Padar and Flores. Adult males average 8 feet in length and weigh 175–200 lbs. Lengths up to 23 feet (*sic*) have been quoted for this species, but the largest specimen to be accurately measured was a male presented to an American zoologist in 1928 by the Sultan of Bima which then taped 10 feet 0.8 inches. In 1937, this animal was put on display in the St. Louis Zoological Gardens for a short period. It then measured 10 feet 2 inches in length and weighed 365 lbs.

Oldest. The greatest age recorded for a lizard is more than 54 years for a male slow worm (*Anguis fragilis*) kept in the Zoological Museum in Copenhagen, Denmark, from 1892 until 1946.

Chelonians

Largest. The largest of all chelonians is the Pacific leatherback turtle (*Dermochelys coriacea schlegelii*). The average adult measures 6–7 feet in overall length (length of carapace 4–5 feet) and weighs between 660 and 800 lbs. The greatest weight reliably recorded is 1,908 lbs. for a specimen captured off Monterey, California, in 1961, which is now on permanent display at the Wharf Aquarium, Fisherman's Wharf, Monterey.

The largest living tortoise is *Geochelone gigantea* of Aldabra Island in the Indian Ocean. Adult males sometimes exceed 500 lbs. in weight, and a specimen weighing 900 lbs. was collected in 1847.

Longest-Lived. Tortoises are the longest-lived of all vertebrates. Reliable records over 100 years include a common box tortoise (*Testudo carolina*) of 138 years and a European pond tortoise (*Emys orbicularis*) of 120+years. The greatest proven age of a continuously observed tortoise is 116+years for a Mediterranean spur-thighed tortoise (*Testudo graeca*) which died in Paignton Zoo, Devon, England, in 1957. On May 19, 1966, the death was reported of "Tu'imalilia" or "Tui Malela" the famous but much battered Madagascar radiated tortoise (*Testudo radiata*) reputedly presented to the King of Tonga by Captain James Cook in 1773, but this record of almost 200 years lacks proper documentation.

Slowest-Moving. Tests on a giant tortoise (*Geochelone gigantea*) in Mauritius show that even when hungry and enticed by a cabbage it

LARGEST LIVING TORTOISE: A native of Aldabra Island in the Indian Ocean, this creature weighs in excess of 500 lbs.

cannot cover more than 5 yards in a minute (0.17 m.p.h.) on land. Over longer distances its speed is greatly reduced.

Snakes

Longest. The longest (and heaviest) of all snakes is the anaconda (*Eunectes murinus*) of South America. In 1944, a length of 37½ feet was reliably reported for a specimen shot on the upper Orinoco River in eastern Colombia. It was accurately measured but later recovered and escaped. Another anaconda killed on the lower Rio Guaviare, in southeastern Colombia, in November, 1956, reportedly measured 33 feet 7½ inches in length, but nothing of this snake was preserved.

The longest snake ever kept in a zoo was probably "Colossus," a female reticulated or regal python (*Python reticulatus*) who died of tuberculosis on April 15, 1963, in the Highland Park Zoological Gardens, Pittsburgh. She measured 22 feet on August 10, 1949, when she arrived there from Singapore, and was measured at 28 feet 6 inches on November 15, 1956, when she was growing at the rate of about 10 inches per year. Her girth, before a feed, was measured at 36 inches on March 2, 1955, and she weighed 320 lbs. on June 12, 1957. She was probably at least 29 feet long at the time of her death in 1963.

A long-standing reward of $2,000, offered by the New York

Zoological Society, Bronx Park, New York City, for the skin or vertebral column of a snake measuring more than 30 feet has never been collected.

The longest venomous snake in the world is the king cobra (*Ophiophagus hannah*), also called the hymadryad. A specimen was collected near Fort Dickson in Malaya in April, 1937, and grew to 18 feet 9 inches in the London Zoo.

Shortest. The shortest known snake is the thread snake (*Leptotyphlops bilineata*), found on the Caribbean islands of Martinique, Barbados and St. Lucia. It has a maximum recorded length of 4.7 inches.

The shortest venomous snake is probably Peringuey's adder (*Bitis peringueyi*) of southwest Africa which has a maximum recorded length of 12 inches.

Heaviest. The heaviest snake is the anaconda (*Eunectes murinus*). The 37½-foot specimen (see *Longest Snake*) was also the heaviest, probably weighing nearly 1,000 lbs.

The heaviest venomous snake is the Eastern diamond-back rattlesnake (*Crotalus adamanteus*), found in the southeastern United States. A specimen 7 feet 9 inches in length weighed 34 lbs. Less reliable measurements of 40 lbs. for an 8-foot-9-inch specimen have been reported.

Oldest Snake. The greatest irrefutable age recorded for a snake is 34 years 1 month in the case of an Indian python (*Python molurus*) at Philadelphia Zoological Gardens, which was still alive on January 1, 1971.

Fastest-Moving. The fastest-moving land snake is probably the

LONGEST VENOMOUS SNAKE: The hymadryad, 18 feet 9 inches long.

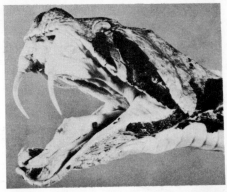

slender black mamba (*Dendroaspis polylepis*). On April 23, 1906, an angry black mamba was timed at a speed of 7 m.p.h. over a measured distance of 47 yards near Mbuyuni on the Serengeti Plains, Kenya. Stories that black mambas can overtake galloping horses (maximum speed 43.26 m.p.h.) are wild exaggerations, though a speed of 15 m.p.h. may be possible for short bursts over level ground.

Most Venomous. Authorities differ on which of the world's 300 venomous snakes possesses the most toxic venom. That of the Tiger snake (*Notechis scutatus*) of southern Australia is perhaps matched by the Javan krait (*Bungarus javincus*), and more likely by the beaked sea snake (*Enhydrina schistosa*) of the Indo-Pacific region. The beaked sea snake has a minimal lethal dose for man of only 1.5 mg. (1/22,000th of an ounce).

It is estimated that between 30,000 and 40,000 people die from snakebite each year, 75 per cent of them in densely populated India. Burma has the highest mortality rate with 15.4 deaths per 100,000 population per annum.

Longest Fangs. The longest fangs of any snake are those of the Gaboon viper (*Bitus gabonica*), of tropical Africa. In a 6-foot-long specimen, the fangs measured 1.96 inches. A Gaboon viper bit itself to death on February 12, 1963, in the Philadelphia Zoological Gardens. Keepers found the dead snake with its fangs deeply embedded in its own back. It was the only one of that species in the zoo.

4. Amphibians *(Amphibia)*

(Salamanders, toads, frogs, newts, caecilians, etc.)

Largest

The largest species of amphibian is the Chinese giant salamander (*Megalobatrachus davidianus*), which lives in the cold mountain streams and marshy areas of northeastern, central and southern China. The average adult measures 39.37 inches in total length and weighs 24.2 to 28.6 lbs. One huge individual collected in Kweichow (Guizhou)

Province in southern China in the early 1920's measured 5 feet in total length and weighed nearly 100 lbs. The Japanese giant salamander (*Megalobatrachus japonicus*) is slightly smaller, but one captive specimen weighed 88 lbs. when alive and 99 lbs. after death, the body having absorbed water from the aquarium.

Newt. The largest newt in the world is the Pleurodele or Ribbed newt (*Pleurodeles waltl*), which is found in Morocco and on the Iberian Peninsula. Specimens measuring up to 15.74 inches in total length and weighing over 1 lb. have been reliably reported.

Frog. The largest known frog is the rare Goliath frog (*Rana goliath*) of Cameroon and Spanish Guinea, West Africa. A female weighing 7 lbs. 4.5 oz. was caught in the rapids of the River Mbia, Spanish Guinea, on August 23, 1960. It had a snout-vent length of 13.38 inches and measured 32.08 inches overall with legs extended. In December, 1960, another giant frog known locally as "agak" or "carn-pnag" and said to measure 12–15 inches snout to vent and to weigh over 6 lbs. was reportedly discovered in central New Guinea, but further information is lacking. In 1969, a new species of giant frog was discovered in Sumatra.

Tree Frog. The largest species of tree frog is *Hyla vasta*, found only on the island of Hispaniola (Haiti and the Dominican Republic) in the West Indies. The average snout-vent length is about 3.54 inches, but a female collected from the San Juan River, Dominican Republic, in March, 1928, measured 5.63 inches.

The largest toad in the world is probably the Marine toad (*Bufo marinus*) of tropical South America. An enormous female collected on November 24, 1965, at Miraflores Vaupes, Colombia, and later exhibited in the Reptile House at the Bronx Zoo, New York City, had a snout-vent length of 9.37 inches and weighed 2 lbs. 11¼ oz. at the time of its death in 1967.

Smallest

The smallest species of amphibian is believed to be an arrow-poison frog *Sminthillus limbatus*, found in Cuba. Fully-grown specimens have a snout-vent length of 0.33–0.48 inches.

Newt. The smallest newt in the world is believed to be the striped newt (*Notophthalmus perstriatus*) of the southeastern United States. Adult specimens average 2.01 inches in total length.

Tree frog. The smallest tree frog in the world is the Least tree frog (*Hyla ocularis*), found in the southeastern United States. It has a maximum snout-vent length of 0.62 inches.

Toad. The smallest toad in the world is the subspecies *Bufo taitanus beiranus*, first discovered in *c.* 1906 near Beira, Mozambique, East Africa. Adult specimens have a maximum recorded snout-vent length of 0.94 inches.

Salamander. The smallest species of salamander is the Pygmy salamander (*Desmognathus wrighti*), which is found only in Tennessee, North Carolina and Virginia. Adult specimens measure from 1.45 to 2.0 inches in total length.

Longest-Lived. The greatest authentic age recorded for an amphibian is about 55 years for a male Japanese giant salamander (*Megalobatrachus japonicus*) which died in the aquarium at Amsterdam Zoological Gardens on June 3, 1881. It was brought to Holland in 1829, at which time it was estimated to be 3 years old.

Highest and Lowest. The common toad (*Bufo vulgaris*) is said to have been found at an altitude of 26,246 feet in Tibet, and at a depth of 1,115 feet in a coal mine.

Most Poisonous. The most active known venom is the batracho-toxin of an arrow poison frog (*Phyllobates latinasus*), or kokoi, of the Chocó in western Colombia, South America. Only about 1/100,000th of a gram (0.0000004 of an ounce) is enough to kill a man.

Longest Frog Jump. The record for three consecutive leaps is 32 feet 3 inches by a 2-inch-long South African sharp-nosed frog (*Rana oxyrhyncha*), recorded by Dr. Walter Rose of the South African Museum on Green Point Common, Cape Town, on January 16, 1954. It was named "Leaping Lena" (but later found to be a male). At the annual Calaveras County Jumping Frog Jubilee at Angels Camp, California, May, 1955, another male of this species made an unofficial *single* leap of over 15 feet when being retrieved for place-ment in its container.

5. Fishes *(Pisces, Bradyodonti, Selachii and Marsipobranchii)*

Largest—Sea. The largest species of fish is the whale-shark (*Rhinodon typus* or variously *Rhineodon typus*) first discovered off Cape Town, South Africa, in April, 1828. It is not, however, the largest aquatic animal, since it is smaller than the larger species of whales (mammals). A whale-shark measuring 59 feet long and weighing about 90,000 lbs. was caught in a bamboo fish-trap at Koh Chik, in the Gulf of Siam, in 1919.

The plankton-feeding whale-shark, grayish or dark brown with white or yellow spots, is extremely docile and lives in the warmer areas of the Atlantic, Pacific and Indian Oceans. Unlike mammals, fish continue to grow with age.

LARGEST FISH: The whale-shark (not a mammal) grows to 45 feet long and lays the largest eggs of any living creature.

The largest carnivorous fish (excluding plankton eaters) is the great white shark (*Carcharadon carcharias*), also called the man-eater, which is found mainly in tropical and sub-tropical waters. In June, 1930, a specimen measuring 37 feet in length was found trapped in a herring weir at White Head Island, New Brunswick, Canada. Another great white shark which ran aground in False Bay, near the Cape of Good Hope, South Africa many years ago reportedly measured 43 feet, but further information is lacking.

The longest of the bony or "true" fishes (Pisces) is the Russian sturgeon (*Acipenser huso*), also called the Beluga, which is found in the temperate areas of the Adriatic, Black and Caspian Seas, but enters large rivers like the Volga and the Danube for spawning. Lengths up to 26 feet 3 inches have been reliably reported, and a gravid female taken in the estuary of the Volga in 1827 weighed 3,250½ lbs.

The heaviest bony fish in the world is the ocean sunfish (*Mola mola*), which is found in all tropical, sub-tropical and temperate waters. On September 18, 1908, a huge specimen was accidentally struck by the S.S. *Fiona* off Bird Island about 40 miles from Sydney, New South Wales, Australia, and towed to Port Jackson. It measured 14 feet between the anal and dorsal fins and weighed 4,928 lbs.

Largest—Fresh-water. The largest fish which spends its whole life in fresh water is the European catfish or wels (*Silurus glanis*). In September, 1918, a specimen weighing 564.74 lbs. and measuring 11 feet long was caught in Desna River, U.S.S.R. Another specimen allegedly weighing 660 lbs. was caught in the Dneiper River, near Kremenchug, U.S.S.R. The arapaima (*Arapaima gigas*), also called the pirarucu, found in the Amazon and other South American rivers and often claimed to be the largest fresh-water fish averages 6½ feet and 150 lbs. The largest "authentically recorded" measured 8 feet 1½ inches and weighed 325 lbs. It was caught in the Rio Negro, Brazil, in 1836.

Smallest—Fresh-water. The shortest recorded fresh-water fish and the shortest of all vertebrates is the dwarf pygmy goby (*Pandaka pygmaea*), almost transparent and colorless, found in streams and lakes on Luzon, the Philippines. Adult males measure only 0.29 to 0.38 of an inch long and weigh only 4 to 5 milligrams (0.00014 to 0.00017 of an ounce).

Smallest—Marine. The shortest recorded marine fishes are the Marshall Islands goby (*Eviota zonura*), measuring 0.47 to 0.63 of an inch, and *Schindleria praematurus* from Samoa, measuring 0.47 to 0.74 of an inch, both in the Pacific Ocean. Mature specimens of the latter, largely transparent and first identified in 1940, have been known to weigh only 2 milligrams, equivalent to 17,750 to the ounce—the lightest of all vertebrates and the smallest catch possible for any fisherman.

Fastest. The sailfish (*Isiophorus platypterus*) is generally considered to be the fastest species of fish, although the practical difficulties of measurement make data extremely difficult to secure. A figure of 68.18 m.p.h. (100 yards in 3 seconds) has been cited for one off Florida. The swordfish (*Xiphias gladius*) has also been credited with very high speeds, but the evidence is based mainly on bills that have been found deeply embedded in ships' timbers. A speed of 50 knots

(57.6 m.p.h.) has been calculated from a penetration of 22 inches by a bill into a piece of timber, but 30 to 35 knots (35 to 40 m.p.h.) is the most conceded by some experts. Speeds in excess of 35 knots (40 m.p.h.) have also been attributed to the marlin (*Tetrapturus sp.*), the wahoo (*Acanthocybium solandri*), the great blue shark (*Prionace glauca*), and the bonefish (*Albula vulpes*), and the bluefin tuna (*Thunnus thynnus*) has been scientifically clocked at 43.4 m.p.h. in a 20-second dash. The four-winged flying fish (*Cypselurus heterurus*) may also exceed 40 m.p.h. during its rapid rush to the surface before take-off (the average speed in the air is about 35 m.p.h.). Record flights of 42 seconds, 36 feet in altitude and 1,200 feet in length have been recorded in the tropical Atlantic.

Longest-Lived. Aquaria are of too recent origin to be able to establish with certainty which species of fish can fairly be regarded as the longest-lived. Early indications are that it is the lake sturgeon (*Acipenser fulvescens*). One specimen 6 feet 7 inches long, caught in the Lake Winnebago region of Wisconsin, was believed to be 82 years old based on a count of the growth rings (*annuli*) in the marginal ray of the pectoral fin. Another lake sturgeon 6 feet 9 inches long and weighing 215 lbs., caught in the Lake of the Woods, Kenora, Ontario, Canada, on July 15, 1953, was believed to be 150 years old based on a growth ring count, but this extreme figure has been questioned by some authorities. A figure of 150 years has also been attributed to the mirror carp (*Cyprinus carpion*), but the greatest authoritatively accepted age is "more than 50 years." Other long-lived fish include the European sterlet (*Acipenser ruthenus*) with 69 years, the European catfish (*Silurus glanis*) with 60+ years, the European fresh-water eel (*Anguilla anguilla*) with 55 years, and the American eel (*Anguilla chrisypa*) with 50 years.

Oldest Goldfish. The exhibition life of a goldfish (*Carassius auratus*) is normally about 17 years, but much greater ages have been reliably reported. On August 22, 1970, Mrs. I. M. Payne of Dawlish, Devon, England, announced that her pet goldfish had just celebrated its 34th birthday. There is also a record of a goldfish living for 40 years.

Shortest-Lived. There are several contenders for the title of shortest-lived fish. One of them is the transparent or white goby (*Latrunculus pellucidus*), which hatches, grows, reproduces and dies in less than a year. Other "annuals" include the top minnow (*Gambusia holbrookii*), the sea horse (*Hippocampus husonius*), the dwarf pygmy goby (*Pandaka pygmaea*) and the ice fishes (family *Chaenichthyidae*) of the Antarctic.

Deepest. The greatest depth from which a fish has been recovered is 23,392 feet for a 6¾-inch-long brotulid of the genus *Bassogigas*, sledge-trawled by the Royal Danish research vessel *Galathea* in the Sunda Trench, south of Java, in September, 1951. Dr. Jacques Piccard and Lieutenant Don Walsh, U.S. Navy, reported they saw a sole-like fish about 1 foot long (tentatively identified as *Chascanopsetta lugubris*) from the bathyscaphe *Trieste* at a depth of 35,802 feet in the Challenger Deep (Mariana Trench) in the western Pacific on January 24, 1960. This sighting, however, has been questioned by some authorities, who still regard the brotulids of the genus *Bassogigas* as the deepest-living vertebrates.

Most Eggs. The ocean sunfish (*Mola mola*) produces up to 300,000,000 eggs, each of them measuring about 0.05 in. in diameter. The egg yield of the guppy, *Lebistes reticulatus*, is usually only 40–50, but one female measuring 1¼ inches in length had only four in her ovaries.

Most Venomous. The most venomous fish in the world are the stonefish (*Synanceja verrucosa, S. torrida* and *S. trachynis*) of the tropical Indo-Pacific oceans. Contact with the spines of their fins often proves fatal.

Most Electric. The most powerful electric fish is the electric eel (*Electrophorus electricus*), which is found in the rivers of Brazil, Colombia, Venezuela and Peru. An average-sized specimen can discharge 400 volts at 1 ampere, but measurements up to 650 volts have been recorded.

6. Starfishes *(Asteroidea)*

Largest. The largest of the 1,600 known species of starfish is probably the five-armed *Evasterias echinosomo* of the North Pacific. One specimen collected by a Russian expedition in the flooded crater of a volcano in Broughton Bay, Semushir, one of the Kurile Islands, in June, 1970, measured 37.79 inches in total diameter and weighed more than 11 lbs.

Smallest. The smallest recorded starfish is the North Pacific deep-sea species *Leptychaster propinquus*, which has a maximum total diameter of 0.72 inches.

Deepest. The greatest depth from which a starfish has been recovered is 25,032 feet for a specimen of *Eremicaster tenebrarius* collected by the Galathea Deep Sea Expedition in the Kermadec Trench in the central Pacific in 1951.

7. Arachnids *(Arachnida)*

Spiders (Order Araneae)

Largest. The world's largest known spider is the South American "bird eating" spider (*Theraphosa leblondi*). A male specimen with a body 3½ inches long and a leg span of 10 inches, when fully extended, was collected in April, 1925, at Montagne la Gabrielle, French Guiana. It weighed nearly 2 ounces. (See photograph.)

The heaviest spider ever recorded was a female of the genus *Lasiodora*, collected at Manaos, Brazil, in 1945. It measured 9½ inches across and weighed almost 3 ounces.

Smallest. The smallest known spider in the world is *Microlinypheus bryophilus* (family Argiopidae) discovered in Lorne, Victoria, Australia in January, 1928. The adult male has a body length of 0.023 of an inch, and the adult female 0.031 of an inch.

Largest and Smallest Webs. The largest webs are the aerial

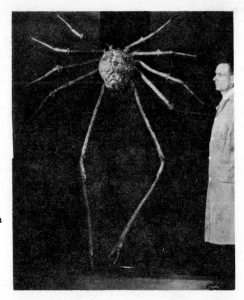

LARGEST SPIDER (left):
The Theraphosa leblondi has a
leg span of 10 inches.
LARGEST CRAB (right):
The Japanese spider crab has
legs that span up to 12½ feet.

ones spun by the tropical orb weavers of the genus *Nephila*, which have been measured up to 18 feet 9¾ inches in circumference.

The smallest webs are spun by spiders like *Glyphesis cottonae*, etc. which are about the size of a small postage stamp.

Most Venomous. The most venomous spider in the world is probably *Latrodectus mactans* of the Americas, which is better known as the "black widow." Females of this species (the much smaller males are harmless) have a bite capable of killing a human being, but deaths are rare. The funnel web spider (*Atrax robustus*) of Australia, the jockey spider (*Latrodectus hasseltii*) of Australia and New Zealand, the button spider (*Latrodectus indistinctus*) of South Africa, the podadora (*Glyptocranium gasteracanthoides*) of Argentina and the brown recluse spider (*Loxosceles reclusa*) of the central and southern United States have been credited with fatalities.

Rarest. The most elusive of all spiders are the primitive atypical tarantulas of the genus *Liphistius*, which are found in southeast Asia.

Fastest. The highest speed measured for a spider on a level surface is 1.73 feet per second (1.17 m.p.h.) in the case of a specimen of *Tegenaria atrica*.

Longest-Lived. The longest-lived of all spiders are the primitive *Mygalomorphae* (tarantulas and allied species). One mature female tarantula collected at Mazatlan, Mexico, in 1935 and estimated to be 12 years old at the time, was kept in a laboratory for 16 years, making a total of 28 years.

8. Crustaceans *(Crustacea)*

(Crabs, lobsters, shrimps, prawns, crayfish, barnacles, water fleas, fish lice, wood lice, sand hoppers and krill, etc.)

Largest. The largest of all crustaceans (although not the heaviest) is the giant spider crab (*Macrocheira kaempferi*), also called the stilt crab, which is found in deep waters off the southeastern coast of Japan. Mature specimens usually have a 12–14-inch-wide body and a claw span of 8–9 feet, but unconfirmed measurements up to 19 feet have been reported. A specimen with a claw span of 12 feet 1½ inches weighed 14 lbs. (See photograph on previous page.)

The largest species of lobster, and the heaviest of all crustaceans, is the American or North Atlantic lobster (*Homarus americanus*). One weighing 42 lbs. 7 oz. and measuring 4 feet from the end of the tail-fan to the tip of the claw was caught by the smack *Hustler* in a deep-sea trawl off the Virginia coast in 1934 and is now on display in the Museum of Science, Boston. Another specimen allegedly weighing 48 lbs. was caught off Chatham, Massachusetts, in 1949. Less reliable weights of up to 60 lbs. have been reported.

Smallest. The smallest known crustaceans are water fleas of the genus *Alonella*, which may measure less than 1/100th of an inch long. They are found in British waters.

The smallest known lobster is the cape lobster (*Homarus capensis*) of South Africa which measures 3.93–4.72 inches in total length.

The smallest crabs in the world are the pea crabs (family Pinnotheridae). Some species have a shell diameter of only 0.25 in., including *Pinnotheres pisum* which is found in British waters.

Longest-Lived. The longest-lived of all crustaceans is the American lobster (*Homarus americanus*). Very large specimens may be as much as 50 years old.

Deepest. The greatest depth from which a crustacean has been recovered is 32,119 feet for an amphiopod (order Amphiopoda) collected by the Galathea Deep Sea Expedition in the Philippine Trench in 1951.

9. Insects (*Insecta or Hexapoda*)

Heaviest. The heaviest insect in the world is the Goliath beetle *Goliathus giganteus*, of equatorial Africa. One specimen measuring 5.85 inches in length (jaw to tip of abdomen) and 3.93 inches across the back, weighed 3.52 ounces. The longhorn beetles *Titanus giganteus* of South America and *Xinuthrus heros* of the Fiji Islands are also massive insects, and both have been measured up to 5.9 inches in length.

Longest. The longest insect in the world is the tropical stick-insect *Pharnacia serratipes*, females of which have been measured up to 12.99 inches in body length. The longest beetle known (excluding antennae) is the Hercules beetle (*Dynastes hercules*) of Central and South America, which has been measured up to 7.08 inches, but over half of this length is accounted for by the "prong" from the thorax. The longhorn beetle *Batocera wallacei* of New Guinea has been measured up to 10.5 inches, but 7.5 inches of this was antenna.

Smallest. The smallest insects recorded so far are the "hairy-winged" beetles of the family Trichopterygidae and the "battledore-wing fairy flies" (parasitic wasps) of the family Mymaridae. They measure only 0.008 of an inch in length, and the fairy flies have a wing span of only 0.04 of an inch. This makes them smaller than some of the protozoa (single-celled animals).

The male bloodsucking banded louse (*Enderleinellus zonatas*), un-gorged, and the parasitic wasp *Caraphractus cinctus* may each weigh as little as 0.005 of a milligram, or 1/5,670,000 of an ounce. The eggs of the latter each weigh 0.0002 of a milligram, or 1/141,750,000 of an ounce.

Fastest-Flying. Experiments have proved that a widely pub-licized claim by an American entomologist in 1926 that the deer bot-fly could attain a speed of 818 m.p.h. was wildly exaggerated.

Acceptable modern experiments have now established that the highest maintainable air speed of any insect is 24 m.p.h., rising to a maximum of 36 m.p.h. for short bursts. A relay of bees (maximum speed 14 m.p.h.) would use only a gallon of nectar in cruising 3,300,000 miles at 7 m.p.h.

Longest-Lived. The longest-lived insects are queen termites (*Isoptera*), which have been known to lay eggs for up to 50 years.

Loudest. The loudest of all insects is the male cicada (family Cicadidae). At 7,400 pulses per second its tymbal (sound) organs produce a noise (officially described by the U.S. Department of Agriculture as "Tsh-ee-EEEE-e-ou") detectable over a quarter of a mile distance.

Largest Locust Swarm. The greatest swarm of desert locusts (*Schistocerea gregaria*) ever recorded was one covering an estimated 2,000 square miles, observed crossing the Red Sea in 1889. Such a swarm must have contained about 250,000,000,000 insects weighing about 500,000 tons.

LOCUST SWARM: When the insects leave, the area is left bare.

Southernmost. The furthest south at which any insect has been found is 77°S (900 miles from the South Pole) in the case of a spring-tail (order Collembola).

Fastest Wing Beat. The fastest wing beat of any insect under natural conditions is 62,760 a minute by a tiny midge of the genus *Forcipomyia*. In experiments with truncated wings at a temperature of 98.6°F., the rate increased to 133,080 beats per minute. The muscular contraction-expansion cycle in 0.00045 or 1/2,218th of a second, further represents the fastest muscle movement ever measured.

Slowest Wing Beat. The slowest wing beat of any insect is 300 a minute by the swallowtail butterfly (*Papilo machaon*). Most butter-flies beat their wings at a rate of 460 to 636 a minute.

Largest Ant. The largest ant in the world is the driver ant (*Dinoponera grandis*) of Africa, workers of which measure up to 1.31 inches in length.

Smallest Ant. The smallest is the thief ant (*Solenopsis fugax*), whose workers measure 0.059–0.18 of an inch.

Largest Grasshopper. The bush-cricket with the longest wing span is the New Guinean grasshopper *Siliquoferg grandis* with some females measuring more than 10 inches. The *Pseudophyllanax imperialis*, found on the island of New Caledonia, in the south-western Pacific Ocean, has antennae measuring up to 8 inches.

Largest Dragonfly. The largest dragonfly is *Tetracanthagyne plagiata* of northeastern Borneo, which is known only from a single specimen preserved in the British Museum of Natural History, London. This dragonfly has a wing span of 7.63 inches and an overall length of 4.25 inches.

Flea Jumps. The champion jumper among fleas is the common flea (*Pulex irritans*). In one American experiment carried out in 1910 a specimen allowed to leap at will performed a long jump of 13 inches and a high jump of 7¾ inches. In jumping 130 times its own height a flea subjects itself to a force of 200 g. Siphonapterologists recognize about 1,830 varieties.

Butterflies and Moths (**Order** Lepidoptera)

Largest. The largest known butterfly is the giant birdwing *Troides victoriae* of the Solomon Islands in the southwestern Pacific. Females may have a wing span exceeding 12 inches and weigh over 0.176 oz.

The largest moth in the world is the Hercules emperor moth (*Coscinoscera hercules*) of tropical Australia and New Guinea. Females measure up to 10½ inches across the outspread wings and have a wing area of up to 40.8 square inches. The rare owlet moth (*Thysania agrippina*) of Brazil has been measured up to 11.81 inches in wing span, and the Atlas moth (*Attacus atlas*) of southeast Asia up to 11.02 inches, but both these species are less bulky than *C. hercules*.

Smallest. The smallest of the estimated 140,000 known species of Lepidoptera is the moth *Nepticula microtheiella*, with a wing span of

0.11–0.15 of an inch and a body length of 0.078 of an inch. The smallest known butterfly is the dwarf blue (*Brephidium barberae*) from South Africa. It is 0.55 of an inch from wing tip to wing tip.

Rarest. The rarest of all butterflies (and the most valuable) is the giant birdwing *Troides allottei*, which is found only on Bougainville in the Solomon Islands. A specimen was sold for $1,800 at an auction in Paris on October 24, 1966.

Fastest. The highest speeds recorded for Lepidoptera are: for moths, 33 m.p.h. by the hawk-head moth (family Sphingidae); and for butterflies, 20 m.p.h. by the great monarch butterfly (*Danaus plexippus*).

Most Acute Sense of Smell. The most acute sense of smell exhibited in nature is that of the male silkworm moth (*Bombyx mori*), which, according to German experiments in 1961, can detect the sex signals of the female at the almost unbelievable range of 6.8 miles upwind. This scent has been identified as one of the higher alcohols ($C_{16}H_{29}OH$) of which the female carries less than 0.0001 of a milligram.

10. Centipedes *(Chilopoda)*

Longest. The longest recorded species of centipede is the giant scolopender *Scolopendra gigantea*, found in the rain forests of Central and South America. It has 23 segments (46 legs) and specimens have been measured up to 10.43 inches long and 1 inch in diameter.

Shortest. The shortest recorded centipede is an unidentified species which measures only 0.19 of an inch.

Most Legs. The centipede with the greatest number of legs is *Himantarum gabrielis* of southern Europe which has 171–177 pairs when adult.

Fastest. The fastest centipede is probably *Scutiger coleoptrata* of southern Europe which can travel at a rate of 19.68 inches a second or 4.47 m.p.h.

11. Millipedes *(Diplopoda)*

Longest. The longest species of millipede known are the *Graphidostreptus gigas* of Africa and *Scaphistostreptus seychellarum* of the Seychelles Islands in the Indian Ocean, both of which have been measured up to 11.02 inches in length and 0.78 of an inch in diameter.

Shortest. The shortest millipede in the world is the British species *Polyxenus lagurus*, which measures 0.082–0.15 of an inch in length.

Most Legs. The greatest number of legs reported for a millipede is 355 pairs (710 legs) for an unidentified South African species.

12. Segmented Worms *(Annelida or Annulata)*

Longest Earthworm. The longest species of earthworm known is probably *Megascolides australis*, found in the Gippsland region of eastern Victoria, Australia, in 1868. An average specimen measures

4 feet in length (2 feet when contracted) and nearly 7 feet when *naturally* extended. The longest accurately measured *Megascolides* on record was one collected before 1930 in southern Gippsland which measured 7 feet 2 inches in length and over 13 feet when naturally extended. The eggs of this worm measure 2–3 inches in length and 0.75 of an inch in diameter.

In November, 1967, a specimen of the African giant earthworm *Microchaetus rappi* (= *M. microchaetus*) measuring 11 feet in length and 21 feet when naturally extended was found on the road between Alice and King William's Town, Eastern Cape Province, South Africa. The *average* length of this species, however, is 3 feet 6 inches and 6–7 feet when naturally extended.

Shortest. The shortest segmented worm known is *Chaetogaster annandalei*, which measures less than 0.0019 of an inch in length.

13. Mollusks *(Mollusca)*

(Squids, octopuses, snails, shellfish, etc.)

Largest. The heaviest of all invertebrate animals is the Atlantic giant squid (*Architeuthis sp.*). The largest specimen ever recorded was one measuring 55 feet in total length (head and body 20 feet, tentacles 35 feet), captured on November 2, 1878, after it had run aground in Thimble Tickle Bay, Newfoundland. Its eyes were 9 inches in diameter. The total weight was calculated to be 4,480 lbs.

The rare Pacific giant squid (*Architeuthis longimanus*) is much less bulky, but the longest recorded specimen was one measuring 57 feet overall, with a head and body length of 7 feet 9 inches and tentacles of 49 feet 3 inches, found in Lyall Bay, New Zealand, in 1888.

Largest Octopus. The largest known octopus is the common Pacific octopus (*Octopus apollyon*). One specimen trapped in a

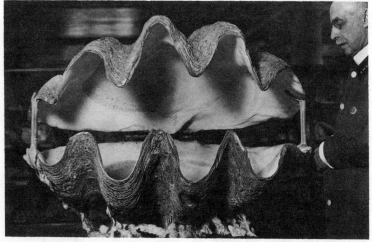

LARGEST SHELL: This giant clam shell weighs 579½ pounds.

fisherman's net in Monterey Bay, California, had a radial spread of over 20 feet and scaled 110 lbs. A weight of 125 lbs. has been reported for another individual. In 1874, a radial spread of 32 feet was reported for an octopus (*Octopus hongkongensis*) speared in Illiuliuk Harbour, Unalaska Island, Alaska, but the body of this animal only measured 12 inches in length and it probably weighed less than 20 lbs.

Most Ancient. The longest existing living creature is *Neopilina galatheae*, a deep-sea worm-snail which had been believed extinct for about 320,000,000 years, but which was found at a depth of 11,400 feet off Costa Rica by the Danish research vessel *Galathea* in 1952. Fossils found in New York State, in Newfoundland, and in Sweden show that this mollusk was also living about 500,000,000 years ago.

Shells

Largest. The largest of all existing bivalve shells is the marine giant clam (*Tridacna desera*), found on the Indo-Pacific coral reefs. A specimen measuring 43 inches by 29 inches and weighing 579½ lbs. was collected from the Great Barrier Reef in 1917, and now belongs to the American Museum of Natural History, New York City. (See photograph.)

Smallest. Probably the smallest bivalve shell in the world is *Neolepton skysi*, which measures less than 0.629 of an inch in length. This species is only known from a few specimens collected off Guernsey in the Channel Islands in 1894.

Rarest. The most highly prized of all shells in the hands of conchologists is the white-tooth cowrie (*Cypraea leucodon*), measuring 3 inches long and found in deep water off the Philippines. Only three examples are known, one in the British Museum (Natural History), London, and another at Harvard University.

The most highly prized of all molluscan shells in the hands of conchologists is the three-inch long white-toothed cowrie (*Cypraea leucodon*), which is found in the deep waters off the Philippines. Only three examples are known, including one in the British Museum. The highest price ever paid for a seashell is $2,510 in a sale at Sotheby's, London, on March 4, 1971, for one of the four known examples of *Conus bengalensis*. This 4-inch long shell was trawled by fishermen off northwestern Thailand in December, 1970.

Longest-Lived. The longest-lived of all mollusks is probably the fresh-water mussel (*Margaritan margaritifera*) which has been credited with a potential maximum longevity of 100 years. The giant clam (*Tridacna derasa*) lives about 30 years.

Snails

Largest. The largest known species of snail is the sea hare (*Tethys californicus*) found in coastal waters off California. The average weight is 7 to 8 lbs., but a specimen has been recorded at 15 lbs. 13 oz. The largest known land snail is the African giant land snail (*Achatina fulica*), measuring up to 10¾ inches long and weighing up to 1 lb. 2 oz.

Speed. The fastest-moving species of land snail is probably the common snail (*Helix aspersa*). On February 13, 1972, a specimen named Henry covered a distance of 2 feet across glass at Truro, Cornwall, England, giving him a speed of 103 hours per mile.

A snail's pace varies from as slow as 0.00036 m.p.h., or 23 inches per hour, up to 0.0313 m.p.h. (or 55 yards per hour) for the common garden snail (*Helix aspersa*). Tests were carried out in the United States.

14. Ribbon Worms *(Nemertina or Rhynchopods)*

Longest Worm. The longest of the 550 recorded species of ribbon worms, also called nemertines (or nemerteans), is the "living fishing-line worm" (*Lineus longissimus*), a highly elastic boot-lace worm found in the shallow waters of the North Sea. A specimen washed ashore at St. Andrews, Fifeshire, Scotland, in 1864 after a severe storm, measured more than 180 feet in length, making it easily the longest recorded worm of any variety.

15. Jellyfishes *(Scyphozoa or Scyphomedusia)*

Largest and Smallest. The longest jellyfish (in fact, the longest animal) ever recorded is *Cyanea arctica*. One specimen washed up on the coast of Massachusetts, *c.* 1865, had a bell $7\frac{1}{2}$ feet in diameter and tentacles measuring 120 feet, thus giving a theoretical tentacular span of some 245 feet.

Some true jellyfishes have a bell diameter of less than 0.78 of an inch.

Most Venomous. The most venomous are the box jellies of the genera *Chiropsalmus* and *Chironex* of the Indo-Pacific region, which carry a neurotoxic venom similar in strength to that found in the Asiatic cobra. These jellyfish have caused the deaths of at least 60 people off the coast of Queensland, Australia, in the past 25 years.

16. Sponges *(Parazoa, Porifera or Spongiida)*

Largest and Smallest. The largest sponges are the barrel-shaped loggerhead (*Spheciospongia vesparium*), found in the Caribbean and Florida, measuring $3\frac{1}{2}$ feet high and 3 feet in diameter, and the Neptune's cup or goblet (*Poterion patera*) of Indonesia, standing up to 4 feet in height, but it is not such a bulky animal. In 1909, a wool sponge (*Hippospongia canaliculatta*) measuring 6 feet in circumference was collected off the Bahama Islands. When first taken from the water it weighed between 80 and 90 lbs., but after it had been dried and relieved of all excrescences it scaled 12 lbs. (This sponge is now preserved in the Smithsonian Institution, Washington, D.C.)

The smallest known sponge is the widely distributed *Leucosolenia blanca*, which measures 0.11 of an inch in height when fully grown.

Deepest. Sponges have been taken from depths of up to 18,500 feet.

17. Extinct Animals

Largest. The first dinosaur to be scientifically described was *Megalosaurus bucklandi*, a 20-foot-long bipedal theropod, in 1824.

LARGEST PREHISTORIC MAMMAL (left): Leg of the giant fossil rhinoceros and (right) the full reconstructed body of the Baluchitherium now in a Moscow museum.

The bones of this animal had been discovered before 1818 in a slate quarry at Stonesfield, near Woodstock, Oxfordshire, England. It stalked across southern England about 130,000,000 years ago. The word "dinosaur" (great lizard) was not used for such reptiles until 1842. The longest recorded dinosaur was *Diplodocus carnegiei*, an attenuated sauropod which wallowed in the swamps of western North America about 150,000,000 years ago. A mounted skeleton in the Carnegie Museum, Pittsburgh, measures 87½ feet in length (neck 22 feet, body 15 feet, tail 50½ feet) and stands 11 feet 9 inches at the pelvis (the highest point on the body). This animal weighed an estimated 11.63 tons in life.

The heaviest of all prehistoric animals was the swamp-dwelling *Brachiosaurus*, which lived in East Africa and Colorado between 135,000,000 and 165,000,000 years ago. A complete skeleton excavated near Tendaguru Hill, southern Tanganyika (Tanzania) in 1909 and mounted in the Museum fur Naturkunde in East Berlin, Germany, measures 74 feet 6 inches in total length and 21 feet at the shoulder. This reptile weighed a computed 87.65 tons in life, but isolated bones have since been discovered in East Africa which indicate that some specimens may have weighed as much as 111 tons and measured over 90 feet in total length.

Largest Predator. The largest was thought to be *Tyrannosaurus rex*, which lived about 75,000,000 years ago in what are now Montana and Wyoming (bones found in 1900) and also in Mongolia. It measured up to 47 feet in overall length, had a bipedal height of 18½ feet, and weighed a calculated 8 tons. Its 4-foot-long skull contained serrated teeth up to 6 inches long.

It is now known that some other carnosaurs were just as large or even larger than *Tyrannosaurus*. In 1930, the British Museum Expedition to East Africa dug up the pelvic bones and part of the vertebrae of another huge carnosaur at Tendaguru Hill, Tanzania, which must have measured about 54 feet in total length when alive. During the summers of 1963–65, a Polish-Mongolian expedition discovered the remains of a carnosaur in the Gobi Desert which had 8½-foot-long forelimbs! It is not yet known, however, whether the rest of this dinosaur was built on the same colossal scale.

Longest Tusks. The longest tusks of any prehistoric animal were those of the straight-tusked elephant *Hesperoloxodon antiquus germanicus*, which lived in what is now northern Germany about 2,000,000 years ago. The average length in adult bulls was 16 feet 4¾ inches. A single tusk of a woolly mammoth (*Mammonteus primigenius*) preserved in the Franzens Museum at Brno, Czechoslovakia, measures 16 feet 5½ inches along the outside curve. In *c.* August, 1933, a single tusk of an Imperial mammoth (*Archidiskodon imperator*) measuring 16+ feet (anterior end missing) was unearthed near Post, Texas. In 1934, this tusk was presented to the American Museum of Natural History in New York City.

Heaviest Tusks. The heaviest tusk on record is one weighing 330 lbs., with a girth of 35 inches, now preserved in the Museo Archeologico, Milan, Italy. It measures 11 feet 9 inches in length.

The heaviest recorded mammoth tusks are a pair in the Peabody Museum of Archeology and Ethnology at Harvard University, Cambridge, Massachusetts, which have a combined weight of 498 lbs. and measure 13 feet 9 inches and 13 feet 7 inches respectively.

Longest Horns. The prehistoric giant deer (*Megaceros giganteus*), erroneously called the Irish elk, which lived in Northern Europe and Northern Asia as recently as 50,000 B.C. stood 7 feet at the shoulder and had greatly palmated antlers measuring up to 14 feet across.

Most Brainless. The *Stegosaurus* ("plated reptile"), which measured up to 30 feet in length, 8 feet in height at the hips and weighed up to 2 tons, had a walnut-sized brain weighing only 2½ ounces. It represented 0.004 of one per cent of its body weight compared with 0.074 of one per cent for an elephant and 1.88 per ce it for a human. It roamed widely across the Northern Hemisphere about 150,000,000 years ago, trying to remember where it had been.

Largest Mammal. The largest prehistoric mammal, and the largest land mammal ever recorded, was *Baluchitherium* (= *Indricotherium, Paraceratherium, Aceratherium, Thaumastotherium, Aralotherium* and *Benaratherium*), a long-necked hornless rhinoceros which lived in Europe and central and western Asia between 20,000,000 and 40,000,000 years ago. It stood up to 17 feet 9 inches to the top of the shoulder hump (27 feet to the crown of its head), measured 28 feet in length and weighed at least 22 tons. The bones of this gigantic browser were first discovered in 1907–08 in the Bugti Hills in east Baluchistan, Pakistan.

Largest Dinosaur Eggs. The largest dinosaur eggs discovered were those of a *Hypselosaurus priseus* in the valley of the Durance, near Aix-en-Provence, in southern France. The eggs of this 30-foot-long sauropod, believed to be 80,000,000 years old, would have had, uncrushed, a length of 12 inches and a diameter of 10 inches.

LONGEST EARTHWORM (left): This species measures 4 feet in length, 7 feet when naturally extended. (See page 87-88.) TALLEST PREHISTORIC BIRD (right): The flightless moa of New Zealand, shown here in a reconstruction, stood over 13 feet tall.

Largest Flying Creature. The extinct winged reptile *Pteranodon ingens*, which soared over what is now Kansas, about 80,000,000 years ago, probably a dynamic sea-soarer, had a wing span of up to 27 feet and weighed an estimated 40 lbs.

Largest Bird. The largest prehistoric bird was the elephant bird (*Aepyornis maximus*), also known as the roc bird, which lived in southern Madagascar. It was a flightless bird standing 9 to 10 feet in height and weighing nearly 1,000 lbs. It also had the largest eggs of any known animal. One example preserved in the British Museum of Natural History, London, measures $33\frac{3}{4}$ inches around the long axis with a circumference of $28\frac{1}{2}$ inches, giving a capacity of 2.35 gallons—seven times that of an ostrich egg. A more cylindrical egg preserved in the Academie des Sciences, Paris, measures $12\frac{7}{8}$ inches by $15\frac{3}{8}$ inches, and probably weighed about 27 lbs. with its contents. This bird may have survived until *c.* 1660. The flightless moa *Dinornis giganteus* of North Island, New Zealand, was taller, attaining a height of over 13 feet, but probably weighed about 500 lbs.

In May, 1962, a single fossilized ankle joint of an enormous flightless bird was found at Gainesville, Florida. The largest actually to fly was probable the condor-like *Teratornis incredibilis*, which lived in North America about 100,000,000 years ago. Fossil remains of one of this species, discovered in Smith Creek Cave, Nevada, in 1952, indicate a wing span of 16 feet $4\frac{1}{4}$ inches, and the bird must have weighed at least 50 lbs. Another gigantic flying bird named *Osteodontornis*, which lived in what is now California, about 20,000,000 years ago, had a wing span of 16 feet and was probably even heavier. It was related to the pelicans and storks. The albatross-like *Gigantornis eaglesomei* has been credited with a wing span of 20 feet on the evidence of a single fossilized breastbone. It flew over what is now Nigeria between 34,000,000 and 58,000,000 years ago.

A wing span measurement of 16 feet 4¼ inches has also been reported for another flying bird named *Ornithodesmus latidens*, which flew over what is now Hampshire and the Isle of Wight, England, about 90,000,000 years ago.

Largest Marine Reptile. The largest marine reptile ever recorded was the short-necked pliosaur *Kronosaurus queenlandicus*, which swam in the seas around what is now Australia about 100,000,000 years ago. It measured about 55 feet in length, with a skull 11½ feet long.

Largest Crocodile. The largest recorded crocodile was *Phobosuchus* ("horror crocodile"), which lived in the lakes and swamps of what are now the states of Montana and Texas 75,000,000 years ago. It measured up to 50 feet in length and had a skull 6 feet long. The gavial *Rhamphosuchus*, which lived in northern India about 7,000,000 years ago, also reached a length of 50 feet, but was not nearly so bulky.

Southernmost. The two southernmost fossil discoveries have been a piece of the jaw of the fresh-water amphibian *labyrinthodont* and, on November 23, 1969, the skull of the extinct reptile *Lystrosaurus* at Coalsack Bluff some 400 miles from the South Pole.

Chelonians. The largest prehistoric marine turtle was *Archelon ischyros*, which lived in Kansas and South Dakota when they were shallow seas about 80,000,000 years ago. An almost complete skeleton with a carapace (shell) 6½ feet long was discovered in August, 1895, near the south fork of the Cheyenne River in Custer County, South Dakota. The skeleton, which has an overall length of 11 feet 4 inches (20 feet across the outstretched flippers), is now in the Peabody Museum of Natural History at Yale University, New Haven, Connecticut. This specimen is estimated to have weighed 6,000 lbs. when it was alive.

The fossil remains of another giant marine turtle (*Cratochelone berneyi*) which must have measured at least 12 feet in overall length when alive were discovered in 1914 at Sylvania Station, 20 miles west of Hughenden, Queensland, Australia.

The largest prehistoric tortoise was *Colossochelys atlas*, which lived in northern India between 7,000,000 and 12,000,000 years ago. An almost complete skeleton with a carapace 5 feet 5 inches long (7 feet 4 inches over the curve) and 2 feet 11 inches high was discovered in 1923. This animal had an overall length of 8 feet and is computed to have weighed about 2,100 lbs. when it was alive.

Largest Amphibian. The largest amphibian ever recorded was the alligator-like *Eogyrinus* which lived between 280,000,000 and 345,000,000 years ago. It measured nearly 15 feet in length.

Longest Snake. The longest prehistoric snake was the python-like *Gigantophis garstini*, which inhabited what is now Egypt about 50,000,000 years ago. Parts of a spinal column discovered at El Faiyûm indicate a total length of about 42 feet.

Largest Fish. The largest fish ever recorded was the great shark *Carcharodon megalodon*, which lived between 1,000,000 and 25,000,000 years ago. In 1909, the American Museum of Natural History undertook a restoration of the jaws of this giant shark, basing the size on 4-inch-long fossil teeth, and found that the jaws measured 9 feet

JAWS OF THE LARGEST FISH: This shark, which lived about 25,000,000 years ago, must have been 80 feet long.

across and had a gape of 6 feet. The length of this fish was estimated at 80 feet. (See photo.)

Other fossil teeth measuring up to 6 inches in length and weighing 12 ounces have since been discovered near Bakersfield, California.

Earliest Animals by Type

Type and year of discovery	Location	Estimated years before present
Ape (1966)	Fayum, U.A.R.	28,000,000
Primate		
tarsier-like	Indonesia	70,000,000
lemur	Madagascar	70,000,000
Social insect (1967)	New Jersey	100,000,000
Bird (1861)	Bavaria, W. Germany	140,000,000
Mammal (1966)		
shrew-like	Pokane, Lesotho	190,000,000
Reptiles	Nova Scotia	290,000,000
Amphibian		
first quadruped	Greenland	350,000,000
Spider	Scotland	370,000,000
Insect	Scotland	370,000,000
Vertebrates		
jawless fish	near Leningrad	480,000,000
Mollusk (1952)	off Costa Rica	500,000,000
Crustacean		
12-legged	Sayan Mts., U.S.S.R.	c. 650,000,000

The earliest known primates originated about 70,000,000 years ago and were similar in form to the tarsier of Indonesia and the lemur of Madagascar. The earliest known bird was the glider *Archaeopteryx* of about 140,000,000 years ago. The earliest known mammal was a shrew-like animal between 1 and 2 inches long, whose fossilized remains, estimated to be 190,000,000 years old, were found at Pokane, in Lesotho (formerly called Basutoland), in December, 1966. The earliest known reptiles were *Hylonomus*, *Archerpeton*, *Romericus* and *Protoclepsybrops*, which all lived in Nova Scotia, Canada, about 290,000,000 years ago. The earliest amphibian and the earliest known four-legged creature was *Ichthyostega*, measuring 4 feet long, which lived in Greenland about 350,000,000 years ago. The earliest spider, *Palaeocteniza crassipes*, and the earliest insect, *Rhyniella praecursor*, a springtail, occur in a fossil peat of Middle Devonian age (about 370,000,000 years old) in Aberdeenshire, Scotland. The earliest vertebrates were agnathans, or jawless fishes, the first fragments of which occur in the Lower Ordovician period (about 480,000,000 years ago) near Leningrad, in the U.S.S.R. The most archaic living mollusk is *Neopilina galatheae*, found in 1952 off Costa Rica, belonging to a group which has survived almost unchanged for 500,000,000 years. The earliest known crustacean was the 12-legged shelled *Karagassiema*, measuring 2 feet long, found in pre-Cambrian rock in the eastern Sayan Mountains of Siberia, U.S.S.R. This animal lived about 650,000,000 years ago.

Largest Arachnid. The largest arachnid ever recorded was *Pterygotus buffaloensis*, a sea scorpion (eurypterid) which lived about 400,000,000 years ago. It grew to a length of 9 feet.

Largest Insect. The largest prehistoric insect was *Meganeura monyi*, a dragonfly of the Upper Carboniferous period (between 280,000,000 and 325,000,000 years ago), with a wing span reaching $27\frac{1}{2}$ inches.

Largest Shelled Mollusk. The Cretaceous fossil ammonite (*Pachydiscus seppenradensis*) of about 75,000,000 years ago, had a shell measuring up to 8 feet 5 inches in diameter.

Protista and Microbes

Protista. Protista were first discovered in 1676 by Anton van Leeuwenhoek (1632–1723), a Dutch microscopist. Among Protista, characteristics common to both plants and animals are exhibited. The more plant-like are termed Protophyta (protophytes) and the more animal-like are placed in the phylum Protozoa (protozoans).

Largest. The largest protozoans which are known to have existed were the now extinct Nummulites, which each had a diameter of 0.95 of an inch. The largest existing protozoan is *Pelomyxa palustris*, which may attain a length of up to 0.6 of an inch.

Smallest. The smallest of all free-living organisms are the pleuropneumonia-like organisms (P.P.L.O.) called *Mycoplasma*. One of these, *Mycoplasma laidlawii*, first discovered in sewage in 1936, has a diameter during the early part of its life of only 100 millimicrons, or 0.000004 of an inch. Examples of the strain known as H.39 has a maximum diameter of 300 millimicrons and weighs an estimated 1.0×10^{-15} of a gram. The smallest of all protophytes is *Micromonas pusilla*, with a diameter of less than 2 microns.

Longest-Lived. A culture of the protozoan *Euglena gracilis* has been kept alive for more than 20 years in King's College, London, England. Cysts of *Mastigamoeba* and *Oikomonas* have also been observed to live for more than 20 years.

Fastest-Moving. The protozoan *Monas stigmatica* has been measured to move a distance equivalent to 40 times its own length in a second. No human can cover even seven times his own length in a second.

Fastest Reproduction. The protozoan *Glaucoma*, which reproduces by binary fission, divides as frequently as every three hours. Thus in the course of a day it could become a "six greats grandparent" and the progenitor of 510 descendants.

Densest. The most densely existing species in the animal kingdom is the sea water dino-flagellate *Gymnodinium breve*, which exists at a density of 240,000,000 per gallon of sea water in certain conditions of salinity and temperature off the coast of Florida.

Bacteria

Largest. The largest of the bacteria is the sulphur bacterium *Beggiatoa mirabilis*, which is from 16 to 45 microns in width and which may form filaments several millimeters long.

Highest. In April, 1967, the U.S. National Aeronautics and Space Administration reported that bacteria had been discovered at an altitude of 135,000 feet (more than 25 miles).

Longest-Lived. The oldest deposits from which living bacteria are claimed to have been extracted are salt layers near Irkutsk. U.S.S.R., dating from about 600,000,000 years ago. The discovery of their survival was made on February 26, 1962, by Dr. H. J. Dombrowski of Freiburg University, West Germany, but it is not accepted internationally.

Toughest. The bacterium *Micrococcus radiodurans* can withstand atomic radiation 10,000 times greater than radiation that is fatal to the average man (i.e. 650 röntgens).

Viruses

Largest. The largest true viruses are the brick-shaped pox viruses (e.g. smallpox, vaccinia, orf, etc.), measuring *c.* 250 × 300 millimicrons (mμ) or 0.0003 of a millimeter.

Smallest. Of more than 1,000 identified viruses, the smallest is the potato spindle tuber virus measuring less than 20 mμ in diameter.

Sub- and Ultra-Viral Infective Agents

In January, 1967, evidence was announced from the Institute of Research on Animal Diseases at Compton, Berkshire, England, of the existence of a form of life more basic than both the virus and nucleic acid. It was named SF or Scrapie factor, from the sheep disease. If proven, this will become the most fundamental replicating particle known. Its diameter is believed to be not more than 7 millionths of a millimeter. Having now been cultured, it has been allocated back to its former status of an ultra-virus.

PLANT KINGDOM (*PLANTAE*)

Earliest Life. If one accepts the definition of life as the ability of an organism to make replicas of itself by taking as building materials the simpler molecules in the medium around it, life probably appeared on earth about 3,200,000,000 years ago. In April, 1969, minute spherical bluish fluorescent organisms up to 0.000008 of an inch in diameter were reported found in Swaziland, Southern Africa.

The oldest known living life form was announced in December, 1970, by Drs. Sanford and Barbara Siegel of Harvard University, to be a microscopic organism, similar in form to an orange slice, first collected near Harlech, Merionethshire, Wales, in 1964. It has been named *Kakabekia barghoorniana* and has existed from 2,000,000,000 years ago.

Earliest Flower. The oldest fossil of a flowering plant with palm-like imprints was found in Colorado in 1953 and dated about 65,000,000 years old.

Largest Forest. The largest afforested areas are the vast coniferous forests of the northern U.S.S.R., lying mainly between latitude 55°N. and the Arctic Circle. The total wooded areas amount to 2,700,000,000 acres (25 per cent of the world's forests), of which 38 per cent is Siberian larch. The U.S.S.R. is 34 per cent afforested.

Plant Life

Rarest. Plants thought to be extinct are rediscovered each year and there are thus many plants of which specimens are known in but a single locality.

Commonest Plants. The most widely distributed flowering plant in the world is *Cynodon dactylon*, a toothed grass found as far apart as Canada, Argentina, New Zealand, Japan and South Africa.

Northernmost. The yellow poppy (*Papaver radicatum*) and the Arctic willow (*Salix arctica*) survive the latter in an extremely stunted form, on the northernmost land (83°N.).

Southernmost. The most southerly plant life recorded is seven species of lichen found in 1933–34 by the second expedition of Rear Admiral Richard E. Byrd, U.S. Navy, in latitude 86° 03′ S in the Queen Maud Mountains, Antarctica. The southernmost recorded flowering plant is the carnation (*Colobanthus crassifolius*), which was found in latitude 67° 15′ S on Jenny Island, Margaret Bay, Graham Land (Palmer Peninsula), Antarctica.

Highest Altitude. The *Stellaria decumbens* is the flowering plant found at the highest altitude—20,130 feet up in the Himalayas.

Deepest Roots. The greatest recorded depth to which roots have penetrated is a calculated 150 feet in the case of a species of *Acacia*, probably *Acacia giraffae*, in a borehole on Okapanje Farm, about 60 miles east of Windhoek, in South-West Africa, reported in 1948.

Largest Blooms. The mottled orange-brown and white parasitic stinking corpse lily (*Rafflesia arnoldi*) has the largest of all blooms. These attach themselves to the cissus vines of the jungle in southeast Asia. They measure up to 3 feet across and ¾ of an inch thick, and attain a weight of 15 lbs.

The largest known inflorescence is that of *Puya raimondii*, a rare Bolivian plant with an erect panicle (diameter 8 feet) which emerges to a height of 35 feet. Each of these bears up to 8,000 white blooms. (See also Slowest-Flowering Plant, below.)

The world's largest blossoming plant is the giant Chinese wisteria at Sierra Madre, California. It was planted in 1892 and now has branches 500 feet long. It covers nearly an acre, weighs 252 tons and has an estimated 1,500,000 blossoms during its blossoming period of five weeks, when up to 30,000 people pay admission to visit.

Largest Leaves. The largest leaves of any plant belong to the raffia palm (*Raphia raffia*) of the Mascarene Islands, in the Indian Ocean, and the Amazonian bamboo palm (*R. toedigera*) of South America, whose leaf blades may measure up to 65 feet in length with petioles up to 13 feet.

The largest undivided leaf is that of *Alocasia macrorrhiza*, found in Sabah, East Malaysia. One found in 1966 measured 9 feet 11 inches long and 6 feet 3½ inches wide, and had an area of 34.2 square feet on one side.

Smallest Flowering Plant. The smallest of all flowering plants are duckweeds, seen on the surface of ponds. Of these, the rootless *Wolffia punctata* has fronds only 1/50th to 1/35th of an inch long.

Slowest-Flowering Plant. The slowest-flowering of all plants is the rare *Puya raimondii*, the largest of all herbs, discovered in Bolivia in 1870. The panicle emerges after about 150 years of the plant's life. It then dies. (See also above under Largest Blooms.)

Most and Least Nutritive Fruit. An analysis of the 38 commonly eaten fruits shows that the one with by far the highest calorific value is avocado (*Persea drymifolia*) with 1,200 calories per lb. That with the lowest value is rhubarb (*Rheum rhaponticum*), which is 94.9 per cent water, at 80 calories per lb. The fruit with the highest percentage of invert sugar by weight is plantain or cooking banana (*Musa paradisiaca*) with 25.3 per cent, and that with the lowest is rhubarb with 0.4 of one per cent. Apple (*Malus pumila*) and quince (*Cydonia oblonga*) are the least proteinous, at 0.3 of one per cent.

Largest Rose Tree. A "Lady Banksia" rose tree at Tombstone, Arizona, has a trunk 40 inches thick, stands 9 feet high and covers an area of 5,380 square feet, supported by 68 posts and several thousand feet of iron piping. This enables 150 people to be seated under the arbor. The original cutting came from Scotland in 1884.

Largest Rhododendron. The largest species of rhododendron is the scarlet *Rhododendron arboreum*, examples of which reach a height of 60 feet at Mangalbaré, Nepal.

Largest Aspidistra. The aspidistra (*Aspidistra elatior*) was introduced as a parlor palm to Britain from Japan and China in 1822. The biggest aspidistra in the world is one 49¾ inches tall, grown by George Munns at Perth University, Western Australia, and measured in January, 1972.

Largest Vine. The largest recorded grape vine was one planted in 1842 at Carpinteria, California. By 1900 it was yielding more than 9 tons of grapes in some years, and averaging 7 tons per year. It died in 1920.

LARGEST CACTUS: The saguaro grows to a height of 53 feet, about 10 times as high as the woman standing beneath it.

Tallest Hedge. The world's tallest hedge is the Meikleour beech hedge in Perthshire, Scotland. It was planted in 1746 and has now attained a trimmed height of 85 feet. It is 600 yeards long.

The tallest yew hedge in the world is in Earl Bathurst's Park, Cirencester, Gloucestershire, England. It was planted in 1720, runs for 130 yards, reaches 35 feet and takes 30 man-days to trim.

The tallest box hedge is one 35 feet in height at Birr Castle, Offaly, Ireland.

Largest Cactus. The largest of all cacti is the saguaro (*Cereus giganteus* or *Carnegiea gigantea*), found in Arizona, New Mexico, California, and Sonora, Mexico. The green fluted column is surmounted by candelabra-like branches rising to a height of 53 feet in the case of a specimen found in 1950 near Madrona, New Mexico. They have waxy white blooms which are followed by edible crimson fruit. A cardon cactus in Baja California, Mexico was reputed to reach 58 feet and a weight of 10 tons.

Worst Weeds. The most intransigent weed is the mat-forming water weed *Salvinia auriculata*, found in Africa. It was detected on the filling of Kariba Lake in May, 1959, and within 11 months had choked an area of 77 sq. miles, rising by 1963 to 387 sq. miles. The world's worst land weeds are regarded as purple nut sedge, Bermuda grass, barnyard grass, junglerice, goose grass, Johnson grass, Guinea grass, cogon grass and lantana.

Longest Seaweed. Claims made that seaweed off Tierra del Fuego, South America, grows to 600 and even 1,000 feet in length have gained currency. More recent and more reliable records indicate that the longest species of seaweed is the Pacific giant kelp (*Macrocyctis pyrifera*), which does not exceed 195 feet in length. It can grow 17¾ inches in a day.

Most-Spreading. The greatest area covered by a single clonal growth is that of the wild box huckleberry (*Gaylussacia brachyera*), a mat-forming evergreen shrub first reported in 1796. A colony covering 8 acres was discovered in 1845 near New Bloomfield, Pennsylvania. Another colony, covering about 100 acres, was "discovered" on July 18, 1920, near the Juniata River in Pennsylvania. It has been estimated that this colony began 13,000 years ago.

Ten-Leafed Clover. A certified ten-leafed clover (*Trifolium pratense*) found by Phillipa Smith in Woodborough, Nottinghamshire, England, in 1966 was exhibited on T.V. on July 8, 1971.

Trees

Largest Living Thing. The most massive living thing on earth is a California "big tree" (*Sequoiadendron giganteum*) named the "General Sherman," standing 272 feet 4 inches tall, in Sequoia National Park, California. It has a true girth of 79.1 feet (at 5 feet above the ground). The "General Sherman" has been estimated to contain the equivalent of 600,120 board feet of timber, sufficient to make 40 five-roomed bungalows. The foliage is blue-green, and the red-brown tan bark may be up to 24 inches thick in parts. In 1968, the official published figure for its estimated weight was 2,145 tons.

The seed of a "big tree" weighs only 1/6,000th of an ounce. Its growth to maturity may therefore represent an increase in weight of over 250,000,000,000,000 fold.

Tallest. The world's tallest known species of tree is the coast redwood (*Sequoia sempervirens*), now growing indigenously only in northern California and southern Oregon. The tallest example is now believed to be the Howard Libbey Tree in Redwood Creek Grove, Humboldt County, California, announced at 367.8 feet in 1964 but discovered to have an apparently dead top and re-estimated at 366.2 feet in 1970. The nearby tree announced to a Senate Committee by Dr. Rudolf W. Becking on June 18, 1966, to be 385 feet proved on re-measurement to be no more than 311.3 feet tall. It has a girth of 44 feet.

The tallest non-sequoia is a Douglas fir at Quinault Lake Park, Washington, of *c.* 310 feet.

The identity of the tallest tree of all time has never been satisfactorily resolved. In 1872 a mountain ash (*Eycalyptus regnans*) found in Victoria, Australia, measured 435 feet from its roots to the point where the trunk had been broken off by its fall. At this point the trunk's diameter was 3 feet, so the overall height was probably at least 500 feet. Its diameter was 18 feet at 5 feet above the ground. Another specimen, known as the "Baron Tree," was reported to be 464 feet in 1868.

Modern opinion tends to the view that the highest accurately measured Australian "big gum" tree is one 346 feet tall felled near

Colac, Victoria, in 1890. Claims for a Douglas fir (*Pseudotsuga taxifolia*) of 417 feet with a 77-foot circumference felled in British Columbia in 1940 remain unverified. The most probable claimant was thus a coast redwood of 367 feet 8 inches, felled in 1873 near Guerneville, California, this being almost exactly the same height as the Howard Libbey redwood as originally measured.

Greatest Girth. The Santa Maria del Tule tree, in the state of Oaxaca, in Mexico, is a Montezuma cypress (*Taxodium mucronatum*) with a girth of 112–113 feet at a height of 5 feet above the ground in 1949.

A figure of 204 feet in circumference was reported for the European chestnut (*Castanea sativa*) known as the "Tree of the 100 Horse" on the edge of Mount Etna, Sicily, Italy, in 1770.

Earliest. The earliest species of tree still surviving is the maidenhair tree (*Ginkgo biloba*) of China, which first appeared about 160,000,000 years ago, during the Jurassic era. It was "re-discovered" by Kaempfer (Netherlands) in 1690 and reached England *c.* 1754. It has been grown in Japan since *c.* 1100 where it is known as *Yin Kou.*

Most Expensive. The highest price ever paid for a tree is $51,000 for a single Starkspur golden delicious apple tree from near Yakima, Washington, bought by a nursery in Missouri in 1959.

Fastest-Growing. Discounting bamboo, which is not botanically classified as a tree, but as woody grass, the fastest-growing tree is *Eucalyptus deglupta*, which has been measured to grow 35 feet in 15 months in New Guinea. The youngest recorded age for a tree to reach 100 feet is 7 years for *E. regnans* in Rhodesia, and for 200 feet is 40 years for a Monterey pine in New Zealand.

Slowest-Growing. The speed of growth of trees depends largely upon conditions, although some species, such as box and yew, are always slow-growing. The extreme is represented by a specimen of Sitka spruce which required 98 years to grow to 11 inches tall, with a diameter of less than one inch, on the Arctic tree-line. The growing of miniature trees or *bonsai* is an Oriental cult mentioned as early as *c.* 1320.

Oldest. The oldest recorded living thing is a bristlecone pine (*Pinus longalva*) designated WPN-114, growing at 10,750 feet above sea level on the northeast face of Wheeler Peak (13,063 feet) in eastern Nevada. During studies in 1963 and 1964 it was found to be about 4,900 years old. The oldest dated California "big tree" (*Sequoiadendron giganteum*) is a 3,212-year-old stump felled in 1892, but larger standing specimens are estimated to be between 3,500 and 4,000 years as in the case of the "General Sherman" tree from a ring count from a core drilled in 1931. Dendrochronologists estimate the *potential* life span of a bristlecone pine at nearly 5,500 years, but that of a "big tree" at perhaps 6,000 years. Ring count dating extends back to 5,150 B.C. by examination of fallen bristlecone pine wood. Such tree-ring datings have led archeologists to realize that some radiocarbon datings could be 1,000 years or more too young.

OLDEST TREE: This bristlecone pine is estimated to be 4,900 years old.

Wood

Heaviest. The heaviest of all woods is black ironwood (*Olia laurifolia*), also called South African ironwood, with a specific gravity of up to 1.49, and weighing up to 93 lbs. per cubic foot.

Lightest. The lightest wood is *Aeschynomene hispida*, found in Cuba, which has a specific gravity of 0.044 and a weight of only 2¾ lbs. per cubic foot. The wood of the balsa tree (*Ochroma pyramidale*) is of very variable density—between 2½ and 24 lbs. per cubic foot. The density of cork is 15 lbs. per cubic foot.

Bamboo

Tallest. The tallest recorded species of bamboo is *Dendrocalamus giganteus*, native to southern Burma. It was reported in 1904 that there were specimens with a culm-length of 100 to 115 feet in the Botanic Gardens at Peradeniya, Ceylon.

Fastest-Growing. Some species of the 45 genera of bamboo have attained growth rates of up to 36 inches per day (0.00002 m.p.h.), on their way to reaching a height of 100 feet in less than three months.

Mosses

The smallest of mosses is the pygmy moss (*Ephemerum*), and the longest is the brook moss (*Fontinalis*), which forms streamers up to 3 feet long in flowing water.

Fungi

Largest. The largest recorded ground fungus was a specimen of the giant puff ball (*Calvatia gigantea*), which was 5 feet 3 inches long,

4 feet 5 inches wide and 9½ inches high. It was discovered in New York State in 1884.

Largest Tree Fungus. The largest officially recorded tree fungus was a specimen of *Oxyporus* (*Fomes*) *nobilissimus*, measuring 56 inches by 37 inches and weighing at least 300 lbs., found by J. Hisey in Washington State in 1946.

Most Poisonous Toadstool. The yellowish-olive death cap (*Amanita phalloides*) is regarded as the world's most poisonous fungus. From 6 to 15 hours after tasting, the effects are vomiting, delirium, collapse and death. Among its victims was Cardinal Giulio de' Medici, Pope Clement VII (1478–1534).

Ferns

Largest. The largest of all the more than 6,000 species of fern is the tree-fern (*Alsophila excelsa*) of Norfolk Island, in the South Pacific, which attains a height of up to 80 feet.

Smallest. The world's smallest ferns are *Hecistopteris pumila*, found in Central America, and *Azolla caroliniana*, which is native to the U.S.

Orchids

Largest. The largest of all orchids is *Grammatophyllum speciosium*, native to Malaysia. A specimen recorded in Penang, West Malaysia, in the 19th century had 30 spikes up to 8 feet tall and a diameter of more than 40 feet. The largest orchid flower is that of *Selenipedium caudatum*, found in tropical areas of America. Its petals are up to 18 inches long, giving it a maximum outstretched diameter of 3 feet. The flower is, however, much less bulky than that of the stinking corpse lily (see Largest Blooms).

Tallest. The tallest of all orchids is the terrestrial tree-orchid (*Angraecum infundibulare*) which grows in the swamps of Uganda to a height of 12 feet.

Smallest. The smallest orchid plant is believed to be *Notylia norae*, found in Venezuela. The smallest orchid flower is that of *Bulbophyllum minutissium*, found in Australia.

Highest-Priced. The highest price ever paid for an orchid is £1,207 10s. (then $6,000), paid by Baron Schröder to Sanders of St. Albans for an *Odontoglossu crispum* (variety *pittianum*) at an auction by Protheroe & Morris of Bow Lane, London, England, on March 22, 1906.

Seeds

Largest. The largest seed in the world is that of the double coconut or Coco de Mer (*Lodoicea seychellarum*), the single-seeded fruit of which may weigh 40 lbs. This grows only in the Seychelles Islands, in the Indian Ocean.

Smallest. The smallest seeds are those of epiphytic orchids, at 35,000,000 to the ounce (*cf.* grass pollens at up to 6,000,000,000 grains per ounce). A single plant of the American ragweed can generate 8,000,000,000 pollen grains in five hours.

LARGEST SEED: The Coco de Mer seed may weigh 40 lbs. It grows only in the Seychelles Islands in the Indian Ocean.

Most Durable. The most durable of all seeds are those of the Arctic lupin (*Lupinus arcticus*) found in frozen silt at Miller Creek in the Yukon, Canada, in July, 1954. They were germinated in 1966 and dated by the radio-carbon method to at least 8,000 B.C. and more probably to 13,000 B.C.

Parks, Zoos, Aquaria and Oceanaria

Largest Park. The world's largest park is the Wood Buffalo National Park in Alberta, Canada, which has an area of 11,172,000 acres (17,560 square miles).

Smallest Park. The smallest park in the world is Mill Ends Park on a safety island on S.W. Front Avenue, Portland, Oregon. It measures 452.4 square inches and was designated in 1948 at the behest of the city journalist Dick Fagan (died 1969) for snail races and as a colony for leprechauns.

Smallest Reserve. The world's smallest nature reserve is believed to be the Badgeworth Nature Reserve (346 square yards), near Cheltenham, Gloucestershire, England. Owned by the Society for the Promotion of Nature Reserves, it is leased to the Gloucestershire Trust for Nature Conservation to protect the sole site in the British Isles of the adder's-tongue spearwort (*Ranunculus ophioglossifolius*).

Largest Zoo. It has been estimated that throughout the world there are some 500 zoos with an estimated annual attendance of 330,000,000. The largest zoological preserve in the world is the Etosha Reserve, South-West Africa, with an area which grew between 1907 and 1970 to 38,427 square miles. (It was thus larger than Ireland.) In 1970 it was announced that the Kaokoveld section of 26,000 square miles had been de-proclaimed in the interests of the 10,000 Ovahimba and Ovatjimba living in the area.

Largest Collection. The largest collection in any zoo is that in the Zoological Gardens of West Berlin, Germany. At January 1, 1972, the zoo had a total of 12,653 specimens from 2,399 species. This total included 1,057 mammals (230 species), 2,801 birds (746 species), 575 reptiles (289 species), 148 amphibians (67 species), 2,863 fishes (782 species) and 5,209 invertebrates (285 species).

Oldest. The oldest known zoo is that at Schönbrunn, Vienna, Austria, built in 1752 by the Holy Roman Emperor Franz Josef for his wife Maria Theresa. The oldest privately owned zoo in the world is that of the Zoological Society of London, founded in 1826. Its collection is housed partly in Regent's Park, London (36 acres) and partly at Whipsnade Park, Bedfordshire (541 acres, opened 1931).

The earliest known collection of animals (not a public zoo) was that set up by Wu-Wang, the first Emperor of the famous Chou Dynasty in China, about 1050 B.C. This "Park of Intelligence" contained tigers, deer, rhinoceroses, birds, snakes, tortoises and fish.

Most Valuable Zoo Animal. The most valuable animal is Chi-Chi, the giant panda (*Ailuropoda melanoleuca*) in the London Zoo, worth $33,500. She was captured in China on July 4, 1957, when aged probably six months, and died in July, 1972.

Largest Aquarium. The world's largest is the John G. Shedd Aquarium, 12th Street and Grant Park, Chicago, completed in November, 1929, at a cost of $3,250,000. The total capacity of its display tanks is 450,000 gallons, with reservoir tanks holding 2,000,000 gallons. Exhibited are 10,000 specimens from 350 species. Salt water is brought in road and rail tankers from Key West, Florida, and a tanker barge from the Gulf of Mexico. The record attendances are 78,658 in a day on May 21, 1931, and 4,689,730 visitors in the single year of 1931.

Earliest Oceanarium. The world's first oceanarium is Marineland of Florida, opened in 1938 at a site 18 miles south of St. Augustine. Up to 7,000,000 gallons of sea water are pumped daily through two major tanks, one rectangular (100 feet long by 40 feet wide by 18 feet deep) containing 450,000 gallons and one circular (233 feet in circumference and 12 feet deep) containing 400,000 gallons. The tanks are seascaped, including coral reefs and even a shipwreck.

Largest Oceanarium. The largest salt water tank in the world is that at the Marineland of the Pacific, Palos Verdes Peninsula, California. It is $251\frac{1}{2}$ feet in circumference and 22 feet deep, with a capacity of 640,000 gallons. The total capacity of the whole oceanarium is 2,200,000 gallons.

WORST RECENT EARTHQUAKE: When Alaska was hit in 1964, boats at Anchorage were lifted far inland.

Chapter Three

THE NATURAL WORLD

1. Natural Phenomena

EARTHQUAKES

It is estimated that each year there are some 500,000 detectable seismic or micro-seismic disturbances of which 100,000 can be felt and 1,000 cause damage.

Greatest. Using the comparative scale of Mantle Wave magnitudes (defined in 1968), the world's largest earthquake since 1930 has been the cataclysmic Alaska or Prince William Sound earthquake (epicenter Latitude 61° 10′ N., Longitude 147° 48′ W.) of March 28, 1964, with a magnitude of 8.9. The Kamchatka, U.S.S.R., earthquake (epicenter Lat. 52° 45′ N., Long. 159° 30′ E.) of November 4, 1952, and the shocks around Lebu, south of Concepción, Chile, on May 22, 1960, are both now assessed at a magnitude of 8.8. Formerly the largest earthquake during this period had been regarded as the submarine shock (epicenter Lat. 39° 30′ N., Long. 144° 30′ E.) about 100 miles off the Sanriku coast of northeastern Honshu, Japan, on March 2, 1933, estimated at 8.9 on the Gutenberg-Richter scale (1956).

It is possible that the earthquake in Lisbon, Portugal, on November 1, 1755, would have been accorded a magnitude of between 8.75 and 9, if seismographs, invented in 1853, had been available then to record traces. The first of the three shocks was at 9:40 a.m. and lasted for between 6 and 7 minutes. Lakes in Norway were disturbed. The energy of an earthquake of magnitude 8.9 is about 5.6×10^{24} ergs, which is equivalent to an explosion of 140 megatons (140,000,000 tons of trinitrotoluene $[C_7H_5(NO_2)_3]$, called T.N.T.).

Worst. The greatest loss of life occurred in the earthquake in Shensi Province, China, on January 23, 1556, when an estimated 830,000 people were killed. The greatest material damage was in the earthquake on the Kwanto plain, Japan, at 11:58 a.m. on September 1, 1923 (magnitude 8.2, epicenter in Lat. 24°48′N., Long. 139°21′E.). In Sagami Bay, the sea bottom in one area sank 1,310 feet. The official total of persons killed and missing in this earthquake called the *Shinsai* or Great 'Quake, and the resultant fires was 142,807. In Tokyo and Yokohama 575,000 dwellings were destroyed. The cost of the damage was estimated at $2,800,000,000.

VOLCANOES

The total number of known active volcanoes in the world is 455 with an estimated 80 more submarine. The greatest concentration is in Indonesia, where 77 of its 167 volcanoes have erupted within historic times.

Greatest Eruption. The total volume of matter discharged in the eruption of Tambora, a volcano on the island of Sumbawa, in Indonesia, on April 7, 1815, has been estimated as 36.4 cubic miles. The energy of this eruption was 8.4×10^{26} ergs. The volcano lost about 4,100 feet in height and a crater 7 miles in diameter was formed. This compares with a probable 15 cubic miles ejected by Santoríni and 4.3 cubic miles ejected by Krakatoa (see next entry). The internal pressure causing the Tambora eruption has been estimated at 46,500,000 lbs. per square inch.

Greatest Explosion. The greatest known volcanic explosion was the eruption in *c.* 1470 B.C. of Thíra (Santoríni), a volcanic island in the Aegean Sea. It is highly probable that this explosion destroyed the centers of the Minoan civilization in Crete, about 80 miles away, with a tsunami (tidal wave) 165 feet high. Evidence was published in December, 1967, of an eruption that spewed lava over 100,000 square miles of Oregon, Idaho, Nevada and Northern California about 3,000,000 years ago.

The greatest explosion since Santoríni occurred at 9:56 a.m. (local time), or 2:56 a.m. G.M.T., on August 27, 1883, with an eruption of Krakatoa, an island (then 18 square miles) in the Sunda Strait between Sumatra and Java, in Indonesia. A total of 163 villages were wiped out, and 36,380 people killed by the wave it caused. Rocks were thrown to a height of 34 miles and dust fell 10 days later at a distance of 3,313 miles. The explosion was recorded four hours later on the island of Rodrigues, 2,968 miles away, as "the roar of heavy guns" and was heard over 1/13th part of the surface of the globe. This explosion has been estimated to have had about 26 times the

HIGHEST DORMANT VOLCANO: Llullaillaco in the Andes is 22,058 feet above sea level.

power of the greatest H-bomb test detonation, but was still only a fifth the size of the Santoríni cataclysm (see above).

Highest—Extinct. The highest extinct volcano in the world is Cerro Aconcagua (22,834 feet), on the Argentine side of the Andes. It was first climbed on January 14, 1897, and was the highest mountain climbed until June 12, 1907.

Highest—Dormant. The highest dormant volcano is Volcán Llullaillaco (22,058 feet), on the frontier between Chile and Argentina.

Highest—Active. The highest volcano regarded as active is Volcán Antofalla (20,013 feet) in Argentina, though a more definite claim is made for Volcán Guayatiri or Guallatiri (19,882 feet), in Chile, which erupted in 1959.

Northernmost. The northernmost volcano is Beeren Berg (7,470 feet) on the island of Jan Mayen (71°05′N.) in the Greenland Sea. The island was possibly discovered by Henry Hudson in 1607 or 1608, but definitely visited by Jan Jacobsz May (Netherlands) in 1614. It was annexed by Norway on May 8, 1929.

Southernmost. The most southerly known active volcano is Mount Erebus (12,450 feet) on Ross Island (77°35′S.), in Antarctica. It was discovered on Janaury 28, 1841, by the expedition of Captain (later Rear-Admiral Sir) James Clark Ross (1800–62) of the British Royal Navy, and first climbed at 10 a.m. on March 10, 1908, by a British party of five, led by Professor (later Lieut.-Col. Sir) Tannatt William Edgeworth David (1858–1934).

Largest Crater. The world's largest *caldera* or volcano crater is that of Mt. Aso (5,223 feet) in Kyushu, Japan, which measures 17 miles north to south, 10 miles east to west and 71 miles in circumference. The longest lava flows, known as *pahoehoe* (twisted cord-like solidifications), are 60 miles in length and are in Iceland.

TALLEST GEYSER: After erupting to more than 1,000 feet high in 1909, the Waimangu geyser in New Zealand has not been active since 1917.

GEYSERS

Tallest. The Waimangu geyser, in New Zealand, erupted to a height in excess of 1,000 feet in 1909, but has not been active since it erupted violently in 1917. Currently the world's tallest active geyser is the "Giant" in the Yellowstone National Park, Wyoming, discovered in 1870, which erupts at intervals varying from 7 days to 3 months, throwing a spire 200 feet high at a rate of 700,000 gallons per hour. The *Geysir* ("gusher") near Mt. Hekla in south-central Iceland, from which all others have been named, spurts, on occasions, to 180 feet.

2. Structure and Dimensions

The earth is not a true sphere, but flattened at the poles and hence an ellipsoid. The polar diameter of the earth (7,899.809 miles) is 25.576 miles less than the equatorial diameter (7,926.385 miles). The earth also has a slight ellipticity of the equator since its long axis (about longitude 37° W.) is 174 yards greater than the short axis. The greatest departures from the reference ellipsoid are a protuberance of 266 feet in the area of New Guinea, and a depression of 371 feet south of Ceylon in the Indian Ocean.

The greatest circumference of the earth, at the equator, is 24,901.47 miles, compared with 24,859.75 miles at the meridian. The area of the surface is estimated to be 196,937,600 square miles. The period of axial rotation, *i.e.* the true sidereal day, is 23 hours 56 minutes 4.0996 seconds, mean time.

Earth's Structure

The mass of the earth is 6,588,000,000,000,000,000,000 tons and its density is 5.517 times that of water. The volume is an estimated 259,875,424,000 cubic miles. The earth picks up cosmic dust but estimates vary widely with 40,000 long tons a day being the upper limit. Modern theory is that the earth has an outer shell or lithosphere about 25 miles thick, then an outer and inner rock layer or mantle extending 1,800 miles deep, below which there is an iron-nickel core at an estimated temperature of 3,700°C. and at a pressure of 27,400 tons per square inch or 3,400 kilobars. If the iron-nickel core theory is correct, iron must be by far the most abundant element in the earth.

Rocks

The age of the earth is generally considered to be within the range 4,600 ±100 million years, by analogy with directly measured ages of meteorites and of the moon. However, no rocks of this great age have yet been found on the earth, since geological processes have presumably destroyed the earliest record.

Oldest. The greatest recorded age for any reliably dated rock is 3,800 ±50 million years for the Amitsoq Gneiss from the Godthaab area of West Greenland, as measured by the rubidium-strontium method by workers at Oxford University, England. A date of 3,550 million years has been reported for the Morton Gneiss of Minnesota, measured by the uranium-lead method by American workers, while a number of dates in the general range 3,200—3,400 million years have been reported from Africa, India and the U.S.S.R.

Largest. The largest exposed rocky outcrop is the 1,237-foot-high Mount Augustus (3,627 feet above sea level), discovered on June 3, 1858, about 200 miles east of Carnarvon, Western Australia. It is an up-faulted monoclinal gritty conglomerate 5 miles long and 2 miles across and thus twice the size of the celebrated monolithic arkose Ayer's Rock (1,100 feet), 250 miles southwest of Alice Springs, in Northern Territory, Australia.

OCEANS

Largest. The area of the earth covered by the sea is estimated to be 139,670,000 square miles, or 70.92 per cent of the total surface. The mean depth of the hydrosphere was commonly assumed to be 12,450 feet, but recent surveys suggest a lower estimate, closer to 11,660 feet. The total weight of the water is estimated as 1.45×10^{18} tons, or 0.022 per cent of the earth's total weight. The volume of the oceans is estimated to be 308,400,000 cubic miles, compared with only 8,400,000 cubic miles of fresh water.

LARGEST EXPOSED ROCK: Mount Augustus in Western Australia is 5 miles long by 2 miles wide.

The largest ocean in the world is the Pacific. Excluding adjacent seas, it represents 45.8 per cent of the world's oceans and is about 63,800,000 square miles in area.

Most Southerly. The most southerly point in the oceans is 85°34'S., 154°W., at the snout of the Robert Scott Glacier, 305 miles from the South Pole, in the Pacific sector of Antarctica.

Deepest. The deepest part of the ocean was first discovered in 1951 by the British survey ship *Challenger* in the Marianas Trench in the Pacific Ocean. The depth was measured by sounding and by echo-sounder and published as 5,960 fathoms (35,760 feet). Subsequent visits to the Challenger Deep have resulted in claims by echo-sounder only, culminating in one of 36,198 feet by the U.S.S.R.'s research ship *Vityaz* in March, 1959. A metal object, say a pound-ball of steel, dropped into water above this trench would take nearly 63 minutes to fall to the sea bed 6.85 miles below. The average depth of the Pacific Ocean is 14,000 feet.

Remotest Spot

The world's most distant point from land is a spot in the South Pacific, approximately 48°30'S., 125°30'W., which is about 1,660 miles from the nearest points of land, namely Pitcairn Island, Ducie Island and Cape Dart, Antarctica. Centered on this spot, therefore, is a circle of water with an area of about 8,657,000 square miles—about 7,000 square miles larger than the U.S.S.R., the world's largest country (see Chapter 10).

Sea Temperature

The temperature of the water at the surface of the sea varies from —2°C. (28.5°F.) in the White Sea to 35.6°C. (96°F.) in the Persian Gulf in summer. A freak geothermal temperature of 56°C. (132.8°F.) was recorded in February, 1965, by the survey ship *Atlantis II*, near the bottom of Discovery Deep (7,200 feet) in the Red Sea. The normal sea temperature in the area is 22° C. (71.6° F.).

Largest Sea

The largest of the world's seas (as opposed to oceans) is the South China Sea, with an area of 1,148,500 square miles. The Malayan Sea comprising the waters between the Indian Ocean and the South Pacific, south of the Chinese mainland, covering 3,144,000 square miles, is not now an entity accepted by the International Hydrographic Bureau.

Largest Gulf

The largest gulf in the world is the Gulf of Mexico, with a shoreline of 3,100 miles from Cape Sable, Florida, to Cabo Catoche, Mexico.

Largest Bay

The largest bay in the world is the Bay of Bengal, with a shoreline of 2,250 miles from southeastern Ceylon to Pagoda Point, Burma. Its mouth measures 1,075 miles across.

Highest Sea-Mountain

The highest known submarine mountain is one discovered in 1953 near the Tonga Trench between Samoa and New Zealand. It rises 28,500 feet from the sea bed, with its summit 1,200 feet below the surface.

Straits

Longest. The longest straits in the world are the Malacca Straits between West Malaysia (formerly called Malaya) and Sumatra, in Indonesia, which extend for 485 miles.

Broadest. The broadest straits in the world are the Mozambique Straits, between Mozambique and Madagascar, which are at one point 245 miles across.

Narrowest. The narrowest navigable straits are those between the Aegean island of Euboea and the mainland of Greece. The gap is only 45 yards wide at Chalkis. The Seil Sound, Argyllshire, Scotland, narrows to a point only 20 feet wide where a bridge joins the island of Seil to the mainland and is thus said to span the Atlantic.

Highest Wave

The highest officially recorded sea wave was measured from the U.S.S. *Ramapo* proceeding from Manila, Philippines, to San Diego, California, on the night of February 6–7, 1933, during a 68-knot (78.3 m.p.h.) gale. The wave was computed to be 112 feet from trough to crest. A stereo-photograph of a wave calculated to be 81.7 feet high was taken from the U.S.S.R.s' diesel-electric vessel *Ob'* in the South Pacific Ocean, about 370 miles south of Macquarie Island, Australia, on April 2, 1956.

The highest instrumentally measured wave was one calculated to be exactly 77 feet high, recorded by the British ship *Weather Reporter* on station Juliette in the North Atlantic at noon on February 17, 1968. Its length was 1,150 feet and its period was 15 seconds. It has been calculated on the statistics of the Stationary Random Theory that one wave in more than 300,000 may exceed the average by a factor of 4.

On July 9, 1958, a landslip caused a wave to wash 1,740 feet high along the shore of Lituya Bay, Alaska.

"Tidal" Wave. The highest recorded seismic sea wave, or *tsunami*, was one of 220 feet which appeared off Valdez, southwest Alaska, after the great Prince William Sound earthquake of March 27, 1964. *Tsunami* (a Japanese word which is singular and plural) have been observed to travel at 490 m.p.h. Between 479 B.C. and 1967 there were 286 instances of devastating *tsunami*.

Greatest Current. The greatest current in the oceans of the world is the Antarctic Circumpolar Current, which was measured in 1969 in the Drake Passage between South America and Antarctica to be flowing at a rate of 9,500,000,000 cubic feet per second—nearly three times that of the Gulf Stream. Its width ranges from 185 to 620 miles and has a surface flow rate of $\frac{3}{4}$ of a knot.

Strongest Current. The world's strongest currents are the Saltstraumen in the Saltfjord, near Bodo, Norway, which reach 15.6 knots (18.0 m.p.h.). The flow rate through the 500-foot-wide channel surpasses 500,000 cu/secs.

Greatest Tides. The greatest tides in the world occur in the Bay of Fundy, which separates Nova Scotia from Maine and the Canadian province of New Brunswick. Burncoat Head in the Minas Basin, Nova Scotia, has the greatest mean spring range with 47.5 feet, and an extreme range of 53.5 feet. (See photographs.)

Icebergs

Largest. The largest iceberg on record was an Antarctic tabular berg of over 12,000 square miles (208 miles long and 60 miles wide) sighted 150 miles west of Scott Island, in the South Pacific Ocean, by the U.S.S. *Glacier* on November 12, 1956. This iceberg was thus larger than Belgium.

The 200-foot-thick Arctic ice island T.1 (140 square miles) was discovered in 1946, and was still being plotted in 1963.

Most Southerly Arctic. The most southerly Arctic iceberg was sighted in the Atlantic in 30°50′N., 45°06′W., on June 2, 1934.

Most Northerly Antarctic. The most northerly Antarctic iceberg was a remnant sighted in the Atlantic by the ship *Dochra* at Lat. 26°30′S., Long. 25°40′W., on April 30, 1894.

Tallest. The tallest on record was an iceberg carved off northwest Greenland with 550 feet showing above the surface.

LAND

There is satisfactory evidence that at one time the earth's land surface comprised a single primeval continent of 80,000,000 square miles, now termed Pangaea, and that this split about 190,000,000 years ago, during the Jurassic period, into two super-continents, termed Laurasia (Eurasia, Greenland and North America) in the north and Gondwanaland, named after Gondwana, India (comprising Africa, Arabia, India, South America, Oceania and Antarctica) in the south. The South Pole was apparently in the area of the Sahara as recently as the Ordovician period of *c.* 450 million years ago.

Largest and Smallest Continents. Only 29.08 per cent, or an estimated 57,270,000 square miles, of the earth's surface is land, with a mean height of 2,480 feet above sea level. The Eurasian land mass is the largest with an area (including islands) of 21,053,000 square miles.

The smallest is the Australian mainland, with an area of about 2,940,000 square miles, which, together with Tasmania, New Zealand, New Guinea and the Pacific Islands, is described as Oceania. The total area of Oceania is about 3,450,000 square miles, including West Irian (formerly West New Guinea) which is politically in Asia.

Remotest Land. There is an unpinpointed spot in the Dzoosotoyn Elisen (desert), northern Sinkiang, China, that is more than 1,500 miles from the open sea in any direction. The nearest large town to this point is Wulumuchi (Urumchi) to its south.

Peninsula. The world's largest peninsula is Arabia, with an area of about 1,250,000 square miles.

GREATEST TIDAL CHANGE: In the Bay of Fundy, between Nova Scotia and Maine, the tide may rise or drop 53½ feet, as shown by the above two views of the same ship at the dock, at high tide (top) and low tide (below).

Islands

Largest. Discounting Australia, which is usually regarded as a continental land mass, the largest island in the world is Greenland (Kingdom of Denmark), with an area of about 840,000 square miles. There is some evidence that Greenland is in fact several islands overlaid by an ice-cap.

The largest island surrounded by fresh water is the Ilha de Marajó (1,553 square miles), in the mouth of the Amazon River, Brazil. The largest island in a lake is Manitoulin Island (1,068 square miles) in the Canadian (Ontario) section of Lake Huron. This island itself has on it a lake of 41.09 square miles called Manitou Lake, in which there are several islands.

Remotest. The remotest island in the world is Bouvet Oya (formerly Liverpool Island), discovered in the South Atlantic by J. B. C. Bouvet de Lozier on January 1, 1739, and first landed on by Capt. George Norris on December 16, 1825. Its position is 54°26'S., 3°24'E. This uninhabited Norwegian dependency is about 1,050 miles from the nearest land—the uninhabited Queen Maud Land coast of eastern Antarctica.

The remotest inhabited island in the world is Tristan da Cunha, discovered in the South Atlantic by Tristão da Cunha, a Portuguese admiral, in March, 1506. It has an area of 38 square miles (habitable area 12 square miles) and was annexed by the United Kingdom on August 14, 1816. The island's population was 235 in August, 1966. The nearest inhabited land is the island of St. Helena, 1,320 miles to the northeast. The nearest continent, Africa, is 1,700 miles away.

Newest. The world's newest island is a volcanic one about 100 feet high, which began forming in 1970 south of Gatukai Island in the British Solomon Islands, South-West Pacific.

Greatest Archipelago. The world's greatest archipelago is the 3,500-mile-long crescent of over 3,000 islands which forms Indonesia.

Northernmost Land. The most northerly land is Kaffeklubben Øyen off the northeast of Greenland, 440 miles from the North Pole, discovered in 1921, but determined only in June, 1969, to be in latitude 83° 40' 6".

Longest Reef. The longest reef in the world is the Great Barrier reef off Queensland, northeastern Australia, which is 1,260 geographical miles in length. Between 1959 and 1969 a large section between Cooktown and Townsville was destroyed by the proliferation of the Crown of Thorns starfish (*Acanthaster planci*).

Largest Atoll. The largest atoll in the world is Kwajalein in the Marshall Islands, in the central Pacific Ocean. Its slender 176-mile-long coral reef encloses a lagoon of 1,100 square miles. (See photograph.)

The atoll with the largest land area is Christmas Island, in the Line Islands, in the central Pacific Ocean. It has an area of 184 square miles. Its two principal settlements, London and Paris, are 4 miles apart.

Mountains

Highest. An eastern Himalayan peak of 29,028 feet above sea level on the Tibet-Nepal border (in an area first designated Chu-mu lang-ma on a map of 1717) was discovered to be the world's highest mountain in 1852 by the Survey Department of the Government of India, from theodolite readings taken in 1849 and 1850. In 1860 its height was computed to be 29,002 feet. The 5½-mile-high peak was named Mount Everest after Sir George Everest (1790–1866),

LARGEST ATOLL: Kwajalein, inhabited island of the Marshall group in the central Pacific, encloses a lagoon of 1,100 square miles.

formerly Surveyor-General of India. After a total loss of 11 lives since the first reconnaisance in 1921, Everest was finally conquered at 11:30 a.m. on May 29, 1953. (For details of ascents, see under Mountaineering in Chapter 12.)

The mountain whose summit is farthest from the earth's center is the Andean peak of Chimborazo (20,561 feet), 98 miles south of the equator in Ecuador.

On May 7, 1949, the Clark Expedition claimed an unacceptable altitude of 29,661 feet for Amne Machin (23,491 feet) in western China, first climbed by a Chinese party on June 2, 1960.

The highest insular island in the world is Mt. Sukarno (Carstensz Pyramide) (17,096 feet) in West Irian (formerly New Guinea), Indonesia.

Highest Unclimbed. Excluding subsidiary summits, the highest separate unclimbed mountain in the world is Gasherbrum III (26,090 feet) in the Karakoram, followed by Kangbachen (25,925 feet) in the Himalaya. These rank, respectively, 15th and 19th in height. (See photograph on next page.)

Largest. The world's tallest mountain measured from its submarine base (3,280 fathoms) in the Hawaiian Trough to peak is Mauna Kea (Mountain White) on the island of Hawaii, with a combined height of 33,476 feet, of which 13,796 feet are above sea level. Another mountain whose dimensions, but not height, exceed those of Mount Everest is the Hawaiian peak of Mauna Loa (Mountain Long) at 13,680 feet. The axes of its elliptical base, 15,000 feet below sea level, have been estimated at 74 miles and 53 miles. It should be noted that Cerro Aconcagua (22,834 feet) is more than 38,800 feet above the 16,000-foot-deep Pacific abyssal plain or 42,824 feet above the Peru-Chile Trench, which is 180 miles distant in the South Pacific.

Greatest Ranges. The world's greatest land mountain range is the Himalaya-Karakoram, which contains 96 of the world's 108 peaks of over 24,000 feet. The greatest of all mountain ranges is, however, the submarine mid-Atlantic range, which is 10,000 miles long and 500 miles wide, with its highest peak being Mount Pico in

HIGHEST UNCLIMBED MOUNTAIN: Gasherbrum III (26,090 feet) in the Karakoram range, Kashmir, is the 15th highest peak in the world.

the Azores, which rises 23,615 feet from the ocean floor (7,615 feet above sea level).

Greatest Plateau. The most extensive high plateau in the world is the Tibetan Plateau in Central Asia. The average altitude is 16,000 feet and the area is 77,000 square miles.

Highest Halites. Along the northern shores of the Gulf of Mexico for 725 miles there exist 330 subterranean "mountains" of salt, some of which rise more than 60,000 feet from bed rock and appear as the low salt domes first discovered in 1862.

Sand Dunes. The world's highest measured sand dunes are those in the Saharan sand sea of Isaouane-N-Tiferine of east central Algeria in Lat. 26° 42′ N, Long. 6° 43′ E. They have a wave-length of nearly 3 miles and attain a height of 1,410 feet.

Depressions

Deepest. The deepest depression so far discovered is beneath the Hollick-Kenyon Plateau in Marie Byrd Land, Antarctica, where, at a point 5,900 feet above sea level, the ice depth is 14,000 feet, hence indicating a bed rock depression 8,100 feet below sea level.

The deepest exposed depression on land is the shore surrounding the Dead Sea, 1,291 feet below sea level. The deepest point on the bed of the lake is 2,600 feet below the Mediterranean. The deepest part of the bed of Lake Baykal in Siberia, U.S.S.R., is 4,872 feet below sea level.

The greatest submarine depression is a large area of the floor of the northwest Pacific which has an average depth of 15,000 feet.

Largest. The largest exposed depression in the world is the Caspian Sea basin in the Azerbaijan, Russian, Kazakh, and Turkmen republics of the U.S.S.R. and northern Iran (Persia). It is more than 200,000 square miles, of which 143,550 square miles is lake area. The preponderant land area of the depression is the Prikaspiyskaya Nizmennost', lying around the northern third of the lake and stretching inland for a distance of up to 280 miles.

Rivers

The river systems of the world are estimated to contain 55,000 cubic miles of fresh water.

Longest. The two longest rivers in the world are the Amazon (*Amazonas*), flowing into the South Atlantic, and the Nile (*Bahr-el-Nil*) flowing into the Mediterranean. Which is the longer is a matter of definition rather than measurement.

The true source of the Amazon was discovered in 1953 to be a stream named Huarco, rising near the summit of Cerro Huagra (17,188 ft.) in Peru. This stream progressively becomes the Toro, then the Santiago, then the Apurímac, which in turn is known as the Ene, and then the Tambo before its confluence with the Amazon prime tributary, the Ucayali. The length of the Amazon from this source to the South Atlantic *via* the Canal do Norte was measured in 1969 to be 4,007 miles (usually quoted to the rounded-off figure of 4,000 miles).

If, however, a vessel navigating down river turns to the south of Ilha de Marajó through the straits of Breves and Boiuci into the Pará, the total length of the waterway becomes 4,195 miles. The Pará is not however a tributary of the Amazon, being hydrologically part of the basin of the Tocantins.

The length of the Nile waterway, as surveyed by M. Devroey (Belgium) before the loss of a few miles of meanders due to the formation of Lake Nasser, behind the Aswan High Dam, was 4,145 miles. This course is the hydrologically acceptable one from the source in Ruanda of the Luvironza branch of the Kagera feeder of the Victoria Nyanza *via* the White Nile (*Bahr-el-Jebel*) to the delta.

Greatest Flow. The greatest flow of any river in the world is that of the Amazon, which discharges an average of 4,200,000 cubic feet of water per second into the Atlantic Ocean, rising to more than 7,000,000 "cusecs" in full flood. The lowest 900 miles of the Amazon average 300 feet in depth.

Largest Basin. The largest river basin in the world is that drained by the Amazon (4,195 miles). It covers about 2,720,000 square miles. It has about 15,000 tributaries and sub-tributaries, of which four are more than 1,000 miles long. These include the Madeira, the longest of all tributaries, with a length of 2,100 miles, which is surpassed by only 14 rivers.

The longest sub-tributary is the Pilcomayo (1,000 miles long) in South America. It is a tributary of the Paraguay (1,500 miles long), which is itself a tributary of the Paraná (2,500 miles).

Submarine River. In 1952 a submarine river 250 miles wide, known as the Cromwell current, was discovered flowing eastward 300 feet below the surface of the Pacific for 3,500 miles along the equator. Its volume is 1,000 times that of the Mississippi.

Subterranean River. In August, 1958, a crypto-river was tracked by radio-isotopes flowing under the Nile, with a mean annual flow six times greater—560,000 million cubic meters (20 million million cubic feet).

Longest Estuary. The world's longest estuary is that of the Ob', in the northern U.S.S.R., at 450 miles.

Largest Delta. The world's largest delta is that created by the Ganga (Ganges) and Brahmaputra in East Pakistan and West Bengal, India. It covers an area of 30,000 square miles.

Greatest River Bores. The bore on the Ch'ient'ang-kiang (Hang-chou-fe) in eastern China is the most remarkable in the world. At spring tides, the wave attains a height of up to 25 feet and a speed of 13 knots. It is heard advancing at a range of 14 miles. The bore on the Hooghly branch of the Ganges travels for 70 miles at more than 15 knots. The annual downstream flood wave on the Mekong River of Southeast Asia sometimes reaches a height of 46 feet. The greatest volume of any bore is that of the Canal do Norte (10 miles wide) in the mouth of the Amazon.

Fastest Rapids. The fastest rapids which have ever been navigated are the Lava Falls on the Colorado River. At times of flood these attain a speed of 30 m.p.h. with waves boiling up to 12 feet high.

Lakes and Inland Seas

Largest. The largest inland sea or lake in the world is the Kaspiskoye More (Caspian Sea) in southern U.S.S.R. and Iran (Persia). It is 760 miles long and its total area is 143,550 square miles. Of the total area, 55,280 square miles (38.6 per cent) is in Iran, where the lake is named the Darya-ye-Khazar. Its maximum depth is 3,215 feet and its surface is 92 feet below sea level. Since 1930 it has diminished 15,000 square miles in area with a fall of 62 feet, while the shore line has retreated more than 10 miles in some places.

The freshwater lake with the greatest surface area is Lake Superior, one of the Great Lakes. The total area is about 31,800 square miles, of which 20,700 square miles are in the U.S. and 11,100 square miles in Ontario, Canada. It is 600 feet above sea level. The freshwater lake with the greatest volume is Baykal (see Deepest, below) with an estimated volume of 5,750 cubic miles.

Lake in a Lake. The largest lake in a lake is Manitou Lake (41.09 square miles) on Manitoulin Island (1,068 square miles) in the Canadian part of Lake Huron.

Deepest. The deepest lake in the world is Ozero (Lake) Baykal in central Siberia, U.S.S.R. It is 385 miles long and between 20 and 46 miles wide. In 1957 the Olkhon Crevice was measured to be 6,365 feet deep and hence 4,872 feet below sea level.

Highest. The highest steam-navigated lake in the world is Lago Titicaca (maximum depth 1,214 feet), with an area of about 3,200 square miles (1,850 square miles in Peru, 1,350 square miles in Bolivia), in South America. It is 130 miles long and is situated at 12,506 feet above sea level.

There is a small unnamed lake north of Mount Everest in the Changtse Glacier, Tibet, at an altitude of 20,230 feet above sea level.

Waterfalls

Highest. The highest waterfall in the world is Angel Falls, in Venezuela, on a branch of the Carrao River, an upper tributary of the Caroní, with a total drop of 3,212 feet and the longest single drop 2,648 feet (see photograph, next page.) It was discovered in 1935

HIGHEST WATERFALL: Angel Falls in Venezuela has a total drop of 3,212 feet; the first drop is 2,648 feet. Jimmy Angel, American pilot, was the discoverer. Note airplane passing in front of falls. LARGEST ICE CAVE (right): The Eisriesenwelt in Austria is 24.8 miles long.

by a U.S. pilot named Jimmy Angel (died December 8, 1956), who crashed nearby.

HIGHEST WATERFALLS—BY COUNTRIES

Country	Drop in feet	Name and Location
Venezuela	3,212	Angel Falls, Carrao River
South Africa	3,110	Tugela, Natal
Norway	2,625	Utigardsfossen
United States	2,425	Yosemite, California
New Zealand	1,904	Sutherland Falls, River Arthur
Guyana	1,600	King George VI, Utshi
Australia	1,580	Wollomombi, N.S.W.
Tanzania-Zambia	1,400	Kalambo
France	1,384	Gavarnie, Gave de Pau
Brazil	1,325	Glass Fall, Iguazi
Austria	1,280	Krimmler Fälle
Congo (Kinshasa)	1,259	Lofoi
Canada	1,248	Takkakaw, Yoho River, B.C.
Italy	1,033	Serio, Lombardy
Switzerland	978	Staubbach

Greatest. On the basis of the average annual flow, the greatest waterfall in the world is the Guaíra (374 feet high), known also as the Salto das Sete Quedas, on the Alto Paraná River between Brazil and Paraguay. Although attaining an average height of only 110 feet, its estimated annual average flow over the lip (5,300 yards wide) is 470,000 cubic feet per second. It has a peak flow of 1,750,000 cubic feet per second. The seven cataracts of Stanley Falls in the Congo (Kinshasa) have an average annual flow of 600,000 cubic feet per second.

Widest. The widest waterfalls in the world are Khône Falls (50 to 70 feet high) in Laos, with a width of 6.7 miles and a flood flow of 1,500,000 cubic feet per second.

Natural Phenomena

Longest Fjords. The world's longest fjord is the Nordvest fjord arm of the Scoresby Sund in eastern Greenland, which extends inland 195 miles from the sea. The longest of Norwegian fjords is the Sogne Fjord, which extends 113.7 miles inland from Sygnefest to the head of the Lusterfjord arm at Skjolden. It averages barely 3 miles in width and has a deepest point of 4,085 feet. If measured from Huglo along the Bømlafjord to the head of the Sørfjord arm at Odda, the Hardengerfjorden can also be said to extend 113.7 miles.

Longest Glaciers. It is estimated that 6,020,000 square miles, or about 10.4 per cent of the earth's land surface, is permanently glaciated. The world's longest known glacier is the Lambert Glacier, discovered by an Australian aircraft crew in Australian Antarctic Territory in 1956–57. It is up to 40 miles wide and, with its upper section known as the Mellor Glacier, it measures at least 250 miles in length. With the Fisher Glacier limb, the Lambert forms a continuous ice passage about 320 miles long. The longest Himalayan

NATURAL BRIDGE: The size of this double arch in Arches National Monument, Utah, can be judged by the size of the man in the center.

LONGEST STALACTITES: Free-hanging, 38 feet long (left) in County Clare, Ireland. (Right): Wall-supported, 195 feet long, near Málaga, Spain.

glacier is the Siachen (47 miles) in the Karakoram range, though the Hispar and Biafo combine to form an ice passage 76 miles long.

Natural Bridge. The longest natural bridge in the world is the Landscape Arch in the Arches National Monument, Utah. This natural sandstone arch spans 291 feet and is set about 100 feet above the canyon floor. In one place erosion has narrowed its section to 6 feet. (See photograph.)

Greatest Avalanches. The greatest avalanches, though rarely observed, occur in the Himalaya, but no estimates of their volume have been published. It was estimated that 3,500,000 cubic meters (120,000,000 cubic feet) of snow fell in an avalanche in the Italian Alps in 1885. (See also Disasters, end of Chapter 11.)

Largest Desert. Nearly an eighth of the world's land surface is arid with an annual rainfall of less than 9.8 inches. The Sahara Desert in North Africa is the largest in the world. At its greatest length, it is 3,200 miles from east to west. From north to south it is between 800 and 1,400 miles. The area covered by the desert is about 3,250,000 square miles. The land level varies from 436 feet below sea level in the Qattâra Depression, United Arab Republic (formerly Egypt), to the mountain Emi Koussi (11,204 feet) in Chad. The diurnal temperature range in the western Sahara may be more than 80°F.

Caves

Longest Stalactite. The longest known stalactite in the world is a wall-supported column extending 195 feet from roof to floor in the Cueva de Nerja, near Málaga, Spain. The rather low tensile strength of calcite (calcium carbonate) precludes very long free-hanging stalactites, but one of 38 feet exists in the Poll on Ionian cave in County Clare, Ireland. (See photographs.)

Tallest Stalagmite. The tallest known stalagmite in the world is La Grande Stalagmite in the Aven Armand cave, Lozère, France, which has attained a height of 98 feet from the cave floor. It was found in September, 1897.

DEEPEST CAVES BY COUNTRIES

These depths are subject to continuous revisions.

Feet below entrance	Cave and mountain range	Country
4,300	Gouffre de la Pierre Saint-Martin, Pyrenees	France/Spain
3,750	Gouffre Berger, Sornin Plateau, Vercors	France
2,906	Spulga della Preta, Lessinische Alps	Italy
2,427	Hölloch, Moutatal, Schwyz	Switzerland
2,329	Gruberhorn Höhle, Hoher Göll, Salzburg	Austria
2,099	Sniezna, Tatra	Poland
2,040	Gouffre de Faour Dara	Lebanon
2,006	Sotano del San Agustin	Mexico
1,969	Gouffre Juhue	Spain
1,885	Ragge favreraige	Norway
1,770	Abisso Vereo, Istria	Yugoslavia
1,690	Anou Boussouil, Djurdjura	Algeria
>1,300	Provetina, Mount Astraka	Greece
1,184	Neffs Cave, Utah	U.S.
1,115	Izvorul Tausoarclor, Rodna	Rumania
850	Ogof Ffynnon Du, Breconshire	Wales
653	Oxlow Cavern, Giant's Hole, Derbyshire	England
527	Growling Swallet Cave, Tasmania	Australia
330	Pollnagollum-Poulelva, Country Clare	Ireland

LONGEST CAVE SYSTEMS BY COUNTRIES

These surveyed lengths are subject to continuous revision.

Miles		Country
72.9	Flint Ridge Cave System, Kentucky	U.S.
67.2	Hölloch, Schwyz	Switzerland
32.74	Sistema Cavernavio de Cuyaguatega	Cuba
*26.10	Eisriesenwelt, Werfen, Salzburg	Austria
22.74	Peschtschera Optimistitshcheskaya, Pololien	U.S.S.R.
22.48	Complejo Palomera-Dolencias, Burgos	Spain
20.3	Ogof Ffynnon Du, Breconshire	Wales
17.00	Postojnska Jama, Slovenia	Yugoslavia
15.98	Réseau de la Dent de Crolles	France
13.67	Baradla Barlang-Jaskyna Domica, Magyarország	Hungary
12.5	Lancaster Hole—Easegill Caverns, Westmorland	England
7.39	Poulnagollum-Poulelva Caves, County Clare	Ireland
>6	Mullamullang Cave	Australia

Longest ice caves, discovered in 1879. Now rank as eighth longest known.

Largest. The largest known underground chamber in the world is the Big Room of the Carlsbad Caverns (1,320 feet deep) in New Mexico. It is 4,270 feet long, and reaches 328 feet in height and 656 feet in width.

The most extensive cave system in the world is said to be the Flint Ridge Cave system, discovered in 1799 in Kentucky. Its total length is reputed to be more than 150 miles, but it contains only 72.9 miles of actual mapped passageways.

The world's largest ice caves are the Eisriesenwelt, discovered in 1879 at Werfen, Austria, with a length of 24.8 miles. (See photograph on page 121.)

Gorge

Largest. The largest gorge in the world is the Grand Canyon on the Colorado River in north-central Arizona. It extends from

Marble Gorge to the Grand Wash Cliffs, over a distance of 217 miles. It varies in width from 5 to 15 miles and is up to 7,000 feet deep.

Deepest. The deepest visible canyon in the world is Hell's Canyon, dividing Oregon and Idaho. It plunges 7,900 feet from the Devil Mountain down to the Snake River. The deepest submarine canyon yet discovered is one 25 miles south of Esperance, Western Australia, which is 6,000 feet deep and 20 miles wide.

Sea Cliffs

The location of the highest sea cliffs in the world has yet to be established. These may be in northwest Greenland. Coastal terrain at Dexterity Fjord, northeast Baffin Island, Canada, rises to 4,000 feet.

3. Weather

The meteorological records given below necessarily relate largely to the last 125 to 145 years, since data before that time are both sparse and unreliable. Reliable registering thermometers were introduced as recently as *c.* 1820.

Greatest Temperature Ranges

The world's extremes of temperature have been noted progressively thus:

World's Maximum Shade Temperatures

127.4°F.	Ouargla, Algeria	Aug. 27, 1884
130°F.	Amos and Mammoth Tank, California	Aug. 17, 1885
134°F.	Death Valley, California	July 10, 1913
136.4°F.	Al 'Aziziyah (el-Azizia), Libya*	Sept. 13, 1922†‡

World's Minimum Screen Temperatures

− 73°F.	Floeberg Bay, Ellesmer Island, Canada ...	1852
− 90.4°F.	Verkhoyansk, Siberia, U.S.S.R.	Jan. 3, 1885
− 90.4°F.	Verkhoyansk, Siberia, U.S.S.R.	Feb. 5 & 7, 1892
− 90.4°F.	Oymyakon, Siberia, U.S.S.R.	Feb. 6, 1933
−100.4°F.	South Pole, Antarctica	May 11, 1957
−102.1°F.	South Pole, Antarctica	Sept. 17, 1957
−109.1°F.	Sovietskaya, Antarctica	May 2, 1958
−113.3°F.	Vostok, Antarctica	June 15, 1958
−113.8°F.	Sovietskaya, Antarctica	June 19, 1958
−117.4°F.	Sovietskaya, Antarctica	June 25, 1958
−122.4°F.	Vostok, Antarctica	Aug. 7–8, 1958
−124.1°F.	Sovietskaya, Antarctica	Aug. 9, 1958
−125.3°F.	Vostok, Antarctica	Aug. 25, 1958
−126.9°F.	Vostok, Antarctica	Aug. 24, 1960

* Obtained by the National Geographical Society but not officially recognized by the Libyan Ministry of Communications. (See photograph, next page.)

† A reading of 140°F. at Delta, Mexico, in August, 1953, and one of 136.4°F. at San Luis, Sonora, Mexico, on August 11, 1933, are not now accepted because of over-exposure to roof radiation.

‡ A freak heat flash struck Coimbra, Portugal, in September, 1933, when the temperature rose to 70°C. (158°F.) for 120 seconds.

The greatest recorded temperature ranges in the world are around the Siberian "cold pole" in the eastern U.S.S.R. Olekminsk has ranged 189°F. from −76°F. to 113°F. and Verkhoyansk (67°33′N, 133°23′E) has ranged 192°F. from −94°F. (unofficial) to 98°F.

The greatest temperature variation recorded in a day is 100°F. (a fall from 44°F. to −56°F.) at Browning, Montana, on January

HOTTEST SPOT ON EARTH: Al Aziziyah, Libya, where a temperature of 136.4°F. was recorded in the shade in 1922.

23–24, 1916. The most freakish rise was 49°F. in 2 minutes at Spearfish, South Dakota, from −4°F. at 7:30 a.m. to 45°F. at 7:32 a.m. on January 22, 1943.

Atmospheric Temperature

The lowest temperature ever recorded in the atmosphere is −225.4°F. at an altitude of about 50 to 60 miles, during noctilucent cloud research above Kronogård, Sweden, from July 27 to August 7, 1963.

Upper Atmosphere

A jet stream moving at 408 m.p.h. at 154,200 feet (29.2 miles) was recorded by Skua rocket above South Uist, Outer Hebrides, Scotland on December 13, 1967.

Most Equable Temperature

The location with the most equable recorded temperature over a short period is Garapan, on Saipan, in the Mariana Islands, Pacific Ocean. During the nine years from 1927 to 1935, inclusive, the lowest temperature recorded was 67.3°F. on January 30, 1934, and the highest was 88.5°F. on September 9, 1931, giving an extreme range of 21.2°F. Between 1911 and 1966 the Brazilian offshore island of Fernando de Noronha had a minimum temperature of 65.5°F. on November 17, 1913, and a maximum of 89.6°F. on March 2, 1965, an extreme range of 24.1°F.

Deepest Permafrost

The greatest recorded depth of permafrost is 4,921 feet, reported in April, 1968, in the basin of the Lena River, Siberia, U.S.S.R.

Humidity and Discomfort

Human discomfort depends not merely on temperature but on the combination of temperature, humidity, radiation and wind speed. The U.S. Weather Bureau uses a Temperature-Humidity Index, which equals two-fifths of the sum of the dry and wet bulb thermometer readings plus 15. When the THI in still air reaches 75, at least half of the people will be uncomfortable while at 79 few, if any, will be comfortable. A reading of 92 (shade temperature 119°F., relative humidity 22 per cent) was recorded at Yuma, Arizona, on July 31, 1957, but even this must have been surpassed in Death Valley, California.

Most Intense Rainfall

Difficulties attend rainfall readings for very short periods but the figure of 1.23 inches in one minute at Unionville, Maryland, at 3:23 p.m. on July 4, 1956, is regarded as the most intense recorded in modern times. The cloudburst of "near two foot . . . in less than a quarter of half an hour" at Oxford, England, on the afternoon of May 31 (Old Style), 1682, is regarded as unacademically recorded.

Lightning

The visible length of lightning strokes varies greatly. In mountainous regions, when clouds are very low, the flash may be less than 300 feet long. In flat country with very high clouds, a cloud-to-earth flash sometimes measures four miles, though in extreme cases such flashes have been measured at 20 miles. The intensely bright central core of the lightning channel is extremely narrow. Some authorities suggest that its diameter is as little as half an inch. This core is surrounded by a "corona envelope" (glow discharge) which may measure 10 to 20 feet in diameter.

The speed of a lightning discharge varies from 100 to 1,000 miles per second for the downward leader track, and reaches up to 87,000 miles per second (nearly half the speed of light) for the powerful return stroke.

Every few million strokes there is a giant discharge, in which the cloud-to-earth and the return lightning strokes flash from the top of the thunder clouds. In these "positive giants" energy of up to 3,000 million joules (3×10^{16} ergs) is sometimes recorded. The temperature reaches about 30,000° C, which is more than five times greater than that of the surface of the sun.

Waterspouts

The highest waterspout of which there is reliable record was one observed on May 16, 1898, off Eden, New South Wales, Australia. A theodolite reading from the shore gave its height as 5,014 feet. It was about 10 feet in diameter.

Cloud Extremes

The highest standard cloud form is cirrus, averaging 27,000 feet and above, but the rare nacreous or mother-of-pearl formation sometimes reaches nearly 80,000 feet. The lowest is stratus, below 3,500 feet. The cloud form with the greatest vertical range is cumulonimbus, which has been observed to reach a height of nearly 68,000 feet. Noctilucent "clouds," a manifestation of which was observed from Hampshire, England, on June 30, 1950, are believed to pass at a height of over 60 miles.

WEATHER RECORDS

Highest Shade Temperature: 136.4°F., Al 'Aziziyah, Libya, September 13, 1922.

Lowest Screen Temperature: −126.9°F., Vostok, Antarctica, August 24, 1960[1].

Greatest Rainfall (24 hours): 73.62 in., Cilaos, La Réunion, Indian Ocean, March 15–16, 1952[2].

(Month): 366.14 in., Cherrapunji, Assam, India, July, 1861.

(12 months): 1,041.78 in., Cherrapunji, Assam, August 1, 1860 to July 31, 1861.

Greatest Snowfall (24 hours): 76 in., Silver Lake, Colorado, April 14–15, 1921[3].

(12 months): 1,014.5 in., at 5,400 ft. on Mt. Rainier, Washington, 1970–71.

Maximum Sunshine (Year): 97%+ (over 4,300 hours), eastern Sahara. 768 days, February 9, 1967–May 17, 1969, St. Petersburg, Florida.

Minimum Sunshine: Nil at North Pole—for winter stretches of 186 days.

Barometric Pressure (Highest): 1,083.8 mb. (32 in.), Agata, Siberia, U.S.S.R., December 31, 1968.

(Lowest): 877 mb. (25.91 in.), about 600 miles northwest of Guam, Pacific Ocean, September 24, 1958.

Highest Surface Wind-speed:[4] 231 m.p.h., Mt. Washington (6,288 ft.), New Hampshire, April 12, 1934.

Thunder Days (Year):[5] 322 days, Bogor (formerly Buitenzorg), Java, Indonesia (average, 1916–19).

Hottest Place (Annual mean):[6] Dallol, Ethiopia, 94°F., 1960–66.

Coldest Place (Annual mean): Pole of Cold (78°S, 96°E), Antarctica, −72°F. (16°F. lower than Pole).

Wettest Place (Annual mean): Mt. Waialeale (5,080 ft.), Kauai, Hawaii, 486.1 in. (average, 1920–58). About 335 days per year during which rain falls.

Driest Place (Annual mean): Calama, in the Desierto de Atacama, Chile.

Longest Drought: c. 400 years to 1971, Desierto de Atacama, Chile.

Most Rainy Days (Year): Bahía Félix, Chile, 348 days in 1916 (annual average 325 days).

Largest Hailstones:[7]	1.67 lbs. (7½ in. diameter, 17½ in. circumference), Coffeyville, Kansas, March 9, 1970.
Longest Fogs (Visibility less than 1,000 yards):	Fogs persist for weeks on the Grand Banks, Newfoundland, Canada, and the average is more than 120 days per year.
Windiest Place:	The Commonwealth Bay, George V Coast, Antarctica, where gales reach 200 m.p.h. (See photo.)

[1] The coldest permanently inhabited place is the Siberian village of Oymyakon (63°16′N., 143°15′E.), in the U.S.S.R., where the temperature reached −96°F. in 1964.

[2] This is equal to 8327.2 tons of rain per acre. Elevation 3,937 feet.

[3] The record for a single snowstorm is 175.4 inches at Thompson Pass on December 26–31, 1955.

[4] The highest speed yet measured in a tornado is 280 m.p.h. at Wichita Falls, Texas, on April 2, 1958.

[5] At any given moment there are 2,200 thunderstorms in the world, some of which can be heard at a range of 18 miles.

[6] In Death Valley, California, maximum temperatures of over 120°F. were recorded on 43 consecutive days—July 6 to August 17, 1917. At Marble Bar, Western Australia (maximum 121°F.), 160 consecutive days with maximum temperatures of over 100°F. were recorded—October 31, 1923 to April 7, 1924. At Wyndham, Western Australia, the temperature reached 90°F. or more on 333 days in 1946.

[7] Much heavier hailstones are sometimes reported. These are usually not single but coalesced hailstones.

WINDIEST PLACE: The hut at Commonwealth Bay, Antarctica, where gales reach 200 m.p.h.

Chapter Four

THE UNIVERSE AND SPACE

LIGHT-YEAR—that distance traveled by light (speed 186,282.42 ± 0.06 miles per second, or 670,616,722.8 m.p.h., *in vacuo*) in one tropical (or solar) year (365.24219878 mean solar days at January 0, 12 hours Ephemeris time in 1900 A.D.) and is 5,878,500,600,000 miles. The unit was first used in March, 1888.

MAGNITUDE—a measure of stellar brightness such that the light of a star of any magnitude bears a ratio of 2.511886 to that of a star of the next magnitude. Thus a fifth magnitude star is 2.511886 times as bright, while one of the first magnitude is exactly 100 (or 2.511886^5) times as bright, as a sixth magnitude star. In the case of such exceptionally bright bodies as Sirius, Venus, the moon (magnitude −11.2) or the sun (magnitude −26.7), the magnitude is expressed as a minus quantity.

PROPER MOTION—that component of a star's motion in space which, at right angles to the line of sight, constitutes an apparent change of position of the star in the celestial sphere.

The universe is the entirety of space, matter and anti-matter. An appreciation of its magnitude is best grasped by working outward from the earth, through the solar system and our own Milky Way galaxy, to the remotest extra-galactic nebulae.

Meteoroids

Meteor Shower

Meteoroids are mostly of cometary origin. A meteor is the light phenomenon caused by the entry of a meteoroid into the earth's atmosphere. The greatest meteor "shower" on record occurred on the night of November 16–17, 1966, when the Leonid meteors (which recur every $33\frac{1}{4}$ years) were visible over North America. It was calculated that meteors passed over Arizona at a rate of 2,300 per minute for a period of 20 minutes from 5 a.m. on November 17, 1966.

Meteorites

Largest. When a meteoroid penetrates to the earth's surface, the remnant is described as a meteorite. The largest known meteorite is one found in 1920 at Hoba West, near Grootfontein in South-West Africa. This is a block about 9 feet long by 8 feet broad, weighing 132,000 lbs. (See photograph, next page.)

The largest meteorite exhibited by any museum is the "Tent" meteorite, weighing 68,085 lbs., found in 1897 near Cape York, on the west coast of Greenland, by the expedition of Commander (later Rear-Admiral) Robert Edwin Peary (1856–1920). It was known to the Eskimos as the Abnighito and is now exhibited in the Hayden Planetarium in New York City.

The largest piece of stony meteorite recovered is a piece of the Norton County meteorite which fell in Nebraska, on February 18, 1948. The greatest amount of material recovered from any non-

LARGEST KNOWN METEORITE: The 66-ton Hoba West stone, found in South West Africa in 1920.

metallic meteorite is from the Allende fall of more than 1 ton in Chihuahua, Mexico, on February 8, 1969.

There was a mysterious explosion of about 35 megatons in latitude 60° 55′ N., longitude 101° 57′ E., in the basin of the Podkamennaya Tunguska river, 40 miles north of Vanavara, in Siberia, U.S.S.R., at 00 hours 17 minutes 11 seconds G.M.T. on June 30, 1908. The energy of this explosion was about 10^{24} ergs and the cause has been variously attributed to a meteorite (1927), a comet (1930), a nuclear explosion (1961) and to anti-matter (1965). This devastated an area of about 1,500 square miles and the shock was heard more than 600 miles away.

Largest Craters. Aerial surveys in Canada in 1956 and 1957 brought to light a gash, or astrobleme, $8\frac{1}{2}$ miles across near Deep Bay, Saskatchewan, possibly attributable to a very old and very oblique meteorite. There is a possible crater-like formation 275 miles in diameter on the eastern shore of Hudson Bay, where the Nastapoka Islands are just off the coast.

U.S.S.R. scientists reported in December, 1970, an astrobleme with a 60-mile diameter and a maximum depth of 1,300 feet in the basin of the River Popigai.

The largest proven crater is called Barringer Crater or Meteor Crater, formerly called Coon Butte, discovered in 1891 near Winslow, northern Arizona. It is 4,150 feet in diameter and now about 575 feet deep, with a parapet rising 130 to 155 feet above the surrounding plain. It has been estimated that an iron-nickel mass with a diameter of 200 to 260 feet, and weighing about 2,240,000 tons, gouged this crater in *c.* 25,000 B.C., with an impact force equivalent to an explosion of 33,600,000 tons of trinitrotoluene $C_7H_5(NO_2)_3$, called T.N.T.

Evidence published in 1963 discounts a meteoric origin for the crypto-volcanic Vredefort Ring (diameter 26 miles), to the southwest of Johannesburg, South Africa, but this has now been reasserted.

The New Quebec (formerly the Chubb) "Crater," first sighted on June 20, 1943, in northern Ungava, Canada, is 1,325 feet deep and measures 6.8 miles around its rim.

Tektites. The largest tektite of which details have been published was one of 7.04 lbs. found *c*. 1932 at Muong Nong, Saravane Province, Laos, and now in the Paris Museum.

Aurora

Most Frequent. Polar lights, known as Aurora Borealis or Northern Lights in the northern hemisphere and Aurora Australis in the southern hemisphere, are caused by electrical solar discharges in the upper atmosphere and occur most frequently in high latitudes. The maximum auroral frequencies, of up to 240 displays per year, have occurred in the Hudson Bay area of northern Canada.

Altitude. The extreme height of auroras has been measured at 620 miles, while the lowest may descend to 45 miles.

Southernmost "Northern Lights." On September 25, 1909, a display was witnessed as far south as Singapore (1° 25' N.).

The Moon

The earth's closest neighbor in space and only natural satellite is the moon, at a mean distance of 238,856 statute miles center to center or 233,813 miles surface to surface. Its closest approach (perigee) and most extreme distance away (apogee) measured surface to surface are 216,420 and 247,667 miles respectively. It has a diameter of 2,159.9 miles in the plane of the sky and has a mass of 7.23×10^{19} long tons with a mean density of 3.34. The average orbital speed is 2,287 m.p.h.

The first direct hit on the moon was achieved at 2 minutes 24 seconds after midnight (Moscow time) on September 14, 1959, by the Soviet space probe *Lunik II* near the *Mare Serenitatis*. The first photographic images of the hidden side were collected by the U.S.S.R.'s *Lunik III* from 6:30 a.m. on October 7, 1959, from a range of up to 43,750 miles, and transmitted to the earth from a distance of 292,000 miles. The first "soft" landing was made by the U.S.S.R.'s *Lunik IX*, launched at about 11 a.m. G.M.T. on January 31, 1966. It landed in the area of the Ocean of Storms (*Oceanus Procellarum*) at 18 hours 45 minutes 30 seconds G.M.T. on February 3, 1966.

"Blue Moon." Owing to sulphur particles in the upper atmosphere from a forest fire covering 250,000 acres between Mile 103 and Mile 119 on the Alaska Highway in northern British Columbia, Canada, the moon took on a bluish color, as seen from Great Britain, on the night of September 26, 1950. The moon also appeared blue after the Krakatoa eruption of August 27, 1883 (see Volcanoes).

THE EARTH AS
SEEN FROM THE
MOON by Apollo XI
astronauts, the first to
land on the moon.

(Right) FIRST
FOOTPRINT on the
moon.

Crater

Largest. Only 59 per cent of the moon's surface is directly visible from the earth because it is in "captured rotation" *i.e.* the period of revolution is equal to the period of orbit. The largest wholly visible crater is the walled plain Bailly, toward the moon's South Pole, which is 183 miles across, with walls rising to 14,000 feet. Partly on the averted side the Orientale Basin measures more than 600 miles in diameter.

Deepest. The deepest crater is the nearby Newton crater, with a floor estimated to be between 23,000 and 29,000 feet below its rim and 14,000 feet below the level of the plain outside. The brightest directly visible spot on the moon is *Aristarchus*.

Highest Mountains

As there is no water on the moon, the heights of mountains can be measured only in relation to lower-lying terrain near their bases. The highest lunar mountains were, until 1967, thought to be in the Leibnitz and Doerfel ranges, near the lunar South Pole with a height of some 35,000 feet. On the discovery from lunar orbiting spacecraft of evidence that they were merely crater rims, the names have been withdrawn. Currently it is believed that such an elevation would be an exaggerated estimate for any feature of the moon's surface.

Temperature Extremes

When the sun is overhead, the temperature on the lunar equator reaches 243°F. (31°F. above the boiling point of water). By sunset the temperature is 58°F., but after nightfall it sinks to −261°F.

Moon Rocks

The age attributed to the oldest of the first moon rocks brought back to earth by the *Apollo XV* crew on August 7, 1971, was the "genesis rock" aged 4,200,000,000 years. It was picked up on the Apennine Front on August 1.

The Sun

Distance Extremes

The earth's 66,690 m.p.h. orbit of 584,000,000 miles around the sun is elliptical, hence our distance from the sun varies. The orbital speed varies between 65,600 m.p.h. (minimum) and 67,800 m.p.h. The average distance of the sun is 92,955,840 miles. The closest approach (perihelion) is 91,395,000 miles, and the farthest departure (aphelion) is 94,513,300 miles. The solar system is revolving around the center of the Milky Way at a speed of 481,000 m.p.h. and has a velocity of 42,500 m.p.h. relative to stars in our immediate region such as Vega, toward which it is moving.

Temperature and Dimensions

The sun has in internal temperature of about 20,000,000°K., a core pressure of 560,000,000 tons per square inch and uses up nearly 4,500,000 tons of hydrogen per second, thus providing a luminosity of 3×10^{27} candlepower, or 1,500,000 candlepower per square inch. The sun has the stellar classification of a "yellow dwarf" and, although its density is only 1.41 times that of water, its mass is 333,430 times as much as that of the earth. It has a mean diameter of 865,370 miles. The sun with a mass of $2,096 \times 10^{27}$ tons represents more than 99 per cent of the total mass of the solar system. (K. stands for the Kelvin absolute scale of temperatures. See pages 168–9.)

Sunspots

Largest. To be visible to the *protected* naked eye, a sunspot must cover about one two-thousandth part of the sun's hemisphere and thus have an area of about 500,000,000 square miles. The largest recorded sunspot occurred in the sun's southern hemisphere on April 8, 1947. Its area was about 7,000 million square miles, with an extreme longitude of 187,000 miles and an extreme latitude of 90,000 miles. Sunspots appear darker because they are more than 1,500°C. cooler than the rest of the sun's surface temperature of 5,660°C. The largest observed solar prominence was one measuring 70,000 miles across its base and protruding 300,000 miles, observed on June 4, 1946.

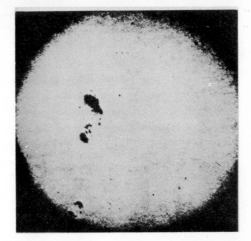

LARGEST SUNSPOTS:
The area of the spot was about 7,000 million square miles.

Most Frequent. In October, 1957, a smoothed sunspot count showed 263, the highest recorded index since records started in 1755 (*cf.* previous record of 239 in May, 1778). In 1943 a sunspot lasted for 200 days from June to December.

Eclipses

Earliest Recorded. The earliest extrapolated eclipses that have been identified are 1361 B.C. (lunar) and 2136 B.C. (solar). For the Middle East only, lunar eclipses have been extrapolated to 3450 B.C. and solar ones to 4200 B.C.

Longest Duration. The maximum possible duration of an eclipse of the sun is 7 minutes 58 seconds. This could occur only at the equator, but the longest actually occurring since 717 A.D. was on June 20, 1955 (7 minutes 8 seconds), seen from the Philippines. An annular eclipse may last for 12 minutes 24 seconds. The longest totality of any lunar eclipse is 104 minutes. This has occurred many times.

Most and Least Frequent. The highest number of eclipses possible in a year is seven, as in 1935, when there were five solar and two lunar eclipses; or four solar and three lunar eclipses, as will occur in 1982. The lowest possible number in a year is two, both of which must be solar, as in 1944 and 1969.

Comets

Earliest Recorded. The earliest records of comets date from the 7th century B.C. The speeds of the estimated 2,000,000 comets vary from 700 m.p.h. in outer space to 1,250,000 m.p.h. when near the sun.

The successive appearances of Halley's Comet have been traced to 466 B.C. It was first depicted in the Nuremberg Chronicle of 684 A.D. The first prediction of its return by Edmund Halley (1656–1742) proved true on Christmas Day, 1758, 16 years after his death. Its next appearance should be at 9:30 p.m. Greenwich Mean Time on February 9, 1986, exactly 75.81 years after the last, which was on April 19, 1910.

Closest Approach. On July 1, 1770, Lexell's Comet, traveling at a speed of 23.9 miles per second (relative to the sun), came within 1,500,000 miles of the earth. However, the earth is believed to have passed through the tail of Halley's Comet, most recently on May 19, 1910.

Largest

Comets are so tenuous that it has been estimated that even the head of one rarely contains solid matter greater than 1 kilometer in diameter. In the tail 10,000 cubic miles contain less than a cubic inch of solid matter. These tails, as in the case of the Great Comet of 1843, may trail for 200,000,000 miles.

Period

Shortest. Of all the recorded periodic comets (these are members of the solar system), the one which most frequently returns is Encke's Comet, first identified in 1786. Its period of 1,206 days (3.3 years) is the shortest established. Not one of its 48 returns (up to May, 1967) has been missed by astronomers. Now increasingly faint, it is expected to "die" by February, 1994. The most frequently observed comets are Schwassmann-Wachmann I, Kopff and Cterma, which can be observed every year between Mars and Jupiter.

Longest. The path of the comet 1910a has not been accurately determined, but it is not expected to return for perhaps 4,000,000 years.

Planets

Planets (including the earth) are bodies which belong to the solar system and which revolve around the sun in definite orbits.

Largest. Jupiter, with an equatorial diameter of 88,070 miles and a polar diameter of 82,720 miles, is the largest of the nine major planets, with a mass 317.83 times and a volume 1,293 times that of the earth. It also has the shortest period of rotation, with a "day" of only 9 hours 50 minutes 30.003 seconds in its equatorial zone.

Smallest. Of the nine major planets, Mercury is the smallest with a diameter of 3,033 miles and a mass only 0.0555 of that of the earth or 326,000,000,000,000,000,000 long tons. Mercury, which orbits the Sun at an average distance of 35,983,100 miles, has a period of revolution of 87.9686 days, so giving the highest average speed in orbit of 107,030 m.p.h.

Hottest. The U.S.S.R. probe *Venera 7* recorded a temperature of 885°F. on the surface of Venus on December 17, 1970. The surface temperature of Mercury has now been calculated to be 790°F. on its daylight side at perihelion (28,566,000 miles).

Most Equable. The planet with a surface temperature closest to earth's average figure of 59°F. is Mars with a value of 55°F. for the sub-solar point at a mean solar distance of 141,636,000 miles.

Coldest. The coldest planet is, not unnaturally, the one which is remotest from the sun, namely Pluto, which has an estimated surface

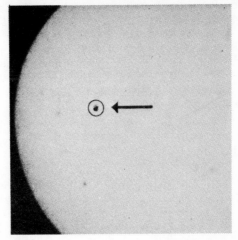

SMALLEST PLANET:
Mercury, closest to the sun,
is only about 5 per cent of
the size of the earth.

temperature of −420°F. (40°F. above absolute zero). Its mean distance from the sun is 3,675,300,000 miles and its period of revolution is 248.62 years. Its diameter is about 3,400 miles and it has a mass about one twentieth that of the earth. Pluto was first recorded by Clyde William Tombaugh (born February 4, 1906) at Lowell Observatory, Flagstaff, Arizona, on February 18, 1930, from photographs taken on January 23 and 29. Because of its orbital eccentricity, Pluto will move closer to the sun than Neptune between January 21, 1979, and March 14, 1999.

Nearest. The fellow planet closest to the earth is Venus, which is, at times, about 25,700,000 miles inside the earth's orbit, compared with Mars' closest approach of 34,600,000 miles outside the earth's orbit. Mars, known since 1965 to be cratered, has temperatures ranging from 85°F. to −130°F. but in which infusorians of the genus *Colpoda* could survive.

The first object from the earth to reach another planet was the U.S.S.R.'s *Venus III*, weighing 2,116 lbs., which was launched on November 16, 1965, and impacted on Venus at 6:56 a.m. G.M.T. on March 1, 1966.

Surface Features. Mariner 9 photographs have revealed a canyon in the Tithonias Lacus region of Mars which is 62 miles wider and 4,000 feet deeper than the 13-mile-wide 5,500-foot-deep Grand Canyon on earth. The volcanic pile Nix Olympica is 305 miles across with a 40-mile-wide crater probably 19,500 feet deep.

Brightest and Faintest. Viewed from the earth, by far the brightest of the five planets visible to the naked eye is Venus, with a maximum magnitude of −4.4. The faintest is Pluto, with a magnitude of 14. Uranus at magnitude 5.7 is only marginally visible.

Densest and Least Dense. Earth is the densest planet with an average figure of 5.51 times that of water, while Saturn has an average density only about one eighth of this value or 0.705 times that of water.

Longest "Day." The planet with the longest period of rotation is

Venus, which spins on its axis once every 243.16 days, so its "day" is longer than its "year" (224.7007 days). The shortest "day" is that of Jupiter (see Largest Planet).

Conjunctions. The most dramatic recorded conjunction (coming together) of the other seven principal members of the solar system (sun, moon, Mercury, Venus, Mars, Jupiter and Saturn) occurred on February 5, 1962, when 16° covered all seven during an eclipse. It is possible that the seven-fold conjunction of September, 1186, spanned only 12°. The next notable conjunction will take place on May 5, 2000.

Satellites

Most. Of the nine major planets, all but Mercury, Venus and Pluto, have natural satellites. The planet with the most is Jupiter, with four large and eight small moons. The earth is the only planet with a single satellite. The distance of the solar system's 32 known satellites from their parent planets varies from the 5,818 miles of *Phobos* from the center of Mars to the 14,730,000 miles of Jupiter's ninth satellite (Jupiter IX).

Largest and Smallest. The largest satellite is *Ganymede* (Jupiter III) with a diameter of 3,450 miles and a mass 2.11 times that of our moon. The smallest is Mars's outer "moon" *Deimos* discovered on August 18, 1877, by Asaph Hall (U.S.) with a major axis of 8.4 miles and a minor one of 7.5 miles.

Largest Asteroids. In the belt which lies between Mars and Jupiter, there are some 45,000 (only 3,100 charted) minor planets or asteroids which are, for the most part, too small to yield to diameter measurement. The largest of these is *Ceres*, with a diameter of 480 miles. The only one visible to the naked eye is *Vesta*, discovered on March 29, 1807, by Dr. Heinrich Wilhelm Olbers, a German amateur astronomer. The closest measured approach to the earth by an asteroid was 485,000 miles, in the case of *Hermes* on October 30, 1937.

It was announced in December, 1971, that the orbit of *Toro* (discovered 1964), though centered on the sun, is also in resonance with the earth-moon system. Its nearest approach to earth is 9,600,000 miles.

Stars

Largest and Most Massive. Of those measured, the star with the greatest diameter is the "red giant" *Epsilon Aurigae B* at 1,800 million miles. This star is so vast that our own solar system of the sun and the six planets out as far as Saturn could be accommodated inside its hot vacuum. *Alpha Herculis*, consisting of a main star and a double star companion, is enveloped in a cold gas. This system, visible to the naked eye, has a diameter of 170,000 million miles. The fainter component of Plaskett's star discovered by J. S. Plaskett from the Dominion Astrophysical Observatory, Victoria, British Columbia, Canada, c. 1920 is the most massive star known with a mass c. 55 times that of the sun.

Smallest. The smallest known star is LP 327-186, a "white dwarf" with a diameter only half that of the moon, 100 light-years distant and detected in May, 1962, from Minneapolis. The claim that LP 768-500 is even smaller at <1,000 miles is not widely accepted. Some pulsars or neutron stars may however have diameters of only 10–20 miles.

Oldest. The sun is estimated to be about 7,500 million years old and our galaxy between 10,000 million and 12,000 million years old.

Farthest. The solar system, with its sun, nine major planets, 32 satellites, asteroids and comets, was discovered in 1921 to be about 27,000 light-years from the center of the lens-shaped Milky Way galaxy (diameter 100,000 light-years) of about 100,000 million stars. The most distant star in our galaxy is therefore about 75,000 light-years distant.

Nearest. Excepting the special case of our own sun, the nearest star is the very faint *Proxima Centauri*, which is 4.3 light-years (25,000,000,000,000 miles) away. The nearest star visible to the naked eye is the southern hemisphere star *Alpha Centauri*, or *Rigil Kentaurus* (4.33 light-years), with a magnitude of 0.1.

Brightest. Sirius A (*Alpha Canis Majoris*), also known as the Dog Star, is the brightest star in the heavens, with an apparent magnitude of —1.58. It is in the constellation *Canis Major* and is visible in the winter months of the northern hemisphere, being due south at midnight on the last day of the year. Sirius A is 8.7 light-years away and has a luminosity 26 times as much as that of the sun. It has a diameter of 1,500,000 miles and a mass of 51,300,000,000,000,000,000,000,000,000 tons.

Most and Least Luminous. If all stars could be viewed at the same distance, the most luminous would be the apparently faint variable *S. Doradûs*, in the Greater Magellanic Cloud (*Nebecula Major*), which can be 300,000 to 500,000 times brighter than the sun, and has an absolute magnitude of —8.9. The faintest star detected visually is a very red star 30 light-years distant in *Pisces*, with one two-millionth of the sun's brightness.

Coolest. A 16th magnitude star with a surface temperature of only about 425°C. (800°F.) was detected in *Cygnus* in 1965.

Densest. The limit of stellar density is at the neutron state, when the atomic particles exist in a state in which there is no space between them. Theoretical calculations call for a density of 4.7×10^{15} grams per cubic centimeter (75,000 million long tons per cubic inch) in the innermost core of a pulsar.

Constellations

The largest of the 88 constellations is *Hydra* (the Sea Serpent) which covers 1,302.84 square degrees and contains at least 68 stars visible to the naked eye (to 5.5 mag,). The constellation *Centaurus* (Centaur), ranking ninth in area embraces however at least 94 such stars. The smallest constellation is *Crux Australis* (Southern Cross) with an area of 68.477 square degrees compared with the 41,252.96 square degrees of the whole sky.

BRIGHTEST SUPER-NOVA (left): The explosion of the Crab Nebula, which occurred in about 3000 B.C., became visible on earth by day in the year 1054 and its remains are still expanding at the rate of 800 miles per second. REMOTEST VISIBLE BODY (right): The Great Galaxy in Andromeda is 2,200,000 light-years away.

Brightest Super-Nova

Super-novae, or temporary "stars" which flare and then fade, occur perhaps five times in 1,000 years. The brightest "star" ever seen by historic man is believed to be the super-nova close to *Zeta Tauri*, visible by day for 23 days from July 4, 1054. The remains, known as the Crab Nebula, now have a diameter of about 130,000,000,000,000,000 miles and are still expanding at a rate of 800 miles per second. It is about 4,100 light-years away, indicating that the explosion actually occurred in about 3000 B.C. (See photograph.)

Stellar Planets. Planetary companions, with a mass of less than 7 per cent of their parent star, have been found to 61 *Cygni* (1943), Lalande 21185 (1960) *Krüger 60, Ci 2354, BD + 20° 2465* and one of the two components of 70 Ophiuchi. Barnard's Star (Munich 15040) was discovered to have a planet in April, 1963, with 1.1 times the mass of Jupiter and a second planet more recently with 0.8 times this mass.

Listening operations ("Project Ozma") on the *Tau Ceti* and *Epsilon Eridani* were maintained from April 4, 1960 to March, 1961, using an 85-foot radio telescope at Deer Creek Valley, Green Bank, West Virginia. The apparatus was probably insufficiently sensitive for any signal from a distance of 11 light-years to be received. Monitoring has been conducted from Gorkiy, U.S.S.R. since 1969.

The Universe

According to Einstein's Special Theory time dilatation effect (published in 1905), time actually runs more slowly for an object as its speed increases. However, time speeds up for an object as it moves away from a body exerting gravitational force. During their mission the crew of the Apollo VIII circumlunar space flight aged a net 300 microseconds more than earthlings. No formal overtime claim was lodged.

Outside the Milky Way galaxy, which possibly moves around the center of the local super-cluster of 2,500 neighboring galaxies at a speed of 1,350,000 m.p.h., there exist 1,000,000 million other galaxies. These range in size up to 200,000 light-years in diameter. The nearest heavenly body outside our galaxy is its satellite body, the Large Magellanic Cloud near the Southern Cross, at a distance of 160,000 light-years. In 1967, it was suggested by the astronomer G. Idlis (U.S.S.R.) that the Magellanic Clouds were detached from the Milky Way by another colliding galaxy, now in *Sagittarius*, about 3,800,000 years ago.

Farthest Visible Object. The remotest heavenly body visible to the eye is the Great Galaxy in *Andromeda* (Mag. 3.47). This is a rotating nebula of spiral form, and its distance from the earth is about 2,200,000 light-years, or about 13,000,000,000,000,000,000 miles. (See photograph.)

It is just possible, however, that, under ideal seeing conditions, Messier 33, the spiral in Triangulum (Mag. 5.79) is visible to the naked eye at a distance of 2,300,000 light-years.

Heaviest Galaxy

In April, 1971, the heaviest galaxy was found to be 41C 31:04 (a "binary" system) with a mass 45 times that of the Milky Way, thus indicating a figure of 12,000 sextillion (1.2×10^{40}) long tons.

"Quasars"

In November, 1962, the existence of quasi-stellar radio sources ("quasars" or QSO's) was established. No satisfactory model has yet been constructed to account for the immensely high luminosity of bodies apparently so distant and of such small diameter. The diameter of 3C 446 is only about 90 light-days, but there are measurable alterations in brightness in less than one day. It is believed to be undergoing the most violent explosion yet detected, since it has increased 3.2 magnitudes or 20-fold in less than one year.

"Pulsars"

The discovery of the first pulsating radio source or "pulsar" CP 1919 was announced from the Mullard Radio Astronomy Observatory, Cambridge, England, on February 29, 1968. The fastest so far discovered is NP 0532 in the Crab Nebula with a pulse of 33 milliseconds. It is now accepted that a pulsar is a rotating neutron star of immense density.

Remotest Object

The greatest distance yet ascribed to a radio-detected and visibly confirmed body is that claimed for a quasar designated 4C 05.34 (red shift of 2.877) identified in May, 1970, by the Kitt Peak National Observatory, Arizona.

Although the Symposium on Relativistic Astrophysics in New York City in 1967 concluded that quasars "have no agreed distance from the earth," a figure of at least 13,000 million light-years has been ascribed to quasars exhibiting a lesser red shift than the 2.877 measured for this body.

PKS 0237—23, a quasar announced in March, 1967, is the most luminous of observed heavenly bodies. Proponents of the oscillation theory of cosmology believe that the universe is between 15,000 and 20,000 million years advanced on the expanding phase of an 80,000 million year expansion-contraction cycle. The number of cycles which may have previously occurred, if any, is not determinable.

Rocketry and Missiles

Earliest Experiments

The origins of the rocket date from the war rockets propelled by a charcoal-saltpeter-sulphur powder, made by the Chinese as early as *c.* 1100. These early rockets became known in Europe by 1258.

The first launching of a liquid-fuel rocket (patented July 14, 1914) was by Robert Hutchings Goddard (1882–1945) of the U.S., at Auburn, Massachusetts, on March 16, 1926, when his rocket reached an altitude of 41 feet and traveled a distance of 184 feet. The U.S.S.R.'s earliest rocket was the semi-liquid fueled GIRD-IX tested on August 17, 1933.

Longest Ranges

The longest range achieved by a ground-to-surface rocket is 9,000 miles by a U.S. *Atlas*, measuring 85 feet long and weighing 130 tons, fired across the South Atlantic from Cape Canaveral (now Cape Kennedy), Florida, to a point 1,000 miles southeast of the Cape of Good Hope, South Africa, on May 20, 1960. The flight lasted about 53 minutes. The previous record was 7,760 miles by a Soviet rocket in the Pacific on January 20, 1960. On March 16, 1962, Nikita Khrushchev, then the Soviet Prime Minister, claimed in Moscow that the U.S.S.R. possessed a "global rocket" with a range of about 19,000 miles, *i.e.* more than the earth's semi-circumference and therefore capable of hitting any target from either direction.

Most Powerful

It has been suggested that the U.S.S.R. manned spacecraft booster which blew up at Tyuratam in the summer (? July) of 1969 had a thrust of 10,000,000 to 14,000,000 lbs. No further details have been released by the U.S.S.R. nor by the U.S. ELINT (Electronic Intelligence Section).

The most powerful rocket that has been publicized is the *Saturn V*, used for the Project Apollo 3-man lunar exploration mission, on which development began in January, 1962, at the John F. Kennedy Space Center, Merritt Island, Florida. The 6,218,558-lb. rocket is 363 feet 8 inches tall, with a payload of 107,500 lbs., and gulps 15 tons of propellant per second for $2\frac{1}{2}$ minutes. Stage I (S-1C) is 138 feet 6 inches tall and is powered by five Rocketdyne F-1 engines, using liquid oxygen (LOX) and kerosene, each delivering a 1,514,000-lb. thrust. Stage II (S-2) is powered by five LOX and liquid hydrogen Rocketdyne J-2 engines with a total thrust of 1,141,453 lbs., while Stage III (designated S-IV B) is powered by a single 228,290-lb.

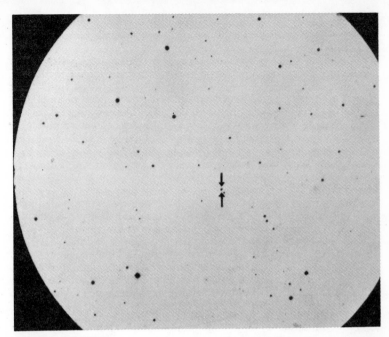

MOST LUMINOUS OBSERVED HEAVENLY BODY: PKS 0237-23, a quasar, found in 1967.

MOST POWERFUL ROCKET: Saturn V, used for the Apollo moon shots, uses 15 tons of propellant per second.

Rocketry and Space Records

	Earth Orbits	Moon Orbits	Solar Orbits
Earliest Satellite	Sputnik I, October 4, 1957	Luna X, March 31, 1966	Luna I, January 2, 1959
Earliest Planetary Contact	Sputnik I rocket—burnt out December 1, 1957	Luna II hit moon, September 13, 1959	Venus III hit Venus, March 1, 1966
Earliest Planetary Touchdown	Discoverer XIII capsule, landed August 11, 1960	Luna IX soft landed on moon February 3, 1966	Venus VII soft landed on Venus, December 15, 1970
Earliest Rendezvous and Docking	Gemini 8 and Agena 8, March 16, 1966	Apollo X and LM 4 docked May 23, 1969	None
Earliest Crew Exchange	Soyuz IV and V, January 14-15, 1969	Apollo X and LM 4, May 18, 1969	None
Heaviest Satellite	34.09 tons, Apollo IV, November 9, 1967	33.98 tons, Apollo XV, July 26, 1971	15.23 tons, Apollo X rocket, May 18, 1969
Lightest Satellite	1.47 lbs. each, Tetrahedron Research Satellites (TRS) 2 and 3, May 9, 1963	150 lbs., Interplanetary Monitoring Probe IMP 6, July 19, 1967	13 lbs., Pioneer IV, March 3, 1959
Longest First Orbit	42 days, Apollo XII rocket, November 14, 1969	720 minutes, Lunar Orbiter 4, May 4, 1967	636 days, Mariner 6 (Mars Probe), February 25, 1969
Shortest First Orbit	86 min. 30.6 sec., Cosmos 169 (rocket), July 17, 1967	114 min., LM 9 ascent stage (Apollo XV), August 2, 1971	195 days, Mariner 5 (Venus Probe), June 14, 1967
Longest Expected Lifetime	>1 million years, Vela 12, April 8, 1970	Unlimited, IMP 6 (see above), July 19, 1967	All unlimited
Nearest First Perigee, Pericynthion or Perihelion	63 miles, Cosmos 169 rocket, July 17, 1967	10 miles, LM 6 ascent stage (Apollo XII), November 20, 1969	50,700 miles Apollo IX rocket, March 3, 1969
Furthest First Apogee, Apocynthion or Aphelion	535,522 miles, Apollo XII rocket, November 14, 1969	4,900 miles, IMP 6 (see above), July 19, 1967	162,900,000 miles Mariner 6 (Mars Probe), February 25, 1969

The highest and lowest speeds in solar orbit are by Apollo IX rocket and Mariner 6 (see above), respectively.

NOTE:—The largest artificial satellite measured by volume has been Echo II (diameter 135 feet), weighing 565 lbs., launched into orbit from Vandenberg Air Force Base, California, on January 25, 1964. It was an inflated sphere, comprising a 535-lb. balloon, whose skin was made of Mylar plastic 0.00035 of an inch thick, bonded on both sides by aluminum alloy foil 0.00018 of an inch thick, together with equipment. Echo II was the brightest of artificial satellites (its magnitude is about −1), and it has been claimed that it became the man-made object seen by more people than any other. Its lifetime was 1,960 days until it burned up on June 7, 1969. (See photo, page 146.)

thrust J-2 engine. The whole assembly generates 175,600,000 horse-power and weighs up to 6,582,000 lbs. fully loaded in the case of Apollo 14. It was first launched on November 9, 1967.

Highest Velocity

The first space vehicle to achieve the third cosmic velocity sufficient to break out of the solar system was *Pioneer X*. The Atlas SLV-3C launcher with a modified Centaur D second stage left the Earth at an unprecedented 31,700 m.p.h. on March 2, 1972.

PROGRESSIVE ROCKET ALTITUDE RECORDS:

Height in miles	Rocket	Place	Launch Date
0.71 (3,762 ft.)	A 3-inch rocket	near London, England	April, 1750
1.24 (6,560 ft.)	Rheinhold Tiling[1] (Germany) solid fuel rocket	Osnabruck, Germany	April, 1931
nearly 3	OR-2 liquid-fuel rocket (U.S.S.R.)	U.S.S.R.	Aug. 17, 1932
8.1	U.S.S.R. "Stratosphere" rocket	U.S.S.R.	1935
52.46	A.4 rocket (Germany)	Peenemünde, Germany	Oct. 3, 1942
c. 85	A.4 rocket (Germany)	Heidelager, Poland ...	early 1944
118	A.4 rocket (Germany)	Heidelager, Poland ...	mid-1944
244	V-2/W.A.C. Corporal (2-stage Bumper), No. 5 (U.S.)	White Sands, N.M. ...	Feb. 24, 1949
250	M.104 *Raketa* (U.S.S.R.)......	? Tyuratam, U.S.S.R.	1954
682	Jupiter C (U.S.)..................	Cape Canaveral (now Kennedy), Fla.	Sept. 20, 1956
>2,700	Farside (4 stage) (U.S.)	Eniwetok Atoll	Oct. 20, 1957
70,700	Pioneer I-B Lunar Probe (U.S.)	Cape Canaveral (now Kennedy), Fla.	Oct. 11, 1958
215,300,000*	Lunik I or Planet X (U.S.S.R.)	Kapustin, Yar U.S.S.R................	Jan. 2, 1959
242,000,000*	Mars I (U.S.S.R.)	U.S.S.R.	Nov. 1, 1962
1,800,000,000[2]	Pioneer X (U.S.)...............	Cape Kennedy, Fla.....	Mar. 2, 1972

* Apogee in solar orbit.

[1] There is some evidence that Tiling may shortly after have reached 31,000 ft. (5.90 miles) with a solid fuel rocket at Wangerooge, East Friesian Islands, West Germany.

[2] This distance will be reached by 1980 after which it will pass out of the solar system's gravitational field.

Ion Rockets

Speeds of up to 100,000 m.p.h. are envisaged for rockets powered by an ion discharge. It was announced on January 13, 1960, that caesium vapor discharge had been maintained for 50 hours at the Lewis Research Center in Cleveland, Ohio. Ion rockets were first used in flight by the U.S.S.R.'s Mars probe *Zond II*, launched on November 30, 1964.

Artificial Satellites

The dynamics of artificial satellites were first propounded by Sir Isaac Newton (1642–1727) in his *Philosophiae Naturalis Principia Mathematica* ("Mathematical Principles of Natural Philosophy"), begun in March, 1686, and first published in the summer of 1687.

The first artificial satellite was successfully put into orbit at an altitude of 142/588 miles and a velocity of more than 17,500 m.p.h. from Tyuratam, a site located 170 miles east of the Aral Sea on the night of October 4, 1957. This spherical satellite, *Sputnik* ("Fellow Traveler") *I*, officially designated "Satellite 1957 Alpha 2," weighed 184.3 lbs., with a diameter of 22.8 inches, and its lifetime is believed to have been 92 days, ending on January 4, 1958. It was designed under the direction of Dr. Sergey Pavlovich Korolyov (1906–66).

Terrestrial escape velocity (25,022 m.p.h. at the surface but less at altitude) was first achieved by the U.S.S.R.'s solar satellite *Lunik I* (or *Planet X*), fired from Kapustin Yar on January 2, 1959. This is sometimes termed "second cosmic velocity."

Solar escape velocity (36,800 m.p.h.) was first achieved in a limited way over the Holloman Air Base, New Mexico, on October 16, 1957, when aluminum pellets were fired at about 40,000 m.p.h. by a "shaped charge" from an Aerobee rocket at an altitude of 55 miles. The speed necessary for escape from the Milky Way galaxy is 815,000 m.p.h.

Earliest Successful Manned Satellites

The first successful manned space flight began at 9:07 a.m. (Moscow time), or 6:07 a.m. G.M.T., on April 12, 1961. Flight Major (later Colonel) Yuriy Alekseyevich Gagarin (born March 9, 1934) completed a single orbit of the earth in 89.34 minutes in the U.S.S.R.'s space vehicle *Vostok* ("East") *I* (10,417 lbs.). The take-off

WORLD'S LARGEST ARTIFICIAL SATELLITE: The U.S. Echo II undergoing inspection before pre-orbit test at Lakehurst, New Jersey. The 565-lb. balloon was made of Mylar plastic. Its lifetime aloft was 1,960 days from 1964 to 1969.

was from Tyuratam in Kazakhstan and the landing was 108 minutes later near the village of Smelovka, near Engels in the Saratov region of the U.S.S.R. The maximum speed was 17,560 m.p.h. and the maximum altitude 203.2 miles. Major Gagarin was invested a Hero of the Soviet Union and awarded the Order of Lenin and the Gold Star Medal and was killed in a jet plane crash near Moscow on March 27, 1968.

First Woman in Space

The first woman to orbit the earth was Jr. Lt. (now Flight Major) Valentina Vladimirovna Tereshkova (born March 6, 1937), who was launched in *Vostok VI* from Tyuratam, U.S.S.R., at 9:30 a.m. G.M.T. on June 16, 1963, and landed at 8:16 a.m. on June 19, after a flight of 2 days 22 hours 46 minutes, during which she completed over 48 orbits (1,225,000 miles) and came to within 3 miles of *Vostok V*. On November 3, 1963, she was formally married in Moscow to Flight Major (now Lt.-Col.) Andreyan Grigoryevich Nikolayev (born September 5, 1929), who completed 64 orbits (1,640,200 miles) in *Vostok III* during a voyage of 94 hours 25 minutes on August 11–15, 1962.

First Admitted Fatality

Col. Vladimir Komarov, U.S.S.R. (born March 16, 1927), was launched in *Soyuz* ("Union") *I* at 00:35 a.m. G.M.T. on April 23, 1967. The spacecraft was in orbit for about $25\frac{1}{2}$ hours, but he impacted on descent due to parachute failure and was thus the first man indisputably known to have died during space flight.

First "Walk" in Space

The first person to leave an artificial satellite during orbit was Lt.-Col. Aleksey Arkhipovich Leonov (born May 30, 1934), who left the Soviet satellite *Voskhod II* at about 8:30 a.m. G.M.T. on March 18, 1965. Lt.-Col. Leonov was "in space" for about 20 minutes, and for 12 minutes 9 seconds he "floated" at the end of a line 16 feet long.

Longest Manned Space Flight

The longest space flight has been that of Soviet Commander Georgyi Timofeyevitch Dobrovolskiy, Test Engineer Viktor Nikolayevitch Patsayev and Fl. Eng. Vladislav Volkov in *Soyuz XI* lasting 23 days 18 hours 15 minutes, June 6–29, 1971. The crew died of hypoxia 30 minutes before landing in Kazakhstan, when the capsule suffered a hatch-sealing failure.

Captain James Arthur Lovell (U.S.N.) has the overall space duration record away from earth between December 4, 1965 and his return from his fourth mission, the abortive *Apollo XIII* flight on March 17, 1970, with 715 hours 4 minutes 57 seconds.

Splashdown Record

The most accurate recovery from space was the splashdown of *Gemini IX* on June 6, 1966, only 769 yards from the *U.S.S. Wasp* in the western Atlantic.

Oldest and Youngest Astronauts

The oldest of the 57 people in space has been Col. Georgiy T. Beregovoiy (U.S.S.R.) who was 47 years and 6 months when launched in *Soyuz III* on October 26, 1968. The youngest was Major Gherman Stepanovich Titov (U.S.S.R.), aged 25 years 11 months when launched in *Vostok II* on August 6, 1961.

First Moon Flights

The first manned spaceflight around the moon was by Astronauts Frank Borman, James A. Lovell, and William Anders in *Apollo VIII* on December 21–27, 1968. The first landing on the moon was by Astronauts Neil A. Armstrong and Edwin Aldrin Jr. from the Apollo XI spacecraft on July 20–21, 1969. (For more details, see Chapter 11.)

Extra-Terrestrial Vehicles

The first wheeled vehicle landed on the moon was the Soviet *Lunokhod I* which began its travels on November 17, 1970. It moved a total of 6.54 miles on gradients up to 30 degrees in the Mare Imbrium and did not become non-functioning until October 4, 1971.

The lunar speed and distance record was set by the *Apollo XVI* Rover with 11 m.p.h. and 18.4 miles.

Longest Lunar Mission

The longest duration of any manned lunar orbit was the *Apollo XV*'s command module *Endeavor*, which set a record of manned lunar orbit with 6 days 1 hour 13 minutes during a mission of 12 days 7 hours 12 minutes from July 26 to August 7, 1971.

Duration Record on the Moon

The crew of *Apollo XVI*'s lunar exploration module *Orion*, manned by U.S.N. Capt. John Watts Young, 41, and Lt.-Col. Charles M. Duke, Jr., 36, was on the lunar surface for 71 hours 2 minutes on April 22–24, 1972. The crew collected a record 245 lbs. of rock and soil during their 20 hours 15 minutes "extra-vehicular activity."

Most Expensive Project

The total cost of the U.S. space program up to and including the projected lunar mission of *Apollo XVII* has been estimated at $25,541,400,000.

Chapter Five

THE SCIENTIFIC WORLD

Elements

All known matter in the solar system is made up of chemical elements. The total of naturally occurring elements so far detected is 94, comprising, at ordinary temperature, two liquids, 11 gases and 81 solids. The so-called "fourth state" of matter is plasma, when negatively charged electrons and positively charged ions are in flux.

Lightest and Heaviest Sub-Nuclear Particles

The number of fundamental sub-nuclear particles catered for by the 1964 Unitary Symmetry Theory or SU (3) was 34. The SU (6) system caters for 91 particles, while the even newer SU(12) system caters for an infinite number, some of which are expected to be produced by higher and higher energies, but with shorter and shorter lifetimes and weaker and weaker interactions. Of SU(3) particles the one with the highest mass is the omega minus, discovered before February 24, 1964, at the Brookhaven National Laboratory, near Upton, Long Island, N.Y. It has a mass of $1,672.5 \pm 0.5$ MeV/c^2 and a lifetime of 1.3×10^{-10} of a second. Of all sub-atomic concepts only the neutrino calls for masslessness. There is experimental proof that the mass, if any, of an electron neutrino, first observed in June, 1956, cannot be greater than one ten-thousandth of that of an electron, which itself has a rest mass of 9.109558 (± 0.000054) $\times 10^{-28}$ of a gram, *i.e.* it has a weight of less than 1.07×10^{-31} of a gram.

By 1971, some 400 particles and resonances had been recorded.

Fastest Particles

A search for the existence of particles, named tachyons (symbol T+ and T−), with a speed *in vacuo* greater than c, the speed of light, was instituted in 1968 by Dr. T. Alvager and Dr. M. Kriesler of Princeton University. Such particles would create the conceptual difficulty of disappearing before they exist. Quarks and anti-quarks (q and $\bar{q}$) have similarly evaded proof of detection.

Elements

Commonest. The commonest element in the universe is hydrogen, which has been calculated to comprise 90 per cent of all matter and over 99 per cent of matter in interstellar space.

Most and Least Isotopes. The element with the most isotopes is the colorless gas xenon (Xe) with 23 and that with the least is hydrogen with three. The metallic element with the most is platinum (Pt) with 29 and that with the least is lithium (Li) with five. Of stable and naturally occurring isotopes, tin (Sn) has the most with 10, while 20 elements exist in nature only as single nuclides.

Longest and Shortest Half-Lives. The half-life of a radioactive substance is the period taken for its activity to fall to half of its original value. The longest recorded is $>2 \times 10^{18}$ years for bismuth 209, while the shortest is 2.4×10^{-21} of a second for helium 5.

Gases

Lightest. Hydrogen, a colorless gas discovered in 1766 by the Hon. Henry Cavendish (1731–1810), a British millionaire, is less than 1/14th the weight of air, weighing only 0.005611 of a pound per cubic foot, or 89.88 milligrams per liter.

Heaviest. Radon, the colorless isotope Em 222 of the gas emanation, was discovered in 1900 by Friedrich Ernst Dorn (1848–1916) of Germany, and is 111.5 times as heavy as hydrogen. It is also known as niton and emanates from radium salts.

Melting and Boiling Points—Lowest. Of all substances, helium has the lowest boiling point ($-268.94°C.$). This element, which at normal temperatures is a colorless gas, was discovered in 1868 by Sir Joseph Norman Lockyer (1836–1920) working with Sir Edward Frankland (1825–99) (both U.K.), and the French astronomer Pierre Jules Cesar Janssen (1824–1907), working independently. Helium was first liquefied in 1908 by Heike Kamerlingh Onnes (1853–1926), a Dutch physicist. Liquid helium, which exists in two forms, can only be solidified under pressure of 26 atmospheres. This was first achieved in 1926 by Wilhemus H. Keesom (born Netherlands, 1876). At this pressure helium will melt at $-272°C.$

Melting and Boiling Points—Highest. Of the elements that are gases at normal temperatures, chlorine has the highest melting point ($-101.0°C.$) and the highest boiling point ($-34.1°C.$) This yellow-green gas was discovered in 1774 by the German-born Karl Wilhelm Scheele (1742–86) of Sweden.

Rarest. The earth's atmosphere weighs an estimated 5,809,-000,000,000,000 tons, of which nitrogen constitutes 78.09 per cent by volume in dry air. The heavy hydrogen isotope, tritium, exists in the atmosphere to an extent of only 5×10^{-23} of one per cent by volume.

Metals

Lightest. The lightest of all metals is lithium (Li), light golden brown (*in vacuo*) metal discovered in 1817 by Johan August Arfvedson (1792–1841) of Sweden. It has a density of 0.5333 of a gram per c.c. or 33.29 lbs. per cubic foot. The isotope Li 6 (7.56 per cent of naturally occurring lithium) is still lighter with a density of only 0.4616 of a gram per c.c.

Densest. The densest of all metals and hence the world's most effective paperweight is osmium (Os), a gray-blue metal of the platinum group, discovered in 1804 by Smithson Tennant (1761–1815) of the United Kingdom. It has a density at 20°C. of 22.59 grams per c.c. or 1,410 lbs. per cubic foot. A cubic foot of uranium would weigh 220 lbs. less than a cubic foot of osmium. During the period of 1955–70, iridium was thought by some inorganic chemists to be the densest metal but has a density of 22.56.

Melting and Boiling Points—Lowest. Excluding mercury, which is liquid at normal temperatures, caesium (Cs), a silvery-white metal discovered in 1860 by Robert Wilhelm von Bunsen (1811–99) and Gustav Robert Kirchhoff (1824–87) of Germany, has the lowest metallic melting point at 28.5°C. (83.3°F.).

Excluding mercury which vaporizes at 356.66°C., the metal which vaporizes at the lowest temperature and hence has the lowest boiling point, is caesium at 669°C. (1,236°F.).

Melting and Boiling Points—Highest. The highest melting point of any pure element is that of tungsten or wolfram (W), a gray metal discovered in 1783 by the Spanish brothers, Juan José d'Elhuyar and Fausto d'Elhuyar (1755–1833). It melts at $3,417°C. \pm 10°C.$

The most refractory substances known are tantalum carbide ($TaC_{0.88}$), a black solid, and the hafnium carbide ($HfC_{0.95}$), which melt at $4,010°C. \pm 75°C.$ and $3,960°C. \pm 20°C.$ respectively.

Expansion. The highest normal linear thermal expansion of a metal is that of caesium which, at 20°C., is 9.7×10^{-5} of a centimeter per cm. per one degree C. The trans-uranic metal plutonium will however expand and contract by as much as 8.9 per cent of its volume when being heated to its melting point of $639.5°C. \pm 2°C.$

The lowest linear expansion is that of the alloy invar, containing 35 per cent nickel, the remainder being iron, with one per cent carbon and manganese. This has a linear thermal expansion of 9×10^{-7} of an inch per inch per one degree C. at ordinary temperatures. It was first prepared in about 1930 by Charles Edouard Guillaume of Switzerland (1861–1938).

Highest Ductility. The most malleable, or ductile, of metals is gold. One ounce (avoirdupois) of gold can be drawn in the form of a continuous wire thread (diameter 2×10^{-4} of an inch) to a length of 43 miles. A cubic inch can be beaten into a leaf five millionths of an inch thick, so as to cover nearly 1,400 square feet. It has been estimated that all gold mined since 1500 A.D. could be stored in a vault $55 \times 55 \times 55$ feet.

Highest Tensile Strength. The material with the highest known UTS (ultimate tensile strength) is sapphire whisker (Al_2O_3) at 6.2×10^6 lbs./in.^{2}. This is equivalent to a whisker the thickness of a human hair (an as yet unachieved 70 microns) which could support a weight of 621 lbs. Amorphous boron has a maximum cohesive strength of 3.9×10^6 lbs./in.^{2} and thus theoretically a wire 189.4 miles long could be suspended without parting.

Rarest. Fourteen of the fifteen "rare earth" or "lanthanide" elements which have naturally-occurring isotopes (this includes lutetium) have now been separated into metallic purity exceeding 99.9 per cent. The highly radioactive element promethium (Pm) has been produced artificially with a purity exceeding only 99.8 per cent. The radioactive elements 43 (technetium) and 61 (promethium) were chemically separated from pitchblende ore in 1961 and 1968 respectively. Because of their relatively short half-lives, their existence in nature is due entirely to the "spontaneous fission" radioactive decay of uranium.

The rarest naturally-occurring element is astatine (element 85) first produced artificially in 1940 and identified in nature three years later. It has been calculated that only 0.3 of a gram exists in the earth's crust to a depth of 10 miles.

The isotope polonium 213 (Po 213) is, however, rarer by a factor of 5×10^{10} which is equivalent to one atom in 3.5×10^{37}.

Several of the trans-uranium elements have been produced on an atom-to-atom basis so that at any one moment only single atoms of these elements may have existed.

Commonest. Though ranking behind oxygen (46.60 per cent) and silicon (27.72 per cent) in abundance, aluminum is the commonest of all metals, constituting 8.13 per cent by weight of the earth's crust.

Most Magnetic and Non-Magnetic. The most magnetic material, at ordinary temperatures, is a cobalt-copper-samerium compound $Co_3 Cu_2 Sm$ with a coercive force of 10,500 oersted. The most non-magnetic alloy yet discovered is 963 parts of copper to 37 parts of nickel.

Newest. The newest trans-uranium element, number 105, was synthesized in the HILAC heavy-ion linear accelerator in the Lawrence Radiation Laboratory, University of California in Berkeley, by an American-Finnish team led by Dr. Albert Ghiorso. The element, for which the name "hahnium" has been proposed, was first produced on March 5, 1970, with a mass of 260 and a half-life of 1.6 seconds.

Attempts initiated in November, 1968, at Berkeley, to find traces of elements 110 (eka-platinum) to 114 (eka-lead) have so far proved inconclusive. The U.S.S.R. claims to have detected elements 108 and 114 in the earth's crust have not been substantiated. Element 110 was apparently recorded by the Physics Department of Bristol University, England, on emulsion plates sent aloft in a balloon 25 miles above Palestine, Texas, in September, 1968, but the evidence must be regarded as being very tenuous.

The heaviest isotope for which there is definite evidence is that of mass 262 of element 105 (Hahnium 262) synthesized by Ghiorso and others and announced in 1971.

Dr. Glenn Theodore Seaborg (born April 19, 1912), Chairman of the U.S. Atomic Energy Commission, estimated in June, 1966, that elements up to 126 would be produced by the year 2000.

Purest. The purest yet achieved is the gray-white metal germanium by the zone refining technique, first mooted in 1939 and published by William G. Pfann of Bell Laboratories in 1952. By 1967, a purity of 99.99999999% had been achieved, which has been likened to one grain of salt in a freight carload of sugar.

Most Expensive Substance

In October, 1968, the U.S. Atomic Energy Commission announced that miniscule amounts of californium 252 (Element 98) were on sale at $100 per tenth of a microgram. A fanciful calculation would indicate that the price of an ingot weighing 1 lb. (if such were available) would at this rate be $530 billion. It was announced in August, 1970, that the price might be reduced to only $10 per microgram.

Hardest Substances

Prof. Naoto Kawai of Osaka University, Japan, announced in June, 1967, the production by dint of a pressure of 168 tons/cm^2 5,300,000 p.s.i.) of a single crystal of 1 part silica, 1 part magnesium and 4 parts oxygen which was "twice as hard as diamond."

Plastics

The plastic with the best temperature resistance is modified polymide which can withstand temperatures of up to 500°C. (930°F.) for short periods. The plastics with the greatest tensile strength are polyvinyl alcoholic fibers which have been tested to 1.5×10^5 lb./in.^{2}.

Finest Powder

The finest powder produced is aluminum dust with an average diameter of 0.03 of a micron and a surface area of 75 square meters (807 square feet) per gram. It was first marketed in the U.S. at $30 per ounce in February, 1959. Some particles measure only 0.005 of a micron.

Smelliest Substance

The most pungent of the 17,000 smells so far classified is 4-hydroxy-3-methaxy benzaldehyde or vanillaldehyde. This can be detected in a concentration of 2×10^{-8} of a milligram per liter of air. Thus 9.7×10^{-5} (about one ten-thousandth) of an ounce completely volatilized would still be detectable in an enclosed space with a floor the size of a large football field (360 feet $\times$ 300 feet) and a roof 45 feet high. Only 2.94 ounces would be sufficient to permeate a cubic mile of atmosphere. The most evil smelling substance must be a matter of opinion, but ethyl mercaptan (C_2H_5SH) and butyl seleno-mercaptan (C_4H_9SeH) are powerful claimants, each with a smell reminiscent of a combination of rotting cabbage, garlic, onions and sewer gas.

Most Expensive Perfume

The costliest perfume in the world is "Adoration," manufactured by Nina Omar of Puerto Real, Cadiz, Spain, and distributed in the U.S. at a retail price of $185 per half-ounce. Its most expensive ingredient is a very rare aromatic gum from Asia.

The biggest and most expensive listed bottle of perfume is the two-liter (3.52 pint) size of Chanel No. 5. Made in France, it is not sold in the U.S.

Sweetest Substance

The sweetest naturally occurring substance is exuded from the red serendipity berry (*Dioscoreophyllum cumminsii*) from Nigeria, which was announced in September, 1967, to be 1,500 times as sweet as sucrose. The chemical 1-n-propoxy-2-amino-4-nitrobenzene was determined by Verkade in 1946 to be 5,600 times as sweet as 1 per cent sucrose.

Bitterest Substance

The bitterest known substance is Bitrex, the proprietary name for benzyldiethyl (2:6-xylylcarbamoyl methyl) ammonium benzoate

$(C_{23}H_{34}N_2O_3)$, first reported from Macfarlan Smith Ltd. of Edinburgh, Scotland. This can be detected in solution at a concentration of one part in 20,000,000 and is thus about 200 times as bitter as quinine sulphate $((C_{22}H_{24}N_2O_2)_2, H_2SO_4, 2H_2O)$.

Strongest Acid

The strength of acids and alkalis is measured on the pH scale. The pH of a solution is the logarithm to the base 10 of the reciprocal of the hydrogen-ion concentration in gram ions per liter. The strongest simple acid is perchloric acid $(HClO_4)$. Assessed on its power as a hydrogen ion donor, the most powerful acid is a solution of antimony pentafluoride in fluosulphonic acid $(SbF_5 + FSO_3H)$.

Strongest Alkali

The strength of alkalis is expressed by pH values rising above the neutral 7.0. The strongest bases are caustic soda or sodium hydroxide (NaOH), caustic potash or potassium hydroxide (KOH) and tetramethylammonium hydroxide $(N(CH_3)_4OH)$, with pH values of 14 in normal solutions. True neutrality, pH7, occurs in pure water at 22°C.

Most Powerful Fuel

The greatest specific impulse of any rocket propulsion fuel combination is 435 lbs./f./sec. per lb. produced by lithium fluoride and hydrogen. This compares with a figure of 300 for liquid oxygen and kerosene.

Poison

Quickest. The barbiturate thiopentone, if given as a large intracardiac injection, will cause permanent cessation of respiration in one to two seconds.

Most Potent. The typhus-like disease, Q-fever, can be instituted by a single micro-organism (*Rickettsia*), transmitted by air, but is only fatal in 1 in 1,000 cases. Effectually the most poisonous substance yet discovered is the toxin of the bacterium *Pasteurella tularensis*. About 10 organisms can institute tulaeremia, variously called alkali disease, Francis disease or deerfly fever, and this is fatal in 50 to 80 cases in 1,000.

Most Powerful Nerve Gas

The nerve gas Sarin or GB, a lethal colorless and odorless gas, has been developed since 1945 in the U.S. and is reputedly 30 times as toxic as phosgene $(COCl_2)$ used in World War I. In the early 1950s, even more toxic substances known as V-agents were developed at the Chemical Defence Experimental Establishment, Porton Down, Wiltshire, England, which are lethal at 1 milligram per man.

Drugs

Most Powerful. The most potent and, to an addict, the most expensive of all naturally derived drugs is heroin, which is a chemically processed form of opium from the juice of the unripe seed capsules of the poppy (*Papaver somniferum*). An ounce, which suffices for up to 1,800 hypodermic shots or "fixes," may sell for up to $9,000 in the U.S., affording a 70,000 per cent profit over the raw material price in Turkey. The most potent analgesic drug is Etorphine or M99, announced in June, 1963, by Dr. K. W. Bentley and D. G. Hardy of Reckitt & Sons Ltd. in Kingston-upon-Hull, Yorkshire, England. The drug has almost 10,000 times the potency of morphine.

The U.S. had, according to President Nixon, 180,000 heroin addicts in 1971.

Drink

Most Alcoholic

The strength of liquor is gauged by degrees proof. In the U.S., proof spirit is that mixture of ethyl alcohol (C_2H_5OH) and water which contains one half its volume of alcohol of a specific gravity of 0.7939 at 60°F., referred to water at 60°F. as unity. Pure or absolute alcohol is thus 200 proof. A "hangover" is due to toxic congenerics such as amyl alcohol ($C_5H_{11}OH$).

The highest strength spirits which can be produced are raw rum and some Polish vodkas, up to 194 proof or 97.2 per cent alcohol. The strongest drink sold commercially is Polish White Spirit Vodka, produced by the State Spirits Monopoly of Poland. This is 160 proof.

Beer

Strongest Beer. The world's strongest beer is Thomas Hardy's ale brewed in July, 1968, by the Dorchester Brewery, Dorset, England, with 10.15 per cent alcohol by weight and 12.58 per cent by volume.

Weakest Beer. The weakest liquid ever marketed as beer was a sweet ersatz beer which was brewed in Germany by Sunner, Colne-Kalk, in 1918. It had an original gravity of 1,000.96°.

Wine

Most Expensive. The highest price ever paid for a bottle of wine of any size is $9,200 for a Jeroboam of *Château Mouton* Rothschild 1929 sold by Michael Noble, Britain's Minister for Trade, at Parke-Bernet Galleries, New York City, on May 23, 1972. This bottle contained the equivalent of *five* normal bottles and was thus equivalent to about $300 per glass or $25 a sip.

A bottle of *Château Lafite* Rothschild 1846 was sold at auction by Michael Broadbent of Christie's in San Francisco, on May 26, 1971, on behalf of Hueblein's and was bought by Laurence H. Bender for $5,000. This thus works out at an even higher price per fluid ounce.

Liqueurs

The most expensive liqueur in France is the orange-flavored *Le Grand Marnier Coronation* at 44 francs ($8.88) per bottle.

Ancient *Chartreuse* (before 1903) has been known to sell for more than $42.00 per liter bottle. An 1878 bottle was sold in 1954.

The most expensive brandy sold is *Grande Fine Champagne Arbellot* 1794 which retails at Fauchon's in Paris at 667 francs ($136.12) per bottle.

Largest Bottles

The largest bottle normally used in the wine and spirit trade is the Jeroboam or double magnum, with a capacity of up to 4 liters (8.45 pints), which is used only for liqueur brandy and champagne. A complete set of Monopole champagne bottles from the ¼ bottle, through the ½ bottle, bottle, magnum, Jeroboam, Rehoboam, Methuselah, Salmanezer and Balthazar, to the Nebuchadnezzar, which has a capacity of 16 liters (33.8 pints), is owned by Miss Denise Joan Wardle of Cleveleys, near Blackpool, Lancashire, England. In May, 1958, a 5-foot-tall sherry bottle with a capacity of 196.9 pints was blown in Stoke-on-Trent, Staffordshire, England. This bottle, with the capacity of 131 normal bottles, was named an "Adelaide."

Smallest Bottles

The smallest bottles of liquor sold are the 24 minim bottles of Scotch whisky marketed by the Cumbrae Supply Co. of Scotland. They contain $\frac{1}{20}$ of a fluid ounce.

Champagne Cork Flight

The longest distance for a champagne cork to fly from an untreated and unheated bottle 4 feet from level ground is 73 feet 10½ inches, popped by A. D. Beaty at Hever, Kent, England, on July 20, 1971.

Gems

Most Precious. From 1955, the value of rubies rose, due to a drying up of supplies from Ceylon and Burma. A flawless natural ruby of good color was carat for carat more valuable than emerald, diamond or sapphire and, in the case of a 6-carat ruby, brought $30,000. The ability to produce very large corundum prisms of 12 inches or over in length in the laboratory for use in lasers must now have a bearing on the gem market.

Largest. The largest recorded stone of gem quality was a 520,000-carat (229-lb.) aquamarine ($Al_2Be_3[Si_6O_{18}]$) found near Marambaia, Brazil, in 1910. It yielded over 200,000 carats of gem quality stones.

Rarest. Only two stones are known of the pale mauve gem Taaffeite ($Be_4Mg_4Al_{16}O_{32}$), first discovered in a cut state in Dublin, Ireland, in November, 1945. The larger of the two examples weighs 0.84 of a carat. There are minerals of which only single examples are known.

Hardest. The hardest of all gems, and the hardest known naturally occurring substance, is diamond, which is, chemically, pure carbon. Diamond is 90 times as hard as the next hardest mineral, corundum (Al_2O_3), and those from Borneo, in Indonesia, and New South Wales, Australia, have a particular reputation for hardness. Hardnesses are compared on Mohs' scale, on which talc is 1, a

LARGEST DIAMONDS: The Star of Africa No. 1 in the British Royal Sceptre (left) was cut, with 74 facets, from the 1¼-pound Cullinan diamond. The Hope diamond (right), the largest known blue diamond, is in the Smithsonian Institution, Washington, D.C.

fingernail is 2½, window glass 5, topaz 8, corundum 9, and diamond 10. Diamonds average 7,000 on the Knoop scale, with a peak value of 8,400. This index represents a micro-indentation index based on kilograms per one hundredth of a square millimeter $(kg/(mm^2)^{-2})$.

Densest Gem Mineral. The densest of all gem minerals is stibotantalite $[(SbO)_2 (Ta,Nb)_2 O_6]$, a rare brownish-yellow mineral found in San Diego County, California, with a density of 7.46 grams per c.c.

Diamonds

The largest diamond ever discovered was a stone of 3,106 metric carats (over 1¼ lbs.) found by Captain M. F. Wells in the Premier Mine, Pretoria, South Africa, on January 26, 1905. It was named after Mr. (later Sir) Thomas Major Cullinan (1862–1936), discoverer of the mine in 1902 and chairman of the mining company. It was purchased by the Transvaal government in 1907 and presented to King Edward VII of the United Kingdom. The Star of Africa No. 1 in the British Royal Sceptre, cut from it by Jak Asscher in Amsterdam in 1908, is the largest cut diamond in the world with 74 facets and a weight of 530.2 metric carats.

The rarest colored diamonds are blue and pink. The largest known are the 44.4-carat vivid blue Hope diamond, probably part of a 112½-carat stone found in the Killur mines, Golconda, India, and purchased in 1642 by Jean Baptiste Tavernier (1605–89); and a 24-carat pink diamond, worth an estimated $1,250,000, presented to the Queen of the United Kingdom in 1947 by Dr. John Thoburn

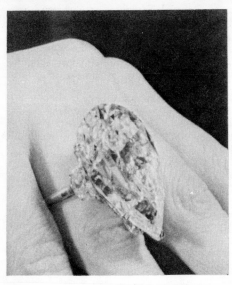

HIGHEST-PRICED DIAMOND ever sold at auction was this 69.42-carat flawless diamond ring which sold to Cartier's, New York, for $1,050,000, and which was almost immediately resold to actor Richard Burton for his wife, in October, 1969. The previous record was $385,000 for a necklace.

Williamson (1907–58), a Canadian geologist. In November, 1958, the Hope diamond was presented to the Smithsonian Institution, Washington, D.C., by Mr. Harry Winston, a jeweler, who had paid a sum variously reported between $700,000 and $1,500,000. (See photograph on previous page.)

Highest Auction Price. The highest price ever paid in an auction was $1,050,000 for a 69.42-carat flawless diamond set in a ring, at the Parke-Bernet Galleries, New York City, on October 23, 1969. The purchaser was the Fifth Avenue jeweler, Cartier's. The next day Cartier's sold the ring to the man who had been the next highest bidder, the actor Richard Burton, provided Cartier's could exhibit the ring on a nationwide tour before delivering it. Mr. Burton has, since then, had the diamond set into a pendant for his wife, Elizabeth Taylor.

Emeralds

Emerald is green beryl. Hexagonal prisms measuring up to 15¾ inches long and 9¾ inches in diameter, and weighing up to 125 lbs. have been recorded from the Ural mines in the U.S.S.R. An 11,000-carat emerald was reported to have been found by Charles Kempt and J. Botes at Letaba, northern Transvaal, South Africa, on October 16, 1956. The largest cut green beryl crystal is the Austrian Government's 2,680-carat unguent jar carved by Dionysio Miseroni in the 17th century. Of gem quality emeralds, the largest known is the Devonshire stone of 1,350 carats from Muso, Colombia.

Sapphires

Sapphire is blue corundum (Al_2O_3). The largest cut gem sapphire in existence is the "Black Star Sapphire of Queensland," weighing 1,444 carats, carved in 1953–55 from a rough stone of 2,097 carats.

It is in the form of a bust of General Dwight David Eisenhower (1890–1969), former President of the United States. A carved dark blue sapphire of the head of President Abraham Lincoln (1809–65), weighing 1,318 carats, is also in the custody of the Kazanjian Foundation of Los Angeles. It was cut in 1949–51 from a 2,302-carat stone also found at Anakie, Queensland, Australia, in *c.* 1935.

Rubies

Ruby is red corundum (Al_2O_3) with chromic oxide impurities. The largest natural gem stone known was a 1,184-carat stone of Burmese origin. In July, 1961, a broken red corundum of an original 3,421 carats was reported to have been found in the U.S. The largest piece weighed about 750 carats. Laboratory-made ruby prisms for laser technology reach over 12 inches in length.

Pearls

Pearls are protective secretionary bodies produced by bivalved mollusks. Gem pearls come chiefly from the western Pacific genus *Pinctada* and the freshwater mussel, genus *Quadrula*. The largest known natural pearl is the "Pearl of Allah," also called the "Pearl of Lao-tze," measuring $9\frac{1}{2}$ inches long, $5\frac{1}{2}$ inches in diameter, and weighing 14 lbs. 1 oz. It was discovered in the shell of a giant clam (*Tridacna gigas*), the largest of all bivalves, in the Philippines on May 7, 1934. Since 1936 the pearl has been owned by Wilburn Dowell Cobb of California. It was valued at $3,500,000 in 1939.

Opals

The largest known opal is a yellow-orange one of 220 troy oz. unearthed by a bulldozer at Anda Mooka, South Australia, in January, 1970, and valued at $A168,000 ($210,000). The largest gem opal is the 17,700 carat "Olympic Australis" found at Coober Pedy, South Australia, in August, 1956.

Crystals

The largest crystal ball is the Warner sphere ($106\frac{3}{4}$ lbs., $12\frac{7}{8}$ inches in diameter) of Burmese quartz (originally a 1,000-lb. piece) in the Smithsonian Institution Museum in Washington, D.C. A single rock crystal weighing 1,728 lbs. was placed in the Ural Geological Museum in Sverdlovsk, U.S.S.R., in November, 1968. A piezo-quartz crystal weighing 78 tons was found in Kazakhstan, U.S.S.R., in September, 1958.

Topaz

The largest known topaz is a low quality transparent crystal weighing 596 lbs., from a pegmatite in the province of Minas Geraes, Brazil. Since 1951 it has been on exhibition at the American Museum of Natural History, New York City.

Largest Slab of Marble

The largest piece of used marble in the world is the coping stone of the Tomb of the Unknown Soldier in Arlington National Cemetery, Arlington, Virginia. It weighs more than 50 tons and was cut from a 100-ton slab, the largest single slab ever found, taken from a quarry at Yule, Colorado.

Precious Stone Records

	Largest	Largest Cut Stone	Other Records
Diamond (pure crystallized carbon)	3,106 metric carats (over 1¼ lbs.) —*The Cullinan*, found by Capt. M. F. Wells, Jan. 26, 1905, in the Premier Mine, Pretoria, South Africa.	530.2 metric carats. Cleaved from *The Cullinan* in 1908, in Amsterdam by Jak Asscher and polished by Henri Koe. Known as *The Star of Africa* No. 1 and now in the British Royal Sceptre.	Diamond is the *hardest* known naturally occurring substance, being 90 times as hard as the next hardest mineral, corundum (Al_2O_3). The peak hardness value on the Knoop scale is 8,400 compared with an average diamond of 7,000. The rarest colors for diamond are blue (record—44.4 carat *Hope* diamond) and pink (record—24 carat diamond presented by Dr. John Thoburn Williamson to H.M. The Queen of the U.K. in 1958). Auction record: $1,050,000 for a 69.42-carat stone bought by Cartier and sold to Richard Burton at $1,200,000 for Elizabeth Taylor on Oct. 24, 1969. The largest uncut diamond is *The Star of Sierra Leone* found at Kono, Sierra Leone, Africa, on Feb. 14, 1972, weighing 969.8 carats.
Emerald (green beryl) [$Be_3Al_2(SiO_3)_6$]	125 lbs. (up to 15¾ inches long and 9¾ inches in diameter) from a Ural, U.S.S.R. mine.	2,680-carat unguent jar carved by Dionysio Miseroni in the 17th century owned by the Austrian Government. 1,350 carats of *gem* quality, the *Devonshire* stone from Muso, Columbia.	An 11,000-carat emerald was reported to have been found by Charles Kempt and J. Botes at Letaba, northern Transvaal, South Africa, Oct. 16, 1956.
Sapphire (blue corundum) (Al_2O_3)	2,302-carat stone found at Anakie, Queensland, Australia, in c. 1935, now a 1,318-carat head of President Abraham Lincoln (1809–65).	1,444-carat *Black Star Sapphire of Queensland* carved in 1953–55 into a bust of General Dwight David Eisenhower (1890–1969).	*Note:* Both the sapphire busts are in the custody of the Kazanjian Foundation of Los Angeles.
Ruby (red corundum) (Al_2O_3)	3,421-carat broken stone reported found in July, 1961, (largest piece 750 carats).	1,184-carat natural gem stone of Burmese origin.	Since 1955 rubies have been the world's most precious gem attaining a price of up to $10,000 per carat by 1969. The ability to make corundum prisms for laser technology up to over 12 inches in length must now have a bearing on the gem market.

Records for other Precious Materials

	Largest	Where Found	Notes on Present Location, etc.
Pearl (Molluscan concretion)	14 lbs. 1 oz., 9½ in. long by 5½ in. in diameter—*Pearl of Lao-tze*	At Palawan, Philippines, May 7, 1934, in shell of giant clam.	In a San Francisco bank vault. It is the property since 1936 of Wilburn Dowell Cobb and was valued at $3,500,000 in 1939.
Opal ($SiO_2 \cdot nH_2O$)	220 troy oz. (yellow-orange) Gem stone: 17,700 carats (*Olympic Australis*)	Anda Mooka, South Australia, Jan. 1970, Coober Pedy, South Australia, Aug., 1956.	The Anda Mooka specimen was unearthed by a bulldozer.
Crystal (SiO_2)	70 tons (piezo-quartz crystal) Ball: 106¾ lbs., 12⅞ in. diameter, the *Warner* sphere	Kazakhstan, U.S.S.R., Sept., 1958. Burma, (originally a 1,000-lb. piece).	Note: There is a single rock crystal of 1,728 lbs. placed in the Ural Geological Museum, Sverdlovsk, U.S.S.R., November, 1968. Smithsonian Institution Museum in Washington, D.C.
Topaz $[Al_2(OH,F)SiO_4]$	596 lbs. Gem stone: 7,725 carats	Minas Gerais, Brazil.	American Museum of Natural History, New York City, since 1951. Also at the American Museum of Natural History.
Amber (coniferous fossil resin)	33 lbs. 10 oz.	Reputedly from Burma, acquired in 1860.	Bought by John Charles Bowring (d. 1893) for £300 in Canton, China. Natural History Museum, London, since 1940.
Jade $[NaAl(Si_2O_6)]$	Submarine boulder of 5 tons (valued at $180,000)	Off Monterey, California. Landed June 5, 1971.	Reputedly worth $50,000. Jadeite can be virtually any color. The less precious nephrite is $[Ca_2(Mg,Fe)_5(OH)_2(Si_4O_{11})_2]$
Marble (Metamorphosed $CaCO_3$)	100.8 tons (single slab)	Quarried at Yule, Colorado.	A piece of over 45 tons was dressed from this slab for the coping stone of the Tomb of the Unknown Soldier in Arlington National Cemetery, Virginia.
Nuggets— Gold (Au)	7,560 oz. (472½ lbs.) (reef gold) *Holtermann Nugget*	Beyers & Holtermann Star of Hope Gold Mining Co., Hill End, N.S.W., Australia, Oct. 19, 1872.	The purest large nugget was the *Welcome Stranger*, found at Tarnagulla, near Moliagul, Victoria, Australia, which yielded 2,248 troy oz. of pure gold from 2,280½ oz.
Silver (Ag)	2,750 lbs. troy	Sonora, Mexico	Appropriated by the Spanish Government before 1821.

LARGEST GOLD NUGGET: Weighing more than 117 lbs. (2,280¼ oz. troy), "Welcome Stranger" was discovered in 1869 in Australia.

Nuggets

Gold. The largest lump of gold ever found *in situ* was the Holtermann Reef, weighing 7,560 oz. (472½ lbs.), taken from Hill End, New South Wales, Australia, in 1872. It was interlaced with quartz and had a total weight of 10,080 oz. (630 lbs.). A nugget weighing 2,280¼ oz. troy, named the "Welcome Stranger," was discovered in 1869 at Tarnagulla, near Moliagul, in Victoria, Australia. It yielded 2,248 oz. of pure gold.

Silver. The largest silver nugget ever recorded was one of 2,750 lbs. troy (2,263 lbs. avoirdupois), found in Sonora, Mexico, and appropriated by the Spanish government before 1821.

Amber

The largest piece of amber ever reported was a piece weighing 33 lbs. 10 oz., reputedly found in Burma in 1860, and bought by John Charles Bowring (d. 1893) for $1,500 in Canton, China. Since 1944 it has been in the Natural History Museum, London, England.

Jade

The largest piece of gem quality jade recorded is a 5-ton boulder found under water off Monterey, California, and landed on June 5, 1971. It is reputedly worth $50,000.

Telescopes

Earliest. Although there is evidence that early Arabian scientists understood something of the magnifying power of lenses, the first use of lenses to form a telescope has been attributed to Roger Bacon (*c.* 1214–92) in England. The prototype of modern refracting telescopes was completed by Johannes Lippershey for the Dutch government on October 2, 1608.

Largest Refractor. The largest refracting (*i.e.* magnification by lenses) telescope in the world is the 62-foot-long 40-inch telescope completed in 1897 at the Yerkes Observatory, Williams Bay, Wisconsin, and belonging to the University of Chicago.

Largest Reflector. The largest operational telescope in the world is the 236.2-inch telescope sited near Zelenchukskaya in the Caucasus Mountains, U.S.S.R., at an altitude of 6,830 feet. The mirror, weighing 78 tons, was assembled in October, 1970. The overall weight of the 80-foot-long assembly is 935 tons. Being the most powerful of all telescopes, its range, which includes the location of objects down to the 25th magnitude, represents the limits of the observable universe. Its light-gathering power would enable it to detect the light from a candle at a distance of 15,000 miles.

Solar

The world's largest solar telescope is the 480-foot-long McMath telescope at Kitt Peak National Observatory near Tucson, Arizona. It has a focal length of 300 feet and an 80-inch heliostat mirror. It was completed in 1962 and produces an image measuring 33 inches in diameter.

Highest Observatory

The highest altitude observatory in the world is the Mauna Kea Observatory, Hawaii, at an altitude of 13,824 feet, opened in 1969. The principal instrument is an 88-inch telescope.

Oldest Observatory

The earliest astronomical observatory in the world is the Chomsongdae built in 632 A.D. in Kyongju, South Korea, and still extant.

Radio-Telescopes

The world's first fully steerable radio-telescope is the Mark I telescope at the University of Manchester Department of Radio Astronomy, Nuffield Radio Astronomy Laboratories, Jodrell Bank, Macclesfield, Cheshire, England, on which work began in September, 1952. The 840-ton 250-foot diameter bowl of steel plates and 180-foot-high supports weighs 2,240 tons. Its cost is believed to have been about £750,000 ($2,100,000) when it was completed in 1957.

Largest. The first $3,000,000 installment for the building of the world's largest and most sensitive radio-telescope was included by the National Science Foundation in its federal budget for the fiscal year 1973. The instrument termed the VLA (Very Large Array) will be Y-shaped with each arm 13 miles long with 27 mobile antennae on rails. The site selected will be 50 miles west of Socorro in the Plains of San Augustin, New Mexico, and the completion date will be 1979 to 1981 at a total cost of $74,000,000.

LARGEST DISH RADIO-TELESCOPE: The 1,000-foot-diameter U.S. Army installation at Arecibo, Puerto Rico.

Largest Steerable Dish. The world's largest trainable dish-type radio-telescope is the 328-foot diameter, 3,360-ton assembly at the Max Planck Institute for Radio Astronomy of Bonn in the Effelsberger Valley, West Germany; it became operative in May, 1971. The cost of the installation, begun in November, 1967, was $36,920,000. The Manchester University Mark V radio-telescope at Meiford, Montgomeryshire, England, will have a diameter of 400 feet and is due for completion at a cost of some $13,000,000 in 1975.

The world's largest dish-type radio-telescope is the partially-steerable ionospheric assembly built over a natural bowl at Arecibo, Puerto Rico, completed in November, 1963, at a cost of about $9,000,000. It has a diameter of 1,000 feet and the dish covers 18½ acres. Its sensitivity is being raised by a factor of 2,000 and its range to 15,000 million light-years by the fitting of new aluminum plates at a cost of $7,000,000.

The RATAN-600 radio-telescope being built in the northern Caucasus, U.S.S.R. will have a dish 1,968.5 feet in diameter.

Planetaria

The ancestor of the planetarium is the rotatable Gottorp Globe, built by Andreas Busch in Denmark between 1654 and 1664 to the orders of Duke Frederick III of Holstein's court mathematician Olearius. It is 34.6 feet in circumference, weighs 4 tons and is now preserved in Leningrad, U.S.S.R. The stars were painted on the inside.

The earliest optical installation was not until 1923 in the Deutsches Museum, Munich, by Zeiss of Jena, Germany.

The world's largest planetarium, with a diameter of 85 feet, is the Washington Planetarium and Space Center, built at a total construction cost of $5,000,000, on Dangerfield Island, in the Potomac, Washington, D.C.

Photography

It is estimated that the total expenditure on photography in the U.S. in 1970 was $3,802,176,896 and that 70,135,000 still cameras and 8,275,000 movie cameras were in use.

Cameras

Largest. The largest camera ever built was the Anderson Mammoth camera, built in Chicago in 1900. When extended, it measured 9 feet high, 6 feet wide and 20 feet long. Its two lenses were a wide-angle Zeiss with a focal length of 68 inches and a telescope Rapid Rectilinear of 120 inches focal length. Exposures averaged 150 seconds and 15 men were required to work it.

Smallest. Apart from cameras built for intra-cardiac surgery and espionage, the smallest camera generally marketed is the Japanese Kiku 16 Model II, which measures $2\frac{3}{8}$ inches $\times$ 1 inch $\times$ $\frac{5}{8}$ of an inch.

Earliest. The earliest photograph was taken in the summer of 1826 by Joseph Nicéphore Niépce (1765–1833), a French physician and scientist. It showed the courtyard of his country house at Gras,

LARGEST CAMERA: When extended, the Anderson Mammoth, built in Chicago in 1900, is 20 feet long, 9 feet high and 6 feet wide.

near St. Loup-de-Varennes. It probably took eight hours to expose and was taken on a bitumen-coated polished pewter plate measuring 8 inches by 6½ inches.

One of the earliest photographs taken was one of a diamond window pane in Lacock Abbey, Wiltshire, England, taken in 1835 by William Henry Fox Talbot (1800–1877), the inventor of the negative-positive process.

The world's earliest aerial photograph was taken in 1858 by Gaspard Félix Tournachon (1820–1910), *alias* Nadar, from a balloon near Villacoublay, on the outskirts of Paris.

Fastest. A paper on a camera of highly limited application with a time resolution of 1.0×10^{-11} of a second has been published by Butslov *et al.* of the U.S.S.R. Academy of Sciences.

In June, 1969, a U.S.S.R. camera was demonstrated at N.P.L. Teddington, England, with "events" moving across image tubes at 167 million m.p.h., or one quarter the speed of light.

Most Expensive. The most expensive "amateur" roll-film cameras in the world are those of the F-1 35 mm. system made by Canon Amsterdam N.V. of Schiphol, Netherlands. The 40 lenses offered range from the Fish Eye 7.5-mm. F/5.6 to the FL 1200-mm. F/11, while the accessories available number 180.

Fastest Lens. The world's fastest lens is the Canon $\times$ 200 mm. F/0.56 mirror lens used for X-ray work. The fastest lens available in television cameras is the Canon F/0.65.

Largest Print

The largest photographic print ever produced was an enlargement of a hand-drawn map of Europe, measuring over 4,000 square feet, made for the British Broadcasting Corporation by the Newbold Wells Organisation Ltd. of London. In 1964, this company produced the largest color transparency, a hand-colored transparency of the London skyline, measuring 212 feet long by 12½ feet high for the Sydney Exhibition in Australia.

Largest X-ray

The largest X-ray ever made was of a 17-foot-long Mercedes 280 SL car using Agfa-Gevaert Structurix D4 film and a 50-hour exposure in September, 1959.

Numeration

In dealing with large numbers, scientists use the notation of 10 raised to various powers, to eliminate a profusion of zeros. For example, 19,160,000,000,000 miles would be written 1.916×10^{13} miles. Similarly, a very small number, for example 0.0000154324 of a grain, would be written 1.54324×10^{-5} of a grain. Of the prefixes used before numbers the smallest is "atto-," from the Danish *atten* for 18, indicating a million million millionth part (10^{-18}) of the unit, and the highest is "tera-" (Greek, *teras*=monster), indicating a million million (10^{12}) fold.

Numbers

Prime Numbers. A prime number is any positive integer (excluding 1) having no integral factors other than itself and unity, *e.g.* 2, 3, 5, 7, or 11. The lowest prime number is 2. The highest known prime number is $2^{19937} - 1$, received by the American Mathematical Society on March 18, 1971, and calculated on an I.B.M. 360/91 computer in 39 minutes 26.4 seconds by Dr. Bryant Tuckerman at Yorktown Heights, New York.

Perfect Numbers. A number is said to be perfect if it is equal to the sum of its divisors other than itself, *e.g.* $1+2+4+7+14=28$. The lowest perfect number is 6 $(1+2+3)$. The highest known, and the 24th so far discovered, is $(2^{19937} - 1) \times 2^{19936}$ which has 12,003 digits.

Highest. The highest generally accepted named number is the centillion, which is 10 raised to the power 600, or one followed by 600 zeros. Higher numbers are named in linguistic literature, the most extreme of which is the milli-millimillillion (10 raised to the power 6,000,000,000) devised by Rudolf Ondrejka. The number Megiston written with symbol 10 is a number too great to have any physical meaning. The highest named number outside the decimal notation is the Buddhist *asankhyeya*, which is equal to 10^{140} or 100 quinto-quadragintillions.

The number 10^{100} (10,000 sexdecillion) is designated a Googol while 10 raised to the power of a Googol is described as a Googolplex. Some conception of the magnitude of such numbers can be gained when it is said that the number of atoms in some models of the observable universe probably does not exceed 10^{85}. Factorial 10^{85} approximates 10 to the power of $43 + 85 \times 10^{85}$.

The largest number to have become sufficiently well known in mathematics to have been named after its begetter is the larger of the two Skewes numbers which is 10 to the power 10 to the power 10 to the power 3, obtained by Prof. Stanley Skewes, Ph.D., now of Cape Town University, South Africa, and published in two papers of 1933 and 1955 concerning the occurrence of prime numbers.

Most Primitive. The lowest limit in enumeration among primitive peoples is among the Yancos, an Amazon tribe who cannot count beyond *poettarrarorincoaroac*, which is their word for "three." The Temiar people of West Malaysia (formerly called Malaya) also stop at three. Investigators have reported that the number "four" is expressed by a look of total stupefaction indistinguishable from that for any other number higher than three. It is said that among survivors of the Aimores, naked nomads of eastern Brazil, there is no apparent word for "two."

Earliest Measures. The earliest known measure of weight is the *beqa* of the Amratian period of Egyptian civilization *c.* 3,800 B.C. found at Naqada, United Arab Republic. The weights are cylindrical with rounded ends from 188.7 to 211.2 grams and are the basis of the troy ounce. The unit of length used by the megalithic tomb-builders in Britain *c.* 1700 B.C. appears to have been 2.72 ± 0.003 feet.

Smallest Units

The shortest unit of length is the atto-meter, which is 1.0×10^{-16} of a centimeter. The smallest unit of area is a "shed," used in sub-atomic physics and first mentioned in 1956. It is 1.0×10^{-48} of a square centimeter. A "barn" is equal to 10^{24} "sheds." The reaction of a neutrino occurs over the area of 1×10^{-43} of a square centimeter.

Most Accurate Version of "Pi." The greatest number of decimal places to which *pi* (π) has been calculated is 500,000 by the French mathematicians, Jean Guilloud and Michele Dichampt, of the *Commissariat* à l'Energie Atomique, published on February 26, 1967. The published value to 500,000 places was 3.141592653589793 . . . (omitting the next 499,975 places) . . . 5138195242.

In 1897 the State legislature of Indiana came within a single vote of declaring that pi should be *de jure* 3.2.

Time Measure

Longest. The longest measure of time is the *kalpa* in Hindu chronology. It is equivalent to 4,320 million years. In astronomy a cosmic year is the period of rotation of the sun around the center of the Milky Way galaxy, *i.e.* about 200,000,000 years. In the Late Cretaceous Period of *c.* 85 million years ago, the earth rotated faster so resulting in 370.3 days per year.

Shortest. Owing to variations in the length of a day, which is estimated to be increasing irregularly at the average rate of about 2 milliseconds per century, due to the moon's tidal drag, the second has been redefined. Instead of being 1/86,400th part of a mean solar day, it is now reckoned as 1/31,556,925.9747th part of the solar (or tropical) year at 1900 A.D., January 0 at 12 hours, Ephemeris time. In 1958 the second of Ephemeris time was computed to be equivalent to $9,192,631,770 \pm 20$ cycles of the radiation corresponding to the transition of a caesium 133 atom when unperturbed by exterior fields. In a nano-second (1.0×10^{-9} of a second) light travels 11.7 inches.

Physical Extremes

Temperatures

Highest. The highest man-made temperatures yet attained are those produced in the center of a thermonuclear fusion bomb, which are of the order of 300,000,000° to 400,000,000°C. Of controllable temperatures, the highest effective laboratory figure reported is 50,000,000°C. for 2/100ths of a second, Prof. Lev A. Artsimovich at Tokamuk in the U.S.S.R., in 1969. At very low particle densities, even higher figures are obtainable. Prior to 1963, a figure of 3,000 million °C. was reportedly achieved in the U.S.S.R. with Ogra injection-mirror equipment.

Lowest. The lowest temperature reached is 5×10^{-7} degree Kelvin, achieved by Professor A. Abragam (b. 1914) in collaboration with M. Chapellier, M. Goldman, and Vu Hoang Chau at the

Centre d'Etudes Nucléaires, Saclay, France, in 1969. Absolute or thermodynamic temperatures are defined in terms of ratios rather than as differences reckoned from the unattainable absolute zero, which on the Kelvin scale is $-273.15°C$. or $-459.67°F$. Thus the lowest temperature ever attained is 1 in 1.8×10^9 of the melting point of ice (0°C. or 273.15 K. or 32°F.).

Highest Pressures

The highest sustained laboratory pressures yet reported are of 5,000,000 atmospheres (36,700 tons per square inch), achieved in the U.S.S.R. and announced in October, 1958. Using dynamic methods and impact speeds of up to 18,000 m.p.h., momentary pressures of 75,000,000 atmospheres (550,000 tons per square inch) were reported from the U.S. in 1958.

Highest Vacuum

The highest vacuums obtained in scientific research are of the order of 1.0×10^{-16} of an atmosphere. This compares with an estimated pressure in interstellar space of 1.0×10^{-19} of an atmosphere. At sea level there are 3×10^{19} molecules per cubic centimeter in the atmosphere, but in interstellar space there are probably less than 10 per c.c.

Fastest Centrifuge

The highest man-made rotary speed ever achieved is 1,500,000 revolutions per second, or 90,000,000 revolutions per minute, on a steel rotor with a diameter of about 1/100th of an inch suspended in a vacuum in an ultra-centrifuge installed in March, 1961, in the Rouss Physical Laboratory at the University of Virginia in Charlottesville, Virginia. This work is led by Prof. Jesse W. Beams. The edge of the rotor is traveling at 2,500 m.p.h. and is subject to a pressure of 1,000,000,000 g.

Highest Note

The highest note yet attained is one of 60,000 mega-hertz (MHz) (60,000,000,000 vibrations) per second, generated by a "laser" beam at the Massachusetts Institute of Technology, Cambridge, Massachusetts, in September, 1964. This is 3,000,000 times as high in pitch as the upper limit of adult human audibility.

Loudest Noise

The loudest noise created in a laboratory is 210 decibels or 400,000 acoustic watts reported by NASA in the U.S. in October, 1965. The noise came from a 48-foot steel and concrete horn. Holes can be bored in solid material by this means.

Most Powerful Sound System

The world's most powerful sound system is that installed at the Ontario Motor Speedway, California, in July, 1970. It has an output of 30,800 watts, connectable to 355 horn speaker assemblies and thus able to communicate the spoken word to 230,000 people above the noise of 50 screaming racing cars.

Quietest Place

The "dead room," measuring 35 feet by 28 feet, in the Bell Telephone System Laboratory at Murray Hill, New Jersey, is the most anechoic room in the world, eliminating 99.98 per cent of reflected sound.

Most Powerful Adhesive

The most powerful adhesive known is epoxy resin, which, after being supercooled to −450°F., can withstand a shearing pull of 8,000 lbs. per square inch.

Finest Balance

The most accurate balance in the world is the Q01 quartz fiber decimicro balance made by L. Oertling Ltd. of Orpington, Kent, England, which has a read-out scale on which one division corresponds to 0.0001 of a milligram. It can weigh to an accuracy of 0.0002 of a milligram, which is equivalent to little more than one-third of the weight of ink on this period dot. (See photo.)

Lowest Viscosity

The California Institute of Technology announced on December 1, 1957, that there was no measurable viscosity, *i.e.* perfect flow, in liquid helium II, which exists only at temperatures close to absolute zero (−273.15°C. or −459.67°F.).

Lowest Friction

The lowest coefficient of static and dynamic friction of any solid is 0.02, in the case of polytetrafluoroethylene ($(C_2F_4)n$), called P.T.F.E. —equivalent to wet ice on wet ice. It was first manufactured in quantity by E. I. du Pont de Nemours & Co. Inc. in 1943, and is marketed as Teflon.

At the University of Virginia (see above, Fastest Centrifuge) a 30-lb. rotor magnetically supported has been spun at 1,000 revolutions per second in a vacuum of 10^{-6} mm. of mercury pressure. It loses only one revolution per second per day, thus spinning for years.

Most Powerful Electric Current

The most powerful electric current generated is that from the Zeus capacitor at the Los Alamos Scientific Laboratory, New Mexico. If fired simultaneously the 4,032 capacitors would produce for a few microseconds twice as much current as that generated elsewhere on earth.

Largest Bubble Chamber

The largest bubble chamber in the world is at the Argonne National Laboratory, Illinois. It is 12 feet in diameter and contains 6,398 gallons of liquid hydrogen at a temperature of −247°C. (−476.6°F.). The magnet is 40,000 kilogauss and the plant went into operation in October, 1969, after an expenditure of $18,000,000. (See photograph.)

A 30,000-liter chamber (7,925 gallons) is being built at CERN, near Geneva, Switzerland.

FINEST BALANCE:
This is the Q01, which
can weigh to 0.0002 of a
milligram.

LARGEST BUBBLE CHAMBER: This $18,000,000 plant at the Argonne
National Laboratory in Illinois has a capacity of 6,398 gallons of liquid hydrogen
at a temperature of −476.6°F.

Strongest Magnet

The heaviest magnet in the world is one measuring 200 feet in diameter, with a weight of 40,000 tons, for the 10 GeV synchrophasotron in the Joint Institute for Nuclear Research at Dubna, near Moscow, U.S.S.R.

The largest super-conducting magnet is a niobium-zirconium magnet, weighing 15,675 lbs., completed in June, 1966, by Avco Everett Research Laboratory, Massachusetts. It produces a magnetic field of 40,000 gauss and the windings are super-cooled with 6,000 liters (1,585 gallons) of liquid helium.

Strongest Magnetic Field

The strongest recorded magnetic fields are ones of 10 megagauss (1,000,000 gauss), fleetingly produced by explosive flux compression devices, reported in 1968. The first megagauss field was announced in March, 1967.

The strongest steady magnetic field yet achieved is one of 225,000 gauss in a cylindrical bore of 1.25 inches, using 10 megawatts of power, called the "IJ" magnet, designed by D. Bruce Montgomery, which was put in operation at the Francis Bitter National Magnet Laboratory at Massachusetts Institute of Technology in 1964.

Most Powerful Microscopes

Electron microscopes have now reached the point at which individual atoms are distinguishable. In March, 1958, the U.S.S.R. announced an electronic point projector with a magnification approaching $\times 2,000,000$, in which individual atoms of barium and molecules of oxygen can be observed. In 1970, a resolution of 0.88 Ångström units diameter was achieved by Dr. K. Yada (Japan), using a Hitachi Model H U-11B.

In February, 1969, it was announced from Pennsylvania State University, that the combination of the field ion microscope invented by their Prof. Erwin Muller in 1956 and a spectrometer enabled single atoms to be identified.

The most powerful electron microscope in the world is the 3,500 kV installation at the National Scientific Research Center, Toulouse, France, which reached testing stage in October, 1969. The high voltage generator and accelerator fill a cylinder 15 feet in diameter and 30 feet high. Its six lenses form a column 3 feet by 11 feet and weigh 22.4 tons.

Smallest. The smallest high power microscope in the world is the 2,000 $\times$ 18 oz. McArthur microscope measuring $4 \times 2\frac{1}{2} \times 2$ inches. It provides immersion dark ground, phase contrast, polarizing and incident illumination and is produced at Landbeach, Cambridge, England.

Most Powerful Particle Accelerator

The 1.24-mile diameter proton synchrotron at the National Accelerator Laboratory at Weston, Illinois, is the largest and most powerful "atom-smasher" in the world. An energy of 200 GeV was attained on March 1, 1972. The plant cost $250,000,000.

The construction of the CERN II 1.37-mile diameter proton

LARGEST WIND TUNNEL: At Ames Research Center, Moffett Field, California

synchroton on the French-Swiss border at Megrin near Geneva was authorized on February 19, 1971 and should attain 300 GeV by 1979.

The $72,000,000 CERN intersecting storage rings (ISR) project, started on January 27, 1971, using two 28 GeV proton beams, is designed to yield the equivalent of 1,700 GeV in its center of mass experiments.

Wind Tunnels

The world's largest wind tunnel is a low-speed tunnel with a closed test section measuring 40 feet by 80 feet, built in 1944, at Ames Research Center, Moffett Field, California. The tunnel encloses 900 tons of air and cost approximately $7,000,000. The maximum volume of air that can be moved is 60,000,000 cubic feet per minute. (See photograph.)

The most powerful is the 216,000-h.p. installation at the Arnold Engineering Test Center at Tullahoma, Tennessee. The highest mach number attained with air is mach 27 at the plant of the Boeing Company, Seattle, Washington. For periods of microseconds, shock mach numbers of the order of 30 have been attained in impulse tubes at Cornell University, Ithaca, N.Y.

Finest Cut

Biological specimens embedded in epoxy resin can be sectioned by a glass knife microtome under ideal conditions, to a thickness of 1/875,000th of an inch or 290 Ångström units.

Brightest Light

The brightest artificial light sources are "laser" beams (see below), with a luminosity exceeding the sun's 800,000 candles per square inch by a factor of well in excess of 1,000. Of continuously burning

HOME OF THE LASER: Bell Telephone Laboratories, where the maser and its relative, the laser, were devised and developed. This photo shows the way cohesive light is amplified by reflection.

sources, the most powerful is a 200-kilowatt high pressure xenon arc lamp of 600,000 candle-power, reported from the U.S.S.R. in 1965. In May, 1969, the U.S.S.R. Academy of Sciences announced blast waves traveling through a luminous plasma of inert gases heated to 90,000°K. The flare-up for up to 3 microseconds shone at 50,000 times the brightness of the sun, *viz.* 40,000 million candles per square inch.

The most powerful searchlight ever developed was one produced during the 1939–45 war by the General Electric Company Ltd. at the Hirst Research Centre in Wembley, Greater London, England. It had a consumption of 600 kilowatts and gave an arc luminance of 300,000 candles per square inch and a maximum beam intensity of 2,700,000,000 candles from its parabolic mirror (diameter 10 feet).

The world's most powerful beacon is on top of the Playboy (formerly Palmolive) Building (36 stories) in Chicago, with a reported capacity of 2,100,000,000 candle-power.

Most Durable Light

The electric light *bulb* was invented in New York City, in 1860, by Heinrich (later Henry) Goebel (1818–93) of Springe, Germany. The average bulb lasts for 750 to 1,000 hours. There is some evidence that a carbide filament bulb burning in the Fire Department, Livermore, South Alameda County, California, has been burning since 1901.

"Laser" Beams

The first illumination of another celestial body was achieved on May 9, 1962, when a beam of light was successfully reflected from the moon by the use of an optical "maser" (microwave amplification by stimulated emission of radiation) or "laser" (light amplification by stimulated emission of radiation) attached to a 48-inch telescope at the Massachusetts Institute of Technology, Cambridge, Massachusetts. The spot was estimated to be 4 miles in diameter on the moon. A "maser" light flash is focused into a liquid nitrogen-cooled ruby crystal. Its chromium atoms are excited into a high energy state in which they emit a red light which is allowed to escape only in the direction desired. The maser was devised in 1958 by Dr. Charles Hard Townes (born 1915) of Bell Telephone Laboratories. Such a flash for 1/5,000th of a second can bore a hole through a diamond by vaporization at 10,000°C., produced by 2×10^{23} photons.

Computers

Largest Computer

The world's most powerful computer is the Control Data Corporation CDC 7600 first delivered in January, 1969. It can perform 36 million operations in one second and has an access time of 27 nano-seconds. It has two internal memory cores of 655,360 and 5,242,880 characters (6 bits per character) supplemented by a Model 817 disc file of 800,000,000 characters. Commercial deliveries have been scheduled from 1972 at a cost of $9,000,000-$15,000,000, depending on peripherals.

The most capacious storage device is the Ampex Terabit Memory which can store 2.88×10^{12} bits.

Chapter Six

THE ARTS AND ENTERTAINMENTS

Painting

Earliest

Evidence of Paleolithic art in a cave was found in 1834 at Chaffaud, Vienne, France, by Brouillet when he recognized an engraving of two deer on a piece of flat bone from the cave, dating to about 20,000 B.C. The number of stratigraphically-dated examples of cave art is very limited. The oldest known dated examples came from La Ferrassie, near Les Eyzies in the Périgord region, where large blocks of stone engraved with animal figures and symbols were found in the Aurignacian II layer (*c.* 25,000 B.C.); similarly engraved blocks and with traces of paint possibly representing a cervid (a deer-like form) came from the Aurignacian III layer (*c.* 24,000 B.C.).

Largest

Panorama of the Mississippi, completed by John Banvard (1815–91) in 1846, showing the river scene for 1,200 miles in a strip probably 5,000 feet long and 12 feet wide, was the largest painting in the world, with an area of more than 1.3 acres. The painting is believed to have been destroyed when the rolls of canvas, stored in a barn at Cold Spring Harbor, Long Island, New York, caught fire shortly before Banvard's death on May 16, 1891.

The largest painting now in existence is probably *The Battle of Gettysburg*, completed in 1883, after 2½ years of work, by Paul Philippoteaux (France) and 16 assistants. The painting is 410 feet long, 70 feet high and weighs 12,000 lbs. It depicts the climax of the Battle of Gettysburg, in central Pennsylvania, on July 3, 1863. In 1964, the painting was bought by Joe King of Winston-Salem, North Carolina.

The largest "Old Master" is *Il Paradiso*, painted between 1587 and 1590 by Jacopo Robusti, *alias* Tintoretto (1518–94), and his son Domenico on Wall "E" of the Sala del Maggior Consiglio in the Palazzo Ducale (Doge's Palace) in Venice, Italy. The work is 72 feet 2 inches long and 22 feet 11½ inches high and contains more than 100 human figures.

Most Valuable

It is not possible to state which is the most valuable painting in the world since many very valuable works are permanent museum and gallery acquisitions unlikely to come on to the market. Neither can they have an insurance replacement value. Valuations thus tend to be hypothetical. The "Mona Lisa" (*La Gioconda*) by Leonardo da Vinci (1452–1519) in the Louvre, Paris, was assessed for insurance purposes at $100,000,000 for its move for exhibition in Washington, D.C., and New York City, from December 14, 1962, to March 12, 1963. However, insurance was not concluded because the cost of the closest security precautions was less than that of the premiums. It was painted in *c.* 1503–07 and measures 3 feet by 2 feet 4 inches. It is believed to portray Mona (short for Madonna) Lisa Gherardini, the

HIGHEST-PRICED PAINTINGS: (Left) One of nine undisputed Leonardos, this was purchased for $5-6 million by the National Gallery of Art, Washington, in 1967. (Right) For a work by a living artist, Picasso, $532,000 was paid for his "Mère et enfant de profil."

wife of Francesco del Gioconda of Florence. The husband is said to have disliked it and refused to pay for it. Francis I, King of France, bought the painting for his bathroom for 4,000 gold florins (now equivalent to $600,000) in 1517. The painting was once stolen from the Louvre by Vicenzo Peruggia (born 1881) on August 21, 1911, but was recovered in Italy in 1913.

HIGHEST PRICED PAINTINGS—PROGRESSIVE RECORDS

Price	Painter, title, sold by and sold to	Date
$32,500	Correggio's *The Magdalen, Reading* (in fact spurious) to Elector Friedrich Augustus II of Saxony.	1746
$42,500	Raphael's *The Sistine Madonna* to Elector Friedrich Augustus II of Saxony.	1759
$80,000	Van Eyck's *Adoration of the Lamb*, 6 outer panels of Ghent altarpiece by Edward Solby to the Government of Prussia.	1821
$123,000*	Murillo's *The Immaculate Conception* by estate of Marshall Soult to the Louvre (against Czar Nicholas I) in Paris.	1852
$350,000	Raphael's *Ansidei Madonna* by the 8th Duke of Marlborough to the National Gallery, London.	1885
$500,000	Raphael's *The Colonna Altarpiece* by Sedelmeyer to J. Pierpoint Morgan.	1901
$514,400	Van Dyck's *Elena Grimaldi-Cattaneo* (portrait) by Knoedler to Peter Widener (1834–1915).	1906
$514,400	Rembrandt's *The Mill* by 6th Marquess of Lansdowne to Peter Widener.	1911
$582,500	Raphael's smaller *Panshanger Madonna* by Joseph (later Baron) Duveen (1869–1939) to Peter Widener.	1913
$1,572,000	Leonardo da Vinci's *Benois Madonna* to Czar Nicholas II in Paris.	1914
$2,000,000	Vermeer's *Girl's Head* by Prince d'Arenburg to Charles Wrightsman (U.S.).	1959
$2,300,000*	Rembrandt's *Aristotle Contemplating the Bust of Homer* by Mrs. Alfred Erickson to New York Metropolitan Museum of Art.	1961
$5,000,000–$6,000,000	Leonardo da Vinci's *Ginevra de' Benci* by Prince Franz Josef II of Liechtenstein to National Gallery, Washington.	1967
$5,544,000*	Velázquez *Portrait of Juande Pareja*, sometimes known as *The Slave of Velázquez* by the Earl of Radnor (U.K.) to Wildenstein Gallery, New York.	1970

* indicates price at auction, otherwise prices were by private treaty.

Highest Price

Old Master. On February 6, 1967, the National Gallery of Art in Washington, D.C., acquired for an undisclosed amount, the oil painting *Ginevra de' Benci*, a portrait of a young Florentine woman, painted in *c.* 1480 by Leonardo da Vinci (1452–1519) of Italy. It was reported on February 19, 1967, that the price was between $5,000,000 and $6,000,000, paid to Prince Franz Josef II of Liechtenstein. The painting, on poplar wood, measures 15⅛ inches by 14½ inches. Said to portray "sombreness without dejection," it is one of the only nine undisputed Leonardos in existence.

Auction Price. The highest price ever bid in a public auction was $5,544,000 for a portrait by Diego Velázquez, of his mulatto assistant and servant, called variously *Portrait of Juan de Pareja* and *The Slave of Velázquez*, painted in Rome in 1649, and sold on November 27, 1970, at Christie's salesrooms, London, to the Wildenstein Gallery of New York. When the same painting was sold at Christie's at auction in 1801, it went for 39 guineas (about $200). It remained in the possession of the Earls of Radnor from 1811 until 1970. It was reported at the time Velázquez made this painting that he chose to portray his servant "by way of exercise" before he attempted to fulfill his "important assignment" of painting the portrait of Pope Innocent X.

Miniature Portrait. The highest price ever paid for a portrait miniature is $169,260 by an anonymous buyer at a sale held by Christie's, London, on June 8, 1971, for a miniature of Frances Howard, Countess of Essex and Somerset by Isaac Oliver, painted *c.* 1605. This miniature, sent for auction by Lord Derby, measured 5⅛ inches in diameter.

Modern Painting. The highest price paid for a modern painting is $1,550,000 paid by the Norton Simon Foundation of Los Angeles, at the Parke-Bernet Galleries, New York City on October 9, 1968, for *Le Pont des Arts* painted by Pierre-Auguste Renoir (1841–1919) in 1868. Renoir sold the picture to the Paris dealer Durand-Ruel for about $80.

"Pop" Painting. The highest price paid for an item of Pop Art was $79,200 for *Big Painting No. 6* (1965) by Roy Lichtenstein (U.S.), sold at Parke-Bernet Galleries, New York City, on November 18, 1970.

Living Artist. The highest price paid for paintings in the lifetime of the artist is $1,950,000 paid for the two canvases *Two Brothers* (1905) and *Seated Harlequin* (1922) by Pablo Diego José Francisco de Paula Juan Nepomuceno Crispín Crispiano de la Santisima Trinidad Ruiz y Picasso (born October 25, 1881, in Spain). This was paid by the Basle City government to the Staechelin Foundation to enable the Basle Museum of Arts to retain the painting after an offer of $2,560,000 had been received from the U.S. in December, 1967.

The highest price for a single work at auction for a living artist is the $532,000 paid by the New York dealer David Mann for the blue period Picasso *Mère et enfant de profil*. Picasso's lifetime output was valued at $250,000,000 in 1966 but a more detailed survey now shows that this valuation could be safely doubled.

The highest price for a single work for a living artist is $520,000

HIGHEST PRICE PAID AT AUCTION: "Portrait of Juan de Pareja" (sometimes known as "The Slave of Velázquez," sold for $5,544,000 in 1970 to the Wildenstein Gallery of New York. Velázquez painted it in 1649 "by way of exercise" before attempting a portrait of the Pope.

paid by the Cleveland Museum, Ohio, for his *Bottle, Glass and Fork* (painted in 1912) on March 22, 1972.

Drawing. The highest price ever attached to any drawing was £804,361 ($2,252,210) for the cartoon *The Virgin and Child with St. John the Baptist and St. Anne,* measuring 54¼ inches by 39¼ inches. drawn, probably in 1499–1500, by Leonardo da Vinci (1452–1519) of Italy. On July 31, 1962, the United Kingdom Government announced that it would add £350,000 ($980,000) to the £404,361 ($1,132,211) collected by public subscription and the £50,000 ($140,000) grant from the National Art-Collections Fund to ensure that the work would remain as a national treasure under the trustee-

HIGHEST PRICE FOR A MODERN PAINTING: Renoir sold this work for $80 in 1868, and it cost the Norton Simon Foundation $1,550,000 to buy it in 1968.

ship of the National Gallery, London. Three U.S. bids of over $4,000,000 were reputed to have been made for the cartoon.

Largest Gallery

The world's largest art gallery is the Winter Palace and the neighboring Hermitage in Leningrad, U.S.S.R. One has to walk 15 miles to visit each of the 322 galleries, which house nearly 3,000,000 works of art and archeological remains.

Upside Down Duration Record

The longest period of time for which a modern painting has hung upside down in a public gallery unnoticed is 47 days. This occurred to *Le Bateau,* by Henri Émile Benoît Matisse (1869–1954) of France, in the Museum of Modern Art, New York City, between October 18 and December 4, 1961. In this time 116,000 people had passed through the gallery.

Most Prolific Painter

Antoine Joseph Wiertz (1806–1865) of Belgium painted 131 canvases 50 feet wide and 30 feet high, totaling over 4.5 acres. This is believed to be the greatest area covered by any painter of any note.

Painting—Endurance Record

The marathon record for painting is 60 hours by 60 students of the St. Albans College of Art, Hertfordshire, England, on a 3-mile-long roll of paper on July 1–3, 1971.

Murals

Earliest. The earliest known murals on man-made walls are those at Çatal Hüyük in southern Anatolia, Turkey, dating from *c.* 5850 B.C.

Largest. The world's largest mural is *The March of Humanity,* a mural of 54 panels, covering 48,000 square feet, by David Alfaro Siqueiros, which was unveiled in 1968 in the Olimpico Hotel, Mexico City. A mural stretching nearly 300 feet up the sides of the Rainbow Tower of the Hawaiian Village Hotel, Waikiki, Honolulu, Hawaii, was completed in 1968.

Largest Mobile

The largest mobile in the world is one measuring 45 feet by 17 feet and weighing 600 lbs., suspended in December, 1957, in the main terminal building of the John F. Kennedy International Airport (formerly Idlewild), New York City. It was created by Alexander Calder (born 1898), who invented this art form in 1930 as a reaction to sculptures or "stabiles." The heaviest of all mobiles is *Spirale,* weighing 4,000 lbs., outside the UNESCO headquarters in Paris, France. The word "mobile" was coined by Marcel Duchamp in 1932.

Largest Mosaic

The world's largest mosaic is on the walls of the central library of the Universidad Nacional Autónoma de México, Mexico City.

LARGEST MOBILE: Created by Alexander Calder, the "father" of the art, this 600-lb. movable sculpture hangs in the Arrivals Building at John F. Kennedy International Airport, Long Island, N.Y.

There are four walls; the two largest measuring 12,949 square feet each represent the pre-Hispanic past.

Museums

Oldest. The oldest museum in the world is the Ashmolean Museum in Oxford, England, built in 1679.

Largest. The largest museum in the world is the American Museum of Natural History between 77th and 81st Streets on Central Park West, New York City. Founded in 1874, it comprises 19 interconnected buildings with 23 acres of floor space.

Sculptures

Earliest. The earliest known examples of sculpture are the so-called Venus figurines from Aurignacian sites, dating to *c.* 25,000–22,000 B.C., *e.g.* the famous Venus of Willendorf from Austria and the Venus of Brassempouy (Landes, France).

Largest. The world's largest sculptures are the mounted figures of Jefferson Davis (1808–89), Gen. Robert Edward Lee (1807–70) and Gen. Thomas Jonathan ("Stonewall") Jackson (1824–63). covering 1.33 acres on the face of Stone Mountain, near Atlanta, Georgia. They are 20 feet higher than the more famous Rushmore sculptures. (See photograph, next page.)

When completed the world's largest sculpture will be that of the Indian chief Tashunca-uitco, known as Crazy Horse, of the Oglala tribe of the Dakota or Nadowessioux (Sioux) group. He is believed to have been born in about 1849, and he died at Fort Robinson, Nebraska, on September 5, 1877. The sculpture was begun on June 3, 1948, near Mount Rushmore, South Dakota. A projected 561 feet high and 641 feet long, it will require the removal of 5,500,000 tons of stone and is the life work of one man, Korczak Ziolkowski. It is estimated that the work will take until at least 1978.

LARGEST SCULPTURE: Three Confederate figures—Jefferson Davis. Robert E. Lee and Stonewall Jackson—are being carved on Stone Mountain, Georgia. Note the size of the workmen (top left).

Most Expensive. The highest price ever paid for a sculpture is the $380,000 given at the New York salesroom, of Parke-Bernet, on May 5, 1971, for Edgar Degas' (1834–1917) bronze *Petite Danseuse de Quatorze Ans*, executed in an edition of about 12 casts in 1880.

Ground Figures. In the Nazca Desert, south of Lima, Peru, there are straight lines (one 5 miles long), geometric shapes and plants and animals drawn on the ground by still unknown persons for an unknown purpose.

Language

Earliest. Anthropologists have evidence that the truncated pharanx of Neanderthal man precluded his speaking anything akin to a modern language any more than an ape or a modern baby. Cro-Magnon man of 40,000 B.C. had however developed an efficient vocal tract. Clay tablets of the neolithic Danubian culture discovered in December, 1966, at Tartaria, Moros River, Rumania have been dated to the fifth or fourth millennium B.C. The tablets bear symbols of bows and arrows, gates and combs. In 1970, it was announced that writing tablets bearing an early form of the Elamite language dating from 3,500 B.C. had been found in southeastern Iran. The scientist, Alexander Marshack (U.S.), maintains that marked Upper Paleolithic artifacts, such as a Cro-Magnon bone from 30,000 B.C. in the Musée des Antiquités Nationales, outside Paris, with 69 marks with

24 stroke changes, are not random but of possibly lunar or menstrual cycle significance.

Commonest. The language spoken by more people than any other is Northern Chinese, or Mandarin, by an estimated 615,000,000 people at mid-1972. The so-called national language (*guoyu*) is a standardized form of Northern Chinese as spoken in the Peking area. This was alphabetized into *zhuym zimu* of 39 letters in 1918. In 1958, the *pinyin* system, using a Latin alphabet, was introduced. The next most commonly spoken language and the most widespread is English, with an estimated 340,000,000 in mid-1972. English is spoken by 10 per cent or more of the population in 29 sovereign countries. Today's world total of languages and dialects still spoken is about 5,000 of which some 845 come from India.

Most Complex. The following extremes of complexity have been noted: Chippewa, the North American Indian language of Minnesota, has the most verb forms with up to 6,000; Tillamook, the North American Indian language of Oregon, has the most prefixes with 30; Tabassaran, a language in Daghestan, U.S.S.R., uses the most noun cases with 35; the Eskimo language uses 63 forms of the present tense and simple nouns have as many as 252 inflections.

In Chinese, the *Chung-wen Ta Tz'u-tien* Dictionary lists 49,905 characters. The fourth tone of "i" has 84 meanings, varying as widely as "dress," "hiccough" and "licentious." The written language provides 92 different characters for "i⁴." The most complex written character in Chinese is that representing the sound of thunder which has 52 strokes and is somewhat surprisingly pronounced *ping*. The most complex in current use consists of 36 strokes representing a blocked nose and less surprisingly pronounced *nang*.

Rarest and Commonest Sounds. The rarest speech sound is probably the sound written ř in Czech which occurs in very few languages and is the last sound mastered by Czech children. The *l* sound in Arabic as in *Allah* is seemingly unique as it occurs in no other word in the language. The commonest sound is the vowel *a* (as in the English father); no language (even Wishram) is known to be without it.

Most and Least Regular Verbs. Esperanto was devised in 1887 without irregular verbs. It is now estimated from textbook sales to have a million speakers. Swahili has a strict 6-class pattern of verbs and no verbs which are irregular to this pattern. According to more daunting grammars published in West Germany, English has 194 irregular verbs, though there are arguably 214.

Largest Vocabulary. The English language contains about 490,000 words, plus another 300,000 technical terms, the most in any language, but it is doubtful if any individual uses more than 60,000. "Basic English," devised in 1930 by C. K. Ogden, consists of 850 words. Written English contains about 10,000 words, while spoken English among the better educated has about 5,000 words.

Oldest Words in English. Recent research indicates that several river names date from pre-Celtic times (*ante*-550 B.C.) in Britain. These include Ayr, Hayle and Nairn. This ascendant, Indo-Germanic tongue, which was spoken from *c.* 3000 B.C. on the Great Lowland Plain of Europe, now has only fragments left in Old Lithuanian, from which the modern English word *eland* derives. The word *land* is traceable to the Old Celtic *landa*, a heath, and therefore must have been in use on the continent before the Roman Empire grew powerful in the 6th century B.C.

English became the language of court proceedings in October, 1362, and the language for teaching in universities in *c.* 1380. Henry IV (1399–1413) was the first post-Conquest monarch (after 1066) whose mother tongue was English. The earliest surviving document in English is the proclamation by Henry III, known as the Oxford Provision dated 1258.

GREATEST LINGUIST:
Cardinal Mezzofanti who lived in the 19th century, could translate 186 languages and dialects.

Greatest Linguist

The most accomplished linguist ever known was Cardinal Giuseppe Caspar Mezzofanti (1774–1849), the former chief keeper of the Vatican library in Rome, Italy. He could translate 114 languages and 72 dialects, and spoke 39 languages fluently, 11 others passably and understood 20 others along with 37 dialects. (See photo.)

The greatest living linguist is probably Georges Schmidt (b. Strasbourg, France, in 1915) of the United Nations Translation Department in New York City, who can speak fluently in 30 languages and can translate 66.

Alphabet

Oldest. The development of the use of an alphabet in place of pictograms occurred in the Siniatic world between 2000 and 1700 B.C. This northern Semitic language developed the consonantal system based on phonetic and syllabic principles. Its "O" has remained unchanged and is thereby the oldest of all letters in the 65 alphabets now in use.

Longest and Shortest. The language with most letters is Cambodian with 74. Rotakas, spoken in the center of Bougainville Island in the South Pacific, has least with 11 (just A, b, E, G, I, K, O, P, r, T and U). Amharic has 231 formations from 33 basic syllabic forms, each of which has seven modifications, so this Ethiopian language cannot be described as alphabetic.

Most and Least Consonants and Vowels. The language with most consonants is the Caucasian mountain language, Ubyx, with 80 and that with the least is Rotakas (see above) with only 6 consonants. The language with the most vowels is Sedang, a central Vietnamese language with 55 distinguishable vowel sounds. The languages with the least (2 vowels) are the Caucasian languages Abuza and Kabardian. The Hawaiian word for "certified" has 8 consecutive vowels—hooiaioia.

Most Frequently Used Letters. In English the most frequently used letters are in order: e, t, a, i, s, o, n, h, r, d and u. The most frequent initial letters are s, e, p, a, t, b, m, d, r, f and h.

Largest Letter. The largest permanent letters in the world are the giant 600-foot letters spelling READYMIX on the ground in the Nullarbor near East Balladonia, Western Australia. This was constructed in December, 1971.

In sky-writing (normally at *c.* 8,000 feet) a 7-letter word may stretch for 6 miles in length and can be read from 50 miles. The world's earliest example was over Epsom racecourse, England, on May 30, 1922, when Cyril Turner "spelt out" "London Daily Mail" from an S.E.5A biplane.

Longest Words

World. The longest word ever to appear in literature occurs in *The Ecclesiazusae*, a comedy by Aristophanes (448–380 B.C.). In the Greek it is 170 letters long but transliterates into 182 letters in English, thus: lopadotemachoselachogaleokranioleipsanodrimhypotrimmatosilphioparaomelitokatakechymenokichlepikossyphophattoperisteralektryonoptekephalliokigklopeleiolagoiosiraiobaphetraganopterygon. The term describes a fricassee of 17 sweet and sour ingredients, including mullet, brains, honey, vinegar, pickles, marrow (the vegetable) and ouzo (a Greek drink laced with anisette).

English. The longest word in the Oxford English Dictionary is floccipaucinihilipilification (alternatively spelt in hyphenated form with "n" in seventh place), with 29 letters, meaning "the action of estimating as worthless," first used in 1741, and later by Sir Walter Scott (1771–1832). Webster's Third International Dictionary lists among its 450,000 entries pneumonoultramicroscopicsilicovolcanoconiosis (45 letters), the name of a miner's lung disease.

The longest word in an English classic is the nonce word honorificabilitudinitatibus (27 letters), occurring in Act V, scene I of *Love's Labour's Lost* by William Shakespeare (1564–1616), but used with the ending "-tatatibus," making 29 letters, in *The Water Poet* by John Taylor (1580–1653).

In this category may also be placed the 52-letter word used by

Dr. Edward Strother (1675–1737) to describe the spa waters at Bristol—aequeosalinocalcalinoceraceoaluminosocupreovitriolic. In his novel *Headlong Hall*, Thomas Love Peacock (1785–1866) described the human physique as "osseocarnisanguineoviscericartilaginonervomedullary"—51 letters.

The longest regularly formed English word is praetertranssubstantiationalistically (37 letters), used by Mark McShane in his novel *Untimely Ripped*, published in 1963. The medical term hepaticocholangiocholecystenterostomies (39 letters) refers to the surgical creations of new communications between gall bladders and hepatic ducts and between intestines and gall bladders. The longest in common use is disproportionableness (21 letters).

Longest Chemical Name. The longest chemical term is that describing tryptophan synthetase A protein, which has the formula $C_{1289} H_{2051} N_{343} O_{375} S_8$ and the 1,913-letter name:

Methionylglutaminylarginyltyrosylglutamylserylleucylphenylalanylalanylglutaminylleucyllysylglutamylarginyllysygultamylglycylalanylphenylalanylvalylprolylphenylalanylvalylthreonylleucylglycylaspartylprolylglycylisoleucylglutamylglutaminylserylleucyllysylisoleucylaspartylthreonylleucylisoleucylglutamylalanylglycylalanylaspartylalanylleucylglutamylleucylglycylisoleucylprolylphenylalanylserylaspartylprolylleucylalanylaspartylglycylprolylthreonylisoleucylglutaminylasparaginylalanylthreonylleucylarginylalanylphenylalanylalanylalanylglycylvalylthreonylprolylalanylglutaminylcysteinylphenylalanylglutamylmethionylleucylalanylleucylisoleucylarginylglutaminyllysylhistidylprolylthreonylisoleucylprolylisoleucylglycylleucylleucylmethionyltyrosylalanylasparaginylleucylvalylphenylalanylasparaginyllysylglycylisoleucylaspartylglutamylphenylalanyltyrosylalanylglutaminylcysteinylglutamyllysylvalylglycylvalylaspartylserylvalylleucylvalylalanylaspartylvalylprolylvalylglutaminylglutamylserylalanylprolylphenylalanylarginylglutaminylalanylalanylleucylarginylhistidylasparaginylvalylalanylprolylisoleucylphenylalanylisoleucylcysteinylprolylprolylaspartylalanylaspartylaspartylaspartylleucylleucylarginylglutaminylisoleucylalanylseryltyrosylglycylarginylglycyltyrosylthreonyltyrosylleucylleucylserylarginylalanylglycylvalylthreonylglycylalanylglutamylasparaginylarginylalanylalanylleucylprolylleucylasparaginylhistidylleucylvalylalanyllysylleucyllysylglutamyltyrosylasparaginylalanylalanylprolylprolylleucylglutaminylglycylphenylalanylglycylisoleucylserylalanylprolylaspartylglutaminylvalyllysylalanylalanylisoleucylaspartylalanylglycylalanylalanylglycylalanylisoleucylserylglycylserylalanylisoleucylvalyllysylisoleucylisoleucylglutamylglutaminylhistidylasparaginylisoleucylglutamylprolylglutamyllysylmethionylleucylalanylalanylleucyllysylvalylphenylalanylvalylglutaminylprolylmethionyllysylalanylalanylthreonylarginylserine.

Longest Palindromic Words. The longest known palindromic word (same spelling backwards as forwards) is *saippuakauppias* (15 letters), the Finnish word for a soap-seller. The longest in the English language are *evitative* and *redivider* (each nine letters), while another nine-letter word, *Malayalam*, is a proper noun given to the language of the Malayali people in Kerala, southern India. The contrived chemical term *detartrated* has 11 letters, as does *kinnikinnik* (sometimes written *kinnik-kinnik*, a 12-letter palindrome), the word for the dried leaf and bark mixture which was smoked by the Cree Indians of North America.

Some baptismal fonts in Greece and Turkey bear the circular 25-letter inscription NII ON ANOMHMATA MHMONAN OI IN meaning "wash (my) sins not only (my) face."

The longest palindromic composition devised is one of 242 words by Howard Bergeson of Oregon. It begins "Deliver no evil, avid diva" . . . and hence predictably ends . . . "avid diva live on reviled."

Commonest Words. In written English, the most frequently used words are in order: the, of, and, to, a, in, that, is, I, it, for *and* as. The most used in conversation is I.

Most Meanings. The most overworked word in English is the word *jack* which has 10 main substantive uses with 40 sub-uses and two verbal uses.

Most Homophones. The most homophonous sound in English is rōz which has 7 meanings: roes (deer); roes (fish); rose (flower); rose (past tense of rise); rows (boats); rows (of houses) or rhos (plural of the Greek letter).

Most Accents. The word with most accents is the French word *hétérogénéité*, meaning heterogeneity. An atoll in the Pacific Ocean 320 miles east southeast of Tahiti is named Héréhérétué.

Worst Tongue-Twisters. The most difficult tongue-twister is deemed by Ken Parkin of Teesside to be "The sixth sick sheik's sixth sheep's sick"—especially when spoken quickly.

Perhaps more difficult is the Xhosa (from Transkei, South Africa) for "The skunk rolled down and ruptured its larynx": "Iqaqa laziqikaqika kwaze kwaqhawaka uqhoqhoqha." The last word contains three "clicks." A European rival is the vowelless *Strch prst skrz krk*, the Czech for "stick a finger in the throat."

Longest Abbreviation. The longest known abbreviation is S.O.M.K.H.P.B.K.J.C.S.S.D.P.M.W.D.T.B., the initials of the Sharikat Orang-Orang Melayu Kerajaani Hilir Perak Berkerjasama-Serkerjasama Kerama Jimat Chermat Serta Simpanan Dan Pinjam Meminjam Wang Dengan Tanggonan Berhad. This is the Malay name for the Lower Perak Malay Government Servants' Co-operative Thrift and Loan Society Limited, in Telok Anson, Perak State, West Malaysia (formerly called Malaya). The abbreviation for this abbreviation is not recorded.

Longest Anagrams. The longest regular English words which can form anagrams are the 16-letter pair "interlaminations" and "internationalism" along with "conservationists" and "conversationists."

Shortest Holo-alphabetic Sentence. The shortest English sentence containing all the 26 letters of the alphabet is "Jackdaws love my big sphinx of quartz" with 31 letters.

The contrived headline describing the annoyance of an eccentric in finding inscriptions on the side of a fjord in a rounded valley as "Cwm fjord-bank glyphs vext quiz" represents the ultimate in containing all 26 letters in 26 letters.

Longest Sentence. The longest in classical Western literature is one in *Les Misérables* by Victor Marie Hugo (1802–85) which runs to 823 words punctuated by 93 commas, 51 semi-colons and 4 dashes. A sentence of 958 words appears in "Cities of the Plain" by Marcel Proust, while some authors such as James Joyce (1882–1941) eschew punctuation altogether. The first 40,000 words of the Gates of Paradise by George Andrzeyevski (Panther) appear to lack any punctuation.

The Report of the President of Columbia University, 1942–43, contained a sentence of 4,284 words.

Place Names

Longest. The official name for Bangkok, the capital city of Thailand, consists of the Thai words Krungt'ep ("city of the divine messenger"), plus a long list of Pali titles, as proclaimed at the city's foundation in 1782. A *shortened version* of this name is Krungtepmahanakornbowornratanakosinmahintarayudhayamahadilokpopnoparatanarajthaniburiromudomrajniwesmahasatarnamornpimarnavatarsatitsakatattiyavisanukamprasit (158 letters). The longest place name now in use in the world is Taumatawhakatangihangakoauauotamatea(turipukakapikimaungahoronuku)pokaiwhenuakitanatahu, the unofficial 85-letter version of the name of a hill (1,002 feet above sea level) in the Southern Hawke's Bay district of North Island, New Zealand. This Maori name means "the place where Tamatea, the man with the big knee who slid, climbed and swallowed mountains, known as Land-eater, played on his flute to his loved one." The official version has 57 letters (1 to 36 and 65 to 85).

Shortest. The shortest place names in the world are the French village of Y (population 143), so named since 1241, in the Somme, the Norwegian village of Å (pronounced "Aw"), and U in the Caroline Islands of the Pacific. There was once a 6 in West Virginia.

LONGEST PLACE NAME IN USE: A 57-letter Maori name for a hill in New Zealand. In 1959 the first letter in the third line was changed from "A" to "O".

Today in the U.S., there are seven two-lettered place names, including Ed and Uz, both in Kentucky.

Personal Names

Earliest. The earliest personal name which has survived is uncertain. Some experts believe that it is En-lil-ti, a word which appears on a Sumerian tablet dating from *c.* 3300 B.C., recovered before 1936 from Jamdat Nasr, 40 miles southeast of Baghdad, Iraq. Other antiquarians regard it purely as the name of a diety, Lord of the air, and claim that the names Lahma and Lahamu, Sumer gods of silt, are older still. N'armer, the father of Men (Menes), the first Egyptian pharaoh, dates from about 2900 B.C.

Longest. The longest name used by anyone is Adolph Blaine Charles David Earl Frederick Gerald Hubert Irvin John Kenneth Lloyd Martin Nero Oliver Paul Quincy Randolph Sherman Thomas Uncas Victor William Xerxes Yancy Zeus Wolfeschlegelstein-hausenbergerdorffvoralternwarengewissenhaftschaferswessenschafe-warenwohlgepflegeundsorgfaltigkeitbeschutzenvonangreifendurch-ihrraubgierigfeindewelchevoralternzwolftausendjahresvorandieersch-einenvanderersteerdemenschderraumschiffgebrauchlichtalsseinursp-rungvonkraftgestartseinlangefahrthinzwischensternartigraumaufder-suchenachdiesternwelchegehabtbewohnbarplanetenkreisedrehensic-hundwohinderneurassevonverstandigmenschlichkeitkonntefortpflan-zenundsicherfreuenanlebenslanglichfreudeundruhemitnichteinfurch-tvorangreifenvonandererintelligentgeschopfsvonhinzwischensternart-igraum, Senior, who was born at Bergedorf, near Hamburg, Germany, on February 29, 1904. On printed forms, he uses only his eighth and second Christian names and the first 35 letters of his surname. He lives in Philadelphia, and has recently shortened his surname to Wolfe+590, Senior.

The longest Christian or given name on record is Napuamahal-aonaonekaurehiwehionakuahiweanenawawakehoonkakehoaalek-eeaonanainananiakeao' Hawaiikawao (93 letters), in the case of Miss Dawn Lee of Honolulu, so named in February, 1967. The name means "the abundant, beautiful blossoms of the mountains and valleys begin to fill the air with their fragrance throughout the length and breadth of Hawaii."

Most Christian Names. The daughter of Arthur Pepper of West Derby, Lancashire, England, born on December 19, 1882, was christened Ann Bertha Cecilia Diana Emily Fanny Gertrude Hypatia Inez Jane Kate Louisa Maud Nora Orphelia Quince Rebecca Starkey Teresa Ulysis Venus Winifred Xenophen Yetty Zeus Pepper.

Commonest. The commonest surname in the world is the Chinese name Chang which is borne, according to estimates, by between 9.7 per cent and 12.1 per cent of the Chinese population, so indicating even on the lower estimate that there are at least some 75,000,000 Changs—more than the entire population of all but 7 of the 145 other sovereign countries of the world.

The commonest surname in the English-speaking world is Smith. There are over 800,000 Smiths in England and Wales alone, of

whom 90,000 are called A. Smith. There were an estimated
1,678,815 Smiths in the United States in 1964.

There are, however, estimated to be 1,600,000 persons in Britain
with M', Mc or Mac (Gaelic "son of") as part of their surnames.
The commonest of these is Macdonald which accounts for about
55,000 of the Scottish population.

Most Contrived Name. The palm for the most determined
attempt to be last in the local telephone directory must be awarded
to Mr. Zeke Zzzypt of Chicago. He outdid the previous occupant
who was a mere Mr. Zyzzy Zzyryzxxy. In September, 1970, Mr.
Zero Zzyzz (rhymes with "fizz") was ousted by Mr. Vladimir Zzzyd
(rhymes with outdid) in the Miami directory.

The Written Word

Smallest Handwriting on Paper

The smallest writing achieved is a density of 85 letters per square
millimeter with an engraving tool on a metal flap by Dr. Anto
Leikola of Helsinki, Finland.

In 1968, Mr. C. N. Swift of Edgbaston, Birmingham, England,
wrote the Lord's Prayer 25 times on a piece of paper half the size of
a standard postage stamp, measuring 0.87 of an inch by 0.71 of an
inch, with a density of nearly 37 letters per square millimeter.

Texts

Oldest. The oldest known written text is the pictograph expression
of Sumerian speech, dating from *c.* 3500 B.C. In 1952, some clay tablets of this writing were unearthed from the Uruk IV level of the
Sumerian temple of Inanna (*c.* 3300 B.C.) at Erech (called Uruk in
Sumerian), now Warka, Iraq. The earliest known vellum document
dates from the 2nd century A.D.; it contains paragraphs 10 to 32 of
Demosthenes' *De Falsa Legatione.* Demosthenes died in the 4th
century B.C.

Oldest Printed. The oldest surviving printed work is a Korean
scroll or *sutra*, printed from wooden blocks found in the foundations
of the Pulguk Sa pagoda, Kyongju, Korea, on October 14, 1966. It
has been dated no later than 704 A.D.

Oldest Mechanically Printed. It is generally accepted that the
earliest mechanically printed book was the 42-line Gutenberg Bible,
printed at Mainz, Germany, in *c.* 1455 by Johann zum Gensfleisch
zur Laden, called "zu Gutenberg" (*c.* 1398–*c.* 1468). Recent work on
watermarks published in 1967 indicates a copy of a surviving printed
Latin grammar was made from paper made in *c.* 1450. The earliest
exactly dated printed work is the Psalter completed on August 14,
1457, by Johann Fust (*c.* 1400–1466) and Peter Schöffer (1425–
1502), who had been Gutenberg's chief assistant.

Manuscripts

The highest price ever paid for any manuscript is £100,000
($280,000), paid in December, 1933, by the British Museum,
London, to the U.S.S.R. Government for the manuscript Bible

Codex Sinaiticus originally from the Monastery of St. Catherine on Mt. Sinai (the Sinai peninsula is now occupied by Israel). It consists of 390 of the original 730 leaves, measuring 16 inches by 28 inches, of the book, dictated in Greek and written by three scribes in about 350 A.D. and rescued from a wastepaper basket in May, 1844, by Lonegott Friedrich Konstantin von Tischendorf (1815–74), a German traveler and Biblical critic.

The highest price paid at auction is 1,100,000 New Francs ($225,000 including tax) paid by H. P. Krauss, the New York dealer, at the salesroom of Rheims et Laurin, Paris, on June 24, 1968, for the late 13th century North Italian illuminated vellum manuscript of the Apocrypha.

Books

Largest. The largest book in the world is *The Little Red Elf*, a story in 64 verses by William P. Wood, who designed, constructed and printed the book. It measures 7 feet 2 inches high and 10 feet across when open. The book is at present on show in a cave at the foot of Beinn Ruadh ("The Red Elf Cave"), Ardentinny, near Dunoon, Scotland. The largest art book ever produced was 82.7 inches high and 31.5 inches wide, first shown in Amsterdam, the Netherlands, in May, 1963. It contained five "pages," three the work of Karel Appel (born 1921), an abstract painter, and two with poems by Hugo Claus. The price was $5,225.

Largest Publication. The largest publication in the world is the 1,200-volume set of *British Parliamentary Papers* of 1800–1900 by Irish University Press in 1967–1971. A complete set weighs 3.64 tons, costs $65,000 and would take 6 years to read at 10 hours per day. The binding of the edition involved the death of 34,000 Indian goats and $39,000 worth of gold ingots. Further volumes are planned.

Smallest. The smallest book in the world is a handwritten one— *Poems by Edgar Guest*. It was written in 1942 by Burt Randle. It is less than ⅛ of an inch square and is held by a metal clasp.

The smallest book printed in metal type as opposed to any microphotographic process is one printed for the Gutenberg Museum, Mainz, West Germany. It measures 3.5 millimeters by 3.5 millimeters (0.13 of an inch square) and consists of the Lord's Prayer in seven languages.

Most Valuable. The most valuable printed books are the three surviving perfect vellum copies of the Gutenberg Bible (see above). The Library of Congress copy, bound in three volumes, was obtained in 1930 from Dr. Otto Vollbehr, who paid about $330,000 for it. During 1970, a paper edition in the hands of the New York book dealer, H. P. Kraus, was privately bought for $2,500,000.

Highest-Priced Printed Document. The highest price ever paid for a broadsheet was $404,000 for one of the 16 known copies of *The Declaration of Independence*, printed in Philadelphia in 1776 by Samuel T. Freeman & Co., and sold to a Texan in May, 1969.

Longest Novel. The longest important novel ever published is *Les hommes de bonne volonté* by Louis Henri Jean Farigoule (born

August 26, 1885), *alias* Jules Romains, of France, in 27 volumes in 1932–46. The English version, *Men of Good Will*, was published in 14 volumes in 1933–46 as a "novel-cycle." The novel *Tokuga-Wa Ieyasu* by Sohachi Yamaoka has been serialized in Japanese daily newspapers since 1951. When completed it will run to 40 volumes.

Encyclopaediae

Earliest. The earliest known encyclopaedia was compiled by Speusippas (*post* 408–*c.* 388 B.C.) a nephew of Plato, in Athens *c.* 370 B.C.

Most Comprehensive. The most comprehensive present day encyclopaedia is the *Encyclopaedia Britannica*, first published in Edinburgh, Scotland, in December, 1768. A group of booksellers in the U.S. acquired reprint rights in 1898 and complete ownership in 1899. In 1943, the *Britannica* was given to the University of Chicago. The current 24-volume edition contains 28,380 pages, 34,696 articles and 2,247 other entries, 36,674,000 words and 22,670 illustrations. It is now edited in Chicago and in London. There are 10,326 contributors.

Largest. The largest encyclopaedia ever compiled was the *Great Standard Encyclopaedia* of Yung-lo of 22,937 manuscript books (370 still survive), written by 2,000 Chinese scholars in 1403–08.

Top Selling. The world's top selling encyclopaedia is The World Book Encyclopaedia published by Field Enterprises Educational Corporation of Chicago. Since 1961, the annual average sales have exceeded 450,000 sets per year.

Largest Dictionary

The largest dictionary now published is the 12-volume Royal quarto *The Oxford English Dictionary* of 15,487 pages published between 1884 and 1928 with a first supplement of 963 pages in 1933 with a further 2-volume supplement, edited by R. W. Burchfield, due in 1974. The work contains 414,825 words, 1,827,306 illustrative quotations and reputedly 227,779,589 letters and figures.

Bible

Oldest. The oldest known Bible is the Yonan manuscript of the complete New Testament, written in Syriac-Aramaic in about 350 A.D. and presented to the Library of Congress, on March 27, 1955. The earliest Bible printed in English was one edited by Miles Coverdale (*c.* 1488–1569), printed in 1535 at Marberg in Hesse, Germany. The longest of the Dead Sea scrolls is the Temple Scroll, measuring 28 feet. It first became available for study in June, 1967.

Longest and Shortest Books. The longest book in the Bible is the Book of Psalms, while the longest prose book is the Book of the Prophet Isaiah, with 66 chapters. The shortest is the Third Epistle of John, with 294 words in 14 verses. The Second Epistle of John has only 13 verses but 298 words.

Longest Psalm, Verse, Sentence and Name. Of the 150 Psalms, the longest is the 119th, with 176 verses, and the shortest is the 117th, with two verses. The shortest verse in the English language version of the Bible is verse 35 of Chapter XI of the Gospel according to St. John, consisting of the two words "Jesus wept." The longest is verse 9 of Chapter VIII of the Book of Esther, which extends to a 90-word description of the Persian empire. The total number of letters in the Bible is 3,566,480. The total number of words depends on the method of counting hyphenated words, but is usually given as between 773,692 and 773,746. The word "and" appears 46,399 times-The longest name in the Bible is Maher-shalal-hash-baz, the symbolic name of the second son of Isaiah (Isaiah, Chapter VIII, verses 1 and 3). Longer by 2 letters is the title in the caption of Psalm 22, however, sometimes rendered Al-'Ayyeleth Hash-Shahar (20 letters).

Most Prolific Writers

The most prolific writer for whom a word count has been published was Charles Hamilton, *alias* Frank Richard (1875–1961), the Englishman who created Billy Bunter. At the height of his career in 1908 he wrote the whole of the boys' comics *Gem* (founded 1907) and *Magnet* (founded 1908) and most of two others, totaling 80,000 words a week. His lifetime output was at least 72,000,000 words. He enjoyed the advantage of being unmarried. (See photo, next page.)

The Belgian writer Georges Simenon (born Georges Sim in Liège on February 13, 1903), creator of Inspector Maigret, writes a novel of 200 pages in 8 days and in February, 1969, completed his 200th under his own name of which 74 were about Inspector Maigret. He has also written 300 other novels under 19 other pen-names. These are published in 31 countries in 43 languages and have sold more than 300,000,000 copies. He hates adverbs and has had his children's playroom soundproofed.

Since 1931 the British novelist John Creasey (born 1908) has, under his own name and 13 *aliases*, written 564 books totaling more than 40,000,000 words. The authoress with the greatest total of published books is Ursula Bloom (Mrs. A. C. G. Robinson), with 420 full-length works, including the best sellers *The Ring Tree* (novel) and *The Rose of Norfolk* (non-fiction).

Short Stories. The highest established record for published short stories is 3,500 held by Michael Hervey (born London, 1914) of Henley, New South Wales, Australia. Aided by his wife, Lilyan Brilliant, he has also written 60 detective novels and 80 stage and television plays.

Fastest Novelist. The world's fastest novelist was Erle Stanley Gardner (1889–1970), the popular mystery writer who created Perry Mason. He dictated up to 10,000 words per day and worked with his staff on as many as seven novels simultaneously. His sales on 140 titles reached 170,000,000 by his death.

The British novelist John Creasey (see above) has an output of 15 to 20 novels per annum, with a record of 22. He once wrote two books in a week with a half-day off.

Fastest Playwright. British writer and playwright Edgar Wallace (1875–1932) began his play *On the Spot* on a Friday and finished it by lunchtime on the following Sunday. This included the stage directions and, unusually, after the production the prompt

YOUNGEST AUTHOR: Janet Aitchison (left) wrote a children's book when aged 5½, and it was published when she was 6½. MOST PROLIFIC WRITER: Frank Richard (right) wrote comics and is credited with a lifetime output of at least 72 million words.

copy was identical to his original. The shortest time in which he wrote a novel was in the case of *The Three Oaks Mystery* which he started on a Tuesday and delivered typed to his publishers on the following Friday.

Oldest Authoress

The oldest authoress in the world is Mrs. Alice Pollock (*née* Wykeham-Martin) (b. July 2, 1868) of Haslemere, Surrey, England, whose book "Portrait of My Victorian Youth" (Johnson Publications) was published in March, 1971, when she was aged 102 years 8 months.

Youngest Author

The youngest recorded commercially-published author is Janet Aitchison who wrote *The Pirate's Tale* when aged 5½ years. It was published as a Puffin Book by Penguin Books, England, in April, 1969, when she was 6½.

Highest-Paid Writer

The highest rate ever offered to a writer was $30,000 to Ernest Miller Hemingway (1899–1961) for a 2,000-word article on bull-fighting by *Sports Illustrated* in January, 1960. This was a rate of $15 per word. In 1958, a Mrs. Deborah Schneider of Minneapolis, Minnesota, wrote 25 words to complete a sentence in a competition for the best blurb for Plymouth cars. She won from about 1,400,000 entrants the prize of $500 every month for life. On normal life expectations she will collect $12,000 per word. No known anthology includes Mrs. Schneider's deathless prose.

Top-Selling Author

It was announced on March 13, 1953, that 672,058,000 copies of the works of Marshal Iosif Vissarionovich Dzhugashvili, *alias* Stalin (1879–1953), had been sold or distributed in 101 languages.

Among writers of fiction, sales alone of over 300,000,000 have been claimed for Georges Simenon (see above) and for the British authoress Agatha Christie (born Agatha Mary Clarissa Miller), now Mrs. Max Mallowan (formerly Mrs. Archibald Christie). The paperback sales in the U.K. alone of her total of 80 novels are 1,500,000 per annum.

Longest Literary Gestation

Brig.-Gen. Sir Harold Hartley (U.K.) (b. September 3, 1878) made an agreement with Oxford University Press to publish "Studies in the History of Chemistry" on February 22, 1901. The book appeared in April, 1971—more than 70 years later.

Best Sellers

The world's best seller is the Bible, portions of which have been translated into 1,315 languages. It has been estimated that between 1800 and 1950 some 1,500,000,000 were printed of which 1,100,000,000 were handled by Bible Societies. The total production of Bibles or parts of the Bible in the United States in the year 1963 alone was reputed to be 50,000,000.

It has been reported that 800,000,000 copies of the red-covered booklet *Quotations from the Works of Mao Tse-Tung* were sold or distributed between June, 1966, when possession became virtually mandatory in China, up to November, 1970. The name of Mao Tse-Tung (born December 26, 1893) means literally "Hair Enrich-East."

The total disposal through non-commercial channels by Jehovah's Witnesses of the 190-page hardbound book, *The Truth That Leads to Eternal Life*, published by the Watchtower Bible and Tract Society of Brooklyn, New York, on May 8, 1968, reached 46,000,000 in 67 languages by February, 1972.

Non-Fiction. The commercially best selling non-fiction book is *The Common Sense Book of Baby and Child Care* by Dr. Benjamin McLane Spock (born May 2, 1903) of New Haven, Connecticut. It was first published in New York in May, 1946, and the total sales were more than 23,000,000 by January, 1972. Dr. Spock's book was written with a ball-point pen and typed by his wife, a silk heiress.

Slowest Seller. The accolade for the world's slowest selling book (known in publishing as slooow-sellers) probably belongs to David Wilkin's Translation of the New Testament into Coptic published by Oxford University Press in 1716 in 500 copies. Selling an average of one each 139 days it was in print for 191 years.

Fiction. The novel with the highest sales has been *Peyton Place* (first published in 1956) by Mrs. Grace de Repentigny Metalious (1924–64) of the U.S., with a total of 11,919,660 copies by November, 1970. Six million of these were sold in the first six months.

Post Card. The top-selling post card of all time is reputed to be a drawing by Donald McGill (1875–1962) with the caption: He: "How do you like Kipling?" She: "I don't know, you naughty boy, I've never Kippled." It sold about 6,000,000. Between 1904 and his death McGill sold more than 350,000,000 cards to users and deltiologists (picture post card collectors).

The world's first postcards were issued in Vienna on October 1, 1869. Pin-up girls came into vogue in 1914 having been pioneered in

1900 by Raphaël Kirchner (1876–1917). The most expensive on record were ones made in ivory for an Indian prince which involved the killing of 60 elephants.

Poetry

Poets Laureate. The earliest official Poet Laureate was John Dryden (1631–1700), appointed in April, 1668. It is recorded that Henry I (1100–1135) had a King's versifier named Wale. The youngest Poet Laureate was Laurence Eusden (1688–1730), who received the bays on December 24, 1718, at the age of 30 years and 3 months. The greatest age at which a poet has succeeded is 73 in the case of William Wordsworth (1770--1850) on April 6, 1843. The longest-lived Laureate was John Masefield, O.M., who died on May 12, 1967, aged 88 years 11 months. The longest which any poet has worn the laurel is 41 years 322 days, in the case of Alfred (later the 1st Lord) Tennyson (1809–92), who was appointed on November 19, 1850, and died in office on October 6, 1892.

Longest Poem. The longest poem ever written was the *Mahabharata* which appeared in India in the period *c.* 400 to 150 B.C. It runs to 220,000 lines and nearly 3,000,000 words. The longest poem ever written in the English language is *Poly-Olbion* or *A Chorographicall Description of Tracts, Rivers, Mountains, Forests, etc.*, written in Alexandrines in 30 books, comprising nearly 100,000 lines, by Michael Drayton (1563–1631) between 1613 and 1622.

Shortest Poem. The shortest poem in the *Oxford Dictionary of Quotations* is *On the Antiquity of Microbes* and consists of the 3 words: "Adam, Hae 'em."

Most Successful Slogan. "Think Mink" invented by John Gasnick in 1929 has sold in metal, celluloid and ribbon 50,000,000 since 1950. His *"Cross at the Green . . . not in Between Enterprises"* of New York City has sold 55,000,000 buttons, badges and tabs and 40,000,000 other pieces.

Largest Publishers

The largest publisher in the world is the U.S. Government Printing Office in Washington, D.C. The Superintendent of Documents Division dispatches more than 150,000,000 items every year. The annual list of new titles and annuals is about 6,000.

Fastest Publishing

The shortest interval between the receipt of a manuscript and the publication of a book is 66½ hours, in the case of *The Pope's Journey to the United States—the Historic Record*, a paperback of 160 pages. costing 75 cents, written by 51 editors of the strike-bound *New York Times* and published by Bantam Books, Inc. of New York City. It was printed by the W. F. Hall Printing Co. of Chicago. The first article reached the publishers at 1:30 p.m. on October 4, 1965, and completed copies came off the printers' presses at 8:00 a.m. on October 7, 1965.

Largest Printers

The largest printers in the world are R. R. Donnelly & Co. of Chicago. The company, founded in 1864, has plants in seven main centers, turning out $200,000,000 worth of work per year from 180 presses, 125 composing machines and more than 50 binding lines. Nearly 18,000 tons of inks and 450,000 tons of paper and board are consumed every year.

Largest Cartoon

The largest cartoon ever published was one covering two floors (35 feet by 30 feet) on a building opposite the United Nations Headquarters in New York City, depicting the enslavement by the U.S.S.R. of eight Eastern European nations.

Longest-Lived Comic Strip

The most durable newspaper comic strip has been the Katzenjammer Kids (Hans and Fritz) first published in the U.S. in 1897 and currently drawn by Joe Musial. The most read is believed to be "Peanuts" by Charles M. Schultz (born 1922) which since 1950 has grown to be syndicated in 1,000 U.S. newspapers with a total readership of 90,000,000.

Letters

Longest. Physically, the longest letter ever written was one of 3,696 feet 10 inches (about ⅔ of a mile) in length. It was written on adding machine rolls by Miss Terry Finch of Southsea, Hampshire, England, and posted on June 11, 1969, to her boy friend, Sergeant Jerry Sullivan at Goodfellow Air Base, Texas.

A letter of 325,000 words by Anton van Dam of Arnhem, Netherlands, to his pen pal Clementi (now Mrs. H. Randolph Holder) between June 24, 1940, and July 15, 1945, is believed to be the most voluminous.

To the Editor. The longest recorded letter to an editor was one of 13,000 words (a third of a modern novel) written to the editor of the *Fishing Gazette* by A.R.I.E.L. and published in 7-point type spread over two issues in 1884.

Shortest. The shortest correspondence on record was that between Victor Marie Hugo (1802–85) and his publisher, Hurst and Blackett, in 1862. The author was on holiday and anxious to know how his new novel *Les Misérables* was selling. He wrote "?". The reply was "!"

Autographs

Earliest. Not counting attested crosses in a few charters of the early Norman kings ostensibly affixed by their own hands, the earliest

HIGHEST-PRICED AUTOGRAPH: The signature of Button Gwinnett on the Declaration of Independence.

English sovereign whose handwriting is known to have survived is Henry III (1207–72). The earliest signature to have survived is that of Richard II (dated July 26, 1386). The Magna Carta does not bear even the mark of King John (reigned 1199–1216), but carries his seal. In 1932, an attested cross of William I (reigned 1066–87) was sold in London.

Most Expensive Autographs. The highest price ever paid on the open market for a single letter is $51,000, paid in 1927 for a letter written by Button Gwinnett (1732–77), one of the three men from Georgia to sign the Declaration of Independence on July 4, 1776. Such an item would probably attract bids of up to $250,000 today. (See photo, previous page.)

If one of the six known signatures of William Shakespeare (1564–1616) were to come on the market or if a new one were discovered the price would doubtless set a record.

Crossword Puzzles

The earliest crossword was one with 32 clues invented by Arthur Wynne (born Liverpool, England) and published in the *New York World* on December 21, 1913.

Largest. The largest crossword ever published was one with 3,185 clues across and 3,149 clues down, compiled by Robert M. Stilgenbauer of Los Angeles in 7½ years of spare time between May 15, 1938 and publication in 1949. Despite the 125,000 copies distributed, not one copy has been returned worked out or even partially worked out.

Slowest. In May, 1966, *The Times* of London received an announcement from a Fijian woman that she had just succeeded in completing their crossword No. 673 in the issue of April 4, 1932.

Oldest Map

The oldest known map is the Turin Papyrus, showing the layout of an Egyptian gold mine, dated about 1320 B.C.

Christmas Cards

The greatest number of personal Christmas cards sent out is believed to be 40,000 in 1969 by President and Mrs. Nixon to friends and others.

Libraries

Largest. The largest library in the world is the Library of Congress (founded on April 24, 1800), on Capitol Hill, Washington, D.C. On June 30, 1969, it contained more than 59,000.000 items, including 14,846,000 books and pamphlets. The two buildings cover six acres and contain 327 miles of book shelves.

The Lenin State Library in Moscow, U.S.S.R., claims to house more than 20,000,000 books, but this total is understood to include periodicals. (See photo.)

The largest non-statutory library in the world is the New York Public Library (founded 1895) on Fifth Avenue, New York City, with a floor area of 525,276 square feet. The main part of its collection is in a private research library which has 4,666,326 volumes on 80 miles of shelves, 9,000,000 manuscripts, 120,000 prints, 150,000

LARGEST LIBRARY (next to the Library of Congress, which is the depository for copyright works in the U.S.) is the Lenin State Library in Moscow, U.S.S.R. Its 20,000,000-copy total includes periodicals, as well as books.

phonograph records, and 275,000 maps. There are also 81 tax-supported branch libraries with more than 3,231,696 books and 4,000,000 pictures.

Overdue Books. It was reported on December 7, 1968, that a book on febrile diseases (London, 1805, by Dr. J. Currie) checked out in 1823 from the University of Cincinnati Medical Library was returned by the borrower's great-grandson Richard Dodd. The fine was calculated as $22,646, but waived.

Newspapers

Most. It has been estimated that the total circulation of newspapers throughout the world averaged 320,000,000 copies per day in 1966. The country with the greatest number is the U.S.S.R., with 7,967 in 1966. Their average circulation in 1966 was 110,400,000.

The U.S. had 1,749 English-language daily newspapers on January 1, 1968. They had a combined net paid circulation of 61,397,000 copies per day at September 30, 1966. The peak year for U.S. newspapers was 1910, when there were 2,202. The leading newspaper readers in the world are the people of Sweden, where 515 newspapers were sold for each 1,000 of the population in 1967–68.

Oldest. The oldest existing newspaper in the world is the Swedish official journal *Post och Inrikes Tidningar*, founded in 1644. It is published by the Royal Swedish Academy of Letters. The oldest existing commercial newspaper is the *Haarlems Dagblad/Oprechte Haarlemsche Courant*, published in Haarlem, in the Netherlands. The *Courant* was first issued as the *Weeckelycke Courante van Europa* on January 8, 1656, and a copy of issue No. 1 survives.

Largest. The most massive single issue of a newspaper was *The New York Times* of Sunday, October 10, 1971. It comprised 15 sections with a total of 972 pages, including about 1,200,000 lines of advertising. Each copy weighed 7½ lbs. and sold for 50 cents locally.

The largest page size ever used has been 51 inches by 35 inches for *The Constellation*, printed in 1895 by George Roberts as part of the Fourth of July celebrations in New York City. The largest page size of any present newspaper is 30 inches by 22 inches in *The Nantucket*

Inquirer and Mirror, published every Friday in Nantucket, on Nantucket Island, Massachusetts.

The smallest recorded page size has been $3\frac{1}{2}$ inches by $4\frac{1}{2}$ inches, as used in *Diario di Roma*, an issue of which, dated February 28, 1829, survives.

Highest Circulation. The first newspaper to achieve a circulation of 1,000,000 was *Le Petit Journal*, published in Paris, which reached this figure in 1886, when selling at 5 centimes (fractionally more than one cent) per copy.

The claim exercised for the world's highest circulation is that by the *Ashashi Shimbun* (founded 1879) of Japan with a figure which attained more than 10,000,000 copies in October, 1970. This, however, has been achieved by totaling the figures for editions published in various centers with a morning figure of 6,100,000 and an evening figure of 3,900,000.

The highest circulation of a *single* newspaper is the Sunday *News of the World*, printed in Bouverie Street, London, England. Single issues have attained a sale of 9,000,000 copies, with an estimated readership of more than 19,000,000. The paper first appeared on October 1, 1843, averaged 12,971 copies per week in its first year and surpassed the million mark in 1905. To provide sufficient pulp for the 1,500 reels used per week, each measuring 5 miles long, more than 780,000 trees have to be felled each year. The latest sales figure is 6,085,680 copies per issue (average for July 1 to December 31, 1971), with an estimated readership of 16,208,000.

The highest circulation of any daily newspaper is that of the U.S.S.R. government organ *Izvestia* (founded in Leningrad on March 12, 1917, as a Menshevik newssheet) with a figure of 8,670,000 in March, 1967. The daily tabloid *Pionerskaya Pravda* had an average circulation of 9,181,000 copies per issue in 1966. This is the news organ of the Pioneers, a Communist youth organization founded in 1922.

The highest circulation of any evening newspaper is that of the *Evening News*, established in London in 1881. The average daily net sale reached 1,752,166 in the first six months of 1950. The latest figure is 1,876,182 copies per issue (average for July 1 to December 31, 1971), with an average readership of 2,644,000 in 1968.

Most Read. The newspaper which achieves the closest to a saturation circulation is *The Sunday Post*, established in Glasgow, Scotland, in 1914. In 1971, its total estimated readership of 2,947,000 represented more than 79 per cent of Scotland's entire population aged 15 and over.

Periodicals

Largest Circulation. The largest circulation of any weekly periodical was that of *This Week Magazine*, produced until 1969 in the U.S. to circulate with 43 newspapers which found it uneconomical to run their own colored Sunday magazine section. The circulation was 11,889,211 copies in 1967.

In its 30 international editions the *Reader's Digest* (established February, 1922) circulates more than 29,000,000 copies monthly, in 13 languages, including a U.S. edition of 17,500,000 copies (average for July to December, 1971).

Advertising Rates. The highest price asked for advertising space *pro rata* was $98,200 for a four-color center spread in *This Week*. The highest price for a single page has been $84,100 for a four-color back cover in *Life* magazine (circulation 8,500,000 per week) from January, 1969, to January, 1971.

The highest expenditure ever incurred on a single advertisement in a periodical is $950,000 by Uniroyal, Inc. for a 40-page insert in the May, 1968, issue of the U.S. edition of the *Reader's Digest*.

Music

Instruments

Oldest. The world's oldest surviving musical notation is a heptonic scale deciphered from a clay tablet by Dr. Duchesne-Guillemin in 1966–67. The tablet has been dated to *c.* 1800 B.C. and was found at a site in Nippur, Sumeria, now Iraq. Musical history is, however, able to be traced back to the 3rd millennium B.C., when the yellow bell (*huang chung*) had a recognized standard musical tone in Chinese temple music. It is possible that either a flute or a mouth bow is the object depicted in a painting from the Magdalenian period (*c.* 18,000 B.C.) in the Trois Frères Caves in the Pyrenees. Rock-gongs probably existed even earlier.

Earliest Piano. The earliest pianoforte in existence is one built in Florence, Italy, in 1720, by Bartolommeo Cristofori (1655–1731) of Padua, and now preserved in the Kraus Museum of Florence.

WORLD'S OLDEST MUSIC: Dating back to 1800 B.C., this clay tablet, found in Iraq, contains the notation of a heptonic scale.

Organs. The largest and loudest musical instrument ever constructed is the Auditorium Organ in Atlantic City, New Jersey. Completed in 1930, this heroic instrument has two consoles (one with seven manuals and another movable one with five), 1,477 stop controls and 33,112 pipes ranging from $\frac{3}{16}$ of an inch to 64 feet in length. It is powered with blower motors of 365 horse-power, cost $500,000 and has the volume of 25 brass bands, with a range of seven octaves. It is now only partially functional. The world's largest church organ is that in Passau Cathedral, Germany. It was completed in 1928 by D. F. Steinmeyer & Co. It has 16,000 pipes and five manuals.

The grand organ at John Wanamaker's department store in Philadelphia, installed in 1911, was enlarged until by 1930 it had six manuals and 30,067 pipes including a 64-foot Gravissima.

The loudest organ stop in the world is the Ophicleide stop of the Grand Great in the Solo Organ in the Atlantic City Auditorium (see above). It is operated by a pressure of 100 inches of water ($3\frac{1}{2}$ lbs. per square inch) and has a pure trumpet note of earsplitting volume, more than six times the volume of the loudest locomotive whistles.

Organ Marathons. The longest organ recital ever sustained was one of $43\frac{1}{4}$ hours at Handsworth College Chapel, Birmingham, England, by the Rev. Ian Yates on May 9–11, 1970.

The duration for playing an electric organ is 64 hours by James A. Barron at the Sundale Shopping Complex, Southport, Queensland, Australia, on November 16–19, 1971. An entirely non-stop record of 50 hours was set by Jeremy Cody, aged 15, from April 10–12, 1971, at Pontypridd, Glamorgan, Wales.

The longest recorded non-stop harmonium (small organ) marathon is 72 hours by Iain Stinson and John Whiteley, both of the Royal Holloway College at Englefield Green, Surrey, England, on February 6–9, 1970.

Brass Instruments. The largest recorded brass instrument is a tuba standing $7\frac{1}{2}$ feet tall, with 39 feet of tubing and a bell 3 feet 4 inches across. This contrabass tuba was constructed for a world tour by the band of John Philip Sousa (1854–1932), the "march king," in c. 1896–98, and is still in use. This instrument is now owned by Mr. Ron Snyder (Great Britain).

Longest Alphorn. The longest Swiss alphorn, which is of wooden construction, is $26\frac{1}{2}$ feet long and was constructed before June, 1968, in Maine.

String Instruments. The largest stringed instrument ever constructed was a pantaleon with 270 strings stretched over 50 square feet, used by George Noel in 1767.

Largest Guitar. The largest and presumably also the loudest playable guitar in the world is one 8 feet 10 inches tall, weighing 80 lbs. and with a volume of 16,000 cubic inches (cf. the standard 1,024 cubic inches) built by The Harmony Company of Chicago and completed in April, 1970.

Largest Double Bass. The largest bass viol ever constructed was an octo-bass 10 feet tall, built in c. 1845 by J. B. Vuillaume (1798–

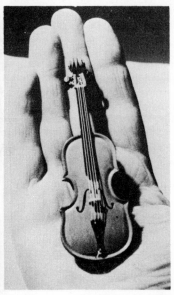

WORLD'S LARGEST BRASS INSTRUMENT (left): A tuba 7½ feet tall with 39 feet of tubing, constructed for a John Philip Sousa band. SMALLEST VIOLIN: Fully functional, this 5½-inch instrument fits neatly into one's palm.

1875) of France. Because the stretch was too great for any musician's finger-span, the stopping was effected by foot levers. It was played in London in 1851.

Most Valuable Violin. The highest recorded auction price for a violin is the £84,000 ($201,600) paid by W. E. Hill & Son, London, at Sotheby's on June 3, 1971 for the Lady Anne Blunt Stradivarius, made in 1721. On this valuation the "Messie" Stradivarius in the Ashmolean Museum at Oxford, England, is now worth some £200,000 ($520,000).

Smallest Violin. The smallest fully functional violin made is one 5½ inches overall, constructed by Mr. T. B. Pollard of Rock Ferry, Birkenhead, England.

Largest Drum. The largest drum in the world is the Disneyland Big Bass Drum with a diameter of 10 feet 6 inches and a weight of 450 lbs. It was built in 1961 by Remo, Inc., of North Hollywood, California, and is mounted on wheels and towed by a tractor.

Most Players for an Instrument. The greatest number of musicians required to operate a single instrument was the six required to play the gigantic orchestrion, known as the Apollonican, built in 1816 and played until 1840.

Orchestras

Most. The greatest number of professional orchestras maintained in one country is 94 in West Germany. The total number of symphony orchestras in the U.S., including "community" orchestras, was estimated to be 1,436, including 30 major and 66 metropolitan orchestras, as of August, 1970.

Largest. The vastest "orchestras" ever recorded were those assembled on Band Day at the University of Michigan, Ann Arbor. In some years between 1958 and 1965 the total number of instrumentalists reached 13,500.

On June 17, 1872, Johann Strauss the younger (1825–99) conducted an orchestra of 2,000, supported by a choir of 20,000, at the World Peace Jubilee in Boston, Massachusetts. The number of violinists was more than 350.

Greatest Classical Attendance. The greatest attendance at any classical concert was 90,000 for a presentation by the New York Philharmonic Orchestra, conducted by Leonard Bernstein, at Sheep Meadow in Central Park, New York City, on August 1, 1966.

Pop Festival Attendance. The greatest estimated attendance at a Pop Festival was 400,000 for the Woodstock Music and Art Fair at Bethel, New York, on August 15–17, 1969. According to one press estimate "at least 90 per cent" were smoking marijuana. The attendance at the third Pop Festival at East Afton Farm, Freshwater, Isle of Wight, England on August 30, 1970, was claimed by its promoters, Fiery Creations, also to be 400,000.

Highest and Lowest Notes. The extremes of orchestral instruments (excluding the organ) range between the piccolo or octave flute, which can reach e′′′′′ or 5,274 cycles per second, and the subcontrabass clarinet, which can reach C_{iii} or 16.4 cycles per second. The highest note on a standard pianoforte is 4,186 cycles per second which is also the violinist's limit. In 1873, a sub double bassoon able to reach $B_{iii}\sharp$ or 14.6 cycles per second was constructed, but no surviving specimen is known. The extremes for the organ are g′′′′′′ (12,544 cycles per sec.) and C_{iii} (8.12 cycles per sec.) obtainable from ¾-inch and 64-foot pipes, respectively.

Composers

Most Prolific. The most prolific composer of all time was probably Georg Philipp Telemann (1681–1767) of Germany. He composed 12 complete sets of services (one cantata every Sunday) for a year, 78 services for special occasions, 40 operas, 600 to 700 orchestral suites, 44 Passions, plus concertos and chamber music.

The most prolific symphonist was Johann Melchior Molter (c. 1695–1765) of Germany who wrote 169. Joseph Haydn (1732–1809) of Austria wrote 104 numbered symphonies, some of which are regularly played today.

Most Rapid. Among classical composers the most rapid was Wolfgang Amadeus Mozart (1756–91) of Austria, who wrote 600 operas, operettas, symphonies, violin sonatas, divertimenti, serenades, motets, concertos for piano and many other instruments, string quartets, other chamber music, masses and litanies, of which only 70 were published before he died, aged 35. His opera *The Clemency of Titus* (1791) was written in 18 days and three symphonic masterpieces, *Symphony No. 39 in E flat major, Symphony in G minor* and the *Jupiter Symphony in C*, were reputedly written in the space of 42 days in 1788. His overture to *Don Giovanni* was written in full score at one sitting in Prague in 1787 and finished on the day of its opening performance.

National Anthems

The oldest national anthem is the *Kimigayo* of Japan, in which the words date from the 9th century. The anthem of Greece constitutes the first four verses of the Solomos poem, which has 158 verses. The shortest anthems are those of Japan, Jordan and San Marino, each with only four lines. The anthems of Bahrain and Qatar have no words at all.

Longest Rendering

"God Save the King" was played non-stop 16 or 17 times by a German military band on the platform of Rathenau Railway Station, Brandenburg, on the morning of February 9, 1909. The reason was that King Edward VII was struggling inside the train to get into his German Field-Marshal uniform before he could emerge.

Longest Symphony

The longest of all orchestral symphonies is No. 3 in D minor by Gustav Mahler (1860–1911) of Austria. This work, composed in 1895, requires a contralto, a women's and a boys' choir and an organ, in addition to a full orchestra. A full performance requires 1 hour 34 minutes, of which the first movement alone takes 45 minutes.

At least equally long is the Symphony No. 2 (the Gothic, now renumbered as No. 1), composed in 1919–22 by Havergal Brian, which has been performed only twice, on June 24, 1961 and October 30, 1966. The total *ensemble* included 55 brass instruments, 31 wood wind, six kettledrummers playing 22 drums, four vocal soloists, four large mixed choruses, a children's chorus and an organ. The symphony is continuous and required, when played as a recording on November 27, 1967, 100 minutes. Brian has written an even vaster work based on Shelley's *Prometheus Unbound* lasting 4 hours 11 minutes but the full score has been missing since 1961. He wrote 27 symphonies, 4 grand operas and 7 large orchestral works between 1948 when he was 72 and 1968.

Longest Piano Composition

The longest non-repetitious piece for piano ever composed was the Opus Clavicembalisticum by Kaikhosru Shapurji Sorabji (born 1892). The composer himself gave it its only public performance on December 1, 1930, in Glasgow, Scotland. The work is in 12 movements with a theme and 49 variations and a Passacaglia with 81 and a playing time of 2¾ hours.

The longest piano piece of any kind is *Vexations* by Erik Satie which consists of a 180-note composition which, on the composer's orders, must be repeated 840 times so that the whole performance lasts 18 hours 40 minutes. Its first reported public performance in September, 1963, in the Pocket Theatre, New York City, required a relay of ten pianists. The *New York Times* critic fell asleep at 4 a.m.

and the audience dwindled to six masochists. At the conclusion a sado-masochist shouted "Encore." Richard Toop, played the first solo rendition in London, on October 10–11, 1967 in 25 hours.

Longest Silence

The most protracted silence in a modern composition is one entitled *4 minutes 33 seconds* in a totally silent *opus* by John Cage (U.S.). Commenting on this trend among modern composers, Igor Fyodorovich Stravinsky (1882–1971) said that he now looked forward to their subsequent compositions being "works of major length."

Highest-Paid Musician

Pianist. The highest-paid concert pianist was Ignace Jan Paderewski (1860–1941), Prime Minister of Poland in 1919–21, who accumulated a fortune estimated at $5,000,000, of which $500,000 was earned in a single season in 1922–23. He once received $33,000 for a concert in Madison Square Garden, New York City, the highest fee ever paid for a single performance.

Singers. Of great fortunes earned by singers, the highest on record are those of Enrico Caruso (1873–1921), the Italian tenor, whose estate was about $9,000,000, and the Italian-Spanish coloratura soprano Amelita Galli-Curci (1889–1963), who received about $3,000,000. In 1850, up to $653 was paid for a single seat at the concerts given in the U.S. by Johanna ("Jenny") Maria Lind (1820–87), the "Swedish Nightingale." She had a range of nearly three octaves, of which the middle register is still regarded as unrivaled.

Violinist. The Austrian-born Fritz Kreisler (1875–1962) is reputed to have received more than $3,000,000 during his career.

Drummer. The most highly paid drummer, or indeed "side man" of any kind, is Bernard ("Buddy") Rich, (born 1917), in the band of Harry James, at more than $75,000 per annum.

Opera

Longest. The longest of commonly performed operas is *Die Meistersinger von Nurnberg* by Wilhelm Richard Wagner (1813–83) of Germany. A normal uncut performance of this opera as performed by the Sadler's Wells company between August 24 and September 19, 1968, entailed 5 hours 15 minutes of music. *William Tell* by Rossini, never now performed uncut, would according to the *tempi* require some 7 or more hours if performed in full.

Aria. The longest single aria, in the sense of an operatic solo, is Brunnhilde's immolation scene in Wagner's *Götterdämmerung*. A well-known recording has been precisely timed at 14 minutes 46 seconds.

Cadenza. The longest recorded cadenza in operatic history occurred in *c.* 1815, when Crevilli, a tenor, sang the two words *felice ognora* ("always happy") as a cadenza for 25 minutes in the Milan Opera House, Italy.

LONGEST PLAY (left): The Passion Play, performed to Oberammergau, Germany, every 10 years since 1633, takes 5½ to 8½ hours. WEALTHIEST SINGER (right) was Enrico Caruso, the Italian tenor, who left an estate of $9,000,000 when he died in 1921 at the age of 48. His recording of "Vesti la giubba" from "I Pagliacci" was the first to sell a million copies (see page 219).

Opera House—Largest. The largest opera house in the world is the Metropolitan Opera House, Lincoln Center, New York City, completed in September, 1966, at a cost of $45,700,000. It has a capacity of 3,800 seats in an auditorium 451 feet deep. The stage is 234 feet in width and 146 feet deep. The tallest opera house is one housed in a 42-story building on Wacker Drive in Chicago.

Opera Houses—Most Tiers. The Teatro della Scala (La Scala) in Milan, Italy, shares with the Bolshoi Theatre in Moscow, U.S.S.R., the distinction of having the greatest number of tiers. Each has six, with the topmost in Moscow being termed the Galurka.

Opera Singers—Youngest and Oldest. The youngest opera singer in the world has been Jeanette Gloria (Ginetta) La Bianca, born in Buffalo, New York, on May 12, 1934, who made her debut as Rosina in *The Barber of Seville* at the Teatro dell'Opera, Rome, on May 8, 1950, aged 15 years 361 days. Miss La Bianca was taught by Lucia Carlino and managed by Angelo Carlino.

Giacomo Lauri-Volpi (Spain) gave a public performance on January 26, 1972, aged 79.

HEAVIEST BELL: Tsar Kolokol, 216 tons and cracked (on the side not seen), has stood in the Kremlin, Moscow, since 1836.

Bells

Oldest. The oldest bell is reputed to be that found in the Babylonian Palace of Nimrod in 1849 by Mr. (later Sir) Austen Henry Layard (1817–94). It dates from *c.* 1000 B.C.

Largest Carillon. The largest carillon in the world is the Laura Spelman Rockefeller Memorial carillon in Riverside Church, New York City. It consists of 72 bells with a total weight of 114 tons.

Bell Ringing. Eight bells have been rung to their full "extent" (a complete "Bob Major" of 40,320 changes) only once without relays. This took place in a bell foundry at Loughborough, Leicestershire, England, beginning at 6:52 a.m. on July 27, 1963, and ending at 12:50 a.m. on July 28, after 17 hours 58 minutes. The peal was composed by Kenneth Lewis of Altrincham, Cheshire, and the eight ringers were conducted by Robert B. Smith, aged 25, of Marple, Cheshire. Theoretically it would take 37 years 355 days to ring 12 bells (maximus) to their full extent of 479,001,600 changes.

Heaviest. The heaviest bell in the world is the Tsar Kolokol, cast in 1733 in Moscow, U.S.S.R. It weighs 216 tons, measures 22 feet 8 inches in diameter, is over 19 feet high, and its greatest thickness is 24 inches. The bell is cracked, and a fragment, weighing about 12 tons, is broken from it. The bell has stood on a platform in the Kremlin, in Moscow, since 1836. (See photo.)

The heaviest bell in use is the Mingoon bell, weighing 97 tons, in Mandalay, Burma, which is struck by a teak boom from the outside. The heaviest swinging bell in the world is the Kaiserglock in Cologne Cathedral, Germany, which was recast in 1925 at 28 tons.

The heaviest tuned bell is the bourdon bell of the Laura Spelman Rockefeller Memorial carillon in Riverside Church, New York City. It weighs 40,926 lbs. and is 10 feet 2 inches in diameter.

Song

Oldest. The oldest is the *chadouf* song, which has been sung since time immemorial by irrigation workers on the man-powered treadwheel Nile water mills (or *saqiyas*) in Egypt (now the United Arab Republic). The English song *Sumer is icumen in* dates from *c.* 1240.

Top Songs of All Time. The most frequently sung songs in English are *Happy Birthday to You* (based on the original *Good Morning to All*, by Mildred and Patty S. Hill of New York, published in 1936 and in copyright until 1992); *For He's a Jolly Good Fellow* (originally the French *Malbrouk*), known at least as early as 1781, and *Auld Lang Syne* (originally the Strathspey *I fee'd a Lad at Michaelmass*), some words of which were written by Robert Burns (1759–96). *Happy Birthday* was sung in space by the Apollo IX astronauts on March 8, 1969.

Most Monotonous. The longest song sung on one note is *Ein Ton*, written in 1859 by Peter Cornelius (1824–74) of Germany. The single note (the B above middle C) is repeated 80 times for 30 bars.

Top Selling Sheet Music. Sales of three non-copyright pieces are known to have exceeded 20,000,000, namely *The Old Folks at Home, Listen to the Mocking Bird* (1855) and *The Blue Danube* (1867). Of copyright material, the two top-sellers are *Let Me Call You Sweetheart* (1910, by Whitson Friedman) and *Till We Meet Again* (1918, by Egan Whiting) each with some 6,000,000 by 1967.

Most Successful Song Writers. In terms of sales of single records, the most successful of all song writers have been John Lennon and Paul McCartney of The Beatles. Between 1962 and 1970 together they wrote 30 songs which sold more than 1,000,000 records each.

Hymns

Earliest. There are believed to be more than 500,000 Christian hymns in existence. "Te Deum Laudamus" dates from about the 5th century, but the earliest exactly datable hymn is the French one "Jesus soit en ma teste et mon entendement" from 1490, translated into the well-known "God be in my head" in 1512.

Longest and Shortest. The longest hymn is "Hora novissima tempora pessima sunt; vigilemus" by Bernard of Cluny (12th century), which runs to 2,966 lines. In English the longest is "The Sands of Time are Sinking" by Mrs. Anne Ross Cousin, *née* Cundell

LARGEST THEATRE:
Completed in 1959, this
building in Peking, China,
covers 12.9 acres and seats
10,000.

(1824–1906), which is in full 152 lines, though only 32 lines in the Methodist Hymn Book. The shortest hymn is the single verse in Long Metre "Be Present at our Table, Lord," anonymous but attributed to "J. Leland."

Most Prolific Hymnists. Mrs. Frances Jan Van Alstyne, *née* Crosby (U.S.) (1820–1915) wrote more than 8,000 hymns although she had been blinded at the age of 6 weeks. She is reputed to have knocked off one hymn in 15 minutes. Charles Wesley (1707–88) wrote about 6,000 hymns. In the seventh (1950) edition of *Hymns Ancient and Modern* the works of John Mason Neale (1818–66) appear 56 times.

Longest Hymn-in. The Cambridge University Student Methodist Society (England) sang through the 984 hymns in the Methodist Hymn Book in 45 hours 42 minutes, and completed 1,000 hymns with 16 more requests in 88 minutes on February 7–9, 1969, in the Wesley Church, Cambridge.

Theatre

Origins. Theatre as we know it has its origins in Greek drama performed in honor of a god, usually Dionysus. The earliest amphitheatres date from the 5th century B.C. The largest of all known *orchestras* is one at Megalopolis in central Greece, where the auditorium reached a height of 75 feet and had a capacity of 17,000.

Oldest. The oldest indoor theatre in the world is the Teatro Olimpico in Vicenza, Italy. Designed in the Roman style by Andrea di Pietro, *alias* Palladio (1508–80), it was begun three months before his death and finished in 1582 by his pupil Vicenzo Scamozzi (1552–1616). It is preserved today in its original form.

Largest. The largest building used for theatre is the National People's Congress Building (*Ren min da hui tang*) on the west side of Tian an men Square, Peking, China. It was completed in 1959 and covers an area of 12.9 acres. The theatre seats 10,000 and is occasionally used as such, as in 1964 for the play "The East is Red."

The largest regular theatre is the Radio City Music Hall in Rockefeller Center, New York City. It seats more than 6,200 people and the average annual attendance is more than 8,000,000. The stage is 144 feet wide and 66 feet 6 inches deep, equipped with a revolving turntable 43 feet in diameter and three elevator sections, each 70 feet long.

The greatest seating capacity of any theatre in the world is that of the "Chaplin" (formerly the "Blanquita") in Havana, Cuba. It was opened on December 30, 1949, and has 6,500 seats.

Largest Amphitheatre. The largest amphitheatre ever built is the Flavian amphitheatre or Colosseum of Rome, Italy, completed in 80 A.D. Covering 5 acres and with a capacity of 87,000, it has a maximum length of 612 feet and maximum width of 515 feet.

Longest Runs. The longest run of any show at one theatre anywhere in the world was of the play *The Drunkard*, written by W. H. Smith and "a gentleman." First produced as a moral lesson in 1844 by Phineas Taylor Barnum (1810–91), an American showman, it was not performed commercially again until it was revived on July 6, 1933, at the Theatre Mart in Los Angeles. From that date it ran continuously, one show a night, for 7,510 performances, until September 3, 1953. Starting on September 7, 1953, a new musical adaptation of *The Drunkard*, called *The Wayward Way*, started to play alternate nights with the original version. On October 17, 1959, it played its 9,477th and final time. It was seen by more than 3,000,000 people.

The Broadway record is 3,242 performances by *Fiddler on the Roof*, which opened on September 22, 1964, and closed on July 2, 1972. Based on stories by Sholom Aleichem, the play had a book by Joseph Stein and music by Jerry Bock and Sheldon Harnick. It surpassed the previous records for both plays and musical comedies on Broadway.

The longest continuous run of any show still running at one theatre is of *The Mousetrap* by Agatha Christie (now Lady Mallowan) at the Ambassadors Theatre (capacity 453), London. This thriller opened on November 25, 1952, and has broken the record with 7,511 performances on December 23, 1970. So far 111 actors have played its 8 roles. More than 2,600,000 people have seen the play.

One-Man Show. The longest run of any one-man show has been 327 performances of *Comedy Tonight* by James Young at the Ulster Group Theatre, Belfast, Northern Ireland, from April 7, 1969, to March 22, 1970. Mr. Young was on stage for 2 hours 15 minutes each performance.

Shortest Runs. The shortest run on record was that of *The Intimate Revue* at the Duchess Theatre, London, on March 11, 1930. Anything which could go wrong did. With scene changes taking up to 20 minutes apiece, the management scrapped seven scenes to get the finale on before midnight. The run was described as "half a performance." Even this fractional first night was surpassed by *As You Like It* by William Shakespeare (1564–1616) at the Shaftesbury Theatre, London, in 1888. On the opening night the fire curtain was let down, jammed, and did not rise again that night, or ever again on this production.

Of the many Broadway and off-Broadway shows for which the opening and closing nights coincided the most costly was *Kelly*, a musical costing $700,000 which suffered its double ceremony on February 6, 1965.

Longest Play. The Oberammergau *Passionsspiel* ("Passion Play"), performed every ten years since 1633, was performed, with 125 speaking parts, 97 times in 1970, each performance occupying $5\frac{1}{2}$ or $8\frac{1}{2}$ hours, including intervals. The audience for this 37th presentation was 530,000. (See photo, page 207.)

Shakespeare. The first all-amateur company to have staged all 37 of Shakespeare's plays was The Southsea Shakespeare Actors, Hampshire, England, when in October, 1966, they presented *Cymbaline*.

Longest Title. The longest title of any play was *The Fire of London* plus another 118 words. It was presented at The Mermaid Theatre, London, on September 4, 1966. This 17th century documentary was written by Peter Black, TV critic of the *Daily Mail*.

Longest Chorus Line. The world's longest permanent chorus line is formed by the Rockettes in the Radio City Music Hall, New York City. The 36 girls dance precision routines across the 144-foot-wide stage. The whole troupe, which won the *Grand Prix* in Paris in July, 1937, is 46 strong, but 10 girls are always on alternating vacation or are recuperating. The troupe is sometimes augmented to 64.

Shortest Criticism. The shortest dramatic criticism in theatrical history was that attributed to Wolcott Gibbs (died 1958), writing about the farce "Wham!" He wrote the single word "Ouch!"

Radio Broadcasting

Most Stations. The country with the greatest number of radio transmitters is the U.S., where there were 6,980 authorized transmitting stations in 1971 of which 4,346 were AM (amplitude modulation) and 2,634 FM (frequency modulation).

Radio Sets. There were an estimated 620,000,000 radio sets in use throughout the world at June 30, 1970, equivalent to 192 for each 1,000 people. Of these about 336,000,000 were in the U.S. (including Puerto Rico and the U.S. Virgin Islands) at December 31, 1970. Of the U.S. total, 85,000,000 were in cars.

Origins. The earliest description of a radio transmission system was written by Dr. Mahlon Loomis (born New York State, 1826) on July 21, 1864, and demonstrated between two kites at Bear's Den, Loudoun County, Virginia, in October, 1866. He received a U.S. Patent entitled Improvement in Telegraphing, in 1872.

Earliest Patent. The first patent for a system of communication by means of electro-magnetic waves, numbered No. 12039, was granted on June 22, 1896, to the Italian-Irish Marchese, Guglielmo Marconi (1874–1937). The first permanent wireless installation was at The Needles on the Isle of Wight, Hampshire, England, by Marconi's Wireless Telegraph Co., Ltd., in November, 1896.

A prior public demonstration of wireless transmission of speech was given in the town square of Murray, Kentucky, in 1892 by Nathan B. Stubblefield. He died, destitute, on March 28, 1928.

Earliest Broadcast. The first advertised broadcast was made on December 24, 1906, by Prof. Reginald Aubrey Fessenden (1868–1932) from the 420-foot mast of the National Electric Signalling Company at Brant Rock, Massachusetts. The transmission included the *Largo* by Georg Friedrich Händel (1685–1759) of Germany. Fessenden had achieved the broadcast of highly distorted speech as early as November, 1900.

Transatlantic Transmissions. The earliest transatlantic wireless signals (the letter S in Morse Code) were sent by Marconi from a 10-kilowatt station at Poldhu, Cornwall, England, and received by Percy Wright Paget and G. S. Kempon at St. John's, Newfoundland, Canada, on December 11, 1901. Human speech was first heard across the Atlantic in November, 1915, when a transmission from the U.S. Navy station at Arlington, Virginia, was received by U.S. radio-telephone engineers up in the Eiffel Tower, Paris.

Longest Broadcast. The longest B.B.C. broadcast was by Radio Station ELBC, Monrovia, on November 23, 1961, when a transmission of 14 hours 20 minutes was devoted to the coverage of Queen Elizabeth II's visit to Liberia.

Television

Invention. The invention of television, the instantaneous viewing of distant objects, was not an act but a process of successive and interdependent discoveries. The first commercial cathode ray tube was introduced in 1897 by Karl Ferdinand Braun (1850–1918), but was not linked to "electric vision" until 1907 by Boris Rosing of Russia in St. Petersburg (now Leningrad). The earliest public demonstration of television was given on January 26, 1926, by John Logie Baird (1888–1946) of Scotland, using a development of the mechanical scanning system suggested by Paul Nipkov in 1884. A patent application for the Iconoscope (No. 2,141,059) had been filed on December 29, 1923, by Vladimir Kosma Zworykin (born in Russia in 1889, became a U.S. citizen in 1924), and a short-range transmission of a model windmill had been made on June 13, 1925, by C. Francis Jenkins in Washington, D.C.

Earliest Service. The first high-definition television broadcasting service was opened from Alexandra Palace, London, N.22, on November 2, 1936, when there were about 100 sets in the United Kingdom. A television station in Berlin, Germany, began low-definition broadcasting on March 22, 1935. The transmitter burned out in August, 1935.

Most Transmitters and Sets. In 1971, the total estimated number of television transmitters in use or under construction was 6,400 serving 270,500,000 sets (75 for each 1,000 of the world population). Of these, about 92,700,000 were estimated to be in use in the U.S. where 96 per cent of the population is reached. The number of color sets in the U.S. has grown from 200,000 in 1960 to 31,300,000 in January, 1971.

Transatlantic Transmission. The first transatlantic transmission by satellite was achieved at 1 a.m. on July 11, 1962, *via* the active satellite *Telstar I* from Andover, Maine, to Pleumeur Bodou, France. The picture was of Frederick R. Kappel, chairman of the American Telephone and Telegraph Company, which owned the satellite. The first "live" broadcast was made on July 23, 1962. The earliest satellite transmission was one of 2,700 miles from California to Massachusetts, *via* the satellite *Echo I*, on May 3, 1962. The picture showed the letters "M.I.T."

Greatest Audience. The greatest number of viewers for a televised event is an estimated 600,000,000 for the live and recorded transmissions of man's first lunar landing with the *Apollo XI* mission on July 20–21, 1969. This total was reportedly matched by the viewership of the near-disaster of the *Apollo XIII* space mission of April 11–17, 1970.

Largest TV Prizes. The greatest amount won by an individual in TV prizes was $264,000 by Teddy Nadler on quiz programs in the United States up to September, 1958. In March, 1960, he failed a test to become a census enumerator because of his inability to distinguish between east and west. His comment was, reportedly, "Those maps threw me."

Largest Contract. The largest TV contract ever signed was one, for $34,000,000 in a three-year no-option contract between Dino Paul Crocetti (Dean Martin, b. June 7, 1917) and N.B.C. Martin was acclaimed in September, 1968, as the top earning show business personality of all time with $5,000,000 in a year. Television's highest-paid interviewer has been Garry Moore (born Thomas Garrison Morfit on January 31, 1915), who was earning $43,000 a week in 1963, equivalent to $2,236,000 per year.

Highest Hourly Rate. The world's highest-paid television performer based on an hourly rate is Perry Como (born Pierino Como, Canonsburg, Pennsylvania, on May 18, 1912), who began as a barber. In May, 1969, he signed a contract with N.B.C. to star in four one-hour video specials at $5,000,000. At the rate of $1,250,000 per hour, he was paid $20,833 per minute.

Longest Program. The longest pre-scheduled telecast on record was a non-stop transmission of *The Forsyte Saga* lasting 23 hours 50 minutes on U.S. stations in November, 1971.

**EARLIEST CINEMATO-
GRAPH:** Louis Lumière,
with one of the Lumière
Brothers' first projectors.

Motion Pictures

Earliest. The greatest impetus in the development of cinematography came from the inventiveness of Étienne Jules Marey (1830–1903) of France.

The earliest demonstration of a celluloid cinematograph film was given at Lyon, France, on March 22, 1895, by Auguste Marie Louis Nicolas Lumière (1862–1954) and Louis Jean Lumière (1864–1948), French brothers. The first public showing was at the Indian Salon of the Hotel Scribe, on the Boulevard des Capucines, in Paris, on December 28, 1895. The 33 patrons were charged 1 franc each and saw ten short films, including *Baby's Breakfast, Lunch Hour at the Lumière Factory* and *The Arrival of a Train.*

The earliest sound-on-film motion picture was demonstrated by Joseph Tykociner of the University of Illinois in 1922. The event is more usually attributed to Dr. Lee de Forest (1873–1961) in New York City, on March 13, 1923. The first all-talking picture was *Lights of New York,* shown at the Strand Theatre, New York City, on July 6, 1928.

Highest Production. Japan annually produces most full-length films, with 607 films of 4,921 feet or more completed in 1967, compared with 367 films of 11,155 feet or more approved by the censor in India in 1969. This compares, however, with Japan's production of 1,000 films in 1928. The average seat price in Japan is 70 yen (20 cents).

Movie-Going. The people of Taiwan go to the movies more often than those of any other country in the world, with an average of 66 attendances per person in 1967. The Soviet Union has the most movie theatres in the world, with 146,400 in 1969, including those projecting only 16 mm. film.

Most Movie Theatre Seats. The Falkland Islands (off South America's Straits of Magellan) have more seats per total population than any other country, with 250 for each 1,000 inhabitants.

Largest Theatre. The largest open-air movie theatre in the world is in the British Sector of West Berlin, Germany. One end of the Olympic Stadium, converted into an amphitheatre, seats 22,000 people.

Oldest Theatre. The earliest was the "Electric Theatre," part of a tented circus in Los Angeles. It opened on April 2, 1902. The oldest building designed as a movie theatre is the Biograph Cinema in Wilton Road, Victoria, London. It was opened in 1905 and originally had seating accommodation for 500 patrons. Its present capacity is 700.

Most Expensive Film. The most expensive film ever made is *War and Peace*, the U.S.S.R. government adaptation of the masterpiece of Tolstoy produced by Sergei Bondarchuk (born 1921) over the period 1962–67. The total cost has been officially stated to be more than $96,000,000. More than 165,000 uniforms had to be made. The re-creation of the Battle of Borodino involved 12,000 men and 800 horses on a location near Smolensk in 1964.

The highest price ever paid for film rights is $5,500,000, paid on February 6, 1962, by Warner Brothers for *My Fair Lady*, which cost $17,000,000, thus making it the most expensive musical film made up to that time.

Longest Film. The longest film ever shown is *The Human Condition*, directed in three parts by Masaki Kobayashi of Japan. It lasts 8 hours 50 minutes, excluding two breaks of 20 minutes each. It was shown in Tokyo in October, 1961, at an admission price of 250 yen (70 cents).

The longest film ever released was * * * * by Andy Warhol, which lasted 24 hours. It proved, not surprisingly, except reportedly to its creator, a commercial failure, and was withdrawn and re-released in 90-minute form as *The Loves of Ondine*.

Longest Title. The longest film title is: *Persecution and Assassination of Jean-Paul Marat as performed by the Inmates of the Asylum of Charenton under the direction of the Marquis de Sade*, made by the United Artists in March, 1967.

Highest Earnings by an Actor. The greatest earnings by any film star for one film is expected to be that of Elizabeth Taylor in *Cleopatra*. Her undisputed share of the earnings is $3,000,000 and could reach $7,000,000.

Highest Box Office Gross. The film with the highest world gross earnings (amount paid by theatre owners) is *The Sound of Music* (released in February, 1965), which reached $112,481,000 by

HIGHEST-PAID FILM STAR: Elizabeth Rosamond Taylor-Hilton-Wilding-Todd-Fisher-Burton, with Richard Burton, later her fifth husband, in the film "Cleopatra," from which her share is expected to reach $7,000,000.

September, 1969, having cost 20th Century Fox $8,100,000 to produce.

The fastest-earning film has been *Diamonds Are Forever*, one of a series of films based on stories of James Bond (Agent 007 in the Secret Service) by Ian Lancaster Fleming (1908–64). The film grossed $36,647,251 in the 31 days from December 17, 1971.

Oscars. Walter (Walt) Elias Disney (1901–1966) won more "Oscars"—the awards of the Academy of Motion Picture Arts and Sciences, instituted on May 16, 1929, for 1927–28—than any other person. His total was 35 from 1931 to 1969. The films with most awards have been *Ben Hur* (1959) with 11, followed by *West Side Story* (1961) with 10. The film with the highest number of nominations was *All About Eve* (1950) with 14.

The only performer to win three Oscars for the starring roles has been Katherine Hepburn (born November 9, 1909), in *Morning Glory* (1933), *Guess Who's Coming to Dinner* (1967) and *The Lion in Winter* (1968).

Oscars are named after Oscar Pierce of Texas.

Phonograph

The phonograph was first described on April 30, 1877, by Charles Cros (1842–88), a French poet and scientist. The first successful machine was constructed by Thomas Alva Edison (1847–1931), who gained his first patent on February 19, 1878. It was on August 15, 1877, that he shouted onto a record "Mary had a little lamb." The first practical hand-cranked foil cylinder phonograph was manufactured in the U.S. by Chichester Bell and Charles Sumner Tainter in 1886.

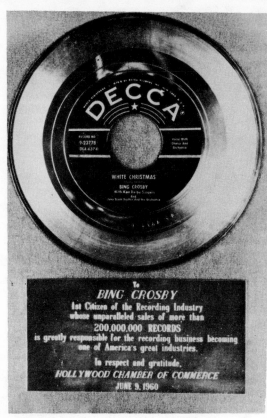

UNIQUE PLATINUM DISC which was awarded to Bing Crosby to commemorate the sale of 200,000,000 of his records in 1960. He received a second platinum disc in 1970 after 300,000,000 of his records had been sold.

The country with the greatest number of record players is the U.S., with more than 60,000,000 by mid-1969. A total of more than half a billion dollars is spent annually on 500,000 juke boxes in the U.S.

World sales of records for 1968 have been estimated at close to 1,141 million. Sales in the U.S. of discs and tapes reached $1,660,000,000 in 1970. This compares with $48,000,000 in 1940.

Oldest Record. The oldest record in the British Broadcasting Corporation's library is a record made by Émile Berliner (born Berlin, 1851) of himself reciting the Lord's Prayer. It was made in 1884. Berliner invented the flat disc to replace the cylinder in 1888. The B.B.C. library, the world's largest, contains over 750,000 records, including 5,250 with no known matrix.

The earliest jazz record made was *Indiana* and *The Dark Town Strutters Ball*, recorded for the Columbia label in New York City, on or about January 30, 1917, by the Original Dixieland Jazz Band, led by Dominick (Nick) James La Rocca (born April 11, 1889). This was released on May 31, 1917. The first jazz record to be released was the O.D.J.B.'s *Livery Stable Blues* (recorded February 24), backed by *The Dixie Jazz Band One-Step* (recorded February 26), released by Victor on March 7, 1917.

Most Successful Recording Artist. On June 9, 1960, the Hollywood Chamber of Commerce presented Harry Lillis (*alias* Bing) Crosby, Jr. (born May 2, 1904, at Tacoma, Washington) with a platinum disc to commemorate his 200,000,000th record sold from 2,600 singles and 125 albums he had recorded. On September 15, 1970, he received a second platinum disc when 300,650,000 records had been sold by Decca. It was then estimated that his global lifetime sales on 88 labels in 28 countries totaled 362,000,000.

His first commercial recording was *I've Got the Girl* recorded on October 10, 1926 (master number W142785 (Take 3) issued on the Columbia label).

Most Successful Group. The singers with the greatest sales of any group are The Beatles. This group from Liverpool, Lancashire, comprises George Harrison (born February 25, 1943), John Ono (formerly John Winston) Lennon (born October 9, 1940), James Paul McCartney (born June 18, 1942) and Richard Starkey, *alias* Ringo Starr (born July 7, 1940). Between February, 1963, and September, 1970, their sales in single units or equivalents was more than 420,000,000.

Golden Discs

Earliest. The first recorded piece to sell a million copies and become a "golden disc" were performances by Enrico Caruso (born Naples, Italy, 1873 and died 1921) of the aria *Vesti la giubba* (*On with the Motley*) from the opera *I Pagliacci* by Ruggiero Leoncavallo (1858–

RECORD RECORD-BREAKERS: As singers and disc sellers, The Beatles (left to right: Paul McCartney, George Harrison, "Ringo" Starr, John Lennon) broke many records in 1963-69.

1919), the earliest version of which was recorded on November 12, 1902.

The first single recording to surpass the million mark was Alma Gluck's rendition of *Carry Me Back to Old Virginny* on the Red Seal Victor label on a 12-inch single-faced (later backed) record (No. 74420).

The first literally golden disc was one sprayed by RCA Victor for presentation to Glen Miller for his *Chattanooga Choo Choo* on February 10, 1942.

Most. The singer claiming the most golden discs is Elvis Aron Presley (born at Tupelo, Mississippi, January 8, 1935). By January 1, 1971, he had 101 golden discs (78 for singles, 1 E.P. and 7 for L.P.'s) which are said to mark each sale of each 1,000,000 copies and each million dollar sale among his 65 best-selling records. His total global sales were estimated at 160,000,000 discs by that date, representing 300,000,000 singles equivalents.

The only *audited* measure of million-selling records is certification by the Record Industry Association of America (R.I.A.A.) introduced in 1958. By this yardstick Presley has 10 golden discs with an additional 11 for million dollar sales. The champions for R.I.A.A. awards are The Beatles with 21 singles and 17 for L.P.'s each of which sold more than $1,000,000 worth by September 1, 1970. The Beatles' global total of million copy sellers was believed to stand at 59 by January 1, 1971.

Youngest. The youngest age at which an artist has achieved sales of 1,000,000 copies of a record is 6 years by Osamu Minagawa of Tokyo, Japan, for his single *Kuro Neko No Tango* (*Black Cat Tango*) released on October 5, 1969.

Most Recorded Song. Two songs have each been recorded between 900 and 1,000 times in the U.S. alone—*St. Louis Blues*, written in 1914 by W. C. (William Christopher) Handy (born Memphis, Tennessee, in 1873 and died 1958), and *Stardust*, written in 1927 by Hoagland ("Hoagy") Carmichael (born Bloomington, Indiana, November 22, 1899).

Biggest Sellers. The greatest seller of any record to date is *White Christmas* by Irving Berlin (born Israel Bailin, at Tyumen, Russia, May 11, 1888). First recorded in 1941, it became, in 1970 the first record to reach 100,000,000 in sales.

The top-selling "pop" record has been *Rock Around the Clock* by William John Clifton Haley, Jr. (born Detroit, Michigan, March, 1927) and the Comets, recorded on April 12, 1954, with sales of 16,000,000 by January, 1972.

Most Recordings. Miss Lata Mangeshker (born 1928) has reportedly recorded between 1948 and 1971 not less than 20,000 solo, duet and chorus-backed songs in 20 Indian languages. She frequently has 5 sessions in a day.

Best-Seller Chart Duration Record. The longest stay in *Billboard's* best-seller chart has been 490 weeks from late 1958 to July, 1968, for the Columbia album *Johnny's Greatest Hits* by Johnny Mathis.

CLAIMANT TO MOST GOLDEN DISCS: Elvis Presley's records have sold the equivalent of 300,000,000 single discs.

Long-Players. The best-selling L.P. is the 20th Century Fox album *Sing We now of Christmas*, issued in 1958 and re-entitled *The Little Drummer Boy* in 1963. Its sales were reported to be more than 13,000,000 by January 1, 1972.

The all-time best-seller among long-playing records of musical film shows is the *Sound of Music* album, released by RCA Victor on March 2, 1965, with over 14,000,000 to January 1, 1972.

The first classical long-player to sell a million was a performance featuring the pianist Harvey Lavan (Van) Cliburn, Jr. (born in Kilgore, Texas, July 12, 1934) of the *Piano Concerto No. 1* by Pyotr Ilyich Tchaikovsky (1840–93) of Russia. This recording was made in 1958 and sales reached 1,000,000 by 1961, 2,000,000 by 1965 and about 2,500,000 by January, 1970.

The longest long-playing record is the 137-disc set of the complete works of William Shakespeare (1564–1616). The recordings, which were made in 1957–64, cost £260 12s. 6d. ($729.75) per set, and are by the Argo Record Co. Ltd., London. The Vienna Philharmonic's playing of Wagner's "Ring" covers 19 L.P.'s, was 8 years in the making and requires 14½ hours playing time.

Fastest Seller. The fastest selling record of all time is *John Fitzgerald Kennedy—A Memorial Album* (Premium Albums), an L.P. recorded on November 22, 1963, the day of Mr. Kennedy's assassination, which sold 4,000,000 copies at 99 cents in six days (December 7–12, 1963), thus ironically beating the previous speed record set by the humorous L.P. *The First Family* about the Kennedys in 1962–63.

Advance Sales. The greatest advance sale was 2,100,000 for *Can't Buy Me Love* by The Beatles, released in the U.S. on March 16, 1964.

Highest Fee

The highest fee ever paid to recording artists for a single performance is $189,000, paid to The Beatles for a performance in the William A. Shea baseball stadium, New York City, on August 23, 1966.

Longest Title

The song with the longest title is *I'm a Cranky Old Yank in a Clanky Old Tank on the Streets of Yokohama with my Honolulu Mama Doin' Those Beat-o, Beat-o, Flat-On-My-Seat-o, Hirohito Blues*, by "Hoagy" Carmichael, released in about 1943. Mr. Carmichael later claimed that the title ended with the word *Yank*, and that the rest was a joke.

TELEVISION PIONEER: John Logie Baird of Scotland put on the earliest public demonstration of the new medium in 1926 (see page 213).

Chapter Seven

THE BUSINESS WORLD

1. Commerce

Oldest Industry

Agriculture is often described as "the oldest industry in the world," whereas in fact there is no evidence that it was practiced before *c.* 7000 B.C. The oldest industry is believed to be flint knapping, involving the production of chopping tools and hand axes, dating from about 1,750,000 years ago.

Oldest Company. The oldest company in the world is the Faversham Oyster Fishery Co. of England, referred to in an Act of Parliament of 1930 as existing "from time immemorial," *i.e.* from before 1189.

Greatest Assets. The business with the greatest amount in physical assets is the Bell System, which comprises the American Telephone and Telegraph Company, with headquarters at 195 Broadway, New York City, and its subsidiaries. The group's total assets on the consolidated balance sheet at December 31, 1971, were valued at $54,547,929,000. The plant involved included 100,366,000 telephones. The number of employees was 1,000,600. The shareholders at January 1, 1971, numbered more than those of any other company, namely 3,009,768. A total of 20,109 attended the annual meeting in April, 1961, thereby setting a world record. The total of operating revenues and other income in 1971 was $18,949,000,000. The first company to have assets in excess of $1 billion was the United States Steel Corporation with $1,400,000,000 at the time of its creation by merger in 1900.

The manufacturing company with the greatest total assets employed is Imperial Chemical Industries, Ltd., with headquarters in England. It had £1,774,000,000 ($4,612,400,000) on December 31, 1971, and more than 400 U.K. and overseas subsidiaries.

Greatest Sales and Capital. The first company to surpass the $1 billion mark in annual sales was the United States Steel Corporation in 1917. Now there are 65 corporations with sales exceeding $2,500,000,000 (43 U.S., 17 European and 5 Japanese). The list is headed by General Motors with sales in 1971 of $28,263,918,443.

Greatest Profit and Loss. The greatest net profit made by one company in a year is $2,125,606,440 by General Motors Corporation of Detroit in 1965. The greatest loss ever sustained by a commercial concern in a year was $431,200,000 by the Penn Central Transportation Co. in 1970—a rate of $13.67 per second.

Biggest Work Force. The greatest payroll of any civilian organization is that of the U.S. Post Office with 716,782 on July 1, 1971.

LARGEST AIRCRAFT MANUFACTURER: From the Boeing plants in Seattle, Washington, and elsewhere, more than $3 billion worth of planes were sold in 1971.

Advertising Agency

The largest advertising agency in the world is J. Walter Thompson Co., which in 1971 had total billings of $779,000,000, which were $64,000,000 more than the Interpublic Group of Companies, also headquartered in New York City.

Biggest Advertiser

The world's biggest advertiser is the Unilever group of companies, the Anglo-Dutch group formed in 1929 whose origins go back to 1884. The group has more than 500 companies in more than 70 countries and employs 324,000 people, mainly in the production of food, detergents and toiletries. The advertising bill for over 1,000 branded products was £110,000,000 ($286,000,000) in 1971.

Aircraft Manufacturer

The world's largest aircraft manufacturer is the Boeing Company of Seattle, Washington. (See photo.) The corporation's sales totaled $3,040,000,000 in 1971, and it had 56,300 (down from a 120,500 top) employees and assets valued at $2,464,424,000 on December 31, 1971.

Airlines

Largest. The largest airline in the world is the U.S.S.R. State airline "Aeroflot," so named since 1932. This was instituted on February 9, 1923, with the title of Civil Air Fleet of the Council of Ministers of the U.S.S.R., abbreviated to "Dobrolet." It operates about 1,300 aircraft over about 373,000 miles of routes, employs

400,000 people and carried 74,000,000 passengers in 1970 to 57 countries.

The commercial airline carrying the greatest number of passengers in 1971 was United Air Lines of Chicago (formed 1931), with 26,048,293 passengers. The company had 46,552 employees and a fleet of 381 jet planes.

The commercial airline serving the greatest mileage of routes is Air France, with 258,000 miles of unduplicated routes in 1971. In 1971, the company carried 6,386,882 passengers.

Oldest. The oldest commercial airline is Koninklijke Luchtvaart Maatschappij N.V. (KLM) of the Netherlands, which opened its first scheduled service (Amsterdam-London) on May 17, 1920, having been established in 1919. One of the original constituents of B.O.A.C., Aircraft Transport and Travel Ltd., was founded in 1918 and merged into Imperial Airways in 1924; and one of the holding companies of S.A.S., Det Danske Luftfahrtselskab, was established on October 29, 1918, but operated a scheduled service only between August, 1920, and 1946.

Aluminum Producer

The world's largest producer of aluminum is Alcan Aluminium Limited, of Montreal, Quebec, Canada. With its affiliated companies, the company had an output of 1,865,000 tons and record consolidated revenues of $1,449,000 in 1971. The company's principal subsidiary, the Aluminum Company of Canada, Ltd., owns the world's largest aluminum smelter, at Arvida, Quebec, with a capacity of 458,500 tons per annum.

Art Auctioneering

The largest and oldest firm of art auctioneers is Sotheby and Co. of New Bond Street, London, England, founded in 1744. Their turnover in 1970 was £45,211,484 ($108,507,562) including their Parke-Bernet Galleries in New York City.

The highest total of any single art sale was $5,852,250 paid at Parke-Bernet on February 25, 1970, for 73 Impressionist and modern paintings.

Bicycle Factory

The 54-acre plant of Raleigh Industries Ltd. at Nottingham, England, is the largest factory in the world producing complete bicycles. The factory employs 10,000 and in 1972 has targets to make 800,000 wheeled toys and 1,700,000 bicycles.

Bookshop

The world's largest single bookshop is that of W. & G. Foyle, Ltd., of London, W.C.2. First established in 1904 in a small shop in Islington, the company is now at 119–125 Charing Cross Road, which has an area of 75,825 square feet. The largest single display of books in one room in the world is in the Norrington Room at Blackwell's Bookshop, Oxford, England. This subterranean adjunct was opened on June 16, 1966, and contains 160,000 volumes on 2½ miles of shelving in 10,000 square feet of selling space.

Brewery

The oldest brewery is the Weihenstepan Brewery in Freising, near Munich, West Germany, founded in 1040.

The largest brewery is Anheuser-Busch, Inc. of St. Louis, Missouri. In 1971, the company sold 24,308,794 barrels, the greatest annual volume ever produced by a brewing company. The company's St. Louis plant covers 95 acres and has a capacity of 9,300,000 barrels.

The largest brewery in Europe is the Guinness Brewery at St. James's Gate, Dublin, Ireland, which extends over 58.03 acres. The business was founded in 1759. Arthur Guinness Son & Co., Ltd., is the largest exporter of beer, ale and stout in the world. Exports of Guinness from the Republic of Ireland in 1971 were 1,210,490 bulk barrels, which is equivalent to 1,915,501 half-pint glasses per day.

Brickworks

The largest brickworks in the world is the London Brick Company plant at Stewartby, Bedford, England. The works, established in 1898, now cover 221 acres and produce 17,000,000 bricks and brick equivalent every week.

Car Manufacturer

The largest car manufacturing company in the world (and largest manufacturer of any kind) is General Motors Corporation of Detroit. During its peak year of 1971 worldwide sales totaled $28,263,918,443, including 7,779,225 cars and trucks. Its assets at December 31, 1971, were valued at $18,241,900,040. Its total 1971 payroll was $8,015,071,514 to an average of 773,352 employees. The greatest total of dividends ever paid for one year was $1,509,740,939 by General Motors for 1965.

The largest single automobile plant in the world is the Volkswagen-werk, Wolfsburg, West Germany, with more than 60,000 employees turning out 5,000 cars daily. The surface area of the factory buildings is 353.5 acres and that of the whole plant 1,730 acres with 45 miles of rail sidings.

Chemical Company

The world's largest chemical company is Imperial Chemical Industries Ltd. (See *Greatest Assets*, page 223).

Chocolate Factory

The world's largest chocolate factory is that built by Hershey Foods, Inc. of Hershey, Pennsylvania, in 1905. In 1971, sales were $401,879,817 and the payroll was over 8,000 employees.

Department Stores

The largest department store chain, in terms of number of stores, is J. C. Penney Company, Inc., founded in Wyoming, in 1902. The company operates almost 2,000 retail units in the U.S., Belgium and Italy, with net selling space of 45,400,000 square feet. Its turnover was $4,812,238,548 in the year ending January 29, 1972, the sixteenth consecutive year of record sales.

LARGEST SINGLE CAR MANUFACTURING PLANT: The Volkswagenwerk in Wolfsburg, West Germany, covers 1,730 acres. Inside (right) the car's rear end is added to the chassis on a "merry-go-round."

Largest Single Store. The world's largest store is R. H. Macy & Co. Inc. at Broadway and 34th Street, New York City. It has a floor space of 46.2 acres, and 11,000 employees who handle 400,000 items. Macy's has an average of 150,000 customers a day who make 4,500,000 transactions a year. The sales of the company and its subsidiaries was $1,000,000,000 in 1971/72. Mr. Rowland Hussey Macy's sales on his first day at his fancy goods store on 6th Avenue, on October 27, 1858, were recorded as $11.06.

Most Profitable. The department store with the fastest-moving stock in the world is the Marble Arch store of Marks & Spencer Ltd. at 458 Oxford Street, London, England. The figure of more than $625-worth of goods per square foot of selling space per year is believed to have become an understatement when the selling area was raised to 72,000 square feet in October, 1970. The company has 250 branches in the U.K. and over 5,000,000 square feet of selling space.

Distillery

The world's largest distilling company is Distillers Corporation-Seagrams Limited of Canada. Its sales in the year ending July 31, 1971, totaled $1,512,246,000, of which $1,219,018,000 were from sales by Joseph E. Seagram & Sons, Inc. in the United States. The group employs about 15,000 people, including about 8,000 in the United States.

The largest of all Scotch whisky distilleries is Carsebridge at Alloa, Clackmannanshire, Scotland, owned by Scottish Grain Distillers Limited. This distillery is capable of producing more than 12,000,000 proof gallons per annum. The largest establishment for blending and bottling Scotch whisky is owned by John Walker & Sons Limited at Kilmarnock, Ayrshire, with a potential annual output of 120,000,000 bottles. "Johnnie Walker" is the world's largest-selling brand of Scotch whisky. The world's largest-selling brand of gin is Gordon's.

Drug Store Chain

The largest chain is that of Boots the Chemist, which has 1,400 retail branches. The firm was founded in England by Jesse Boot (1850–1931).

Fisheries

The highest recorded catch of fish was 59,540,000 long tons in 1967. The highest proportion of the world catch was that of Peru, with 17.4 per cent of the 1969 catch. The world's largest fishmongers are MacFisheries, a subsidiary of Unilever Ltd., England, with 303 retail outlets in March, 1972.

Games Manufacturer

The largest company manufacturing games is Parker Bros. Inc. of Salem, Massachusetts. The company's top-selling line is the real estate game "Monopoly," acquired in 1935. More than 65,000,000 sets were sold by January, 1972. The daily print of "money" is equivalent to 215,000,000 "dollars," thus exceeding the dollar output of the U.S. Treasury. The most protracted non-stop "Monopoly" session was one of $127\frac{1}{2}$ hours by four students of Dundee (Scotland) University in April, 1972.

General Merchandise

The largest general merchandising firm in the world is Sears, Roebuck and Co. (founded by Richard W. Sears in the Redwood North railroad station in Minnesota in 1886) of Chicago. The net sales were $10,006,145,548 in the year ending January 31, 1972, when the corporation had 864 retail stores and 2,507 catalogue, retail and telephone sales offices and total assets valued at $8,312,355,925.

Grocery Stores

The largest grocery chain in the world is The Great Atlantic and Pacific Tea Company, Inc., of New York City. On February 27, 1971, the company owned 4,427 stores, including more than 3,000 super-markets. It operates 24 bakeries plus laundries for the uniforms of its 115,000 employees. The total sales, including subsidiary companies, for the 52 weeks ending February 27, 1971, were $5,664,000,000.

Hotel Chain

The top revenue-earning hotel business is Holiday Inns, Inc., with 1971 revenues of $707,876,910 from 1,371 inns (200,464 rooms) in 21 countries. The business was founded by Charles Kemmons Wilson with his first inn on Summer Avenue in Memphis, Tennessee, in 1952.

The Hilton chain is the largest luxury hotel group in the world. Hilton Hotels Corporation operates 39 hotels, with 30,809 rooms, in continental U.S.A.; Hilton International Co. operates 54 hotels in 37 countries (51 cities), with 18,133 rooms. In 1971, Hilton Hotels Corporation had an operating revenue of more than $210,000,000 and 20,000 employees. Hilton International Co. had an operating revenue of $222,753,577 and 20,000 employees. In May, 1967, Hilton International Co. became a wholly-owned subsidiary of Trans World Airlines Inc., operated, however, by Hilton management. The original Hilton corporation was founded by Conrad Nicholson Hilton (born December 25, 1887) who started in 1919 in Cisco, Texas.

Insurance Company

The company with the highest volume of insurance in force in the world is the Prudential Insurance Company of America, with headquarters in Newark, New Jersey. The life insurance in force on January 1, 1971, was $91,119,263,748.

Largest Association. The largest single association in the world is the Blue Cross, the medical insurance organization with a membership at January 1, 1971, of 78,715,111. Benefits paid out exceeded $5,300,000,000.

Largest Life Policy. The largest life insurance policy ever written was one of $10,800,000 reported on March 18, 1969, as taken out on Michael Davis, 34, of Hollywood, California, who is chairman of NEBRA International, Inc., a chain of sandwich stands.

Marine Insurance. The greatest insured value of any ship lost has been $16,500,000 on the *Torrey Canyon* which was loaded with oil when it split apart in 1967. The Cunard liner *Queen Elizabeth 2* was insured on its sea trials in 1969 for $61,200,000.

High Life Insurance Pay-out. Mrs. Linda Mullendore, wife of a murdered Oklahoma rancher, is reported to have received $14,000,000 on November 14, 1970, the largest pay-out on a single life. Her husband paid $300,000 in premiums in 1969.

Mineral Water

The world's largest mineral water firm is Source Perrier near Nîmes, France, with an annual production of more than 1,400,000,000 bottles, of which more than 330,000,000 come from the single spring near Nîmes. The net profits for 1971 were $5,340,000. The French drink 40 liters of mineral water per person per year.

Oil Company and Refinery

The world's largest oil company is the Standard Oil Company (New Jersey), with 143,000 employees and assets valued at

LARGEST OIL REFINERY: With a distilling capacity of 25,000,000 long tons per year, the Pernis Refinery and chemical plant belonging to Shell has a waterfront nearly 4 miles long, with 29 jetties.

$20,315,249,000 on January 1, 1972. The world's largest refinery is the Pernis Refinery, Netherlands, operated by the Royal Dutch/Shell Group with a capacity of 25,000,000 long tons annually.

Paper Mill

The world's largest paper mill is that established in 1936 by the Union Camp Corporation at Savannah, Georgia, with an output of 903,124 tons.

Popcorn Plant

The largest popcorn plant is Clarks Cereal Products Ltd. of Dagenham, Essex, England (instituted in 1933), which in 1971–72 produced an unrivaled 21,000,000 packets of "Butter Kist."

Public Relations

The world's largest public relations firm is Hill and Knowlton, Inc. of 150 East 42nd Street, New York City. The firm employs a full-time staff of more than 325 and also maintains offices of wholly-owned subsidiary companies in Brussels, Frankfurt, Geneva, London, Paris, Milan, Rome and Tokyo.

Publishing

The publishing company generating most revenue is Time, Inc., of New York City with $606,800,000 in 1971, of which $130,000,000 came from *Time* magazine.

Restaurant Chain

The largest restaurant chain is that operated by F. W. Woolworth and Co., with 2,074 (mostly lunch counters) in six countries.

Shipbuilding

In 1968 there were 24,859,701 gross tons of ships, excluding sailing ships, barges, and vessels of less than 100 tons launched throughout the world, excluding the U.S.S.R. and China (mainland). Japan launched 11,992,495 gross tons (48.2 per cent of the world's total), the greatest tonnage launched in peacetime by any single country.

The world's leading shipbuilding firm in 1971 was the Ishikawa-jima-Harima Co. of Japan, which launched 49 ships of 2,229,128 gross tons from five shipyards.

Shipping Line

The largest shipping group in the world is the Royal Dutch/Shell Group, which on March 31, 1972, owned and managed 189 ships of 10,215,001 deadweight tons and had on charter 251 ships of 16,989,254 deadweight tons. Many of the vessels of the combined fleet of 440 ships of 27,204,255 d.w.t. were mammoth tankers.

Shoe Shop

The largest shoe shop in the world is that of Lilley & Skinner, Ltd. at 356/360 Oxford Street, London, W.1. The shop has a floor area of 76,000 square feet, spread over four floors. With a total staff of more than 350 people it offers, in ten departments, a choice of 250,000 pairs of shoes. Every week, on average, over 45,000 people visit this store.

Shopping Center

The world's largest shopping center is the Lakewood (Calif.) Shopping Center, built on a 165-acre site with parking for 12,500 cars. The total selling space is 2,191,000 square feet (50.2 acres). The Center has 140 stores and services and a mall 2,640 feet in length. The Woodfield Shopping Center in Schaumburg, Illinois, when completed in September, 1973, will have 2,203,454 square feet of selling space on its current 191-acre site.

LARGEST PAPER MILL: The Union Camp Corporation's plant in Savannah, Georgia.

LARGEST STEEL MILL: Bethlehem's plant at Sparrows Point, Maryland, has a 9,000,000-ton annual capacity.

Soft Drinks

The world's top-selling soft drink is Coca-Cola with over 110,000,000 bottles per day at the end of 1971 in more than 130 countries. "Coke" was invented by Dr. John S. Pemberton of Atlanta, Georgia, in 1886, and the company was formed in 1892. The fastest bottling line is the plant at Tama, Tokyo, Japan, which can fill, crown and pack bottles of Coca-Cola at the rate of 90,000 per hour.

Steel Company

The world's largest steel company is the United States Steel Company, with headquarters in Pittsburgh, with sales of $4,963,200,000 in 1971. The company had an average of 183,940 employees in 1971, and net assets valued at $5,282,800,000 on December 31, 1971. The largest producer of steel by weight is Japan's largest company, Nippon Steel Corp., whose sales were $3,750,000,000.

The largest steelworks in the world is the Bethlehem Steel Corporation's plant at Sparrows Point, Maryland, with an annual ingot steel capacity of more than 9,000,000 tons.

Tobacco Company

The world's largest tobacco company is the British-American Tobacco Company Ltd. (founded 1902), of London. The group's assets were £832,800,000 ($2,082,000,000) at September 30, 1971. Sales for 1970–71 were £1,632,640,000 ($4,081,600,000). The group has more than 140 factories and 120,000 employees.

Toy Manufacturer

The largest toy manufacturer is Mattel, Inc. of Hawthorne, California, founded in 1945. Its sales in 1971 were $272,358,000.

Toy Store

The world's biggest toy store is F.A.O. Schwarz, 745 Fifth Avenue at 58th Street, New York City, with 50,000 square feet on three floors; also 16 branch stores with a further 150,000 square feet.

Wine Company

The oldest champagne firm is Ruinart Père et Fils, founded in 1729. The oldest cognac firm is Augier Frères & Cie., established in 1643.

LAND

The world's largest land owner is the United States Government, with a holding of 761,301,000 acres (1,189,000 square miles), including 527,000 acres outside the U.S. The total value at cost was $78,813,000,000.

Land Values

Highest. Currently the most expensive land in the world is that in the City of London. Prime freehold attained £500 ($1,250) per square foot in mid-1972. The 600-foot National Westminster Bank on a 2¼-acre site off Bishopsgate will become the world's highest valued building. At rents of £10 ($25) per square foot on 500,000 net square feet and on 18-year purchase, it will, by 1972, be worth £90,000,000 ($225,000,000). The value of the whole site of 6½ acres will be £225,000,000 ($562,500,000).

On February 1, 1926, a parcel of land of 1,275 square feet on Wall Street, New York City, was bought by the One Wall Street Realty Corporation for $1,000 per square foot.

In February, 1964, a woman paid $510 for a triangular piece of land measuring 3 inches by 6½ inches by 5¾ inches at a tax lien auction in North Hollywood, California—equivalent to $365,182,470 per acre.

The real estate value per square meter of the four topmost French vineyards has not been recently estimated.

Lowest. The historic example of low land values is the Alaska Purchase of March 30, 1867, when William Henry Seward (1801–72), the Secretary of State, agreed that the U.S. should buy the whole territory from the Russian Government of Czar Alexander II for $7,200,000, equivalent to 1.9 cents per acre. When Willem Verhulst (c. 1580–1638) bought Manhattan Island, New York, before June, 1626, by paying the Brooklyn Indians (Canarsees) with trinkets and cloth valued at 60 guilders (equivalent to $39), he was buying land now worth up to $425 per square foot for 0.2 of a cent per acre—a capital appreciation of 9,000,000,000-fold.

Greatest Auction

The greatest auction ever was that at Anchorage, Alaska, on September 11, 1969, for 179 tracts of 450,858 acres of the oil-bearing

North Slope, Alaska. An all-time record bid of $72,277,133 for a 2,560-acre lease was made by the Amerada Hess Corporation-Getty Oil consortium. The bid indicated a price of $28,233 per acre.

Highest Rent. The highest recorded rentals are about £17 ($42.50) per square foot for office accommodation in the prime areas of the City of London in mid-1972.

Most Directorships

A London real estate financier named Harry O. Jasper set a record for directorships in September, 1959, with 451. If he had attended all the annual directors' meetings, this would have involved him, in normal business hours, in one every 4 hours 33 minutes.

STOCK EXCHANGES

The oldest Stock Exchange in the world is that in Amsterdam, in the Netherlands, founded in 1602. There were 126 throughout the world as of June 13, 1972.

Highest and Lowest Values

The highest price quoted was for a share of F. Hoffmann-La Roche of Basel, Switzerland, at £17,250 ($43,125). The lowest price was one penny (2½ cents) for a share of each of the following: City of San Paolo Improvements, Freehold Land Co. Ltd., and Acorn Securities Co. Ltd. All quotations are from London trading.

New York Stock Exchange Records

The highest index figure on the Dow Jones average (instituted October 8, 1896) of selected industrial stocks at the close of a day's trading was 995.15 on February 9, 1966, when the average of the daily "highs" of the 30 component stocks was 1,001.11.

The old record trading volume in a day on the New York Stock Exchange of 16,410,030 shares on October 29, 1929, the "Black Tuesday" of the famous "crash" was not surpassed until the first 20-million-share day (20,410,000) was achieved on April 10, 1968, and the ticker tape fell 47 minutes behind.

The Dow Jones industrial average, which had reached 381.17 on September 3, 1929, plunged 48.31 points in the day, on its way to the Depression's lowest point of 41.22 on July 8, 1932. The total lost in security values was $125,000 million. World trade slumped 57 per cent from 1929 to 1936.

The greatest paper loss in a year was $62,884,000,000 in 1969.

The record daily increase of 28.40 on October 30, 1929, was beaten on August 16, 1971, when the index increased 32.93 points. The day's trading was also a record 31,730,960 shares.

The largest transaction on record "share-wise" was on March 14, 1972, for 5,245,000 shares of American Motors at $7.25 each.

The record dollar value for one block was $76,135,026 for 730,312 shares of American Standard Class A Preferred shares at $104.25 a share.

The largest deal "value-wise" was for two 2,000,000 blocks of Greyhound shares at $20 each sold to Goldman Sachs and Saloman Brothers.

Largest Issue

The largest security offering in history was one of $1,375,000,000 in American Telephone and Telegraph Company stock in a rights offer on 27,500,000 shares of convertible preferred stock on June 2, 1971.

Greatest Appreciation

It is impossible to state categorically which shares have enjoyed the greatest appreciation in value. Spectacular "growth stocks" include the International Business Machines Corporation (IBM), in which 100 shares, costing $5,250 in July, 1932, grew to 13,472 shares with a market value of $4,230,000 on March 28, 1969. In addition, $233,100 were paid in dividends. The greatest aggregate market value of any corporation is $35.5 billion assuming the closing price of $314 for IBM multiplied by the 113,116,613 shares extant on March 28, 1969.

Largest Investment House

The largest investment company in the world, and also once the world's largest partnership (124 partners, and 61,200 stockholders at the end of 1971), is Merrill Lynch, Pierce, Fenner & Smith, Inc. (founded January 6, 1914, went public in 1971) of New York City. It has 21,177 employees, 273 offices and 1,800,000 separate accounts. The firm is referred to as "We, the people" or "The Thundering Herd." The company's assets totaled $2,867,558,000 on December 31, 1971.

Largest Bank

The International Bank for Reconstruction and Development (founded December 27, 1945), the United Nations "World Bank" at 1818 H Street N.W., Washington, D.C., has an authorized share capital of $27,000 million. There were 117 members with a

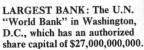

LARGEST BANK: The U.N. "World Bank" in Washington, D.C., which has an authorized share capital of $27,000,000,000.

subscribed capital of $24,046,300,000 on January 1, 1972. The International Monetary Fund in Washington, D.C., has 120 members with total quotas of $28,807,800,000 on February 29, 1972.

The private bank with the greatest deposits is the Bank of America National Trust and Savings Association, of San Francisco, with $29,073,301,000 on December 31, 1971. Its total resources on that date were $33,985,906,000.

The bank with the most branches internationally is Barclays Bank of England (with Barclays Bank International and other subsidiary companies) with nearly 5,000 branches in 40 countries (over 3,150 in the U.K.) at the end of 1971.

Largest Bank Building

The largest bank building in the world is the 813-foot-tall Chase Manhattan Building, completed in May, 1961, in New York City. It has 64 stories and contains the largest bank vault in the world, measuring 350 feet × 100 feet × 8 feet and weighing 879 tons. Its six doors weigh up to 40 tons apiece, but each can be closed by the pressure of a forefinger.

The First National Bank of Chicago building is 60 stories and 850 feet tall.

MANUFACTURED ARTICLES

Largest Antique

The largest antique ever sold has been the London Bridge in March, 1968. The sale was made by Ivan F. Luckin of the Court of Common Council of the Corporation of London to the McCulloch Corporation of Los Angeles, California, for $2,460,000. Over 10,000 tons of elevational stonework were re-assembled at Lake Havasu City, Arizona, and "re-dedicated" on October 10, 1971.

Armor

The highest price paid for a suit of armor is £25,000 ($125,000) paid in 1924 for the Pembroke suit of armor, made in the 16th century for the Earl of Pembroke.

Largest Beds

In Bruges, Belgium, Philip, Duke of Burgundy, had a bed 12½ feet wide and 19 feet long erected for the perfunctory *coucher officiel* ceremony with Princess Isabella of Portugal in 1430. The largest bed in existence is the Great Bed of Ware, dating from *c.* 1580, from the Crown Inn, Ware, Hertfordshire, England, now preserved in the Victoria and Albert Museum, London. It is 10 feet 8½ inches wide, 11 feet 1 inch long and 8 feet 9 inches tall. The largest standard bed currently marketed is the London Bedding Centre's "King Size" bed, 7 feet wide by 7 feet long, with 1,600 springs, sold for £170 ($425).

The most massive beds are waterbeds, which first became a vogue in California in 1970, when merchandised by Michael V. Zamaro, 53. When filled with water, king-sized versions measuring 8 feet square weigh 1,568 lbs. and are advisedly used on the ground floor.

Stuffed Bird

The highest price ever paid for a stuffed bird is £9,000 ($23,400). This was given in 1972 in the salesrooms of Sotheby & Co., London, by the Iceland Natural History Museum for a specimen of the Great Auk (*Alca impennis*) in summer plumage, which was taken in Iceland *c*. 1821; this particular specimen stood 22½ inches high. The Great Auk was a flightless North Atlantic seabird, which was finally exterminated on Eldey, Iceland, in 1844, becoming extinct through hunting.

Candle

The biggest candle is Western Candle Co.'s 50-foot-high, 18-foot-diameter candle alongside U.S. Highway 30, near Scappoose, Oregon, erected on May 9, 1971.

Carpets and Rugs

Earliest. The earliest carpet known (and still in existence) is a white bordered black hair pelt from Pazyryk, U.S.S.R., dated to the 5th century B.C. now preserved in Leningrad. Of ancient carpets the largest on record was the gold-enriched silk carpet of Hashim (dated 743 A.D.) of the Abbasid caliphate in Baghdad, Iraq. It is reputed to have measured 180 feet by 300 feet.

Largest. The world's largest carpet now consists of 88,000 square feet (over two acres) of maroon carpeting in the Coliseum exhibition hall, Columbus Circle, New York City. This was first used for the International Automobile Show on April 28, 1956.

Most Expensive. The most magnificent carpet ever made was the Spring carpet of Khusraw made for the audience hall of the Sassanian palace at Ctesiphon, Iraq. It was about 7,000 square feet of silk and gold thread, encrusted with emeralds. It was cut up as booty by a Persian army in 635 A.D. and from the known realization value of the pieces must have had an original value of some $200,000,000.

It was reported in March, 1968, that a 16th-century Persian silk hunting carpet was sold "recently" to an undisclosed U.S. museum by a member of the Rothschild family for "about $600,000."

Most Finely Woven. The most finely woven carpet known is one with more than 2,490 knots per square inch from a fragment of an Imperial Mughal prayer carpet of the 17th century, now in the Altman collections in the Metropolitan Museum of Art, New York City.

Chair

The largest chair is claimed to be an American ladderback, located outside the Hayes and Kane furniture store, Bennington, Vermont, which is 19 feet 1 inch tall and weighs 2,200 lbs.

Christmas Present

The most expensive Christmas present listed in any store's catalogue was in the 1971 Neiman-Marcus, Dallas, Texas, offering a vehicle called a "Fortress of the Freeway" for $845,300. This Total Transportational Security Environment features anti-theft device hood ornament, closed-circuit dual-lens infrared scanning camera, infrared periscope, 360° vision indestructible cockpit bubble, telephoto periscope, radar, dual-exhaust anti-pollution device, highway signal markers, signals "Stop"—"Too Close," marine prop, retractable tires, tank tracks, loudspeakers to warn off passing motorists, multilevel terrain stabilizer, safety air bumpers and padded safety bumpers—absolutely one of a kind.

Cigars

Largest and Most Expensive. The largest cigar in existence is one 5 feet 4½ inches long and 10½ inches in circumference, made by Abraham & Gluckstein, London, England, and now housed at the Northumbrian University Air Squadron.

The largest standard brand of cigar in the world is the 9¾-inch-long "Partagas Visible Immensas." The Partagas factory in Havana, Cuba, manufactures special gift cigars 19.7 inches long for gift purposes, which retail in Europe for more than $12 each, making them also the most expensive cigars.

Most Voracious Smoker. The only man to master the esoteric art of smoking 13 full-size cigars while simultaneously whistling, talking and giving bird imitations is Simon Argevitch of Oakland, California. He performed his feat in 1972 before a national television audience on the Johnny Carson show.

Cigarettes

Consumption. The heaviest smokers in the world are the people of the U.S. where about 533,000 million cigarettes (an average of nearly 4,000 per adult) were consumed at a cost of more than $10,000,000,000 in 1971.

Most Expensive. The most expensive cigarettes in the world are the gold-tipped "Royal Dragoons," made by Simon Arzt of Cairo, in the United Arab Republic (formerly Egypt). They have been retailed in Europe for more than 12 cents each.

Most Popular. The world's most popular cigarette is "Winston," a filter cigarette made by the R. J. Reynolds Tobacco Co., which sold 82,000 million of them in 1969.

Longest and Shortest. The longest cigarettes ever marketed were "Head Plays," each 11 inches long and sold in packets of five in the U.S. in about 1930, to save tax. The shortest were "Lilliput" cigarettes, each 1¼ inches long, made in Great Britain in 1956.

Largest Collection. The world's largest collection of cigarettes is that of Robert E. Kaufman, M.D., of 950 Park Avenue, New York City 10028. In March, 1972, he had 6,404 different brands of cigarettes from 159 countries. The oldest brand represented is "Lone Jack," made in the U.S. in c. 1885. Both the longest and shortest (see above) are represented. (See photograph.)

Cigarette Packs. The world's largest collection of cigarette packs is that of Niels Ventegodt of Copenhagen, Denmark. He had 46,188 different packets from 202 countries by March, 1972. The countries supplying the largest numbers were the United Kingdom

LARGEST CIGARETTE COLLECTION: Dr. Robert E. Kaufman of New York (left) shows some of the 6,404 different brands he owns. He has cigarettes from 159 countries. RAREST PACK is the Riga packet (right) celebrating the 700th anniversary of that Latvian city.

(6,258) and the United States (3,734). The earliest is the Finnish "Petit Cannon" packet for 25, made by Tollander & Klärich in 1860. The rarest is the Latvian 700-year-anniversary (1201–1901) Riga packet, believed to be unique.

Cigarette Cards. The earliest known and most valuable cigarette card is that bearing the portrait of the Marquess of Lorne published in the United States *c.* 1879. The only known specimen is in the Metropolitan Museum of Art, New York City.

The earliest dated cigarette cards were those of the four U.S. Presidential candidates of 1880, produced by Thomas H. Hall of New York City. The most expensive card is the John Peter ("Honus") Wagner card in the American Tobacco Co. Baseball Player series of 1912, withdrawn because Wagner was opposed to smoking. Examples are now worth $250.

Earliest Abstention. The earliest recorded case of a man giving up smoking was on April 5, 1679, when Johan Kastu, Sheriff of Turku, Finland, wrote in his diary "I quit smoking tobacco." He died one month later.

Clock

The highest price ever paid for a clock was £16,800 ($43,680) for a longcase or Grandfather clock at the London Salesrooms of Christie, Manson & Woods on March 16, 1972. The clock, made in England by Joseph Knibb, *c.* 1675, has a walnut case and stands 6 feet 5 inches high. It was purchased by Ronald A. Lee, a London dealer.

LARGEST FIREWORKS (left): Bouquet of Chrysanthemums is the name given to this Japanese-made display which is fired 3,000 feet in the air from a 36-inch caliber mortar. LARGEST FLAG (right): Displayed annually on the Woodward Avenue side of J. L. Hudson's store in Detroit, it is 104 feet by 235 feet and weighs 1,500 lbs.

Finest Cloth

The finest of all cloths is Shahtoosh (or Shatusa), a brown-gray wool from the throats of Indian goats. It is sold by Neiman-Marcus of Dallas, at $18.50 per square foot and is both more expensive and finer than vicuña. A simple hostess gown in Shahtoosh costs up to $5,000.

Largest Curtain

The largest curtain ever built was the bright orange 4-ton 250,000-square-foot curtain suspended across the Rifle Gap, Grand Hogback, Colorado, by the Bulgarian-born sculptor Christo, 36 (né Javacheff) in the summer of 1971.

Dinner Service

The highest price ever paid for a silver dinner service is $579,600 for the Berkeley Louis XV Service of 168 pieces, made by Jacques Roettiers between 1736 and 1738, sold at the salesrooms of Sotheby & Co., London, in June, 1960.

Most Expensive Fabric

The most expensive fabric obtainable is an evening-wear fabric 40 inches wide, hand embroidered and sequinned on a pure silk ground in a classical flower pattern. It has 194,400 tiny sequins per yard, and is designed by Alan Hershman of London; it costs $260 per yard.

Largest Fireworks

The most powerful firework obtainable is the Bouquet of Chrysanthemums *hanabi*, marketed by the Marutamaya Ogatsu Fireworks Co. Ltd., of Tokyo, Japan. It is fired to a height of over 3,000 feet from a 36-inch caliber mortar. Their chrysanthemum and peony flower shells produce a spherical flower with "twice-thrice changing colors," 2,000 feet in diameter. (See photograph.)

Flags

Largest. The largest flag in the world is the Stars and Stripes displayed annually on the Woodward Avenue side of the J. L. Hudson main store in Detroit. The flag, 104 feet by 235 feet and weighing 1,500 lbs., was unfurled on June 14, 1949. The 50 stars are each 5½ feet high and each stripe is 8 feet wide. It is displayed every Flag Day (June 14). (See photo.)

Oldest. The oldest national flag in the world is that of Denmark (a large white cross on a red field), known as the Dannebrog ("Danish Cloth"), dating from 1219, adopted after the Battle of Lindanissa in Estonia, now part of the U.S.S.R. The crest in the center of the Austrian flag has its origins in the 11th century. The origins of the Iranian flag, with its sword-carrying lion and sun are obscure, but "go beyond the 12th century."

Largest Float

The largest float used in any street carnival is the 200-foot-long dragon *Sun Loon* used in Bendigo, Victoria, Australia. It has 65,000 mirror scales. Six men are needed to carry its head alone.

Most Expensive Fur Coats

The most expensive fur coats are made of solid white and solid black chinchilla mutations, sea otter or mink-sable cross breeds. In February, 1969, single pelts of the last named realized $2,700 at auction.

Most Expensive Furniture

The highest price ever paid for a single piece of furniture is 165,000 guineas ($415,800) at auction at Christie's, London, on June 24, 1971, for a Louis XVI *bureau plat* (writing table) by Martin Carlin in 1778 which once belonged to the Grand Duchess (later Czarina) Marie-Feodorovna of Russia in 1784. It was sold by the estate of Mrs. Anna Thompson Dodge (widow of Horace Dodge, the car manufacturer) and bought by Henri Sabet of Teheran, Iran. It is 51½ inches wide, 24½ inches deep and 30 inches high in veneered pale tulipwood with a tooled and gilded black leather top. It is decorated with 14 Sèvres porcelain plaques in ormolu frames. The price paid was more than twice the previous world record price.

Gold Plate

The world's highest auction price for a single piece of gold plate is £40,000 ($112,000) for a 20-oz. George II teapot made by James Ker for the King's Plate horserace for 100 guineas at Leith, Scotland, in 1736. The sale was by Christie's of London on December 13, 1967, to a dealer from Boston, Massachusetts.

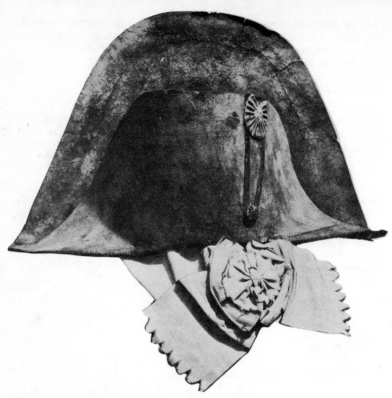

Most Expensive Hat

The highest price ever paid for a hat is 165,570 francs (including tax) ($29,471) at an auction by Maitres Liery, Rheims et Laurin, France, on April 23, 1970, for one last worn by Emperor Napoleon I (1769–1821) on January 1, 1815. It was bought by Moet et Chandon, a champagne house. (See photo.)

Most Expensive Jade

The highest price ever paid for jade was £42,000 ($117,600) for four Imperial spinach-green jade screens measuring 24½ × 13 inches each from the Summer Palace, Peking, China, sold at the salesrooms of Christie, Manson & Woods, London, on July 16, 1963. The screens were emblematic of the Four Seasons.

Largest Jig-Saw Puzzle

The largest jig-saw puzzle ever made is believed to be one of 10,400 pieces, measuring 15 feet by 10 feet, made in 1954, at the special request of a man in Texas, by Panda Puzzle Products, Ltd., of St. Leonards-on-Sea, Sussex, England.

Knife with Most Blades

The penknife with the greatest number of blades is the Year Knife made by the world's oldest firm of cutlers, Joseph Rodgers & Sons

Ltd., of Sheffield, England, whose trademark was granted in 1682. The knife was built in 1822 with 1,822 blades, but now has 1,972, and will continue to match the year of the Christian era until 2000 A.D., beyond which there will be no further space.

Matchbox Labels

The oldest matchbox label is that of John Walker, Stockton-on-Tees, County Durham, England, in 1827. Collectors of labels are phillumenists, of bookmatch covers philliberumenists, and of matchboxes cumyxaphists. The world's longest and perhaps dullest set is one in the U.S.S.R. comprising 600 variations on interior views of the Moscow Metro.

Longest Menu

The restaurant with the world's longest menu is Oskar Davidsen's in Copenhagen, Denmark. The menu, which lists 177 dishes, is 3 feet 9½ inches long.

Sheerest Nylon

The lowest denier nylon yarn ever produced is the 6-denier used for stockings exhibited at the Nylon Fair in London in February, 1956. The sheerest stockings normally available are 9 denier. An indication of the thickness is that a hair from the average human head is about 50 denier.

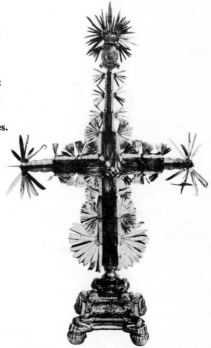

MOST-BLADED KNIFE: The Year Knife now has 1,972 blades. It was built in 1822 with 1,822 blades, and each year another blade was added. After the year 2000 there will be no more space for new blades.

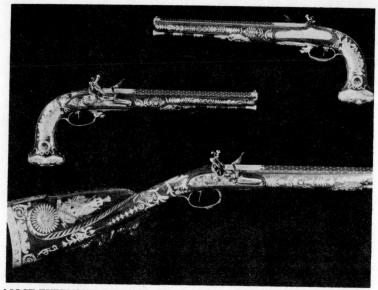

MOST EXPENSIVE PISTOLS: These pistols and the matching rifle were sold at auction for $103,320 in London in 1970. They had been made for Napoleon.

Paperweight

The highest price ever paid for a paperweight is £8,500 ($20,040) at Sotheby & Co., London, England, on March 16, 1970, for a Clichy Lily-of-the-Valley weight.

Most Expensive Pipe

The most expensive smoker's pipe is the Charatan *Summa cum Laude* straight-grain briar root pipe available in limited number in New York City at $2,500.

Longest Pipe

In the Braunschweig Museum, Germany, there is exhibited an outsize late 19th century pipe, 15 feet in length, the bowl of which can accommodate 3 lbs. of tobacco. (See photo.)

Most Expensive Pistols

The highest price ever paid for a pair of pistols at auction is £43,050 ($103,320) bought together with a matching rifle at the salesrooms of Christie, Manson and Woods, Ltd., London, on July 8, 1970. They were bought by Frank Partridge & Sons, Ltd., London, and date from between 1798 and 1809. The three pieces were made by Nicolas Boutet of Versailles, France, who was gunsmith to Emperor Napoleon I. (See photograph.)

Porcelain and Pottery

The highest price ever paid at auction for a single piece of porcelain is £220,500 ($573,300) at the salesrooms of Christie's,

London, on June 5, 1972, for a 14th-century Chinese porcelain wine jar in blue and white with a red underglaze decoration, 13½ inches high, previously used as an umbrella stand. It was bought by a Japanese dealer.

The most priceless example of the occidental ceramic art is usually regarded as the Portland Vase which dates from late in the first century B.C. or 1st century A.D. It was made in Italy and was in the possession of the Barberini family in Rome from at least 1642. It was eventually bought by the Duchess of Portland in 1792, but smashed while in the British Museum in 1847.

Largest Rope

The largest rope ever made was a coir fiber launching rope with a circumference of 47 inches, made in 1858 for the British liner *Great Eastern* by John and Edwin Wright. It consisted of four strands, each of 3,780 yards.

Most Expensive Shoes

The most expensive standard shoes obtainable are the shawl-tongued custom golf shoes, Style 5591, made by Brockton Footwear, Inc. of Massachusetts, which retail for $220 per pair.

The largest shoes ever sold, excluding those made for cases of elephantiasis, are a pair of size 42 built for the giant, Harley Davidson, of Avon Park, Florida.

LONGEST PIPE: Preserved in Germany, this 15-foot-long specimen holds 3 lbs. of tobacco in its bowl.

HIGHEST-PRICED SILVER: This unique silver ink stand belonged to Charles I, was hallmarked for 1639, and sold at auction on July 1, 1970, for £78,000 ($187,200) at Cristie's of London. It weighs 172 oz. and had previously been sold at Christie's in 1893 for £446 (about $2,230).

Silver

The highest price ever paid for any kind of silver is $187,200.00 at the salesrooms of Christie, Manson and Woods, Ltd., London, on July 1, 1970, for a unique silver Charles I ink stand hallmarked for 1639 weighing 172 oz.

English Silver. The highest price for English silver is £56,000 ($134,400) paid by the London dealer, Wartski, for the Brownlow James II Tankards at Christie's, London, on November 20, 1968. This pair, made in 1686, was in mint condition and weighed nearly 7½ lbs.

Snuff Box

The highest price ever paid for a snuff box is the 825,570 francs ($148,600) given in a sale in 1972, held by Maîtres Ader and Picard at the Palais Galliera in Paris for a gold and lapis-lazuli example by J. A. Meissonnier (d. 1750), dated Paris 1728. This is the only signed example of a snuff box by Meissonnier to have survived although he is known to have been one of the most patronized of French 18th-century goldsmiths. It was made for Marie-Anne de Vaviere-Neubourg, wife of Charles II of Spain. It measures 84 × 29 millimeters and was put up for sale by the estate of D. David Weill. It was purchased by the London dealer, Wartski of Regent Street.

Apostle Spoons

The highest price ever paid for a set of 13 apostle spoons is $30,000, paid by the Clark Institute of Williamstown, Massachusetts. There are only six other complete sets known.

Sword

The highest price recorded for a European sword is £21,000 ($50,400) paid at Sotheby & Co., London, on March 23, 1970, for a swept-hilt rapier 48½ inches long, made by Israel Schuech in 1606 probably for Elector Christian II or Duke Johann Georg of Saxony. The hilt is inset with pearls and semi-precious stones. It should be noted that prices as high as £60,000 ($150,000) have been reported in Japan for important swords by master Japanese swordsmiths, such as the incomparable 13th-century master Masamune.

Tapestry

Earliest. The earliest known examples of tapestry-woven linen are three pieces from the tomb of Thutmose IV, the Egyptian pharaoh, which date to 1483 to 1411 B.C.

Most Expensive. The highest price paid for a set of tapestries is £200,000 ($560,000) for four Louis XV pieces at Sotheby & Co., London, on December 8, 1967.

Largest. The largest single piece of tapestry ever woven is "Christ in Glory," measuring 74 feet 8 inches by 38 feet, designed by Graham Vivian Sutherland (b. August 24, 1903), for an altar hanging in Coventry Cathedral, Warwickshire, England. It cost $29,400 and was delivered from Pinton Frères of Felletin, France, on March 1, 1962.

Longest. The longest of all antique tapestries is Queen Matilda of England's famous Bayeux tapestry of embroidery, a hanging 19½ inches wide by 231 feet in length. It depicts events of the period 1064–66 in 72 scenes and was probably worked in Canterbury, Kent, in c. 1086. It was "lost" from 1476 until 1724.

Tablecloth

The world's largest tablecloth is one 60 yards long by 2¼ yards wide woven in linen in Belfast, Northern Ireland, in January, 1972, for King Bhumibol of Thailand, whose titles include Brother of the Moon and Half-Brother of the Sun.

Earliest Tartan

The earliest evidence of tartan is the so-called Failkirk tartan, found stuffed in a jar of coins in Bells Meadow, north of Callendar Park, Scotland. It is a dark and light brown pattern and dates from c. 245 A.D. The earliest reference to a specific named tartan has been to a Murray tartan in 1618.

Teapot

The largest recorded teapot is one of 9 Imperial gallons capacity (290 cups) with a girth of 4 feet 9½ inches, weighing 47 lbs., made at Corsham, Wiltshire, England, in July, 1971.

Most Expensive Vase

The highest price ever paid for a vase is 23,000,000 yen ($65,712), obtained by Sotheby & Co. of London, England, at a sale held at the department store of Mitsukoshi in Tokyo, Japan, on October 2, 1969. This was for a 16th century Chinese Kinrade double-gourd green and orange vase 15½ inches tall.

Largest Wig

The largest wig yet made is that made by Jean Leonard, owner of a salon in Copenhagen, Denmark. It is intended for bridal occasions, is made from 24 tresses, measures nearly 8 feet in length and costs $1,000.

Wreaths

The most expensive wreath on record was that sent to the funeral of President Kennedy in Washington, D.C. on November 25, 1963, by the civic authority of Paris. It was handled by Interflora Inc. and cost $1,200. The only rival was a floral tribute sent to the Mayor of Moscow in 1970 by Umberto Farmichello, general manager of Interflora, which is never slow to scent an opportunity. The largest wreath on record is a Christmas wreath 61 feet 4 inches in diameter, weighing 750 lbs., built for the Park Plaza, Oshkosh, Wisconsin, in November, 1971.

Writing Paper

The most expensive writing paper in the world is that sold by Cartier, Inc., on Fifth Avenue, New York City at $1,904 per 100 sheets with envelopes. It is of handmade paper from Finland with deckle edges and a "personalized" portrait watermark.

2. Agriculture

Origins. It has been estimated that only 21 per cent of the world's land surface is cultivatable and that only two-fifths of this is cultivated. The earliest attested evidence of cultivated grain is that from Jarmo, Iraq, dated *c.* 6750 B.C. The earliest evidence of animal husbandry comes from sheep at Zawi Chemi Shanidar, Iraq, dating from *c.* 8800 B.C. The order in which animals have been domesticated appears to be: sheep (*c.* 8800 B.C.); dog (*c.* 7700 B.C. in Yorkshire, England); goats (at Jarmo and Jericho, *c.* 6500 B.C.); pigs (at Jarmo, *c.* 6500 B.C.) and cattle (at Banahilk, northern Iraq, before 5000 B.C.). Reindeer may have been domesticated as early as *c.* 18,000 B.C., but definite evidence is lacking.

Farms

The largest farms in the world are collective farms in the U.S.S.R. These have been reduced in number from 235,500 in 1940 to only 39,000 in 1969, and have been increased in size so that units of over 60,000 acres are not uncommon.

Largest Wheat Field. The world's largest single wheat field was probably one of more than 35,000 acres, sown in 1951 near Lethbridge, Alberta, Canada.

LARGEST MUSHROOM FARM is a disused limestone mine in Pennsylvania. A trailer train is used to carry trays of mushroom spawn to their growing areas.

Largest Hop Field. The largest hop field in the world is one of 710 acres at Toppenish, Washington, owned by John I. Haas, Inc., the world's largest hop growers, with hop farms in British Columbia (Canada), California, Idaho, Oregon and Washington, with a total net area of 3,065 acres.

Largest Cattle Station. The world's largest cattle station was Alexandria Station, Northern Territory, Australia, selected in 1873 by Robert Collins, who rode 1,600 miles to reach it. It now has 66 wells, a staff of 90 and originally extended over 7,207,608 acres. The present area is 6,500 square miles which is stocked with 58,000 shorthorn cattle. Until 1915 the Victoria River Downs Station, Northern Territory, was over three times larger, with an area of 22,400,000 acres (35,000 square miles).

Largest Sheep Station. The largest sheep station in the world is Commonwealth Hill, in the northwest of South Australia. It grazes between 70,000 and 90,000 sheep in an area of 3,640 square miles (2,329,600 acres). The largest sheep move on record occurred when 27 horsemen moved a mob of 43,000 sheep 40 miles from Barealdine to Beaconsfield Station, Queensland, Australia, in 1886.

Mushroom Farm. The largest mushroom farm in the world is Butler County Mushroom Farm, Inc., founded in 1937 in a disused limestone mine near West Winfield, Pennsylvania. It has 900 employees working underground, in a maze of galleries 110 miles long, producing about 32,000,000 lbs. of mushrooms per year.

Crop Yields

Wheat. Crop yields for highly tended small areas are of little significance. The greatest recorded wheat yield is 169.9 bushels (91 cwts.) per acre from 27.7 acres in 1964 by Yoshino Brothers Farms at Quincy, Washington.

Barley. A yield of 69¾ cwt. per acre of variety Pallas was reported in 1962 from a field of 20 acres by Col. K. C. Lee of Blaco Hill Farm, Mattersey, Doncaster, Yorkshire, England.

Potato. In 1968 it was reported that Tom Cooke of Funtington, West Sussex, England, dug 1,190 lbs. 10 oz. of potatoes from six seed potatoes.

Dimensions and Prolificacy

Cattle. Of heavyweight cattle the heaviest on record was a Hereford-Shorthorn named "Old Ben," owned by Mike and John Murphy of Miami, Indiana. When he died at the age of 8, in February, 1910, he had attained a length of 16 feet 2 inches from nose to tail, a girth of 13 feet 8 inches, a height of 6 feet 4 inches at the forequarters and a weight of 4,720 lbs. The stuffed and mounted steer is displayed in Highland Park, Kokomo, Indiana, as proof to all who would otherwise have said "there ain't no such animal."

The highest recorded birthweight for a calf is 225 lbs. from a British Friesian cow at Rockhouse Farm, Bishopston, Swansea, Glamorganshire, Wales, in 1961.

On April 25, 1964, it was reported that a cow named "Lyubik" had given birth to seven calves at Mogilev, U.S.S.R. A case of five live calves at one birth was reported in 1928 by T. G. Yarwood of Manchester, Lancashire, England. The lifetime prolificacy record is 30 in the case of a cross-bred cow owned by G. Page of Warren Farm, Wilmington, Sussex, England, which died in November, 1957, aged 32. A cross-Hereford calved in 1916 and owned by A. J. Thomas of West Hook Farm, Marloes, Pembrokeshire, Wales, produced her 30th calf in May, 1955, and died in May, 1956, aged 40.

Pigs. The highest recorded number of piglets in one litter is 34, thrown on June 25–26, 1961, by a sow owned by Aksel Egedee of Denmark.

Sheep. The highest recorded birthweight for a lamb is 26 lbs., in the case of a lamb delivered on February 9, 1967, by Alan F. Baldry from a ewe belonging to J. L. H. Arkwright of Winkleigh, Devonshire, England. A case of eight lambs at a birth was reported by D. T. Jones of Priory Farm, Monmouthshire, Wales, in June, 1956, but none lived.

Egg-Laying

The highest authenticated rate of egg-laying by a hen is 361 eggs in 364 days by a Black Orpington in an official test at Taranki, New Zealand, in 1930. The largest egg reported is one of 16 ounces, with double yolk and double shell, laid by a white Leghorn at Vineland, New Jersey, on February 25, 1956.

Milk Yields

The world lifetime record yield of milk is 334,292 lbs. by the Holstein cow "College Ormsby Burke," which died at Fort Collins, Colorado, in August, 1966.

The greatest recorded yield for one lactation (365 days) is 45,081 lbs. by R. A. Pierson's British Friesian "Bridge Birch" in England in 1947–48.

The hand milking record for cows is 17 lbs. 11 oz. in two minutes from two cows by Manuel Dutra of Stockton, California, at the Cow Palace, San Francisco, on October 27, 1970. Dutra proclaimed, "I credit my cows with the victory."

The highest recorded milk yield for any goat is 6,661 pints in 365 days by "Malpas Melba," owned by Mr. J. R. Egerton of Bramford, England, in 1931.

Butter Fat

The world record butter fat yield in a lifetime is 13,607 lbs. from 308,569 lbs. by the Brown Swiss cow named "Ivetta" (1954–71) in the herd of W. E. Naffziger of Pekin, Illinois, in 4,515 days.

The world's lactation (365-day) record is 1,866 lbs. by the U.S. Holstein-Friesian "Princess Breezewood R.A. Patsy."

Cheese

The most active cheese-eaters are the people of France, with an annual average in 1969 of 29.98 lbs. per person. The world's biggest producer is the United States with a factory production of 998,800 tons in 1970.

Oldest. The oldest and most primitive cheeses are the Arabian *kishk*, made of the dried curd of goat's milk. There are today 450 named cheeses of 18 major varieties, but many are merely named after different towns and differ only in shape or the method of packing. France has 240 varieties.

Most Expensive. The most expensive of all cheeses is the small goat cheese Crottin de Chavignol, from the Berri area of France, which is marketed in Paris, at times, for 30 francs per kilogram ($2.76 per lb.).

Largest. The largest cheese ever made was a cheddar of 34,591 lbs., made in 43 hours, January 20–22, 1964, by the Wisconsin Cheese Foundation for exhibition at the New York World's Fair. It was transported in a specially designed 45-foot-long refrigerated tractor trailer "Cheese-Mobile."

Livestock Prices

Bull. The highest nominal value ever placed on a bull is $1,050,000, implicit in the $350,000 paid in April, 1967, for a one-third share in the Aberdeen-Angus bull "Newhouse Jewror Eric," aged 7, by the Embassy Angus Farm of Mississippi.

Cow. The highest price ever paid for a cow is Can. $62,000 for the Holstein-Friesian "Oak Ridges Royal Linda" by Mr. E. L. Vesley of Lapeer, Michigan, at the Oak Ridges, Canada, dispersal sale on November 12, 1968.

Sheep. The highest price ever paid for a sheep is $A27,200 ($30,600) for a Merino ram from John Collins & Sons, Mount Bryan, South Australia, by L. W. Gare & Sons of Burra, South Australia, at Adelaide in September, 1970.

The highest price ever paid for wool is 1,800 Australian pence ($16.76) per lb. for a bale from 120 selected sheep of the Hillcrest Merino stud, bought for Illingworth, Morris & Co. of Shipley,

Yorkshire, at an auction at Goulbourn, New South Wales, Australia, on December 3, 1964.

Pig. The highest price ever paid for a pig is $10,200, paid in 1953 for a Hampshire boar "Great Western" by a farm in Byron, Illinois.

Horse. The highest price ever paid for a farm horse is £9,500 ($27,930), paid for the Clydesdale stallion "Baron of Buchlyvie" by William Dunlop at Ayr, Scotland, in December, 1911.

Donkey. Perhaps the lowest price ever for livestock was at a sale at Kuruman, Cape Province, South Africa, in 1934, where donkeys were sold for less than 4d. (4 cents) each.

Turkey. The highest price ever paid for a turkey is $990 for a 33-lb. stag bird bought at the Arkansas State Turkey Show at Springdale, Ark., on December 3, 1955.

Sheep Shearing

The highest recorded speed for lamb shearing in a working day was that of Steve Morrell, who machine-sheared 585 lambs (average 65 per hour) in 9 hours at Ashburton, New Zealand, on December 29, 1971.

The feminine record is held by Mrs. Pamela Warren, aged 21, who machine-sheared 337 Romney Marsh ewes and lambs at Puketutu, near Piopio, North Island, New Zealand, on November 25, 1964.

Piggery

The world's largest piggery is at Sljeme, Yugoslavia, which is able to process 300,000 pigs in a year. Even bigger units may exist in Rumania, but details are lacking.

Plowing

The world championship (instituted 1953) has been staged in 15 countries and won by plowmen of eight nationalities of which the United Kingdom has been most successful with 6 champions. The only man to take the title three times has been Hugh Barr of Northern Ireland in 1954–55–56. The fastest recorded time for plowing an acre (minimum 32 right-hand turns and depth 9 inches) is 17 minutes 52.5 seconds by Mervyn Ford using a 6-furrow 14-inch Ransomes plow towed by a Roadless 114 four-wheel drive tractor at Bowhay Farm, Ide, Exeter, Devon, England, on September 25, 1970. The greatest recorded acreage plowed in 24 hours is 84.1 acres by five farmers of the Exeter and District Young Farmers' Club near Ide, Exeter, Devon, England, on September 25–26, 1970.

Chicken Plucking

The fastest recorded time for plucking chickens was set in the 1970 contest at Masaryktown, Florida, on November 15 when a team of four women plucked 3 birds each naked in 6 mins. 31 secs., so averaging 2 mins. 10.4 secs. apiece. Leaving a single feather produces the cry "Fowl!"

Chapter Eight

THE WORLD'S STRUCTURES

Earliest Structures

The earliest known human structure is a rough circle of loosely piled lava blocks found in 1960 on the lowest cultural level at the Lower Paleolithic site at Olduvai Gorge in Tanganyika (now part of Tanzania). The structure was associated with artifacts and bones and may represent a work-floor, dating to *circa* 1,750,000 B.C. (see Chapter 1, *Earliest Man*). The earliest evidence of *buildings* yet discovered is that of 21 huts with hearths or pebble-lined pits and delimited by stake holes found in October, 1965, at the Terra Amata site in Nice, France, originally dated to 300,000 B.C. but now thought to be more likely belonging to the Acheulian culture of 120,000 years ago. Excavation carried out between June 28 and July 5, 1966, revealed one hut with palisaded walls with axes of 49 feet and 20 feet.

1. Buildings for Working

Largest Buildings

Scientific. The most capacious scientific building in the world is the Vehicle Assembly Building (VAB) at Complex 39, the selected site for the final assembly and launching of the Apollo moon space-craft on the Saturn V rocket, at the John F. Kennedy Space Center (KSC), near Cape Kennedy (formerly Cape Canaveral), Florida. It is a steel-framed building measuring 716 feet in length, 518 feet in width and 525 feet high. The building contains four bays, each with its own door 460 feet high. Construction began in April, 1963,

MOST CAPACIOUS BUILDING: The Boeing Company main assembly plant for the 747 jet airliners at Everett, Washington.

TALLEST INHABITED BUILDINGS: Even though the Wall Street district of New York City includes many skyscrapers, they are dwarfed by the twin towers of the World Trade Center, built on the banks of the Hudson River. Each building, upon completion in 1973 (now occupied in part as work continues) will have 21,800 windows and 104 elevators.

by the Ursam Consortium. Its floor area is 343,500 square feet (7.87 acres) and its capacity is 129,482,000 cubic feet. The building was "topped out" on April 14, 1965, at a cost of $108,700,000.

Manufacturing. The largest ground area covered is by the main assembly building at the Boeing Company's works at Everett, Washington. It has a capacity of 200,000,000 cubic feet. Construction was begun in August, 1966, and parts were in use by late 1967. The building, constructed for the manufacture of Boeing 747 jet airliners, has a maximum height of 115 feet and encloses a floor area of 1,565,000 square feet (36.0 acres).

Administrative. The largest ground area covered by any office building is that of the Pentagon, in Arlington, Virginia. Built to house the U.S. Defense Department's offices, it was completed on January 15, 1943, and cost about $83,000,000. Each of the outermost sides of the Pentagon is 921 feet long and the perimeter of the building is about 1,500 yards. The five stories of the building enclose a floor area of 6,500,000 square feet. During the day 29,000 people work in the building. The telephone system of the building has more than 44,000 telephones connected by 160,000 miles of cable and its 220 staff members handle 280,000 calls a day. Two restaurants, six cafeterias and ten snackbars and a staff of 675 form the catering department of the building. The corridors measure 17 miles in length and there are 7,748 windows to be cleaned.

Commercial. The largest commercial and office buildings in the world are the twin towers comprising the World Trade Center in New York City, with a total of 9,000,000 square feet (206.6 acres) of rentable space. (See *Tallest Buildings*, below.)

Fair Hall. The largest fair hall is in Hanover, West Germany, completed on April 1, 1970, at a cost of DM 55,000,000($16,500,000) with dimensions of 1,180 feet by 885 feet and a floor area of 877,500 square feet.

Tallest Buildings

The tallest inhabited buildings in the world are those of the Port of New York Authority's World Trade Center with twin towers of 110 stories, each standing 1,353 feet tall. Work started in August, 1966, on Barclay and Liberty Streets, New York City, and the North Tower was topped out on December 14, 1970, having surpassed the Empire State Building on October 21, 1970. The total cost is estimated at $650,000,000. A 365-foot antenna tower will bring the total height of the North Tower to 1,718 feet. Completion will be in 1973. Each tower will have 21,800 windows and 104 elevators. (See photograph on front cover.)

The World Trade Center will be overtopped by the Sears Tower, the national headquarters of Sears Roebuck & Co. on Wacker Drive, Chicago. It will have 109 stories, rising to 1,451 feet. It is due for completion in 1974.

Most Stories. The World Trade Center (see above) has 110 stories—eight more than the Empire State Building. The projects for the 1,300-foot Schaumburg (Illinois) Planet Corporation Building with a 250-foot antenna, and the 1,610-foot Barrington Space Needle, Barrington, Illinois, call for 113 and 120 stories respectively.

TALLEST STRUCTURES IN THE WORLD—PROGRESSIVE RECORDS

Height in feet	Structure	Location	Material	Building or Completion Dates
204	Djoser step pyramid (earliest Pyramid)	Saqqâra, Egypt	Tura limestone	c. 2650 B.C.
294	Pyramid of Meidun	Meidun, Egypt	Tura limestone	c. 2600 B.C.
c. 336	Snefru Bent pyramid	Dahshûr, Egypt	Tura limestone	c. 2600 B.C.
342	Snefru North Stone pyramid	Dahshûr, Egypt	Tura limestone	c. 2600 B.C.
480.9[1]	Great Pyramid of Cheops (Khufu)	El Gizeh, Egypt	Tura limestone	c. 2580 B.C.
525[2]	Lincoln Cathedral, Central Tower	Lincoln, England	lead sheathed wood	c. 1307–1548
489[3]	St. Paul's Cathedral	London, England	lead sheathed wood	1315–1561
465	Minster of Notre Dame	Strasbourg, France	vosges sandstone	1420–1439
502[4]	St. Pierre de Beauvais	Beauvais, France	lead sheathed wood	–1568
475	St. Nicholas Church	Hamburg, Germany	vosges sandstone	1846–1874
485	Rouen Cathedral	Rouen, France	cast iron	1823–1876
513	Köln Cathedral	Cologne, West Germany	stone	–1880
555	Washington Memorial	Washington, D.C.	stone	1848–1884
985.9[5]	La Tour Eiffel	Paris, France	steel	1887–1889
1,046	Chrysler Building	New York City	steel and concrete	1929–1930
1,250[6]	Empire State Building	New York City	steel and concrete	1929–1930
1,572	KWTV Television Mast	Oklahoma City	steel	Nov. 1954
1,610[7]	KSWS Television Mast	Roswell, N. Mex.	steel	Dec. 1956
1,619	WGAN Television Mast	Portland, Maine	steel	Sept. 1959
1,676	KFVS Television Mast	Cape Girardeau, Missouri	steel	June 1960
1,749	WTVM & WRBL TV Mast	Columbus, Georgia	steel	May 1962
1,749	WBIR-TV Mast	Knoxville, Tennessee	steel	Sept. 1963
2,063	KTHI-TV Mast	Fargo, North Dakota	steel	Dec. 1963
2,100	Polish National TV Service Tower	Plock, Poland	tubular steel	due 1974

[1] Original height. With loss of pyramidion (topmost stone) height now 449 ft. 6 in.
[2] Fell in a storm.
[3] Struck by lightning and destroyed in August 1561.
[4] Fell April 1573, shortly after completion.
[5] Original height. With addition of T.V. antenna in 1957, now 1,052 ft. 4 in.
[6] Original height. With addition of T.V. tower on May 1, 1951, now 1,472 ft.
[7] Fell in gale in 1960.

Skyscrapers of up to 3,000 feet in height with 400 stories are now regarded as feasible by the "suspend-arch" principle developed by the U.S. engineer Chelazzi.

Habitations

Greatest Altitude. The highest inhabited buildings in the world are those in the Chilean mining village of Aucanquilca, at 17,500 feet above sea level. During the 1960–61 Himalayan High Altitude Expedition, the "silver hut," a prefabricated laboratory, was inhabited for four months in the Ming Bo Valley at 18,765 feet.

A formerly occupied 3-room dwelling was discovered in April, 1961, at 21,650 feet on Cerro Llullaillaco (22,058 feet), on the Argentine-Chile border, believed to date from the late pre-Columbian period *c.* 1480. (See photo, page 109.)

Northernmost. The most northerly habitation in the world is the Danish scientific station set up in 1952 in Pearyland, northern Greenland, more than 900 miles north of the Arctic Circle. The U.S.S.R. and the U.S. have maintained research stations on the Arctic ice-cap, which have drifted close to the North Pole. The U.S.S.R.'s "North Pole 15," which drifted 1,250 miles, passed within 1¼ miles of the North Pole in December, 1967. The 1969 Pearyland research group from Britain reported signs of Eskimo habitation above the 83rd latitude N. apparently dating from earlier than 1000 B.C.

Southernmost. The most southerly permanent human habitation is the United States' Scott-Amundsen I.G.Y. (International Geophysical Year) base 800 yards from the South Pole.

Largest Embassy. The largest embassy in the world is the U.S.S.R. embassy on Bei Xiao Jie, Peking, China, in the northeastern corner of the northern walled city. The whole 45-acre area of the old Orthodox Church mission (established 1728), now known as the *Bei guan,* was handed over to the U.S.S.R. in 1949.

Plants

Atomic. The largest atomic plant in the world is the Savannah River Project, South Carolina, extending 27 miles along the river and over a total area of 315 square miles. The plant, comprising 280 permanent buildings, cost $1,400,000,000. Construction was started in February, 1951, and by September, 1952, the labor force had reached 38,500. The present operating strength is 8,500.

Underground. The world's largest underground factory was the Mittelwerk Factory, near Nordhausen in the Kohnstein Hills, south of the Harz Mountains, Germany. It was built with concentration camp labor during World War II and had a floor area of 1,270,000 square feet and an output of 900 V-2 rockets per month.

Tallest Chimney. The world's tallest chimney is the $5,500,000 International Nickel Company's stack, 1,250 feet 9 inches tall, at Copper Cliff, Sudbury, Ontario, Canada, completed in 1970. It was built by the M. W. Kellogg Company and the diameter tapers from 116.4 feet at the base to 51.8 feet at the top. It weighs 38,390 tons and became operational in 1971.

LARGEST HANGAR: The Goodyear Airship hangar at Akron, Ohio, covers 364,000 sq. ft. and has a capacity of 55,000,000 cu. ft.

LARGEST HOUSE: Biltmore House in Asheville, North Carolina, has 250 rooms and is surrounded by 119,000 acres. When it was built by a Vanderbilt in the early 1890's, it cost $4,100,000, but today is worth $55,000,000.

Largest Hangars. The largest hangar is the Goodyear Airship hangar at Akron, Ohio, which measures 1,175 feet long, 325 feet wide and 200 feet high. It covers 364,000 square feet (8.35 acres) and has a capacity of 55,000,000 cubic feet.

The largest single fixed-wing aircraft hangar is the Lockheed-Georgia engineering test center at Marietta, Georgia, measuring 630 feet by 480 feet (6.94 acres) completed in 1967.

The largest group of hangars is at the U.S. Air Force Base near San Antonio, Texas. These, including covered maintenance bays, cover 23 acres.

Grain Elevator. The world's largest single-unit grain elevator is that operated by the C-G-F Grain Company at Wichita, Kansas. Consisting of a triple row of storage tanks, 123 on each side of the central loading tower or "head house," the unit is 2,717 feet long and 100 feet wide. Each tank is 120 feet high, with an inside diameter of 30 feet, giving a total storage capacity of 20,000,000 bushels of wheat. The largest collection of elevators in the world is at Thunder Bay, Ontario, Canada, on Lake Superior, with a total capacity of 3,300,000,000 bushels.

Largest Garage. The largest garage is probably that completed in September, 1961, for the Austin Motor Works at Longbridge, near Birmingham, England. It has nine stories and cost $1,400,000. It has a capacity of 3,300 cars.

The largest private garage ever built was one for 100 cars at the Long Island, New York, mansion of William Kissam Vanderbilt (1849–1920).

Largest Glass Greenhouse. The largest glasshouse is 826 feet long and 348 feet wide, covering 6.5 acres at Brough, East Yorkshire, England, completed in 1971. A total of 420 tons of glass was used in glazing it.

Largest Sewerage Works. The largest single sewerage works is the West-Southwest Treatment Plant, opened in 1940 on a site of 501 acres in Chicago. It serves an area containing 2,940,000 people. It treated an average of more than 685,000,000 gallons of wastes per day in 1971. The capacity of its sedimentation and aeration tanks is 1,125,000,000 cubic meters.

Largest Warehouses. The largest warehouse is the Eurostore, built by the Garoner warehousing firm on a 240-acre site near Le Bourget, in northeast Paris, France. The building provides 5,400,000 square feet (124 acres) of floor space.

2. Buildings for Living

Wooden Buildings. The oldest wooden building in the world is the Temple of Horyu (Horyu-ji), built at Nara, Japan, in 708–715 A.D. The largest wooden building in the world is the Daibutsuden, built also at Nara in 1704–11. It measures 285.4 feet long, 167.3 feet wide and 153½ feet tall.

The municipal building occupied by the Department of Education

LARGEST CASTLE (above): The Citadel in Aleppo, Syria, has a surrounding wall 1,230 feet long and 777 feet across. MOST MASSIVE CASTLE (left): The 13th-century château at Coucy-le-Château-Auffrique, France, which has walls 22½ feet thick.

in Wellington, New Zealand, built in 1876, has the largest floor area of any wooden building, with 101,300 square feet.

Castles

Earliest. Castles in the sense of unfortified manor houses existed in all the great early civilizations, including that of ancient Egypt from 3000 B.C. Fortified castles in the more accepted sense only existed much later. The oldest in the world is that at Gomdan, in the Yemen, which originally had 20 stories and dates from before 100 A.D.

Largest. The largest castle in the world is the Qila (Citadel) at

Halab (Aleppo) in Syria. It is oval in shape and has a surrounding wall 1,230 feet long and 777 feet across. It dates, in its present form, from the Humanid dynasty of the 10th century A.D. (See photograph.)

The largest inhabited castle in the world is the British Royal residence of Windsor Castle at New Windsor, Berkshire. It is primarily of 12th century construction and is in the form of a parallelogram, 1,890 feet by 540 feet.

The most massive keep in the world is that in the 13th-century château at Coucy-le-Château-Auffrique, in the Department of L'Aisne, France. It is 177 feet high, 318 feet in circumference and has walls over 22½ feet in thickness. It was leveled to its foundations by the Germans in 1917. (See photograph.)

The walls of Babylon, Iraq, built in 600 B.C. were up to 85 feet in thickness.

Largest Palace. The largest palace in the world is the Imperial Palace (*Gu gong*) in the center of Peking (*Bei jing*, the northern capital), China, which covers a rectangle 1,050 yards by 820 yards, an area of 177.9 acres. The outline survives from the construction of the third Ming emperor Yong le of 1307–20, but due to constant rearrangements most of the intramural buildings are 18th century. These consist of 5 halls and 17 palaces of which the last occupied by the last Empress was the Palace of Accumulated Elegance (*Chu xia gong*) until 1924.

The largest residential palace in the world is the Vatican Palace, in the Vatican City, an enclave in Rome, Italy. Covering an area of 13½ acres, it has 1,400 rooms, chapels and halls, of which the oldest date from the 15th century.

The world's largest moats are those which surround the Imperial Palace in Peking. From plans drawn by French sources it appears to measure 54 yards wide and have a total length of 3,600 yards.

The oldest Throne Room in existence is in the restored Bronze Age palace of Knossos, Crete, dating to the Middle Minoan III or Late Minoan I phase of the Great Palaces (*c.* 1500 B.C.).

Apartments

Largest. The largest single apartment building is Dolphin Square, London, covering a site of 7½ acres. The building occupies the four sides of a square enclosing gardens of about 3 acres. Dolphin Square contains 1,220 separate and self-contained flats, an underground garage for 300 cars with filling and service station, a swimming pool, 8 squash courts, a tennis court and an indoor shopping center. It cost £1,750,000 ($8,750,000) to build in 1936 but was sold to Westminster City Council for £4,500,000 ($12,600,000) in January, 1963. Its nine stories house 3,000 people.

The Hyde Park development in Sheffield, Yorkshire, England, comprises 1,322 dwellings and an estimated population of 4,675 persons. It was built between 1959 and 1966.

Tallest. The tallest block of apartments in the world is Lake Point Towers of 70 stories, 645 feet high in Chicago.

Hotels

Largest. The world's largest hotel is the Hotel Rossiya in Moscow, U.S.S.R., with 3,200 rooms providing accommodation for 6,000 guests, in three buildings, each of 14 stories. It was completed in December, 1967. (See photograph.)

The largest hotel in a single building is the Conrad Hilton (formerly the Stevens) on Michigan Avenue, Chicago. Its 25 floors contain 2,600 (originally 3,000) guest rooms. It would thus take more than seven years to spend one night in each room of the hotel. The hotel employs about 2,000 people, of whom more than 70 are telephone operators and supervisors. The laundry of the hotel, with 195 employees, handles 600 tons of flat work each month.

The largest hotel building in the world, on the basis of volume, is the Waldorf Astoria, on Park Avenue, between 49th and 50th Streets, New York City. It occupies a complete block of 81,337 square feet (1.87 acres) and reaches a maximum height of 625 feet 7 inches. The Waldorf Astoria has 47 stories and 1,900 guest rooms and maintains the largest hotel radio receiving system in the world. The Waldorf can accommodate 10,000 people at one time and has a staff of 1,700. The restaurants have catered for parties up to 6,000 at a time. The coffee-makers' daily output reaches 1,000 gallons. The electricity bill is about $360,000 each year.

Tallest. The world's tallest hotel is the 34-story Ukraine in Moscow, U.S.S.R., which, including its tower, is 650 feet tall. The highest hotel rooms in the world are those on the topmost (50th) story of the 509-foot-tall Americana Hotel, opened on September 24, 1962, on 7th Avenue at 52nd Street, New York City.

Most Expensive. The world's costliest hotel is the Mauna Kea Beach Hotel on Hawaii Island, which was built at a cost of $15,000,000 and has only 154 rooms. The Presidential Suite of 8 rooms in the New York Hilton cost $500 per night in 1963.

Spas

The largest spa in the world measured by number of available hotel rooms is Vichy, Allier, France, with 14,000 rooms. Spas are named after the watering place in the Liège province of Belgium where hydropathy was developed from 1626. The highest French spa is Barèges, Hautes-Pyrénées, at 4,068 feet above sea level.

Largest House

The largest private house in the world is 250-room Biltmore House in Asheville, North Carolina. It is owned by George and William Cecil, grandsons of George Washington Vanderbilt II (1862–1914). The house was built between 1890 and 1895 on an estate of 119,000 acres, at a cost of $4,100,000, and is now valued at $55,000,000 with 112 acres. (See photo, page 258.)

The most expensive private house ever built is La Cuesta Encantada at San Simeon, California. It was built 1922–39 for William Randolph Hearst (1863–1951), at a total cost of more than $30,000,000. It has more than 100 rooms, a 104-foot-long heated swimming pool, an 83-foot-long assembly hall and a garage for 25 limousines. The house would require 60 servants to maintain it.

LARGEST HOTEL: The new Hotel Rossiya in Moscow has 3,200 rooms in its three buildings of 14 stories each.

3. Buildings for Entertainment

Night Clubs

Oldest. The oldest night club (*boîte de nuit*) is "Le Bal des Anglais" at 6 Rue des Anglais, Paris 5me, France. It was founded in 1843.

Largest. The largest night club in the world is that in the Imperial Room of the Concord Hotel in the Catskill Mountains, New York, with a capacity of 3,000 patrons.

In the more classical sense the largest night club in the world is "The Mikado" in the Akasaka district of Tokyo, Japan, with a seating capacity of 2,000. It is "manned" by 1,250 hostesses, some of whom earn $10,300 per annum. Long sight is an essential to an appreciation of the floor show.

Loftiest. The highest night club will be that on the 52nd story of the Antigone Building, now under construction, in Montparnasse, Paris, at 613.5 feet above street level.

Lowest. The lowest night club is the "Minus 206" in Tiberias, Israel, on the shores of the Sea of Galilee. It is 676 feet below sea level. An alternative candidate is "Outer Limits," opposite the Cow Palace, San Francisco, which was raided for the 151st time on August 1, 1971. It has been called both "The Most Busted Joint" and "The Slowest to Get the Message."

LARGEST INDOOR ARENA: The Astrodome in Houston has a capacity of 45,000 for baseball and 66,000 maximum for boxing. It belongs to Harris County, Texas, and cost $38,000,000, not including repairs.

Largest Stadiums

The world's largest stadium is the Strahov Stadium in Praha (Prague), Czechoslovakia. It was completed in 1934 and can accommodate 240,000 spectators for mass displays of up to 40,000 Sokol gymnasts.

The largest football stadium in the world is the Maracanã Municipal Stadium in Rio de Janeiro, Brazil, which has a normal capacity of 205,000, of whom 155,000 may be seated. A crowd of 199,854 was accommodated for the World Cup soccer final between Brazil and Uruguay on July 1, 1950. A dry moat, 7 feet wide and over 5 feet deep, protects players from spectators and *vice versa*. The stadium also has facilities for indoor sports, such as boxing, and these provide accommodation for an additional 32,000 spectators.

The largest covered stadium in the world is the Empire Stadium, Wembley, London, opened in April, 1923. It was the scene of the 1948 Olympic Games and the final of the 1966 World Cup. In 1962–63 the capacity under cover was increased to 100,000, of whom 45,000 may be seated. The original cost was $3,500,000.

Largest One-Piece Roof. The transparent acryl glass "tent" roof over the Munich Olympic Stadium, West Germany, measures 914,940 square feet in area. It rests on a steel net supported by masts.

Largest Indoor Arena. The world's largest indoor stadium is the Harris County Sports Stadium, or Astrodome, in Houston, Texas. It has a capacity of 45,000 for baseball and 66,000 (maximum) for boxing. The domed stadium covers $9\frac{1}{2}$ acres and is so large that an 18-story building could be built under the roof (208 feet high). The total cost was $38,000,000. In some conditions of humidity it would rain if the air-conditioning equipment, which has a cooling capacity of 79,200,000 b.t.u. per hour, were turned off. (See also Largest Dome.) (See photograph.)

The architects of the $150,000,000 superdome, due to be completed in New Orleans by mid-1974 say that the Astrodome could comfortably fit inside it. Its capacity will be 103,402 people, and the dome will rise 280 feet.

Largest Amusement Resort

The largest amusement resort is Disney World on 27,443 acres of Orange and Osceola Counties, near Orlando in central Florida. It was opened on October 23, 1971.

Miniature Village

The largest miniature village in the world is Legoland on an $8\frac{1}{4}$-acre site at Billund, Denmark, opened in June, 1968, and now attended by 750,000 visitors a year. It is built of 9,000,000 Lego bricks and has 30,000 lights at night.

Pleasure Beach

The largest pleasure beach in the world is Virginia Beach, Virginia. It has 28 miles of beach front on the Atlantic and 10 miles of estuary frontage. The area embraces 255 square miles and contains 134 hotels and motels.

Largest Circus

The world's largest permanent circus is Circus Circus, Las Vegas, Nevada, opened on October 18, 1968, at a cost of $15,000,000. It covers an area of 129,000 square feet capped by a 90-foot-high tent-shaped plexiglass roof.

Longest Pleasure Pier

The longest pleasure pier in the world is Southend Pier at Southend-on-Sea in Essex, England. It is 1.33 miles in length, and was built in 1889, with final extensions made in 1929. It is decorated with more than 75,000 lamps.

Fairs

Earliest. The earliest major international fair was the Great Exhibition of 1851 in the Crystal Palace, Hyde Park, London, which in 141 days attracted 6,039,195 admissions.

Largest. The largest fair grounds were for the New York World's Fair, covering $1,216\frac{1}{2}$ acres of Flushing Meadow Park, Queens, New York City, in 1939 and 1940. There were 25,817,265 admissions. An attendance of 51,607,037 was recorded for the 1964–65 Fair held on the same grounds.

Record Attendance. The record attendance for any fair was 65,000,000 for Expo '70 held on an 815-acre site at Osaka, Japan, from March to September 13, 1970. It made a profit of more than $30,000,000. (See photograph, next page.)

Ferris Wheel. The original Ferris Wheel, named after its constructor, George W. Ferris (1859–96), was erected in 1893 at the Midway, Chicago, at a cost of $300,000. The wheel was 250 feet in diameter, 790 feet in circumference, weighed 1,070 tons, and carried 36 cars each seating 40 people, making a total of 1,440 passengers. The structure was removed in 1904 to St. Louis, and was eventually sold as scrap for $1,800. In 1897, a Ferris Wheel with a diameter of 300 feet was erected for the Earls Court Exhibition, London. The largest wheel now operating is the Riesenrad in Prater Park, Vienna, Austria, with a diameter of 197 feet. It was built in 1896 and carried 15,000,000 people in its first 75 years.

Fastest Roller Coaster. The world's fastest gravity roller coaster was the Bobs in the Belle Vue Amusement Park, Manchester,

MOST POPULAR WORLD'S FAIR: Expo '70 in Osaka, Japan, attracted 65,000,000 visitors in 183 days. The roof that looks like a flying saucer in this helicopter view covered the U.S. Pavilion.

GREATEST FERRIS WHEEL:
300 feet in diameter, the Earls
Court wheel, London, was
erected in 1897.

Lancashire, England. The cars attained a peak speed of 61 m.p.h.
The track was 862 yards long and the maximum height 76 feet.

Bars

The largest beer-selling establishment in the world is the Mathäser,
Bayerstrasse 5, Munich, West Germany, where the daily sale reaches
84,470 pints. It was established in 1829, was demolished in World
War II, rebuilt by 1955, and now seats 5,500 people. Consumption
at the Dube beer halls in the Bantu township of Soweto, Johannesburg, South Africa, may, however, be higher on some Saturdays
when the average of 6,000 gallons (48,000 pints) is far exceeded.

Longest Bar. The longest bar with beer pumps was built in 1938
at the Working Men's Club, Mildura, Victoria, Australia. It has a
counter 287 feet in length, served by 32 pumps. Temporary bars
have been erected of greater length. The Falstaff Brewing Corp.
put up a temporary bar 336 feet 5 inches in length on Wharf St.,
St. Louis, Missouri, on June 22, 1970.

Wine Cellar. The largest wine cellars in the world are at Paarl,
those of the Ko-operative Wijnbouwers Vereeniging (K.W.V.),
near Cape Town, in the center of the wine district of South Africa.
They cover an area of 25 acres and have a capacity of 36,000,000
gallons. The largest blending vats have a capacity of 54,880 gallons.

4. Major Civil Engineering Structures

Tallest Structure

The tallest structure in the world is a stayed television transmitting
tower, 2,063 feet tall, between Fargo and Blanchard, North Dakota.
It was built at a cost of about $500,000 for Channel 11 of KTHI-TV,
owned by the Pembina Broadcasting Company of North Dakota, a

TALLEST SELF-SUPPORTING TOWER (left): Built of reinforced concrete, this 1,749-foot-tall television tower in Moscow has a 3-story restaurant near the top. HIGHEST DAM (right): The Grand Dixence in Switzerland is 932 feet high and 2,310 feet long.

subsidiary of the Polaris Corporation from Milwaukee, Wisconsin. The tower was erected in 30 days (October 2 to November 1, 1963), by 11 men of the Kline Iron and Steel Company of Columbia, South Carolina, who designed and fabricated the tower. The cage elevator in the center rises to 1,948 feet. The tower is built to allow for a sway of up to 13.9 feet in a wind gusting to 120 m.p.h. and is so tall that anyone falling off the top would no longer be accelerating just before hitting the ground.

Uncompleted. Work was begun in July, 1970, on a tubular steel guyed TV tower near Plock, northwest Poland, which will rise to 2,100 feet. The structure, designed by Jan Polak, will weigh 550 tons and is due for completion in 1974.

Tallest Tower

The tallest self-supporting tower (as opposed to a guyed mast) in the world is the 1,749-foot-tall tower at Ostankino, Greater Moscow, U.S.S.R., "topped out" in May, 1967. It is of reinforced concrete construction and weighs over 22,000 tons. A 3-story restaurant revolves near the top. In a high wind the TV antennae may sway up to 26 feet, but the restaurant only 3.14 inches. The tower was designed by N. V. Nikitin.

The tallest tower built before the era of television masts is the Tour Eiffel (Eiffel Tower), in Paris, France, designed by Alexander Gustav Eiffel (1832–1923) for the Paris exhibition and completed on March 31, 1889. It was 985 feet 11 inches tall, now extended by a TV antenna to 1,052 feet 4 inches, and weighs 7,728 tons. The maximum sway in high winds is 5 inches. The whole iron edifice, which has 1,792 steps, took 2 years, 2 months, and 2 days to build and cost 7,799,401 francs 31 centimes. The 352nd suicide committed from the tower occurred by January 1, 1970.

The architects André and Jean Polak put forward a design in February, 1969, for a tower 2,378.6 feet in height to be erected at La Défense in Paris.

Bridges

Oldest. Arch construction was understood by the Sumerians as early as 3200 B.C., but the oldest surviving bridge in the world is the slab stone single arch bridge over the River Meles in Smyrna (now Izmir), Turkey, which dates from c. 850 B.C.

Longest Suspension. The world's longest single span bridge is the Verrazano-Narrows Bridge stretching across the entrance to New York Harbor from Staten Island to Brooklyn. Work on the $305,000,000 project began on August 13, 1959, and the bridge was opened to traffic on November 21, 1964. It measures 6,690 feet between supports and carries two decks, each with six lanes of traffic. The center span is 4,260 feet and the tops of the main towers (each 690 feet tall) are $1\frac{5}{8}$ inches out of parallel, to allow for the curvature of the earth. The traffic in the first 12 months was 17,000,000 vehicles, and is rising to 48,000,000 per year. The bridge was designed by Othmar H. Ammann (1879–1965), a Swiss-born engineer. (See photograph, next page.)

The Mackinac Straits Bridge between Mackinaw City and St. Ignace, Michigan, is the longest suspension bridge in the world measured between supports (8,344 feet) and has an overall length, including viaducts of the bridge proper measured between abutment faces, of 19,203 feet 4 inches. It was completed in November, 1957 (opened June 28, 1958) at a cost of $100 million and has a main span of 3,800 feet.

Detailed plans have been published for the building of a $333,000,000 suspension bridge with a central span of 4,265 feet, across the Akashi Straits, west of Kobe, Japan. It will have an overall length of 16,076 feet or 3.04 miles, including all main and side spans. The distance between the main anchors will be 8,530 feet and the cables will be 50 inches in diameter. Even longer main spans are planned for completion in 1976 across the Humber Estuary, England (4,580 feet), a bridge of 4,600 feet across Tokyo Bay, Japan, and one of 9,000 feet, with piers 400 feet deep, across the Messina Straits, Italy.

Longest Cantilever. The Québec Bridge (Pont de Québec) over the St. Lawrence River in Canada has the longest cantilever span of any in the world—1,800 feet between the piers and 3,239 feet overall. It carries a railway track and two roadways. Begun in 1899,

WORLD'S LONGEST BRIDGE: With a span of 4,260 feet, the Verrazano-Narrows Bridge crosses the entrance to New York Harbor, connecting Brooklyn and Staten Island. The two 690-foot-high towers are 5 inches out of parallel to allow for the curvature of the earth.

LARGEST STEEL ARCH BRIDGE: 172 feet above the water, the Sydney Harbour Bridge in Australia has eight lanes for cars, two for trains and two footways.

it was finally opened to traffic on December 3, 1917, at a cost of Can. $22,400,000 and 87 lives.

Largest. The largest steel arch bridge in the world is the Sydney Harbour Bridge in Sydney, Australia. Its main arch span is 1,650 feet long and it carries two electric overhead railway tracks, eight lanes of roadway, a cycleway and two footways, 172 feet above the waters of Sydney Harbour. It took seven years to build and was officially opened on March 19, 1932 at a cost of $12,600,000. Its total length is 3,770 feet, excluding viaducts.

Longest Steel Arch. The longest steel arch bridge in the world is the Bayonne Bridge over the Kill Van Kull, which has connected Bayonne, New Jersey, to Staten Island, New York, since its completion in November, 1931. Its span is 1,652 feet 1 inch—25 inches longer than the Sydney Harbour Bridge, Australia.

Railroad. The longest railroad bridge in the world is the Huey P. Long Bridge, New Orleans, Louisiana, with a railroad section 22,996 feet (4.35 miles) long. It was completed on December 10, 1935, with a longest span of 790 feet.

Widest. The bridge with the widest roadway is the Crawford Street Bridge in Providence, Rhode Island, with a width of 1,147 feet.

LONGEST BRIDGE SPANS IN THE WORLD—BY TYPE

	feet		opened
Suspension	4,260	Verrazano-Narrows, New York City	1964
Cantilever	1,800	Québec Railway Bridge, Québec, Canada	1917
Tied arch (steel)	1,652	Bayonne (Kill Van Kull), New Jersey—N.Y.	1931
Continuous truss	1,232	Astoria, Columbia River, Oregon	1966
Cable-stayed	1,148	Duisberg-Neuenkamp, West Germany	1970
Chain suspension	1,114	Florianopolis, Santa Catarina, Brazil	1926
Steel arch (concrete)	1,000	Gladesville, Sydney, Australia	1964
Plate and box girder	984	Rio Niterói, Rio de Janeiro, Brazil	1971

HIGHEST BRIDGE:
1,053 feet below this
suspension bridge is the
water level in the Royal
Gorge of the Arkansas
River in Colorado.

Highest. The highest suspension bridge in the world is the bridge over the Royal Gorge of the Arkansas River in Colorado. It is 1,053 feet above the water level. It has a main span of 880 feet and was constructed in 6 months, ending on December 6, 1929. The highest railroad bridge in the world is at Fades, outside Clermont-Ferrand, France. It was built in 1901–09 with a span of 472 feet and is 430 feet above the River Sioule.

Deepest Foundation. The deepest foundations of any structure are those of the 3,323-foot-span Ponte de Salazar, which was opened on August 6, 1966, at a cost of $75,000,000, across the Rio Tejo (the River Tagus), at Lisbon, Portugal. One of the 625-foot-tall towers extends 240 feet down.

PROGRESSIVE RECORD OF WORLD'S LONGEST BRIDGE SPANS

Feet	Location	Type	Completion
121	Martorell, Spain	Stone Arch	219 B.C.
142	Nera River, Lucca, Italy	Stone Arch	14 A.D.
170	Trajan's Bridge, Danube River	Timber Arch	104
251	Trezzo, Italy	Stone Arch	1377
390	Wettingen, Switzerland	Timber Arch	1758
408	Schuylkill Falls, Philadelphia, Pa.	Suspension	1816
449	Union Bridge, Berwick, England	Chain	1820
580	Menai Straits, Wales	Chain	1826
870	Fribourg, Switzerland	Suspension	1834
1,010	Wheeling-Ohio Bridge	Suspension	1849
1,043	Lewiston Bridge, Niagara River	Suspension	1851
1,057	Covington-Cincinnati Bridge (rebuilt 1898)	Suspension	1867
1,268	Clifton Bridge, Niagara Falls	Suspension	1869
1,595½	Brooklyn Bridge, New York City	Suspension	1883
1,706	Forth Bridge, Scotland	Cantilever	1889
1,800	Québec Bridge, Canada	Cantilever	1917
1,850	Ambassador Bridge, Detroit	Suspension	1929
3,500	George Washington Bridge, New York City	Suspension	1931
4,200	San Francisco Golden Gate	Suspension	1937
4,260	Verrazano-Narrows Bridge, New York City	Suspension	1965

Floating. The longest floating bridge in the world is the Second Lake Washington Bridge in Seattle, Washington. Its total length is 12,596 feet and its floating section measures 7,518 feet (1.42 miles). It was built at a cost of $15,000,000, and completed in August, 1963.

Longest Aqueduct. The greatest of ancient aqueducts was the Aqueduct of Carthage in Tunisia, which ran 87.6 miles from the springs of Zaghouan to Djebel Djougar. It was built by the Romans during the reign of Publius Aelius Hadrianus (117–138 A.D.). By 1895, 344 arches still survived. Its original capacity has been calculated at 8,400,000 gallons per day. The triple-tiered aqueduct Pont du Gard, built in 19 A.D. near Nîmes, France, is 160 feet high. The tallest of the 14 arches of the Aguas Livres Aqueduct, built in Lisbon, Portugal, in 1748, is 213 feet 3 inches.

The world's longest aqueduct, in the modern sense of a water conduit, is the Colorado River Aqueduct in southeastern California. The system, complete with aqueduct conduit, tunnels and siphons, is 242 miles long and was completed in 1939. The California Aqueduct due for completion in 1973 will be 444 miles long.

Longest Viaduct. The world's longest viaduct is the second Lake Ponchartrain Causeway, opened on March 23, 1969, joining Mandeville and Jefferson, Louisiana. Its length is 126,055 feet (23.87 miles). It was completed at a cost of $29,900,000 and is 228 feet longer than the adjoining First Causeway completed in 1956.

The longest railroad viaduct in the world is the rock-filled Great Salt Lake Viaduct, carrying the Southern Pacific Railroad 11.85 miles across the Great Salt Lake, Utah. It was opened as a pile and trestle bridge on March 8, 1904, and converted to rock fill in 1955–1960.

TALLEST ANCIENT AQUEDUCT: Built by the Romans in 19 A.D. near Nîmes, France, this triple-tiered structure is 160 feet high.

LONGEST CANAL OF THE ANCIENT WORLD: Completed in the 13th century, the Grand Canal of China extended 1,107 miles from Peking to Hangchow. Now filled with silt, it is reported to have been reconstructed.

Canals

Relics of the oldest canals in the world, dated by archeologists to 5000 B.C., were discovered near Mandali, Iraq, early in 1968.

Longest. The largest canalized system in the world is the Volga-Baltic Canal opened in April, 1965. It runs 1,850 miles from Astrakhan up the Volga, *via* Kuybyshev, Gor'kiy and Lake Ladoga, to Leningrad, U.S.S.R. The longest canal of the ancient world was the Grand Canal of China from Peking to Hangchow. It was begun in 540 B.C. and not completed until the 13th century by which time it extended for 1,107 miles. Having been allowed by 1950 to silt up to the point that it was in no place more than 6 feet deep, it is reported to have been reconstructed. (See photo.)

The Beloye More (White Sea)-Baltic Canal from Belomorsk to Povenets, in the U.S.S.R., is 141 miles long with 19 locks. It was completed with the use of forced labor in 1933 and cannot accommodate ships of more than 16 feet in draught.

The world's longest big ship canal is the still inoperative (since June, 1967) Suez Canal in the United Arab Republic, opened on November 16, 1869, by the Khedive, Isma'il Pasha, and officially inaugurated on the following day by a procession of 68 vessels, headed by the French imperial yacht *L'Aigle*, with the Empress Marie Eugénie Ignace Augustine (1826–1920) on board. The canal was planned by the French diplomatist Ferdinand de Lesseps (1805–1894) and work began on April 25, 1859. It is 100.6 miles in length from Port Said lighthouse to Suez Roads, 197 feet wide and dredged to 34 feet.

Seaway. The world's longest artificial seaway is the St. Lawrence Seaway (189 miles long) along the New York State-Ontario border from Montreal to Lake Ontario, which enables 80 per cent of all ocean-going ships, and bulk carriers with a capacity of 26,000 tons, to sail 2,342 miles from Québec, Canada, up the St. Lawrence Estuary and across the Great Lakes to Duluth, Minnesota, on Lake Superior (602 feet above sea level). The project cost $470,000,000 and was opened on April 25, 1959.

Irrigation. The longest irrigation canal in the world is the Kara-kumskiy Kanal, stretching 546 miles from Haun-Khan to Ash-khabad, Turkmenistan, U.S.S.R. In September, 1971, the navigable length was reported to have reached 280 miles.

Locks

Largest. The world's largest locking system is the Miraflores lock system in the Panama Canal, opened on August 15, 1914. The two lower locks are 1,050 feet long, 110 feet wide and have gates 82 feet high, 65 feet long and 7 feet thick, with doors weighing 730–780 tons each. The largest ship ever to transit was the S.S. *Bremen* (51,730 gross tons), with a length of 899 feet, a beam of 101.9 feet and a draught of 48.2 feet, on February 15, 1939. A swimmer named Albert H. Oshiver was charged a toll of 45 cents to swim through the locks in December, 1962.

The world's largest single lock is that connecting the Schelde with the Kanaaldok system at Zandvliet, west of Antwerp, Belgium. It is 1,640 feet long and 187 feet wide and is an entrance to an impounded sheet of water 11.2 miles long.

Deepest. The world's deepest lock is the Wilson dam lock at Muscle Shoals, Alabama, on the Tennessee River, completed in November, 1959. It can raise or lower barges 100 feet, and has twin-leaf gates weighing 1,400 tons.

Highest Lock Elevator. The world's highest lock elevator is the Arzwiller-Saint Louis, France, lift completed in 1969 to replace 17 locks on the Marne-Rhine canal system. It drops 146 feet over a ramp 383.8 feet long on a 41° gradient.

Largest Cut. The Gaillard Cut (known as "the Ditch") on the Panama Canal is 270 feet deep between Gold Hill and Contractor's Hill with a bottom width of 300 feet. In one day in 1911 as many as 333 dirt trains each carrying 400 tons left this site. The total amount of earth excavated for the whole Panama Canal was 9,980,000 tons, which total will be raised by the widening of the Gaillard Cut to 500 feet. In 1968, there were a record 14,807 transits.

Dams

Earliest. The earliest dam ever built was the Sadd al-Kafara, 7 miles southeast of Helwan, United Arab Republic (formerly Egypt). It was built in the period 2950–2750 B.C. and had a length of 348 feet and a height of 37 feet.

Most Massive. Measured by volume, the largest dam in the world is the Fort Peck Dam, completed in 1940 across the Missouri River in Montana. It contains 125,628,000 cubic yards of earth and rock fill, and is 21,026 feet (3.98 miles) long and up to 251 feet high. It maintains a reservoir with a capacity of 19,100,000 acre-feet.

Work started in December, 1967, on the Tarbela Dam, in the Sind, West Pakistan. The total expenditure before completion in 1975 on the 485-foot-tall, 9,000-foot-long construction is expected to reach $815 million including the $623 million contract awarded to the Impregilo Consortium. The total volume of the dam will be 186,000,000 cubic yards.

Largest Concrete. The world's largest concrete dam, and the largest concrete structure in the world, is the Grand Coulee Dam on the Columbia River, Washington. Work on the dam was begun in 1933, it began working on March 22, 1941, and was completed in 1942 at a cost of $56,000,000. It has a crest length of 4,173 feet and is 550 feet high. It contains 10,585,000 cubic yards of concrete, and weighs about 21,600,000 tons. The hydroelectric power plant (completed in 1951) has a capacity of 1,974,000 kilowatts.

Highest. The highest dam in the world is the Grand Dixence in Switzerland, completed in September, 1961, at a cost of $372,000,000. It is 932 feet from base to rim, 2,296 feet long and the total volume of concrete in the dam is 7,792,000 cubic yards. (See photograph, page 268.)

The earth-fill Nurek Dam on the Vakhsh-Amu Darya River, U.S.S.R., will be 1,017 feet high, have a crest length of 2,280 feet and a volume of 75,900,000 cubic yards. The concrete Ingurskaya dam in western Georgia, U.S.S.R., is planned to have a final height of 988 feet, a crest length of 2,240 feet and a volume of 3,920,000 cubic yards. (See photograph, next page.)

Longest. The longest river dam in the world is the Hirakud Dam on the Mahanadi River, near Sambalpur, Orissa, India. It consists of a main concrete and masonry dam (3,768 feet), an Earth Dam (11,980 feet), the Left Dyke (five sections of 32,275 feet) and the Right Dyke (35,500 feet), totaling 15.8 miles altogether.

The longest sea dam in the world is the Afsluitdijk stretching 20.195 miles across the mouth of the Zuider Zee in two sections of 1.553 miles (mainland of North Holland to the Isle of Wieringen) and 18.641 miles (Wieringen to Friesland). It has a sea-level width of 293 feet and a height of 24 feet 7 inches.

Largest Reservoir

The largest man-made reservoir is Bratsk Lake on the Angara River, U.S.S.R., with a volume of 137,214,000 acre-feet. A volume of 149,000,000 acre-feet has been quoted for Kariba Lake, the reservoir at Kariba Gorge on the Zambesi River on the border between Zambia and Rhodesia, but is now more reliably estimated at 130,000,000 acre-feet, with a shoreline of 860 miles. The Volta Lake, Ghana, which filled behind the Akosombo dam from May, 1964, to late 1968, also often referred to as the world's largest man-made lake, has a capacity of 120,000,000 acre-feet.

The completion in 1954 of the Owen Falls Dam near Jinja, Uganda, across the northern exit of the White Nile River from the lake, Victoria Nyanza, marginally raised the level of that lake by adding 166,000,000 acre-feet, and technically turned it into a reservoir with a surface area of 17,169,920 acres (26,828 square miles).

NEW DAM WILL BE HIGHEST: The Nurek Dam in the U.S.S.R., now nearing completion, is an earth-fill project that will reach a crest of 1,017 feet.

The most grandiose reservoir project planned is the Xingu-Araguaia river scheme in central Brazil for a reservoir behind a dam at Ilha da Paz with a volume of 780,000 million cubic yards extending over 22,800 square miles. A dam at Obidos on the Amazon would produce a 744-mile-long back-up and a 68,400-square-mile reservoir at an estimated cost of $3,000 million.

Largest Polder

The largest of the five great polders in the old Zuider Zee, Netherlands, will be the 149,000-acre (232.8 square-mile) Markerwaard. Work on the 66-mile-long surrounding dyke was begun in 1957. The water area remaining after the erection of the 1927–32 dam is called IJssel Meer, which will have a final area of 487.5 square miles.

Largest Levees

The most massive earthworks ever carried out are the Mississippi levees begun in 1717 and vastly augmented by the U.S. Government after the disastrous floods of 1927. These extend for 1,732 miles along the main river from Cape Girardeau, Missouri, to the Gulf of Mexico and comprise more than 1,000,000,000 cubic yards of earthworks. Additional levees on the tributaries comprise an additional 2,000 miles.

LONGEST TUNNEL: Inside the 85-mile-long tunnel which supplies New York City with its water. Recently the supply has been found inadequate when rainfall declines.

Tunnels

Longest. The world's longest tunnel of any kind is the New York City-West Delaware water supply tunnel begun in 1937 and completed in 1945. It has a diameter of 13 feet 6 inches and runs for 85.0 miles from the Rondout Reservoir into the Hillview Reservoir, near the northern city line of New York City. (See photo.)

Vehicular. The world's longest continuous vehicular tunnel is the London Transport Board underground railway line from Morden to East Finchley, *via* Bank, in London. In use since 1939, it is 17 miles 528 yards long. The diameter of the tunnel is 12 feet and the station tunnels 21 feet $2\frac{1}{2}$ inches.

Bridge-Tunnel. The world's longest bridge-tunnel system is the Chesapeake Bay Bridge-Tunnel, extending 17.65 miles from Cape Charles to Cape Henry, Virginia, near Norfolk. It cost $200,000,000, took 42 months to complete, and opened on April 15, 1964. The longest bridged section is Trestle C (4.56 miles long) and the longest tunnel is the Thimble Shoal Channel Tunnel (1.09 miles).

Canal-Tunnel. The world's longest canal-tunnel is that on the Rove Canal between the port of Marseille, France, and the Rhône River, built in 1912–27. It is 4.53 miles long, 72 feet wide and 50 feet high, involving 2,250,000 cubic yards of excavation.

Railroad. The world's longest main-line tunnel is the Simplon II Tunnel, completed after 4 years' work on October 16, 1922. Linking Switzerland and Italy under the Alps, it is 12 miles 559 yards long. Over 60 were killed boring this and the Simplon I (1896–1906), which is 22 yards shorter. Its greatest depth below the surface is 7,005 feet.

Sub-aqueous. The world's longest sub-aqueous road tunnel is the Kanmon Tunnel, completed in 1958, which runs 6.01 miles from Shimonseki, Honshu, to Kyushu, Japan. The Seikan Tunnel (38.6 miles), 460 feet beneath the sea bed of the Tsugara Strait between Tappi Saki, Honshu, and Fukushima, Hokkaido, Japan, is due to be completed in 1977. Tests started on the sub-aqueous section (14.5 miles) in 1963. In 1966, the United Kingdom and French governments reached agreement on an English Channel Tunnel for electric trains. It would run in two passages, each 35.6 miles long, 21 miles being sub-aqueous, between Westenhanger, near Dover, Kent, and Sangatte, near Calais. The project now known as the "Chunnel," was first discussed in 1802. It will cost about $870,000,000 if completed.

Road. The world's longest road tunnel is 7.2 miles long under Mont Blanc (15,771 feet) from Pèlerins, near Chamonix, France, to Entrèves, near Courmayeur in Valle d'Aosta, Italy, on which work began in January, 1959. The holing through was achieved on August 14, 1962, and it was opened to traffic on July 16, 1965, after an expenditure of $63,840,000. The 29½-foot-high tunnel with its carriageway of two 12-foot lanes is expected to carry 600,000 vehicles a year. There were 23 deaths during tunneling.

The largest diameter road tunnel in the world was blasted through Yerba Buena Island in San Francisco Bay. It is 76 feet wide, 58 feet high and 540 feet long. Up to 35,000,000 vehicles pass through on its two decks every year.

Hydroelectric. The longest hydroelectric tunnel in the world will be the 51.5-mile-long Orange-Fish Rivers Tunnel, South Africa, begun in 1967 at an estimated cost of $625,000,000. A 30-mile-long tunnel joining the River Arpa with Lake Sevan at an altitude of

LONGEST BRIDGE-TUNNEL stretches 17.65 miles across four man-made islands in Chesapeake Bay between the Delmarva Peninsula, Va., and the Virginia mainland.

6,500 feet in the Armenian Mountains, U.S.S.R. was also reported under construction in 1967.

Tunneling. The record for rapid tunneling was set on March 18, 1967, in the 8.6-mile-long Blanco Tunnel, in Southern Colorado, when the "mole" (giant boring machine) crew advanced the 10-foot diameter heading 375 feet in one day.

5. Specialized Structures

Seven Wonders of the World

The Seven Wonders of the World were first designated by Antipater of Sidon in the 2nd century B.C. They included the Pyramids of Giza, built by three Fourth Dynasty Egyptian Pharaohs, Hwfw (Khufu or Cheops), Kha-f-Ra (Khafre, Khefren or Chephren) and Menkaure (Mycerinus) near El Giza (El Gizeh), southwest of El Qahira (Cairo) in Egypt (now the United Arab Republic). The Great Pyramid ("Horizon of Khufu") was built in *c.* 2580 B.C. Its original height was 480 feet 11 inches (now, since the loss of its topmost stones or pyramidion, reduced to 449 feet 6 inches) with a base line of 756 feet and thus originally covering slightly more than 13 acres. It has been estimated that a work force of 4,000 required 30 years to maneuver into position the 2,300,000 stone blocks averaging $2\frac{3}{4}$ tons each, totaling about 7,225,000 tons and a volume of 90,700,000 cubic feet.

Of the other six wonders, only fragments remain of the Temple of Artemis (Diana) of the Ephesians, built in *c.* 350 B.C. at Ephesus, Turkey (destroyed by the Goths in 262 A.D.), and of the Tomb of King Mausolus of Caria, built at Halicarnassus, now Bodrum, Turkey, in *c.* 325 B.C. No trace remains of the Hanging Gardens of Semiramis, at Babylon, Iraq (*c.* 600 B.C.); the 40-foot-tall marble, gold and ivory statue of Zeus (Jupiter), by Phidias (5th century B.C.) at Olympia, Greece (lost in a fire at Istanbul); the 117-foot-tall statue by Chares of Lindus of the figure of the god Helios (Apollo), called the Colossus of Rhodes (sculptured 292–280 B.C., destroyed by an earthquake in 224 B.C.); or the 400-foot-tall lighthouse built by Soscratus of Cnidus during the 3rd century B.C. (destroyed by earthquake in 1375 A.D.) on the island of Pharos (Greek, *pharos*= lighthouse), off the coast of El Iskandarîya (Alexandria), Egypt (now the United Arab Republic).

Pyramids

Largest. The largest pyramid, and the largest monument ever constructed, is the Quetzalcóatl at Cholula de Rivadahia, 63 miles southeast of Mexico City. It is 177 feet tall and its base covers an area of nearly 45 acres. Its total volume has been estimated at 4,300,000 cubic yards, compared with 3,360,000 cubic yards for the Pyramid of Cheops (see above). The pyramid-building era here was between the 6th and 12th centuries A.D.

Oldest. The oldest known pyramid is the Djoser step pyramid at Saqqâra, Egypt, constructed to a height of 204 feet of Tura limestone in *c.* 2650 B.C. The oldest New World pyramid is that on the island of La Venta in southeastern Mexico built by the Olmec

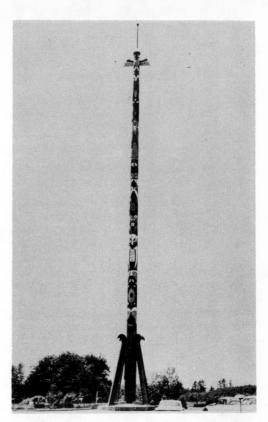

TALLEST TOTEM POLE: This 160-foot-tall pole was carved from a 500-year-old tree, and weighs 57,000 lbs.

people *c.* 800 B.C. It stands 100 feet tall with a base diameter of 420 feet.

Obelisks

Oldest. The longest an obelisk has remained *in situ* is that at Heliopolis (now Masr-el-Gedîda) United Arab Republic (Egypt), erected by Senusret I *c.* 1750 B.C.

Largest. The largest standing obelisk in the world is that in the Piazza of St. John in Lateran, Rome, erected in 1588. It came originally from the Circus Maximus (erected 357 A.D.) and before that from Heliopolis, Egypt (erected *c.* 1450 B.C.). It is 110 feet in length and weighs 450 long tons.

Tallest Totem Pole

The tallest totem pole in the world is 160 feet tall in McKinleyville, California. It weighs 57,000 lbs. and was carved from a 500-year-old tree. It was erected in May, 1962.

Tallest Flagpole

The tallest flagpole ever erected was outside the Oregon Building at the 1915 Panama-Pacific International Exposition in San Fran-

TALLEST MONUMENT: This Gateway Arch at the edge of the Mississippi River in St. Louis was designed by Eero Saarinen, is 630 feet high, and has a span of 630 feet.

cisco. Trimmed from a Douglas fir, it stood 299 feet 7 inches in height. The tallest unsupported flagpole in the world is a 220-foot-tall metal pole weighing 28,000 lbs., erected in 1955 at the U.S. Merchant Marine Academy in King's Point, New York. The pole, built by Kearney-National Inc., tapers from 24 inches to 5½ inches at the jack.

Monuments

Tallest. The world's tallest monument is the stainless steel Gateway Arch in St. Louis, Missouri, completed on October 28,

1965, to commemorate the westward expansion after the Louisiana Purchase of 1803. It is a sweeping arch of stainless steel, spanning 630 feet and rising to a height of 630 feet, and costing $29,000,000. It was designed by Eero Saarinen (died 1961).

The tallest monumental column in the world commemorates the battle of San Jacinto (April 21, 1836), on the bank of the San Jacinto River near Houston, Texas. General Sam Houston (1793–1863) and his force of 743 Texan troops killed 630 Mexicans (out of a total force of 1,600) and captured 700 others, for the loss of nine men killed and 30 wounded. Constructed in 1936–39, at a cost of $1,500,000, the tapering column is 570 feet tall, 47 feet square at the base, and 30 feet square at the observation tower, which is surmounted by a star weighing 220 tons. It is built of concrete, faced with buff limestone, and weighs 35,150 tons.

Largest Prehistoric. The largest monolithic prehistoric monuments in Britain are the 28½-acre earthworks and stone circles of Avebury, Wiltshire, rediscovered in 1646. This is believed to be the work of the Beaker people of the later Neolithic period of *c.* 1700 to 1500 B.C. The whole work is 1,200 feet in diameter with a 40-foot ditch around the perimeter. The largest trilithons exist at Stonehenge, to the south of Salisbury Plain, Wiltshire, with single sarsen blocks weighing over 45 long tons and requiring over 550 men to drag them up a 9° gradient. The dating of the ditch was, in 1969, revised to 2180 B.C. $\pm$ 105.

Largest Tomb

The largest tomb in the world is that of Emperor Nintoku (died *c.* 428 A.D.) south of Osaka, Japan. It measures 1,594 feet long by 1,000 feet wide by 150 feet high.

Ziggurat (Temple Tower)

The largest surviving ziggurat (from the verb *zigguratu,* Babylonian, to build high) is the Ziggurat of Ur (now Muqqayr, Iraq) with a base 200 feet by 150 feet built to at least three stories of which only the first and part of the second now survive to a height of 60 feet. It was built by the Akkadian King Ur-Nammu (*c.* 2113–2006 B.C.).

Tallest Columns

The tallest columns in the world are the sixteen 82-foot-tall pillars in the Palace of Labor in Torino (Turin), Italy, for which the architect was Pier Luigi Nervi (born June 21, 1891). They were built of concrete and steel in only 8 days. The tallest load-bearing stone columns are those measuring 69 feet in the Hall of Columns of the Temple of Amun at Al Karnak, the northern part of the ruins of Thebes, the Greek name for the ancient capital of Upper Egypt (now the United Arab Republic). They were built in the 19th dynasty in the reign of Rameses II in *c.* 1270 B.C.

Largest Dome

The world's largest dome is the "Astrodome" of the Harris County Sports Stadium, in Houston, Texas. It has an outside diameter of 710 feet and an inside diameter of 642 feet. (See photo, page 264.)

The largest dome of ancient architecture is that of the Pantheon, built in Rome in 112 A.D., with a diameter of 142½ feet.

Tallest Statue. The tallest free-standing statue in the world is that of the "Motherland," an enormous female figure on Mamayev Hill, outside Volgograd, U.S.S.R., designed in 1967 by Yevgenyi Vuchetich, to commemorate victory in the Battle of Stalingrad (1942–43). The statue from its base to the tip of a sword clenched in her right hand measures 270 feet.

Near Bamiyan, Afghanistan, there are the remains of the recumbent Sakya Buddha, built of plastered rubble, which was "about 1,000 feet" long and is believed to date from the 3rd or 4th century A.D.

Docks

Drydock—Largest. The largest drydock in the world is the Belfast Harbour Commission and Harland and Wolff building dock at Belfast, Northern Ireland. It has been excavated by Wimpey's to a length of 1,825 feet and a width of 305 feet and can accommodate tankers of 1,000,000 deadweight tons. Work was begun on January 26, 1968 and completed on November 30, 1969. It involved the excavation of 400,000 cubic yards. (See also *Largest Crane.*)

Work started at Nagasaki, Japan, on September 16, 1970, on a building dock capable of taking a tanker of 1,200,000 d.w.t. for Mitsubishi Heavy Industries Co. at a cost of $80,000,000.

Floating Dock. The largest floating docks ever constructed are the U.S. Navy's advanced base sectional docks (A.B.S.D.). These consist of 10 sectional units giving together an effective keel block length of 827 feet and clear width of 140 feet, with a lifting capacity of 71,000 tons. One designated AFDB3 at Green Cove Springs, Florida, has a normal lifting capacity of 80,000 tons.

The largest single unit floating dock is Admiralty Floating Dock (AFD) 35, which was towed from the British Royal Navy's dockyard in Malta to the Cantieri Navali Santa Maria of Genoa, Italy, in May, 1965. It has a lifting capacity of 65,000 tons and an overall length of 857 feet 8 inches. It had been towed to Malta from Bombay, India, where it was built in 1947.

Longest Jetty

The longest deep-water jetty in the world is the Quai Hermann du Pasquier at Le Havre, France, with a length of 5,000 feet. Part of an enclosed basin, it has a constant depth of water of 32 feet on both sides.

Longest Pier

The world's longest pier is the Dammam Pier at El Hasa, Saudi Arabia, on the Persian Gulf. A rock-filled causeway 4.84 miles long joins the steel trestle pier 1.80 miles long, which joins the Main Pier (744 feet long), giving an overall length of 6.79 miles. The work was begun in July, 1948, and completed on March 15, 1950.

Longest Breakwater

The world's longest breakwater system is that which protects the Ports of Long Beach and Los Angeles, California. The combined length of the four breakwaters is 43,602 feet (8.26 miles) of which the Long Beach section, built between 1941 and February, 1949, is the longest at 13,350 feet (2.53 miles). The north breakwater at Tuticorin, Madras Province, Southern India, on which construction began in 1968 will extend when complete to 13,589 feet.

Lighthouses

Brightest. The lighthouse with the most powerful light in the world is Créac'h d'Ouessant lighthouse, established in 1638 and

MOST POWERFUL LIGHTHOUSE: On the coast of Brittany, France, the Créac'h d'Ouessant, built in 1638, has a light equal to 500,000,000 candles.

last altered in 1939 on l'Île d'Ouessant, Finistère, Brittany, France. It is 163 feet tall and, in times of fog, has a luminous intensity of up to 500,000,000 candles.

The lights with the greatest visible range are those 1,092 feet above the ground on the Empire State Building, New York City. Each of the four-arc mercury bulbs has a rated candlepower of 450,000,000, visible 80 miles away on the ground and 300 miles away from aircraft. They were switched on on March 31, 1956.

Tallest. The world's tallest lighthouse is the steel tower 348 feet tall near Yamashita Park in Yokohama, Japan. It has a power of 600,000 candles and a visibility range of 20 miles.

Remotest. The most remote lighthouse is The Smalls, about 16 sea miles (18.4 statute miles) off the Pembrokeshire coast of Wales.

Windmills

The earliest recorded windmills are those used for grinding corn in Iran (Persia) in the 7th century A.D.

The oldest Dutch mill is the towermill at Zedden, Gelderland, built in *c.* 1450.

The largest Dutch windmill is the Dijkpolder in Maasland, built in 1718. The sails measure 95¾ feet from tip to tip.

The tallest windmill in the Netherlands is De Walvisch in Schiedam built to a height of 108 feet in 1794.

Waterwheel

The largest waterwheel is the Mohammadieh Noria wheel at Hama, Syria, with a diameter of 131 feet. It dates from Roman times.

LONGEST STAIRS: Built of wood, these 3,875 steps at a power station in Norway are 4,101 feet long.

Largest Windows

The largest sheet of glass ever manufactured was one of 538.2 square feet, or 65 feet 7 inches by 8 feet $2\frac{1}{2}$ inches, exhibited by the Saint Gobain Company in France at the *Journées Internationales de Miroiterie* in March, 1958. The largest windows in the world are the three in the Palace of Industry and Technology at Rond-point de la Défense, Paris, with an extreme width of 715.2 feet and a maximum height of 164 feet.

Longest Stairs

The world's longest stairs are reputedly at the Mar power station, Overland, western Norway. Built of wood in 1952, these are 4,101 feet in length, rising in 3,875 steps at an angle of 41° inside the pressure shaft. The length of a very long, now discontinuous, stone stairway in the Rohtang Pass, Manali, Kulu, Northern India, is still under investigation.

Longest Wall

The Great Wall of China, completed during the reign of Shih Huang-ti (246–210 B.C.), is 1,684 miles in length, with a height of from 15 to 39 feet and up to 32 feet thick. Its erection is the most massive masonry construction job ever undertaken by the human race. It runs from Shanhaikuan, on the Gulf of Pohai, to Chiayukuan in Kansu and was kept in repair up to the 16th century.

Longest Fence

The longest fence in the world is the dingo-proof fence enclosing the main sheep areas of Queensland, Australia. The wire fence is 6 feet high, goes one foot underground, and stretches for 3,437 miles.

Largest Doors

The largest doors in the world are the four in the Vertical Assembly Building near Cape Kennedy, Florida, with a height of 460 feet. (See *Largest Buildings—Scientific.*)

Tallest Fire Ladder

The world's tallest mobile fire ladder is a 250-foot-tall turntable ladder built in 1962 by Magirus, a German firm.

Largest Marquee

The largest ever erected was a tent covering an area of 188,368 square feet (4.32 acres) put up by the firm of Deuter from Augsburg, Germany, for the 1958 "Welcome Expo" in Brussels, Belgium.

Largest Nudist Camp

The first nudist camps were established in Germany in 1912. The largest such camp in the world was at l'Ile du Levant, southern France, which had up to 15,000 *adeptes* before it was taken over for defense purposes by the French Navy in 1965.

Largest today is Naked City in Rose Lawn, Indiana, which covers 386 acres and caters to as many as 8,400 customers on pageant days.

Largest Vat

The world's largest fermentation vessel is the giant stainless steel container, No. 26M, built by the A.P.V. Co. Ltd. of Crawley,

GREATEST ADVERTISING SIGN EVER ERECTED (left): The Citroën sign which appeared on the Eiffel Tower from 1925 to 1936. The letter "N" alone measured over 68 feet in height. HIGHEST ADVERTISING SIGN (right): The letters "RCA" rise 825 feet above Rockefeller Plaza in the heart of New York City.

Sussex, England, for the Guinness Brewery, St. James's Gate, Dublin, Ireland. This has a nominal capacity of 8,000 barrels, and dimensions of 63 feet long by 28 feet 9 inches wide by 29 feet 7 inches high.

Advertising Signs

Largest. The greatest advertising sign ever erected was the electric Citroën sign on the Eiffel Tower, Paris. It was switched on on July 4, 1925, and could be seen 24 miles away. It was in six colors with 250,000 lamps and 56 miles of electric cables. The letter "N" which terminated the name "Citroën" between the second and third levels measured 68 feet 5 inches in height. The whole apparatus was taken down after 11 years in 1936. (See photo.)

The world's largest neon advertising sign was owned by the Atlantic Coast Line Railroad Company at Port Tampa, Florida. It measured 387 feet 6 inches long and 76 feet high, weighed 175 tons and contained about 4,200 feet of red neon tubing. It was demolished on February 19, 1970.

Broadway's largest current billboard is 11,426 square feet in area—equivalent to 107 feet by 107 feet. The world's largest working sign was that in Times Square between 44 & 45th Streets, New York City, in 1966. It showed two 42½-foot-tall "bottles" of Haig Scotch Whisky and an 80-foot-long "bottle" of Gordon's Gin being "poured" into a frosted glass.

Highest. The highest advertising sign in the world is the "RCA" on the Radio Corporation of America Building in Rockefeller Plaza, New York City. The top of the 25-foot-tall illuminated letters is 825 feet above street level. (See photo.)

The tallest free-standing advertising sign is the 188-foot-high 93-foot-wide sign of the Stardust Hotel, Las Vegas, Nevada, completed in February, 1968. It uses 25,000 light bulbs and 2,500 of neon tubing, and has letters up to 22 feet tall.

Cemetery

The world's largest cemetery is one in Leningrad, U.S.S.R., which contains over 500,000 of the 1,300,000 victims of the German army's siege of 1941–42.

The largest crematorium is at the Nikolo-Arkhangelskoye Cemetery, East Moscow, completed to a British design in March, 1972. It has seven twin furnaces and several Halls of Farewell for atheists.

Tallest Fountain

The world's tallest fountain is the "Delacorte Geyser" in Welfare Park, at the southern tip of Welfare Island, in the East River, New York City, which can attain a height of 600 feet. It was installed in June, 1969, at a cost of $350,000 and given to the city by George T. Delacorte, founder of the Dell Publishing Co. (See photograph.)

TALLEST FOUNTAIN (left) is the new 600-foot-high Delacorte Geyser at the tip of Welfare Island in New York's East River. The Chrysler Building's spire seems hardly any higher. GREATEST GUSHER (right): This 1,160-foot-deep wildcat oil well near Beaumont, Texas, yielded 800,000 barrels in 1901 in 9 days before it could be capped.

Borings

Deepest. Man's deepest penetration into the earth's crust is the Baden No. 1 gas wildcat well, Beckham County, Oklahoma. After 546 days of drilling, the Loffland Brothers Drilling Co. reached 30,050 feet (5.69 miles) on February 29, 1972. The hole temperature at the bottom was 420° F. A conception of the depth of this hole can be gained by the realization that it was sufficient in depth to lower the Empire State Building down it 24 times.

The most recent in a succession of announcements from the U.S.S.R. of intentions to drill down 15 kilometers (49,213 feet) was in February, 1972, from the Baku Scientific Research Institute. A depth of 21,620 feet has been reached at the Kura River Valley site in Southern Azerbaijan. The target here remains 48,000 feet (9.09 miles).

Oil Fields

Largest. The largest oil field in the world is one at Oktyabr'skiy, U.S.S.R., which extends over 1,800 square miles (60 miles by 30 miles). It has been asserted that the Groningen gas field in the Netherlands is the largest yet discovered.

It was estimated in 1968 that the United Kingdom's segment of the North Sea gas field contains 2.5 by 10^{13} cubic feet of almost pure methane of which the Leman Field (discovered April, 1966), operated by the Shell-Esso-Gas Council-Amoco group, accounts for about half.

Greatest Gusher. The most prolific wildcat recorded is the 1,160-foot-deep Lucas No. 1, at Spindletop, about 3 miles north of Beaumont, Texas, on January 10, 1901. The gusher was heard more than a mile away and yielded 800,000 barrels during the 9 days it was uncapped. The surrounding ground subsequently yielded 142,000,000 barrels. (See photograph, previous page.)

Greatest Flare. The greatest gas fire was burnt at Gassi Touil in the Algerian Sahara from noon on November 13, 1961 to 9:30 a.m. on April 28, 1962. The pillar of flame rose 450 feet and the smoke 600 feet. It was eventually extinguished by Paul Neal ("Red") Adair, aged 47, of Houston, Texas, using 550 lbs. of dynamite. His fee was understood to be about $1,000,000.

Largest Gas Tank. The world's largest gas tank is that at Fontaine l'Evêque, Belgium, where disused mines have been adapted to store up to 500 million cubic meters (17,650 million cubic feet) of gas at ordinary pressure. Probably the largest conventional gas tank is that at Wien-Simmering, Vienna, Austria, completed in 1968, with a height of 274 feet 8 inches and a capacity of 10.59 million cubic feet.

Well

The world's deepest water well is the Stensvad Water Well 11-W1 7,320 feet deep drilled by the Great Northern Drilling Co. Inc. in Rosebud County, Montana, in October–November, 1961.

The largest hand-dug well is one 32 feet in diameter, 100 feet in circumference and 109 feet deep dug in 1877–78 in Greensburg, Kansas.

Depth in ft.	Location	Date
475	Duck Creek, Ohio (brine)...............	1841
550	Perpignan, France (artesian).............	1849
5,735	Schladebach, Germany	1886
6,570	Schladebach, Germany	1893
7,230	Schladebach, Germany	1909
8,046	Olinda, Calif.	1927
8,523	Big Lake, W. Texas........................	1928
9,280	Long Beach, Calif...........................	1929
9,753	Midway, Calif.	1930
10,030	Rinconfield, Calif.	1931
10,585	Vera Cruz, Mexico.........................	1931
10,944	Kettleman Hills, Calif......................	1933
11,377	Belridge, Calif.	1934
12,786	Gulf McElroy, W. Texas..................	1935
15,004	Wasco, Calif.	1938
15,279	Pecos County, W. Texas..................	1944
16,246	S. Coles Levee, Calif.......................	1944
16,655	Brazos County, Texas	1945
16,668	Miramonte, Calif.	1946
17,823	Caddo County, Oklahoma	1947
18,734	Ventura County, Calif.	1949
20,521	Sublette County, Wyoming	1949
21,482	Bakersfield, Calif.	1953
22,570	Plaquemines, Louisiana....................	1956
25,340	Pecos County, W. Texas	1958
25,600	St. Bernard Parish, Louisiana	1970
28,500	Pecos County, W. Texas	1972
30,050	Beckham County, Oklahoma	1972

Mines

Earliest. The earliest known mining operations were in the Ngwenya Hills of the Hhohho District of northwestern Swaziland where hematite (iron ore) was mined for body paint *c.* 41,000 B.C.

Deepest. The world's deepest mine is the East Rand Proprietary Mine at Boksburg, Transvaal, South Africa. In November, 1959, a depth of 11,246 feet (2.13 miles) below the ground and 5,875 feet below sea level was first attained. Mining does not now proceed below 10,788 feet where the rock temperature is two degrees cooler at 124°F.

The deepest terminal below any vertical mine shaft in the world is No. 3 sub-vertical main shaft on the Western Deep Levels Mine reaching 9,783 feet below the surface. The longest vertical shaft is No. 3 Ventilation Shaft at the mine which measures 9,673 feet in one continuous hole. The longest sub-incline shaft is the Angelo Tertiary at E.R.P.M. with a length of 6,656 feet (1.26 miles).

Gold. The largest gold-mining area in the world is the Witwatersrand gold field extending 30 miles east and west of Johannesburg, South Africa. Gold was discovered there in 1886 and by 1944 more than 45 per cent of the world's gold was mined there by 320,000 Bantu and 44,000 Europeans. Currently 74 per cent of the free world's supply comes from this area, which now has a total labor force of 650,000.

The largest gold mine in area is the East Rand Proprietary Mines Ltd. (see above), whose 8,785 claims cover 12,100 acres. The largest, measured by volume extracted, is Randfontein Estates Gold Mine Co. Ltd. with 170 million cubic yards—enough to cover Manhattan

LARGEST EXCAVATION: The Bingham Canyon Copper Mine near Salt Lake City has had removed from it five times the amount of material that was excavated for the Panama Canal. It was the most productive copper mine in history.

Island to a depth of 8 feet. The main tunnels if placed end to end would stretch a distance of 2,600 miles.

Richest. The richest gold mine has been Crown Mines with nearly 45 million ounces and still productive. The richest in yield per year was West Driefontein which averaged more than 2,500,000 ounces per year until disrupted in November, 1968, by flooding. The only large mine in South Africa yielding more than one ounce per ton milled is Free State Geduld.

Iron. The world's largest iron mine is at Lebedinsky, U.S.S.R., in the Kursk Magnetic Anomaly which has altogether an estimated 20,000 million tons of rich (45–65 per cent) ore and 10,000,000 million tons of poorer ore in seams up to 2,000 feet thick. The world's greatest reserves are, however, those of Brazil, estimated to total 58,000 million tons, or 35 per cent of the world's total surface stock.

Copper. Historically the world's most productive copper mine has been the Bingham Canyon Mine (see photo) belonging to the Kennecott Copper Corporation with over 9,000,000 tons in the 65 years 1904–68. Currently the most productive is the Chuquicamata mine of the Anaconda Company 150 miles north of Antofagasta, Chile, with 334,578 tons in 1966.

The world's largest underground copper mine is at El Teniente, 50 miles southeast of Santiago, Chile, with more than 200 miles of underground workings and an annual output of nearly 11,000,000 tons of ore.

Silver, Lead and Zinc. The world's largest lead, zinc and silver mine is the Sullivan Mine at Kimberley, British Columbia, Canada, with 248 miles of tunnels. The mines at Broken Hill, New South Wales, Australia, found in September, 1883, produce annually

2,300,000 tons of ore, from which is extracted some 10 per cent of the world's output of lead. The world's largest zinc smelter is the Cominco Ltd. plant at Trail, British Columbia, Canada, which has an annual capacity of 263,000 tons of zinc and 800 tons of cadmium.

Quarries

The world's deepest open pit is the Kimberley Open Mine in South Africa (the "Big Hole") dug over a period of 43 years (1871 to 1914) to a depth of nearly 1,200 feet and with a diameter of about 1,500 feet and a circumference of nearly a mile, covering an area of 36 acres. Some 3.36 tons (14,504,566 carats) of diamonds were extracted from the 28,000,000 tons of earth dug out. The inflow of water has now made the depth 845 feet to the water surface. The "Big Hole" was dug by pick and shovel.

Largest Stone. The largest mined slab of quarried stone is one measuring 68 feet by 14 feet by 14 feet, weighing about 1,780 tons, at Ba'labakk (Baalbeck), in the Lebanon. The largest able to be moved from this mine were slabs of 900 tons for the trilithon of the nearby Temple of Jupiter.

Excavation

The world's largest excavation is the Bingham Canyon Copper Mine, 30 miles south of Salt Lake City, Utah. From 1906 to mid-1969 the total excavation has been 2,736,400,000 tons over an area of 2.08 square miles to a depth of 2,280 feet. This is five times the amount of material moved to build the Panama Canal. Three shifts of 900 men work around the clock with 38 electric shovels, 62 locomotives hauling 1,268 wagons and 18 drilling machines for the 28 tons of explosive used daily. The average daily extraction is 106,620 tons of ore and 252,000 tons of overburden.

Dump Heap

The world's largest artificial heap is the sand dump on the Randfontein Estates Gold Mines, South Africa, which comprises 42 million long tons of crushed ore and rock waste and has a volume six times that of the Great Pyramid.

Chapter Nine

THE MECHANICAL WORLD

1. Ships

Earliest. The earliest known vessel which is still sea-worthy is a 102-foot-long sailing vessel dated to the Egyptian sixth dynasty from *c.* 2420 B.C. Oars found in bogs at Magle Mose, Sjaelland, Denmark, and Star Carr, Yorkshire, England, have been dated to *c.* 8000 B.C.

Earliest Power Vessels

The earliest experiments with marine steam engines date from those on the Seine River in France, in 1775. Propulsion was first achieved when the Marquis Jouffroy d'Abbans ascended a reach of the Saône River near Lyons, France, in 1783, in the 180-ton paddle steamer *Pyroscaphe.*

The tug *Charlotte Dundas* was the first successful power-driven vessel. She was a paddlewheel steamer built in Scotland in 1801–02 by William Symington (1763–1831), using a double-acting condensing engine constructed by James Watt (1736–1819).

The earliest regular steam run was by the *Clermont*, built by Robert Fulton (1765–1815), a U.S. engineer, which maintained a service from New York to Albany from August 17, 1807. The oldest steamer is believed to be the *Skiblandner* (206 gross tons), which was built in Motala, Sweden, in 1856, and sank on Lake Mjøsa, Norway, in February, 1967. By June, 1967, she was raised and fitted for re-commission. G. H. Pattinson's 40-foot steam launch, raised from Ullswater, England, in 1962 and now on Lake Windermere, may date from a year or two earlier.

Earliest Turbine

The first turbine ship was the *Turbinia*, built in 1894 at Wallsend-on-Tyne, Northumberland, England, to the design of the Hon. Sir Charles Algernon Parsons (1854–1931). The *Turbinia* was 100 feet long and of $44\frac{1}{2}$ tons displacement with machinery consisting of three steam turbines totaling about 2,000 shaft horsepower. At her first public demonstration in 1897 she reached a speed of 34.5 knots (39.7 m.p.h.).

Atlantic Crossings

Earliest. The earliest crossing of the Atlantic by a power vessel, as opposed to an auxiliary-engined sailing ship, was a 22-day voyage, begun in April, 1827, from Rotterdam, Netherlands, to the West Indies by the *Curacao*. She was a wooden paddle boat of 438 registered tons, built in Dundee, Angus, Scotland, in 1826, and purchased by the Dutch Government for the West Indian mail service. The earliest Atlantic crossing entirely under steam (with intervals for desalting the boilers) was by H.M.S. *Rhadamanthus* from Plymouth,

England, to Barbados in 1832. The earliest crossing of the Atlantic under continuous steam power was by the condenser-fitted packet ship *Sirius* (703 tons) from Queenstown (now Cobh), Ireland, to Sandy Hook, New Jersey, in 18 days 10 hours on April 4–22, 1838.

Fastest. The fastest Atlantic crossing was made by the *United States* (then 51,988, later 38,216, gross tons), flagship of the United States Lines Company. On her maiden voyage between July 3 and 7, 1952, from New York City, to Le Havre, France, and Southampton, England, she averaged 35.59 knots, or 40.98 m.p.h., for 3 days 10 hours 40 minutes (6:36 p.m. G.M.T. July 3, to 5:16 a.m. July 7) on a route of 2,949 nautical miles from the Ambrose Light Vessel to the Bishop Rock Light, Isles of Scilly, Cornwall, England. During this run, on July 6–7, 1952, she steamed the greatest distance ever covered by any ship in a day's run (24 hours)—868 nautical miles, hence averaging 36.17 knots (41.65 m.p.h.). Her maximum speed is 41.75 knots (48 m.p.h.) on a full power of 240,000 shaft horsepower. The s.h.p. figure was only revealed by the U.S. Defense Department in 1968.

Submerged. The fastest disclosed submerged Atlantic crossing is 6 days 11 hours 55 minutes by the U.S. nuclear-powered submarine *Nautilus*, which traveled 3,150 miles from Portland, Dorset, England, to New York City, arriving on August 25, 1958.

Most Crossings

Between 1856 and June, 1894, Captain Samuel Brooks (1832–1904) crossed the North Atlantic 690 times—equal to 2,437,712 statute miles. In 1850–51 he had sailed in the brig *Bessie* as an able-bodied seaman around Cape Horn to Panama, coming home to Liverpool as her master. His lifetime sailing distance was at least 2,513,000 miles.

Pacific Crossing

The fastest crossing of the Pacific Ocean (Yokohoma, Japan, to San Francisco) is 8 days 35 minutes achieved by the 14,114-ton diesel cargo liner *Italy Maru* in August, 1967.

Northernmost

The farthest north ever attained by a surface vessel is 86° 39′ N. in 47° 55′ E. by the drifting U.S.S.R. icebreaker *Sedov* on August 29, 1939. She was locked in the Arctic ice floes from October 23, 1937, until freed on January 13, 1940.

Southernmost

The farthest south ever reached by a ship was achieved on January 3, 1955, by the Argentine icebreaker *General San Martin* in establishing the General Belgrano Base, Antarctica, on the shores of the Weddell Sea at 78° S., 39° W., 830 miles from the South Pole.

Fastest Warship

The world's fastest warship is the H.M.C.S. *Bras d'Or*, the more than 180-ton-150.8-foot-long Canadian Navy Hydrofoil commissioned in 1967. On July 17, 1969, outside Halifax Harbor, Nova Scotia, she attained 61 knots (70.2 m.p.h.).

PROGRESSIVE LIST OF WORLD'S LARGEST LINERS

Gross Tonnage	Name	Propulsion	Overall Length in Feet	Dates
1,340	Great Western (U.K.)...............	Paddle wheels......	236	1838–1856
1,862	British Queen (U.K.)..............	Paddle wheels......	275	1839–1844
2,360	President (U.K.).....................	Paddle wheels......	268	1840–1841
3,270	Great Britain (U.K.)..............	Single screw	322	1845–1937
4,690	Himalaya (U.K.)....................	Single screw	340	1853–1927
18,914[5]	Great Eastern (U.K.)............	Paddles and screw	692	1858–1888
10,650	City of New York (later Harvard, Pittsburgh) (U.S.)	Twin screw.........	528	1888–1923
17,274	Oceanic (U.K.).........................	Twin screw.........	705	1899–1914
20,904	Celtic (U.K.)	Twin screw.........	700	1901–1933
21,227	Cedric (U.K.)	Twin screw.........	700	1903–1932
23,884	Baltic (U.K.)	Twin screw.........	726	1904–1933
31,550	Lusitania (U.K.)	4 screws	790	1907–1915
31,938	Mauretania (U.K.)	4 screws	787	1907–1935
45,300	Olympic (U.K.)	Triple screw	892	1911–1935
46,328	Titanic (U.K.)	4 screws	882.5	1912–1912
52,022	Imperator (Germany) (later Berengaria) (U.K.)	4 screws	919	1913–1938
54,282[1]	Vaterland (later Leviathan) (Germany)	4 screws	950	1914–1938
56,621	Bismarck (later Majestic) (Germany)	4 screws	954	1914–1940
79,280[2]	Normandie (France) (later U.S.S. Lafayette)	4 screws	1,029	1935–1946
80,774[3]	Queen Mary (U.K.)	4 screws	1,019.5	1936–
83,673[4]	Queen Elizabeth (U.K.)...........	4 screws	1,031	1940–1972
66,348	France (France)	4 screws	1,035.2	1961–

[1] Listed as 59,957 gross tons under U.S. registration, 1922–31, but not internationally accepted as such.

[2] Gross tonnage later raised by enclosure of open deck space to 83,423 gross tons.

[3] Later 81,237 gross tons. Later sold to U.S. interests.

[4] Later 82,998 gross tons. Later sold to U.S. interests.

[5] Originally 22,500 tons.

Largest Battleship

The Japanese battleships *Yamato* (sunk in the Bungo Strait by U.S. planes on April 7, 1945) and *Musashi* (sunk in the Philippine Sea by 11 bombs and 16 torpedoes on October 24, 1944) were the largest battleships ever constructed, each with a full load displacement of 72,809 tons. With an overall length of 863 feet, a beam of 127 feet and a full load draught of $35\frac{1}{2}$ feet, they mounted nine 18.1-inch guns in three triple turrets. Each gun weighed 181 tons and was 75 feet in length, firing a 3,200-lb. projectile.

The largest battleships now are the U.S.S. *Iowa* (completed February 22, 1943) and U.S.S. *Missouri* (completed June 11, 1944), each of which has a full load displacement of 57,950 tons and mounts nine 16-inch and twenty 5-inch guns. The U.S.S. *New Jersey* (57,216 tons full load displacement) is, however, longer than either by 9 inches, with an overall length of 888 feet. She was the last battleship on active service in the world and was decommissioned on December 17, 1969.

Largest Passenger Liner

When in operation, the *Queen Elizabeth* (82,998 but formerly 83,673 gross tons), of the Cunard fleet, was the largest passenger vessel ever built and also had the largest displacement of any liner in the world. She had an overall length of 1,031 feet and was 118 feet 7 inches in breadth. She was powered by steam turbines which

developed 168,000 h.p. The *Queen Elizabeth's* normal sea speed was
28½ knots (32.8 m.p.h.). Her last passenger voyage ended on
November 15, 1968. In 1970, she was removed to Hong Kong to
serve as a floating marine university and renamed *Seawise University*.
On January 9, 1972, she caught fire and was gutted.

The longest (1,035.2 feet) and largest (66,348 gross tons) liner
now, the *France*, owned by the Compagnie Générale Transatlantique,
made her official maiden voyage from Le Havre, France, to New
York City, on February 3, 1962. She cost $81,250,000. (See photo.)

Largest Aircraft Carrier

The warship with the largest full load displacement in the world
is the aircraft carrier U.S.S. *Nimitz* at 95,100 tons. She was launched
in April, 1972, and will be commissioned in September, 1973.
U.S.S. *Enterprise* is, however, 1,101½ feet long and thus 65½ feet
longer. U.S.S. *Nimitz*, which will have a speed well in excess of
30 knots, cost $536,000,000. She will be followed by a sister ship,
U.S.S. *Eisenhower*, which will be only 9½ feet shorter than the
Enterprise.

Most Landings. The pilot who has made the greatest number of
deck landings is British Royal Navy Capt. Eric M. Brown, C.B.E.,
D.S.C., A.F.C., with 2,407. Capt. Brown, who retired in 1970,
flew a record 325 types of aircraft during his career and also set
a world record with 2,721 catapult launchings.

Most Powerful Cruiser

The Fleet Escort Ships (formerly cruisers) with the greatest
fire power are the three Albany class ships, U.S.S. *Albany*, *Chicago*
and *Columbus* of 13,700 tons and 673 feet overall. They carry 2 twin
Talos and 2 twin Tartar surface-to-air missiles and an 8-tube Asroc
launcher.

LONGEST AND MOST EXPENSIVE PASSENGER LINER: The "France,"
a two-class ship, cost $81,250,000, on launching in 1961.

Fastest Destroyer

The highest speed attained by a destroyer was 45.02 knots (51.84 m.p.h.) by the 3,750-ton French destroyer *Le Terrible* in 1935. She was powered by four Yarrow small-tube boilers and two geared turbines giving 100,000 shaft horsepower. She was removed from the active list at the end of 1957.

Submarines

Largest. The world's largest submarines are believed to be the 18 nuclear-powered U.S.S.R. "Y" Class submarines with a submerged displacement of 9,000 tons and an overall length of 426.5 feet.

Fastest. The world's fastest submarines are the 35-knot U.S. Navy's tear-drop hulled nuclear vessels of the *Skipjack* class. They have been listed semi-officially as capable of a speed of 45 knots (51.8 m.p.h.) submerged. In November, 1968, the building of attack submarines with submerged speeds in the region of 50 knots was approved for the U.S. Navy.

Deepest. The greatest depth recorded by a true submarine was 8,310 feet by the *Sea Quest* off California, on February 29, 1968. The 51-foot-long *Aluminaut* launched by the Reynolds Metals Co. on September 2, 1964, is designed for depths of up to 15,000 feet, but is prevented from descending below 6,250 feet by prohibitive insurance costs. The U.S. Navy's nuclear-powered NR-1 being built by General Dynamics Inc. will be able to operate at a "very great" but classified depth, which is assumed to be lower than the published figure of 20,000 feet for the first 7-man Deep Submergence Search Vehicle Vessel DSSV due in service in 1973.

Largest Fleet. The largest submarine fleet in the world is that of the U.S.S.R. Navy or *Krasni Flot*, which numbers 401 boats, of which 83 (18 ballistic) are nuclear-powered and 318 conventional. The U.S. Navy has 41 nuclear submarines in service.

Largest and Longest Tankers

The world's largest tankers are the six of the *Universe* class, tankers with a deadweight tonnage of 326,500 tons. Of these the *Universe Portugal* has by a slight margin the highest gross registered tonnage with 149,623 and together with the *Universe Japan* the greatest overall length of 1,135 feet 2 inches. The whole class has a beam of 175 feet 2 inches, a summer draught of 81 feet 5 inches, and a capacity of 2,500,000 barrels of crude oil. Each cost more than $20,000,000 from Japanese shipyards. They carry three anchors each of 22.7 tons with seven-tenths of a mile of chain cable weighing 425.6 tons. The full load displacement of these tankers is believed to be about 400,000 tons.

The longest tanker and the longest ship of any kind are the Esso class tankers, which have a length of 1,141 feet 1 inch—106 feet longer than the world's longest liner, *France*. They have a deadweight tonnage of 253,000 tons, a gross registered tonnage of 127,150 and a beam of 170 feet 2 inches.

Largest Cargo Vessel

The largest vessel in the world capable of carrying dry cargo is *La Loma* (129,961 gross) (U.K.). She is 1,069 feet 8 inches in length and has a beam of 170 feet 8 inches.

The world's largest ore carrier is the *Niizuru Maru* of 165,196 deadweight tons, which made her maiden voyage in October, 1971.

Fastest-Built. During the Second World War "Liberty Ships" of prefabricated welded steel construction were built at seven shipyards on the Pacific coast, under the management of Henry J. Kaiser (1882–1967). The record time for assembly of one ship of 7,200 gross tons (10,500 tons deadweight) was 4 days 15½ hours. In January, 1968, some 900 Liberty ships were still in service.

Largest Cable Ship

The world's largest cable-laying ship is the American Telephone & Telegraph Co.'s German-built *Long Lines* (11,200 gross tons), completed by Deutsche Werft of Hamburg, Germany, in April, 1963, at a cost of $19,040,000. She has a fully-laden displacement of about 17,000 tons, measures 511 feet 6 inches overall and is powered by twin-turbine electric engines.

Largest Whale Factory

The largest whale factory ship is the U.S.S.R.'s *Sovietskaya Ukraina* (32,034 gross tons), with a summer deadweight of 46,000 tons, completed in October, 1959. She is 714.6 feet in length and 94 feet 3 inches in the beam.

Most Successful Trawler

The greatest tonnage of fish ever landed from any trawler in a year is 4,169 tons in 1969 from the British freezer stern trawler *Lady Parkes* owned by Boston Deep Sea Fisheries Ltd. (est. 1894).

Most Powerful Tug

The world's largest and most powerful tugs are the two 17,500 i.h.p. *Oceanic* class boats of 2,046 gross tons, 284 feet 5 inches long, 46 feet 11 inches in the beam, a speed of 22 knots (25 m.p.h.) and a range of 20,000 miles.

Towing

The largest ship ever to take another in tow is S.S. *Ardlui*, the 214,180-deadweight-ton tanker which towed S.S. *British Architect* (22,729 gross tons) 73 miles in the China Sea on June 16, 1970.

H.M.S. *Scylla* (Commander A. F. C. Wemyss, R.N.) towed her sister ship, H.M.S. *Penelope*, in the western Mediterranean on September 25, 1970 with an 11-inch mile-long nylon rope (breaking strain 165 tons) at a speed of 24 knots. The $25,000 Viking Nylon Braidline hawser, made by British Ropes, stretched 38 per cent to 7,325 feet.

Largest Car Ferry

The world's largest car and passenger ferry is the 502-foot-long *Finlandia* (8,100 gross tons), delivered by Wärtsilä Ab. of Helsinki in

LARGEST CONVERTED ICEBREAKER: On her first try, the S.S. "Manhattan" made a double voyage through the Northwest Passage of Canada to Alaska. She has a specially designed bow on which the ship rides upon ice floes until its weight causes the ship to break through.

May, 1967, for service between Helsinki, Finland, and Copenhagen, Denmark, with Finska Ångfartygs Ab. She can carry 321 cars and up to 1,200 passengers. She achieved a speed of 22 knots (25 m.p.h.) during trials.

Largest Hydrofoil

The world's largest naval hydrofoil is the 212-foot-long *Plainview* (310 tons full load), launched by Lockheed Shipbuilding and Construction Company at Seattle, Washington, on June 28, 1965. She has a service speed of 50 knots (57 m.p.h.).

A larger commercial hydrofoil, carrying 150 passengers and 8 cars at 40 knots to ply the Göteborg-Åbborg crossing, between Sweden and Denmark, came into service in June, 1968. She was built by Westermoen Hydrofoil Ltd. of Mandal, Norway.

Largest Dredger

The world's largest dredger is one reported to be operating in the lower Lena basin of the U.S.S.R. in May, 1967, with a rig more than 100 feet tall and a cutting depth of 165 feet. The pontoon is 750 feet long.

The largest dredging grabs in the world are those of 635 cubic feet capacity built in 1965 by Priestman Bros. Ltd. of Hull, Yorkshire, England, for the dredging pontoon *Biarritz*.

Most Powerful Icebreaker

The world's most powerful icebreaker and first atomic-powered ship is the U.S.S.R.'s 44,000 s.h.p. *Lenin* (16,000 gross tons), which was launched at Leningrad on December 2, 1957, and began her maiden voyage on September 18, 1959. In 1971–72, mystery surrounded her continued existence. She is or was 439¾ feet long, 90½ feet in the beam, and has a maximum speed of 18 knots (20.7 m.p.h.). In March, 1970, the U.S.S.R. announced the building of a more powerful atomic-powered icebreaker to be named *Arctika*, able to go through ice 7 feet thick at 4 knots.

The largest converted icebreaker is the 1,007-foot-long S.S. *Manhattan* (43,000 s.h.p.), which was converted by the Humble Oil Co. into a 150,000-ton icebreaker with an armored prow 69 feet 2 inches long. She made a double voyage through the Northwest Passage in arctic Canada to Alaska from August 24 to November 12, 1969. (See photo.) The Northwest Passage was first navigated in 1906.

Wooden Ship

The heaviest wooden ship ever built was British Royal Navy Battleship *Lord Clive* at 7,750 tons. She was completed at Pembroke Dock, Wales, on June 2, 1866. She measured 280 feet in length and was sold in 1875. (See photo.)

Sailing Ships

Largest. The largest sailing vessel ever built was the *France II* (5,806 gross tons), launched at Bordeaux in 1911. The *France II* was a steel-hulled, five-masted barque (square-rigged on four masts and fore and aft rigged on the aftermost mast). Her hull measured 418 feet overall. Although principally designed as a sailing vessel with a stump top-gallant rig, she was also fitted with two steam engines. She was wrecked in 1922.

HEAVIEST WOODEN SHIP: Built in 1866, the H.M.S. "Lord Clive" was a battleship, 280 feet long with a displacement of 7,750 tons.

The only 5-masted full-rigged ship ever built was the *Preussen*, built in 1902, of 5,548 gross tons and 410 feet overall.

Largest Junks. The largest junk on record was the seagoing *Cheng Ho* of *c*. 1420, with a displacement of 3,100 tons and a length variously estimated at from 300 feet to 440 feet.

A river junk 361 feet long, with treadmill-operated paddlewheels, was recorded in 1161 A.D. In *c*. 280 A.D. a floating fortress 600 feet square, built by Wang Chün on the Yangtze, took part in the Chin-Wu river war. Modern junks do not, even in the case of the Chiang-su traders, exceed 170 feet in length.

Longest Day's Run under Sail. The longest day's run by any sailing ship was one of 465 nautical miles (535.4 statute miles) in 23 hours 17 mins. by the *Champion of the Seas* (2,722 registered tons) on her maiden voyage on December 11–12, 1854. She was on passage in the south Indian Ocean under Capt. Alex. Newlands, running before a northwesterly gale. She averaged 19.97 knots.

The highest recorded speed by a sailing ship is 22 knots (25.3 m.p.h.) in 4 consecutive watches, by *Lancing* (ex *La Péreire*) when "running her easting down" on a passage to Melbourne in 1890–91. She was the last 4-masted full-rigged ship (36 sails) and at 405 feet the longest. Her main and mizzen masts were 203 feet from keelson to truck with yards 98 feet 9 inches across.

Slowest Voyage. Perhaps the slowest passage on record was that of the *Red Rock* (1,600 tons), which was posted missing at Lloyd's of London after taking 112 days for a 950-mile passage across the Coral Sea from February 20 to June 12, 1899, at an average speed of less than 0.4 of a knot.

Largest Sails. The largest spars ever carried were those in the British Royal Navy battleship *Temeraire*, completed at Chatham, Kent, on August 31, 1877. The fore and main yards measured 115 feet in length. The mainsail contained 5,100 feet of canvas, weighing 2 tons, and the total sail area was 25,000 square feet. At 8,540 tons the *Temeraire* was the largest brig ever built. The main masts of the British Royal Navy warships *Achilles*, *Black Prince* and *Warrior* all measured 175 feet from truck to deck.

Largest Propeller

The largest ship's propeller will be one of 30 feet 2 inches diameter from blade tip to blade tip, built for the 477,000-ton tanker *Globtik Tokyo*, due to be delivered in February, 1973.

Largest Dracones

The largest dracones (flexible plastic containers used for bulk transport of liquids) ever built were completed by Frankenstein and Sons Ltd., Manchester, England, in July, 1962. They are 300 feet in length and can transport 1,200 tons (250,000 gallons) of water.

Deepest Anchorage

The deepest anchorage ever achieved is one of 24,600 feet in the mid-Atlantic Romanche Trench by Capt. Jacques-Yves Cousteau's research vessel *Calypso*, with a 5½-mile-long nylon cable, on July 29, 1956.

Largest Oil Rigs

The largest oil drilling rigs are those under construction for the Humble Oil & Refinery Co. for their Santa Barbara Channel, California, oil field. Each 4-legged structure will tower 775 feet and weigh more than 20,000 tons.

Wrecks

The largest ship ever wrecked was the 206,60-ton tanker, *Marpessa*, belonging to Royal Dutch/Shell, which sank empty and without casualties on the second leg of her maiden voyage from Rotterdam at a point 50 miles northwest of Dakar, Senegal, on December 15, 1969. The *Marpessa* had been built in Japan, and was 1,067 feet 5 inches long. A tank explosion ripped her open the day before she sank.

The oldest wreck regarded as salvageable is the carrack *Mary Rose* of 1509, which sank off Ryde, Isle of Wight, in 1545. On September 18, 1970, a 448-lb. 8-foot-long breech-loader was recovered from her hull, which appears to have been preserved in a blue clay layer of the sea bed.

Greatest Roll

The ultimate in rolling was recorded in heavy seas off Coos Bay, Oregon, on November 13, 1971, when the U.S. Coast Guard motor lifeboat *Intrepid* made a 360-degree roll.

2. Road Vehicles

Coaches. Before the advent of the Macadam road surfaces in *c.* 1815 coach-riding was slow and hazardous. The zenith in speed was reached on July 13, 1888, when J. Selby, Esq., drove the "Old Times" coach 108 miles from London to Brighton and back with 8 teams and 14 changes in 7 hours 50 minutes to average 13.79 m.p.h. Four-horse carriages could maintain a speed of $21\frac{1}{4}$ m.p.h. for nearly an hour.

CARS

Earliest Automobile. The earliest car of which there is record is a two-foot-long model constructed by Ferdinand Verbiest (died 1687), a Belgian Jesuit priest, described in his *Astronomia Europaea*. His model was possibly inspired either by Giovanni Branca's description of a steam turbine, published in 1629, or by writings on "fire carts" during the Chu dynasty (*c.* 800 B.C.) in the library of the Emperor Khang-hi of China, to whom he was an astronomer during the period *c.* 1665–80.

A 3-wheeled model steam locomotive was built at Redruth, Cornwall, England, by William Murdoch (1754–1839) in 1785–6.

The earliest mechanically-propelled passenger vehicle was the first of two military steam tractors completed in Paris in 1770 by Nicolas Joseph Cugnot (1725–1804). This reached about $2\frac{1}{4}$ m.p.h. Cugnot's second, larger tractor, completed in 1771, today survives in the *Conservatoire National des Art et Metiers* in Paris.

The first true internal-combustion engined vehicle was built by a Londoner, Samuel Brown, whose 4-h.p. 2-cylinder-engined carriage climbed Shooters Hill, Blackheath, Kent, England, in 1824.

FASTEST PRODUCTION MODEL: This German-made Porsche 917L reached a speed of 238 m.p.h. during practice in 1971.

Earliest Gasoline-Driven Cars. The first successful gasoline-driven car, the Motorwagen, built by Karl-Friedrich Benz (1844–1929) of Karlsruhe, ran at Mannheim, Germany, in late 1885. It was a 560-lb. 3-wheeler reaching 8–10 m.p.h. Its single-cylinder chain-drive engine (bore 91.4 mm., stroke 150 mm.) delivered 0.85 h.p. at 200 r.p.m. It was patented on January 29, 1886. Its first 1-kilometer road test was reported in the local newspaper, the *Neue Badische Landeszeitung*, of June 4, 1886, under the heading "Miscellaneous." Two were built in 1885 of which one has been preserved in "running order" at the Deutsche Museum, Munich, since 1959. (See photo.)

The oldest internal-combustion engine car still in running order is the Danish "Hammel." Designed by Albert Hammel, who took out the original patents in 1886, it was completed in 1887. As recently as 1954 it completed the 54-mile London-to-Brighton run in England in 12½ hours, averaging 4½ m.p.h. The engine is a twin-cylinder, horizontal water-cooled four-stroke with a capacity of 2,720 c.c., bore and stroke 104.5 mm. × 160 mm., and a compression ratio of 3.5:1.

Most Durable Car. An automotive writer, Boyd Eugene Taylor of Atlanta, Georgia, in 1956 surpassed the 1,000,000 mile mark in his 1936 Ford 2-door car. The "clock" on its 11th trip around showed (1 million and) 37,000 miles.

Earliest Registrations. The world's first plates were probably introduced by the Parisian police in France in 1893. The first American plates were in 1901 in New York State. Registration plates were introduced in Britain in 1903. The original A1 plate was secured by the 2nd Earl Russell (1865–1931) for his 12 h.p. Napier. This plate, willed to Mr. Trevor Laker of Leicester, was sold in August, 1959, for £2,500 ($7,000) in aid of charity. The Rolls-Royce bearing the registration plate RR1 was sold by tender to R. H. Owen Ltd. by the executors of Sydney Black on July 22, 1968 for £10,800 ($25,920)—£3,300 ($7,920) more than the price of the Silver Shadow to which the number plate was affixed.

Fastest Cars

Rocket-Engined. The highest speed attained by any wheeled land vehicle is 631.368 m.p.h. over the first measured kilometer by *The Blue Flame*, a liquid natural gas-powered 4-wheeled vehicle driven by Gary Gabelich on the Bonneville Salt Flats, Utah, on October 23, 1970. Momentarily Gabelich exceeded 650 m.p.h. The tires were made by Goodyear. The car was powered by a liquid natural gas/hydrogen peroxide rocket engine delivering 22,000 lbs.s.t. maximum, and theoretically capable of 900 m.p.h.

Jet. The highest speed attained by any jet-engined car is 613.995 m.p.h. over a flying 666.386 yards by the 34-foot-7-inch-long 9,000-lb. *Spirit of America—Sonic I*, driven by Norman Craig Breedlove (born March 23, 1938, Los Angeles) on Bonneville Salt Flats, Utah, on November 15, 1965. The car was powered by a General Electric J79 GE-3 jet engine, developing 15,000 lbs. static thrust at sea level.

Wheel-Driven. The highest speed attained is 429.311 m.p.h. over a flying 666.386 yards by Donald Malcolm Campbell (1921–67), a British engineer, in the 30-foot-long *Bluebird*, weighing 9,600 lbs., on the salt flats at Lake Eyre, South Australia, on July 17, 1964. The car was powered by a Bristol-Siddeley 705 gas-turbine engine developing 4,500 s.h.p. Its peak speed was *c.* 440 m.p.h. It was rebuilt in 1962, after a crash at about 360 m.p.h. on September 16, 1960.

Piston-Engined. The highest speed attained is 418.504 m.p.h. over a flying 666.386 yards by Robert Sherman Summers (born April 4, 1937, Omaha, Nebraska) in *Goldenrod* at Bonneville Salt Flats, Utah, on November 12, 1965. The car, measuring 32 feet long and weighing 5,500 lbs., was powered by four fuel-injected Chrysler Hemi engines (total capacity 27,924 c.c.) developing 2,400 b.h.p.

Fastest Production Model. The world's fastest and most powerful production car (more than 25 examples produced within 12 months) ever produced was the German Porsche 4.9 liter Type 917 built in 1970 and 1971. It had a flat 12-cylinder air-cooled 4.99 liter engine developing 600 b.h.p. at 8,600 r.p.m. A Type 917L reached a speed calculated to be 238 m.p.h. during practice on the Le Mans Mulsanne straight on April 18, 1971.

Longest in Production

The longest any car has been in production is 42 years (1910–52), including wartime interruptions, in the case of the Jowett "Flat Twin," produced in Britain.

The Ford Model T production record of 15,007,033 cars (1908–1927) was surpassed by the Volkswagen "Beetle" series when their 15,007,034th car came off the production line on February 17, 1972.

LARGEST CAR EVER BUILT: The Bugatti "Royale" of which only six were made, measured over 22 feet in length, and the hood alone was over 7 feet long.

Largest Car

Of cars produced for private road use, the largest ever was the Bugatti "Royale," type 41, known as the "Golden Bugatti," of which only six (not seven) were made, and some survive. First built in 1927, this machine has an 8-cylinder engine of 12.7-liter capacity, and measures over 22 feet in length. The hood is over 7 feet long.

The longest present-day limousine is the Stageway Coaches Inc. (U.K.) 10-door Travelall 18-seat model, announced in 1970, and measuring 25 feet 4½ inches overall.

The widest standard production car is the U.S.S.R.'s Zil 114, measuring 6 feet 8.3 inches across. The Rolls-Royce Phantom V is 6 feet 7 inches wide.

(For cars not intended for private use, see *Largest Engines*.)

Most Expensive Car

The most expensive car ever built is the Presidential 1969 Lincoln Continental Executive delivered to the U.S. Secret Service on October 14, 1968. It has an overall length of 21 feet 6.3 inches with a 13-foot-4-inch wheelbase and, with the addition of two tons of armor plate, weighs 12,000 lbs. The cost for research, development and manufacture was estimated at $500,000, but it is rented at $5,000 per annum. Even if all four tires were shot out it can travel at 50 m.p.h. on inner rubber-edged steel discs.

The most expensive standard car now available is the 19-foot-10-inch-long 7-seat Rolls-Royce Phantom VI (V8, 6,230 c.c. engine) with coachwork by Park Ward at £14,145 ($36,777) including purchase tax. The cost of a 4.9-liter Series 2 Porsche Type 917 (see above) would have been about $92,000 if any had been exported.

The all-time dollar record was a Bugatti Royale in 1931 for $55,000.

The greatest price paid for any vintage car has been $65,000 for a 1905 Rolls-Royce paid in the U.S. in January, 1969. A bid of $70,000 was refused for a 1932 Dusenberg, reserved at $75,000 by Joe Kaufman at Auburn, Indiana, on September 6, 1971. The greatest collection of vintage cars is the William F. Harrah Collection of 1,440, estimated to be worth $3,000,000 in Reno, Nevada. Mr. Harrah is still looking for a Chalmers Detroit 1909 Tourabout, an Owen car of 1910–12, and a Nevada truck of 1915.

Most Inexpensive. The cheapest car of all-time was the U.S. 1908 Brownicker, made for children, but designed for road use, which sold for $150. The Kavan of 1905, also of U.S. manufacture, was listed at $200. The early models of the King Midget cars were sold in kit form for self-assembly for as little as $100 as late as 1948.

Largest Engines

Cars are compared on the basis of engine capacity. Distinction is made between those designed for normal road use and machines specially built for track racing and outright speed records.

The highest engine capacity of a production car was $13\frac{1}{2}$ liters (824 cubic inches), in the case of the Pierce-Arrow 6–66 Raceabout of 1912–18, the Peerless 6–60 of 1912–14 and the Fageol of 1918. The largest currently available is the V8 engine of 500.1 cubic inches (8,195 c.c.), developing 235 b.h.p. net, used in the 1972 Cadillac Fleetwood Eldorado.

The largest car ever used was the "White Triplex," sponsored by J. H. White of Philadelphia. Completed early in 1928, after two years' work, the car weighed about $4\frac{1}{2}$ tons and was powered by three Liberty V12 aircraft engines with a total capacity of 81,188 c.c., developing 1,500 b.h.p. at 2,000 r.p.m. It was used to break the world speed record, but crashed at Daytona, Florida, on March 13, 1929.

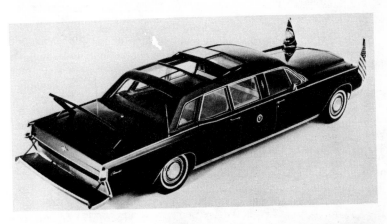

MOST EXPENSIVE CAR: Costing $500,000, this Presidential Lincoln Continental Executive (1969) was rented to the U.S. Secret Service at $5,000 per year. It weighs 12,000 lbs. including its armor plate of 2 tons.

LARGEST CAR: The Quad A 1, built in California in 1965, intended for drag racing, is powered by 4 aircraft engines.

The largest car ever built is the "Quad A 1," constructed in 1965 in California. Intended for drag racing, the car has four-wheel drive and is powered by four V12 Allison V-1710 aircraft engines with a total capacity of 112,088 c.c. developing 12,000 b.h.p. It was first shown in January, 1966, at the San Mateo Auto Show in California, but was unable to move under its own power. (See photo.)

The largest racing car was the "Higham Special," which first raced at Brooklands racing circuit, Surrey, England, in 1923. It was driven by its owner, Count Louis Vorow Zborowski, the younger (killed 1924) and was powered by a V12 Liberty aircraft engine with a capacity of 27,059 c.c., developing 400 to 500 b.h.p. at 2,000 r.p.m. J. G. Parry Thomas renamed the car "Babs" and used it to break the land speed record. The car was wrecked, and Thomas killed, during an attempt on this record at Pendine Sands, South Wales, on March 3, 1927.

Gasoline Consumption

The world record for fuel economy on a closed circuit course (one of 14.08 miles) was set by R. J. (Bob) Greenshields, C. A. (Skeeter) Hargrave, Jan Evans and Earl Elmqvist in a highly modified 1956 Austin Healey in the annual Shell Research Laboratory contest at Wood River, Illinois, on September 19, 1970. They achieved 302.7 ton-miles per gallon and 145.5 miles on one gallon of gasoline.

The best recorded figure in an unmodified car using pump gas is 96.59 m.p.g. by a Fiat 500 driven on an out-and-home course from Cheltenham to Evesham, Gloucestershire, England, by W. (Featherfoot Joe) Dembowski on July 1, 1965.

Buses

Largest. The longest buses in the world are the 65-foot-long articulated buses for 160 passengers built by Bus Bodies (S.A.) Ltd. of Port Elizabeth, South Africa for use in Johannesburg.

Largest Trolley-Buses. The largest trolley-buses in the world are the articulated vehicles put into service in Moscow, U.S.S.R., in May, 1959, with a length of 57 feet and a capacity of 200.

Longest Route. The longest regularly scheduled bus route is Greyhound's "Supercruiser" Miami-to-San Francisco route over

3,240 miles in 81 hours 50 minutes (average speed of travel 39.59 m.p.h.). The total Greyhound fleet numbers 5,500 buses.

Largest Truck

The world's largest truck is the V-Con End Dump Truck built by the Vehicle Constructors division of Peerless Manufacturing Co. of Dallas, Texas, with a capacity of 285 tons. It is powered by a 12-cylinder locomotive engine which develops 2,600 h.p. regularly and can reach 3,000 h.p. It is 43 feet long and 28 feet wide. A prototype is operating at the Pima Mining Company near Tucson, Arizona. The advertised price is $700,000.

Most Massive Vehicle

The most massive vehicle ever constructed is the Marion 8-caterpillar crawler used for conveying *Saturn V* rockets to their launching pads at the John F. Kennedy Space Center, Florida (see *Most Powerful Rocket*). It measures 131 feet 4 inches by 114 feet and cost $12,300,000. The loaded train weight is 9,000 tons. Its windshield wipers with 42-inch blades are the world's largest. Two vehicles were built.

Longest Vehicle

The longest vehicle in the world was the 572-foot-long, 54-wheeled U.S. Army Overland Train Mk. II, built by R. G. Le Tourneau Inc. of Longview, Texas. Its gross weight was 450 tons and it had a top speed of 20 m.p.h. It was driven by a 6-man crew, who controlled

LARGEST TRUCK: Capable of hauling 285 tons, this V-Con End Dump Truck has an engine that can develop 3,000 h.p. It sells for about $700,000, and one is in operation in Arizona.

4 engines with a combined s.h.p. of 4,680, which require a capacity of 7,828 gallons of fuel. Despite a cost of $3,755,000, it was sold for scrap for $47,900 in 1971.

Largest Bulldozers

The world's largest bulldozer is the Caterpillar SXS D9G with a 24-foot dozer blade weighing 95 tons. The largest road grader in the world is the 28-ton 31-foot 5-inch-long CMI Corporation Autograde 55 with a 325-h.p. engine.

Fastest Trailer

The world record for towing a house trailer in 24 hours is 1,689 miles (average speed 70.395 m.p.h.) by a Ford Zodiac Mark IV, towing a Sprite Major 5-berth trailer, 16 feet long and weighing 1,680 lbs., at Monza Autodrome near Milan, Italy, on October 15–16, 1966. The drivers were Ian Mantle, John Risborough and Michael Bowler, all of Great Britain.

The longest trailer tour on record is one of 68,000 miles carried out in a 1966 Commer Highwayman through 69 sovereign countries between December 27, 1966 and October 20, 1971, by Sy Feldman, his wife Christine, and two sons, Greg and Tim.

Largest Road Load

The tallest load ever conveyed by road comprised two 98-foot-tall cableway towers, each weighing 78.4 tons, which were taken 25 miles from Ohakuri to Aratiatia, New Zealand, in June, 1961. The loads were carried on a 68-wheel trailer, towed by a 230-h.p. Leyland Buffalo tractor, for George Dale and Son Ltd.

Amphibious Vehicle

The only transatlantic crossing by an amphibious vehicle was achieved by Ben Carlin (U.S.) in an amphibious jeep called "Half-Safe." He completed the leg across the English Channel from France on August 24, 1951.

Largest Taxi Fleet

The largest taxi fleet was that of New York City, which amounted to 29,000 cabs in October, 1929, compared with the 1969 figure of

LONGEST SKID MARKS: When Craig Breedlove was attempting to set a land speed record in his jet-powered "Spirit of America" at Bonneville Salt Flats, Utah, in 1964, he skidded for nearly 6 miles.

ONLY AMPHIBIOUS CROSSING OF THE ATLANTIC: In this jeep, the "Half-Safe" Ben Carlin of the U.S. arrived in London after crossing the English Channel on the first leg of his journey.

11,500. The drivers refer to poor tippers as "flap jacks" and non-tippers as "fish balls."

Largest Tires

The world's largest tires are the 4000-57 OR tires built in 1971 by Bridgestone Tire Co. of Japan which have a diameter of 11 feet 10 inches and weigh 7,275 lbs. (3.24 tons).

Largest Tractor

The most powerful tractor in the world is the 160-ton K-205 Pacemaker with a 1,260 horsepower rating. It is built by R. G. Le Tourneau, Inc., of Longview, Texas.

Longest Skid Marks

The longest recorded skid marks on a public road were 950 feet long, left by a Jaguar car involved in an accident on the M.1 near Luton, Bedfordshire, England, on June 30, 1960. Evidence given in the High Court case *Hurlock v. Inglis and others* indicated a speed "in excess of 100 m.p.h." before the application of the brakes.

The skid marks made by the jet-powered *Spirit of America*, driven by Craig Breedlove, after the car went out of control at Bonneville Salt Flats, Utah, on October 15, 1964, were nearly 6 miles long.

MOTORCYCLES

Earliest. The earliest internal combustion-engined motorized bicycle was a wooden machine built in 1885 by Gottlieb Daimler

(1834–1900) of Germany. It had a top speed of 12 m.p.h. and developed one-half of one horsepower from its single cylinder 264-c.c. engine at 700 r.p.m. The earliest factory which made motorcycles in quantity was opened in 1894 by J. Hildebrand and A. Wolfmüller at München (Munich), Germany. In its first two years this factory produced over 1,000 machines, each having a water-cooled 1488-c.c. twin-cylinder engine developing about 2.5 b.h.p. at 600 r.p.m.

Fastest Motorcycle. The fastest standard motorcycle ever produced is the Dunstall Norton Commando powered by a twin-cylinder 810-c.c. engine developing 70 b.h.p. at 7,000 r.p.m. and capable of 135 m.p.h.

Fastest Track Motorcycle. The fastest racing motorcycle ever built has been the 748-c.c. 105-b.h.p. Kawasaki 3-cylinder 2-stroke, produced in December, 1971 and capable of 185 m.p.h. (see also *Motorcycle Racing*, Chapter 12).

Largest Motorcycle. The largest motorcycle ever put into production was the 1,301-c.c. in-line 4-cylinder Henderson, manufactured in the U.S. in the period 1926–29.

Most Expensive Motorcycle. The most expensive motorcycles in current production are the Harley-Davidson FLHB and FLHFB Super Sports Electra Glide machines, with an engine capacity of 1,213 c.c. Extensively used for highway patrol work by State Police Departments, they weigh 661 lbs. and sell for $3,240 overseas.

BICYCLES

Earliest. Though there were many velocipedes before that time, the term bicycle was first used in 1868. The earliest portrayal of such a vehicle is in a stained glass window, dated 1642, in Stoke Poges Church, Buckinghamshire, England, depicting a man riding a hobby horse or celeripede.

The first machine propelled by cranks and pedals, with connecting rods, was invented in 1839 by Kirkpatrick Macmillan (1810–78) of Dumfries, Scotland. It is now in the Science Museum, South Kensington, London.

Longest Bicycle. The longest tandem bicycle ever built is the 31-man 50-foot-long trigintapede built in Queanbeyan, Australia, in November, 1971.

Smallest Bicycle. The world's smallest rideable bicycle is a 5½-inch-high 3-inch-wheel model made and ridden by Alfred G. Tabb (b. March 5, 1883) of Kidderminster, Worcestershire, England.

Largest Tricycle. The largest tricycle ever made was manufactured in 1897 for the Woven-Hose and Rubber Company of Boston, Massachusetts. Its side wheels were 11 feet in diameter and it weighed over 2,000 lbs. It could carry eight riders.

Tallest Unicycle. The tallest unicycle ever mastered is one 32 feet tall, ridden by Steve McPeak of Seattle Pacific College, in 1969. McPeak set a duration record when on November 26, 1968, he completed a 2,000-mile journey from Chicago to Las Vegas in 6 weeks on a 13-foot unicycle. He covered 80 miles on some days.

Lawn Mowers

Largest. The widest gang mower on record is one of 15 overlapping sections manufactured by Lloyds & Co. of Letchworth Ltd., Hertfordshire, England, used by The Jockey Club to mow 2,500 acres on Newmarket Heath. Its cutting width is 41 feet 6 inches and has a capacity, with a 15 m.p.h. tractor, of up to 70 acres per hour.

Longest Journey. In an endurance trial over 306.6 miles from Washington, D.C. to New York City on September 9–21, 1971, three Gravely machines (a 12-h.p. walking model, an 8-h.p. lawn tractor and a 16.5-h.p. riding tractor) each covered 144.1 miles, mowing 47 per cent of the time.

3. Railroads

Earliest. Railed trucks were used for mining as early as 1550 at Leberthal, Alsace, near the French-German border, and by Ralph Wood from Coombe Down to Avon, England, in 1731, but the first self-propelled locomotive ever to run on rails was built by Richard Trevithick (1771–1833) and demonstrated over 9 miles with a 10-ton load and 70 passengers in Penydarren, Glamorganshire, Wales, on February 21, 1804.

The earliest established railway to have a steam-powered locomotive was the Middleton Colliery Railway, set up by an Act of 1758 running between Middleton Colliery and Leeds Bridge, Yorkshire, England. This line went over to the use of steam locomotives, built by Matthew Murray, in 1812. The Stockton and Darlington colliery line, County Durham, England, which ran from Shildon through Darlington to Stockton, opened on September 27, 1825. The 7-ton *Locomotion I* (formerly *Active*) could pull 48 tons at a speed of 15 m.p.h. It was designed and driven by George Stephenson (1781–1848).

The first regular steam passenger run was inaugurated over a one-mile section on the $6\frac{1}{4}$-mile track from Canterbury to Whitstable, Kent, England, on May 3, 1830, hauled by the engine *Invicta*.

The first electric railway was Werner von Siemen's 300-yard-long Berlin electric tramway opened for the Berlin Trades Exhibition on May 31, 1879.

Fastest

Electric. The world rail speed record is held jointly by two French Railway electric locomotives, the CC7107 and the BB9004. On March 28 and 29, 1955, hauling three carriages of a total weight of 112 tons, they each achieved a speed of 205.6 m.p.h. The runs took place on the 1,500-volt D.C. Bordeaux-Dax line, from Facture to Morcenx, and the top speed was maintained by the drivers, H. Braghet and J. Brocca, for nearly $1\frac{1}{4}$ miles. The CC7107 weighs 119 tons and has a continuous rating of 4,300 h.p. at 1,500 volts, but developed 12,000 h.p. over the timing stretch. The BB9004 weighs 91 tons and has a continuous rating of 4,000 h.p.

Steam. The highest speed ever recorded by a steam locomotive is 126 m.p.h. by the London & North Eastern Railway 4-6-2 No. 4468 *Mallard* (later numbered 60022), which hauled seven coaches

FASTEST TRAIN: The Japanese "New Tokaido" travels at 112 m.p.h. between Osaka and Okayama and is expected to travel eventually at 159 m.p.h.

weighing 268.8 tons gross, near Essendine, down Stoke Bank, between Grantham, Lincolnshire, and Peterborough, Northamptonshire, England, on July 3, 1938. Driver Duddington was at the controls with Fireman T. Bray.

Fastest Regular Run. The fastest point-to-point schedule in the world is that of the "New Tokaido" service of the Japanese National Railways from Osaka to Okayama, inaugurated on March 15, 1972. The train covers 112.03 miles in exactly 1 hour. The maximum speed is being raised from 130.5 to 159 m.p.h. The 60-ton 12-car unit has motors generating 8,880 kilowatts on a single-phase 25,000-volt A.C. system.

Longest Non-stop Run. The world's longest daily non-stop run is that of the "Florida Special" from New York City to Miami (1,377 miles) of which the 936-mile stretch from Washington, D.C. to Winter Haven, Florida, contains only conditional stops.

Most Powerful Locomotive. The world's most powerful compound-type steam locomotive was No. 700, a triple articulated or triplex 2-8-8-8-4 six-cylinder engine which the Baldwin Locomotive Co. built in 1916 for the Virginian Railway. It had a tractive force of 166,300 lbs. working compound and 199,560 lbs. working simple. In 1918, this railway operated a 4-cylinder compound 2-10-10-2 engine, built by the American Locomotive Co., with a starting (*i.e.* working simple) tractive effort of 176,000 lbs. Probably the heaviest train ever hauled by a single engine was one of 17,136 tons made up of 250 freight cars stretching 1.6 miles by the Matt H. Shay (No. 5014), a 2-8-8-8-2 engine which ran on the Erie Railroad from May, 1914, until 1929.

Steepest Grade

The world's steepest standard gauge gradient by adhesion is 1:11. This figure is achieved by the Guatemalan State Electric Railway between the Samala River Bridge and Zunil.

PROGRESSIVE RAILROAD SPEED RECORDS

Speed m.p.h.	Engine	Place	Date
29¼	The Rocket (Stephenson).........	Great Britain......................	1829
59	*Lucifer*...............................	Madeley Bank, Staffordshire, England	11.13.1839
85.1	Compressed air train	Kingstown (now Dun Laóghaire) to Dalkey, Ireland	8.19.1843
89.48	Crampton No. 604	France.............................	6.21.1890
98.4*	*Philadelphia & Reading R. Engine 206*	*Skillmans to Belle Mead, New Jersey*	*July 1890*
102.8*	*N.Y. Central & Hudson River Railway*	*Grimesville, N.Y.*	*5.9.1893*
112.5*†	*Empire State Express No. 999...*	*Crittenden West, N.Y.*	*5.11.1893*
90.0	Midland Rly. 7 ft. 9 in. single...	Melton Mowbray, Nottingham, England	1897
130*	*Burlington Route*	*Siding to Arion, Iowa............*	*1.1899*
101.0	Siemens und Halske Electric...	near Berlin, Germany.........	1901
120.0*‡	*Savannah, Florida and Western Rly. mail train*	*Screven, Florida..................*	*3.1.1901*
124.89	Siemens und Halske Electric...	Marienfeld-Zossen, nr. Berlin	10.6.1903
128.43	Siemens und Halske Electric...	Marienfeld-Zossen, nr. Berlin	10.23.1903
130.61	Siemens und Halske Electric...	Marienfeld-Zossen, nr. Berlin	10.27.1903
143.0	Kruckenberg (propeller-driven)	Karstädt-Dergenthin, Germany	6.21.1931
150.9	Co-Co S.N.C.F. No. 7121......	Dijon-Beaune, France	2.21.1953
205.6	Co-Co S.N.C.F. No. 7107.......	Facture-Morceux, France......	3.28.1955
205.6	Bo-Bo S.N.C.F. No. 9004	Facture-Morceux, France......	3.29.1955
235	*Aerotrain* (jet aero engine and rockets) (see photograph)	Gométz le Chatel, France......	12.5.1967

* Not internationally regarded as authentic.

† Later alleged to be unable to attain 82 m.p.h. on this track when hauling 4 coaches.

‡ 5 miles in 2½ minutes to a stop, hence ludicrous.

Busiest Railroad

The world's most crowded rail system is the Tokyo subway service of the Japanese National Railways, which in 1970 carried 6,129,000 passengers daily. Professional pushers are employed to squeeze in passengers before the doors can be closed. Among articles reported lost in the crush in 1970 were 419,929 umbrellas, 250,630 eyeglasses and hats, 172,106 shoes, and also an assortment of false teeth and artificial eyeballs.

The world's busiest stations are Tokyo Central, which in 1970, handled an average of 2,600 trains, and Shinjuku, which handled 2,200,000 passengers daily.

FASTEST THING ON TRACKS: This "Aerotrain" made in France can go 235 m.p.h. It has jet airplane engines.

Widest Gauge

The widest gauge in standard use is 5 feet 6 inches. This width is used in India, Pakistan, Ceylon, Spain, Portugal, Argentina and Chile. In 1885, there was a lumber railway in Oregon with a gauge of 8 feet.

Longest Straight Length. The longest straight in the world is on the Commonwealth Railways Trans Australian line over the Nullarbor Plain from Mile 496 between Nuringa and Loongana, Western Australia, to Mile 793 between Ooldea and Watson, South Australia, 297 miles dead straight although not level.

Longest Electric Line

The world's longest stretch of electrified line is the 3,240 miles between Moscow and Irkutsk in Siberia, U.S.S.R., reported completed in late 1960.

Highest Track

The highest standard gauge (4 feet 8½ inches) track in the world is on the Central Railway of Peru (owned by the Peruvian Corporation Ltd.) at La Cima, where a branch siding rises to 15,844 feet above sea level. The highest point on the main line is 15,688 feet in the Galera tunnel.

Stations

Largest. The world's biggest railroad station is Grand Central Terminal, New York City, built 1903–13. It covers 48 acres on two levels with 41 tracks on the upper level and 26 on the lower. On average, more than 550 trains and 180,000 people per day use it, with a peak of 252,288 on July 3, 1947.

Highest. The highest station in the world on standard gauge railways is Ticlio, at 15,685 feet above sea level, on the Central Railway of Peru, in South America.

Waiting Rooms. The world's largest waiting rooms are in Peking Station, Changan Boulevard, Peking, China, opened in September, 1959, with a capacity of 14,000.

Longest Platform. The longest railroad platform in the world is the Kharagpur platform, Bihar, northeastern India, which measures 2,733 feet in length. The State Street Center subway platform staging in "The Loop" in Chicago, measures 3,500 feet in length.

Freight Trains

Longest. The longest and heaviest freight train on record was one about 4 miles in length, consisting of 500 coal cars with three 3,600-h.p. diesels pulling, with three more placed 300 cars from the front on the Iaeger, West Virginia, to Portsmouth, Ohio, stretch of 157 miles on the Norfolk and Western Railway on November 15, 1967. The total weight was more than 47,000 tons.

Greatest Load. The heaviest single piece of freight ever conveyed by rail was a 1,230,000-lb. 106-foot-tall hydrocracker reactor which was carried from Birmingham, Alabama, to Toledo, Ohio, on November 12, 1965.

LONGEST ELECTRIFIED LINE: The track between Moscow and Irkutsk, Siberia, is 3,240 miles long.

Most Expensive Freight Rate. In accordance with British Rail regulations the correct charge for a domestic animal accompanying a passenger is the same as the 2nd class child fare. Thus in traveling from Paddington, London, to Plymouth (225¾ miles) a Miss Harries on May 7, 1968, had to pay 30s. 6d. ($4.27) for a budgerigar weighing 1 oz. This was equivalent to more than £238 ($666) per ton-mile.

Subways

The most extensive and oldest (opened January 10, 1863) underground railway system in the world is that of the London Transport Executive, with 257 miles of route, of which 80 miles is bored tunnel and 24 miles is "cut and cover." This whole system is operated by a staff of 20,000 serving 278 stations. The 500 trains comprising 4,350 cars carried 654,000,000 passengers in 1971. The record for a day is 2,073,134 on VE Day, May 8, 1945. The greatest depth is 192 feet at Hampstead. The record for touring 277 stations (all at that time) was 15 hours precisely, by Leslie V. R. Burwood on September 3, 1968. The record for the Paris Metro's 270 stations (7 closed) is 11 hours 13 minutes by Alan Jenkins (G.B.) on August 30, 1967.

The busiest subway in the world is operated by the New York City Transit Authority with a total of 237.22 miles of track and 2,081,810,464 passengers in 1970, a new high. The stations are close set and total 475. The record for traveling the whole system is 22 hours 11½ minutes by Morgan Chu and 6 others on August 3, 1967.

FASTEST TRACKED VEHICLE: This jet-powered aerotrain, seen here from the rear, is actually a hovercraft invented by Jean Bertin of France to travel on land, and has attained a speed of 235 m.p.h. Its engines are the same as used on jet planes.

Monorail

Highest Speed. The highest speed ever attained on rails is 3,090 m.p.h. (Mach 4.1) by an unmanned rocket-powered sled on the 6.62-mile-long captive track at the U.S. Air Force Missile Development Center at Holloman, New Mexico, on February 19, 1959. The highest speed reached carrying a chimpanzee is 1,295 m.p.h.

The highest speed attained by a tracked vehicle is 235 m.p.h. by the jet-powered *L'Aerotrain*, invented by Jean Bertin.

Speeds as high as Mach 0.8 (608 m.p.h.) are planned in 1973 from the Onsoku Kasotai (sonic speed sliding vehicle), a wheelless rocket-powered train running on rollers designed by Prof. H. Ozawa (Japan) and announced in March, 1968.

Model Railway

The record run for a model train was set at Nuremberg, West Germany, in 1971, when the Fleischmann *Black Elephant* HO gauge engine pulled a 62-axle train 1,053 actual miles. The run was equivalent, at scale, to 11,600 miles averaging 123.9 m.p.h.

4. Aircraft

Note.—The use of the Mach scale for aircraft speeds was introduced by Prof. Acherer of Zürich, Switzerland. The Mach number is the ratio of the velocity of a moving body to the local velocity of sound. This was first employed by Dr. Ernst Mach (1838–1916) of Austria in 1887. Thus Mach 1.0 equals 760.98 m.p.h. at sea level at 15° C. (590°F.) and is assumed, for convenience, to fall to a constant 659.78 m.p.h. in the stratosphere, *i.e.* above 11,000 meters (36,089 feet).

Earliest Flight. The first controlled and sustained power-driven flight occurred near Kill Devil Hills, Kitty Hawk, North Carolina, at 10:35 a.m. on December 17, 1903, when Orville Wright (1871–1948) flew the 16-h.p. chain-driven *Flyer I* at an airspeed of 30–35 m.p.h., a ground speed of less than 8 m.p.h. and an altitude of 8–12 feet for 12 seconds, watched by his brother Wilbur (1867–1912) and five members of the Coast Guard. Both brothers, from Dayton, Ohio, were bachelors because, as Orville put it, they had not the means to "support a wife as well as an airplane." The plane is now in the Smithsonian Institution, Washington, D.C.

The first man-carrying powered airplane to fly, but not entirely under its own power, was a monoplane with a hot-air engine built by Félix du Temple de la Croix (1823–90), a French naval officer, and piloted by a young sailor who made a short hop after taking off, probably down an incline, at Brest, France, *c.* 1874. The first hop by a man-carrying airplane entirely under its own power was made when Clément Ader (1841–1925) of France flew in his *Eole* for about 164 feet at Armainvilliers, France, on October 9, 1890.

Cross-Channel Flight. The earliest flight across the English Channel by an airplane was made on July 25, 1909, when Louis Blériot (1872–1936), of France, flew his *Blériot XI* monoplane, powered by a 23-h.p. Anzani engine, from Les Baraques, France, to a meadow near Dover Castle, England, in 37 minutes, after taking off at 4:41 a.m.

Transatlantic Flight. The first crossing of the North Atlantic by air was made by Lt.-Cdr. (later Rear Admiral) Albert C. Read (1887–1967) and his crew (Stone, Hinton, Rodd, Rhoads and Breese) in the Curtiss flying boat NC-4 of the U.S. Navy, from Newfoundland, Canada, *via* the Azores, to Lisbon, Portugal, on May 16 to 27, 1919. The whole flight of 3,936 miles originating from Rockaway Air Station, Long Island, N.Y., on May 8, required 53 hours 58 minutes, terminating at Plymouth, England, on May 31.

The first non-stop transatlantic flight was achieved from 4:13 p.m. G.M.T. on June 14, 1919, from Trepassy Harbour, St. John's, Newfoundland, 1,960 miles to Derrygimla bog near Clifden, County Galway, Ireland, at 8:40 a.m. June 15, when Capt. John William Alcock, D.S.C. (1892–1919), and Lt. Arthur Whitten-Brown (1886–1948) flew across in a Vickers *Vimy*, powered by two Rolls-Royce

THE FIRST NON-STOP TRANSATLANTIC FLIGHT was made in this Vickers biplane from Newfoundland to Ireland in 1919. The pilots, Alcock and Brown, are looking everything over before starting.

Eagle engines. Both men were given knighthoods on June 29, 1919, when Alcock was only 26 years 286 days old. They won a £10,000 (then $50,000) prize given by a London newspaper.

The first solo transatlantic flight was achieved by Capt. (later Colonel) Charles Augustus Lindbergh, who took off in his 220-h.p. Ryan monoplane *Spirit of St. Louis* at 12:52 p.m. G.M.T. on May 20, 1927, from Roosevelt Field, Long Island, New York. He landed at 10:21 p.m. G.M.T. on May 21, 1927, at Le Bourget airfield, Paris, France. His flight of 3,610 miles lasted 33 hours 29½ minutes and he won a prize of $25,000.

The present New York-Paris transatlantic record is 3 hours 19 minutes 44.5 seconds by a General Dynamics/Convair B-58A *Hustler* "Firefly," piloted by Major William R. Payne (U.S.A.F.), on May 26, 1961. The 3,626 miles were covered at an average of 1,089 m.p.h. The B-58 aircraft was withdrawn from service in January, 1970.

The fastest time between New York and London (3,570 miles) is 4 hours 36 minutes 30.4 seconds by Lt.-Cdr. Brian Davies, 35, and Lt.-Cdr. Peter M. Goddard, 32, of the British Royal Navy, on May 11, 1969, flying a McDonnell Douglas F-4K *Phantom II* with Rolls-Royce Spey engines. Goddard won a prize of $12,000 for winning a race from the top of the Empire State Building to the top of the Post Office Tower in London. His time was 5 hours 11 minutes 22 seconds.

Earliest Circumnavigation. The earliest flight around the world was achieved by two U.S. Army Air Service Douglas amphibian aircraft "Chicago" (Lt. Lowell H. Smith) and "New Orleans" (Lt. Erik H. Nelson) between April 24 and September 28, 1924. The 175-day flight of 26,100 miles began and ended at Seattle, Washington, and involved 57 "hops" and a flying time of 351 hours 11 minutes. These aircraft had interchangeable wheels and floats.

The earliest solo flight around the world was made from July 15 to 22, 1933, by Wiley Hardeman Post (U.S.) in the Lockheed *Vega* "Winnie Mae" starting and finishing at Floyd Bennett Field, New York City. He flew the 15,596 miles eastwards in 7 days 18 hours 49 minutes—in 10 hops with a flying time of 115 hours 36 minutes.

Fastest Circumnavigation. The fastest circumnavigation of the globe was achieved by three U.S.A.F. B-52 Stratofortresses, led by Maj.-Gen. Archie J. Old, Jr., chief of the U.S. 15th Air Force. They took off from Castle Air Force Base, Merced, California, at 1 p.m. on January 16, and flew eastwards, arriving 45 hours 19 minutes later at March Air Force Base, Riverside, California, on January 18, 1957, after a flight of 24,325 miles. The planes averaged 525 m.p.h. and were refueled four times in flight by KC-97 aerial tankers.

Circumpolar Flight. Capt. Elgen M. Long, 44, completed at San Francisco International Airport the first ever solo polar circumnavigation in his Piper Navajo in 215 hours. He flew 38,896 miles from November 5 to December 3, 1971. The cabin temperature sank to –40° F. over Antarctica.

Jet-Engine Flight. Proposals for jet propulsion date back to Captain Marconnet (1909) of France, and to the turbojet proposals of Maxime Guillaume in 1921. The earliest test bed run was that of the British Power Jets Ltd.'s experimental W.U. (Whittle Unit) on April 12, 1937, invented by Flying Officer (now Air Commodore Sir) Frank Whittle (born June 1, 1907), who had applied for a patent on jet propulsion in 1930.

FASTEST TRIP NEW YORK-TO-LONDON: Two lieutenant-commanders in the British Navy crossed in just over 4½ hours in a Phantom II in 1969.

The first flight by an airplane powered by a turbojet engine was made by the Heinkel He 178, piloted by Flug Kapitan Erich Warsitz, at Marienehe, Germany, on August 27, 1939. It was powered by a Heinkel S-3b engine (834-lb. s.t. as installed with long tailpipe) designed by Dr. Hans von Ohain and first tested in August, 1937.

Supersonic Flight. The first supersonic flight was achieved on October 14, 1947, by Capt. (now Colonel) Charles ("Chuck") E. Yeager (born February 13, 1923), U.S.A.F., over Edwards Air Force Base, Muroc, California, in a U.S. Bell XS-1 rocket plane ("Glamorous Glennis"), with Mach 1.015 (670 m.p.h.) at a height of 42,000 feet.

Planes

Largest. The aircraft with the largest wing span ever constructed was Howard R. Hughes' H.2 *Hercules* flying boat, which rose 70 feet into the air in a test run of 1,000 yards off Long Beach Harbor, California, on November 2, 1947. The 8-engined 190-ton aircraft had a wing span of 320 feet and a length of 219 feet. It never flew again. The craft cost $40,000,000, and is still in its hangar, but the Hughes Tool Co. has been served notice to remove it by March 4, 1973.

Heaviest. The greatest weight at which an airplane has taken off is 820,700 lbs., achieved by the prototype Boeing Model 747-200 (747B) commercial transport at Edwards Air Force Base, California, in November, 1970. The basic plane weighed 320,000 lbs., the remaining weight representing fuel, flight test equipment and an artificial payload of sand and water. The 747B has a wing span of 195 feet 8 inches, is 231 feet 4 inches long. It is structurally capable of accepting 4 Pratt & Whitney JT9D-7W turbofans, giving a total thrust of 188,000 lbs.

Most Powerful. From October, 1971, the Boeing 747B with its 4 Pratt & Whitney JT 9D-7W turbofans (see *Heaviest*, above) gave a total thrust of 188,000 lbs. s.t., so surpassing the 186,000 lbs. s.t., of the 6-engined North American XB-70A *Valkyrie*.

Smallest. The smallest airplane ever flown is the Stits *Skybaby* biplane, designed, built and flown by Ray Stits at Riverside, California, in 1952. It was 9 feet 10 inches long, with a wing span of 7 feet 2 inches, and weighed 452 lbs. empty. It was powered by an 85-h.p. Continental C85 engine giving a top speed of 185 m.p.h.

Lightest. The lightest plane ever flown is the Whing Ding II, a single seat biplane designed and built by R. W. Hovey of Sangus, California, and first flown in February, 1971. It has a wing span of 17 feet, an empty weight of 120 lbs., and a loaded weight of 310 lbs. It is powered by a 14-h.p. McCulloch Go-Kart engine, driving a pusher propeller. It has a maximum speed of 50 m.p.h. and a range of 20 miles on half a gallon of fuel. The pilot sits on an open seat. A second Whing Ding II was completed in spring, 1972.

Bombers

Heaviest. The world's heaviest bomber is the 8-jet sweptwing Boeing B-52H Stratofortress, which has a maximum takeoff weight of more than 243 tons. It has a wing span of 185 feet and is 157 feet

PLANE WITH LARGEST WINGS: Howard Hughes' mammoth flying boat with a wing span of 320 feet, flew only 1,000 yards when tested in 1947 and never flew again. It had 8 engines and weighed 190 tons.

6¾ inches in length, with a speed of over 650 m.p.h. The B-52 can carry 12 750-lb. bombs under each wing and 84 500-lb. bombs in the fuselage giving a total bomb load of 60,000 lbs. The 10-engined Convair B-36J, weighing 205 tons, has a greater wing span, at 230 feet, but is no longer in service. It had a top speed of 435 m.p.h.

Fastest. The world's fastest operational bombers are the French Dassault Mirage IV, which can fly at Mach 2.2 (1,450 m.p.h.) at 36,000 feet, and the American General Dynamics FB-111A, which also flies above Mach 2. Under development is a swing-wing Russian Tupolev bomber known to NATO as "Backfire," which has an estimated over-target speed of Mach 2.25–2.5 and a range of 4,600 miles. The fastest Soviet bomber is the Tupolev Tu-22 "Blinder," with an estimated speed of Mach 1.4 (925 m.p.h.) at 36,000 feet.

Airliners

Largest. The highest capacity jet airliner is the Boeing 747, "Jumbo Jet," first flown on February 9, 1969, which by November, 1970, had set a record for gross take-off weight with 820,700 lbs. and has a capacity of from 362 to 490 passengers with a cruising speed of 595 m.p.h. Its wing span is 195.7 feet and its length, 231.3 feet. It entered service on January 21, 1970.

Largest Cargo Compartment. The largest cargo compartment of any aircraft is the 3,900 cubic feet of the Super Guppy ZO1 manufactured by Aero Space Lines, which was put into service in September, 1971. The compartment is more than 25 feet in diameter.

LARGEST AIRLINER is the Boeing 747 which began service in January, 1970, and can carry 490 passengers.

Fastest. Fastest airliner in service is the Convair CV-990 *Coronado*, one of which flew at 675 m.p.h. at 22,500 feet (Mach 0.97) on May 8, 1961. Its maximum cruising speed is 625 m.p.h. A Douglas DC-8 Series 40, with Rolls-Royce Conway engines, exceeded the speed of sound in a shallow dive on August 21, 1961. Its true air speed was 667 m.p.h. or Mach 1.012 at a height of 40,350 feet.

The U.S.S.R.'s Tu-144 supersonic airliner, with a capacity of 121 passengers, first flew on December 31, 1968. Its design speed is Mach 2.35 (1,553 m.p.h.) with a ceiling of 65,000 feet and it "went" supersonic on June 5, 1969. It first exceeded Mach 2 on May 26, 1970, and attained 1,565.8 m.p.h. (Mach 2.37) at 59,000 feet in late December, 1971. (See photo.)

The 288-foot-long scale mock-up of the planned Mach 2.7 Boeing SST which cost $10,680,000 was sold to Marks O. Morrison for $31,119 on February 18, 1972, after the U.S. Congress decided not to appropriate more money for its development.

Longest Scheduled Flight. The longest scheduled non-stop flight is the Buenos Aires, Argentina–Madrid, Spain, stage of 6,462 statute miles by Aerolineas Argentinas and Iberia, inaugurated on August 7, 1967. The Boeing 707-320B requires 11½ hours.

Shortest Scheduled Flight. The shortest scheduled flight is made by Loganair between the Orkney Islands (Scotland) of Westray and Papa Westray, which has been flown since September, 1967. Though scheduled for 2 minutes, in favorable wind conditions it is accomplished in 70 seconds.

PROGRESSIVE FIXED-WING AIRCRAFT SPEED RECORDS

m.p.h.	Mach No.	Pilot	Date
2,111	3.19	J. A. Walker	May 12, 1960
2,196	3.31	J. A. Walker	Aug. 4, 1960
2,275	3.50	R. M. White	Feb. 7, 1961
2,905	4.43	R. M. White	Mar. 7, 1961
3,074	4.62	R. M. White	Apr. 21, 1961
3,300	4.90	J. A. Walker	May 25, 1961
3,603	5.27	R. M. White	June 23, 1961
3,614	5.25	J. A. Walker	Sept. 12, 1961
3,620	5.30	F. S. Petersen	Sept. 28, 1961
3,647	5.21	R. M. White	Oct. 11, 1961
3,900	5.74	J. A. Walker	Oct. 17, 1961
4,093	6.04	R. M. White	Nov. 9, 1961
4,104	>6.06	J. A. Walker	June 27, 1962
4,250	6.33	W. J. Knight	Nov. 18, 1966
4,534	6.72	W. J. Knight	Oct. 3, 1967

> more than

Highest Speed

The official air speed record is 2,070.102 m.p.h. by Col. Robert L. Stephens and Lt.-Col. Daniel André (U.S.) in a Lockheed YF-12A over Edwards Air Force Base, California, on May 1, 1965.

The fastest fixed-wing aircraft in the world was a North American Aviation X-15A-2, which flew for the first time (after conversion) on June 28, 1964, powered by a liquid oxygen and ammonia rocket propulsion system. Ablative materials on the airframe have enabled a temperature of 3,000°F. to be withstood. The landing speed was 210 knots (241.8 m.p.h.) momentarily. The highest speed attained

WORLD'S FASTEST FIXED-WING AIRCRAFT: North American Aviation's X-15A-2 attained a speed of Mach 6.70, or more than 4,520 m.p.h., before the experimental program with this plane was suspended.

was 4,520 m.p.h. (Mach 6.70) when piloted by Major William J. Knight, U.S.A.F. (b. 1930) on October 3, 1967. An earlier version piloted by Joseph A. Walker (1920–66) reached 354,200 feet (67.08 miles) also over Edwards Air Force Base, California, on August 22, 1963. The program was suspended after the final flight of October 24, 1968. (See photo.)

Fastest Jet. The world's fastest jet aircraft is the Lockheed SR-71 reconnaissance aircraft (a variant of the YF-12A, above) which first flew on December 22, 1964, and is reportedly capable of attaining a speed of 2,200 m.p.h. and an altitude ceiling of close to 100,000 feet.

FASTEST AIRLINER: The Soviet's Tu-144, with a capacity of 121 passengers, is designed to cruise at 1,553 m.p.h. and has attained 1,565.8 m.p.h. at 59,000 feet.

The SR-71 has a span of 55.6 feet and a length of 107.4 feet and weighs 170,000 lbs. at takeoff. Its reported range is 2,982 miles at Mach 3 at 78,750 feet. Only 23 are believed to have been built and 9 had been lost by April, 1969.

The fastest Soviet jet aircraft in service is the Mikoyan MiG-23 fighter (code name "Foxbat") with a speed of Mach 3.2 (2,110 m.p.h.). It is armed with air-to-air missiles.

Fastest Biplane. The fastest recorded biplane was the Italian Fiat C.R.42B, with 1,010 h.p. Daimler-Benz DB601A engine, which attained 323 m.p.h. in 1941. Only one was built.

Fastest Piston-Engined Aircraft. The fastest speed at which a piston-engined plane has ever been measured was for a cut-down privately owned Hawker *Sea Fury* which attained 520 m.p.h. in level flight over Texas in August, 1966, piloted by Mike Carroll (k. 1969) of Los Angeles. The official record is 482–462 m.p.h. over Edwards Air Force Base, California, by Darryl C. Greenmyer, 33, in a Grumman F8F-2 Bearcat on August 16, 1969. The Republic XF-84M prototype U.S. Navy fighter which flew on July 22, 1955, had a claimed top speed of 670 m.p.h.

Fastest Propeller-Driven Aircraft. The Soviet Tu-114 turbo-prop transport is the world's fastest propeller-driven airplane. It has achieved average speeds of more than 545 m.p.h. carrying heavy payloads over measured circuits. It is developed from the Tupolev Tu-20 bomber, known in the West as the "Bear," and has 14,795-horsepower engines.

PROGRESSIVE FIXED-WING AIRCRAFT ALTITUDE RECORDS

Feet	Miles	Pilot	Date
136,500	25.85	R. M. White	Aug. 12, 1960
169,600	32.13	J. A. Walker	Mar. 30, 1961
217,000	41.11	R. M. White	Oct. 11, 1961
246,700	46.72	J. A. Walker	Apr. 30, 1962
246,700	46.72	R. M. White	June 21, 1962
314,750	59.61	R. M. White	July 17, 1962
347,000	65.88	J. A. Walker	July 19, 1963
354,200	67.08	J. A. Walker	Aug. 22, 1963

Greatest Altitude

The official world altitude-record by an aircraft which took off from the ground under its own power is 113,891 feet (21.57 miles) by Lt.-Col. Geolgiy Mosolov (U.S.S.R.) in a Mikoyan YE-66A aircraft, powered by one turbojet and one rocket engine, on April 28, 1961. Major R. W. Smith of the U.S. Air Force reached an unofficial record height of 118,860 feet (22.15 miles) in a Lockheed NF-104A over Edwards Air Force Base, California, early in November, 1963. (See photo.)

Largest Propeller

The largest aircraft propeller ever used was the 22-foot 7½-inch diameter Garuda propeller, fitted to the Linke-Hofmann R II built in Breslau, Germany, which flew in 1919. It was driven by four 260-h.p. Mercedes engines and turned at only 545 r.p.m.

ALTITUDE RECORD HOLDER is this NF-104A made by Lockheed, which unofficially reached 118,860 feet starting from the ground under its own power in California in 1963.

Flight Duration

The flight duration record is 64 days, 22 hours, 19 minutes and 5 seconds, set up by Robert Timm and John Cook in a Cessna 172 "Hacienda." They took off from McCarran Airfield, Las Vegas, Nevada, just before 3:53 p.m. local time on December 4, 1958, and landed at the same airfield just before 2:12 p.m. on February 7, 1959. They covered a distance equivalent to six times around the world.

Airports

Largest. The world's largest airport is the Dulles International Airport, Washington, D.C., which extends over an area of 9,880 acres (15.59 square miles).

The largest international airport terminal is at John F. Kennedy International Airport (formerly Idlewild), Long Island, New York City. Terminal City covers an area of 840 acres.

Work was started in December, 1968, on Fort Worth/Dallas Regional Airport, Texas, a 17,000-acre complex for completion at a cost of $500 million by June, 1973. The four terminals will have 65 gates.

Busiest. The world's busiest airport is the Chicago International Airport, O'Hare Field, with a total of 628,013 movements (569,199 air carrier movements) in 1970. This represents a takeoff or landing every 50.2 seconds.

The busiest landing area is, however, Bien Hoa Air Base, Republic of Vietnam, which handled more than 1,000,000 takeoffs and landings in 1970. The world's largest "helipad" is An Khe, South Viet-Nam, which services U.S. Army and Air Force helicopters.

Highest and Lowest. The highest airport in the world is El Alto, near La Paz, Bolivia, at 13,599 feet above sea level. Ladakh airstrip in Kashmir has, however, an altitude of 14,270 feet. The highest landing ever made was at 19,947 feet on Dhaulagri in the Nepal Himalayas by a high-wing monoplane, named *Yeti*, supplying the 1960 Swiss Expedition. The lowest landing field is El Lisan on the east shore of the Dead Sea, 1,180 feet below sea level. The lowest international airport is Schiphol, Amsterdam, Netherlands, at 13 feet below sea level.

Longest Runway. The longest runway in the world is 7 miles in length (of which 15,000 feet is concreted) at Edwards Air Force Base on the bed of Rogers Dry Lake at Muroc, California. The whole test center airfield extends over 65 square miles. In an emergency, an auxiliary 12-mile strip is available along the bed of the Dry Lake.

The world's longest civil airport runway is one of 15,510 feet (2.95 miles) at Salisbury, Rhodesia, completed in 1969.

Helicopters

The earliest known representation of the rotating wing principle is a child's toy in a painting of the Madonna and Child, dated *c.* 1460, in Le Mans Museum, France.

Fastest. A Bell Model 533 compound research helicopter, boosted by two auxiliary turbojet engines, attained an unofficial speed record of 316.1 m.p.h. over Arlington, Texas, in April, 1969. The world's official speed record for a pure helicopter, subject to official confirmation, is 220.8 m.p.h. by a Sikorsky S-67 Blackhawk, flown by test pilot Kurt Cannon, between Milford and Branford, Connecticut, on December 19, 1970. In November, 1971 a Lockheed AH-56A Cheyenne reportedly flew at 266 m.p.h.

Largest. The world's largest helicopter is the Soviet Mi-12 ("Homer"), also known as the V-12, which set up an international record by lifting a payload of 88,636 lbs. to a height of 7,398 feet on August 6, 1969. It is powered by four 6,500-h.p. turboshaft engines, and has an estimated span of 219 feet 10 inches, over its rotor tips with a fuselage length of 121 feet and weighs 115.7 tons.

Highest. The altitude record for helicopters is 36,027 feet by Jean Boulet in a Sud-Aviation S.E.3150 *Alouette II* at Brétigny-sur-Orge, France, on June 13, 1958. A claim was made for a U.S. Sikorsky CH-54B (James K. Church) at 36,122 feet on November 4, 1971. The highest landing has been at 23,000 feet below the southeast face of Everest in a rescue sortie in May, 1971.

Flying Boat

The fastest flying-boat ever built has been the Martin XP6M-1, the U.S. Navy 4-jet-engined minelayer, flown in 1955–59 with a top speed of 646 m.p.h. In September, 1946 the Martin Caroline *Mars* flying boat set a payload record of 68,327 lbs. Two Mars flying boats are still working as forest fire protection water bombers in British Columbia, Canada.

Balloons

Distance Record. The record distance traveled is 1,896.9 miles by H. Berliner (Germany) from Bitterfeld, Germany, to Kirgishan in the Ural Mountains, Russia, on February 8–10, 1914.

The official duration record is 87 hours aloft by H. Kaulen (Germany) set on December 13–17, 1913.

Largest. The largest balloon ever to fly is the 800-foot-tall balloon built by G. T. Schjeldal for the U.S.A.F., first tested on July 18, 1966. It was used for a Martian re-entry experiment by N.A.S.A. 130,000 feet above Walter Air Force Base, New Mexico, on August 30, 1966. Its capacity is 260,000,000 cubic feet.

Airships

The earliest flight of an airship was by Henri Giffard from Paris in his hydrogen 88,000-cu. ft. 144-foot-long rigid airship on September 24, 1852.

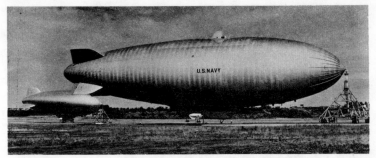

LARGEST NON-RIGID AIRSHIP: The Navy's ZPG 3-W, 403.4 feet long and 85.11 feet in diameter, had a capacity of more than 1½ million cubic feet. It flew from 1958 to 1960.

The largest non-rigid airship ever constructed was the U.S. Navy ZPG 3-W. It had a capacity of 1,516,300 cubic feet, was 403.4 feet long and 85.1 feet in diameter, with a crew of 21. It first flew on July 21, 1958, but crashed into the sea in June, 1960. (See photo.)

The largest rigid airship ever built was the German *Graf Zeppelin II* (LZ130), with a length of 803 feet and a capacity of 7,063,000 cubic feet. She made her maiden flight on September 14, 1938 and in May and August, 1939, made radar spying missions in British air space. She was dismantled in April, 1940.

The most people ever carried in an airship was 207 in the U.S. Navy *Akron* in 1931. The transatlantic record is 117 by the German *Hindenberg* in 1937.

Human-Powered Flight

The earliest successful attempt to fly over half a mile with a human-powered aircraft was made by John C. Wimpenny, who flew 993 yards at an average altitude of 5 feet (maximum 8 feet) and an average speed of 19.5 m.p.h. in a pedal-cranked propeller-driven aircraft called "Puffin I" at Hatfield, Hertfordshire, England, on May 2, 1962.

Hovercraft

The inventor of the ACV (air-cushion vehicle) is Christopher S. Cockerell (born June 4, 1910), a British engineer who had the idea in 1954, published his Ripplecraft Report 1/55 on October 25, 1955, and patented it on December 12, 1955. The earliest patent relating to an air-cushion craft was taken out in 1877 by John I. Thornycroft (1843–1928) of Chiswick, London. The first flight by a hovercraft was made by the 4½-ton Saunders Roe SR-N1 at Cowes, Isle of Wight, on May 30, 1959. With a 1,500-lb. thrust Viper turbojet engine, this craft reached 68 knots in June, 1961. The first hovercraft public service was opened across the Dee Estuary, Great Britain, by the 60-knot 24-passenger Vickers-Armstrong VA-3 in July, 1962.

The largest is the $3,600,000 Westland SR-N4, weighing 185 tons, first run on February 4, 1968. It has a top speed of 77 knots powered by 4 Bristol Siddeley Marine Proteus engines with 19-foot propellers. It carries 34 cars and 174 passengers and is 130 feet 2 inches long with a 76-foot-10-inch beam.

The longest hovercraft journey was one of 5,000 miles through 8 west African countries between October 15, 1969 and January 3, 1970, by the British Trans-African Hovercraft Expedition. The longest non-stop journey on record is one of 550 miles lasting 33 hours by a Denny Mark II piloted by Sir John Onslow around half of England on July 4–5, 1968.

Model Aircraft

The world record for altitude is 26,929 feet by Maynard L. Hill (U.S.) on September 6, 1970, using a radio-controlled model. The speed record is 213.71 m.p.h. by V. Goukoune and V. Myakinin with a motor piston radio-controlled model at Klementyeva, U.S.S.R., on September 21, 1971.

5. Power Producers

Largest Power Plant

The world's largest power station is the U.S.S.R.'s hydro-electric station at Krasnoyarsk on the Yenisey River, U.S.S.R., with a power of 6,000,000 kilowatts. Its third generator turned in March, 1968, and the twelfth became operative by December, 1970. The turbine hall completed in June, 1968, is 1,378 feet long. The turbine hall at the Volga-V.I. Lenin Power Plant, Kuybyshev is more than 2,100 feet long.

The largest non-hydro-electric generating plant in the world is the 2,500,000 kilowatt Tennessee Valley Authority installation under construction at Paradise, Kentucky, with an annual consumption of 8,150,000,000 tons of coal a year. Its total cost: $189,000,000.

When its third power plant is complete the Grand Coulee complex in Washington State will have an added capacity of 7,200,000 kilowatts, making a total of 9,771,000 kilowatts.

WORLD'S LARGEST HYDRO-ELECTRIC GENERATING PLANTS—PROGRESSIVE LIST

Ultimate Kilowattage	First Operational	Location	River
38,400	1898	De Cew Falls No. 1 (old plant)	Welland Canal
132,500	1905	Ontario Power Station	Niagara
403,900	1922	Sir Adam Beck No. 1 (formerly Queenston-Chippawa)	Niagara
1,641,000	1942	Beauharnois, Quebec, Canada	St. Lawrence
2,025,000*	1951	Grand Coulee, Washington	Columbia
2,100,000	1955	Kuybyshev, U.S.S.R.	Volga
2,543,000	1958	Volgograd, U.S.S.R.	Volga
4,500,000	1961	Bratsk, U.S.S.R.	Angara
6,096,000	1967	Krasnoyarsk, U.S.S.R.	Yenisey
6,400,000	—	Sayano-Shushensk, U.S.S.R.	Yenisey
6,500,000†	1967	Guri, Venezuela	Caroni
c. 20,000,000	—	Lower Lena, near Verkhoyansk, U.S.S.R.	Lena

*Ultimate long-term planned kilowattage will be 9,771,000.
†Present kilowattage only 524,000.

Biggest Blackout

The greatest power failure in history struck seven northeastern U.S. states and Ontario, Canada, on November 9–10, 1965. About

THE WORLD'S FIRST ATOMIC PILE was built here in December, 1942, by Enrico Fermi and other scientists, working in a squash court at the University of Chicago that had been abandoned for the duration of the war.

30,000,000 people in 80,000 square miles were plunged into darkness. Only two were killed. In New York City the power failed at 5:27 p.m. Supplies were eventually restored by 2 a.m. in Brooklyn, 4:20 a.m. in Queens, 6:58 a.m. in Manhattan and 7 a.m. in the Bronx.

Atomic Power

The world's first atomic pile was built in an abandoned squash court at the University of Chicago. It "went critical" on December 2, 1942.

The world's largest atomic power station is the 1,180 million watt (MW) plant at Wylfa, Anglesey, North Wales, completed in 1970. It will be overtaken by Hinkley Point "B" (1973) Hartlepool, Durham, England (1974), and Heysham, Lancashire (1976) all at 1,320 MW. The largest atomic plant scheduled in the United States is the Spring City, Tennessee, Unit 1 and Unit 2 (1,169 MW) due to be completed for TVA in 1976 or 1977.

Largest Reactor

The largest single atomic reactor in the world will be the 873 MW Westinghouse Electric Corporation pressurized water-type reactor being installed at Indian Point, New York, on the Hudson River, which became operative in 1969.

Largest Generator

Generators in the 2,000,000 kW (or 2,000 MW) range are now in the planning stages both in the U.K. and the U.S. The largest

FIRST MAJOR TIDAL POWER STATION: Built on the Rance estuary in Brittany, France, it has an annual output of 544,000,000 kWh.

under construction is one of 1,300 MW by the Brown Boveri Co. of Switzerland for the Tennessee Valley Authority.

Tidal Power Station

The world's first major tidal power station is the *Usine marémotrice de la Rance*, officially opened on November 26, 1966, at the Rance estuary in the Golfe de St. Malo, Brittany, France. (See photo, above.) Built in five years, at a cost of $75,600,000, it has a net annual output of 544,000,000 kilowatt-hours. The 880-yard barrage contains 24 turbo-alternators. This harnessing of the tides has imperceptibly slowed the earth's rate of revolution. The $1,000,000,000 Passamaquoddy project for the Bay of Fundy between Maine and New Brunswick, Canada, is not expected to be operative before 1978.

The first tidal power station ever was the Dee Hydro Station, Cheshire, England, with a capacity of 635 kW which began producing in October, 1913.

Biggest Boiler

The largest boilers ever designed are those ordered in the U.S. from the Babcock & Wilcox Company, with a capacity of 1,330 MW so involving the evaporation of 9,330,000 lbs. of steam per hour.

Solar Power Plant

The largest solar furnace in the world is the Laboratoire de L'Energie Solaire, at Mont Louis in the eastern Pyrenees, France. Its parabolic reflector, 150 feet in diameter, is the largest mirror in the world and concentrates the sun's rays to provide a temperature of 5,432°F. (See photo.)

In April, 1958, it was announced that Soviet scientists had designed a solar power station for the Ararat Valley, Armenia, U.S.S.R., using 1,300 moving mirrors, totaling 5 acres in area, to provide 2,500,000 kilowatt-hours in a year. The U.S. Air Force solar furnace at Cloudcroft, New Mexico, has a parabolic mirror 108 feet in diameter and a flat mirror 154 feet square, yielding temperatures of *c*. 8,500°F.

Largest Turbines

Under construction are turbines rated at 820,000 h.p. with an overload capacity of 1,000,000 h.p., 32 feet in diameter, with a 449-ton runner and a 350-ton shaft, for the Grand Coulee "Third Power Plant" (see *Largest Power Plant*).

Largest Gas Turbine

The largest gas turbine in the world is that installed at the Krasnodar thermal power station in August, 1969, with a capacity of 100,000 kilowatts. It was built in Leningrad, U.S.S.R.

Largest Pump Turbine

The world's largest integral reversible pump turbine was made by Allis-Chalmers for the $50,000,000 Taum Sauk installation of the Union Electric Co. in St. Louis, Missouri. It has a rating of 240,000 h.p. as a turbine and a capacity of 1,100,000 gallons per minute as a pump. The Tehachapi Pumping Plant in California will in 1972 pump 18,300,000 gallons per minute over 1,700 feet up.

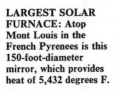

LARGEST SOLAR FURNACE: Atop Mont Louis in the French Pyrenees is this 150-foot-diameter mirror, which provides heat of 5,432 degrees F.

MOST POWERFUL JET ENGINE: This General Electric 4/J5 has a thrust of 69,900 lbs.

Largest Gas Works

The flow of natural gas from the North Sea is diminishing the manufacture of gas by the carbonization of coal and the reforming process using petroleum derivatives.

Most Powerful Jet Engine

The world's most powerful jet engine was the General Electric GE4/J5 turbojet which attained a thrust of 69,900 lbs., with afterburning, on November 13, 1969. The Pratt & Whitney JT 90D-X turbofan first run on January 15, 1972, has a thrust of 62,000 lbs. at 23° F. The thrust of the Thiokol XLR99-RM-2 rocket motor in each of the three experimental U.S. X-15 aircraft was 56,880 lbs. at sea level, reaching 70,000 lbs. at peak altitudes. The Rolls-Royce RB 211-22B powered the Lockheed L-1011-1 Tristar, from April, 1972, and develops 42,000 lbs. The -22X version (45,000 lbs.) may be developed for the L-1011-2.

6. Engineering

The earliest machinery still in use is the dalu—a water-raising instrument known to have been in use in the Sumerian civilization which originated *c.* 3,500 B.C. in Lower Iraq.

Largest Press

The world's two most powerful production machines are forging presses in the U.S. The Loewy closed-die forging press, in a plant leased from the U.S. Air Force by the Wyman-Gordon Company at North Grafton, Massachusetts, weighs 10,600 tons and stands 114 feet 2 inches high, of which 66 feet is sunk below the operating floor. It has a rated capacity of 50,000 tons, and went into operation in October, 1955. The other similar press is at the plant of the Aluminum Company of America at Cleveland, Ohio. There has been a report of a press in the U.S.S.R. with a capacity of 75,000 tons, at Novo Kramatorsk.

Lathe

The world's largest lathe is the 72-foot-long 431-ton giant lathe built by the Dortmunder Rheinstahl firm of Wagner, in Germany, in 1962. The face plate is 15 feet in diameter and can exert a torque of 289,000 feet per lb. when handling objects weighing up to 225 tons.

Excavator

Largest. The world's largest excavator is the 33,400-h.p. Marion 6360 excavator, weighing 14,000 tons. This vast machine can grab nearly 270 tons in a single bite in a bucket of 85 cubic yards capacity.

Dragline

The Ural Engineering Works at Ordzhonikdze, U.S.S.R., completed in March, 1962, has a dragline known as the ES–25(100) with a boom of 100 meters (328 feet) and a bucket with a capacity of 31.5 cubic yards. The world's largest walking dragline is the Bucyrus-Erie 4250W with an all-up weight of 13,440 tons and a bucket capacity of 220 cubic yards on a 310-foot boom. The world's largest mobile land machine is now operating on the Central Ohio Coal Company's Muskingum site in Ohio.

Blast Furnace

The world's largest blast furnace is the No. 3 Blast Furnace at the Nippon Steel Corporation's Kimitsu Steel Works completed in April, 1971. It has a daily pig iron production capacity of 11,200 tons.

Largest Forging. The largest forging on record is one 53 feet long weighing 396,000 lbs. forged by Bethlehem Steel for the Tennessee Valley Authority nuclear power plant at Brown Ferry, Alabama, in November, 1969.

Longest Pipelines

Oil. The longest crude oil pipeline in the world is the Interprovincial Pipe Line Company's installation from Edmonton, Alberta, to Buffalo, New York, a distance of 1,775 miles. Along the length of the pipe 13 pumping stations maintain a flow of 8,280,000 gallons of oil per day.

The eventual length of the Trans-Siberian Pipeline will be 2,319 miles, running from Tuimazy through Omsk and Novosibirsk to Irkutsk. The first 30-mile section was opened in July, 1957.

Natural Gas. The longest natural gas pipeline in the world is the TransCanada Pipeline which by mid-1971 had 3,769 miles of pipe up to 36 inches in diameter. The mileage will be increased to 4,464 miles, some of it in 42-inch pipe, by mid-1973. A system 5,625 miles in length, with a 3,500-mile trunk from northern Russia to Leningrad, is under construction in the U.S.S.R., for completion by 1976.

Largest Cat Cracker

The world's largest catalyst cracker is the American Oil Company's installation at its refinery in Texas City, Texas, with a capacity of 4,000,000 gallons per day.

Largest Nut

The largest nuts ever made weigh 3,304 lbs. each and have an outside diameter of 43½ inches and a 26-inch thread. Known as the Pilgrim Nuts, they are manufactured by Doncaster Moorside Ltd. of Oldham, Lancashire, England, for securing propellers.

Largest Transformer

The world's largest single-phase transformers are rated at 1,500,000 kVa of which 8 are in service with the American Electric Power Service Corporation. Of these five step down from 765 to 345 kV.

Highest Ropeway

The highest and longest aerial ropeway in the world is the Teleferico Mérida (Mérida télépherique) in Venezuela, from Mérida City (5,379 feet) to the summit of Pico Espejo (15,629 feet), a rise of 10,250 feet. The ropeway is in four sections, involving 3 car changes in the 8-mile ascent in one hour. The fourth span is 10,070 feet in length. The two cars work on the pendulum system—the carrier rope is locked and the cars are hauled by means of three pull ropes powered by a 230 h.p. motor. They have a maximum capacity of 45 persons and travel at 32 feet per second (21.8 m.p.h.).

The longest single-span ropeway is the 13,500-foot-long span from the Coachella Valley to Mt. San Jacinto (10,821 feet), California, opened on September 12, 1963.

Largest Cable Cars

The largest cable cars in the world are those at Squaw Valley, California, with a capacity of 121 persons, built by Carrosseriewerke A.G. of Aarburg, Switzerland, they had their first run on Dec. 19, 1968. The breaking strain on the 7,000-foot cable is 312 tons.

Fastest Passenger Elevators

The fastest domestic passenger elevators in the world are those fitted in the 100-story, 1,107-foot-tall John Hancock Building in Chicago. They operate at a speed of 1,600 feet per minute, or about 18 m.p.h.

Much higher speeds are achieved in the winding cages of mine shafts. A hoisting shaft 6,800 feet deep, owned by Western Deep Levels Ltd. in South Africa, winds at speeds of up to 40.9 m.p.h.

Longest Escalators

The world's longest "moving sidewalk" is the Speedwalk Passenger Conveyor System at San Francisco Airport, comprising two conveyors measuring 450 feet each, and each with a capacity of 7,200 passengers per hour. It was opened on May 20, 1964.

Fastest Printer

The world's fastest printer is the Radiation Inc. electro-sensitive system at the Lawrence Radiation Laboratory, Livermore, California. High speed recording of up to 30,000 lines each containing 120 alphanumeric characters is attained by controlling electronic pulses through chemically impregnated recording paper which is rapidly moving under closely spaced fixed styli. It can thus print

LARGEST CABLE CAR: With a capacity of 121 persons, this car operates at Squaw Valley, California.

the wordage of the whole Bible (773,692 words) in 65 seconds—3,333 times as fast as the world's fastest typist.

Transmission Lines

Longest. The longest span between pylons of any power line in the world is that across the Sogne Fjord, Norway, between Rabnaberg and Flatlaberget. Erected in 1955, by the Whitecross Co. Ltd. of Warrington, England, as part of the high-tension power cable from Refsdal power station at Vik, it has a span of 16,040 feet and a weight of 13 tons. In 1967, two further high-tensile steel/aluminum lines 16,006 feet long, and weighing 37 tons, manufactured by Whitecross and British Insulated Callender's Cables Ltd., were erected here.

Highest. The world's highest are those across the Straits of Messina, with towers of 675 feet (Sicily side) and 735 feet (Calabria) and 11,900 feet apart.

Highest Voltages. The highest voltages now carried are 765,000 volts A.C. in the U.S. since 1969. The Swedish A.S.E.A. Company is experimenting with a possible 1,000,000 volt D.C. transmission line.

Longest Conveyor Belt

The world's longest single-flight conveyor belt is one of 9 miles installed near Uniontown, Kentucky, by Cable Belt Ltd. of Camberley, Surrey, England. It has a weekly capacity of 140,000 tons of coal on a 42-inch-wide 800-feet-per-minute belt and forms part of a 12½-mile long system.

LARGEST CRANE: The crane with the greatest lifting capacity is shown as it was installed at Harland and Wolff's shipbuilding dock, Belfast, Northern Ireland.

Longest Wire Rope

The longest wire rope ever spun in one piece was one measuring 46,653 feet (8.83 miles) long and $3\frac{1}{8}$ inches in circumference, with a weight of $31\frac{1}{2}$ tons, manufactured by British Ropes Ltd., of Doncaster, Yorkshire, England.

Smallest Tubing

The smallest tubing in the world is made by Accles and Pollock, Ltd. of Oldbury, Worcestershire, England. It is of pure nickel with an outside diameter of 0.000515 of an inch and a bore of 0.00013 of an inch, and was announced on September 9, 1963. The average human hair measures from 0.002 to 0.003 of an inch in diameter. The tubing, which is stainless, can be used for the artificial insemination of mosquitoes and "feeding" nerves, and weighs only 5 ounces per 100 miles.

Largest Radar Installations

The largest of the three installations in the U.S. Ballistic Missile Early Warning System is that near Thule, Greenland, 931 miles from the North Pole, completed in 1960 at a cost of $500,000,000. Its sister stations are at Cape Clear, Alaska, completed in July, 1961, and a $115,000,000 installation at Fylingdales Moor, Yorkshire, England, completed in June, 1963. A fourth station is being built on an Indian Ocean island site. A 187-mast installation has been erected at Orfordness, Suffolk, England, for the U.S.A.F. and R.A.F.

Cranes

The crane with the greatest lifting capacity is the Goliath crane first installed in 1969 at Harland and Wolff's shipbuilding dock, Belfast, Northern Ireland. The crane spans 460 feet and has a working safe load of 840 long tons, but on a test lifted 1,050 long tons. It was built to the design of Krupper-Ardelt of Wilhelmshaven, West Germany.

A 32-wheeled gantry hydraulic crane with a span of 95 feet with a capacity of 2,000 short tons by R. A. Hanson Co. Inc. is installed at the Grand Coulee Third Power Plant, in Washington.

The highest crane reported is a mobile crane, owned by Van Twist N.V. of Dordrecht, Netherlands, of 350-long-ton capacity, which overtopped a 540-foot-high high-tension power pylon during its erection on the bank of the Scheldt River, near Antwerp, Belgium, in March, 1970.

Largest Hoisting Tackle. The greatest weight lifted by hoisting tackle is 784 tons by The Fluor Corporation of Los Angeles, in the case of an Isomax reactor 90 feet in length at Shuaiba, Kuwait, on August 26, 1968.

Largest Floating Crane. The world's most powerful floating crane is the Dutch vessel *Taklift I* (2,370 long tons gross) completed in 1969. It is capable of lifting objects as heavy as 800 tons.

Clocks

Oldest. The earliest mechanical clock, that is one with an escapement, was completed in China in 725 A.D. by I'Hsing and Liang Ling-tsan.

The oldest surviving working clock in the world is one dating from 1386, or possibly earlier, at Salisbury Cathedral, Wiltshire, England, which was restored in 1956. Earlier dates, ranging back to *c.* 1335, have been attributed to the weight-driven clock in Wells Cathedral, Somerset, England, but only the iron frame is original. A model of Giovanni de Dondi's heptagonal astronomical clock of 1348–64 was completed in 1962.

Largest. The world's most massive clock is the Astronomical Clock in Beauvais Cathedral, France, constructed between 1865 and 1868. It contains 90,000 parts and measures 40 feet high, 20 feet wide and 9 feet deep. The Su Sung clock, built in China at Khaifeng in 1088–92, had a 22-ton bronze armillory sphere for $1\frac{1}{3}$ tons of water. It was removed to Peking in 1126 and was last known to be working in its 40-foot-high tower in 1136.

The largest clock wheel in the world is the World Time Clock installed at 120 Cheapside, London. It has a diameter of 10 feet and enables the zone times in the major cities of the world to be read off. This was commissioned by J. Henry Schroder Wagg & Co. Ltd., from Martin Burgess.

Time Measurer

The most accurate time-keeping devices are the twin atomic hydrogen masers installed in 1964 in the U.S. Naval Research Laboratory, Washington, D.C. They are based on the frequency of

WORLD'S LARGEST FOUR-FACED CLOCK is on the Allen-Bradley Building in Milwaukee. Each face has a diameter of 40 feet 3½ inches.

the hydrogen atom's transition period of 1,420,450,751,694 cycles per second. This enables an accuracy to within one second per 1,700,000 years.

Public Clocks. The largest four-faced clock in the world is that on the building of the Allen-Bradley Company of Milwaukee, Wisconsin. Each face has a diameter of 40 feet 3½ inches with a minute hand 20 feet in overall length. (See photo.)

The tallest four-faced clock in the world is that of the Williamsburgh Savings Bank, Brooklyn, New York City. It is 430 feet above street level.

Most Accurate. The most accurate and complicated clock in the world is the Olsen clock, installed in the Copenhagen Town Hall, Denmark. The clock, which has more than 14,000 units, took 10 years to make and the mechanism of the clock functions in 570,000 different ways. The celestial pole motion of the clock will take 25,700 years to complete a full circle, the slowest moving designed mechanism in the world. The clock is accurate to 0.5 seconds in 300 years.

Most Expensive. The highest auction price for any portable English clock is £16,000 ($40,000) for an ebony bracket clock made by Thomas Tompian (c. 1639–1713) sold at the salesrooms of Sotheby & Co., London, on May 22, 1972.

Watches

Oldest. The oldest watch (portable clockwork timekeeper) is one made of iron by Peter Henlein (or Hele) in Nürnberg (Nuremberg), Bavaria, Germany, in *c*. 1504 and now in the Memorial Hall, Philadelphia, Pennsylvania. The earliest wrist watches were those of Jacquet-Droz and Leschot of Geneva, Switzerland, dating from 1790.

Most Expensive. Excluding watches with jeweled cases, the most expensive standard man's wrist watch is the Swiss *Grande Complication* by Audemars-Piguet, which retails for $25,000.

On June 1, 1964, a record £27,500 ($77,000) was paid for the Duke of Wellington's watch made in Paris in 1807 by Abraham Louis Bréguet, at the salesrooms of Sotheby & Co., London, by the dealers Messrs. Ronald Lee for a Portuguese client.

Smallest. The smallest watches in the world are produced by Jaeger Le Coultre of Switzerland. Equipped with a 15-jeweled movement, they measure just over half-an-inch in length and three-sixteenths of an inch in width. The movement, with its case, weighs under a quarter of an ounce.

MOST EXPENSIVE WATCH: Made by the Swiss firm of Audemars-Piguet, this "Grande Complication" costs $25,000.

Chapter Ten

THE HUMAN WORLD

1. Political and Social

The land area of the earth is estimated at 57,700,000 square miles (including inland waters), or 29.3 per cent of the world's surface area. The permanently inhabited continents (*i.e.*, excluding Antarctica) and island groups have an estimated area of 52,430,000 square miles, including inland waters.

Largest Political Division

The British Commonwealth of Nations, a free association of 32 independent sovereign states together with their dependencies, covers an area of 13,400,000 square miles and had an estimated population of 930,000,000 in 1972.

COUNTRIES

The total number of separately administered territories in the world is 228, of which 148 are independent countries. Of these, 24 sovereign and 65 non-sovereign are insular countries. Only 29 sovereign and 3 non-sovereign countries are entirely without a seaboard. Territorial waters vary between extremes of 3 miles (*e.g.* Australia, France, Ireland, United Kingdom and the U.S.) up to 200 miles (*e.g.* Argentina, Ecuador, El Salvador and Panama).

Largest. The country with the greatest area is the Union of Soviet Socialist Republics (the Soviet Union), comprising 15 Union (constituent) Republics with a total area of 8,649,550 square miles, or 15.0 per cent of the world's total land area, and a total coastline (including islands) of 66,090 miles. The country measures 5,580 miles from east to west and 2,790 miles from north to south.

Smallest. The smallest independent country in the world is the State of the Vatican City (Stato della Città del Vaticano), which was made an enclave within the city of Rome, Italy, on February 11, 1929. It has an area of 108.7 acres.

The smallest colony in the world is Pitcairn Island with an area of 960 acres (1.5 square miles) and a population of 74 on January 1, 1970.

SMALLEST COLONY:
Pitcairn Island in the Pacific has a population of 74, but an 8-man Parliament. Many of the people are descendants of Fletcher Christian of "Mutiny on the Bounty" fame.

The world's smallest republic is Nauru, less than 1 degree south of the equator in the Western Pacific. It became independent on January 31, 1968, has an area of 5,263 acres (8.2 square miles) and a population of 7,000 (estimate mid-1969).

The official residence, since 1834, of the Grand Master of the Order of the Knights of Malta totaling 3 acres and comprising the Villa del Priorato di Malta on the lowest of Rome's seven hills, the 151-foot Aventine, retains certain diplomatic privileges and has accredited representatives to foreign governments. Hence, it is sometimes cited as the smallest state in the world.

On January 19, 1972, the two South Pacific atolls of North and South Minerva (400 miles south of Fiji) were declared to be a sovereign independent Republic under international law by Michael Oliver, formerly of Lithuania.

Frontiers

Most. The country with the most frontiers is the U.S.S.R., with 12—Norway, Finland, Poland, Czechoslovakia, Hungary, Rumania, Turkey, Iran (Persia), Afghanistan, Mongolia, Peoples' Republic of China, and North Korea.

Longest. The longest continuous frontier in the world is that between Canada and the U.S., which (including the Great Lakes boundaries) extends for 3,987 miles (excluding 1,538 miles with Alaska).

Most Frequently Crossed. The frontier which is crossed most frequently is that between the U.S. and Mexico. It extends for 1,933 miles and has more than 120,000,000 crossings every year. The Sino-Soviet frontier extends for 4,500 miles with virtually no crossings.

Most Impenetrable Boundary. The 858-mile-long "Iron Curtain," dividing the Federal Republican (West) and the Democratic Republican (East) parts of Germany, utilizes 2,230,000 land mines and 50,000 miles of barbed wire, in addition to many watchtowers containing detection devices. The whole 270-yard-wide strip occupies 133 square miles of East German territory.

POPULATIONS

Estimates of the human population of the world depend largely on the component figure for the population of the People's Republic of China. The first official figures place the 1970 population at 697,260,000, including Taiwan, which is about 75,000,000 less than previous unofficial estimates.

The world total at mid-1972 can be estimated to be 3,707 miillon, giving an average density of 72.7 people per square mile of land (including inland waters). This excludes Antarctica and uninhabited island groups. The daily increase in the world's population was running at 208,000 in 1972–73. It is estimated that about 245 are born and about 101 die every minute in 1972. The world's population has doubled in the last 50 years and is expected to double again in the next 35 years.

It is now estimated that the world's population in the year 2000 will be more than 6,000 million, and probably closer to 7,000 million. The present population "explosion" is of such a magnitude that it has been fancifully calculated that, if it were to continue unabated, there would be one person to each square yard by 2600 A.D. and humanity would weigh more than Earth itself by 3700 A.D. It is estimated that 75,000,000,000 humans have been born and died in the last 600,000 years.

WORLD POPULATION—PROGRESSIVE MID-YEAR ESTIMATES

Date	Millions	Date	Millions
4000 B.C.	85	1966	3,353
1 A.D.	c. 200–300	1967	3,420
1650	c. 500–550	1968	3,483
1750	750	1969	3,552
1800	960	1970	3,632
1850	1,240	1971	3,706
1900	1,650	1972	3,707
1920	1,862	1973	3,860
1930	2,070	2000	6,493*
1940	2,295	2007	7,600**
1950	2,517	2070	25,000**
1960	3,005	2100	48,000**
1965	3,297		

* U.N. Forecasts made on medium variants.
** Estimated date of future doublings of the present population.

Largest. The country with the largest population in the world is the People's Republic of China. Figures announced in mid-1972 by the Chinese Cartographic Institute give an official 1970 population of 697,260,000. This includes 12,040,000 for Taiwan, which Peking holds is part of China.

Foreign estimates previously ranged from 750,000,000 to 870,000,000. The United Nations had estimated 760,000,000, which is 63,000,000 higher than the official Chinese release. Most of the foreign estimates were based on the 1957 Chinese census. No census has been taken in China since then.

Smallest. The independent state with the smallest population is the Vatican City (see *Smallest Country*), with 880 inhabitants at January 1, 1966.

Densest. The most densely populated territory in the world is the Portuguese province of Macau (or Macao), on the southern coast of China. It has an estimated population of 314,000 (June 30, 1970) in an area of 6.2 square miles, giving a density of about 50,645 per square mile. The population has continued to increase as a result of the influx of Chinese refugees.

Of territories with an area of more than 200 square miles, Hong Kong (398¼ square miles) contains 3,950,802 people (census of March 9, 1971), giving the territory a density of 9,920 per square mile. Hong Kong is only the transcription of the local pronunciation of the Peking dialect version of Xiang gang (a port for incense). About 80 per cent of the population lives in the urban areas of Hong Kong Island (Victoria) and Kowloon, a peninsula of the mainland, and the density there is greater than 200,000 per square mile. At North Point, there are 12,400 people living in 6½ acres, giving an unsurpassed spot density of more than 1,200,000 per square mile. In 1959 it was reported that in one house designed for 12 people the number of occupants was 459, including 104 in one room and 4 living on the roof.

The Principality of Monaco, on the south coast of France, has a population of 24,000 (estimated June 30, 1970) in an area of 369.9

MOST DENSELY POPULATED TERRITORY: Macao on the southern coast of China, a Portuguese province, has 50,645 people per square mile.

acres, giving a density of 41,500 per square mile. This is being relieved by marine infilling which will increase her area to 447 acres.

Singapore has 2,074,507 (mid-1971 census) people in an inhabited area of 73 square miles.

Of countries over 1,000 square miles, the most densely populated is the Netherlands, with a population of 13,194,000 (estimate, July 1, 1971) on 12,978 square miles of land, giving a density of 1,016 people per square mile.

MOST DENSELY POPULATED INDEPENDENT NATION: Monaco contains 39,790 people to the square mile.

The Indonesian islands of Java and Madura (combined area 51,033 square miles) have a population of 73,400,000 (estimate for mid-1969), giving a density of 1,438 per square mile.

Sparsest. Antarctica became permanently occupied by relays of scientists from October, 1956. The population varies seasonally and reaches 1,500 at times.

The least populated territory, apart from Antarctica, is Greenland, with a population of 47,000 (estimate, July 1, 1970) in an area of 840,000 square miles, giving a density of about 0.055 of a person per square mile, or one person to every 17.8 square miles. The ice-free area of the island (now believed to be several islands) is only 132,000 square miles.

Cities

Most Populous. The most populous city in the world is Tokyo, the capital of Japan since 1868. The 23 wards (*ku*) of the Old City contained 8,807,202 people at December, 1971, while Tokyo-to (Tokyo Prefecture) had 11,408,000 in its 823.6 square miles at October 1, 1970. The population of this area had surpassed that of Greater London and New York in early 1957, and in January, 1962, it became the first urban area in history whose recorded population exceeded 10,000,000. At the census of October 1, 1970, the "Keihin Metropolitan Area" (Tokyo-Yokohoma Metropolitan Area) of 1,081 square miles contained 14,034,074.

In December, 1964, the population of Shanghai, China, was

WORLD'S MOST POPULOUS CITY: Tokyo, capital of Japan, has almost 9,000,000 in the Old City and well over 11,000,000 in the Tokyo Prefecture within an area of 824 square miles. The center of the city is shown in the photo.

HIGHEST CAPITAL CITY: La Paz, Bolivia, is located in the Andes Mountains at an altitude of 11,916 feet above sea level.

unofficially reported to be 10,700,000. The city-proper population figure in the 1957 census was 6,900,000.

The world's largest city not built by the sea or on a river is Mexico City (Ciudad de México), the capital of Mexico, with an estimated population of 7,005,855 at July 1, 1970. Greater Mexico City's population was 8,541,070 (1970 census).

Highest. The highest capital city in the world, before the domination of Tibet by China, was Lhasa, at an elevation of 12,087 feet above sea level.

La Paz, the administrative and *de facto* capital of Bolivia, stands at an altitude of 11,916 feet above sea level. The city was founded in 1548 by Capt. Alonso de Mendoza on the site of an Indian village named Chuquiapu. It was originally called Ciudad de Nuestra Señora de La Paz (City of Our Lady of Peace), but in 1825 was renamed La Paz de Ayacucho, its present official name. Sucre, the legal capital of Bolivia, stands at 9,301 feet above sea level.

The new town of Wenchuan, founded in 1955 on the Chinghai-Tibet road, north of the Tangla Range is the highest in the world at 16,732 feet above sea level. The highest village in the world is the Andean mining village of Aucanquilca, in Chile, at 17,500 feet above sea level.

Oldest. The oldest known walled town is Jericho, in Israel-occupied Jordan. Radio-carbon dating on specimens from the lowest levels reached by archeologists indicate habitation there by perhaps 3,000 people as early as 7800 B.C. The village of Zawi Chemi Shanidar, discovered in 1957 in northern Iraq, has been dated to 8910 B.C. The oldest capital city in the world is Dimashq (Damascus), capital of Syria. It has been continuously inhabited since *c.* 2500 B.C.

Towns

Largest in Area. The world's largest town, in area, is Kiruna, in Sweden. Its boundaries have, for fiscal avoidance purposes, been extended to embrace an area of 5,458 square miles.

NORTHERNMOST VILLAGE: Ny Ålesund (78° 55′N), in Vest Spitsbergen, on the world's most northerly railroad.

Northernmost. The world's northernmost town with a population of more than 10,000 is the Arctic port of Dikson, U.S.S.R., at 73° 32′ N.

The northernmost village is Ny Ålesund (78° 55′ N.), a coal mining settlement on King's Bay, Vest Spitsbergen, in the Norwegian territory of Svalbard, inhabited only during the winter season. (See photo.)

The northernmost capital is Reykjavik, Iceland, at 64° 06′ N. Its population was estimated to be 81,288 on July 1, 1969. The northernmost permanent human occupation is the base at Alert (82° 31′ N.), on Dumb Bell Bay, on the northeast coast of Ellesmere Island, northern Canada.

Southernmost. The world's southernmost village is Puerto Williams (population about 350), on the north coast of Isla Navarino, in Tierra del Fuego, Chile, about 680 miles north of Antarctica. Wellington, North Island, New Zealand, is the southernmost capital city at 41° 17′ S. The world's southernmost administrative center is Port Stanley (51° 43′ S.), in the Falkland Islands, off southern South America.

Most Remote from Sea. The large town most remote from the sea is Wulumuchi (Urumchi) formerly Tihwa, Sinkiang, capital of the Uighur Autonomous Region of China, at a distance of about

1,400 miles from the nearest coastline. Its population was estimated to be 275,000 at December 31, 1957 (latest published figure).

Emigration

More people emigrate from the United Kingdom than from any other country. A total of 299,600 emigrated from the U.K. from mid-1969 to mid-1970 (latest available data). The largest number of emigrants in any one year was 360,000 in 1852, mainly from Ireland in the post-famine period.

Immigration

The country which regularly receives the most immigrants is the United States, with 358,579 in 1969. It has been estimated that, in the period 1820–1969, the U.S. received 44,789,312 immigrants.

Most Tourists

In 1971, Italy received 33,230,000 foreign visitors—more than any other country except Canada, which in 1970 received 37,735,000, of whom more than 62 per cent entered and left the same day.

Birth Rate

Highest and Lowest. Based on the latest data available, the highest recorded crude live birth rate is 62 live births per 1,000 of the population in Guinea (Africans only, based on births reported for the 12-month period preceding the sample survey of January 15, to May 31, 1955). The highest 1968 figure is 52.3 for Swaziland. The rate for the whole world was 33 per 1,000 in 1963–69.

The lowest of the latest available recorded rates is 6.8 in Christmas Island.

Death Rate

Highest and Lowest. The highest of the latest available recorded death rates is 40 deaths per each 1,000 of the population in Guinea (Africans only, 12 months preceding 1955 sample survey). The next highest figure is 35 per 1,000 in Burma in 1955 (still latest available). The rate for the whole world was 14 per 1,000 in 1963–69.

The lowest of the latest available recorded rates is 1.3 deaths per 1,000 in Mozambique in 1968. The lowest rate in an independent country in 1967 was 4.1 per 1,000 registered in Iraq and 4.4 in Syria in 1968.

Natural Increase

The highest of the latest available recorded rates of natural increase is 55.0 per 1,000 in Kuwait (births 61.2, deaths 6.2) in 1964. The rate for the whole world was 34 — 14 = 20 per 1,000 in 1965–70.

There are three territories in which the death rate exceeds the birth rate, and which thus have a rate of natural decrease: West Berlin, Germany, 9.9 per 1,000 (birth rate 10.0, death rate 19.9) in 1969; East Berlin 1.9 per 1,000 and the Isle of Man 2.9 per 1,000 (registered births 15.3, registered deaths 18.3) in 1969. The lowest rate of natural increase in an independent country in 1969 was 0.3 per 1,000 in East Germany (birth rate 14.0, death rate 14.3).

Marriage Ages

The country with the lowest average ages for marriage is India, with 20.0 years for males and 14.5 years for females. At the other extreme is Ireland, with 31.4 for males and 26.5 years for females. In the People's Republic of China, marriage for men is reportedly not approved before the age of 28.

Sex Ratio

The country with the largest recorded female surplus is the U.S.S.R., with 1,171.6 females to every 1,000 males at January 15, 1970. The country with the largest recorded woman shortage is Pakistan, with 900.7 to every 1,000 males at February 1, 1961.

Infant Mortality

Based on deaths before one year of age, the lowest of the latest available recorded rates is 9.2 deaths per 1,000 live births in Gibraltar in 1968, compared with 12.9 per 1,000 in Sweden in 1967.

The highest recorded infant mortality rate recently reported has been 259 per 1,000 live births among the indigenous African population of Zambia (then Northern Rhodesia) in the 12 months preceding the sample survey of June 30, 1950. Among more recent estimates, the highest is an annual average of 64.2 per 1,000 for Mexico in 1968.

Many countries do not make returns. Among these is Ethiopia, where the infant mortality rate was estimated to be nearly 550 per 1,000 live births in 1969.

Life Expectation

There is evidence that life expectation in Britain in the 5th century A.D. was 33 years for males and 27 years for females. In the decade 1890–1900 the expectation of life among the population of India was 23.7 years.

Based on the latest available data, the highest recorded expectation of life at birth is 71.85 years for males, and 76.54 years for females, both in Sweden in 1969.

The lowest recorded expectation of life at birth is 27 years for both sexes in the Vallée du Niger area of Mali in 1957 (sample survey, 1957–58). The figure for males in Gabon was 25 years in 1960–61.

At the age of 60, the highest recorded expectation of life for males is in Bolivia, with 20.39 years (1949–51). More reliable figures include 18.64 years in Puerto Rico (1959–61), 18.6 years in Iceland (1961–65). The highest recorded figure for females is 21.66 years in Ryukyu Islands (1960), 20.99 years in Puerto Rico (1959–61) and 20.9 years in Iceland (1961–65).

STANDARDS OF LIVING

National Incomes

The country with the highest income per person in 1968 was Nauru, with nearly $4,000 per head, followed by Kuwait and the U.S. The U.S. in 1967 leads on the basis of major industrial countries measured by real product per head at 190.

Cost of Living

The greatest increase since 1963 (= 100) has been in Djakarta, the capital of Indonesia, where the index figure reached 57,712 (food 62,876) by 1968.

Most and Least Expensive Capital City

According to data published by the U.N. Statistical Office in June, 1970, the world's most expensive capital city is Saigon, South Viet-Nam (122) and the world's cheapest is Damascus, Syria (69). These indices compare with the cost of living in New York of 100 in 1968.

Housing Units

For comparison, a dwelling unit is defined as a structurally separated room or rooms occupied by private households of one or more people and having separate access or a common passageway to the street. The country with the greatest recorded number of private dwelling units is India, with 79,193,602 occupied in 1960. These contain 83,523,895 private households.

Physicians

The country with the most physicians is the U.S.S.R., with 550,389 in 1967, or one to every 427 persons. The country with the highest proportion of physicians is Israel, where there were 6,312 (one for every 420 inhabitants) in 1967. The country with the lowest recorded proportion is Upper Volta, with 68 physicians (one for every 74,320 people) in 1967.

Dentists

The country with the most dentists is the U.S., where 115,000 were registered members of the American Dental Association in 1971.

Psychiatrists and Psychologists

The country with the most psychiatrists is the U.S. The registered membership of the American Psychiatric Association was 18,225 in 1971. The membership of the American Psychological Association was 31,000 in 1971.

Hospitals

Largest. The largest medical center in the world is the District Medical Center in Chicago. It covers 478 acres and includes five hospitals, with a total of 5,600 beds, and eight professional schools with more than 3,000 students.

The largest hospital in the world is Danderyd Hospital in northern Stockholm, Sweden. In 1969, it had 12,000 beds.

The largest mental hospital in the world is the Pilgrim State Hospital, Long Island, New York, with 12,800 beds. It formerly contained 14,200 beds.

The largest maternity hospital in the world is the Kandang Kerbau Government Maternity Hospital in Singapore. It has 239 midwives, 151 beds for gynecological cases, 388 maternity beds and

LARGEST MATERNITY HOSPITAL: In these buildings in Singapore almost 40,000 babies were born in one year—over 109 a day.

an output of 31,255 babies in 1969, compared with the record "birthquake" of 39,856 babies (more than 109 per day) in 1966.

ROYALTY

Oldest Ruling House. The Emperor of Japan, Hirohito (born April 29, 1901), is the 124th in line from the first Emperor, Jimmu Tenno or Zinmu, whose reign was traditionally from 660 to 581 B.C., but probably from *c.* 40 to *c.* 10 B.C.

His Imperial Majesty Muhammad Riza Shah Pahlavi of Iran (born October 26, 1919) claims descent from Cyrus the Great (reigned *c.* 559–529 B.C.).

Reigns

Longest. The longest recorded reign of any monarch is that of Pepi II, a Sixth Dynasty Pharaoh of ancient Egypt. His reign began in *c.* 2272 B.C., when he was aged 6, and lasted 91 years.

Currently the longest reigning monarch in the world is King Sobhuza II (born July, 1899), the *Ngwenyama* (Paramount Chief) of Swaziland, who began his reign at the age of 5 months. The country was placed under United Kingdom protection at that time, December, 1899, and became independent on September 6, 1968. Emperor Hirohito of Japan began his reign on December 25, 1926.

The longest reign in European history was that of King Louis XIV of France, who ascended the throne on May 14, 1643, aged

4 years 8 months, and reigned for 72 years 110 days until his death on September 1, 1715, four days before his 77th birthday.

Musoma Kanijo, chief of the Nzega district of western Tanganyika (now part of Tanzania), reputedly reigned for more than 98 years from 1864, when aged 8, until his death on February 2, 1963.

The 6th Japanese Emperor Koo-an traditionally reigned for 102 years (from 392 to 290 B.C.), but probably his actual reign was from about 110 A.D. to about 140 A.D. The reign of the 11th Emperor Suinin was traditionally from 29 B.C. to 71 A.D. (99 years), but probably was from 259 A.D. to 291.

Shortest. The shortest recorded reign was that of the Dauphin Louis Antoine, who was technically King Louis XIX of France for the 15 minutes between the signature of Charles X (1757–1836) and his own signature to the act of abdication, in favor of Henri V, which was executed at the Château de Rombouillet on August 2, 1830.

Highest Regnal Number. Prince Henry LXXIV of Reuss (1798–1886) boasted the highest post-nominal number (74). All male members of his family were called Henry.

Longest-Lived Royalty. The longest life among the "blood royal" of Europe is the 96 years 8 months of H.R.H. Princess Anna of Battenberg, daughter of Nicholas I of Montenegro, who was born August 18, 1874, and died in Switzerland April 22, 1971.

Oldest and Youngest Heads of State. The oldest head of state in the world is Dr. Eamon de Valera (b. October 14, 1882), President of the Republic of Ireland since June 25, 1959. The youngest head of state is Jean-Claude du Valier (b. July 3, 1951), President of Haiti.

LONGEST REIGNS: Louis XIV (left) was King of France for more than 72 years. The longest current reign is that of King Sobhuza II (right), Paramount Chief of Swaziland since December, 1899, when he was only 5 months old.

British Monarchs

Longest Reign. The longest reign of any King of Great Britain was that of George III, from October 25, 1760, to January 29, 1820 (59 years 96 days) and the longest of a Queen was that of Victoria, from June 20, 1837 to January 22, 1901 (63 years 216 days). James Francis Edward (born June 10, 1688), the Old Pretender, known to his supporters as James III, styled his reign from September 16, 1701, until his death on January 1, 1766, thus lasting over 64 years.

Shortest Reign. The shortest reign of a King of England was that of Edward V, from April 9 until he was deposed on June 25, 1483 (77 days). He died probably between July and September, 1483. The shortest reign of a Queen was that of Jane, who acceded on July 6, 1553, was proclaimed Queen on July 10 and was deposed on July 19, 1553, after a reign of only 13 days (or 9 days from proclamation).

Longest-Lived. Excluding the 8 who suffered violent death, English monarchs have had an average life span of 57 years. The longest-lived British monarchs were King George III, who died on January 29, 1820, aged 81 years 239 days, and Queen Victoria, who, at the time of her death on January 22, 1901, had surpassed his age by four days. The oldest monarch at the time of succession was William IV, who became King on June 26, 1830, aged 64 years 10 months.

Youngest. The youngest English monarch was Henry VI, who was born on December 6, 1421, and came to the throne on September 1, 1422, aged less than 9 months. Scotland's youngest was Queen Mary, born on December 7 or 8, 1542. She succeeded to the Scottish throne on December 14, 1542, aged 6 or 7 days.

England's youngest Queen was Isabella, daughter of King Charles VI of France. She was born on November 9, 1389, and became the second wife of Richard II at Calais, probably on November 4, 1396, when a few days short of her seventh birthday.

Most Children. The King with the most legitimate children was Edward I (1239–1307), who had 16 by his two queens, Eleanor of Castille (died 1290) and Margaret of France (1282–1317).

The monarch with the greatest number of illegitimate children was Henry I (1068–1135), who had at least 20 (9 sons, 11 daughters) and possibly 22 by six mistresses, in addition to one (possibly two) sons and a daughter born legitimately.

The largest number of children born to a Queen regnant was nine to Queen Victoria (1819–1901) and the largest number to a Queen Consort was 15 to Queen Charlotte Sophia (1744–1818), the wife of George III (1738–1820). Before coming to the throne in 1702, Queen Anne (1665–1714) conceived 18 children, of whom only five were live-born and all of these died in infancy. Her Prince William (1689–1700), the Duke of Gloucester, survived to the age of 11 years 6 days.

Most Often Married. The most often married English King was Henry VIII, whose sixth and last wife, Catherine Parr (c. 1512–1548), was England's most married Queen. She was first married to the Hon. Sir Edward Burgh (died 1529 or earlier), secondly to

John Neville, the 3rd Lord Latimer (died 1542 or 1543), thirdly on July 12, 1543, to Henry VIII, and fourthly and finally on March 3, 1547, five weeks after Henry's death, to Thomas, Lord Seymour of Sudeley. She died on September 7, 1548, eight days after giving birth to a daughter.

Tallest and Shortest. England's tallest monarch was Edward IV (reigned 1461–1483), who was between 6 feet 3 inches and 6 feet 4 inches and was regarded as a giant in his time. Charles I (reigned 1625–1649) was, on the evidence of his armor, barely over 5 feet tall. This compares with the 4 feet 9½ inches of the 12-year-old Edward V.

LEGISLATURES

Parliaments

Oldest. The oldest legislative body is the *Alpingi* (Althing) of Iceland, founded in 930 A.D. This body, which originally comprised 39 local chieftains, was abolished in 1800, but restored by Denmark to a consultative status in 1843 and a legislative status in 1874. The legislative assembly with the oldest continuous history is the Tynwald Court of the Isle of Man, in the Irish Channel, which is believed to have originated more than 1,000 years ago.

The earliest known use of the term "parliament" in an official English royal document, in the meaning of a summons to the King's council, dates from December 19, 1241.

Largest. The largest legislative assembly in the world is the National People's Congress of China (mainland). The fourth Congress, which met in March, 1969, had 3,500 members.

Smallest Quorum. The British House of Lords has the smallest quorum, expressed as a percentage of eligible voters, of any legislative body in the world, namely one-third of one per cent. To transact business there must be three peers present, including the Lord Chancellor or his deputy.

Highest Paid Legislators. The most highly paid of all the world's legislators are U.S. Senators, who receive a basic annual salary of $42,500. Of this, up to $3,000 is exempt from taxation. In addition, Senators from large states receive up to $130,000 per annum for office help, with a salary limit of $13,345 per assistant per year. Senators also enjoy free travel to and from Washington, telephones, postage, medical care, telegrams (to a limit of $2,000 per session), flowers and haircuts. They also are charged very low rates for stationery, filming, speech and radio transcriptions and, in the case of women Senators, beauty treatment. When abroad they have access to "counterpart funds" and on retirement to non-contributory benefits.

Filibusters. The longest continuous speech in the history of the U.S. Senate was that of Senator Wayne Morse of Oregon on April 24–25, 1953, when he spoke on the Tidelands Oil Bill for 22 hours 26 minutes without resuming his seat. Senator Strom Thurmond (South Carolina, Democrat) spoke against the Civil Rights Bill for

LONGEST-LIVED POLITICIANS: Christopher Hornsrud (left), Prime Minister of Norway in 1928, lived to be more than 101 years of age. József Madarász (right) of Hungary also lived to the age of 101, and 83 of those years spanned his career in the Parliament.

24 hours 19 minutes on August 28–29, 1957, interrupted only briefly by the swearing-in of a new senator.

The record for a filibuster in any legislature is 42 hours 33 minutes by Texas State Senator Mike McKool, known as Little Hercules, at Austin, Texas, on June 26–28, 1972. He was speaking for inclusion of $17,000,000 for mental health services in the state budget. It took the Senate less than five minutes to ignore his speech.

Longest Membership. The longest span as a legislator was 83 years by József Madarász (1814–1915). He first attended the Hungarian Parliament in 1832–36 as *ablegatus absentium* (*i.e.* on behalf of an absent deputy). He was a full member in 1848–50 and from 1861 until his death on January 31, 1915. (See photo.)

Prime Ministers

Oldest. The longest-lived Prime Minister of any country is believed to have been Christopher Hornsrud, Prime Minister of Norway from January 28 to February 15, 1928. He was born on November 15, 1859 and died on December 13, 1960, aged 101 years 28 days. (See photo.)

El Hadji Mohammed el Mokri, Grand Vizier of Morocco, died on September 16, 1957, at a reputed age of 116 Muslim (*Hijri*) years, equivalent to 112.5 Gregorian years. (See photo, next page.)

Longest Term of Office. Prof. Dr. António de Oliveira Salazar, (1889–1970), was the President of the Council of Ministers (*i.e.* Prime Minister) of Portugal from July 5, 1932, for 36 years and 83 days until superseded on September 27, 1968, eleven days after going into a coma.

Elections

Largest. The largest election ever held was that for the Indian *Lok Sabha* (House of the People) on March 1–10, 1971. About 152,720,000 of the electorate of 272,630,000 chose from 2,785 candidates for 518 seats.

Closest. The ultimate in close general elections occurred in Zanzibar (now part of Tanzania) on January 18, 1961, when the Afro-Shirazi Party won by a single seat, after the seat of Chake-Chake on Pemba Island had been gained by a single vote.

Most One-Sided. North Korea recorded a 100 per cent turn-out of electors and a 100 per cent vote for the Workers' Party of Korea in the general election of October 8, 1962. The previous record had been set in the Albanian election of June 4, 1962, when all but seven of the electorate of 889,875 went to the polls—a 99.9992 per cent turn-out. Of the 889,868 voters, 889,828 voted for the candidates of the Albanian Party of Labor, *i.e.* 99.9955 per cent of the total poll.

The highest personal majority was 157,692 from 192,909 votes cast for H.H. Maharani of Jaipur (born May 23, 1919), in the Indian general election of February, 1962.

Communist Parties. The largest national Communist party outside the U.S.S.R. (which had 14,254,000 members in 1971) and Communist states has been the Partito Comunista Italiano (Italian Communist Party), with a membership of 2,300,000 in 1946. The total fell to 1,500,000 by 1971. The membership in mainland China was estimated to be 17,000,000 in 1970.

MOST DURABLE PRIME MINISTER: (Left) Prof. Dr. António de Oliveira Salazar was Prime Minister of Portugal for 36 years and 83 days. (Right) OLDEST RECORDED EXECUTIVE HEAD of any country: El Hadji Mohammed el Mokri, Grand Vizier of Morocco, who died in 1957, reputedly aged 112.

Most Parties. The country with the greatest number of political parties is Italy, with 73 registered for the elections of May 19, 1968. These included "Friends of the Moon" with one candidate.

2. Military and Defense

WAR

Longest. The longest of history's countless wars was the "Hundred Years War" between England and France, which lasted from 1338 to 1453 (115 years), although it may be said that the Holy War, comprising nine Crusades from the First (1096–1104) to the Ninth (1270–91), extended over 195 years. It has been calculated that in the 3,462 years since 1496 B.C. there have been only 230 years of peace throughout the civilized world.

Shortest. The shortest war on record was that between the United Kingdom and Zanzibar (now part of Tanzania) from 9:02 to 9:40 a.m. on August 27, 1896. The U.K. battle fleet under Rear-Admiral (later Admiral Sir) Harry Holdsworth Rawson (1843–1910) delivered an ultimatum to the self-appointed Sultan Sa'id Khalid to evacuate his palace and surrender. This was not forthcoming until after 38 minutes of bombardment. Admiral Rawson received the Brilliant Star of Zanzibar (first class) from the new Sultan Hamud ibn Muhammad. It was proposed at one time that elements of the local populace should be compelled to defray the cost of the ammunition used. (See photo.)

Bloodiest. By far the most costly war in terms of human life was World War II (1939–45), in which the total number of fatalities, including battle deaths and civilians of all countries, is estimated to have been 54,800,000, assuming 25,000,000 U.S.S.R. fatalities and 7,800,000 Chinese civilians killed. The country which suffered most was Poland with 6,028,000 or 22.2 per cent of her population of 27,007,000 killed.

Most Costly. Although no satisfactory computation has been published, it is certain that the material cost of World War II far transcended that of the rest of history's wars put together. In the case of the United Kingdom the cost was over nine times as great as that of World War I. The total cost of World War II to the Soviet Union was estimated semi-officially in May, 1959, at 2,500,000,000,000 roubles ($280,000 million).

Bloodiest Civil War. The bloodiest civil war in history was the T'ai-p'ing ("Peace") rebellion, in which peasant sympathizers of the Southern Ming dynasty fought the Manchu Government troops in China from 1853 to 1864. The rebellion was led by the deranged Hung Hsiu-ch'üan (poisoned himself in June, 1864), who imagined himself to be a younger brother of Jesus Christ. His force was named *T'ai-p'ing Tien Kuo* (Heavenly Kingdom of Great Peace). According to the best estimates, the loss of life was between 20,000,000 and 30,000,000 including more than 100,000 killed by Government forces in the sack of Nanking on July 19–21, 1864.

VICTOR IN
SHORTEST WAR:
Admiral Sir Harry Rawson
of the British Royal Navy
commanded the battle
fleet that defeated Zanzibar
in 38 minutes.

Bloodiest Battle. The battle with the greatest recorded number of casualties was the First Battle of the Somme from July 1 to November 19, 1916, with more than 1,030,000—614,105 British and French and *c.* 420,000 (*not* 650,000) German. The gunfire was heard as far away as Hampstead Heath, London. The greatest battle of World War II and the greatest conflict ever of armor was the Battle of Kursk of July 5–22, 1943, on the Eastern front, which involved 1,300,000 Red Army troops with 3,600 tanks, 20,000 guns and 3,130 aircraft in repelling a German Army Group which had 2,500 tanks. The final invasion of Berlin by the Red Army in 1945 is, however, said to have involved 3,500,000 men; 52,000 guns and mortars; and 7,750 tanks and 11,000 aircraft on both sides.

Modern historians give no credence to the casualty figures attached to ancient battles, such as the 250,000 reputedly killed at Plataea (Greeks *v.* Persians) in 479 B.C. or the 200,000 allegedly killed in a single day at Châlons-sur-Marne, France, in 451 A.D. This view is on the grounds that it must have been logistically quite impossible to maintain forces of such a size in the field at that time.

Worst Sieges

The longest siege in military history was that of Centa which was besieged by the Moors under Mulai Ismail for 26 years—1674 to 1700. The worst siege in history was the 880-day siege of Leningrad, U.S.S.R., by the German Army from August 30, 1941, until January 27, 1944. The best estimate is that between 1.3 and 1.5 million defenders and citizens died.

Largest Armed Forces

Numerically, the country with the largest regular armed force is the U.S.S.R., with 3,375,000 at mid-1971, compared with the U.S.'s 2,700,000 at the same date. The Chinese People's Liberation Army, which includes naval and air services, has more than 2,900,000 regulars, but there is also a civilian home guard militia claimed to be 200 million strong, but regarded by the Institute of Strategic Studies to have an effective element of not more than 5,000,000.

GREATEST EVACUATION: From Dunkirk, France, in 1940, some 1,200 Allied naval and civil craft removed 338,226 British and French troops from the beachhead.

Greatest Invasion

Seaborne. The greatest invasion in military history was the Allied land, air and sea operation against the Normandy coasts of France on D-day, June 6, 1944. Thirty-eight convoys of 745 ships moved in on the first three days, supported by 4,066 landing craft, carrying 185,000 men and 20,000 vehicles, and 347 minesweepers. The air assault comprised 18,000 paratroopers from 1,087 aircraft. The 42 available divisions possessed an air support from 13,175 aircraft. Within a month 1,100,000 troops, 200,000 vehicles and 750,000 tons of stores were landed. On D-day, 2,132 were killed and 8,592 wounded among the invading force.

Airborne. The largest airborne invasion was the Anglo-American assault of three divisions (34,000 men), with 2,800 aircraft and 1,600 gliders, near Arnhem, in the Netherlands, on September 17, 1944.

Greatest Evacuation

The greatest evacuation in military history was that carried out by 1,200 Allied naval and civil craft from the beachhead at Dunkerque (Dunkirk), France, between May 27 and June 4, 1940. A total of 338,226 British and French troops were taken off.

Defense

The estimated level of spending on armaments throughout the world in 1971 was $185,000 million. This represents $50 per person per annum, or close to 10 per cent of the world's total production of goods and services. It was estimated in 1970 that there were 15,400,000 full-time military and naval personnel and 30,000,000 armament workers.

The expenditure on "defense" by the government of the United States in the year ending June 30, 1971, was $78,783 million, or about 7.9 per cent of the country's gross national product.

The U.S.S.R.'s defense expenditure in 1970 has been estimated to be equivalent to $55,000 million, adopting a conversion rate of 0.9 of a rouble to the U.S. dollar. This represents 11 per cent of the gross national product. Almost certainly, this does not include space research costs or the research and development budget for advanced weapons systems.

At the other extreme is Andorra, whose defense budget, voted in 1970, amounted to $10.

NAVIES

Largest. The largest navy in the world is the U.S. Navy, with manpower at 623,000 and 212,000 Marines at June 30, 1971. The active strength in 1971 included 15 attack and 3 anti-submarine carriers, 99 submarines of which 53 are nuclear-powered, 73 guided missile ships (8 cruisers, 29 destroyers and 30 frigates), and 133 amphibious assault ships. The total number of ships in commission was 645.

Greatest Naval Battles

The greatest number of ships and aircraft ever involved in a sea-air action was 231 ships and 1,996 aircraft in the Battle of Leyte Gulf, in the Philippines. It raged from October 22 to 27, 1944, with 166 U.S. and 65 Japanese warships engaged, of which 26 Japanese and 6 U.S. ships were sunk. In addition, 1,280 U.S. and 716 Japanese aircraft were engaged.

The greatest naval battle of modern times was the Battle of Jutland on May 31, 1916, in which 151 British Royal Navy warships were involved against 101 German warships. The Royal Navy lost 14 ships and 6,097 men and the German fleet 11 ships and 2,545 men.

The greatest of ancient naval battles was the Battle of Lepanto on October 7, 1571, when an estimated 25,000 Turks were lost in 250 galleys, sunk by the Spanish, Venetian and Papal forces of more than 300 ships in the Gulf of Lepanto, now called the Gulf of Corinth, Greece.

ARMIES

Largest. Numerically, the largest army is the People's Republic of China's, with a total strength of about 2,550,000 in mid-1971. The total size of the U.S.S.R.'s army (including the ground elements of the Air Defense Command) in mid-1971 was estimated at 2,000,000 men, believed to be organized into about 160 divisions with a maximum strength of 10,500 each.

Smallest. The smallest army in the world is that of San Marino, with a strength of 11, while Costa Rica, Iceland, Liechtenstein, Monaco and Nauru have no army at all. (See photo, next page.)

Oldest. The oldest army in the world is the 83-strong Swiss Guard in the Vatican City, with a regular foundation dating back to January 21, 1506. Its origins, however, extend back before 1400.

Oldest Old Soldier. The oldest old soldier of all time was probably John B. Salling of the Army of the Confederate States of

WORLD'S SMALLEST ARMY is that of San Marino (left) with a force of 11.
OLDEST ARMY is the Vatican's Swiss Guard (right), established in 1506.

America and the last accepted survivor of the U.S. Civil War
(1861–65). He died in Kingsport, Tennessee, on March 16, 1959,
aged 113 years 1 day. (See photo, page 368.)

Tallest Soldier. The tallest soldier of all time was Väinö
Myllyrinne (1909–63) who was inducted into the Finnish Army
when he was 7 feet 3 inches and later grew to 8 feet 1¼ inches.

Tanks

Earliest. The prototype of all tanks was the "Little Willie," built
by William Forster & Co. Ltd. of Lincoln, England, and first tested
in September, 1915. The tank was first taken into action by the
Machine Gun Corps (Heavy Section), which later became the Royal
Tank Corps, at the battle of Flers, in France, on September 15, 1916.
Known as the Mark I Male, it was armed with a pair of 6-lb. guns
and four machine-guns. It weighed 31 tons and, driven by a motor
developing 105 horse-power, had a maximum road speed of 4 to
5 m.p.h.

Heaviest. The heaviest tank ever constructed was the German
Panzer Kampfwagen Maus II, which weighed 212 tons. By 1945, it
had reached only the experimental stage and was not proceeded with.

The heaviest operational tank used by any army was the 91.3 ton
13-man French Char de Rupture 3C of 1923. It carried a 155 mm.
howitzer and had two 250-h.p. engines giving a maximum speed of
8 m.p.h. On November 7, 1957, in the annual military parade in
Moscow, U.S.S.R., a Soviet tank possibly heavier than the German
Jagd Tiger II (80.3 tons), built by Henschel, and certainly heavier
than the Stalin III, was displayed.

Guns

Earliest. Although it cannot be accepted as proved, the best
opinion is that the earliest guns were constructed in North Africa,

possibly by Arabs, in *c.* 1250. The earliest representation of an English gun is contained in an illustrated manuscript dated 1326 at Oxford. The earliest anti-aircraft gun was an artillery piece on a high-angle mounting used in the Franco-Prussian War of 1870 by the French against Prussian balloons.

Largest. The remains of the most massive guns ever constructed were found near Frankfurt-am-Main, Germany, in 1945. They were "Schwerer Gustav" and "Dora," each of which had a barrel 94 feet 9 inches long, with a caliber of 800 millimeters (31.5 inches), and a breech weighing 121 tons. The maximum charge was 4,409 lbs. of cordite to fire a shell weighing 5.28 tons a distance of 34 miles. The maximum projectile was one of 7.8 tons with a range of 22 miles. Each gun with its carriage weighed 1,481 tons and required a crew of 1,500 men.

Greatest Range. The greatest range ever attained by a gun is by the H.A.R.P. (High Altitude Research Project) gun consisting of two 16.5-inch caliber barrels in tandem in Barbados. In 1968, a 200-lb. projectile has been fired to a height of 400,000 feet ($75\frac{3}{4}$ miles).

The famous "Big Bertha" guns which shelled Paris in World War I were the "Lange Berta" of which seven were built with a caliber of 21 cm. (8.26 inches), a designed range of 79.5 miles and an achieved range of more than 75 miles.

Mortars

The largest mortars ever constructed were Mallets mortar (Woolwich Arsenal, London, England, 1857), and the "Little David" of World War II, made in the U.S. Each had a caliber of $36\frac{1}{4}$ inches (920 mm.), but neither was ever used in action.

Largest Cannon

The highest caliber cannon ever constructed is the *Tsar Puchka* (King of Cannons), now housed in the Kremlin, Moscow, U.S.S.R. It was built in the 16th century with a bore of 36 inches (915 mm.) and a barrel 17 feet long. It was designed to fire cannonballs weighing $2\frac{1}{4}$ tons but was never used.

The Turks fired up to seven shots per day from a bombard 26 feet long, with an internal caliber of 42 inches, against the walls of Constantinople (now Istanbul) from April 12 to May 29, 1453. It was dragged by 60 oxen and 200 men and fired a stone cannonball weighing 1,200 lbs.

Military Engines

The largest military catapults, or onagers, were capable of throwing a missile weighing 60 lbs. a distance of 500 yards.

March

Longest. The longest march in military history was the famous Long March by the Chinese Communists in 1934–35. In 368 days, of which 268 days were of movement, from October to October, their force of 90,000 covered 6,000 miles northward from Kiangsi to Yünnan. They crossed 18 mountain ranges and six major rivers and lost all but 22,000 of their force in continual rear-guard actions against Nationalist Kuo-min-tang (K.M.T.) forces.

FIRST ATOMIC BOMB, the one dropped on Hiroshima, Japan, was called a "Little Boy," and was similar in type to this one—10 feet long and weighing 9,000 lbs.

Most Rapid. The most rapid recorded march by foot-soldiers was one of 42 miles in 26 hours on July 28–29, 1809, by the Light Brigade under Brigadier- (later Major-) General Robert Craufurd (1764–1812), coming to the relief of Lieut.-Gen. Sir Arthur Wellesley, later Field Marshal the 1st Duke of Wellington (1769–1852), after the Battle of Talavera (Talavera de la Reina, Toledo, Spain) in the Peninsular War.

AIR FORCES

The earliest autonomous air force is the Royal Air Force of Great Britain whose origins began with the Royal Flying Corps (created May 13, 1912); the Air Battalion of the Royal Engineers (April 1, 1911) and the Corps of Royal Engineers Balloon Section (1878) which was first operational in Bechuanaland (now Botswana) in 1884.

Largest. The greatest air force of all time was the U.S. Army Air Force (now called the U.S. Air Force), which had 79,908 aircraft in July, 1944, and 2,411,294 personnel in March, 1944. The U.S. Air Force, including strategic air forces, had 757,000 personnel and 6,000 combat aircraft in mid-1971. The U.S.S.R. Air Force, with about 550,000 men in mid-1971, had about 10,000 combat aircraft. In addition, the U.S.S.R.'s Offensive Strategic Rocket Forces had about 350,000 operational personnel in mid-1971.

Bombs

The heaviest conventional bomb ever used operationally was the British Royal Air Force's "Grand Slam," weighing 22,000 lbs. and measuring 25 feet 5 inches long, dropped on Bielefeld railway viaduct, Germany, on March 14, 1945. In 1949, the U.S. Air Force tested a bomb weighing 42,000 lbs. at Muroc Dry Lake, California.

Atomic. The two atom bombs dropped on Japan by the U.S. in 1945 each had an explosive power equivalent to that of 20,000 tons (20 kilotons) of trinitrotoluene, called T.N.T. The one dropped on Hiroshima, known as "Little Boy," was 10 feet long and weighed 9,000 lbs.

The most powerful thermonuclear device so far tested is one with a power equivalent to 57,000,000 tons of T.N.T., or 57 megatons, detonated by the U.S.S.R. in the Novaya Zemlya area at 8:33 a.m. G.M.T. on October 30, 1961. The shock wave was detected to have circled the world three times, taking 36 hours 27 minutes for the first circuit. Some estimates put the power of this device at between 62 and 90 megatons. On August 9, 1961, Nikita Khrushchev, then the Chairman of the Council of Ministers of the U.S.S.R., declared that the Soviet Union was capable of constructing a 100-megaton bomb, and announced the possession of one in East Berlin, Germany, on January 16, 1963. It has been estimated that such a bomb would make a crater 19 miles in diameter and would cause serious fires at a range of from 36 to 40 miles.

The patent for the fusion or H-bomb was filed in the U.S. on May 26, 1946, by Dr. Janos (John) von Neumann (1903–57), a Hungarian-born mathematician, and Dr. Klaus Emil Julius Fuchs (born in Germany, 1911), the physicist who defected to Russia from England.

Largest Nuclear Arsenal

It has been estimated that in 1970 the U.S. total of 1,054 I.C.B.M.s (Inter-Continental Ballistic Missiles) was surpassed by the U.S.S.R. whose 1971 total has been put at more than 1,300. The greatest S.L.B.M. (Submarine Launched Ballistic Missile) armory was in 1971 that of the U.S. with 656 compared with 440 in service in the U.S.S.R. Navy. The U.S.S.R.'s arsenal was estimated at 2,300 including 1,300 I.C.B.M.s.

No official estimate has been published of the potential power of the device known as Doomsday, but this far surpasses any tested weapon. A 50,000-megaton cobalt-salted device has been discussed which could kill the entire human race except those who were deep underground and who stayed there for more than five years.

Largest "Conventional" Explosion. The largest military use of conventional explosive was in tunnels under the German positions of the Messines Ridge, Belgium. These were mined from January, 1916, to June, 1917, by 6,000 men, under Capt. Cropper (Canadian Army), and packed with more than 500 tons of ammonal. The detonation at 3:10 a.m. on June 7, 1917, was heard or felt in London.

3. Judicial

LEGISLATION AND LITIGATION

Statutes

Oldest. The earliest known judicial code was that of King Urnammu during the Third Dynasty of Ur, Iraq, in c. 2145 B.C.

Most. It was computed in March, 1959, that the total number of laws on Federal and State statute books in the U.S. was

1,156,644. The Illinois State Legislature only discovered in April, 1967, that in 1907 it had made the sale of cigarettes illegal and punishable by a $100 fine for a second offense.

Most Protracted Litigation

The longest contested law suit ever recorded ended in Poona, India, on April 28, 1966, when Balasaheb Patloji Thorat received a favorable judgment on a suit filed by his ancestor Maloji Thorat 761 years earlier in 1205. The points at issue were rights of presiding over public functions and precedences at religious festivals.

Most Inexplicable Statute

Certain passages in several laws have always defied interpretation and the most inexplicable must be a matter of opinion. A judge of the Court of Session of Scotland has sent the editors of this book his candidate which reads, "In the Nuts (unground), (other than ground nuts) Order, the expression nuts shall have reference to such nuts, other than ground nuts, as would but for this amending Order not qualify as nuts (unground) (other than ground nuts) by reason of their being nuts (unground)."

Best-Attended Trial

The greatest attendance at any trial was at that of Major Jesús Sosa Blanco, aged 51, for an alleged 108 murders. At one point in the 12½-hour trial (5:30 p.m. to 6 a.m., January 22–23, 1959), 17,000 people were present in the Havana Sports Palace, Cuba.

Highest Bail

The highest amount ever demanded as bail was $46,500,000 against Antonio De Angelis in a civil damages suit by the Harbor Tank Storage Co. filed in the Superior Court, Jersey City, New Jersey, on January 16, 1964. (See *Greatest Swindle.*)

Greatest Damages

Loss of Life. The highest damages ever awarded in any court of law were $14,387,674 following upon the crash of a private aircraft at South Lake Tahoe, California, on February 21, 1967, to the sole survivor Ray Rosendin, 45, by the Santa Clara Superior Court on March 8, 1972. Rosendin received $1,069,374 for the loss of both legs and disabling arm injuries; $1,213,129 for the loss of his wife and $10,500,000 punitive damages against Avco-Lycoming Corporation which allegedly violated Federal regulations when it rebuilt the aircraft engine owned by Rosendin Corporation.

Breach of Contract. The greatest damages ever awarded for a breach of contract were £610,392 ($1,709,000), awarded on July 16, 1930, to the Bank of Portugal against the printers Waterlow & Sons, Ltd., of London, arising from their unauthorized printing of 580,000 five-hundred escudo notes in 1925. This award was upheld in the House of Lords on April 28, 1932. One of the perpetrators, Arthur Virgilio Alves Reis, served 16 years (1930–46) in jail.

Personal Injury. The greatest damages ever awarded for personal injury were $3,600,000 on October 18, 1970, to Keith Bush,

30, of Ely, Nevada, at Reno, against General Electric and Westinghouse Air Brake Co. in connection with an industrial accident which left him blind, speechless and paralyzed.

Divorce. The highest award made to the dispossessed party in a divorce suit was $70,000, awarded to Mr. Demetrius Sophocles Constantinidi against Dr. Henry William Lance for bigamous adultery with his wife, Mrs. Julia Constantinidi. She married Dr. Lance seven days after going through a form of divorce in Sioux Falls, South Dakota, on February 27, 1902.

Highest Settlement

Divorce. The greatest amount ever paid in a divorce settlement is $9,500,000, paid by Edward J. Hudson to Mrs. Cecil Amelia Blaffer Hudson, aged 43. This award was made on February 28, 1963, at the Domestic Relations Court, Houston, Texas. Mrs. Hudson was, reputedly, already worth $14,000,000.

Patent Case. The greatest settlement ever made in a patent infringement suit is $9,250,000, paid in April, 1952, by the Ford Motor Company to the Ferguson Tractor Co. for a claim filed in January, 1948.

Income Tax Reward. The greatest amount paid for information concerning a case of income tax delinquency was $79,999.93, paid by the U.S. Internal Revenue Service to a group of informers. Payments are limited to 10 per cent of the amount recovered as a direct result of information laid. Informants are often low-income accountants or women scorned. The total of payments in 1965 was $597,731.

The greatest lien ever imposed by the U.S. Internal Revenue Service was one of $21,261,818, filed against the California property of John A. T. Galvin in March, 1963, for alleged tax arrears for 1954–57.

Largest Suit

The highest amount of damages ever sought is $675,000,000,000,000,000 (equivalent to the U.S. Government revenue for 3,000 years) in a suit by Mr. I. Walton Bader brought in the U.S. District Court, New York City on April 14, 1971, against General Motors and others for polluting all 50 States.

Wills

Shortest. The shortest valid will in the world is "Vse zene," the Czech for "All to wife," written and dated January 19, 1967, by Herr Karl Tausch of Langen, Hesse, Germany. The shortest will contested but subsequently admitted to probate in English law was the case of *Thorn v. Dickens* in 1906. It consisted of the three words "All for Mother."

Longest. The longest will on record was that of Mrs. Frederica Cook (U.S.), in the early part of the century. It consisted of four bound volumes containing 95,940 words.

WORLD'S OLDEST ACTIVE JUDGE: (Left) Albert R. Alexander (born November 8, 1859) of Plattsburg, Missouri, shown on his 102nd birthday. He retired at the age of 105 years 8 months. OLDEST OLD SOLDIER: (Right) John B. Salling, Confederate veteran, who died in 1959, more than 113 years old. (See page 361).

Oldest Judge

The oldest recorded active judge was Judge Albert R. Alexander (born November 8, 1859), of Plattsburg, Missouri, magistrate and probate judge of Clinton County. He retired on July 9, 1965, at the age of 105 years 8 months, and died on March 30, 1966. (See photo.)

Highest-Paid Lawyer

It was estimated that Jerry Geisler (1886–1962), an attorney in Los Angeles, averaged $50,000 in fees for each case which he handled during the latter part of his career. Currently, the most highly paid lawyer is generally believed to be Louis Nizer of New York City.

CRIME AND PUNISHMENT

Greatest Mass Killings

China. The greatest massacre in human history ever attributed to any group is that of 26,300,000 Chinese during the régime of Mao Tse-tung between 1949 and May, 1965. This accusation was made by an agency of the U.S.S.R. Government in a radio broadcast on April 7, 1969. The broadcast broke down the total into four periods: 2.8 million (1949–52); 3.5 million (1953–57); 6.7 million (1958–60); and 13.3 million (1961–May 1965). The highest reported death figures in single monthly announcements on Peking radio were 1,176,000 in the provinces of Anhwei, Chekiang, Kiangsu, and Shantung, and 1,150,000 in the Central South Provinces. Po I-po, Minister of Finance, is alleged to have stated in the organ *For a lasting peace, for a people's democracy* "in the past three years (1950–52) we have liquidated more than 2 million bandits." General Jacques Guillermaz, a French diplomat, estimated the total executions between February, 1951, and May, 1952, at between 1 million and 3 million. In April, 1971, the Executive *Yuan* or cabinet of the implacably hostile government of The Republic of China in Taipei, Taiwan, announced its official estimate of the mainland death roll in the period 1949–69 as "at least 39,940,000." This figure, however, excluded "tens of thousands" killed in the Great Proletarian Cultural Revolution, which began in late 1966. The Walker Report published by the U.S. Senate Committee of the Judiciary in July, 1971, placed the total death roll since 1949 between 32.25 and 61.7 million.

U.S.S.R. The death roll in the Great Purge, or *Yezhovshchina*, in the U.S.S.R., in 1936–38, has never been published, though evidence of its magnitude may be found in population statistics which show a deficiency of males from before the outbreak of the 1941–45 war. The reign of terror was administered by the *Narodny Kommissariat Vnutrennykh Del* (N.K.V.D.), or People's Commissariat of Internal Affairs, the Soviet security service headed by Nikolay Ivanovich Yezhov (1895–?1939), described by Nikita Khrushchev in 1956 as "a degenerate." S. V. Utechin, an expert on Soviet affairs, regards estimates of 8,000,000 or 10,000,000 victims as "probably not exaggerations."

Nazi Germany. At the S.S. (*Schutzstaffel*) extermination camp called Auschwitz-Birkenau (Oswiecim-Brezinka), near Oswiecim, in southern Poland, where a minimum of 900,000 people (Soviet estimate is 4,000,000) were exterminated from June 14, 1940 to January 29, 1945, the greatest number killed in a day was 6,000. The man who operated the release of the "Zyklon B" cyanide pellets into the gas chambers there during this time was Sergeant Mold. The Nazi Commandant during the period 1940–43 was Rudolf Franz Ferdinand Höss, who was tried in Warsaw from March 11 to April 2, 1947, and hanged, aged 47, at Oswiecim on April 15, 1947. Erich Koch, the wartime *Gauleiter* of East Prussia and *Reichskommissar* for German-occupied Ukraine, was arrested near Hamburg on May 24, 1949, tried in Warsaw from October 20, 1958, to March 9, 1959, and sentenced to death for his responsibility for, or complicity in, the deaths of 4,232,000 people. The death sentence was later commuted to imprisonment. *Obersturmbannführer* (Lt.-Col.) Otto Adolf Eichmann (born 1906) of the S.S. was hanged in a small room inside Ramleh Prison, near Tel Aviv, Israel, at just before midnight (local time) on May 31, 1962, for his complicity in the deaths of 5,700,000 Jews during World War II, under the instruction given in April, 1941, by Adolf Hitler (1889–1945) for the "Final Solution" (*Endlösung*), *i.e.* the extermination of European Jewry.

Forced Labor

No official figures have been published of the death roll in Corrective Labor Camps in the U.S.S.R., first established in 1918. The total number of such camps was known to be more than 200 in 1946, but in 1956 many were converted to less severe Corrective Labor Colonies. An estimate published in the Netherlands puts the death roll between 1921 and 1960 at 19,000,000. The camps were administered by the *Cheka* until 1922, the O.G.P.U. (1922–34), the N.K.V.D. (1934–1946), the M.V.D. (1946–1953) and the K.G.B. since 1953. Inmates have been limited to only 2,400 calories daily since 1961.

Largest Criminal Organization

The largest syndicate of organized crime is the Mafia (meaning "swank," from a Sicilian word) or La Cosa Nostra ("our thing") which is said to have infiltrated the executive, judiciary and legislative branches of the U.S. Government. It consists of some 3,000 to 5,000 individuals in 24 "families" federated under "The Commission," which has a Sicilian base and an estimated annual turnover in vice, gambling, protection rackets and rigged trading of $30,000 million per annum of which some 25 per cent is profit. The biggest Mafia killing was on September 10, 1931, when the topmost man Salvatore Maranzano, *Il Capo di Tutti Capi*, and 40 allies were liquidated.

Murder

Highest Rate. The country with the highest recorded murder rate is Guinea (in equatorial Africa), with 31.1 registered homicides per 100,000 of the population in 1967. It has been estimated that the total number of murders in Colombia during *La Violencia* (1945–62) was about 300,000, giving a rate over a 17-year period of nearly 48 per day. A total of 592 deaths was attributed to one bandit leader, Teófilo ("Sparks") Rojas, aged 27, between 1948 and his death in an ambush near Armenia on January 22, 1963. Some sources attribute 3,500 slayings to him.

Lowest Rate. The country with the lowest officially recorded rate in the world is Spain, with 39 murders (a rate of 1.23 per million population) in 1967, or one murder every 9 days. In the Indian protectorate of Sikkim, in the Himalayas, murder is, however, practically unknown, while in the Hunza area of Kashmir, in the Karakoram, only one definite case has been recorded since 1900.

Most Prolific Murderers. The greatest number of victims ascribed to anyone has been 610 in the case of Countess Erszébet Báthory (1560–1614) of Hungary. At her trial which began on January 2, 1611, a witness testified to seeing a list of her victims in her own handwriting totaling this number. All were alleged to be young girls from the neighborhood of her castle at Csejthe, where she died on August 21, 1614. She was walled up in her room for $3\frac{1}{2}$ years, after being found guilty.

Gilles de Rays (Raies or Retz) (1404–40) was reputed to have ritually murdered between 140 and 200 kidnapped children. Some modern estimates put the total of his victims at 60. He was hanged and burnt at Nantes, France, on October 25, 1440.

The total number of victims of the cannibalistic cave-dwelling Beane family in Galloway, Scotland, in the early 17th century is not known, but may have run as high as 50 per year. Sawney Beane, head of the family, his wife, 8 sons, 6 daughters and 32 grandchildren were taken by an Army detachment to Edinburgh and executed, apparently without trial.

The most prolific murderer known in recent criminal history was Herman Webster Mudgett (born May 16, 1860), better known as H. H. Holmes. It has been estimated that he disposed of some 150 young women "paying guests" in his "Castle" on 63rd Street, Chicago. After a suspicious fire on November 22, 1893, the "Castle" was investigated and found to contain secret passages, stairways and a maze of odd rooms, some windowless or padded, containing hidden gas inlets and electric indicators. There was also a hoist, two chutes, a furnace, an acid bath, a dissecting table, a selection of surgical instruments and fragmentary human remains. Holmes was hanged on May 7, 1896, on a charge of murdering his associate, Benjamin F. Pitezel.

The greatest number of murders ever ascribed to a modern murderess is 16, together with a further 12 possible victims, making a total of 28. This was in the case of Bella Poulsdatter Sorensen Gunness (1859–1908) of La Porte, Indiana. Evidence came to light when her farm was set on fire on April 28, 1908, when she herself was found by a jury to have committed suicide by strychnine poisoning. Her victims, remains of many of whom were dug from her pig pen (her maiden name was Grunt) are believed to comprise two husbands, at least eight and possibly 20 would-be suitors lured by "Lonely Hearts" advertisements, three women and three children. A claim that Vera Renczi murdered 35 persons in Rumania, in this century, lacks authority.

Gang Murders. During the period of open gang warfare in Chicago, the peak year was 1926, when there were 76 unsolved killings. The 1,000th gang murder in Chicago since 1919 occurred on February 1, 1967. Only 13 cases have ended in convictions.

Suicide

The estimated daily total of suicides throughout the world surpassed 1,000 in 1965. The country with the highest recorded suicide rate is Hungary, with 33.1 per each 100,000 of the population in 1969. The country with the lowest recorded rate is Malta, with only 1 suicide in 1967.

Capital Punishment

Capital punishment was first abolished *de facto* in Liechtenstein in 1798.

Last Public Guillotining

The last person to be publicly guillotined in France was the murderer Eugen Weidmann before a large crowd at Versailles, near Paris, at 4:50 a.m. on June 17, 1939. Dr. Joseph Ignace Guillotin (1738–1812) died a natural death. He had advocated the use of the machine designed by Dr. Antoine Louis in 1789 in the French constituent assembly.

MASS MURDERS by strangulation were practiced in the name of the Great Goddess of Thuggee in India between 1550 and 1852. Shown here is the dreaded, revered and renowned Goddess, also known as Bhowani.

Thuggee. It has been estimated that at least 2,000,000 Indians were strangled by Thugs (pronounced Tugs) (*bhurtotes*) during the period of the unsuppressed Thuggee cult in India, from 1550 to 1852. It was established at the trial of Buhram that he had strangled at least 931 victims with his yellow and white cloth strip or *ruhmal* between 1790 and 1830.

"Smelling-Out." The greatest "smelling-out" (ritualistic execution) recorded in African history occurred before Shaka (chief of the Zulu tribes, 1787–1828) and 30,000 of his subjects near the Umhlatuzana River, Zululand (now Natal, South Africa) in March, 1824. After 9 hours, over 300 were "smelt out" as guilty of smearing the Royal *Kraal* with blood. Their "discoverers" were 150 witchfinders led by the hideous female *isangoma* Nobela. The victims were declared innocent when Shaka admitted to having the smearing done himself to expose the falsity of the power of his diviners. Nobela poisoned herself with atropine ($C_{17} H_{23} NO_3$), but the other 149 witchfinders were thereupon skewered or clubbed to death.

Most Hanging Attempts

The only man in Britain to survive three attempts to hang him was John Lee at Exeter Gaol, Devonshire, England, on February 23,

1885. Lee had been found guilty of murdering, on November 15, 1884, Emma Ann Whitehead Keyse of Babbacombe, who had employed him as a footman. The attempts, in which the executioner, James Berry, failed three times to get the trap open, occupied about seven minutes. Sir William Harcourt, the Home Secretary, commuted the sentence to life imprisonment. After release, Lee emigrated to the U.S. in 1917, was married and lived until 1933.

In 1803 it was reported that Joseph Samuels was reprieved in Sydney, Australia, after three unsuccessful attempts to hang him in which the rope broke twice.

Slowest Executions

The longest delay in carrying out a death sentence in recent history is in the case of Sadamichi Hirasawa (born 1906) of Tokyo, Japan, who was sentenced to death in January, 1950, after a trial lasting 16 months, on charges of poisoning 12 people with cyanide in a Tokyo bank. In November, 1962, he was transferred to a prison at Sendai, in northern Honshu, where he was still awaiting execution in May, 1972.

The longest stay on "death row" in the U.S. has been one of more than 14 years by Edgar Labat, aged 44, and Clifton A. Paret, aged 38, in Angola Penitentiary, Louisiana. In March, 1953, they were sentenced to death, after being found guilty of rape in 1950. They were released on May 5, 1967, only to be immediately re-arrested on an indictment arising from the original charge.

Caryl Chessman, aged 39, and convicted of 17 felonies, was executed on May 2, 1960, in the gas chamber at the California State Prison, San Quentin, California. In 11 years 10 months and one week on "death row," Chessman had won eight stays of execution.

Longest Sentences

The longest recorded prison sentences were ones of 7,109 years, awarded to two confidence tricksters in Iran (formerly Persia) on June 15, 1969. The duration of sentences are proportional to the amount of the defalcations involved. A sentence of 384,912 years was demanded at the prosecution of Gabriel March Grandos, 22, at Palma de Mallorca, Spain, on March 11, 1972, for failing to deliver 42,768 letters.

Richard Honeck was sentenced to life imprisonment in the U.S. in 1899, after having murdered his former schoolteacher. It was reported in November, 1963, that Honeck, then aged 84, who was in Menard Penitentiary, Chester, Illinois, was due to be paroled after 64 years in prison, during which time he had received one letter (a four-line note from his brother in 1904) and two visitors, a friend in 1904 and a newspaper reporter in 1963. He was released on December 20, 1963.

Oldest Prisoner

The oldest known prisoner in the U.S. is John Weber, 95, at the Chillicothe Correctional Institute, Ohio, who began his 44th year in prison on October 29, 1970.

Lynchings

The worst year in the 20th century for lynchings in the U.S. was 1901, with 130 lynchings (105 Negroes, 25 Whites), while the first year with no reported cases was 1952.

Longest Prison Escape

The longest recorded escape from prison was that of Leonard T. Fristoe, 77, who escaped from Nevada State Prison, on December 15, 1923, and was turned in by his son on November 15, 1969, at Compton, California. He had 46 years of freedom under the name Claude R. Willis. He had killed two sheriff's deputies in 1920.

Robbery

The greatest robbery on record was that of the German National Bank's (Reichbank's) reserves by a combine of U.S. military personnel and Germans. Gold bars, 728 in number, valued at $9,878,400 were removed from a cache on Klausenkopf mountainside, near Einsiedel, Bavaria, on June 7, 1945, together with six sacks containing $404,840 in dollar bills and 400 pound notes (possibly forged) from a garden in Oberaer. The book "Gold Is Where You Hide It" by W. Stanley Moss named the Town Major of Garmisch-Partenkirken, Capt. Robert Mackenzie, *alias* Ben F. Harpman of the Third U.S. Army, and the local military governor, Captain (later Major) Martin Borg, as the instigators. Mackenzie was reputedly sentenced to 10 years after an F.B.I. investigation, but Borg vanished from Vitznau, Switzerland, on March 30, 1946. In the same area, in which 6 apparently associated murders occurred, 630 cubes of uranium and six boxes of platinum bars and precious stones and 34 forging plates also disappeared. (See, *Industrial Espionage*, below.)

Bank. On March 23, 1962, 150 *plastiqueurs* of the *Organisation de l'Armée Secrète* (O.A.S.) removed by force 23,500,000 francs ($4,770,000) from the Banque d'Algérie in Oran, Algeria, after the collapse of civil order.

The biggest "inside job" was that at the National City Bank of New York, from which an assistant manager, Richard Crowe, removed $883,660. He was arrested on April 11, 1949.

On October 23, 1969, it was disclosed that $13,193,000 of U.S. Treasury bills were inexplicably missing from the Morgan Guaranty Trust Company, Wall Street, New York City.

Industrial Espionage. It has been alleged that a division of the American Cyanamid Company about 1966 lost some papers and vials of micro-organisms through industrial espionage, allegedly organized from Italy, which data had cost them $24,000,000 in research and development. It is arguable that this represents the greatest robbery of all time.

Jewel. The greatest recorded theft of jewels occurred on November 13, 1969, in Freetown, Sierra Leone, when an armed gang stole diamonds belonging to the Sierra Leone Selection Trust, worth $4,200,000.

LARGEST ART ROBBERY: Through a cut-out panel in an unused door, the raiders of the Dulwich College Picture Gallery, London, bypassed the Gallery's electric alarm system and snatched $4,200,000 worth of paintings.

Art. The greatest recorded art robbery was the theft of eight paintings, valued at £1,500,000 ($4,200,000), taken during the night of December 30–31, 1966, from the Dulwich College Picture Gallery in London. The haul included three paintings by Peter Paul Rubens (1577–1640), one by Adam Ehlsheimer (1578–1610), three by Rembrandt van Rijn (1606–69) and one by Gerard Dou (1613–75). Three of the paintings were recovered on January 2, 1967, and the remaining five on January 4, 1967. (See photo.)

It is arguable that the value of the *Mona Lisa* at the time of its theft from The Louvre, Paris, on August 21, 1911, was greater than this figure. It was recovered in Italy in 1913, and Vicenzo Perruggia was charged with its theft.

Train. The greatest recorded train robbery occurred between about 3:10 a.m. and 3:45 a.m. on August 8, 1963, when a General Post Office mail train from Glasgow, Scotland, was ambushed between Sears Crossing and Bridego Bridge at Mentmore, near Cheddington, Buckinghamshire, England. The gang escaped with about 120 mailbags containing £2,595,998 ($7,268,794) worth of bank notes being taken to London for pulping. Only £343,448 ($961,654) had been recovered by December 9, 1966. (See photo, next page.)

Greatest Kidnapping Ransom

Historically, the greatest ransom paid was that for their chief, Atahualpa, by the Incas to the Spanish conquistador, Francisco

LARGEST TRAIN ROBBERY occurred when this Royal Mail train was ambushed in England in 1963. More than $7,000,000 was taken and less than $1,000,000 recovered.

Pizarro, in 1532–33 at Cajamarca, Peru, which constituted a hall full of gold and silver worth in modern money some $170 million. Pizarro killed his prisoner anyway.

The greatest ransom ever extracted in a kidnapping case in modern times has been 7,500,000 D.M. (approx. $2,200,000) for the return after 19 days of Thomas Albrecht, 49, a West German supermarket owner on December 16–17, 1971.

Greatest Hijack Ransom

The highest amount ever paid to hijackers has been $4,800,000 in small denomination notes by the West German government to Popular Front for the Liberation of Palestine representatives 30 miles outside Beirut, Lebanon, on February 23, 1972. In return, a Lufthansa Boeing 747, hijacked an hour out of New Delhi and bound for Athens which had been forced down at Aden, had its 14 crew members released.

Largest Narcotics Haul

The heaviest recorded haul of narcotics was made off St. Louis at Rhones, France, where 78,400 lbs. of floating bales containing unprocessed morphine, opium, heroin and hashish, worth $75 million on the retail U.S. market were found being loaded into canoes by 3 men on February 25, 1971. The most valuable haul was of 937 lbs. of pure heroin worth $975 million retail seized aboard the 60-ton shrimp boat *Caprice des Temps* at Marseilles, France, on March 2, 1972. The captain, Marcel Boucan, 57, tried to commit suicide.

Largest Bribe

An alleged bribe of $84,000,000 offered to Shaikh Zaid ibn Sultan of Abu Dhabi, Trucial Oman, by a Saudi Arabian official in August,

1955, is the highest on record. The affair concerned oil concessions in the disputed territory of Buraimi on the Persian Gulf.

Greatest Forgery

The greatest recorded forgery was the German Third Reich government's forging operation, code name "Bernhard," engineered by Herr Naujocks in 1940–41. It involved £150,000,000 (now about $375,000,000) worth of Bank of England £5 notes.

Greatest Swindle

The greatest commercial swindle ever perpetrated was performed by Antonio (Tino) De Angelis (born 1915), a 5-foot-5-inch 290-lb. ex-hog-cutter from New York City. His Allied Crude Vegetable Oil Refining Corporation (formed November 19, 1955) operated from an uncarpeted office adjoining a converted tank farm in Bayonne, New Jersey. The tanks were rigged with false dipping compartments and were interconnected so that sea water could be pumped to substitute for phantom salad oil which served as collateral for warehouse receipts. The news of a deficiency of 927,000 tons of oil valued at $175,000,000 coincided with the news of President Kennedy's assassination on November 22, 1963. The New York Stock Exchange was then closed at 2:07 p.m.

Welfare Swindle

The greatest welfare swindle yet worked was that of the gypsy, Anthony Moreno, on the French Social Security in Marseille. By forging birth certificates and school registration forms, he invented 197 fictitious families and 3,000 children on which he claimed benefits from 1960 to mid-1968. Moreno, nicknamed "El Chorro" (the fountain), was last reported free of extradition worries and living in luxury in his native Spain having absquatulated with an estimated $6,440,000.

Biggest Fraud

The largest amount of money named in a fraud case has been £12,707,726 (about $30,500,000) in the Old Bailey, London, trial of Ellis Eser Seillon, 60, and Elias Fahimian, 40. A record total of 3,725 documents were involved. They were sentenced on January 14, 1972, by Judge Stanley Price to 5 and 4 years respectively for manipulation of financial accounts and banking loans.

Passing Bad Checks

The record for passing bad checks was set by Frederick Emerson Peters (1886–1959), who, by dint of some 200 impersonations, netted $250,000 with 28,000 bad checks. Among his many philanthropies was a silver chalice presented to a cathedral in Washington, D.C., also paid for with a bad check.

Fines

A fine equivalent to $25,000,000 was imposed on Juan Vila Reyes, president of the Barcelona textile machinery manufacturer,

Matesa, by the Currency Crime Court, Madrid, Spain, on May 19, 1970, for converting export development funds to his own use.

It is a specific offense on Pitcairn Island in the Pacific to shout "Sail Ho!" when no vessel is in sight. The fine is 25p (about 60 cents), which can be commuted to one day's labor on the public roads (there are no cars) or making an oar for the public boat.

Largest Court

The largest judicial building in the world is the Johannesburg Central Magistrate's Court, opened in 1941, at the junction of Fox and West Streets, Johannesburg, South Africa. There are 42 courtrooms (8 civil and 34 criminal), with a further seven criminal courtrooms under construction. The court has a panel of 70 magistrates and deals with an average of 2,500 criminal cases every week, excluding petty cases in which guilt has been admitted in writing.

Penal Camps

The largest penal camp systems in the world were those near Karaganda and Kolyma, in the U.S.S.R., each with a population estimated in 1958 at between 1,200,000 and 1,500,000. The official N.A.T.O. estimate for all Soviet camps was "more than one million" in March, 1960. The largest labor camp in the U.S.S.R. is now reputed to be Potma, 500 miles southeast of Moscow in the Urals, which is surrounded by a minefield. It was estimated in 1966 that the total population of penal camps in China was about 10,000,000.

Devil's Island. The largest French penal settlement was that of St. Laurent du Maroni, which included the notorious Île du Diable, off the coast of French Guiana, South America. It remained in operation for 99 years from 1854 until the last group of repatriated prisoners, including Théodore Rouselle, who had served 50 years, was returned to Bordeaux on August 22, 1953. It has been estimated that barely 2,000 of the 70,000 deportees ever returned. These included the executioner Ladurelle (imprisoned 1921–37), who was murdered in Paris in 1938.

Prisons

Largest. The largest prison in the world is Kharkhov Prison, in the U.S.S.R., which has at times accommodated 40,000 prisoners.

Smallest. The smallest prison in the world is usually cited as that on the island of Sark, in the Channel Islands, which has a capacity of two. In fact, the prison on Herm, a neighboring island, is smaller with a diameter of 13 feet 6 inches, and must rank with other single person lock-ups.

Most Secure. After it became a maximum security Federal prison in 1934, no convict was known to have lived to tell of a successful escape from the prison on Alcatraz ("Pelican") Island in San Francisco Bay. A total of 23 men attempted it, but 12 were recaptured, 5 shot dead, one drowned and 5 presumed drowned. On December 16, 1962, three months before the prison was closed, one man reached the mainland alive, only to be recaptured on the spot. (See photo.)

MOST SECURE PRISON was Alcatraz, on an island in San Francisco Bay, which was closed in 1962. No convict ever escaped although 23 tried. The Golden Gate Bridge is in the background.

4. Economic

MONETARY AND FINANCE

Largest Budget

The greatest annual budget expenditure of any country was $229,233 million by the U.S. Government (federal expenditure) in the fiscal year ending June 30, 1973. The highest budget revenue in the U.S. was $217,593 million in 1972–73. The estimated revenue receipts of the U.S.S.R. Government in 1969 were 139,000 million roubles (*officially* equivalent to $148,800 million).

In the U.S., the greatest surplus was $8,419,469,844 in 1947–48, and the greatest deficit was $57,420,430,365 in 1942–43.

Foreign Aid

The total net foreign aid given by the U.S. Government between July 1, 1945, and December 31, 1970, was $125,061 million, of which $4,586 million has gone into Vietnam, Cambodia (Khmers) and Laos.

The country which received most U.S. aid in 1969 was India, with $432,000,000. U.S. foreign aid began with $50,000 to Venezuela for earthquake relief in 1812. Foreign aid was curtailed drastically by vote of the U.S. Senate on October 29, 1971.

Taxation

Most Taxed. The major national economy with the highest rate of taxation (central and local taxes, plus social security contribution) is that of Sweden, with 46.6 per cent of its Gross National Product in 1967. The lowest proportion for any advanced national economy in 1967 was 20.3 per cent in Japan, which also enjoys the highest economic growth rate.

Highest Surtax. The country with the most confiscatory marginal rate of income tax is Burma, where the rate is 99 per cent for annual incomes exceeding 300,000 kyats ($63,112). The second highest marginal rate is in the United Kingdom, where the topmost surtax level was 97.5 per cent in 1950–51 and 96.25 per cent in 1966–67.

National Debt

The largest national debt of any country in the world is that of the U.S., where the gross federal public debt reached its peak figure of $429,400,000,000, equivalent to $1,834 per person, in the fiscal year 1971–72. This amount in dollar bills would make a pile 25,421 miles high, weighing 398,900 tons.

Gross National Product

The estimated world aggregate of Gross National Products in 1968 exceeded $200,000,000,000,000. The country with the largest Gross National Product is the U.S., with $1,072,900,000,000 for 1971. The long awaited "Trillion Dollars" was attained in 1971.

National Wealth

The richest large nation, measured by Gross National Product per head, has been the U.S. since about 1910. The average G.N.P. in the U.S. was about $4,700 per person in 1970. It has been estimated that the value of all physical assets in the U.S. in 1966 was $2,460,000,000,000 or $12,443 per head.

Gold Reserves

The country with the greatest monetary gold reserve is the U.S. The Treasury had $9,662 million on hand on March 1, 1972, or 23.3 per cent of the world's current monetary stock. The Bullion Depository at Fort Knox, 30 miles southwest of Louisville, Kentucky, is the principal depository. Gold is stored in standard mint bars of 400 troy ounces (439 oz. avoirdupois), measuring 7 inches by $3\frac{5}{8}$ inches by $1\frac{5}{8}$ inches, and each worth $14,000.

The greatest accumulation of gold in the world is now in the Federal Reserve Bank at 33 Liberty Street, New York City. The bank admits to having gold valued at $13,000 million, owned by foreign central banks and stored, 85 feet below street level, in a vault 50 feet by 100 feet behind a steel door weighing 89 tons.

Bank Rate

In 1971, the highest bank interest rate was that of Brazil at 20 per cent, and the lowest, that of Morocco at $3\frac{1}{2}$ per cent.

Currency

Paper money is an invention of the Chinese and, although the date of 119 B.C. has been suggested, the innovation is believed to date from the T'ang dynasty of the 7th century A.D. The world's earliest bank notes were issued by the Stockholms Banco, Sweden, in July, 1661. The oldest surviving note is one for 5 dalers dated December 6, 1662.

Largest and Smallest. The largest paper money ever issued was the one kwan note of the Chinese Ming dynasty issue of 1368–99, which measured 9 inches by 13 inches. The smallest bank note ever issued was the 5 cent note of the Chekiang Provincial Bank (established 1908) in China. It measured 2.16 inches by 1.18 inches.

HIGHEST DENOMINATION CURRENCY is this $10,000 bill with the portrait of Salmon P. Chase. Only 400 are circulating today.

Highest Denominations. The highest denomination of paper currency ever authorized in the world are U.S. gold certificates for $100,000, bearing the head of former President Thomas Woodrow Wilson (1856–1924), issued by the U.S. Treasury in 1934.

The highest denomination notes in circulation are U.S. Federal Reserve Bank notes for $10,000. They bear the head of Salmon Portland Chase (1808–73). None has been printed since July, 1944, and their circulation fell from 4,600 at December 31, 1941, to only 376 at December 31, 1965, but rose to 1,900 by March, 1969. On July 15, 1969, the U.S. Treasury announced that no further notes higher than $100 would be issued. By June, 1972, only 400 $10,000 bills were in circulation.

Most Expensive. The highest price paid for a note no longer valid currency is believed to be $3,600, paid in 1900 for the first Ming note (see *Largest Currency*) ever found.

Highest Denomination Bond

There exists a U.S. Treasury note for $500,000,000 bearing interest at $6\frac{1}{4}$ per cent for 14 years. Each annual interest payment is $31,250,000.

Largest Check

The greatest amount paid by a single check in the history of banking was $960,242,000, paid on January 31, 1961, by the Continental Illinois National Bank and Trust Company of Chicago. This bank headed a group which bought the accounts receivable of Sears, Roebuck & Co., to whom the check was paid.

Worst Inflation

The world's worst inflation occurred in Hungary in June, 1946, when the 1931 gold pengö was valued at 130 trillion (1.3×10^{20}) paper pengös. Notes were issued for 100 trillion or 10^{20} pengös.

Currently the worst inflation is in Brazil, where the cruzeiro

WORLD'S HEAVIEST COIN: Mid-17th century Swedish copper plate money; the 10-daler weighed 43½ lbs.

depreciated 42 times in terms of the U.S. dollar, between February 1, 1957 (64.80 per $) and March, 1967 (2,720 per $). A new cruzeiro, equivalent to 1,000 old cruzeiros, was introduced on February 8, 1967. In 1966–67, there was a further 21.2 per cent inflation.

COINS

Oldest. The earliest certainly dated coins are the electrum (alloy of gold and silver) staters of Lydia, in Asia Minor (now Turkey), which were coined in the reign of King Gyges (c. 685–652 B.C.). Primitive uninscribed "spade" money of the Chou dynasty of China is now believed to date from c. 770 B.C.

Smallest. The smallest coins in the world were the gold "pinhead" coins used in Colpata, southern India, in c. 1800, which weighed as little as one grain, or 480 to the troy ounce. The 1/96th of a silver stater of Ionia c. 6th century B.C. measure $3 \times 4\frac{1}{2}$ millimeters.

Heaviest. The Swedish copper 10 daler coins of 1659 attained a weight of up to 43½ lbs. Of primitive exchange tokens, the most massive are the holed stone discs, or *Fé*, from the Yap Islands, in the western Pacific Ocean, with diameters of up to 12 feet. A medium-sized one was worth one Yapese wife or an 18-foot canoe.

Coinless Countries. Three modern countries without any coins (paper money only) are Paraguay, Laos and Indonesia.

Denominations

Highest. The 1654 Indian gold 200 mohur ($1,400) coin of the Mughal Emperor Khurram Shihab-ud-din Muhammad, Shah Jahan (reigned 1628–57), is both the highest denomination coin, and that of the greatest intrinsic worth ever struck. It weighed

33,600 grains (70 troy oz.) and hence has an intrinsic worth of $2,462. It had a diameter of 5⅜ inches. The only known example disappeared in Patna, Bihar, India, in *c.* 1820, but a plaster cast of this coin exists in the British Museum, London.

Lowest. Lowest in face value today is the 1 aurar piece of Iceland issued in 1971 with a face value equal to 0.0385 of a U.S. cent.

Quarter farthings (sixteen to the British penny) were struck in copper at the Royal Mint, London, in the Imperial coinage for use in Ceylon, in 1839 and 1851–53.

The lowest denomination gold coins ever struck are the Kruger gold 3-penny pieces struck in South Africa at the behest of Mr. Solly Marks. One is dated 1894 and 215 are dated 1898. They are now worth more than $500 each.

Most Expensive

The highest price paid at auction for a single coin is $77,500 for a U.S. 1804 silver dollar, struck in 1834 (*sic*) of which only seven exist, at Stack's in New York City on October 23, 1970. It was sold by the Massachusetts Historical Society and bought by an anonymous collector. This specimen was spotted by Henry C. Young, a teller, in the ordinary course of his work in the Bank of Pennsylvania in 1850.

The two U.S. gold $50 pieces of 1877 in the Smithsonian Institution, Washington, D.C., have been valued at $100,000 each as have the seven surviving examples of the U.S. Brasher Doubloon of 1787.

Among many unique coins, the one that would logically attract the greatest price on the market would be the unique 1873 U.S. dime with the CC mint mark, since dimes are the most avidly collected series of any coins in the world.

MOST VALUABLE COINS: (Top) The Brasher Doubloon, a U.S. coin of which only 7 specimens exist. (Below) The U.S. $50 gold piece of 1877, valued at $100,000 and now in the Smithsonian Institution.

Rarest

More than 100 coins are unique. An example of a unique coin of threefold rarity is one of the rare admixture of bronze with inlaid gold of Kaleb I of Axum (*c.* 500 A.D.) owned by Richard A. Thorud of Bloomington, Minnesota. Only 700 Axumite coins of any sort are known.

Greatest Collection

It was estimated in November, 1967, that the Lilly coin collection of 1,227 U.S. gold pieces now at the Smithsonian Institution, Washington, D.C., had a market value of $5,500,000.

The greatest hoard of gold of unknown ownership ever recovered is one valued at about $3,000,000, from the lost $8,000,000, carried in 10 ships of a Spanish bullion fleet which was sunk by a hurricane off Florida, on July 31, 1715. The biggest single haul was by the diver Kip Wagner on May 30, 1965.

Greatest Hoarders

It was estimated in 1968 that about $22,500 million worth of gold is being retained in personal collections throughout the world and that $4,800 million of this total is held by the population of France.

Largest Treasure Trove

The most valuable hoard ever found was one of more than 1,200 gold coins from the reigns of Kings Richard II to Edward IV, worth more than $1,400,000, found on March 22, 1966, by John Craughwell, aged 47, at Fishpool, near Mansfield, Nottinghamshire, England.

Largest Mint

The largest mint in the world is the U.S. Mint built in 1965–69 on Independence Mall, Philadelphia, covering 500,000 square feet with an annual capacity on a 3-shift 7-day-a-week production of 8,000 million coins. A single stamping machine can produce coins at a rate of 10,000 per minute.

TRADE UNIONS

The world's largest union is the Industrie-Gewerkschaft Metall (Metal Workers' Union) of West Germany, with a membership of 2,070,000 at December 31, 1969. The union with the longest name is probably the F.N.O.M.M.C.F.E.T.M.F., the National Federation of Officers, Machinists, Motormen, Drivers, Firemen and Electricians in Sea and River Transportation of Brazil.

Longest Working Week. The longest working week (maximum possible 168 hours) is up to 139 hours at times by some housemen and registrars in England.

Labor Disputes

Longest. The world's longest recorded strike ended on January 4, 1961, after 33 years. It concerned the employment of barbers' assistants in Copenhagen, Denmark. The longest recorded major strike was one at the plumbing fixtures factory of the Kohler Co. in Sheboygan, Wisconsin, between April, 1954, and October, 1962. The strike is alleged to have cost the United Automobile Workers' Union about $12,000,000 to sustain.

FOOD CONSUMPTION

The figures relating to net food consumption per person are based on gross available food supplies at retail level, less waste, animal feed and that used for industrial purposes, divided by the total population. The figures given are the latest available.

Calories. Of all countries in the world, based on the latest available data, Ireland has the largest available total of calories per person. The net supply averaged 3,450 per day in 1968. The highest calorific value of any foodstuff is that of pure animal fat, with 930 calories per 100 grams (3.5 oz.). Pure alcohol provides 710 calories per 100 grams.

The lowest *reported* figures are 1,720 calories per day in Haiti in 1964–66. The lowest is 29 grams (1.30 oz.) of protein per day in what is now Zaïre in 1961–63.

Protein. New Zealand has the highest recorded consumption of protein per person, an average of 107 grams (3.76 oz.) per day in 1967.

Cereals. The greatest consumers of cereal products—flour, milled rice, etc.—are the people of the United Arab Republic (Egypt), with an average of 510 lbs. per person annually in 1966–67.

Starch. The greatest eaters of starchy food (e.g., bananas, potatoes, etc.) are the people of Gabon, who consumed 4.02 lbs. per head per day in 1964–66.

Sugar. The greatest consumers of refined sugar are the people of Iceland, with an average of 5.29 oz. per person per day in 1964–66. The lowest consumption is 0.70 oz. per day in Burundi in 1964–66.

Meat. The greatest meat eaters in the world—figures include organs and poultry—are the people of Uruguay, with an average consumption of 10.93 oz. per person per day in 1964–66. The lowest consumption is 0.16 oz. in Sri Lanka (formerly Ceylon) in 1968.

Beer

Of reporting countries, the nation with the highest beer consumption per person is West Germany, with 36.72 U.S. gallons per person in 1970. In the Northern Territory of Australia, however, the annual intake has been estimated to be as high as 62.4 U.S. gallons per person. A society for the prevention of alcoholism in Darwin had to disband in June, 1966, for lack of support. The January, 1970, edition of the U.S.S.R. periodical *Sotsialistichekaya Industria* claimed that the Russians invented beer.

Alcohol

The freest alcohol drinkers are the white population of South Africa, with 2.05 U.S. gallons of proof alcohol per person per year, and the most abstemious are the people of Belgium with ⅛th of a

U.S. gallon per person. It was estimated in 1969 that 13 per cent of all males between 20 and 55 years of age in France were suffering from alcoholism.

Largest Dish

The largest single dish in the world is roasted camel, prepared occasionally for Bedouin wedding feasts. Cooked eggs are stuffed in fish, the fish stuffed in cooked chickens, the chickens stuffed into a roasted sheep carcass and the sheep stuffed into a whole camel.

Most Expensive Food

The most expensive food is white truffle of Alba, Italy, which sells for $85 per lb. in the market. Truffles in the Périgord district of France require drought between mid-July and mid-August.

Largest Banquet

The greatest banquet ever staged was that by President Loubet, President of France, in the gardens of the Tuileries, Paris, on September 22, 1900. He invited every one of the 22,000 mayors in France and their deputies.

The largest indoor banquet was one for 10,158 at $15 a plate in support of Mayor Richard J. Daley of Chicago at the McCormick Place Convention Hall on the Lake, March 3, 1971.

The menu for the main 5½-hour banquet at the Imperial Iranian 2,500th anniversary gathering at Persepolis in October, 1971 (see *Party Giving* in Chapter 11), was probably the most expensive ever compiled. It comprised quail eggs stuffed with Iranian caviar, a mousse of crayfish tails in Nantua sauce, stuffed rack of roast lamb, with a main course of roast peacock stuffed with *foie gras*, fig rings, and raspberry sweet champagne sherbet. Wines included *Chateau Lafite Rothschild* 1945 at $100 per bottle from the cellars of Maxim, Paris.

Longest Bread

The longest loaf ever baked was one of 90 feet (2,600 slices) by United Bakeries of London, England, in July, 1971.

Largest Cake

The largest cakes ever baked were a six-sided "birthday" cake weighing 25,000 lbs. made in August, 1962, by Van de Kemp's Holland Dutch Bakers of Seattle, Washington, for the Seattle World's Fair (the "Century 21 Exposition"), and a 26-foot-tall creation of the same weight made for the British Columbia Centennial, cut on July 20, 1971. The Seattle cake was 23 feet high, with a circumference of 60 feet. The ingredients included 18,000 eggs, 10,500 lbs. of flour, 4,000 lbs. of cane sugar, 7,000 lbs. of raisins, 2,200 lbs. of pecans and 100 lbs. of salt.

Largest Easter Egg

The largest Easter egg ever made was one of 550 lbs. and $500 worth of chocolate, made at the Liverpool College of Crafts and Catering in March, 1971.

Largest Hamburger

The largest hamburger on record is one with buns $12\frac{1}{2}$ feet in circumference and 173 lbs. of prime beef, 5 gallons of tomato sauce and a gallon of mustard, made by McDonald's at Yagoona, Australia, on January 20, 1972.

Largest Pizza

The largest pizza ever baked was one measuring 11 feet 8 inches by 3 feet 7 inches at Cambridge, New York, on January 9, 1971.

Longest Sausage

The longest sausage ever recorded was one 3,124 feet long, made on June 29, 1966, by 30 butchers in Scunthorpe, Lincolnshire, England. It was made from $6\frac{1}{2}$ cwt. of pork and $1\frac{1}{2}$ cwt. of cereal and seasoning.

Largest Sundae

The most monstrous ice cream sundae ever concocted is one of 833 lbs. by Bob Bercaw of Wooster, Ohio, built on July 13, 1971. It contained 42 flavors and 50 lbs. of chocolate fudge syrup.

Spices

Most Expensive. The most expensive of all spices is Mediterranean saffron (*Crocus sativus*). It takes 96,000 stigmas and therefore 32,000 flowers to make a pound. Packets of 1.9 grams are retailed in England for about 24 cents—equivalent to $780 per pound.

Hottest. The hottest of all spices is the capsicum hot pepper known as Tabasco, first reported in 1888 by Edmund McIlhenny on Avery Island, Louisiana.

Rarest Condiment. The world's most prized condiment is Ca Cuong, a secretion recovered in minute amounts from beetles in North Vietnam. Owing to war conditions, the price rose to $100 per ounce before supplies virtually ceased.

Candy

The biggest candy eaters in the world are the people of Britain, with 7.8 oz. of confectionery per person per week in 1971. The figure for Scotland alone is more than 9 oz. in 1968.

Tea

The most expensive tea marketed is "Oolong," specially imported by Fortnum and Mason of Piccadilly, London, where it retails for $10 per lb. It is blended from very young Formosan leaves.

The world's largest tea company is Brooke Bond Liebig Limited (a merger of Brooke Bond Tea Ltd. of London, founded 1869 and Liebig's Extract of Meat Co. Ltd. made in May, 1968), with a turnover of $590,400,000 in the year ended June 30, 1971. The company has 40,000 acres of plantations in India, Sri Lanka (formerly Ceylon) and East Africa, and ranches in Argentina, Paraguay and Rhodesia extending over 2,663,000 acres and employing over 70,000 people.

Coffee

The world's greatest coffee drinkers are the people of Sweden, who consumed 29.24 lbs. of coffee per person per year in 1969.

Oldest Canned Food

The oldest canned food known was roast beef canned by Donkin. Hall and Gamble of England in 1823, and salvaged from the British ship H.M.S. *Fury* in the Northwest Passage, Canada. It was opened on December 11, 1958.

Fresh Water

The world's greatest consumers of fresh water are the people of the U.S., whose average daily consumption was 493,440 million gallons in 1970. By December 31, 1967, 40.6 per cent was fluoridized.

ENERGY

To express the various forms of available energy (coal, liquid fuels and water power, etc., but omitting vegetable fuels and peat), it is the practice to convert them all into terms of coal. On this basis the world average consumption was the equivalent of 3,774 lbs. of coal, or its energy equivalents, per person in 1969. The highest consumption in the world is in the U.S., with an average of 22,769 lbs. per person in 1968. The lowest recorded average for 1968 was 15.4 lbs. per person in Burundi.

COMMUNICATION AND TRANSPORTATION

Merchant Shipping

The world total of merchant shipping (excluding vessels of less than 100 tons gross, sailing vessels and barges) was 55,041 vessels of 247,202,634 tons gross on July 1, 1971. The largest merchant fleet in the world as at mid-1969 was under the flag of Liberia with 38,552,240 tons gross.

Largest and Busiest Ports

Physically, the largest port in the world is New York Harbor. The port has a navigable waterfront of 755 miles (460 miles in New York State and 295 miles in New Jersey) stretching over 92 square miles. A total of 261 general cargo berths and 130 other piers give a total berthing capacity of 391 ships at one time. The total warehousing floor space is 18,400,000 square feet (422.4 acres).

The world's busiest port and largest artificial harbor is the Rotterdam-Europoort in the Netherlands, which covers 38.88 square miles. It handled 32,023 sea-going vessels and about 250,000 barges in 1970. It is able to handle 310 sea-going vessels simultaneously, up to 225,000 tons and 65 feet draught. In 1970, 225,000,000 tons of seaborne cargo were handled. (See photo.)

Airlines

The country with the busiest airlines system is the U.S., where 107,324 million revenue passenger miles were flown on scheduled domestic and international services in 1971. This was equivalent to

BUSIEST PORT:
Rotterdam in the
Netherlands is where
most of the barges from
Europe's network of
canals and rivers load
onto ocean-going
vessels.

an annual trip of 518.4 miles for every one of the inhabitants of the
U.S.

Railroads

The country with the greatest length of railroad is the U.S., with
207,005 miles of track on January 1, 1970.

Roads

The country with the greatest length of highway is the U.S (50
states), with 3,710,299 miles of graded roads at January 1, 1969. The
average speed of cars at off-peak times has risen from 45.0 m.p.h. in
1945, to 58.8 m.p.h. by 1966.

The country with the greatest number of motor vehicles per mile
of road is the United Kingdom, with 221,774 miles of road including
800 miles of motorway at April 1, 1971, and 15,826,000 vehicles in
1971. A total of 36,000,000 by 2010 is forecast.

Busiest. The highest traffic volume of any point in the world is at
the Harbor and Santa Monica Freeways interchange in Los Angeles,
with a 24-hour weekday average of 420,000 vehicles in 1970.

The territory with the highest traffic density in the world is Hong
Kong. On May 31, 1970, there were 122,274 motor vehicles on 600
miles of serviceable roads giving a density of 8.64 yards per vehicle.

Widest. The widest street in the world is the Monumental Axis,
running for $1\frac{1}{2}$ miles from the Municipal Plaza to the Plaza of the
Three Powers in Brasilia, the capital of Brazil. The six-lane boulevard
was opened in April, 1960, and is 273.4 yards wide.

The Bay Bridge Toll Plaza has 34 lanes (17 in each direction)
serving San Francisco and Oakland.

Narrowest. The narrowest street in the world is St. John's Lane
in Rome, with a width of 19 inches.

Longest. The longest motorable road in the world is the Pan-
American Highway, which will stretch 13,859 miles from Anchorage,
Alaska, to southern Chile. There remains a gap of 250 miles, known
as the Darien gap, in Panama and Colombia.

The longest street is Figueroa Street which stretches 30 miles from Pasadena at Colorado Blvd. to the Pacific Coast Highway, L.A.

Highest. The highest pass ever used by traffic is the Bódpo La (19,412 feet above sea level), in western Tibet. It was used in 1929 by a caravan from the Shipki Pass to the trade route to Rudok. The highest carriageable road in the world is one 733.2 miles long between Tibet and southwestern Sinkiang, completed in October, 1957, which takes in passes of an altitude up to 18,480 feet above sea level.

Europe's highest pass (excluding the Caucasian passes) is the Col de Restefond (9,193 feet) completed in 1962 with 21 hairpins between Jausiers and Saint-Etienne-de-Tinée, France. It is usually closed between early October and early June.

Biggest Square

The Tian an men (Gate of Heavenly Peace) Square in Peking, described as the navel of China, extends over 98 acres.

Traffic Jams

The worst traffic jams in the world are in Tokyo, Japan. Only 9 per cent of the city area is roadway, compared with London (23 per cent), Paris (25 per cent), New York (35 per cent) and Washington, D.C. (43 per cent).

Traffic Lights

Automatic electric traffic lights were introduced into New York City in 1918. Semaphore-type traffic signals were set up in Westminster Square, London in 1868.

Parking Meters

The earliest parking meters ever installed were those put in the business district of Oklahoma City, Oklahoma, on July 19, 1935. They were the invention of Carl C. Magee (U.S.). (See photo.)

Worst Driver

It was reported that a 75-year-old *male* driver received 10 traffic tickets, drove on the wrong side of the road four times, committed four hit-and-run offenses and caused six accidents, all within 20 minutes, in McKinney, Texas, on October 15, 1966.

Most Failures on Learner's Test

The record for persistence in taking and failing a test for a driver's license is held by Mrs. Miriam Hargrave, 62, of Wakefield, Yorkshire, England, who finally passed her 40th driving test in August, 1970. She spent $720 on driving lessons and could no longer afford to buy a car.

Most Durable Driving Examiner

The most durable examiner is Jack Lord of Allestree, England, who in 33 years (1935–1968) survived 40,639 tests. The only examinee to defeat his acutely developed sense of self-preservation was a driver (woman) who impaled her Buick on a stanchion in 1937.

Oldest Driver

In a survey by the U.S. Social Security Administration of 300 centenarians in 1968, it was discovered that one, identified as a Mr. Dring, drove his car to work every day.

EARLIEST PARKING METERS: In 1935 these were installed in Oklahoma City.

Telephones

There were an estimated 272,700,000 telephones in the world at January 1, 1971. The country with the greatest number was the U.S., with 120,200,000 instruments, equivalent to 583.5 for every 1,000 people.

The territory with fewest telephones is Pitcairn Island with 30.

The country with the most telephones per head of population is Monaco, with 649.8 per 1,000 of the population at January 1, 1971. The countries with the least are Upper Volta with 0.3 of a telephone per 1,000 people at January 1, 1970 (latest figure), and Laos with 0.4 on January 1, 1971.

The greatest total of calls made in any country is in the U.S., with 152,407 million (779.0 calls per person) in 1970.

The lowest recorded figure was Pakistan, with 0.3 of a call per person in 1970.

The city with most telephones is New York City, with 5,904,933 (739 per 1,000 people) at January 1, 1970. In 1970, Washington, D.C., reached the level of 1,169 telephones per 1,000 people, though in some small areas there are still higher densities, such as Beverly Hills, north of Los Angeles, with about 1,600 per 1,000.

Longest Call. The longest telephone connection on record was one of 550 hours from November 28 to December 21, 1966, between co-eds of Ford Hall (7th floor) and the 7th floor of Moore Hall at Kansas State University, Manhattan, Kansas.

Longest Cable. The world's longest submarine telephone cable is the Commonwealth Pacific Cable (COMPAC), which runs for more than 9,000 miles from Australia *via* Auckland, New Zealand, and the Hawaiian Islands to Port Berni, Canada. It cost about $98,000,000 and was inaugurated on December 2, 1963.

Postal Services

The country with the largest mail in the world is the U.S., whose people posted 95,000 million letters and packages in 1970, when the U.S. Postal Service employed 715,970 people.

The U.S. also takes first place in the average number of letters which each person posts during one year. The figure was 460 in 1970. Of all countries, the greatest discrepancy between incoming and outgoing mails is for the U.S. where, in 1969, only 817 million items were mailed abroad in comparison with 1,397 million items received from foreign sources.

Postage Stamps

Earliest. The earliest adhesive postage stamps ever issued were the "Penny Blacks" of the United Kingdom, bearing the head of Queen Victoria, placed on sale on May 1 for use on May 6, 1840. A total of 64,000,000 were printed. The British National Postal Museum possesses a unique full proof sheet of 240 stamps, printed in April, 1840, before the corner letters, plate numbers or marginal inscriptions were added.

Largest. The largest postage stamps ever issued were the 1913 Express Delivery stamps of China, which measured $9\frac{3}{4}$ inches by $2\frac{3}{4}$ inches. The largest standard postage stamps ever issued were the 10 RLS (ten riyal) airmail stamps issued by the Trucial State of Fujeira (Fujairah) measuring $3\frac{1}{4}$ by $5\frac{3}{4}$ inches (18.68 square inches).

Smallest. The smallest stamps ever issued were the 10 cents and 1 peso of the Colombian State of Bolívar in 1863–66. They measured 0.31 of an inch by 0.37 of an inch.

Highest and Lowest Denominations. The highest denomination stamp ever issued was a red and black stamp for £100 ($280) issued in Kenya in 1925–27. Owing to demonetization and inflation it is difficult to determine the lowest denomination stamp but it was probably the 1946 3000 pengö Hungarian stamp, worth at the time 1.6×10^{-14} parts of a cent.

Most Valuable. There are a number of stamps of which but a single specimen is known. Of these the most celebrated is the one cent black on magenta issued in British Guiana (now Guyana) in February, 1856. It was originally bought for 84 cents (6/–) from L. Vernon Vaughan, a schoolboy, in 1873. This is the world's most renowned stamp, for which £A16,000/$35,768 was paid in 1940, when it was sold by Mrs. Arthur Hind. It was insured for £200,000 ($560,000) when it was displayed in 1965 at the Royal Festival Hall, London. It was sold on March 24, 1970, by auction in New York City for $280,000 by Irwin Weinberg. It was alleged in October, 1938, that Hind had, in 1928, purchased and burned his stamp's twin.

Highest Price. The highest price ever paid for a single philatelic item is $380,000 for two 1-penny orange "Post Office" Mauritius stamps of 1847 on a cover bought at H. R. Harmer's Inc., New York

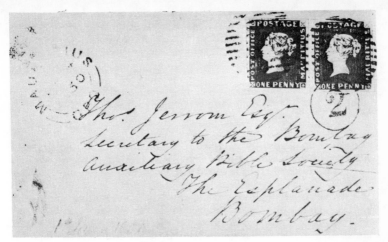

HIGHEST-PRICED PHILATELIC ITEM ever sold was this envelope of 1847, from Mauritius, which realized $380,000 at auction in 1968.

City, by Raymond Weill, Inc. of New Orleans, for an unnamed client from the Lichtenstein-Dale collection on October 21, 1968. The item was discovered in 1897 in an Indian bazaar by a Mr. Charles Williams who paid less than $5 for it. (See photo.)

Largest Collection. The greatest private stamp collection ever auctioned was that of Maurice Burrus (died 1959) of Alsace, France, which realized between $3,250,000 and $4,000,000. He himself valued the collection at $10,000,000.

The largest national collection in the world is that at the British Museum, London, which has had the General Post Office collection on permanent loan since March, 1963. The British Royal collection, housed in 400 volumes, is also believed to be worth more than £1,000,000 ($2,500,000). The collection of the Universal Postal Union (founded October 9, 1874) in Geneva, Switzerland, receives 400 copies of each new issue of each member nation, but the largest international collections are those of the Swiss, Swedish, German, Dutch and U.S. (Smithsonian Institution) postal museums.

Postal Addresses

Highest Numbering. The practice of numbering houses began in 1463 on the Pont Notre Dame, Paris, France. The highest numbered house in the world is No. 81,950 on M-19 in the village of Memphis, near Richmond, Michigan.

Post Boxes. Pillar boxes were introduced at the suggestion of the English novelist Anthony Trollope (1815–82). The oldest original site still in service is one dating from February 8, 1853, at Union Street, St. Peter Port, Guernsey, in the English Channel. The present box is not the original.

Telegrams

The country where most telegrams are sent is the U.S.S.R., whose population sent about 357,000,000 telegrams in 1969.

The world's largest telegraph company is the Western Union Telegraph Company. It had 26,269 employees on January 1, 1969, a total of 11,000 telegraphic offices and agencies and 5,734,792 miles of telegraph channels.

Inland Waterways

The country with the greatest length of inland waterways is Finland. The total length of navigable lakes and rivers is about 31,000 miles.

Longest Navigable River. The longest navigable natural waterway in the world is the Amazon River, which sea-going vessels can ascend as far as Iquitos, in Peru, 2,236 miles from the Atlantic seaboard.

On a National Geographic Society expedition ending on March 10, 1969, Helen and Frank Schreider navigated downstream from San Francisco, Peru, 3,845 miles up the Amazon, by a balsa raft named *Mamuri*, 249 miles to Atalaya, then 356 miles to Pucallpa by outboard motor dug-out canoe, and then the last 3,240 miles towards Belem in the 30-foot gasoline-engined cabin cruiser, *Amazon Queen*.

5. Education

Illiteracy

Literacy is variously defined as "ability to read simple subjects" and "ability to read and write a simple letter." The looseness of definition and the scarcity of data for some countries preclude anything more than approximations, but the extent of illiteracy among adults (15 years old and over) is estimated to have been 39.3 per cent throughout the world in 1961. In 1969, a United Nations' estimate put the level at 810 million out of 2,335 million adults or 34.7 per cent.

The continent with the greatest proportion of illiterates is Africa, where 81.5 per cent of adults were illiterate. The latest figure available for the Niger Republic is 99.1 per cent. A U.S.S.R. source published in June, 1968, affirms that more than 300 million people in China are still "completely illiterate."

University

Oldest. Probably the oldest educational institution in the world is the University of Karueein, founded in 859 A.D. in Fez, Morocco. The European university with the earliest date of foundation is that of Naples, Italy, founded in 1224 by charter of Frederick II (1194–1250), Holy Roman Emperor.

Largest Building. The largest university building in the world is the M. V. Lomonosov State University on the Lenin Hills, south of Moscow, U.S.S.R. It stands 787.4 feet tall, has 32 stories and contains 40,000 rooms. It was constructed in 1949–53. (See photo.)

Greatest Enrollment. The university with the greatest enrollment in the world is the University of Calcutta (founded 1857) in India, with more than 196,257 students (internal and external) and

31 professors in 1968–69. Owing to the inadequacy of the buildings and number of lecturers, the students are handled in three shifts per day.

The enrollment at all branches of the State University of New York, was 155,469 in January, 1971, and is expected to reach 290,400 by 1974.

Richest. The richest university in the world is Harvard University, Cambridge, Massachusetts. Its endowments had a book value of $621,795,041 in 1968.

Professors

Youngest. The youngest at which anybody has been elected to a chair (full professorship) in a major university is 22, in the case of William Rowan Hamilton (born August 4, 1805), Andrews Professor of Astronomy at the University of Dublin Trinity College, Dublin, Ireland, in 1827. He died of alcoholism at the age of 60 on September 2, 1865.

In July, 1967, Dr. Harvey Friedman, Ph.D., was appointed Assistant Professor of Mathematics at Stanford University, California, when aged just 19 years.

Most Durable. The longest period for which any professorship has been held is 63 years in the case of Thomas Martyn (1735–1825), Professor of Botany at Cambridge University, England, from 1762 until his death. His father, John Martyn (1699–1768), had occupied the chair from 1733 to 1762.

Schools

Largest. The largest school in the world was the De Witt Clinton High School in the Bronx, New York City, where the enrollment attained a peak of 12,000 in 1934. It was founded in 1897 and now has an enrollment of 6,000.

Most Expensive. The most expensive school in the world is the Oxford Academy (established 1906) in Pleasantville, New Jersey. It is a private college-preparatory boarding school for boys with "academic deficiencies." The school has 15 masters and each of the 47 boys is taught individually in each course. The tuition fee for the school year is $8,400.

6. Religions

Largest. Religious statistics are necessarily the roughest approximations. The test of adherence to a religion varies widely in rigor, while many individuals, particularly in China and Japan, belong to two or more religions.

Christianity is the world's prevailing religion, with over 985 million adherents in 1971, and probably an additional 150,000,000 Protestants who are not in membership with the church of their baptism. The total of 175,000,000 practicing and 150,000,000 non-practicing Protestants is easily outnumbered by the 590,000,000 who have received baptism into the Roman Catholic Church. The largest non-Christian religion is Islam, with about 475,000,000 adherents in 1971.

Smallest. In New Zealand, the 1966 Census revealed 94 religious sects with just a single follower each. These included a Millenarian Heretic and an Aesthetic Hedonist. Such followers might alternatively be described as leaders.

Largest Clergy. The world's largest religious organization is the Roman Catholic Church, with over 500,000,000 members, 418,000 priests and 946,000 nuns in 1964. The total number of cardinals, patriarchs, metropolitans, archbishops, bishops, abbots and superiors is 2,800. There are about 416,000 churches.

Jews. The total of world Jewry was estimated to be 14,000,000 in 1971. The highest concentration was in the U.S., with 5,870,000 of whom 1,836,000 were in New York City. The total in Israel was 2,530,000, in Britain 450,000 (of whom 280,000 are in Greater London). The total in Tokyo, Japan, is 250.

Largest Temple. The largest religious building ever constructed is Angkor Wat (City Temple), covering 402 acres, in Cambodia, now Khmers. It was built to the God Vishnu by the Khmer King Suryavarman II in the period 1113–1150. Its curtain wall measures 1,400 yards by 1,400 yards and its population, before it was abandoned in 1432, was at times 80,000.

LARGEST RELIGIOUS BUILDING: Angkor Wat in Cambodia (now called Khmers), built in the 12th century, covers 402 acres.

Largest Mosque. The largest mosque ever built was the now ruined al-Malawiya mosque of al-Mutawakil in Samarra, Iraq, built in 842–852 A.D. and measuring 401,408 square feet (9.21 acres) with dimensions of 784 feet by 512 feet.

The world's largest mosque in use is the Jama Masjid (1644–58) in Delhi, India, with an area of more than 10,000 square feet and two 108-foot-tall minarets.

The largest mosque will be the Merdeka Mosque in Djakarta, Indonesia, which was begun in 1962. The cupola will be 147.6 feet in diameter and the capacity in excess of 50,000 people.

Largest Synagogue. The largest synagogue in the world is the Temple Emanu-El on Fifth Avenue at 65th Street, New York City. The temple, completed in September, 1929, has a frontage of 150 feet on Fifth Avenue and 253 feet on 65th Street. The sanctuary proper can accommodate 2,500 people, and the adjoining Beth-El Chapel seats 350. When all the facilities are in use, more than 6,000 people can be accommodated.

Cathedrals

Largest. The world's largest cathedral is the cathedral church of the Episcopalian Diocese of New York, St. John the Divine, with a floor area of 121,000 square feet and a volume of 16,822,000 cubic feet. The cornerstone was laid on December 27, 1892, and the Gothic building was still uncompleted in 1972. In New York it is referred to as "Saint John the Unfinished." The nave is the longest in the world, 601 feet in length, with a vaulting 124 feet in height.

The cathedral covering the largest area is that of Santa María de la Sede in Seville, Spain. It was built in Spanish Gothic style between 1402 and 1519 and is 414 feet long, 271 feet wide and 100 feet high to the vault of the nave.

Churches

The elliptical Basilique of St. Pie X at Lourdes, France, completed in 1957 at a cost of $5,600,000, has a capacity of 20,000 under its giant span arches and a length of 659 feet.

The crypt of the underground Civil War Memorial Church in the Guadarrama Mountains, 28 miles from Madrid, Spain, is 853 feet in length. It took 21 years (1937–58) to build, at a reported cost of $392,000,000 and is surmounted by a cross 492 feet tall.

Smallest. The world's smallest church is the Union Church at Wiscasset, Maine, with a floor area of $31\frac{1}{2}$ square feet (7 feet by $4\frac{1}{2}$ feet). Les Vaubelets Church in Guernsey, Channel Islands, has an area of 16 feet by 12 feet, room for one priest and a congregation of two.

Oldest. The earliest known shrine dates from the proto-neolithic Natufian culture in Jericho, where a site on virgin soil has been dated to the ninth millennium B.C. A simple rectilinear red-plastered room with a niche housing a stone pillar, believed to be the shrine of a pre-pottery fertility cult dating from c. 6500 B.C. was also uncovered in Jericho.

The oldest surviving Christian church in the world is Qal'at es Salihige in eastern Syria, dating from 232 A.D.

Tallest Spires. The tallest cathedral spire in the world is that of the Protestant Cathedral of Ulm in Germany. The building is early Gothic and was begun in 1377. The tower, in the center of the west façade, was not finally completed until 1890 and is 528 feet high.

The world's tallest church spire is that of the Chicago Temple of the First Methodist Church on Clark Street, Chicago. The building consists of a 22-story skyscraper (erected in 1924) surmounted by a parsonage at 330 feet, a "Sky Chapel" at 400 feet and a steeple cross at 568 feet above street level. (See photo.)

Tallest Minaret. The world's tallest minaret is the Qutb Minar, south of New Delhi, India, built in 1194 to a height of 238 feet.

Tallest Pagoda. The world's tallest pagoda is the 288-foot-tall Shwemawdaw in Pegu, Burma. It was restored by April, 1954, having been damaged by an earthquake in 1930. The tallest Chinese temple is the 13-story Pagoda of the Six Harmonies (*Liu he t'a*) outside Hang-chow. It is "nearly 200 feet high."

TALLEST PAGODA (left): The Shwemawdaw in Pegu, Burma, is 288 feet high.
HIGHEST CHURCH SPIRE (right) is on the Sky Chapel of the First Methodist
Church on Clark St., Chicago, which rises 568 feet above street level.

Saints

Most and Least Rapidly Canonized. The shortest interval that
has elapsed between the death of a Saint and his canonization was in
the case of St. Anthony of Padua, Italy, who died on June 13, 1251,
and was canonized 352 days later on May 30, 1252. This was one
day faster than St. Peter of Verona (1206–52) who was canonized on
April 6, 1253.

The other extreme is represented by St. Bernard of Thiron, for
20 years Prior of St. Sabinus, who died in 1117 and was made a
Saint in 1861—744 years later. The Italian monk and painter, Fra
Giovanni da Fiesole (*né* Guido di Pietro), called *Il Beato* ("The
Blessed") Fra Angelico (*c.* 1400–1455), is still in the first stage of
canonization.

Popes

Longest Reign. The longest reign of any of the 262 Popes has
been that of Pius IX (Giovanni Maria Mastai-Ferretti), who reigned
for 31 years 236 days from June 16, 1846, until his death, aged 85,
on February 7, 1878.

Shortest Reign. Pope Stephen II was elected on March 24, 752,
and died two days later, but he is not included in the *Liber pontificalis*
or in the Catalogue of the Popes. The shortest reign of any genuine
Pope is that of Giambattista Castagna (1521–90), who was elected

Pope Urban VII on September 15, 1590, and died twelve days later on September 27, 1590.

Oldest. It is recorded that Pope St. Agatho (reigned 678–681) was elected at the age of 103 and lived to 106, but recent scholars have expressed doubts. The oldest of recent Pontiffs has been Pope Leo XIII (Vincenzo Gioacchino Pecci), who was born on March 2, 1810, elected Pope at the third ballot on February 20, 1878, and died on July 20, 1903, aged 93 years 140 days.

Youngest. The youngest of all Popes was Pope Benedict IX (Theophylact), who had three terms as Pope: in 1032–44; April to May, 1045; and November 8, 1047 to July 17, 1048. It would appear that he was aged only 11 or 12 in 1032, though the Catalogue of the Popes admits only to his "extreme youth."

Last Married. The last married Pope was Adrian II (867–872). Rodrigo Borgia was the father of at least four children before being elected Pope Alexander VI in 1492. The first 37 Popes had no specific obligation to celibacy.

Last Non-Italian, Ex-Cardinalate and English Popes. The last non-Italian Pope was the Utrecht-born Cardinal Priest Adrian Dedel (1459–1523) of the Netherlands. He was elected on January 9, 1522, crowned Pope Adrian VI on August 31, 1522, and died on September 14, 1523. The last Pope elected from outside the College of Cardinals was Bartolomeo Prignano (1318–89), Archbishop of Bari, who was elected Pope Urban VI on April 8, 1378.

Slowest and Fastest Election. After 31 months without declaring "We have a Pope," the cardinals were subjected to a bread and water diet and the removal of the roof of their conclave by the Mayor before electing Teobaldo Visconti (*c.* 1210–76), the Archbishop of Liege, as Pope Gregory X at Viterbo, near Rome, on September 1, 1271. Cardinal Eugenio Maria Giuseppe Giovanni Pacelli (1876–1958), who took the title of Pius XII, was reputedly elected by 61 votes out of 62 at only the third ballot on March 2, 1939, his 63rd birthday. (See photo.)

Cardinals

Oldest. By June, 1972, the College of Cardinals contained 119 declared members—compared with 125 a year earlier. The oldest is Cardinal Bishop Paolo Giobbe of Italy (born January 10, 1880).

Youngest. The youngest Cardinal of all time was Giovanni de' Medici (born December 11, 1475), later Pope Leo X, who was made a Cardinal Deacon in March, 1489, when aged 13 years 3 months. The youngest in 1971 is Cardinal Bishop Stephan Sou Hwan Kim of South Korea (born May 2, 1922). He was named as a cardinal in April, 1969, when aged 46.

Bishops

Oldest. The oldest Roman Catholic bishop in recent years was Mgr. Alfonso Carinci (born November 9, 1862), who was titular Archbishop of Seleucia, in Isauria, from 1945 until his death on

December 6, 1963, at the age of 101 years 27 days. He had celebrated Mass about 24,800 times.

Bishop Herbert Welch of the United Methodist Church who was elected a bishop for Japan and Korea in 1916 died on April 4, 1969, aged 106.

Youngest. The youngest bishop of all time was Hugnes, whose father, the Comte de Vermandois, successfully demanded for him the archbishopric of Reims from the feeble Pope John X (reigned 914–928), when he was only five years old.

Stained Glass

Oldest. The oldest stained glass in the world represents the Prophets in a window of the cathedral of Augsburg, Bavaria, Germany, dating from c. 1050. (See photo.)

Largest. The largest stained glass window is one measuring 300 feet long by 23 feet high at the American Airlines Building at John F. Kennedy International Airport (formerly Idlewild), Long Island, New York City. (See photo, next page.)

Monumental Brasses

The world's oldest monumental brass is that commemorating

Bishop Ysowilpe in St. Andrew's Church, Verden, near Hanover, West Germany, dating from 1231.

Largest Crowd

The greatest recorded number of human beings assembled with a common purpose was more than 5,000,000 at the 21-day Hindu feast of Kumbh-Mela, which is held every 12 years at the confluence of the Yamuna (formerly called the Jumna), the Ganges and the invisible "Sarasviti" at Allahabad, Uttar Pradesh, India, on January 21, 1966. According to the Jacob Formula for estimating the size of crowds, the allowance of area per person varies from 4 square feet (tight) to $9\frac{1}{2}$ square feet (loose). Thus, such a crowd must have occupied an area of more than 700 acres.

Largest Funeral

The greatest attendance at any funeral is the estimated 4 million who thronged Cairo, Egypt (United Arab Republic), for the funeral of President Gamal Abdel Nasser (b. January 15, 1918) on October 1, 1970. (See photo.)

Biggest Demonstrations

A figure of 2.7 million was published from China for the demonstration against the U.S.S.R. in Shanghai on April 3–4, 1969, following border clashes, and one of 10 million for the May Day celebrations of 1963 in Peking.

LARGEST STAINED GLASS WINDOW: Featured in the facade of the American Airlines Building at John F. Kennedy International Airport, New York, this is 300 feet long by 23 feet high.

LARGEST FUNERAL: An estimated 4,000,000 people attended the ceremony when President Nasser of Egypt died in Cairo in 1970.

PROGRESSIVE HUMAN ALTITUDE RECORDS

Feet	Pilot		Place	Date
84	Jean Francois Pilâtre de Rozier (France)	Hot Air Balloon (tethered)	Fauxbourg, Paris	Oct. 15 & 17, 1783
210	J. F. Pilâtre de Rozier (France)	Hot Air Balloon (tethered)	Fauxbourg, Paris ...	Oct. 19, 1783
262	J. F. Pilâtre de Rozier (France)	Hot Air Balloon (tethered)	Fauxbourg, Paris ...	Oct. 19, 1783
c. 330	de Rozier and the Marquis Francois Laurent d'Arlandes	Hot Air Balloon (free flight)	La Muette, Paris ...	Nov. 21, 1783
c. 2,000	Jacques Alexander César Charles and Charles Robert (France)	Hydrogen Balloon	Tuileries, Paris	Dec. 1, 1783
c. 9,000	J. A. C. Charles (France)	Hydrogen Balloon	Nestles, France	Dec. 1, 1783
c. 20,000	E. G. R. Robertson (U.K.) and Loest (Germany)	Hydrogen Balloon	Hamburg, Germany	July 18, 1803
27,950	H. T. Sivel, J. E. Crocé-Spinelli, Gaston Tissandier	Coal gas Balloon Zenith	La Villette, Paris ...	Apr. 15, 1875
31,500	Prof. A. Berson (Germany)	Hydrogen Balloon Phoenix	Strasbourg, France	Dec. 4, 1894
36,565	Sadi Lecointe (France)	Nieuport aircraft	Issy, France	Oct. 30, 1923
43,166	Lt. Apollo Soucek (U.S. Army)	U.S.N. Wright Apache	Washington, D.C.	June 4, 1930
51,961	Prof. Auguste Piccard (Switzerland) and Paul Kipfer	F.N.R.S. I Balloon	Augsburg, Germany	May 27, 1931
53,139	Piccard and Dr. Max Cosyns (Belgium)	F.N.R.S. I Balloon	Dübendorf nr. Zurich	Aug. 18, 1932
72,178[1]	Raul F. Fedoseyenko, A. B. Vasenko and E. D. Ususkin.	Osoaviakhim Balloon	Moscow	Jan. 30, 1934
72,395	Capts. Orvill Anderson and Albert Stevens (U.S. Army)	U.S. Explorer II Helium Balloon	Rapid City, S.D.	Nov. 11, 1935
79,494	William Bridgeman (U.S.)	U.S. Douglas D558-II Skyrocket	California	Aug. 15, 1951
83,235	Lt.-Col. Marion Carl, U.S.M.C.	U.S. Douglas D558-II Skyrocket	California	Aug. 21, 1953
c.93,000	Major Arthur Murray (U.S.A.F.)	U.S. Bell X-1A Rocket Plane	California	Aug. 21, 1954
126,200	Capt. Iven C. Kincheloe (U.S.A.F.)	U.S. Bell X-2 Rocket Plane	California	Sept. 7, 1956
136,500	Major Robert M. White (U.S.A.F.)	U.S. X-15 Rocket Plane	California	Aug. 12, 1960
169,600	Joseph A. Walker (U.S.)	U.S. X-15 Rocket Plane	California	Mar. 30, 1961
Miles 203.2	Fl. Major Yuriy A. Gagarin (U.S.S.R.)	Vostok I capsule	Orbital flight	Apr. 12, 1961
253.6	Col. Vladimir M. Komarov, Lt. Boris B. Yegorov and Konstantin P. Feoktistov (U.S.S.R.)	Voskhod I capsule	Orbital flight	Oct. 12, 1964
309.2	Col. Pavel I. Belyayev and Lt.-Col. Aleksey A. Leonov (U.S.S.R.)	Voskhod II capsule	Orbital flight	Mar. 18, 1965
474.4	Cdr. John W. Young (U.S.N.) and Major Michael Collins (U.S. Army)	U.S. Gemini X capsule	Orbital flight	July 19, 1966
850.7	Cdr. Charles Conrad, Jr., and Lt.-Cdr. Richard F. Gordon, Jr. (U.S. Army)	U.S. Gemini XI capsule	Orbital flight	Sept. 14, 1966
234,473	Col. Frank Borman, Capt. James A. Lovell, William A. Anders (U.S. Army)	U.S. Apollo VIII Command Module	Circum-lunar flight	Dec. 25, 1968
248,433*	Cdr. Eugene A. Cernan (U.S.N.) and Lt.-Col. Thomas P. Stafford (U.S.A.F.)	U.S. Apollo X Lunar Module	Circum-lunar flight	May 22, 1969
248,665	Capt. James Arthur Lovell (U.S.N.), John L. Swigert (U.S.N.), and Frederick W. Haise	U.S. Apollo XIII	Circum-lunar flight	April 15, 1970

1 All died on descent.   *Note: The moon was 6,150 miles less distant at the time of the lunar landing of July 20–21, 1969.

LUNAR CONQUEST:
The greatest human
achievement of the century was
the landing of man on the
moon. This is Col. Edwin Aldrin
stepping down from the lunar
module, as photographed by
Neil Armstrong, fellow
astronaut and the first to land.

Chapter Eleven

HUMAN ACHIEVEMENTS

1. Endurance and Endeavor

Lunar Conquest

Neil Alden Armstrong (born Wapakoneta, Ohio, of Scotch-Irish-German ancestry, on August 5, 1930) command pilot of the Apollo XI mission, became the first man to set foot on the moon on the Sea of Tranquillity at 02:56 and 20 secs. a.m. G.M.T. on July 21, 1969. He was followed out of the Lunar Module *Eagle* by Col. Edwin Eugene Aldrin, Jr. (born Montclair, New Jersey, of Swedish, Dutch and British ancestry, on January 20, 1930), while the Command Module *Columbia* piloted by Lt.-Col. Michael Collins (born Rome, Italy, of Irish and pre-Revolutionary American ancestry, on October 31, 1930) orbited above.

Eagle landed at 20:17 hrs. 42 secs. G.M.T. on July 20 and blasted off at 17:54 G.M.T. on July 21, after a stay of 21 hours 36 minutes.

PROGRESSIVE HUMAN SPEED RECORDS

The progression of the *voluntary* human speed record has been as listed below. It is perhaps noteworthy that the gasoline-engined motor car does not feature in this compilation.

Speed in m.p.h.	Vehicle	Date
<25	Running	before 6500 B.C.
>25	Sledging, southern Finland	c. 6500 B.C.
>35	Skiing, Fenno-Scandia	c. 3000 B.C.
<35	Horse riding, Near East	c. 1400 B.C.
<50	Ice Yachts, Netherlands	c. 1550 A.D.
56¾	*Lucifer* engine, Madeley Bank, Staffordshire, England	Nov. 13, 1839
87.8	Tommy Todd, skier, La Porte, California	March, 1873
89.48	Crompton No. 604 engine, Champigny-Pont sur Yonne, France	June 20, 1890
	(thence 5 further railroad records, 1897–1903)	
130.61	Siemens und Halske electric train, Marienfeld-Zossen, near Berlin	Oct. 27, 1903
c. 150	Frederick C. Marriott in Stanley Steamer automobile at Ormond Beach, Florida. (See photo.)	Jan. 25, 1907
>210	World War I fighters in dives, including Nieuport Nighthawks	1918–19
210.64	Sadi Lecointe (France), Nieuport aircraft	Sept. 26, 1921
	(thence 17 new world air speed records)	
243.94	Brig.-Gen. William Mitchell (U.S. Army) (1879–1936) Curtis R-6, Detroit	Oct. 18, 1922
270.5	Lt. Alford J. Williams (U.S.N.) Curtis R2 C1, Mitchel Field, L.I., N.Y.	Nov. 4, 1923
274.2	Lt. A. Brown (U.S.N.) Curtis H5-D12, Mitchel Field, L.I., N.Y.	Nov. 4, 1923
486	Kapt. Fritz Wendel (Germany) aircraft	Apr. 26, 1939
c. 525	He 176 test flight, Peenemünde, Germany	July 3, 1939
652.6	Turner F. Caldwell (U.S.) Douglas Skystreak*	Aug. 20, 1947
653.4	Marion E. Carl (U.S.) Douglas Skystreak*	Aug. 25, 1947
670	Capt. Charles E. Yeager (U.S.) Bell XS-1	Oct. 14, 1947
967	Capt. Charles E. Yeager (U.S.) Bell XS-1	1948
1,135	Wm. Bridgeman (U.S.)	June, 1951
1,181	Wm. Bridgeman (U.S.)	June 11, 1951
1,221	Wm. Bridgeman (U.S.)	June, 1951
1,238	Wm. Bridgeman (U.S.) ⎫ Douglas Skyrocket	Aug. 7, 1951
1,241	Wm. Bridgeman (U.S.) ⎬ 558-II	Dec., 1951
1,272	A. Scott Crossfield (U.S.)	Oct. 14, 1953
1,328	A. Scott Crossfield (U.S.) ⎭	Nov. 20, 1953
1,612	Maj. Charles Yeager (U.S.) Bell X-1A	Dec. 12, 1953
1,934	Lt.-Col. Frank Everest (U.S.) Bell X-2	July 23, 1956
2,094	Capt. Milburn Apt (U.S.) Bell X-2	Sept. 27, 1956
2,111	Joseph A. Walker, North American X-15	May 12, 1960
2,196	Joseph A. Walker (U.S.) X-15	Aug. 4, 1960
2,275	Major Robert M. White (U.S.) X-15	Feb. 7, 1961
2,905	Major Robert M. White (U.S.) X-15	Mar. 7, 1961
17,560†	Fl. Major Y. A. Gagarin (U.S.S.R.) Vostok I	Apr. 12, 1961
17,558	Cdr. Walter M. Schirra (U.S.N.) Sigma 7	Oct. 3, 1962
17,600†	Komarov, Feoktistov and Yegorov (U.S.S.R.)	Oct. 12–13, 1964
17,750†	Col. Pavel I. Belyayev and Lt.-Col. Aleksey A. Leonov (U.S.S.R.) Voskhod II	Mar. 18–19, 1965
17,943	Cdr. Charles Conrad, Jr., and Lt.-Cdr. Richard F. Gordon, Jr. (U.S.N.) Gemini XI	Sept. 14, 1966
24,226	Col. Frank Borman, Capt. James A. Lovell and William A. Anders (U.S.) Apollo VIII	Dec. 21, 1968
24,752	Same crew on return flight of Apollo VIII	Dec. 27, 1968
24,791	Cdrs. Eugene A. Cernan and John W. Young (U.S.N.), Lt.-Col. Thomas P. Stafford (U.S.A.F.), Apollo X	May 27, 1969

N.B.—New research in the U.S. confirms that ice yacht speeds included in earlier editions are exaggerated.

* Average of two flights in opposite directions, hence one flight is faster.

† Plus or minus 20 m.p.h.   > more than   < less than

SPEED RECORD OF 1907 was set by Fred Marriott in this Stanley Steamer at more than 150 m.p.h.

The *Apollo XI* had blasted off from Cape Kennedy, Florida at 13:32 G.M.T. on July 16 and was a culmination of the U.S. space program, which, at its peak, employed 376,600 people and attained in the year 1966–67 a peak budget of $5,900,000,000.

Altitude

Manned Flight. The greatest altitude attained by man was when the crew of the ill-fated *Apollo XIII* were at apocynthion (*i.e.* their furthest point behind the moon) 158 miles above its surface and 248,665 miles above the earth's surface at 1:21 a.m. B.S.T. on April 15, 1970. The crew were Capt. James Arthur Lovell, U.S.N.; John L. Swigert, U.S.N.; and Frederick W. Haise.

Woman. The greatest altitude attained by a woman is 143.5 miles by Jr. Lt. (now Lt. Col.) Valentina Vladimirovna Tereshkova-Nikolayev (born March 6, 1937), of the U.S.S.R., during her 48-orbit flight in *Vostok VI* on June 16–19, 1963. The record for a woman in an aircraft is 79,842 feet by Natalya Prokhanova (U.S.S.R.) (b. 1940) in an E-33 jet, on May 22, 1965.

Speed

Space

Man. The fastest speed at which any human has traveled is 24,791 m.p.h. when the Command and Service Module (C.S.M.) of Apollo X carrying Col. Thomas P. Stafford, U.S.A.F. (b. Weatherford, Okla., September 17, 1930), and Commanders Eugene Andrew Cernan (b. Chicago, March 14, 1934) and John Watts Young, U.S.N. (b. San Francisco, September 24, 1930) reached their maximum speed on their trans-earth return flight at an altitude of 400,000 feet on May 27, 1969. It was widely but incorrectly reported that the stricken *Apollo XIII* attained the highest recorded speed on its return on April 17, 1970. Its maximum was in fact 24,689.2 m.p.h.

Woman. The highest speed ever attained by a woman is 17,470 m.p.h. by Jr. Lt. (now Lt. Col.) Valentina Vladimirovna Tereshkova-Nikolayev (born March 6, 1937), of the U.S.S.R., during her 48-orbit flight in *Vostok VI* on June 16–19, 1963.

The highest speed ever achieved in an airplane is 1,429.2 m.p.h. by Jacqueline Cochran (now Mrs. Floyd Bostwick Odlum) (U.S.), in a

THE HIGHEST LAND SPEED ever reached is 650 m.p.h. set by Gary Gabelich in this car, "The Blue Flame," on Bonneville Salt Flats, Utah, in October, 1970.

HOLDERS OF WOMEN'S AIRPLANE AND LAND SPEED RECORDS:
Jacqueline Cochran (left) who flew 1,429.2 m.p.h. in 1964, shown with Col. Charles F.
Yeager, first man to fly faster than sound (see table on page 406). Lee (Mrs. Craig)
Breedlove (right) who drove her husband's racing car 335.070 m.p.h. in 1965, is
being embraced by her husband who holds the world land speed record.

F-104G1 *Starfighter* jet over Edwards Air Force Base, California, on
May 18, 1964. (See photo.)

Land

Man. The highest speed ever achieved on land is 650 m.p.h.
momentarily during the 627.287-m.p.h. run of *The Blue Flame*
driven by Gary Gabelich (b. San Pedro, California, August 29,
1940) on Bonneville Salt Flats, Utah, on October 23, 1970 (see
Mechanical World). The car built by Reaction Dynamics Inc. of
Milwaukee, Wisconsin, is designed to withstand stresses up to
1,000 m.p.h. while the tires have been tested to speeds of 850 m.p.h.
(See photo.)

Woman. The highest land speed recorded by a woman is 335.070
m.p.h. by Mrs. Lee Breedlove (*née* Roberts) (born 1937) of Los
Angeles, driving her husband's *Spirit of America—Sonic I* on the
Bonneville Salt Flats, Utah, on November 4, 1965. (See photo.)

Water

The highest speed ever achieved on water is 328 m.p.h. by Donald
Malcolm Campbell (born March 23, 1921), of the U.K., on his last
and fatal run in the turbo-jet-engined $2\frac{1}{4}$-ton *Bluebird* K7, on Conis-
ton water, Lancashire, England, on January 4, 1967.

The official record is 285.213 m.p.h. (average of two 1-mile runs)
by Lee Taylor, Jr. (born 1934) of Downey, California, in the hydroplane *Hustler* on Lake Guntersville, Alabama, on June 30, 1967. (See
photo, next page.)

The world record for propeller-driven craft is 200.42 m.p.h. by
Roy Duby (U.S.) in a Rolls-Royce-engined hydroplane on Guntersville Lake, Alabama, on April 17, 1962.

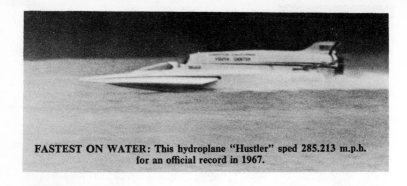

FASTEST ON WATER: This hydroplane "Hustler" sped 285.213 m.p.h. for an official record in 1967.

Most Traveled Man

The man who has most probably visited more countries than anyone is J. Hart Rosdail (born 1915) of Elmhurst, Illinois. Since 1934 he has visited 144 of the 148 sovereign countries and 76 of the 80 non-sovereign territories of the world making a total of 219. He estimates his mileage as 1,170,000 miles by February, 1972. The only sovereign countries which he has not visited are China (Mainland), Cuba, North Korea and North Vietnam.

The most countries visited by a disabled person is 119 by Lester Nixon of Sarasota, Florida, who is confined to a wheelchair.

The most traveled man in space is Capt. James A. Lovell, U.S.N. with 717 hours 4 mins. 16 secs. and an estimated mileage of 7,270,000 miles.

Most Hours Flown

The greatest number of flying hours claimed is more than 40,000 by the light-aircraft pilot Max A. Conrad (b. 1903) of the U.S., who began his flying career on March 13, 1928. Capt. Charles Blair (Pan American World Airways) logged 35,000 flying hours and more than 10,000,000 miles including 1,450 Atlantic crossings up to July 12, 1969. Capt. Gordon R. Buxton (B.O.A.C.) surpassed 8,000,000 miles in 22,750 flying hours in 38 years to May 22, 1966. He retired as Senior Captain, aged 60, after having passed all medical exams.

Polar Conquests

South Pole. The first ship to cross the Antarctic circle (latitude 66° 30′ S.) was the *Resolution* (517 tons), under Capt. James Cook (1728–79), the English navigator, on January 17, 1773.

The first person to sight the Antarctic *mainland*—on the best available evidence and against claims made for British and Russian explorers—was Nathaniel Brown Palmer (U.S.) (1799–1877). On November 17, 1820, he sighted the Orleans Channel coast of the Palmer Peninsular from his 45-ton sloop *Hero*.

The South Pole was first reached on December 14, 1911, by a Norwegian party, led by Roald Amundsen (1872–1928), after a 53-day march with dog sleds from the Bay of Whales, to which he had penetrated in the *Fram*. Olav Bjaaland, the first to arrive, was the last survivor, dying in June, 1961, aged 88. The others were the late Helmer Hanssen, Sverre Hassel and Oskar Wisting. (See photo.)

EVEREST CONQUERED: Tenzing Norkhay (left), a Sherpa, was with Sir Edmund Hillary in 1953 on this historic climb. SOUTH POLE REACHED: Helmer Hanssen (right), one of Roald Amundsen's companions in 1911.

Antarctic Crossing. The first crossing of the Antarctic continent was completed at 1:47 p.m. on March 2, 1958, after a 2,158-mile trek lasting 99 days from November 24, 1957, from Shackleton Base to Scott Base *via* the Pole. The crossing party of 12 was led by Dr. (now Sir) Vivian Ernest Fuchs (born February 11, 1908).

North Pole. The claims of neither of the two U.S. Arctic explorers, Dr. Frederick Albert Cook (1865–1940) nor Civil Engineer

CONQUEST OF NORTH POLE: Commander Robert E. Peary (right) took the picture (left) of his companions after they thought they reached the North Pole on April 6, 1909. Left to right are the Eskimos Ooqueah and Ootah; Matthew Henson, Peary's Negro assistant; and the other two Eskimos Egingwah and Seegloo.

FIRST ARCTIC SEA ICE CROSSING: The British Trans-Arctic Expedition went by sled from Point Barrow, Alaska, to near Spitzbergen, Norway, in 464 days.

Robert Edwin Peary, U.S.N. (1856–1920) in reaching the North Pole is subject to positive proof. Cook, accompanied by the Eskimos, Ah-pellah and Etukishook, two sledges and 26 dogs, struck north from a point 60 miles north of Svartevoeg, on Axel Heiberg Is., Canada, 460 miles from the Pole on March 21, 1908, allegedly reaching Lat. 89° 31′ N. on April 19, and the Pole on April 21. Peary, accompanied by his Negro assistant, Matthew Alexander Henson (1866–1955) and the four Eskimos, Ooqueah, Egingwah, Seegloo, and Ootah (1875–1955), struck north from his Camp Bartlett (Lat. 87° 44′ N.) at 5 a.m. on April 2, 1909. After traveling another 134 miles, he allegedly established his final camp, Camp Jessup, in the proximity of the Pole at 10 a.m. on April 6, and marched a further 42 miles quartering the sea ice before turning south at 4 p.m. on April 7. Peary's longest claimed 3-day march for a record 163 geographical miles must be regarded as highly improbable. Cook's comparative maximum claim was for 68 geographical miles in 3 days.

The earliest indisputable attainment of the North Pole over the sea ice was at 3 p.m. (Central Standard Time) on April 19, 1968, by Ralph Plaisted (U.S.) and three companions after a 42-day trek in four snowmobiles. Their arrival was independently verified 18 hours later by a U.S. Air Force weather aircraft.

Arctic Crossing. The first crossing of the Arctic sea ice was achieved by the British Trans-Arctic Expedition which left Point Barrow, Alaska, on February 21, 1968, and arrived at the Seven Island Archipelago northeast of Spitzbergen 464 days later on May 29, 1969, after a haul of 3,620 miles. The team was Wally Herbert (leader), 34, Major Ken Hedges, 34, R.A.M.C., Allan Gill, 38, and Dr. Roy Koerner (glaciologist), and 34 huskies. This was the longest sustained (sled) journey ever made on polar pack ice.

FIRST ATLANTIC ROW WEST-TO-EAST was made in this 20-foot dory, "Super Silver," by Tom McClean, who rowed for 70 days 17 hours from Newfoundland to Ireland.

Mountaineering

The conquest of the highest point on earth, Mount Everest (29,028 feet) was first achieved at 11:30 a.m. on May 29, 1953, by Edmund Percival Hillary (New Zealand) and the Sherpa, Tenzing Norkhay (see *Mountaineering*, Chapter 12). (See photo, page 411.)

The greatest altitude attained by a woman mountaineer is 26,223 feet by Miss Setsuko Watanabe, 31 (Japan) on Mt. Everest in May, 1970. The highest mountain summit reached by women is Qungur I, (Kongur Tiube Tagh) (*c.* 25,146 feet), climbed in 1961 by Shierab and another (unnamed) Tibetan woman.

FIRST SINGLE-STOP SOLO VOYAGE AROUND WORLD: Sir Francis C. Chichester of England used this 53-foot ketch, "Gipsy Moth IV," for his 274-day trip.

MARINE CIRCUMNAVIGATION RECORDS (Compiled by Sq. Ldr. D. H. Clarke)

A true circumnavigation entails passing through two antipodal points (which are at least 12,429 statute miles apart).

CATEGORY	VESSEL	NAME	START DATE AND PLACE	FINISH DATE AND DURATION
Earliest	*Vittoria* Expedition of Fernão de Magalhães (Magellan) c. 1480–1521	Juan Sebastion de Eleano (d. 1526) and 17 crew	Guadalquivir, Spain Sept. 20, 1519	Sept. 6, 1521, 30,700 miles
Earliest British	*Golden Hind* (ex *Pelican*) 100 tons	Francis Drake (c. 1540–1596) (Knighted April 4, 1581)	Plymouth, England, Dec. 13, 1577	Sept. 26, 1580
Earliest Woman	*La Bordeuse*	Crypto-female valet of M. de Commerson		1764
Earliest Solo	*Spray*, 36¾-foot gaff yawl	Capt. Joshua Slocum, 51 (U.S.) (a non-swimmer)	Newport, Rhode Island, U.S. *via* Magellan Straits, Apr. 24, 1895	July 3, 1898, 46,000 miles
Earliest Solo Eastabout *via* Cape Horn	*Lehg II*, 31¼ foot Bermuda ketch	Vito Dumas (Argentina)	Buenos Aires, June 27, 1942	Sept. 7, 1943 (272 days)
Smallest Boat	*Trekka*, 20½-foot Bermuda ketch	John Guzzwell (G.B.)	Victoria, B.C., Sept. 10, 1955 Westabout *via* Panama	Sept. 12, 1959 (4 years 2 days)
Earliest Submarine	*U.S.S. Triton*	Capt. Edward L. Beach, U.S.N. plus 182 crew	New London, Connecticut, Feb. 16, 1960	May 10, 1960, 30,708 miles
Earliest Solo with One Stop-Over	*Gipsy Moth IV*, 53-foot Bermuda yawl	Sir Francis Chichester (G.B.) (1901–72) (see photo, page 413)	Plymouth, England, to Sydney Aug. 27, 1966	May 28, 1967, 29,626 miles
Earliest Non-stop Solo	*Suhaili*, 32.4-foot Bermuda ketch	Robin Knox-Johnston (G.B.) (b. 1928)	Falmouth, England, June 14, 1968 (unaided repairs at Otago, N.Z.)	Apr. 22, 1969 (313 days)
Fastest Solo	*Victress*, 40-foot Trimaran	Lt.-Cdr. Nigel C. W. Tetley R.N. (G.B.) (South Africa)	Plymouth, England, Sept. 16, 1968	Tied the Knot in 179 days
Earliest Non-stop Solo Westabout	*British Steel*, 59-foot ketch (largest solo)	Charles "Chay" Blyth (G.B.) (b. 1940)	The Hamble, Oct. 18, 1970	Aug. 6, 1971, 292 days

TRANSATLANTIC MARINE RECORDS (Compiled by Sq. Ldr. D. H. Clarke)

CATEGORY	CAPTAIN	VESSEL & SIZE	START	FINISH	DURATION	DATE
Earliest Trimaran	John Mikes+2 crew (U.S.)	*Non Pareil*, 25 ft.	New York (June 4)	Southampton, England	43 days	1868
Earliest Solo Sailing	Alfred Johnson (Denmark)	*Centennial*, 20 ft.	Nova Scotia	Wales	46 days	1876
Earliest Woman Sailing	Mrs. Joanna Crapo (Scotland)	*New Bedford*, 20 ft.	Chatham, Mass.	Newlyn, England	51 days	1877
Earliest Single-handed race	J. W. Lawlor (U.S.)	*Sea Serpent*, 15 ft.	Boston (June 17)	Coverack, England	47 days	1891
Earliest Rowing	George Harbo and Frank Samuelson (U.S.)	*Richard K. Fox*, 18½ ft.	New York City (June 6)	Isles of Scilly (Aug. 1)	55 days	1896
Fastest Solo Sailing West-East	J. V. T. McDonald (G.B.)	*Inverarity*, 38 ft.	Nova Scotia	Ireland	16 days	1922
Earliest Canoe (with sail)	E. Romer (Germany)	*Deutches Sport*, 19¼ ft.	Cape St. Vincent (Apr. 17)	St. Thomas, West Indies	58 days	1928
Fastest Solo Sailing East-West (Shortest Route)	Cdr. R. D. Graham (G.B.)	*Emanuel*, 30 ft.	Bantry, Ireland	St. John's, Newfoundland	24.35 days	1934
Earliest Woman Solo-Sailing	Mrs. Ann Davison (G.B.)	*Felicity Ann*, 23 ft.	Plymouth, Eng. (May 18, 1952)	Miami, Florida (Aug. 13, 1953)	454 days	1952–53
Smallest East-West	John Riding (G.B.)	*Sjø Ág*, 12 ft.	Plymouth, Eng. (July, 1964)	Newport, Rhode Is. (Aug. 17, 1965)	403 days	1964–65
Smallest West-East	William Verity (U.S.)	*Nonoalca*, 12 ft.	Ft. Lauderdale, Florida	Tralee, Ireland (July 12)	68 days	1966
Earliest Rowing (G.B.)	Capt. John Ridgway (G.B.) Sgt. Charles Blyth (G.B.)	*English Rose III*, 22 ft.	Cape Cod (June 4)	Inishmore, Ireland (Sept. 3)	91 days	1966
Fastest Crossing Sailing (Trimaran)	Eric Tabarly (France)+2 crew	*Pen Duick IV*, 63 ft.	Tenerife, Madeira	Martinique	251.4 miles/day (10 days 12 hrs.)	1968
Fastest Solo East-West (Northern)	Geoffrey Williams (G.B.)	*Sir Thomas Lipton*, 57 ft.	Plymouth, Eng. (June 1)	Brenton Point, R.I. (June 27)	25.85 days	1968
Fastest Solo Rowing East-West	Sidney Genders, 51 (G.B.)	*Khaggavisana*, 19¾ ft.	Sennen Cove, Eng.	Miami, Florida via Antigua (June 27)	37.3 miles/day	1970
Earliest Solo Rowing East-West	John Fairfax (G.B.)	*Britannia*, 22 ft.	Las Palmas, Canary Is. (Jan. 20)	Ft. Lauderdale, Florida (July 19)	180 days	1969
Fastest Solo East-West (Southern)	Sir Francis Chichester (G.B.)	*Gipsy Moth V*, 57 ft.	Portuguese Guinea	Nicaragua	171.9 miles/day (22.4 days)	1970
Earliest Solo Rowing West-East	Tom McClean (Ireland) (see photo, page 413)	*Super Silver*, 20 ft.	St. John's, Newfoundland (May 17)	Black Sod Bay, Ireland (July 27)	70.7 days	1969

DEEPEST PLUNGE: The U.S. Navy Bathyscaphe "Trieste," which established the last three ocean depth records culminating in a descent to 35,802 feet.

OCEAN DESCENTS—PROGRESSIVE RECORDS

Feet	Vehicle	Divers	Location	Date
c.245	Steel Sphere	Ernest Bazin (France)	Belle Ile, France	1865
c.830	Diving Bell	Balsamello Bella Nautica (Italy)		1889
c.1,650	Hydrostat	Hartman		1911
1,426	Bathysphere	Dr. C. William Beebe and Dr. Otis Barton (U.S.)	S.E. Bermuda	June 11, 1930
2,200	Bathysphere	Dr. C. W. Beebe and Dr. Otis Barton (U.S.)	S.E. Bermuda	Sept. 22, 1932
2,510	Bathysphere	Dr. C. W. Beebe and Dr. Otis Barton (U.S.)	S.E. Bermuda	Aug. 11, 1934
3,028	Bathysphere	Dr. C. W. Beebe and Dr. Otis Barton (U.S.)	S.E. Bermuda	Aug. 15, 1934
7,850	*Converted U-boat*	*Heinz Sellner (Germany) (unwitnessed)*	*Murmansk, U.S.S.R.*	*Aug.,* 1947
4,500	Benthoscope	Dr. Otis Barton (U.S.)	Santa Cruz, Calif.	Aug. 16, 1949
5,085	Bathyscaphe *F.N.R.S.* 3	Lt.-Cdr. Georges S. Houet and Lt. Pierre-Henri Willm (France)	off Toulon, France	Aug. 12, 1953
6,890	Bathyscaphe *F.N.R.S.* 3	Lt.-Cdr. G. S. Houet and Lt. P.-H. Willm (France)	off Cap Ferrat, Fr.	Aug. 14, 1953
10,335	Bathyscaphe *Trieste*	Prof. Auguste and Jacques Piccard (Switzerland)	Ponza Is., Italy	Sept. 30, 1953
13,287	Bathyscaphe *F.N.R.S.* 3	Lt.-Cdr. G. S. Houet and Eng.-Offr. P.-H. Willm (France)	off Dakar, Senegal	Feb. 15, 1954
18,600	Bathyscaphe *Trieste*	Dr. J. Piccard and Andreas B. Rechnitzer (U.S.)	Marianas Trench	Nov. 14, 1959
24,000	Bathyscaphe *Trieste*	Dr. J. Piccard and Lt. D. Walsh, U.S.N.	Marianas Trench	Jan. 7, 1960
35,802	Bathyscaphe *Trieste*	Dr. J. Piccard and Lt. D. Walsh, U.S.N.	Marianas Trench	Jan. 23, 1960

DEEP DIVING—PROGRESSIVE RECORDS

BREATH-HOLDING

Feet	Divers	Location	Date
c. 50	Mother-of-pearl divers	Mediterranean	c. 3,300 B.C.
c. 120	Sponge and oyster divers (limit)	various	—
c. 200	Stotti Georghios (Greece)	Adriatic	1913
198	Jacques Mayol (France)	off Freeport, Grand Bahama	July, 1966
212½	P.O. Robert Croft, U.S.N.	Florida coast	Feb. 8, 1967
§125	Evelyn Patterson (Zambia) (See photo, next page)	off Freeport, Grand Bahama	1967
217½	P.O. Robert Croft, U.S.N.	off Ft. Lauderdale, Fla.	Dec. 19, 1967
231	Jacques Mayol (France)	Mediterranean	Jan. 14, 1968
240	P.O. Robert Croft, U.S.N.	Florida coast	Aug. 12, 1968
242.7	Enzio Maiorca (Italy)		1969
249.3	Jacques Mayol (France)	off Japanese coast	
250	Enzio Maiorca (Italy)	Syracuse, Sicily	Aug. 11, 1971

BREATHING AIR

Feet	Divers	Location	Date
162[1]	A. Lambert (U.K.)	Grand Canary Is.	1885
190[1]	Greek and Swedish divers	off Patras, Greece	1904
210[1]	Lt. G. C. C. Damant, R.N. (U.K.)	Loch Striven, Scotland	1906
274[2]	Chief Gunner S. J. Drellifsak, U.S.N.	from U.S.S. Walke	Oct. 9, 1914
304[2]	F. Crilley, W. F. Loughman, F. C. L. Nielson, U.S.N.	off Hawaii	1915
344[2]	Diver Hilton, R.N. (U.K.)	British waters	1932
307	Frederick Dumas (France)	Mediterranean	1947
†396[3]	Lt. Maurice Farques (France)	Mediterranean	1947
††400[3]	Hope Root (U.S.)	U.S. waters	1953
350[3]	Jean Clarke-Samazen	off Santa Catalina, Calif.	Aug. 1954
§320[3]	Katherine Troutt (Australia)	Sydney Heads, Australia	Sept. 7, 1964
355[3]	Hal D. Watts and Herb Johnson (U.S.)	off Loo Key, Fla.	Sept. 4, 1966
380[3]	Hal D. Watts and Arthur J. Muns (U.S.)	off Miami Beach, Fla.	Sept. 3, 1967
§325[3]	Kitty Giesler (U.S.) (See photo, next page)	off Freeport, Grand Bahama	Oct. 31, 1967
437[3]	John J. Gruener and R. Neal Watson (U.S.)	off Freeport, Grand Bahama	Oct. 14, 1968

BREATHING GAS MIXTURES

Feet	Divers	Location	Date
420[4]	M. G. Nohl (U.S.)	Lake Michigan	Dec. 1, 1937
440[5]	R. M. Metzger and Claude Conger, U.S.N.	Portsmouth, N.H.	June 22, 1941
†528[5]	A. Zetterström (Sweden)	Baltic	Aug. 7, 1945
450[4]	Wilfred H. Bollard and W. Soper, R.N. (U.K.)	Loch Fyne, Scotland	Aug. 26, 1948
540[4]	W. H. Bollard, R.N. (U.K.)	Loch Fyne, Scotland	Aug. 28, 1948
550	Diver J. E. Johnson	Hauriki Gulf, N.Z.	1949
600[4]	Lt.-Cdr. George A. M. Wookey, R.N. (U.K.)	Oslo Fjord, Norway	Oct. 13, 1956
728[6]	Hannes Keller (Switzerland) and Kenneth MacLeish (U.S.)	Lake Maggiore, Italy	June 30, 1961
*1,000[6]	H. Keller (Switzerland) and Peter Small† (U.K.)	off Santa Catalina, Calif.	Dec. 3, 1962
**1,025[4]	U.S. Navy Aquanauts		Feb. 1968
**1,100[4]	Carl Deckman (Int. Underwater Contractors, Inc.)	Murray Hill, N.J.	Mar. 12, 1968
**1,197[4]	Ralph W. Brauer (U.S.) and Réné Veyrunes (France)	Comex Chamber, France	June 27, 1968
**1,500[4]	John Bevan and Peter Sharphouse (U.K.)	Alverstoke, Hampshire	Mar. 11, 1970
**	Patrice Chemin and Bernard Reiuller (France)	Comex Chamber, Marseille, France	Nov. 19, 1970

§ Female record.
† Died on the ascent.
†† Died on the descent.
* Emerged from a diving bell.
** Simulated chamber dive.

[1] Surface supplied, helmet.
[2] Surface supplied, flexible dress.
[3] Scuba (self-contained underwater breathing apparatus).
[4] Oxygen-helium.
[5] Oxygen-hydrogen.
[6] Oxygen-helium plus an additive.

WOMEN'S DEEP DIVING RECORD HOLDERS: Kitty Giesler (left) in 1967 dove 325 feet using scuba. Evelyn Patterson (above) in 1967 dove 125 feet, holding her breath.

Greatest Ocean Descent

The record ocean descent was achieved in the Challenger Deep of the Marianas Trench, 250 miles southwest of Guam, when the Swiss-built U.S. Navy bathyscaphe *Trieste*, manned by Dr. Jacques Piccard (b. 1914) and Lt. Donald Walsh, U.S.N., reached the ocean bed 35,802 feet (6.78 miles) down, at 1:10 p.m. on January 23, 1960. The pressure of the water was 16,883 lbs. per square inch (1,215.6 tons per square foot), and the temperature 37.4° F. The descent required 4 hours 48 minutes and the ascent 3 hours 17 minutes. (See photo, page 416.)

Deep Sea Diving

The world's record depth for a salvage observation chamber was established by the British Admiralty salvage ship *Reclaim* on June 28, 1956. In an observation chamber measuring 7 feet long and 3 feet internal diameter, Senior Commissioned Boatswain (now Lt.-Cdr.) G. A. M. Wookey, descended to a depth of 1,060 feet in Oslo Fjord, Norway.

Salvaging

Deepest. The deepest salvaging operation ever carried out was on the wreck of the S.S. *Niagara*, sunk by a mine in 1940, 438 feet down off Bream Head, Whangarei, North Island, New Zealand. All but 6 per cent of the $6,300,000 of gold in her holds was recovered in 7 weeks. The record recovery was from the White Star Liner *Laurentic*, which was torpedoed in 114 feet of water off Malin Head, Donegal, Ireland, in 1917, with $14,000,000 of gold ingots in her Second Class baggage room. By 1924, 3,186 of the 3,211 gold bricks had been recovered with immense difficulty.

Largest. The largest vessel ever salvaged was the U.S.S. *Lafayette*, formerly the French liner *Normandie* (83,423 tons), which keeled over during fire-fighting operations at the West 49th Street Pier, Hudson River, New York City, on February 9, 1942. She was righted in October, 1943, at a cost of $4,500,000, and was broken up at Newark, New Jersey, beginning in September, 1946.

Most Expensive. The most expensive salvage operation ever conducted was that by the U.S. Navy off Palomares, southern Spain, for the recovery of a 2,800-lb. 20-megaton H-bomb, between January 17 and April 7, 1966, at a cost of $30,000,000. A fleet of 18 ships and 2,200 men took part. A CURV (Cable-controlled Underwater Research Vehicle) was flown from California and retrieved the bomb, which had been dropped from a crashing B-52 bomber, from a depth of 2,850 feet.

Mining Depths

Man's deepest penetration made into the ground is in the East Rand Proprietary Mine in Boksburg, Transvaal, South Africa. In November, 1959, a level of 11,246 feet or 2.13 miles below ground was attained in a pilot winze in the Hercules section. The rock temperature at this depth was 126° F. Incline shafts to a planned depth of 12,000 feet are being worked at Western Deep Levels mine, Klerksdorp, South Africa.

Shaft-Sinking Record. The one-month (31-day) world record is 1,251 feet for a standard shaft 26 feet in diameter at Buffelsfontein Mine, Transvaal, South Africa, in March, 1962.

Endurance

Running. Mensen Ehrnst (1799–1846), of Norway, is reputed to have run from Istanbul, Turkey, to Calcutta, in West Bengal, India, and back in 59 days in 1836, so averaging an improbable 94.2 miles per day. The longest non-stop run recorded is 121 miles 440 yards in 22 hours 27 minutes by Jared R. Beads, 41, of Westport, Maryland, in October, 1969.

The 24-hour running record is 159 miles 562 yards (6 marathons plus 3,532 yards) by Wally H. Hayward, 45 (South Africa) at Motspur Park, Surrey, England, on November 20–21, 1954.

The greatest distance covered by a man in six days (*i.e.* the 144 permissible hours between Sundays in Victorian times) was 623¾ miles by George Littlewood (England), who required only 139 hours 1 min. for this feat in December, 1888, at the old Madison Square Garden, New York City.

The greatest lifetime mileage recorded by any runner is 151,740 miles by Ken Baily of Bournemouth, England, up to June 21, 1972.

Longest Race. The longest race ever staged was the 1929 Transcontinental Race (3,665 miles) from New York City to Los Angeles. The Finnish-born Johnny Salo (killed October 6, 1931) was the winner in 79 days, from March 31 to June 17. His elapsed time of 525 hours 57 minutes 20 seconds gave a running average of 6.97 m.p.h.

Bruce Tulloh (Great Britain), aged 33, the 1962 European 5,000-meter champion, lowered the North American transcontinental record from Los Angeles to New York (2,876 miles) to 64 days 21 hours 50 minutes (average 44.3 miles per day) from 10 a.m. on April 21 to 11:50 a.m. on June 25, 1969. His weight dropped from 116 lbs. to 110 lbs.

Hottest Run. The traverse of the 120-mile-long Death Valley, California, in both directions was uniquely accomplished by Paul Pfau with ground temperatures reaching 140° F. on January 22–24 (30½ elapsed hours) for the southbound and on March 3–5, 1971 (26 hours 10 minutes), for the northbound traverse.

Walking. The greatest distance ever walked literally non-stop is 230.8 miles in 68½ hours near Napier, New Zealand, on September 11–14, 1971, by John Sinclair, 54, of Great Britain.

Chief Warrant Officer Philippe Latulippe of Canada walked 256.00 miles at Ottawa, Canada, on April 23–26, 1972.

The longest officially controlled walking race was that of 3,415 miles from New York to San Francisco, from May 3 to July 24, 1926, won by A. L. Monteverde, aged 60, occupying 79 days 10 hours 10 minutes. In 1909, Edward Payson Weston walked 7,495 miles on a transcontinental-and-return walk in 181 days.

John Lees, 27, of Brighton, England, between April 13 and June 6, 1972, walked 2,876 miles across the U.S. from City Hall, Los Angeles, to City Hall, New York City in 53 days 12 hours 15 minutes (53.746 miles per day). This betters the time of 54 days (average 53.29 miles a day) for *running* the distance by John Ball (South Africa) in May, 1972.

Walking Backwards. The greatest exponent of reverse pedestrianism has been Plennie L. Wingo of Abilene, Texas, who started on his 8,000-mile transcontinental walks on April 15, 1931. from Fort Worth, Texas, to Istanbul, Turkey. His best distance in a day (12½ hours) was 45 miles.

Longest on a Raft. The longest recorded survival alone on a raft is 133 days (4½ months) by Second Steward Poon Lim (born, Hong Kong) of the U.K. Merchant Navy, whose ship, the S.S. *Ben Lomond*, was torpedoed in the Atlantic 750 miles off the Azores at 11:45 a.m. on November 23, 1942. He was picked up by a Brazilian fishing boat off Salinas, Brazil, on April 5, 1943, and was able to walk ashore. In July, 1943, he was awarded the British Empire Medal.

Swimming. The greatest recorded distance ever swum is 1,826 miles in 176 days, with limited stops, down the Mississippi from Ford Dam, near Minneapolis, to New Orleans, July 6 to December 29, 1933, by Fred P. Newton, then 27, of Clinton, Oklahoma. He was in the water a total of 742 hours, and the water temperature fell as low as 47° F. He protected himself with olive oil and axle grease.

The longest duration swim ever achieved was one of 168 continuous hours, ending on February 24, 1941, by the legless Charles Zibbelman, *alias* Zimmy (born 1894) of the U.S., in a pool in Honolulu, Hawaii.

LONGEST ON A RAFT:
Poon Lim, born in Hong
Kong, a steward in the
British Merchant Navy,
survived alone 4½ months
after being torpedoed in
1942.

The greatest distance covered in a continuous swim is 288 miles by Clarence Giles from Glendive, Montana, to Billings, in the Yellowstone River in 71 hours 3 minutes, June 30 to July 3, 1939.

The longest duration swim by a woman was 87 hours 27 minutes in a pool by Mrs. Myrtle Huddleston of New York City, in 1931.

Cycling. The duration record for cycling on a track is 168 hours (7 days) by Syed Muhammed Nawab, aged 22, of Lucknow, India, in Addis Ababa, Ethiopia, in 1964. The monocycle duration record is 11 hours 21 minutes (83.4 miles) by Raymond Le Grand at Maubeuge, France, on September 12, 1955. The longest cycle tour on record is one of 135,000 miles by Mishreelal Jaiswal (born 1924) of India, through 107 countries from 1950 to April 5, 1964, ending in San Francisco. He wore out five machines.

Marriage and Divorce

Longest Engagement. The longest engagement on record is one of 67 years between Octavio Guillen, 82, and Adriana Martinez, 82. They finally took the plunge in June, 1969, in Mexico City.

Most Divorces and Marriages. Mrs. Beverly Nina Avery, then aged 48, a barmaid from Los Angeles, set a monogamous world record in October, 1957, by obtaining her 16th divorce, this one from Gabriel Avery, her 14th husband. She alleged outside the court that five of the 14 had broken her nose.

In Malaya, Abdul Rahman, aged 55, of Kuala Lumpur, married his 23rd wife, aged 16, in October, 1967, but voluntarily never had more than one wife at a time.

The greatest number of marriages in the monogamous world is 19 by Mr. Glynn de Moss Wolfe (U.S.) (b. 1908) who married, for the 19th time since 1930, his 17th wife Gloria, aged 23, on February 22, 1969. He believes he has 31 children. In 1955, he was reputedly worth $500,000 but recently testified to be living on welfare.

Reports in April, 1959, that Francis Van Wie, a conductor on the street cars of San Francisco, had married his 18th wife, one

Minnie Reardon, were later revised when it was discovered that some of his earlier marriages were undissolved.

The widely publicized story of Bora Micic, 44, of Milesevo, Bosnia, who reputedly married 79 times and divorced 78 times between 1944 and 1970, is not regarded as authentic by Yugoslav diplomatic sources.

The most often-marrying millionaire, Thomas F. Manville (1894–1967), contracted his 13th marriage to his 11th wife Christine Erdlen, aged 20, in New York City, on January 11, 1960, when aged 65. His shortest marriage (to his seventh wife) effectively lasted only 34 minutes. His fortune came from asbestos, which he unfortunately could not take with him.

Oldest Bride and Bridegroom. The oldest bridegroom on record was Ralph Cambridge, 105, who married Mrs. Adriana Kapp, 70, at Knysna, South Africa, on September 30, 1971.

Longest Marriage. The longest recorded marriage is one of 86 years between Sir Temulji Bhicaji Nariman and Lady Nariman from 1853 to 1940 resulting from a cousin marriage when both were five. Sir Temulji (born September 3, 1848) died, aged 91 years 11 months, in August, 1940.

Probably the longest marriage now existing is that between Edd (105) and Margaret (99) Hollen (U.S.) who celebrated their 83rd anniversary on May 7, 1972. They were both living in June, 1972. They were married in Kentucky on May 7, 1889.

Most Married. James and Mary Grady of Illinois have married each other 27 times in the period 1964–69, as a protest against the existence of divorce. They have married in 25 different states, 3 times in a day (December 16, 1968), twice in an hour and twice on television.

Mass Ceremony. The largest mass wedding ceremony was one of 791 couples officiated over by Sun Myung Moon of the Holy Spirit Association for the Unification of World Christianity in Seoul, South Korea, in October, 1970. The response to the question "Will you swear to love your spouse for ever?" is "Ye."

STUNTS AND MISCELLANEOUS ENDEAVORS

Apple Peeling. The longest single unbroken apple peel on record is one of 1,568½ inches peeled by Frank Freer (U.S.) in 8 hours at Wolcott, N.Y., on October 17, 1971. The apple was 15 inches in diameter.

Apple Picking. The greatest recorded performance is 235.8 U.S. bushels picked in 8 hours by Harold Oaks, 21, at his father's ranch, Hood River, Oregon, on October 2, 1971.

Baby Carriage Pushing. The greatest distance covered in 24 hours in pushing a perambulator is 272.8 miles on a track by a 20-man team from Brisbane Boy's College, Toowong, Queensland, Australia, on March 18–19, 1972. A 249.5-mile pushing "safari" was completed at altitudes up to 7,000 feet by 4 Round Table teams from Nairobi and Thika, Kenya, on January 8–9, 1972.

Bagpipes. The longest bagpipe performance was 50 hours by William Donaldson, Donald Grant, John Lovie and William Wotherspoon of Aberdeen University, Scotland, on April 21–23, 1969. The comment of some local inhabitants after the "lang blaw" was "Thank God there's nae smell."

Balancing on One Foot. The longest recorded duration for balancing on one foot is 5½ hours by Olof Hedlund, 19, at Skelleftea, Sweden, on February 3, 1972. The disengaged foot may not be rested on the standing foot nor may any sticks be used for support or balance.

Balloon Racing. The largest balloon release on record has been one of 100,000 helium balloons at the opening of "Transpo 72" at Dulles Airport, Washington, D.C., on May 27, 1972. The longest authenticated balloon flight is one of 1,200 miles from Grantham Football Ground, Lincolnshire, England (released by R. Fenn on August 31, 1971), and found near Skelleftea, northern Sweden, on October 24, 1971.

Ballooning (Hot-Air). The world's endurance and distance records for hot-air ballooning are 8 hours 30 minutes by Matt Wiedertehr, 42, in an AX-5 from St. Paul, Minnesota, 255 miles to Bankston, Iowa, on March 29, 1972. The altitude record is 31,500 feet by Karl H. Stefan, 54, on June 19, 1971. The record-holder for hot-air ballooning records is Ray Munro with 34 ratified records. On February 1, 1970, he flew 158.34 miles across the Irish Sea in 4 hours 52 minutes. He also has 50 honorary citizenships.

Ball Punching. Ron Reunalf (Australia) equaled his own world duration ball-punching record of 125 hours 20 minutes at 10:20 p.m. on December 31, 1955, at the Esplanade, Southport, Queensland, Australia.

BALLOON CHAMPION: Ray Munro (Canada) holds 34 ratified records. He also flew 158.34 miles across the Irish Sea in less than 5 hours.

Band Marathons. The longest recorded "blow-in" is 8 hours by the Harwich Grange Brass Band at Dovercourt, Essex, England, on August 14, 1971. Each bandsman was allowed 5 minutes per hour to regain his wind. The record for a one-man band is 7 hours (no breaks) by Johnny Magoo on drums, harmonica and stylaphone at Strood, Kent, England, on May 22, 1971.

Barrel Jumping. The greatest number of barrels jumped by a skater is 17 (total length 28 feet 8 inches) by Kenneth LeBel at the Grossinger Country Club, Liberty, New York, on January 9, 1965.

Bed of Nails. The duration record for lying on a bed of nails (needle-sharp 6-inch nails, 2 inches apart) is 25 hours 20 minutes by Vernon C. Craig (Komar, the Hindu *fakir*) at Wooster, Ohio, July 22–23, 1971. The greatest weight borne on a bed of nails is also by Komar with 4 persons aggregating 992 lbs. standing on him in Honolulu, Hawaii, on February 7, 1972.

Much longer durations are claimed by unwitnessed *fakirs*—the most extreme case being *Silki* who claimed 111 days in Sao Paulo, Brazil, ending on August 24, 1969.

Bed Pushing. The longest recorded push of a normally stationary object is 604 miles in the case of a wheeled hospital bed by a team of 12 from Box Hill High School, Victoria, Australia, on August 19–24, 1972.

Bed Race. The record time for the annual Knaresborough Bed Race (established 1966) in Yorkshire, England, is 15 minutes 54 seconds for the 2½-mile course across the River Nidd by the Leeds Regional Hospital Board team, from a field of 34, on June 5, 1971.

Best Best Man. The world's champion "best man" is Wally Gant, a bachelor fishmonger from Wakefield, Yorkshire, England, who officiated for the 50th time since 1931 in December, 1964.

Bomb Defusing. The highest reported number of unexploded bombs defused by any individual is 8,000 by Werner Stephan in West Berlin, Germany, in the 12 years from 1945 to 1957. He was killed by a small grenade on the Grünewald blasting site on August 17, 1957.

Bond Signing. The greatest feat of bond signing was performed by L. E. Chittenden (died 1902), the Registrar of the United States Treasury. In 48 hours (March 20–22, 1863), he signed 12,500 bonds worth $10,000,000, which had to catch a steam packet to England. He suffered years of pain thereafter and the bonds were never used.

Boomerang Throwing. Two types of boomerang are used by the natives of Australia: the return type, aimed against birds and used as a plaything, and the war boomerang or throwing stick. The longest measured throws of a return type are ones of 90 yards with an orbital perimeter of 250 yards with 6-oz. vulcanized fiber boomerangs by Bob and Jack Burwell of Slack's Creek, Queensland. These have been kept airborne for 18.4 secs. In November, 1971, Jeff Lewry (Australia) threw well past a steward at 85½ yards at Palmerston, New Zealand, with a 16-inch boomerang.

Brick Carrying. The record for carrying a brick (8¾ lbs.) without dropping or resting is 40 miles by Ronald D. Hamilton of

17 BARRELS: Kenneth LeBel setting the record of 28′ 8″ in 1965.

Arthur River, Western Australia, on October 10, 1970, at Wagga Wagga, New South Wales. The wire-cut semi-pressed brick has to be carried in a downward position with a nominated ungloved hand.

The feminine record for a 7¾-lb. brick is 1.6 miles by Pat McDougall, aged 16, but Jeannette Bartlett of Swindon, Wiltshire, England, carried an 8-lb.-13¾-oz. brick more than 1.49 miles on July 4, 1969.

Bricklaying. The world record for bricklaying was established in 1937 by Joseph Raglon of East St. Louis, Illinois, who, supported by assistants, placed 3,472 bricks in 60 minutes of foundation-work—at a rate of nearly 58 a minute.

The record for constructional bricklaying was set when J. E. Bloxham, of Stratford-upon-Avon, England, laid a 13½-foot wall of 5,188 bricks in 7 hours 35 minutes with two assistants on May 28, 1960.

Brick Throwing. The greatest reported distance for throwing a standard 5-lb. building brick is 135 feet 8 in. by Robert Gardner at Stroud, Gloucestershire, England, on July 18, 1970.

Burial Alive. The longest recorded burial alive is one of 100 days ending on September 17, 1968, in Skegness by Mrs. Emma Smith of Ravenshead, Nottinghamshire, England. The coffin was at a depth of 10 feet.

Largest Circus. The world's largest permanent circus is Circus Circus, Las Vegas, Nevada, opened on October 18, 1968, at a cost of $15,000,000. It covers an area of 129,000 square feet capped by a 90-foot-high tent-shaped flexiglass roof. (See Circus Stunt records, next page.)

The new Moscow Circus, completed in 1968, has a seating capacity of 3,200.

Clapping. The duration record for continuous clapping is 14 hours 6 minutes by Nicholas Willey, 18, and Christopher Floyd, 17,

CIRCUS RECORDS

The following circus acrobatic feats represent the greatest performed, either for the first time or, if marked with an asterisk, uniquely. A "mechanic" is a safety harness.

Category	Feat	Performer	Location	Date
Flying Trapeze	Earliest Act	Jules Leotard (France)	Circus Napoleon, Paris	Nov. 12, 1859
	Double back somersault (female)	Eddie Silbon	Paris Hippodrome	1879
	Triple back somersault (female)	Lena Jordan (Latvia) to Lew Jordan (U.S.)	Sydney, Australia	Apr., 1897
	Triple back somersault (male)	Ernest Clarke to Charles Clarke	Publiones Circus, Cuba	1909
	Triple and a half back somersault	Tony Steele to Lee Strath Marilees	Durango, Mexico	Sept. 30, 1962
	Quadruple back somersault (in practice)	*Ernest Clarke to Charles Clarke	Orrin Bros. Circus, Mexico City, Mexico	1915
	Triple back somersault (bar to bar, practice)	Edmund Ramat and Raoul Monbar	Various	1905–10
	Head to head stand on swinging bar (no holding)	*Ed. and Ira Millette (née Wolf)	Various	1910–20
Horseback	Running leaps on and off	*26 by "Poodles" Hanneford	New York City	1915
	Three-high column without "mechanic"	*Willy, Baby and Rene Fredianis	Nouveau Cirque, Paris	1908
	Double back somersault mounted	(John or Charles) Frederic Clarke	Various	c. 1905
	Double back somersault from a 2-high to a trailing horse with "mechanic"	Aleksandr Sergey	Moscow Circus	1956
Fixed Bars	Pass from 1st to 3rd bar with a double back somersault	Phil Shevette, Andres Atayde	Woods Gymnasium, New York City-European tours	1925–27
	Triple flyaway to ground (male)	Phil Shevette	Folies Bergère, Paris	May, 1896
	Triple flyaway to ground (female)	Loretto Twins, Ora and Pauline	Los Angeles	1914
	Running forward triple back somersault	John Cornish Worland (1855–1933) of the U.S.	St. Louis, Missouri	1874
	Back somersault feet to feet	Richard Risley Carlisle (1814–74) and son (U.S.)	Theatre Royal, Edinburgh.	Feb., 1844
Giant Springboard Risley (Human Juggling) Acrobatics	Quadruple back somersault to a chair	Sylvester Mezzetti (voltigeur) to Butch Mezzetti (catcher)	New York Hippodrome	1915–17
Aerialist	One arm swings 125 (no net) 32 feet up.	Vicky Unus (La Toria) (U.S.)	Ringling Bros., Barnum & Bailey circuit	Nov., 1962
Teeter Board	Seat to seat triple back somersault	The 5 Draytons		1896
	16 hoops (hands and feet)	Ala Naito (Japan) (female)	Madison Square Garden, N.Y.C.	1937
Wire-Juggling		Con Colleano	Empire Theatre, Johannesburg.	1923
Low Wire (7 feet)	Feet to feet forward somersault	Ala Naito (Japan) (female)	Madison Square Garden, N.Y.C.	1937
High Wire (30–40 feet)	Four high column (with mechanic)	*The Solokhin Brothers (U.S.S.R.)	Moscow Circus	1962
	Three layer, 7 man pyramid	Great Wallendas (Germany)	U.S.	1961
	Stationary double back somersault	Francois Gouleau (France)		1905
Ground Acrobatics	Four high column	The Picchianis (Italy)		1905
	Five high pyramids	The Yacopis (Argentina) with 3 understanders, 3 second layer understanders, 1 middleman, 1 upper middleman and a top mounter.	Ringling Bros., Barnum & Bailey circuit	1941

of Canford School, Dorset, England on December 13–14, 1968. They sustained an average of 140 claps per minute and an audibility range of at least 100 yards.

Club Swinging. Bill Franks set a world record of 17,280 revolutions (4.8 per second) in 60 minutes at Webb's Gymnasium, Newcastle, N.S.W., Australia, on August 2, 1934. M. Dobrilla swung continuously for 144 hours at Cobar, N.S.W., Australia, finishing on September 15, 1913.

Coal Carrying. The record time for the annual "World Coal Carrying Championship" over the uphill 1,080-yard course at Ossett cum Gawthorpe, Yorkshire, England, with a 112-lb. sack is 4 minutes 36 seconds by Tony Nicholson, 26, on April 3, 1972.

Coal Shoveling. The record for filling a 1,120-lb. hopper with coal is 56.6 secs. by D. Coghlan of Reefton, New Zealand, on January 3, 1969.

Commuter. Bruno Leuthardt commuted 370 miles each day for 10 years (1957–67) from Hamburg to teach in the Bodelschwingh School, Dortmund, West Germany. He was late only once, due to the 1962 Hamburg floods.

Dancing. Marathon dancing must be distinguished from dancing mania, which is a pathological condition. The worst outbreak of dancing mania was at Aachen, Germany, in July, 1374, when hordes

MARATHON DANCERS: For 22 weeks 3½ days Callum De Villier and Vonnie Kuchinski continued dancing in 1933, the last two weeks with 3 minutes rest per hour, and the last 52½ hours without rest. The prize of $1,000 was the equivalent of 26½ cents per hour.

of men and women broke into a frenzied dance in the streets which lasted for hours till injury or complete exhaustion ensued.

The most severe marathon dance (staged as a public spectacle in the U.S.) was one lasting 3,780 hours (22 weeks 3½ days). This was completed by Callum L. De Villier, now of Minneapolis, and Miss Vonnie Kuchinski in Somerville, Massachusetts, from December 28, 1932, to June 3, 1933. In the last two weeks the rest allowance was cut from 15 minutes per hour to only 3 minutes while the last 52½ hours were continuous. The prize of $1,000 was equivalent to less than 26½ cents per hour. (See photo, previous page.)

Largest. The largest dance ever held was that put on by the Houston Livestock Show at the Astro Hall, Houston, Texas, on February 8, 1969. The attendance was 16,500, with 4,000 turned away.

Dancing, Ballet. Among the world's greatest ballet dancers, Vatslav Fomich Nijinsky (1890–1950), a Russian-born Pole, was alone in being credited with being able to achieve the *entrechat dix—* crossing and uncrossing the feet 10 times in a single elevation. This is not believed by physical education experts, since no high jumper can stay off the ground for more than one second, and no analyzable film exists.

The greatest number of spins called for in classical ballet choreography is the 32 *fouettes en tournant* in "Swan Lake" by Pyotr Ilyich Chaykovskiy (Tschaikovsky) (1840–93). Rowena Jackson, of New Zealand, achieved 121 such turns at her class in Melbourne, Victoria, Australia, in 1940.

The greatest recorded number of curtain calls ever received by ballet dancers is 89 by Dame Peggy Arias, *née* Hookham (born in Reigate, Surrey, England, May 18, 1919) *alias* Margot Fonteyn and Rudolf Hametovich Nureyev (born in a train near Ufa, U.S.S.R., March 17, 1939) after a performance of "Swan Lake" at the Vienna Staatsoper, Austria, in October, 1964. (See photos, next page.)

Dancing, Ballroom. The individual continuous world record is 106 hours 5 minutes 10 seconds by Carlos Sandrini in Buenos Aires, Argentina, in September, 1955. Three girls worked shifts as his partner.

The world's most successful professional ballroom dancing champions have been Bill Irvine and Bobbie Irvine, of London, who have been undefeated as World Professional Champions since 1960.

Dancing, Charleston. The Charleston duration record is 25 hours by Tom Garrett, 23, at Pensacola, Florida, on October 8–9, 1971. (See photo.)

Dancing, Flamenco. The fastest flamenco dancer ever measured is Solero de Jerez, aged 17, who, in Brisbane, Australia, in September, 1967, in an electrifying routine attained 16 heel taps per second or a rate of 1,000 a minute.

Dancing, Go-Go. The duration record for go-go dancing is 108 hours (with 5-minute breaks each hour) by Jane Berins, 16, of Glinton, Peterborough, England, on March 24–28, 1970.

Dancing, Jive. The duration record for non-stop jiving is 40 hours by Gordon Lightfoot and Kathleen Fowler at Penrith, England, on

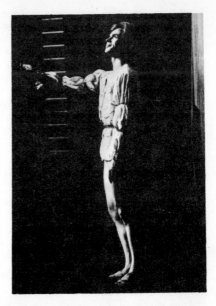

CURTAIN CALL RECORD: Ballet stars, Dame Margot Fonteyn (left) and Rudolf Nureyev (right) taking one of their record 89 curtain calls in the Vienna State Opera House.

CHARLESTON RECORD being set by Tom Garrett of Panama City, Florida, in Pensacola in October, 1971.

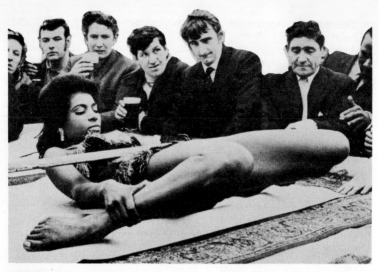

LIMBO DANCER who has sunk the lowest (to 6½ inches) in passing under the bar is Teresa Marquis of the island of St. Lucia in the Caribbean, the area where the dance originated.

April 22–24, 1960. Breaks of 3½ minutes per hour were permitted for massage. This time was equaled by Terry Ratcliffe, aged 16, and Christina Woodcroft, aged 17, at Traralgon, Victoria, Australia, from 10:15 p.m. on May 28 to 2:13 p.m. on May 30, 1965.

Dancing, Limbo. The lowest height for a bar under which a clothed limbo dancer has passed is 6½ inches by Teresa Marquis of St. Lucia, West Indies, at the Guinness Distribution Depot, Grosvenor Road, Belfast, Northern Ireland, on April 15, 1970. Her vital statistics are 35–24–36.

Dancing the Twist. The duration record for the twist is 102 hours by Mrs. Cathie Connelly (now Mrs. Harvey) at Tyldesley, Lancashire, England, on November 29, 1964. She had 5 minutes time out per hour and 20 minutes every 4 hours.

Dancing, Modern. The longest recorded dancing marathon (50 minutes per hour) in popular style is one of 74½ hours by Julia Reece and Vic Jones at the Starlight Ballroom, Crawley, Sussex, England, on July 9–12, 1970.

Dancing, Most Expensive Course. The most expensive dance course was the "Lifetime Executive Course" of Arthur Murray (born Murray Teichmann, April 4, 1895). It comes after the Lifetime Course ($7,300) and the $9,000 "Gold Medal Course" and costs $12,000, making a total of $28,300.

Dance Band. The longest recorded non-stop playing of a dance band was 201 hours on Station WCOH, Yonkers, N.Y. (now WFAS, White Plains, N.Y.), by Wendell G. Merritt and his Music of Merit, starting at 10:03 p.m. on November 6, 1928. Their last two tunes were *Bye Bye Blues* and *Ain't She Sweet*.

The most protracted session of any beat group is one of 321 hours (13 days 9 hours) by the Black Brothers of Bonn, West Germany, ending on January 2, 1969. Never less than a quartet were in action during the marathon.

Disc Jockey. The longest continuous period of acting as a disc jockey is 506 hours by Robert Airbright, 20, at the Sighthill Community Centre, Edinburgh, Scotland, June 4 to 25, 1971. L.P.'s are limited to 50 per cent of total playing time. Jr. Tech. Peter Jackson, R.A.F., played 3,200 singles without rest periods for 144 hours on the Leeming Forces Network, Yorkshire, England, ending on April 14, 1972.

Drumming. The world's duration drumming record is 171 hours 2 minutes by Trevor Mitchell, 20, at Oswald Hotel, Scunthorpe, Lincolnshire, England, July 31 to August 7, 1971. He had a 5-minute rest allowance per hour.

Ducks and Drakes. The best accepted ducks and drakes (stone-skipping) or Gerplunking record is 17 skips by Commander E. F. Tellefson, U.S.N., of Mackinac Island, Michigan, in 1932. The modern video-tape verified record is a 13 skipper (7 plinkers and 6 pitty-pats) by Rolf Anselm in the Open Championship at Mackinac, Michigan, on July 2, 1971.

Egg and Spoon Racing. David Smith and Peter Dilley of Chigwell, Essex, England, completed a local 20-mile fresh egg and dessert spoon marathon in 5 hours 25 minutes on July 27, 1969.

Egg Throwing. The longest recorded distance for throwing a fresh hen's egg without breaking it is 303 feet 6 inches at their 119th exchange by Rauli Rapo and Markku Kuikka at Rilhimäki, Finland, on October 28, 1971.

Escapology. The most renowned of all escape artists has been Ehrich Weiss *alias* Harry Houdini (1874–1926), who pioneered underwater escapes from locked, roped and weighted containers while handcuffed and shackled with irons. Jack Gently performed an escape from a straightjacket when suspended from a crane 135 feet from the ground for English television on August 16, 1971.

Face Slapping. The face-slapping contest duration record was set in Kiev, U.S.S.R., in 1931, when a draw was declared between Vasiliy Bezbordny and Goniusch after 30 hours.

Ferris Wheel Riding. Endurance record for big wheel riding is 14 days 21 hours by David Trumayne, 22, at Ramsgate, Kent, England, ending on June 8, 1969. He completed 62,207 revolutions. Richard Ford, 30, sat for 20 days 16½ hours in a 40-foot Ferris wheel in San Francisco, in January, 1971. It did not, however, revolve at night.

Frisbee Throwing. Competitive Frisbee throwing began in 1958. The longest throw over level ground on record is one of 285 feet by Robert F. May in San Francisco on July 2, 1971.

Grave Digging. It is recorded that Johann Heinrich Karl Thieme, sexton of Aldenburg, Germany, dug 23,311 graves during a 50-year career. In 1826, his understudy dug *his* grave.

Guitar Playing. The longest recorded solo guitar playing marathon is one of 93 hours by Peter Baco, 21, in Winnipeg, Canada, in July, 1970.

Hairdressing. The world record for non-stop barbering is 80 hours (610 heads) by Rolf Elfso at Engelen, Stockholm, Sweden, on November 27–30, 1970. During the same marathon, Gabino Padron dried and blow-waved 442 customers in 51 hours. "Mr. Richard" (the late Richard McGarth) cut, set and styled hair for 80 hours at Raymond's Salon, Colchester, Essex, England, on October 8–11, 1971.

The most expensive men's hairdresser is Tristan of Hollywood, who charges any "client" $100 on a first visit. This consists of a "consultation" followed by "remedial grooming."

Handshaking. The world record for handshaking was set up by President Theodore Roosevelt (1858–1919), who shook hands with 8,513 people at a New Year's Day White House Presentation in Washington, D.C., on January 1, 1907. Outside public life the record has become meaningless because aspirants merely arrange circular queues and shake the same hands repetitively.

High Diving. The highest regularly performed dive is that of professional divers from La Quebrada ("the break in the rocks") at Acapulco, Mexico, a height of 118 feet. The leader of the 25 divers in the exclusive Club de Clavadistas is Raul García (born 1928). The base rocks are 21 feet out from the take-off, necessitating a leap 27 feet out. The water is only 12 feet deep. (See photo.)

On May 18, 1885, Sarah Ann Henley, aged 24, jumped from the Clifton Suspension Bridge across the Avon, England. Her 250-foot fall was slightly cushioned by her voluminous dress and petticoat acting as a parachute. She landed, bruised and bedraggled, in the mud on the Gloucestershire bank and was carried to hospital by four policemen.

On February 11, 1968, Jeffrey Kramer, 24, leaped off the George Washington Bridge 250 feet above the Hudson River, New York City, and survived. Of the 436 people who have made suicide dives from the Golden Gate Bridge, San Francisco, California, 1937–71, only 4 have survived.

On July 10, 1921, a stuntman named Terry leapt from a hydroplane into the Ohio River at Louisville. The alleged altitude was 310 feet.

The celebrated dive, allegedly of 203 feet, made in 1919, by Alex Wickham, from a rock into the Yarra River in Melbourne, Victoria, Australia, was in fact from a height of 96 feet 5 inches. Samuel Scott (U.S.) is reputed to have made a dive of 497 feet at Pattison Fall (now Manitou Falls) in Wisconsin, in 1840, but this would have entailed an entry speed of 86 m.p.h. The actual height was probably 165 feet.

Hiking. The longest recorded hike is one of 18,500 miles through 14 countries from Singapore to London by David Kwan, aged 22, which occupied 81 weeks from May 4, 1957, or an average of 32 miles a day.

Hitchhiking. The title of world champion hitch-hiker is claimed by Devon Smith who from 1947 to 1971 thumbed lifts totaling

HIGHEST DIVE PERFORMED REGULARLY: At Acapulco, Mexico, professional divers fling themselves from La Quebrada ("the break in the rocks") 118 feet above the water to thrill the crowds. The water is only 12 feet deep. Since the base rocks extend 21 feet out from the take-off point, the divers have to jump 27 feet forward.

291,000 miles. In 1957, he covered all the then 48 U.S. states in 33 days. It was not till his 6,013th hitch that he got a ride in a Rolls Royce.

Hoop Rolling. In 1968 it was reported that Zolilio Diaz (Spain) had rolled a hoop 600 miles from Mieres to Madrid and back in 18 days.

House of Cards. The greatest number of stories achieved in building houses of cards is 34 in the case of a tower using 7 packs by R. F. Gompers of the University of Kent, Canterbury, England,

HUMAN CANNONBALLS: Emanuel Zacchini performs this X-15 double rocket act with another member of the Zacchini family in the Ringling Bros.—Barnum & Bailey Circus. He set the men's record for longest distance shot from a cannon in 1940 with 175 feet at a muzzle velocity of 145 m.p.h. On his retirement, the management was fortunate in finding that his daughter-in-law, Florinda, was of the same caliber.

on May 3, 1971. The highest claim authenticated by affidavit for a 7- or 8-card-per-story house is 27 stories by Joe Whitlam of Barnsley, Yorkshire, England, on February 28, 1972.

Human Cannonball. The record distance for firing a human from a cannon is 175 feet in the case of Emanuel Zacchini in the Ringling Bros. and Barnum & Bailey Circus, in 1940. His muzzle velocity was 145 m.p.h. On his retirement the management was fortunate in finding that his daughter-in-law, Florinda, was of the same caliber.

Juggling. The only juggler in history able to juggle—as opposed to "shower"—10 balls or 8 plates was the Italian Enrico Rastelli, who was born in Samara, Russia, on December 19, 1896, and died in Bergamo, Italy, on December 13, 1931.

Kissing. The most prolonged osculatory marathon in cinematic history is one of 185 seconds by Regis Toomey and Jane Wyman in *You're In the Army Now*, released in 1940.

Kite Flying. The greatest reported height attained by kites is 35,530 feet by a train of 19 flown near Portage, Indiana, by 10 Gary high school boys. The flight took 7 hours and was assessed by telescopic triangulation.

The longest recorded flight is one of 44½ hours by Patrick Dunlop, 15, of San Diego, on April 3, 1972.

Knitting. The longest recorded non-stop knitting marathon is one of 90 hours by Mrs. Janice Marwick (with 5-minute time-out allowances per hour), at Pukekohe, New Zealand, August 30–September 3, 1971.

The most prolific hand-knitter of all time is Mrs. Gwen Matthewman (b. 1927) of Featherstone, Yorkshire, England, who retired on December 31, 1970. In her last year she knitted 615 garments involving 438 lbs. 14 oz. of wool (equivalent to the fleece of 57 sheep). She had been timed to average 108 stitches per minute in a 30-minute test. Her technique has been filmed by the world's only Professor of Knitting—a Japanese.

The finest recorded knitting is a piece made with 2,464 stitches per square inch by Douglas Milne of Mount Florida, Glasgow, Scotland, in May, 1969.

Knot Tying. The non-stop knot-tying marathon record is 76,504 links of a drummer's chain knot in ¾-inch tarred sisal rope in 50½ hours by four members of the 9th Beds. (Biggleswade) Scout Troop of England, May 29–31, 1969.

Leap Frogging. Fifteen members of the International Budo Association, Dinnington, Yorkshire, England, covered 40 miles in 6,764 leaps on a 440-yard track on March 25, 1972. An average of more than 40 leaps per lap was maintained.

Lightning-struck. The only living man in the world to be struck by lightning 4 times is Park Ranger Roy "Dooms" C. Sullivan (U.S.), the human lightning-conductor of Virginia. Dooms' attraction for lightning began in 1942 (lost big toe nail), and was resumed in July, 1969 (lost eye brows), in July, 1970 (left shoulder seared) and, *finally* he hopes, on April 16, 1972 (hair set on fire).

Lion Taming. The greatest number of lions mastered and fed in a cage simultaneously by an unaided lion-tamer was 40, by "Captain" Alfred Schneider in 1925. (See photo, next page.)

Clyde Raymond Beatty (1903–65) likewise handled more than 40 "cats" (mixed lions and tigers) simultaneously. Twenty-one lion-tamers have died of injuries since 1900. The youngest legally licensed animal trainer is Carl Ralph Scott Norman (Captain Carl) of Cardforth, Yorkshire, England (b. March 23, 1968) who was licensed on March 13, 1970, aged 1 year 11 months.

Log Rolling. The most protracted log-rolling contest on record was one in Chequamegon Bay, Ashland, Wisconsin, in 1900, when

CHAMPION LION-TAMER: Alfred Schneider is the only man to have tackled 40 lions simultaneously.

Allan Stewart dislodged Joe Oliver from a 24-inch diameter log after 3 hours 15 minutes birling.

Message in a Bottle. The longest voyage recorded for a message in a bottle was one of 25,000 miles, from the Pacific to the shore of the island of Sylt in the North Sea on December 3, 1968. The bottle had been dropped on May 27, 1947.

Morse Code. The highest recorded speed at which anyone has received Morse code is 75.2 words per minute—over 17 symbols per second. This was achieved by Ted R. McElroy (U.S.) in a tournament at Asheville, North Carolina, on July 2, 1939.

Motorcycle Stunting. The greatest number of "bodies" cleared in a motorcycle ramp jump is 41 by Sgt.-Maj. Thomas Gledhill, 41, of the Royal Artillery Motorcycle Display Team on a 441-c.c. B.S.A. Victor G.P. at Woolwich, Greater London, on June 4, 1971. Tony Yeates cleared 84 feet (*equivalent* to 55 men) at Swindon, England, in 1970.

The so-called T-bone dives by motorcycles off ramps over parked cars are measured by the number of cars but, owing to their variable size, distance is more significant. Gary Davis and Rex Blackwell both cleared 21 Datsun cars taking off at 85 m.p.h. in 138-foot jumps in Ontario, California, in March, 1972. Evel Knievel, who jumped over 19 regular-size and compact cars (129 feet), claims that no more than 17 cars were cleared by Blackwell-Davis.

The greatest endurance feat on a "wall of death" was 3 hours 4 minutes by the motorcyclist Louis W. "Speedy" Babbs on a 32-foot diameter silo, refuelling in motion, at the Venice Amusement Pier, California, on October 11, 1929. In 1934, Babbs performed 1,003 consecutive loop-the-loops, sitting side-saddle in an 18-foot diameter globe at Ocean Park Pier, California. In a life of stunting, Babbs, who proclaims "Stuntmen are not fools," has broken 56 bones.

Needle Threading. The record number of strands of cotton threaded through a number 13 needle (eye $\frac{11}{16}$ of an inch by $\frac{1}{16}$ of an inch) in 2 hours is 3,795 by Brenda Robinson of the College of Further Education, Chippenham, Wiltshire, England, on March 20, 1971.

Omelette Making. The greatest number of two-egg omelettes made in 30 minutes is 105 (26 minutes 25 seconds) by Clement Raphael Freud (b. 1924) at The Victoria, Nottingham, England, on July 15, 1971.

The world's largest omelette occurred at Key West, Florida, on October 14, 1971, when a truck carrying 60,000 eggs overturned and caught fire.

Pancake Tossing. Roy Woodward of the Preston Venture Scouts Unit, Wembley, London, succeeded in tossing a pancake 2,105 times at Ealing, England, on February 15, 1972.

Parachute, Earliest Descent. The earliest demonstration of a quasi-parachute was by Sebastien Lenormand (France), with a conical canopy from an observation tower in Montpelier, France, in 1783. The first successful parachute jump from a balloon was by André-Jacques Garnerin (1769–1823) from 2,230 feet over Monceau Park, Paris, France, on October 22, 1797. The earliest descent from an airplane was that of Captain Albert Berry, U.S. Army, over St. Louis, Missouri, on March 1, 1912. The first free fall from an aircraft was by Leslie L. Irvin (1895–1965) of the U.S. on April 19, 1919.

Parachute, Longest Delayed Drop. The longest delayed drop and the greatest altitude for any parachute descent was achieved by U.S. Air Force Captain Joseph W. Kittinger, D.F.C., aged 32, over Tularosa, New Mexico, on August 16, 1960. He stepped out of a balloon at 102,200 feet for a free fall of 84,700 feet (16.04 miles) lasting 4 minutes 38 seconds, during which he reached a speed of 614 m.p.h., despite a stabilizing drogue. He experienced a temperature of −94° F. His 28-foot parachute opened at 17,500 feet and he landed after a total time of 13 minutes 8 seconds. The step by the gondola door was inscribed "This is the highest step in the world."

The women's delayed drop record is 46,250 feet (8.76 miles) by O. Komissarova (U.S.S.R.) on September 21, 1965.

The world record for the greatest number of free-falling parachutists to form a hand-holding circle is 24 over Perris Valley,

LONGEST FREE FALL: When Capt. Kittinger of the U.S.A.F. stepped out of his balloon gondola at 102,200 feet, he was automatically photographed as he dropped 16.04 miles (84,700 feet) before his chute opened.

California (70 seconds of maneuver from 14,500 feet) on January 16, 1972.

Parachute, Highest Escape. The greatest altitude from which a successful parachute *escape* has been made from an aircraft is from a Canberra jet bomber by Flt.-Lt. John de Salis, aged 29, and Fg. Off. Patrick Lowe, aged 23, of the British Royal Air Force, over Monyash, Derbyshire, England, on April 9, 1958. Their plane exploded at 56,000 feet (10.60 miles) and they fell free in a temperature of —70°F. to a height of 10,000 feet at which altitude their parachutes were automatically opened.

The longest descent recorded was one by Lt.-Col. William H. Rankin, U.S.M.C., from an F8U jet fighter at 47,000 ft. on July 26, 1959. His "descent" through a thunderstorm over North Carolina took 40 minutes instead of 11 minutes because of violent upward air currents.

Parachute, Heaviest Load. The greatest single load ever dropped by parachute is 50,450 lbs. of steel plates from a U.S. Air Force C-130 Hercules with 6 chutes near El Centro, California, on January 28, 1970.

The largest parachute made is a U.S. Air Force cargo parachute with a 100-foot diameter, reported in September, 1964.

Parachute, Most Descents. The greatest number of parachute jumps is over 5,000 by Lt.-Col. Ivan Savkin (U.S.S.R.) (born 1913) who reached 5,000 on August 12, 1967. Since 1935, he has spent 27 hours in free fall, 587 hours floating, and has dropped 7,800 miles. The speed record is 81 jumps in 8 hours 22 minutes by Michael Davis, 24, and Richard Bingham, 25, at Columbus, Ohio, on June 26, 1966.

Parachute, Longest Fall Without Parachute. The greatest altitude from which anyone has bailed out without a parachute and survived is 22,000 feet. This occurred in January, 1942, when Lt. (now Lt.-Col.) I. M. Chisov (U.S.S.R.) fell from an Ilyushin 4 which had been severely damaged. He struck the ground a glancing blow on the edge of a snow-covered ravine and slid to the bottom. He suffered a fractured pelvis and severe spinal damage. It is estimated that the human body reaches 99 per cent of its low level terminal velocity after falling 1,880 feet. This is 117–125 m.p.h. at normal atmospheric pressure in a random posture, but up to 185 m.p.h. in a head-down position.

Vesna Vulovic, 23, a Jugoslavenski Aerotransport hostess, survived when her DC-9 blew up at 33,330 feet over the Czechoslovak village of Ceska Kamenice on January 26, 1972. She was found inside a section of tail unit.

Parachute, Greatest Landing Height. The record landing height for parachute jumps is 23,405 feet by 10 U.S.S.R. parachutists onto the summit of Lenina Peak, reported in May, 1969. Four of the ten were killed.

The highest jump ever achieved from a building is from the top of the KTUL-TV tower at Tulsa, Oklahoma, by Herb Schmidt on October 4, 1970. The tower variously claimed to be between 1,800 and 1,984 feet tall.

Parachute, Most Northerly. The most northerly parachute jump was made at 89° 30′ N. on the polar ice cap on March 31, 1969, by Ray Munro, 47, of Lancaster, Ontario, Canada. His eyes were frozen shut instantly in the temperature of —39° F. (See photo, page 423.)

Party Giving. The most expensive private party ever thrown was that of Mr. and Mrs. Bradley Martin of Troy, N.Y. It was staged at the Waldorf-Astoria Hotel, New York City, in February, 1897. The cost to the host and hostess was estimated to be $369,200 in the days when dollars were made of gold.

Piano Playing. The longest piano-playing marathon has been one of 1,091 hours (45 days 11 hours) playing 22 hours every day from October 11 to November 24, 1970, by James Crowley, Jr., 30, in Scranton, Pennsylvania.

The women's world record is 133 hours (5 days 13 hours) by Mrs. Marie Ashton, aged 40, in a theatre at Blyth, Northumberland, England, on August 18–23, 1958.

Piano Smashing. The record time for demolishing an upright piano and passing the entire wreckage through a circle 9 inches in diameter is 2 minutes 26 seconds by six men representing Ireland led by Johnny Leydon of Sligo, at Merton, Surrey, England, on September 7, 1968.

The fastest time in which an upright piano has been sawn in half is 28 minutes 29 seconds by a team of four at the Highland Games, Dronfield Woodhouse, Derbyshire, England, on July 3, 1971, using an Eclipse all-purpose saw.

Pipe Smoking. The duration record for keeping a pipe (3.3 grams of tobacco) continuously alight with only an initial match is 253 minutes 28 seconds by Yrjö Pentikäinen of Kuopio, Finland, on March 15–16, 1968.

Plate Spinning. The greatest number of plates spun simultaneously is 44 by Holley Gray on the *Blue Peter* TV show in London on January 31, 1972.

Pogo Stick Jumping. Stephen Newman, 12, of Great Haywood near Stafford, England, completed 11,052 jumps on June 27, 1971.

Pole Sitting. There being no international rules, the "standards of living" atop poles vary widely. The record squat is 8 months and 4 days by Kenneth Gidge, an unemployed (or resting) actor in a hut on a 30-foot pole at Peabody, Massachusetts, ending on December, 21, 1971.

Modern records do not, however, compare with that of St. Daniel (409–493 A.D.), called Stylites (Greek, *stylos*=pillar), a monk who spent 33 years 3 months on a stone pillar in Syria. This is probably the oldest of all human stunt records.

Pop Group. The duration record for a 5-man pop-playing group is 122 hours 32 minutes at Portsmouth Polytechnic, England, February 14–19, 1972. The group at no time sank below a quartet.

Prize Winning. The largest individual competition prize on record is $307,500 won by Herbert J. Idle, 55, of Chicago, in an encyclopaedia contest run by Unicorn Press Inc., on August 20, 1953.

Psychiatrist, Fastest. The world's fastest "psychiatrist" was Dr. Albert L. Weiner of Erlton, New Jersey, who dealt with up to 50 patients a day in four treatment rooms. He relied heavily on narco-analysis, muscle relaxants and electro-shock treatments. In December, 1961, he was found guilty on 12 counts of manslaughter from using unsterilized needles. He had been trained only in osteopathy.

Quoit Throwing. The world's record for rope quoit throwing is an unbroken sequence of 4,002 pegs by Bill Irby, Sr., of Australia in 1968.

Riding in Armor. The longest recorded ride in full armor is one of 145 miles from Wednesfield to London *via* Birmingham and Oxford, England, in 6 days by Kenneth Quicke in August, 1956.

Riveting. The world's record for riveting is 11,209 in 9 hours by J. Moir at the Workman Clark Ltd. shipyard, Belfast, Northern Ireland, in June, 1918. His peak hour was his seventh with 1,409, an average of nearly 23½ per minute.

Rocking Chair. The longest recorded duration of a "Rockathon" is 150 hours 18 minutes by Rande Dahl, 18, at the Sea Fair, Seattle, Washington, ending on July 30, 1971.

Roller Coasting. The world endurance record for rides on a roller coaster is 465 circuits of the John Collins Pleasure Park roller coaster at Barry Island, Glamorgan, Wales, by a group of 4 men and 2 girls. The test lasted 31 hours on August 15–16, 1968.

Rolling Pin. The record distance for a woman to throw a 2-lb. rolling pin is 140 feet 4 inches by Sheri Salyer at Stroud, Oklahoma, on July 18, 1970.

Rope Tricks. Will Rogers (1879–1935) demonstrated an ability to rope 3 separate objects with 3 lariats at a single throw.

Safari, Longest. The world's longest safari was one mounted in Africa by Peter Parnwell of Johannesburg, South Africa. It lasted 365 days, embraced 37 African countries and territories and extended over 30,000 miles.

See-Saw. The most protracted session for see-sawing is one of 384 hours (16 days) by Ed Garcia, 18, and Steve Pontes, 17, of San Leandro, California, November 29 to December 8, 1971. Total time out was only 6 hours 39 minutes or 1.73 per cent. The "constant motion" record is 200 hours by Tom Adamo and Bob Rowell at Manassa, Virginia, from August 16, 1971.

Sermon. The longest sermon on record was delivered by Clinton Locy of West Richland, Washington, in February, 1955. It lasted 48 hours 18 minutes and ranged through texts from every book in the Bible. A congregation of eight was on hand at the close.

From May 31 to June 10, 1969, the Dalai Lama, the exiled ruler of Tibet, completed a sermon on Tantric Buddhism for five to seven hours per day to total 60 hours.

Sewing Machines. The fastest time recorded for sewing down a piece of tape 9 yards long with a treadle machine is 4 minutes 41.4

seconds by Harry Walgate at the Joint Reading Round Table competition, Reading, Berkshire, England, on November 19, 1969.

Shaving. The fastest barber on record is Gerry Harley, who shaved 130 men in 60 minutes at The Plough, Gillingham, Kent, England, on April 1, 1971. In setting a marathon record he ran out of volunteer subjects.

Sheaf Tossing. The world's best performance for tossing an 8-lb. sheaf is 56 feet by C. R. Wiltshire of Geelong, Victoria, Australia, in 1956. Contests date from 1914.

Shoe Shining. In this category, limited to Boy Scouts, aged 11 to 13, and Cub Scouts, 4 boys shined 707 pairs of shoes in 18 hours in Lincoln, England, on April 8, 1972. They were S. Quiney, P. Gadd, A. Doyle and A. Taylor.

Shorthand, Fastest. The highest recorded speeds ever attained under championship conditions are: 300 words per minute (99.64 per cent accuracy) for five minutes and 350 w.p.m. (99.72 per cent accuracy, that is, two insignificant errors) for two minutes by Nathan Behrin (U.S.), in New York City in December, 1922. Behrin (born 1887) used the Pitman system invented in 1837. Morris I. Kligman of New York City currently claims to be the world's fastest shorthand writer at 300 w.p.m. He has taken 50,000 words in five hours and transcribed them in under five hours.

G. W. Bunbury of Dublin, Ireland, held the unique distinction of writing at 250 w.p.m. for 10 minutes on January 23, 1894. The record for the Gregg system was held by Mr. Leslie Bear at 220 w.p.m. He retired in February, 1972.

Showering. The most prolonged continuous shower bath on record is one of 174 hours by David Hoffman at the Indiana University branch, Gary, Indiana, January 21–27, 1972.

The feminine record is 98 hours 1 minute by Paula Glenn, 18, and Margaret Nelson, 20, in Britain on November 24, 1971.

Singing. The longest recorded solo singing marathon is one of 48 hours and 880 songs by Jerry Cammarata at Nathan's Restaurant, Times Square, New York City, June 12–14, 1972. The longest recorded group marathon was performed by five students (at least four singing at any one time) from Chippenham College of Further Education, Wiltshire, England, who sang for 36 hours 5 minutes on March 10–12, 1972.

Skipping. The greatest number of turns ever performed without a break is variously reported as 32,089 and 32,809 by J. P. Hughes of Melbourne, Victoria, Australia, in 3 hours 10 minutes on October 26, 1953.

Other records made without a break:

Most turns in one jump	5	Katsumi Suzuki (Japan)	Tokyo	early 1968
Most turns in 1 minute	286	J. Rogers (Aust.)	Melbourne	Nov. 10, 1937
		T. Lewis (Aust.)	Melbourne	Sept. 16, 1938
Most turns in 2 hours	22,806	Tom Morris (Aust.)	Sydney	Nov. 21, 1937
Double turns	2,001	K. Brooks (Aust.)	Brisbane	Jan. 1955
Treble turns	70	J. Rogers (Aust.)	Melbourne	Sept. 17, 1951
Duration	1,264 miles	Tom Morris (Aust.)	Brisbane-Cairns	1967

Slinging. The greatest distance recorded for a slingshot is 1,147 feet using a 34-inch-long sling and a 7-oz. stone by Melvin Gaylor on the Newport Golf Course, Shide, Isle of Wight, England, on September 25, 1970.

Smoke-ring Blowing. The highest recorded number of smoke rings formed from a single pull of a cigarette is 86 by Robert Reynard, 46, of George and Pilgrims' Inn, Glastonbury, Somerset, England, on January 1, 1972.

Snowshoe Travel. The fastest time recorded for covering a mile is 5 minutes 18.6 seconds by Clifton Cody (U.S.) at Somersworth, New Haven, Connecticut, on February 19, 1939.

Speech-Listening. The Guild of Professional Toastmasters (founded 1962) has only 12 members. Its founder, Ivor Spencer, has listened to 21,670 speeches to May 7, 1969, including one in excess of 2 hours by the maudlin victim of a retirement luncheon. Winners of the After Dinner Speaker of the Year Trophy (instituted 1967) have been Lord Redcliffe-Maud in 1967, and the Rt. Hon. J. H. Wilson in 1968. The Guild also elects the most boring speaker of the year, but for professional reasons does not publicize the winner's name.

Spinning. The duration record for spinning a clock balance wheel by hand is 5 minutes 26.8 seconds by Philip Ashley, aged 16, of Leigh, Lancashire, England, on May 20, 1968.

Spitting. The greatest distance achieved at the annual classic at Raleigh, Mississippi, is 25 feet 10 inches by Don Snyder, 22, set in August, 1970. He achieved 31 feet 6 inches at Mississippi State University on April 21, 1971. Distance is dependent on the quality of salivation, absence of cross wind and the coordination of the quick hip and neck snap.

The record for projecting a melon seed is 44 feet 1¾ inches by Dale Blaylock of St. Paul's Valley, Oklahoma, achieved at a contest in Neosho, Missouri, in 1971. Serious spitters wear 12-inch boots so practice spits can be measured without a tape.

Stilt Walking. The highest stilts ever successfully mastered were 22 feet from the ankle to the ground by Albert Yelding ("Harry Sloan") of Great Yarmouth, England. (See photo.)

Hop pickers use stilts up to 15 feet. In 1892, M. Garisoain of Bayonne, France, stilt-walked the last 8 km. (4.8 miles) into Biarritz in 42 minutes to average 7.1 m.p.h. In 1891, Sylvain Dornon stilt-walked from Paris to Moscow *via* Vilno in 50 stages for the 1,830 miles. Another source gives his time as 58 days.

Stretcher Bearing. The longest recorded carry of a stretcher case with a 140-lb. "body" is 29.1 miles in 10 hours by a team of 8 from the 4th Ealing Company, London, on December 4, 1971.

Submergence. The longest submergence in a frogman's suit is 100 hours 3 minutes by Mrs. Jane Lisle Baldasare, aged 24, at Pensacola, Florida, ending on January 24, 1960. Mrs. Baldasare also holds the female underwater distance record at 14 miles. Her ex-husband, Fred Baldasare, aged 38, set the underwater distance record of 42 miles in his France-England Channel crossing of 18 hours 1 minute ending on July 11, 1962.

HIGHEST STILTS EVER MASTERED: 22 feet tall from ankle to ground.

Swinging. Jim Anderson and Lyle Hendrickson completed a 100-hour marathon on a swing at the Sea Fair, Seattle, Washington, on August 1, 1971.

Tailoring. The highest speed at which a three-piece man's suit has been made is 84 minutes including measuring and pressing by Wallis and Lennell Ltd. of Kettering, Northamptonshire, England, on December 18, 1969.

Talking. The world record for non-stop talking is 138 hours (5 days 18 hours) by Victor Villimas of Cleveland, Ohio, in Leeds, Yorkshire, England, from October 25–31, 1967.

The longest continuous political speech on record was one of 29 hours 5 minutes by Gerard O'Donnell in Kingston-upon-Hull, Yorkshire, on June 23–24, 1959.

The longest recorded lecture was one of 45 hours on "The Christian Faith and its Response" by the Rev. Roger North, 26, at Hartley Victoria Methodist College, Manchester, England, May 15–17, 1971.

The women's non-stop talking record was set by Mrs. Alton Clapp of Greenville, North Carolina, in August, 1958, with 96 hours 54 minutes 11 seconds in a "gab fest."

Teeth-Pulling. The man with the "strongest teeth in the world" is John Massis of Belgium, who in 1969 demonstrated the ability to pull a 40-ton train along the rails with a bit in his teeth.

Tightrope Walking. The greatest 19th century tightrope walker was Jean François Gravelet, *alias* Charles Blondin (1824–1897), of France, who made the earliest crossing of Niagara Falls on a 3-inch rope, 1,100 feet long, 160 feet above the Falls on July 30, 1855. He also made a crossing with Harry Colcord, pickaback on September 15, 1860. Though it is difficult to believe, Colcord was his agent.

The world tightrope endurance record is 214 hours by Henri Rochetain (born 1926) of France on a wire 4,950 feet long, 1,550 feet above La Seuge River at Le Puy, France, on August 13–21, 1966. The women's record is 34 hours 15 minutes by Francine Pary, aged 17, on a wire 50 feet high at Toulouse, France, in February, 1957.

The longest tightrope walk by any funambulist was achieved by Rochetain on a wire 3,790 yards long slung across a gorge at Clermont Ferrand, France, on July 13, 1969. He required 3 hours 50 minutes to negotiate the crossing.

The highest tightrope walk was over the 750-foot-deep Tallulah Gorge, Georgia, where on July 18, 1970, Karl Wallenda, 65, walked 821 feet in 616 steps with a 35-lb. pole in 20 minutes, including two headstands. (See photo, page 2.)

The highest altitude for a high wire was in the act by the Germans Alfred and Henry Traber on a 520-foot rope stretched from the Zugspitze (9,738 feet) to the Western Peak, Bavaria, Germany, during July and August, 1953.

Tree Climbing. The fastest tree-climbing record is one of 36 secs. for a 90-foot pine by Kelly Stanley (Canada) at the Toowwomba Show, Queensland, Australia, in 1968.

Tree Sitting. The duration record for sitting in a tree is 55 days from 10 a.m., July 22, to 10 a.m., September 15, 1930, by David William Haskell (born 1920) on a 4-foot by 6-foot platform up a backyard walnut tree in Wilmar (now Rosemund), California.

Tunnel of Fire. The longest tunnel of fire (gasoline-soaked hoops of straw) negotiated by a trick motorcyclist is one of 35 feet by Chester Peek at Puyallup Raceway Park, Puyallup, Washington, on February 27, 1972.

Typing, Fastest. The highest recorded speeds attained with a ten-word penalty per error on a manual machine are:

One Minute: 170 words, Margaret Owen (U.S.) (Underwood Standard), New York City, October 21, 1918.

One Hour: 147 words (net rate per minute), Albert Tangora (U.S.) (Underwood Standard), October 22, 1923.

The official hour record on an electric machine is 9,316 words (40 errors) on an I.B.M. machine, giving a net rate of 149 words per minute, by Margaret Hamma, now Mrs. Dilmore (U.S.), in Brooklyn, New York City, on June 20, 1941.

In an official test in 1946, Stella Pajunas, now Mrs. Garnand, has attained a speed of 216 words per minute on an I.B.M. machine.

Typing, Slowest. Chinese typewriters are so complex that even the most skilled operator cannot select characters from the 1,500 offered at a rate of more than 11 words a minute. The Hoang typewriter produced in 1962 now has 5,850 Chinese characters. The keyboard is 2 feet wide and 17 inches high.

Typing, Longest. The world duration record for typing on an electric machine is 150 hours by David J. Carnochan, 22, of the University College. London Union from noon on February 24, to 6 p.m. March 2, 1970. His breaks were 70 minutes less than the permitted 5 minutes per hour. The longest duration typing marathon on a manual machine is 120 hours 15 minutes by Mike Howell, a 23-year-old blind office worker from Greenfield, Lancashire, England, on November 25–30, 1969, on an Olympia manual typewriter in Liverpool. In aggregating 561,006 strokes he performed a weight movement of 2,780 tons plus a further 174 tons on moving the carriage on line spacing. On an electric machine the total figure would have been 633 tons.

Most Traveled Typewriter. The world's most traveled typewriter is the Underwood Noiseless portable (rebuilt 1939) of Britain's most famous sportswriter, Peter Wilson of the *Daily Mirror*. It has accompanied him in covering 45 sports in 51 countries and 60 trans-Atlantic flights for 37 years (1935–1972).

Walking on Hands. The duration record for walking-on-hands is 871 miles by Johann Huslinger, who, in 55 daily 10-hour stints, averaged 1.58 m.p.h. from Vienna to Paris in 1900.

Whip Cracking. The longest stock whip ever "cracked" (*i.e.* the end made to travel above the speed of sound—760 m.p.h.) is one of 55 feet by "Saltbush" Bill Mills of Australia.

Wood Cutting. The world record for cutting six "shoes" to ascend and sever the top of a 16-foot-high 15-inch diameter log is 1 minute 31 seconds set by the Tasmanian axeman, Doug Youd (born 1928), in Tasmania, Australia, on March 12, 1955. His brother, Roy, felled a tree 12 inches in diameter in 1961 in 1 minute 52.3 seconds.

The world record for sawing (hand-bucking) through a 32-inch log is 1 minute 26.4 seconds by Paul M. Searls, aged 46, in Seattle, Washington, on November 5, 1953. The world record for double-handed sawing through an 18-inch white pine log is 10.2 seconds by Bill Donnelly and Ernie Hogg at Southland, South Island, New Zealand, on December 4, 1955, equaled by N. J. Thornburn and M. Reed at Whangarei, New Zealand, on March 3, 1956. Donnelly and Hogg sawed through a 20-inch pine white log in 12.9 seconds at Invercargill, New Zealand, on February 11, 1956. The 24-inch white pine record is 18.8 seconds by Denis Organ and Graham Sanson at Stratford, North Island, New Zealand, on November 27, 1965.

Yo-Yo. The yo-yo originates from a Filipino jungle fighting weapon recorded in the 16th century weighing 4 lbs. with a 20-foot cord. The word means "come-come." The craze was started by the toy manufacturer, Louis Marx (U.S.) in 1929. The most difficult modern yo-yo trick is the double-handed cross-over loop-the-loop. Art Pickles of Shere, Surrey, England, the 1933–53 world champion, once achieved 1,269 consecutive loop-the-loops.

The individual continuous endurance record is 17 hours 4 minutes by Chet Brooks on KRCR, California, on April 7–8, 1972.

GASTRONOMIC RECORDS

Records for eating and drinking by trenchermen do not match those suffering from the rare disease of bulimia (morbid desire to eat) and polydipsia (pathological thirst). Some bulimia patients have to spend 15 hours a day eating, with an extreme consumption of 384 lbs. 2 oz. of food in six days by Matthew Daking, aged 12, in 1743 (known as Mortimer's case). Some polydipsomaniacs have been said to be unsatisfied by less than 96 pints of liquid a day. Miss Helge Andersson (b. 1908) of Lindesberg, Sweden, was reported in January, 1971, to have been drinking 40 pints of water a day since 1922—a total of 87,600 gallons.

The world's greatest trencherman is Edward Abraham ("Bozo") Miller (born 1909) of Oakland, California. He consumes up to 25,000 calories per day, or more than 11 times that recommended. He stands 5 feet 7½ inches tall but weighs from 280 to 300 lbs., with a 57-inch waist. He has been undefeated in eating contests since 1931 (see below).

The bargees (barge sailors) on the Rhine are reputed to be the world's heaviest eaters, with 5,200 calories per day.

Eating Out. The world champion for eating out is Fred E. Magel of Chicago, who, between 1928 and November, 1971, dined in more than 34,509 restaurants in 60 nations as a restaurant grader. He asserts the most expensive restaurant is Voisin, 30 East 65 St., New York City, where a solo lunch cost him $26.50 and the restaurant serving the largest helpings is Zehnder's Hotel, Frankenmuth, Michigan. Mr. Magel's favorite dishes are South African rock lobster and mousse of fresh English strawberries.

While no healthy person has been reported to have succumbed in any contest for eating or drinking non-alcoholic or non-toxic drinks, such attempts, from a medical point of view, must be regarded as *extremely* inadvisable, particularly among young people. *Guinness* will not list any records involving the consumption of more than 2 liters (approximately 2 quarts) of beer nor any at all involving liquor.

Specific records have been claimed as follows:

Baked Beans. 1,220 cold beans one by one, with a cocktail stick in 30 minutes by Clifford Pearce at Gerrards Cross, England, on December 5, 1971.

Bananas. 50½ in 10 minutes by Steyen Nel, 30 (weight 320 lbs.) at Port Elizabeth, South Africa, on July 12, 1970.

Beer. Lawrence Hill (b. 1942) of Bolton, Lancashire, England, drained a 2½-pint yard of ale in 6½ seconds on December 17, 1964. A 3-pint yard was downed in 10.15 seconds by Jack Boyle, 52, at Barrow-in-Furness, England, on May 14, 1971.

Cheese. 16 oz. of hard English cheddar in 4 minutes 30 seconds by John Lombino of Alhambra High School, California, on May 25, 1971.

Chicken. 27 (2-lb. pullets) by "Bozo" Miller (see above) at Trader Vic's, San Francisco, California, in 1963.

Clams. 437 in 10 minutes by Joe Gagnon at Everett, Washington, in January, 1971.

Eggs. (Hard-boiled) 44 in 30 minutes by Georges Grogniet of Belgium on May 31, 1956. (Soft-boiled) 25 in 3 minutes 1.8 seconds by Bill (Dink) Hewit, Bethlehem, Pennsylvania, on October 2, 1971. (Raw) 26 in 9.0 seconds by Leslie Jones on Harlech T.V., Cardiff, Wales, on November 10, 1970. David Taylor at St. Leonards-on-Sea, Sussex, England, ate 16 raw eggs with their shells in 3 minutes 20 seconds on January 8, 1970.

Frankfurters. 18 (2 oz.) in 5 minutes by Mike Wright, 28, at Littlehampton, England, in December, 1971.

Gherkins. 1 lb. in 1 minute 47.5 seconds by Peter L. Citron in Omaha, Nebraska, on May 20, 1971.

Goldfish (Live). 225 by Roger Martinez at St. Mary's University, San Antonio, Texas, on February 6, 1970.

Grapes. 1 lb. (*with* seeds) in 65.0 seconds by Leslie Carter, 24, at Bhisworth Fête, England, on May 20, 1972.

Hamburgers. 77 at a sitting, by Philip Yazdizk, Chicago, on April 25, 1955.

Ice Cream. 7 lbs. 3 oz. (46 2½-oz. scoops) in 30 minutes by Peter Morrow, Brisbane, Australia, on April 27, 1970.

Lemons. 12 quarters (3 lemons) whole (including skin and seeds) in 162 seconds by John Wood at Wakefield Youth Hostel, England, on April 16, 1971.

Meat. One whole roast ox in 42 days by Johann Ketzler of Munich, Germany, in 1880.

Milk. 1.2 quarts in 5.2 seconds by M. Barsby at Corby, Northampton, England, on August 22, 1971.

Oysters. 500 in 60 minutes by Councillor Peter Jaconelli, Mayor of Scarborough, Yorkshire, England, at The Castle Hotel (only 48 minutes 7 seconds required) on August 27, 1972.
The official record for opening oysters is 100 in 3 minutes 37 seconds in Paris in 1954 by le Champion du Monde des Ecaillers M. Williams Bley.

Pickled Onions. 61 in 4 minutes 49 seconds by Ian Davies, 22, at Victoria Hotel, Stoke-on-Trent, England, on March 25, 1972.

Potatoes. 3 lbs. in 8 minutes by Arthur L. Warner at Newcastle, N.S.W., Australia, on April 1, 1971.

Potato Chips. 30 2-oz. bags in 24 minutes 33.6 seconds, without a drink, by Paul G. Tully of Brisbane University, Australia, in May, 1969.

Prunes. 130 (without pits) in 105 seconds by Dave Man at Eastbourne, England, on June 16, 1971.

Ravioli. 324 (first 250 in 70 minutes) by "Bozo" Miller (see page 446) at Rendezvous Room, Oakland, California, in 1963.

Sandwiches. 39 (jam and butter 5×3×½ inch) in 60 minutes by Paul Hughes, 13, at Ruftwood School, Liverpool, England, on July 16, 1971.

Sausages. 89½ Danish 1 oz. sausages in 6 minutes by Lee Hang in Hong Kong, on May 3, 1972.

Spaghetti. 262.6 yards (2.1 lbs.) by Tom L. Cresci at Dino's Restaurant, San Diego, California, on May 20, 1970. 100 yards in 53.0 seconds by Sian Davis and 3 men at The Cafe Royal, London, on June 17, 1972.

SHELLFISH EATING CHAMPION: William Corfield ate 81 unshelled whelks in 15 minutes in England in September, 1969.

Shellfish. 81 (unshelled) whelks in 15 minutes by William Corfield at Helyar Arms, East Coker, Somerset, England, on September 6, 1969.

WEALTH AND POVERTY

Richest Rulers. The Kingdom of Saudi Arabia derived an income of about $500,000,000 from oil royalties in 1964, but the Royal Family's share was understood to be not more than $70,000,000. The Shaikh of Abu Dhabi has become extremely wealthy since the Murban oilfield began yielding in 1963, and in 1966 Abu Dhabi was estimated to have an income of $67,000,000 which if divided equally would result in an income of $3,350 per head. Before World War II, the income of Maj.-Gen. H. H. Maharajadhiraj Raj Rajeshwar Sawai Shree Yeshwant Rao Holkar Bahadure (1908–61), the Maharaja of Indore, was estimated to be as high as $70,000,000 per annum.

The state incomes of the 279 surviving rulers of India's 554 Princely States granted in 1947 were cut off in September, 1970. It had been estimated that the Nizam of Hyderabad (1886–1967) was worth nearly $2,520,000,000 at the time of his death.

The man who once had the highest income in the world was H.H. Shaikh Sir Abdullah as-Salim as-Sabah (1895–1965), the 11th Amir of Kuwait, with an estimated $7,280,000 per week or $378,000,000 a year. The Amir is the Head of State but since January 23, 1963, there has been an elected National Assembly.

Richest Private Citizens. There are currently five proclaimed billionaires in the United States. The dictum of one of them, Jean Paul Getty (b. Minneapolis, Minnesota, December 15, 1892), that, "if you can count your millions, you are not a billionaire" might be extended to saying that the millions are not intended to be countable. The other accepted living billionaires are Howard Robard Hughes (b. Houston, Texas, December 24, 1905); John Donald MacArthur (b. Pittston, Pennsylvania, 1897); Haroldson Lafayette Hunt (b. 1889) of Dallas, Texas and Daniel K. Ludwig (b. South Haven, Michigan, June, 1897).

Fortune magazine which in May, 1968, assessed Mr. Getty at $1.338 billion and Mr. Hughes at $1.373 billion stated in January, 1972, that Mr. Ludwig was richer than either.

Probably the only other billionaires have been John Davison Rockefeller, the first (1839–1937), Henry Ford, the first (1863–1947) and Andrew William Mellon (1855–1937). Rockefeller kept account of his personal expenditure in Ledger No.1 all his life. He referred to competitors, all of whom he regarded as redundant, as "the dear people."

Multi-Millionaires

Fortune magazine in May, 1968, estimated that there were 153 U.S. centimillionaires (*i.e.* those with disposable assets of more than $100 million). The centi-millionaire who achieved his wealth fastest has been Henry Ross Perot (b. Texarkana, Texas, 1930), founder and president of Electronic Data Systems Corporation of Dallas, Texas, in 1962. By 1968, his personal fortune was estimated at $320 million. By December, 1969, it was estimated that the value of his stock holdings might have reached $1,500 million, but he later said he

RICHEST(?) MAN: Jean Paul Getty, an American who lives in England, is personally worth an estimated $1,338,000,000.

GREATEST MISER: Hetty Green, left an estate of $95,000,000, yet saved 4 scraps of soap in her tin box.

could raise $100 million from his own resources to buy the release of 1,361 U.S. P.O.W.'s in North Vietnam.

It was estimated in 1961 that there were 50,000 millionaires in the U.S., of whom 13,500 lived in California. The 1967 total probably surpassed 100,000, of whom 21 succeeded in paying no income tax at all.

Millionairesses. The world's wealthiest woman was probably Princess Wilhelmina Helena Pauline Maria of Orange-Nassau (1880–1962), formerly Queen of the Netherlands (from 1890 to her abdication, September 4, 1948), with a fortune which was estimated at over $550,000,000.

The youngest person ever to accumulate an estate of a million dollars was the child film actress Shirley Temple (born April 23, 1928), now Mrs. Charles Black. Her accumulated wealth was in excess of $1,000,000 before she was 10 years old.

The earliest recorded self-made millionairess was Mrs. Annie M. Pope-Turnbo Malone (died 1957), a laundress from St. Louis, Missouri, who in 1905 perfected the permanent straight treatment for those with crinkly hair.

Greatest Miser. An estate of $95,000,000 was left by the notorious miser Henrietta (Hetty) Howland Green (*née* Robinson) (1835–1916). She had a balance of over $31,400,000 in one bank alone. She was so mean that her son had to have his leg amputated because of the delays in finding a *free* medical clinic. She herself lived off cold oatmeal because she was too mean to heat it, and died of apoplexy in an argument over the virtues of skimmed milk.

Richest Families. In May, 1968, it was estimated that three members of the Mellon family—Mrs. Ailsa Mellon Bruce (1902–1969), Paul Mellon (b. 1907), Richard King Mellon (b. 1900)—were each worth between $500 million and $1,000 million. Another 1968 estimate put the family fortune at more than $3,000 million. It has also been tentatively estimated that the combined wealth of the much larger Du Pont family of some 2,100 members may be in excess of this figure.

Richest Scientist. Probably the wealthiest scientist in the world is Dr. Edwin Land, inventor of the Polaroid camera. His stock (and his family's stock) in the company (15% of the total) is worth roughly $500,000,000.

Biggest Dowry. The largest recorded dowry was that of Elena Patiño, daughter of Don Simon Iturbi Patiño (1861–1947), the Bolivian tin millionaire, who in 1929 bestowed $22,400,000 from a fortune at one time estimated to be worth $350,000,000.

Longest Pension. Miss Millicent Barclay, daughter of Col. William Barclay of Great Britain was born posthumously on July 10, 1872, and became eligible for a Madras Military Fund pension to continue until her marriage. She died unmarried on October 26, 1969, having drawn the pension for every day of her life of 97 years 3 months.

Highest Earnings. In Japan, the National Tax Administration Agency publishes all identities and earnings of the preceding year. The 1971 "Number One Man" was Heima Seki, president of

Sekihei Seibaku Co. of Sendai-shi, with gross income of $10,660,000. Though his company is ostensibly in business for cleaning barley the income was generated by selling forest land to his own real estate company.

The highest salary in the U.S. is that of the chairman of the board and chief executive officer of General Motors Corporation. James Roche (b. 1905) succeeded to this appointment on October 30, 1967. His 1969–70 salary with bonuses was $765,858. In June, 1969, he won a Cadillac in a local drawing but returned it on the grounds that he was already provided.

The record gain from stock options was that of Ralph Cordiner, chairman of General Electric Co., who made a paper profit of $1,262,260 on options exercised in 1957.

Highest Income. The highest gross income ever achieved in a single year by a private citizen is an estimated $105,000,000 in 1927 by the Chicago gangster Alphonse ("Scarface Al") Capone (1899–1947). This was derived from illegal liquor trading and alky-cookers (illicit stills), gambling establishments, dog tracks, dance halls, "protection" rackets and vice. On his business card Capone described himself as a "Second Hand Furniture Dealer." Henry Ford (1863–1947) earned about $70,000,000 per annum at his peak.

Lowest Incomes. The poorest people in the world are the surviving Pintibu (or Bindibu) of whom 42 were found in the Northern Territory of Australia in July, 1957. They subsist with water from soak holes and by eating rats, lizards and yams. In September, 1971, some 20 to 25 were still living. In September, 1957, Chinese Government sources admitted that in some areas of the mainland the average annual income of peasants was 42 yuans ($21.00). In 1964, China's average income per head was estimated at $70 and the daily calorie intake at 2,200.

Return of Cash. The largest amount of cash ever found and returned to its owners was $240,000 in unmarked $10 and $20 bills found in a street in Los Angeles, by Douglas William Johnston, an unemployed Negro, in March, 1961. He received many letters, of which 25 per cent suggested that he was insane.

Greatest Bequests. The greatest bequests in a lifetime of a millionaire were those of the late John Davison Rockefeller (1839–1937), who gave away sums totaling $750,000,000.

The largest bequest made in the history of philanthropy was the $500,000,000 gift, announced on December 12, 1955, to 4,157 educational and other institutions by the Ford Foundation (established 1936) of New York City. The assets of the Foundation had a book value of $2,477,984,000 in 1967.

Best Dressed Women. The longest reign as the "Best Dressed Woman" was 15 years from 1938 to 1953 by the Duchess of Windsor (born Bessie Wallis Warfield, June 19, 1896, formerly Mrs. Spencer, formerly Mrs. Simpson). In January, 1959, the New York Dress Institute put the Duchess and Mrs. William S. "Babe" Paley beyond annual comparison by elevating them to an ageless "Hall of Fame." Also later elevated was Mrs. Jacqueline Bouvier Kennedy Onassis (born July 28, 1929).

Including furs and jewelry, some perennials, such as Mrs. Winston F. C. "Ceezee" Guest, Mrs. Paley and Mrs. Gloria Guinness (*née* Rubio), are reputed to spend up to $100,000 a year on their wardrobes. The published wardrobe of one included 37 nightgowns, 225 pairs of gloves, 45 pairs of earrings, 250 pairs of shoes, and 28 ball gowns.

Mrs. Henry M. Flagler, the chatelaine of her husband's $300,000 establishment, Whitehall, in Palm Beach, Florida, in the era 1902–1914 never wore any dress a second time. Her closets were nonetheless mothproof.

In January, 1960, the Institute decided it was politic to list a Top Twelve, not in order of merit, but alphabetically. The youngest winner was Mrs. Amanda Carter Burden, aged 22, a step-daughter of Mr. William Paley (see page 451), on January 13, 1966. After 1966, rankings were re-established.

2. Honors, Decorations and Awards

Eponymous Record. The largest object to which a human name is attached is the super cluster of galaxies known as Abell 7, after the astronomer Dr. George O. Abell of the University of California. The group of clusters has an estimated linear dimension of 300,000,000 light-years and was announced in 1961.

Orders and Decorations

Oldest. The earliest of the orders of chivalry is the Venetian order of St. Marc, reputedly founded in 831 A.D. The Castilian order of Calatrava has an established date of foundation in 1158. The prototype of the princely Orders of Chivalry is the Most Noble Order of the Garter founded by King Edward III of England in *c.* 1348.

Most Titles. The most titled person in the world is the 18th Duchess of Alba (Albade Termes), Doña María del Rosario Cayetana Fitz-James Stuart y Silva. She is 8 times a duchess, 15 times a marchioness, 21 times a countess and is 19 times a Spanish grandee.

U.S. The highest U.S. decoration is the Congressional Medal of Honor. Five marines received both the Army and Navy Medals of Honor for the same acts in 1918 and 14 officers and men from 1863 to 1915 have received the medal on two occasions. The highest number of repeat awards is to Major Patrick H. Brady (Medal of Honor), who has received the Air Medal with 52 oak leaf clusters.

Top Jet Ace. The greatest number of kills in jet-to-jet battles is 16 by Capt. Joseph Christopher McConnell (U.S.A.F.) in the Korean War (1950–53). He was killed on August 25, 1954. It is possible that an Israeli ace may have surpassed this total in the period 1967–70, but the identity of pilots is subject to strict security.

Top Woman Ace. The record score for any woman fighter pilot is 13 by Jr. Lt. Lila Litvak (U.S.S.R.) in the Eastern Front campaign of 1941–45.

Rarest British Medal. The rarest British medal is the Union of South Africa King's Medal for Bravery in Gold. The unique recipient

WAR ACE WITH HIGHEST HONORS: Captain Edward Rickenbacker (left) who shot down 26 planes in World War I and received Distinguished Service Cross with 9 clusters (see tables below and next page). TOP JET ACE: Captain Joseph McConnell, U.S.A.F. (right) who shot down 16 jets in the Korean War.

MOST CLUSTERS AND GOLD STARS

Navy Cross	4 gold stars	Brig. Gen. Lewis B. Puller, U.S.M.C. Cdr. Ray M. Davenport, U.S.N.
Distinguished Service Cross	9 clusters	Capt. Edward Rickenbacker (see photo).
Silver Star	6 clusters 2 gold stars	Gen. of the Army Douglas MacArthur. Lt. Col. Raymond L. Murray, U.S.M.C. Cdr. Richard H. O'Kane, U.S.N.
Distinguished Flying Cross	8 clusters 8 gold stars	Col. David C. Schilling Capt. Howard J. Finn, U.S.M.C.
Distinguished Service Medal (Army)	4 clusters	Gen. of the Army Douglas MacArthur (also one Naval award)
Distinguished Service Medal (Navy)	3 gold stars	Fleet Admiral William F. Halsey
Legion of Merit	3 gold stars	Major Gen. Field Harris, U.S.M.C.

was Francis C. Drake, aged 14, who rescued a child from a deep well at Parys, in the Orange Free State, on January 6, 1943. The Queen's Fire Services Medal for Gallantry (instituted in 1954), which can only be won posthumously, has yet to be awarded.

U.S.S.R. The U.S.S.R.'s highest award for valor is the Gold Star of a Hero of the Soviet Union. Over 10,000 were awarded in World War II. Among the 109 awards of a second star were those to Marshal Iosif Vissarionovich Dzhugashvili, *alias* Stalin (1879–1953)

Top Scoring Air Aces

Country	World War I 1914–1918	World War II 1939–1945
World	80 Rittm. Manfred, Freiherr (Baron) von Richthofen (Germany)	352[1] Major Erich Hartman (Germany)
U.S.	26 Capt. Edward Vernon Rickenbacker, M.H., D.S.C. (9 o.l.c.), L. d'H., C. de G.	40 Major Richard I. Bong, M.H., D.S.C., S.S., D.F.C. (6 o.l.c.), A.M. (11 o.l.c.).
Canada	72 Lt.-Col. William Avery Bishop, V.C., C.B., D.S.O. and bar, M.C., D.F.C., L. d'H., C. de G.	31½ Sq.-Ldr. George F. Beurling. D.S.O., D.F.C., D.F.M. and bar

[1] Many of these aircraft in this unrivalled total were obsolescent Soviet transport aircraft on the Eastern Front in 1942–45.

---

and Lt.-General Nikita Sergeyevich Khrushchev (born April 17, 1894). The only wartime triple awards were to Marshal Georgiy Konstantinovich Zhukov (born 1896) (subsequently awarded a fourth Gold Star, unique until Mr. Khrushchev's fourth award) and the leading air aces Guards' Colonel (now Aviation Maj.-Gen.) Aleksandr Ivanovich Polkyrshkin and Aviation Maj.-Gen. Ivan Nikitaevich Kozhedub.

Most Bemedalled. The most bemedalled chest is that of H.I.M. Haile Selassie (born, as Ras Tafari Makonnen, July 23, 1892), Emperor of Ethiopia, who had by 1965 over 50 medal ribbons worn in up to 14 rows.

Anti-Submarine Successes. The highest number of U-boat kills attributed to one ship in the 1939–45 war was 13 to H.M.S. *Starling* (Capt. Frederick J. Walker, C.B., D.S.O.***, R.N.). Captain Walker was in overall command at the sinking of a total of 25 U-boats between 1941 and the time of his death in 1944. The U.S. Destroyer Escort *England* sank six Japanese submarines in the Pacific between May 18 and 30, 1944.

Most Successful U-Boat Captain. The most successful of all World War II submarine commanders was Korvetten-Kapitän (now Kapitän zur See) Otto Kretschmer (b. 1911), captain of the U.23 and later the U.99. He sank one Allied destroyer and 43 merchantmen totaling 263,682 gross registered tons in 16 patrols before his capture on March 17, 1941. He is a Knight's Cross of the Iron Cross with Oakleaves and Swords. In World War I, Kapitän Leutnant Lothar von Arnauld de la Periere, in the U.35 and U.139, sank 194 Allied ships totaling 453,716 gross tons.

Greatest Reception. The greatest ticker-tape reception ever given in New York City was that for Lt.-Col. (now Col.) John Herschel Glenn, Jr. (born July 18, 1921), on March 1, 1962, after his return from his tri-orbital flight. (See photo.) The New York Street Cleaning Department estimated that 3,474 tons of paper descended. This total compared with 3,249 tons for General of the Army Douglas MacArthur (1880–1964) in 1951, and 1,800 tons for Col. Charles Augustus Lindbergh (born February 4, 1902), in June, 1927.

GREATEST TICKER-TAPE PARADE: Given on Lower Broadway, New York City, to Lt.-Col. John H. Glenn, Jr. on his return from 3 orbits in space, March, 1962. It was estimated that 3,474 tons of paper were tossed out of windows.

Most Statues. The world record for raising statues to oneself was set by Generalisimo Dr. Rafael Leónidas Trujillo y Molina (1891–1961), former President of the Dominican Republic. In March, 1960, a count showed that there were "over 2,000." The country's highest mountain was named Pico Trujillo (now Pico Duarte). One province was called Trujillo and another Trujillo Valdez. The capital was named Ciudad Trujillo (Trujillo City) in 1936, but reverted to its old name of Santo Domingo on November 23, 1961. Trujillo was assassinated in a car ambush on May 30, 1961, and May 30 is now celebrated annually as a public holiday.

The man to whom most statues have been raised is undoubtedly Vladimir Ilyich Ulyanov, *alias* Lenin (1877–1924), busts of whom have been mass-produced. Busts of Mao Tse-tung (b. December 26, 1893) and Ho Chi Minh (1890–1969) have also been mass-produced.

Most Honorary Degrees. The greatest number of honorary degrees awarded to any individual is 89, given to Herbert Clark Hoover (1874–1964), former President of the United States (1929–33).

Nobel Prizes

The Nobel Foundation of $8,960,000 was set up under the will of Alfred Bernhard Nobel (1833–96), the unmarried Swedish chemist and chemical engineer who invented dynamite in 1866. The Nobel Prizes are presented annually on December 10, the anniversary of Nobel's death and the festival day of the Foundation. Since the first Prizes were awarded in 1901, the highest cash value of the award, in the fields of Physics, Chemistry, Medicine and Physiology, Literature, Peace and Economics was about $80,000 in 1971.

Most Awards by Countries. The U.S. has shared in the greatest number of awards (including those made in 1971) with a total of 79, made up of 20 for Physics, 13 for Chemistry, 24 for Medicine-Physiology, 6 for Literature, 14 for Peace and 2 for Economics.

By classes, the U.S. holds the records for Medicine-Physiology with 24, for Physics with 20 and for Peace with 14; Germany for Chemistry with 21; and France for Literature with 12.

Individuals. Individually the only person to have won two Prizes outright is Dr. Linus Carl Pauling (born February 28, 1901), Professor of Chemistry since 1931 at the California Institute of Technology, Pasadena, California. He was awarded the Chemistry Prize for 1954 and the Peace Prize for 1962. The only other person to have won two prizes was Madame Marie Curie (1867–1934), who was born in Poland as Marja Sklodowska. She shared the 1903 Physics Prize with her husband Pierre Curie (1859–1906) and Antoine Henri Becquerel (1852–1908), and won the 1911 Chemistry Prize outright. The Peace Prize has been awarded three times to the International Committee of the Red Cross (founded October 29, 1863), of Geneva, Switzerland, namely in 1917, 1944 and in 1963, when it was shared with the International League of Red Cross Societies.

Oldest. The oldest prizeman was Professor Francis Peyton Rous (born in Baltimore, Maryland, October 5, 1879), of the Rockefeller Institute, New York City. He shared the Medicine Prize in 1966, at the age of 87.

Youngest. The youngest laureate has been Professor Sir William Lawrence Bragg (born in Adelaide, South Australia, March 31, 1890), of the U.K., who, at the age of 25, shared the 1915 Physics Prize with his father, Sir William Henry Bragg (1862–1942), for work on X-rays and crystal structures. Bragg and also Theodore William Richards (1868–1928) of the U.S., who won the 1914 Chemistry prize, carried out their prize work when aged 23. The youngest Literature prizeman was Rudyard Kipling (U.K.) (1865–1936) at the age of 41, in 1907. The youngest Peace prizewinner was the Rev. Dr. Martin Luther King, Jr. (born January 15, 1929, assassinated April 4, 1968), of the U.S., in 1964.

Who's Who

The longest entry of the 66,000 entries in *Who's Who in America* is that of Prof. Richard Buckminster Fuller (b. 1895) whose all-time record of 139 lines compares with the 23-line sketch on President Nixon.

The longest entry in the British *Who's Who* (founded 1849) was that of the Rt. Hon. Sir Winston Leonard Spencer Churchill, K.G., O.M., C.H., T.D. (1874–1965), who had 211 lines in the 1965 edition. Apart from those who qualify for inclusion by hereditary title, the youngest entry has been Yehudi Menuhin, Hon. K.B.E. (born New York City, April 22, 1916), the concert violinist, who first appeared in the 1932 edition.

"Time" Magazine Cover

The most frequent subject has been President Lyndon B. Johnson with 41 treatments to the end of 1967. The youngest subject for a *Time* (first issued March 3, 1923) cover was Charles Augustus Lindbergh, Jr. (born in June, 1930), during the kidnapping case of 1932. The oldest subject was the veteran sports coach Amos Alonzo Stagg (1862–1965) in the issue of October 20, 1958. He is alleged to have summed up his life's work with the belated discovery that "Nice guys come last," a phrase first mouthed by Leo ("The Lip") Durocher in 1948, while manager of the Brooklyn Dodgers.

Longest Obituary

The obituary of Thomas Edison (February 11, 1847–November 18, 1931) occupied $4\frac{1}{2}$ pages in the *New York Times* of the day after his death.

WORST ACCIDENTS AND DISASTERS IN THE WORLD

	Deaths		
Pandemic	75,000,000	The Black Death (bubonic, pneumonic and septicaemic plague)	1347–51
	21,640,000	Influenza	April–Nov. 1918
Famine	9,500,000[1]	Northern China	Feb. 1877–Sept. 1878
Flood	3,700,000	Yellow (Hwang-ho) River, China	Aug. 1931
Circular Storm	>1,000,000*	Ganges Delta islands, Bangladesh	Nov. 13–14, 1970
Earthquake	830,000	Shensi Province, China	Jan. 23, 1556
Landslide	200,000	Kansu Province, China	Dec. 16, 1920
Conventional Bombing[2]	135,000	Dresden, Germany	Feb. 13–15, 1945
Atomic Bomb	91,223[3]	Hiroshima, Japan	Aug. 6, 1945
Marine (single ship)	c. 7,700	*Wilhelm Gustloff* (25,484 tons) torpedoed off Danzig by U.S.S.R. submarine S-13	Jan. 30, 1945

* The figure published in 1972 of 1,000,000 was from Dr. Afzal, Principal Scientific Officer of the Atomic Energy Authority Centre, Dacca. One report asserted that less than half of the population of the 4 islands of Bhola, Charjabbar, Hatia and Ramagati (1961 Census 1.4 million) survived.

The most damaging hurricane recorded was the billion dollar Betsy (name now retired) in 1965 with an estimated insurance pay-out of $750 million.

Notes. 1.—In 1770 the great Indian famine carried away a proportion of the population estimated as high as one third, hence a figure of tens of millions. The figure for Bengal alone was probably about 10 million.

It has been estimated that more than 5,000,000 died in the post-World War I famine, in the U.S.S.R. The U.S.S.R. government in July, 1923, informed Mr. (later President) Herbert Hoover that the A.R.A. (American Relief Administration) had since August, 1921, saved 20,000,000 lives from famine and famine diseases.

2.—The number of civilians killed by the bombing of Germany has been put variously as 593,000 and "over 635,000." A figure of c. 140,000 deaths in U.S.A.F. fire raids on Tokyo of May 10, 1945, have been attributed.

3.—See next page.

Snow Avalanche	*c.* 5,000[7]	Huaras, Peru	Dec. 13, 1941
Panic	*c.* 4,000	Chungking, China (air raid shelter)	*c.* June 8, 1941
Dam Burst	2,209	Johnstown, Pennsylvania (South Fork dam)	May 31, 1889
Explosion	1,963[5]	Halifax, Nova Scotia, Canada	Dec. 6, 1917
Fire[4] (single building)	1,670	The Theatre, Canton, China	May, 1845
Mining[6]	1,572	Honkeiko Colliery, Manchuria, China (coal dust explosion)	April 26, 1942
Riot	*c.* 1,200	New York City (anti-conscription riots)	July 13–16, 1863
Fireworks	>800	Dauphine's wedding, Seine, Paris	May 16, 1770
Tornado	689	South Central States, U.S.	Mar. 18, 1925
Railroad	543	Modane, France	Dec. 12, 1917
Man-Eating Tigress[9]	436	Champawat district, India, shot by Col. Jim Corbett	1907
Hail	246	Moradabad, Uttar Pradesh, India	April 30, 1888
Aircraft (Civil)[8]	162	Moriora, Japan, All-Nippon Boeing 727	July 30, 1971
Submarine	129	U.S.S. *Thresher* off Cape Cod, Mass.	April 10, 1963

Notes. 3.—United States Casualty Commission figure in 1960 was 79,400, while the Hiroshima Peace Memorial Museum gives a figure of 240,000, excluding later deaths.

4.—The worst ever hotel fire killed 162 at the Hotel Taeyokale, Seoul, South Korea, December 25, 1971.

5.—Some sources maintain that the final death toll was over 3,000.

6.—The worst gold mining disaster in South Africa was 152 killed due to flooding in the Witwatersrand Gold Mining Co. gold mine in 1909.

7.—A total of 10,000 Austrian and Italian troops is reputed to have been lost in the Dolomite valley of Northern Italy on Dec. 13, 1916, in more than 100 avalanches. The total is probably exaggerated though bodies were still being found in 1952.

8.—Collided in mid-air with an F-86F Sabre, whose pilot escaped. All 155 passengers and 7 of the crew of the liner were killed.

9.—In the period 1941–42 *c.* 1,500 Kenyans were killed by a pride of 22 man-eating lions. Eighteen of these were shot by a hunter named Rushby.

10.—The worst year ever for road deaths in the U.S. has been 1969 (about 56,000). In the U.S.A. in 1968 4,400,000 were injured. The world's highest death rate is said to be in Queensland, Australia, but global statistics are not available. The U.S.'s 2 millionth victim since 1899 will probably die in January, 1973.

11.—According to Polish sources, not confirmed by the U.S.S.R. On Mt. Fuji, Japan, 23 died after blizzard and avalanche on March 20, 1972.

Road[10]	>125	Two trucks crashed into a crowd of dancers, Sotouboua, Togo	Dec. 6, 1965
Mountaineering[11]	40	U.S.S.R. Expedition on Mount Everest	Dec., 1952
Space	3	Apollo oxygen fire, Cape Kennedy, Fla.	Jan. 27, 1967
	3	Soyuz II re-entry over U.S.S.R.	June 29, 1971

EVOLUTION OF SPORTS RECORDS IN THE 20TH CENTURY

	Start of First Third—January 1, 1901	*Start of Middle Third—May 1, 1934*	*Start of Final Third—September 1, 1967*
Greatest Weight Lift	4,133 lbs.—Louis Cyr (Canada), 1896	4,133 lbs.—Louis Cyr (Canada), 1896	6,270 lbs.—Paul Anderson (U.S.), 1957
Fastest 100 yards	9.8 secs.—John Owen (U.S.) and 12 others, 1890–1899	9.4 secs.—George Simpson and 5 others, 1929–1933	9.1 secs.—R. L. Hayes (U.S.) and 3 others, 1963–1967
Fastest One Mile	4m 12.8s—W. G. George (U.K.), 1886	4m 07.6s—J. E. Lovelock (N.Z.), 1933	3m 51.1s—J. R. Ryun (U.S.), 1967
One Hour Running	11 miles 932 yds.—W. G. George (U.K.), 1884	11 miles 1,648 yds.—P. J. Nurmi (Finland), 1928	12 miles 1,478 yds.—G. Roelants (Belgium), 1966
Highest High Jump	6′ 5⅝″—M. Sweeney (U.S.), 1895	6′ 9⅛″—W. Marty (U.S.), 1934	7′ 5¾″—V. N. Brumel (U.S.S.R.), 1963
Highest Pole Vault	11′ 10½″—R. Clapp (U.S.), 1898	14′ 9¼″—W. Graber (U.S.), 1932	17′ 8″—P. Wilson (U.S.), 1967
Long Jump	24′ 7¾″—P. O'Conner (U.K.), 1900	26′ 2¼″—C. Nambu (Japan), 1931	27′ 5″—R. H. Boston (U.S.), 1965
Longest Shot Put	48′ 2″—D. Horgan (U.K.), 1897	55′ 1½″—J. Torrance (U.S.), 1934	71′ 5½″—J. R. Matson (U.S.), 1967
Longest Discus Throw	122′ 3½″—R. Sheldon (U.S.), 1899	169′ 8⅞″—P. Jessup (U.S.), 1930	216′ 9″—L. Danek (Czechoslovakia), 1966
Longest Hammer Throw	169′ 4″—J. J. Flanagan (U.S.), 1900	189′ 6½″—P. Ryan (U.S.), 1913	241′ 11½″—G. Zsivótzky (Hungary), 1965
Longest Javelin Throw	161′ 9¾″—E. Lemming (Sweden), 1899	249′ 8½″—M. H. Järvinen (Finland), 1933	300′ 11″—T. O. Pedersen (Norway), 1964
One Hour Walking	8 miles 270 yds.—W. J. Sturgess (U.K.), (Amateur), 1895	8 miles 474 yds.—A. H. G. Pope (U.K.), 1932	8 miles 1,294 yds.—G. Panichkin (U.S.S.R.), 1959
Longest Ski Jump	116½′—O. Tanberg (Norway), 1900	301¾′—B. Rudd (Norway), 1934	505′—R. Bachler (Austria), 1967
Fastest 500 meters Ice Skating	45.2 secs.—P. Ostlund (Norway), 1900	42.5 secs.—H. Engnestangen (Norway), 1933	39.5 secs.—Y. Grishin (U.S.S.R.), 1963
Fastest 100 meters Swim (1 turn)	1m 14.0s (no turn)—J. Nutall (U.K.), 1893	57.4 sec.—J. Weismuller (U.S.), 1924	52.6 sec.—K. Walsh (U.S.), 1967
Cycling (m.p.h.) Paced	62.27—C. M. Murphy (U.S.), 1899	>80—L. Vanderstuyft (Belgium), 1928	127.24—J. Meiffret (France), 1962
Fastest 1 mile Race Horse (excluding straightaways)	1m 35.5s—*Salvator*, in U.S., 1890	1m 34.4s—*Equipoise*, in U.S., 1932	1m 32.6s—*Buckpasser*, in U.S., 1966
Highest Mountain Climbed (feet)	22,834—Aconcagua, Argentina, 1897	25,447—Kamet, Garwhal Himalaya, 1931	29,028—Everest, Nepal-Tibet, 24 men, 1953–1965

Chapter Twelve

SPORTS, GAMES AND PASTIMES

Earliest. The origins of sport stem from the time when self-preservation ceased to be the all-consuming human preoccupation. Archery was a hunting skill in mesolithic times (before 20,000 B.C.), but did not become an organized sport until about 300 A.D., among the Genoese. The earliest dated origin for any sport is *c.* 3000 B.C. for wrestling, depicted on pre-dynastic murals at Ben Hasan, Egypt (now the United Arab Republic), and also from early Sumerian sources at Kyafefe, Iraq.

The oldest known ball game and team game is polo, which, though probably of Tibetan origin as *pula,* was first recorded in Iran (Persia) in *c.* 525 B.C.

Fastest. The governing body for aviation, *La Fédération Aéronautique Internationale,* records maximum speeds in lunar flight of up to 24,791 m.p.h. However, these achievements, like all air speed records since 1923, have been para-military rather than sporting. In shooting, muzzle velocities of up to 7,100 feet per second (4,840 m.p.h.) are reached in the case of a U.S. Army Ordnance Department standard 0.30 caliber M1903 rifle. The highest speed reached in a non-mechanical sport is in sky-diving, in which a speed of 185 m.p.h. is attained in a head-down free falling position, even in the lower atmosphere. In delayed drops, a speed of 614 m.p.h. has been recorded at high rarefied altitudes. The highest projectile speed in any moving ball game is *c.* 160 m.p.h. in pelota (jai-alai). This compares with 170 m.p.h. (electronically-timed) for a golf ball driven off a tee.

Slowest. In amateur wrestling, before the rules were modified toward "brighter wrestling," contestants could be locked in holds for so long that single bouts could last for up to 11 hours. In the extreme case of the 2 hours 41 minutes pull in the regimental tug o'war in Jubbulpore, India, on August 12, 1889, the winning team moved a net distance of 12 feet at an average speed of 0.00084 m.p.h.

Longest. The most protracted sporting test was an automobile duration test of 222,618 miles by Appaurchaux and others in a Ford Taunus. This was contested over 142 days in 1963. The distance was equivalent to 8.93 times around the equator.

The most protracted non-mechanical sporting event is the *Tour de France* cycling race. In 1926, this was over 3,569 miles, lasting 29 days. The total damage to the French national economy of this annual event, now reduced to 23 days, is immense. If it is assumed that one-third of the total working population works for only two-thirds of the time during *Le Tour* this would account for a loss of more than three-quarters of one per cent of the nation's annual Gross National Product. In 1970 this was more than $88,000,000,000 so the loss would have been about $720,000,000.

SWIMMING THE ENGLISH CHANNEL in relay was the achievement of this 8-boy team, the youngest to accomplish the task. From the Royal T. W. Manson Swimming Club of England, the team is here posed in front of the white cliffs of Dover, where they started.

Shortest. Of sports with timed events, the briefest recognized for official record purposes is the quick draw in shooting in which electronic times of 0.02 of a sec. have been returned in self draw events.

Largest Field. The largest field for any ball game is that for polo with 12.4 acres, or a maximum length of 300 yards and a width, without side-boards, of 200 yards.

Most Participants. The annual Nymegen Vierdaages march in the Netherlands over distances up to 50 kilometers (31 miles 120 yards) attracted 16,667 participants in 1968. The greatest number of competitors in any competitive event is for the "Vasa Lopp" Nordic skiing race in Sweden. There were 9,397 entrants on March 4, 1970 over the 52.8 mile course.

Worst Disasters. The worst disaster in recent history was when an estimated 604 were killed after some stands at the Hong Kong Jockey Club race course collapsed and caught fire on February 26, 1918. During the reign of Antoninus Pius (138–161 A.D.) the upper wooden tiers in the Circus Maximus, Rome, collapsed during a gladiatorial combat, killing some 1,100 spectators.

Youngest Sports Record Breaker. The youngest age at which any person has broken a world record is 12 years 328 days in the case of Karen Yvette Muir (born September 16, 1952), of Kimberley, South Africa, who broke the women's 110-yard backstroke world record with 1 minute 08.7 seconds at Blackpool, England, on August 10, 1965. (See photo.)

Youngest and Oldest Internationals. The youngest age at which any person has won international honors is 8 years in the case

YOUNGEST EVER TO SET WORLD RECORD IN SPORTS: Karen Muir of South Africa at the age of 12 years 328 days broke the women's 110-yard backstroke swimming mark.

of Joy Foster, the Jamaican singles and mixed-doubles table tennis champion in 1958. It would appear that the greatest age at which anyone has actively competed for his country is 73 years in the case of Oscar G. Swahn (Sweden), who won a silver medal for shooting in the Olympic Games at Antwerp in 1920.

Youngest and Oldest Champions. The youngest age at which anyone has successfully participated in a world title event is 12 years in the case of Bernard Malvoire (France), coxswain of the winning coxed fours in the Olympic regatta at Helsinki in 1952. The youngest individual Olympic winner was Marjorie Gestring (U.S.), who took the springboard diving title at the age of 13 years 9 months at the Olympic Games in Berlin in 1936. The greatest age at which anyone has held a world title is 60 years in the case of Pierre Etchbaster, who retired in 1955, after 27 years as undefeated world amateur tennis champion from May, 1928.

Longest Reign. The longest reign as a world champion is 27 years by the Basque tennis player, Pierre Etchbaster (see above).

Greatest Earnings. The greatest fortune amassed by an individual in sport is an estimated $47,500,000 by Sonja Henie (1912–69), of Norway, the triple Olympic figure skating champion (1928–32–36) as a professional ice skating promoter starring in her own ice shows and 11 films. The most earned in a single event is the reported $2,500,000 each by Joe Frazier and Muhammad Ali (*née* Cassius Clay) in their world heavyweight boxing title fight in Madison Square Garden, New York City on March 8, 1971. This is at a rate of $925.92½ per second of actual fighting.

Heaviest Sportsmen. The heaviest sportsman of all-time was the wrestler William J. Cobb of Macon, Georgia, who in 1962 was billed as the 802-lb. "Happy Humphrey." The heaviest player of a ball game is Bob Pointer, the 487-lb. tackle, formerly on the 1967 Santa Barbara High School team, and still playing in California.

Most Expensive. The most expensive of all sports is the racing of large yachts—"J" type boats and International 12-meter boats. The owning and racing of these is beyond the means of individual millionaires and is confined to multi-millionaires or syndicates.

Largest Crowd. The greatest number of live spectators for any sporting spectacle is the estimated 1,000,000 (more than 20 per cent of the population) who line the route of the annual San Sylvestre road race of 7,300 meters (4 miles 943 yards) through the streets of São Paulo, Brazil, on New Year's night. However, spread over 23 days, it is estimated that more than 10,000,000 see the annual *Tour de France* along the route.

The largest crowd traveling to any sporting event is "more than 400,000" for the annual *Grand Prix d'Endurance* motor race on the Sarthe circuit near Le Mans, France. The total attendance at the 1969 Stampede at Calgary, Alberta, Canada, was 853,620 from July 9 through 18. The record stadium crowd was one of 199,854 for the Brazil *vs.* Uruguay match in the Maracanã Municipal Stadium, Rio de Janeiro, Brazil, on July 16, 1950.

HOLDER OF THREE FLIGHT-SHOOTING RECORDS: Harry Drake is the master with the footbow, handbow and crossbow. Here he is trying to break his own unlimited footbow record. Drake retired at the end of 1971.

Archery

Earliest References. Paleolithic drawings of archers indicate that bows and arrows are an invention of at least 20,000 years ago. Archery developed as an organized sport at least as early as the 4th century A.D. The world governing body is the *Fédération Internationale de Tir à l'Arc* (FITA), founded in 1931.

Flight Shooting. The longest flight shooting records are achieved in the footbow class. In the unlimited footbow division, the professional Harry Drake holds the record at 2,028 yards, shot on October 24, 1971 in the National Archery Association tournament at Ivanpha Dry Lake, California. The unlimited handbow class (*i.e.* standing stance with bow of any weight) record is 856 yards 20 inches and the crossbow record is 1,359 yds. 29 inches, both held by Drake and set at same venue on October 14–15, 1967.

Highest Scores. The world records for FITA Rounds are: men 1,254 points by Arne Jacobsen (Denmark) in 1971; and women 1,229 points by Miss Irena Szydlowska (Poland) in 1971.

The record for a FITA Double Round is 2,467 points by Jorma Sandelin (Finland) at Varkaus, Finland, on September 2–3, 1969. The feminine record is 2,391 points by Mrs. Doreen Wilber (U.S.) in Moscow, U.S.S.R. on May 27–30, 1971.

Most Titles. The greatest number of world titles (instituted 1931) ever won by a man is four by H. Deutgen (Sweden) in 1947–48–49–50. The greatest number won by a woman is seven by Mrs. Janina Spychajowa-Kurkowska (Poland) in 1931–32–33–34, 1936, 1939 and 1947.

Marathon. The highest recorded score over 24 hours by a pair of archers is 21,700 out of a possible 24,000 during 20 Portsmouth Rounds (60 arrows at 20 yards) shot by Paul Templar and David Dakers of the Heugh Bowmen at Peterlee Community Centre, Peterlee, Co. Durham, England, from 10:30 a.m. to 10:30 a.m. on April 7–8, 1971.

FASTEST CIRCUIT is Francorchamps in Belgium and the fastest road race is the Belgian Grand Prix held on it. Here Pedro Rodriguez, driving a BRM, is setting a record in June, 1970.

Auto Racing

Earliest Races. The first automobile trial was one of 20 miles in France, from Paris to Versailles and back on April 20, 1887, won by Georges Bouton's steam quadricycle in 74 minutes, at an average of 16.22 m.p.h.

The first "real" race was from Paris to Rouen on July 23, 1894 when Count de Dion (France) won in a de Dion Bouton steam car at an average of 11.6 m.p.h.

The oldest auto race in the world, still being regularly run, is the R.A.C. Tourist Trophy (37th race held in 1972), first staged on the Isle of Man on September 14, 1905. The oldest continental races are the Targa Florio in Sicily, first held on May 9, 1906, and the French Grand Prix (50th in 1972) first held on June 26–27, 1906.

Fastest Circuits. The highest average lap speed attained on any closed circuit is 201.105 m.p.h. by Bobby Isaac, driving a 1969

Dodge Charger, powered by a 600-b.h.p., 426-cubic inch V8 engine, at the Alabama International Motor Speedway, Talladega, Alabama, in November, 1970. The race lap average for this 2.66-mile, 33-degree banked tri-oval is also a record. On September 14, 1969, it was lapped at over 195 m.p.h. during a 500-mile race by Richard Brickhouse driving a 1969 Dodge Daytona Charger.

The fastest road circuit is the Francorchamps circuit near Spa, Belgium. It is 14.10 kilometers (8 miles 1,340 yards) in length and was lapped in 3 minutes 14.6 seconds (average speed of 162.080 m.p.h.) during the Francorchamps 1,000-kilometer sports car race on May 9, 1971, by Joseph Siffert (1936–1971) of Switzerland, driving a 4,998-c.c. flat Porsche 917K Group 5 sports car.

Fastest Races. The fastest race in the world was the 50-mile event at the NASCAR Grand National meeting at Daytona International Speedway on February 8, 1964. It was won by Richard Petty of Randleman, North Carolina, in 17 minutes 27 seconds (average speed 171.920 m.p.h.), driving a 405-b.h.p. 1964 Plymouth V8.

The fastest road race is the Belgian Grand Prix held on the Francorchamps circuit (8 miles 1,340 yards) near Spa, Belgium. The record time for this 71-lap (622.055 miles) race is 4 hours, 1 minute 9.7 seconds (average speed 154.765 m.p.h.) by Pedro Rodriguez (1940–67) of Mexico and Keith Jack (Jackie) Oliver (b. 1942) of Great Britain, driving a 4,998-c.c. flat-12 Porsche 917K Group 5 sports car on May 9, 1971.

Toughest Circuits. The Targa Florio (first run 1906) is widely acknowledged to be the most arduous race. Held on the Piccolo Madonie Circuit in Sicily, it now covers eleven laps (492.126 miles) and involves the negotiation of 9,350 corners, over severe mountain gradients, and narrow rough roads.

The record time is 6 hours 27 minutes 48.0 seconds (average speed 76.141 m.p.h.) by Arturo Merzario and Sandro Munari (both Italy) driving a 2,995-c.c. flat-12 Ferrari 312P Group S sports car in the 56th race on May 21, 1972. The lap record is 33 minutes 36.0 seconds (average speed 79.890 m.p.h.) by Leo Kinnunen (born Finland 1943) on lap 11 of this race in a Porsche 908/3 Spyder Group G prototype sports car on May 3, 1970.

The most difficult Grand Prix circuit is generally regarded to be that for the Monaco Grand Prix (first run 1929), run through the streets and harbor of Monte Carlo. It is 3,145 meters (1 mile 1,679 yards) in length and has 10 pronounced corners and several sharp changes of gradient. The race is run over 80 laps (156.377 miles) and involves on average more than 2,000 gear changes.

The record for the race is 1 hour 52 minutes 21.3 seconds (average speed 83.487 m.p.h.) by Jackie Stewart of Scotland driving a 2,933-c.c. Tyrell-Cosworth V8 on May 23, 1971. The race lap record is 1 minute 22.2 seconds (average speed 85.587 m.p.h.) by Stewart on lap 57 of the above race. (See photo, next page.)

Le Mans

The world's most important race for sports cars is the 24-hour *Grand Prix d'Endurance* (first held 1923) on the Sarthe circuit (8 miles

HOLDER OF THE MONACO GRAND PRIX RECORD: Jackie Stewart of Scotland also holds the lap record for the same race, regarded as the most difficult Grand Prix circuit.

641 yards) at Le Mans, France. The greatest distance ever covered is 3,315.210 miles (average speed 138.134 m.p.h.) by Dr. Helmut Marko (b. Austria, April, 1943) and Gijs van Lennep (Netherlands) driving a 4,907-c.c. flat-12 Porsche 917K Group 5 sports car. The race lap record is 3 minutes 18.7 seconds (151.632 m.p.h.) by Pedro Rodriguez (1940–71) driving a Porsche 917L on June 12, 1971. The record practice lap is 3 minutes 13.6 seconds (average speed 155.627 m.p.h.) by Jackie Oliver driving a similar car on April 18, 1971. The pre-war record average speed was 86.85 m.p.h. by a 3.3-liter Bugatti in 1939.

Most Wins. The race has been won by Ferrari cars nine times, in 1949, 1954, 1958 and 1960–61–62–63–64–65. The most wins by one man is four by Oliver Gendebien (Belgium), who won in 1958 and 1960–1–2.

Indianapolis 500

The Indianapolis 500-mile race (200 laps) was inaugurated in 1911. The most successful drivers have been Warren Wilbur Shaw (killed in plane crash in 1954), who won in 1937, 1939, and 1940, Louis Meyer, who won in 1928, 1933 and 1936, and Anthony Joseph Foyt, Jr., who won in 1961, 1964 and 1967. Mauri Rose won in 1947 and 1948 and was the co-driver of Floyd Davis in 1941.

The record time is 3 hours 4 minutes 5.54 seconds (average speed 162.962 m.p.h.) by Mark Donohue (b. Summit, New Jersey, March 18, 1937) driving a 2,605-c.c. 900 b.h.p. turbocharged Sunoco McLaren M16B-Offenhauser on May 27, 1972. He received $218,767.90 from a record prize fund of $1,011,845.94 for winning this, the 56th race. The individual prize record is $271,697.72 by Al Unser (b. Albuquerque, New Mexico, May 29, 1939) on May 30, 1970.

The race lap record is 47.99 seconds (average speed 187.539 m.p.h.) by Mark Donohue on Lap 150 of the 1972 race. The practice lap record is 45.76 (average speed 196.678 m.p.h.) by Bobby Unser driving a 2,589-c.c. Olsonite Eagle 72-Offenhauser on May 14, 1972.

Fastest Pit Stop. A. J. Foyt, Jr.'s first fuel stop on Lap 14 during the Indianapolis 500 on May 29, 1971, took 9 seconds.

Duration Record

The greatest distance ever covered in one year is 400,000 kilometers (248,548.5 miles) by Francois Lecot (1879–1949), an innkeeper from Rochetaillée, France, in a 11-c.v. Citroën (1,900 c.c., 66 b.h.p.), mainly between Paris and Monte Carlo, from July 22, 1935 to July 26, 1936. He drove on 363 of the 370 days.

The world's duration record is 185,353 miles 1,741 yards in 133 days 17 hours 37 minutes 38.6 seconds (average speed 58.07 m.p.h.) by Marchand, Presalé and six others in a Citroën on the Montlhéry track near Paris, during March–July, 1933.

Most Successful Drivers

Based on the World Drivers' Championships, inaugurated in 1950, the most successful driver is Juan-Manuel Fangio y Cia (born

MOST SUCCESSFUL DRIVER: Manuel Fangio of Argentina won the World Drivers' Championship five times and 24 Grand Prix races before retiring in 1958.

Balcarce, Argentina, June 24, 1911), who won five times in 1951–54–55–56–57. He retired in 1958, after having won 24 Grand Prix races (2 shared).

The most successful driver in terms of race wins is Stirling Craufurd Moss (born London, September 17, 1929), with 167 (11 shared) races won, including 16 Grand Prix victories (1 shared), from September 18, 1948 to February 11, 1962. Moss was awarded the annual Gold Star of the British Racing Drivers' Club in 1950–51–52, 1954–55–56–57–58–59 and 1961, a record total of ten awards.

MOST GRAND PRIX VICTORIES IN A YEAR: Jim Clark of Scotland, shown here in his V8-Ford-engined Lotus, won a record 25 in all, and 7 in one year (1963).

The most Grand Prix victories is 25 by Jim Clark (1936–68) of Scotland between June 17, 1962 and January 1, 1968. Clark also holds the record of Grand Prix victories in one year with 7 in 1963. He won 60 Formula One and Formula Libre races between 1959 and 1968.

Oldest and Youngest Grand Prix Winners. The youngest Grand Prix winner was Bruce McLaren (1937–1970) who won the U.S. Grand Prix at Sebring, Florida, on December 12, 1959, aged 22 years 104 days. The oldest Grand Prix winner was Tazio Giorgio Nuvolari (1892–1953) of Italy, who won the Albi Grand Prix at Albi, France, on July 14, 1946 aged 53 years 240 days. The oldest Grand Prix driver was Louis Alexandre Chiron (born Monaco, August 3, 1899), who finished 6th in the Monaco Grand Prix on May 22, 1955, aged 55 years 292 days.

LAND SPEED RECORD-HOLDER: Gary Gabelich with the car in which he set the official mark at 627.287 m.p.h.

Land Speed Records

The highest land speed attained by any wheeled vehicle is 627.287 m.p.h. in the second of two runs of the 37-foot-long 4,959-lb. Reaction Dynamics, *The Blue Flame*, a liquid-natural-gas-powered four-wheeled vehicle driven by Gary Gabelich on the Bonneville Salt Flats, Utah, on October 23, 1970. The earlier run was timed at 617.602 m.p.h. giving an average speed of 622.407 m.p.h. The tires were by Goodyear. During the attempt only 13,000 lbs. static thrust of the 22,000-lb. s.t. available was used and a peak speed of 650 m.p.h. was momentarily attained.

The most successful land speed record breaker was Major Sir Malcolm Campbell (1885–1948) (U.K.). He broke the official record nine times between September 25, 1924, with 146.157 m.p.h. in a Sunbeam, and September 3, 1935, when he achieved 301.129 m.p.h. in the Rolls-Royce-engined *Bluebird*.

WINNER OF FIRST RALLY (1907): The 40-h.p. Italian car, one of the five cars that left Peking on June 10, arriving in Paris exactly two months later.

Dragging

Piston-Engined. The highest terminal velocity recorded by a piston-engined dragster is 240.000 m.p.h. by Donald Glenn "Big Daddy" Garlits (born 1932) of Tampa, Florida, driving his 426-cubic-inch supercharged V8 Dodge "Swamp Rat" on July 13, 1968. The lowest elapsed time is 6.16 seconds (terminal velocity 234.98 m.p.h.) by Clayton Harris of Columbus, Mississippi, driving his rear-engined *New Dimension* AA/F dragster at Lions Drag Strip, Wilmington, California, on February 27, 1972.

Terminal velocity is the speed attained at the end of a 440-yard run made from a standing start and elapsed time is the time taken for the run.

Rocket or Jet-Engined. The highest terminal velocity and lowest elapsed time recorded by any dragster is 311.41 m.p.h. and 5.10 seconds by Victor Wilson of Sydney, Australia, in the 22-foot-long 3-wheeled *Courage of Australia*, powered by a 6,000 lb.-s.t. hydrogen peroxide rocket engine, at Orange County International Raceway, East Irvine, California, in November, 1971.

Stock Car Racing

Richard Petty of Randleman, North Carolina, was the first stock car driver to attain $1,000,000 lifetime earnings on August 1, 1971. In the 1970 Dixie 500 Race on the 1½ mile Atlanta International Raceway he attained a record average speed of 142.712 m.p.h.

Go-Kart Circumnavigation

The only recorded instance of a go-kart being driven around the world was a circumnavigation by Stan Mott, of New York, who drove a Lambretta-engined 175-c.c. "Italkart" with a ground clearance of two inches, 23,300 land miles through 28 countries from February 15, 1961, to June 5, 1964, beginning and finishing in New York.

Pike's Peak Race

The Pike's Peak Auto Hill Climb, Colorado (instituted 1916) has been won by Bobby Unser (b. Colorado Springs, Colorado, 1934) 11 times between 1956 and 1969 (9 championships, 1 stock and 1 sports car). On June 30, 1968 in the 46th race, he set a record of 11 minutes 54.9 seconds in his 336-cubic-inch Chevrolet over the 12.42-mile-course rising from 9,402 to 14,110 feet through 157 curves.

Rallies

Earliest. The earliest long rally was promoted by the Parisian daily *Le Matin* in 1907 from Peking, China, to Paris, over a route of about 7,500 miles. Five cars left Peking on June 10. The winner, Prince Scipione Borghesi, arrived in Paris on August 10, 1907, in his 40 h.p. Italia.

Longest. The world's longest recent rally event was the £10,000 ($24,000) London *Daily Mirror* World Cup Rally run over 16,243 miles starting from London, England, on April 19, 1970, to Mexico city via Sofia, Bulgaria and Buenos Aires, Argentina, passing through 25 countries. It was won on May 27, 1970, by Hannu Mikkola (born Joensuu, Finland, May 24, 1942) and Gunnar Palm (b. Kristinehamn, Sweden, February 25, 1937) in an 1834-c.c. Ford Escort. The longest held annually is the East African Safari (first run 1953), run through Kenya, Tanzania and Uganda, which is up to 3,874 miles long, as in the 17th Safari held on April 8–12, 1971.

Smallest Car. The smallest car to win the Monte Carlo rally (founded 1911) was an 841-c.c. Saab driven by Erik Carlsson (born Sweden, 1929) and Gunnar Häggbom of Sweden on January 25, 1962, and by Carlsson and Gunnar Palm on January 24, 1963.

Badminton

Origins. The game was devised *c.* 1863 at Badminton Hall in Gloucestershire, England, the seat of the Dukes of Beaufort.

International Championships. Malaysia and Indonesia have each won the International Championship or Thomas Cup (instituted 1948) four times: Malaya (now a part of Malaysia) won in 1948–49, 1951–52 and 1954–55, and as Malaysia, by the default of Indonesia in the final, in 1966–67; Indonesia won in 1957–58, 1960–61, 1963–64 and 1970–71.

The inaugural Ladies International Championship or Uber Cup (instituted 1956) has been most often won by Japan with a fourth victory in 1972.

MOST TITLES WON BY A WOMAN: Judy Hashman of the U.S. shares the record at 17 with 10 singles and 7 doubles victories in the All-England championship.

Most Titles Won. The record number of All-England Championship (instituted 1899) titles won is 21 by Sir George Thomas (1903–1928). The record for men's singles is 7 by Erland Kops of Denmark (1958–67). The most, including doubles, by women is 17, a record shared by Miss M. Lucas (1899–1910) and Mrs. G. C. K. Hashman (*née* Judy Devlin) (U.S.) from 1954 to 1967, who won 10 singles titles.

Longest Hit. Frank Rugani drove a shuttlecock 79 feet 8½ inches in tests at San Jose, California, on February 29, 1964.

Baseball

Origins. Baseball is a totally American derivative of the English game of cricket (first recorded in the U.S. in 1747) and the now-little-played English game of rounders. The game evolved about the end of the eighteenth century; as early as 1786, "baste-ball" was banned at Princeton, N.J. Haphazard versions of the so-called Town Ball Game grew up in Boston, New York and Philadelphia during the period 1820–33. Rules were first codified in 1845 in New York by Alexander Cartwright.

On February 4, 1962, it was claimed in *Nedelya*, the weekly supplement to the Soviet newspaper *Izvestia*, that "Beizbol" was an old Russian game.

Individual Batting

Highest percentage, lifetime (5,000 at-bats)
.367 Tyrus R. Cobb, AL: Det. 1905–26; Phil. 1927–28

Highest percentage, season (500 at-bats)
.438 Hugh Duffy, NL: Bos. 1894
.422 Napoleon Lajoie, AL: Phil. 1901

Most games played
3,033 Tyrus R. Cobb, Det. (2,804) AL, 1905–26; Phil. (229) AL, 1927–28 (24 years)

Most consecutive games played
2,130 Henry Louis Gehrig, N.Y. AL, June 1, 1925 through Apr. 30, 1939

Most runs, lifetime
2,244 Tyrus R. Cobb, Det. AL, 1905–1926; Phil. AL, 1927–28; 24 years

Most runs, season
196 William R. Hamilton, Phil. NL, 131 games, 1894

Most runs batted in, lifetime
2,209 George H. (Babe) Ruth, Bos. 1914–19, N.Y. (2,197) AL, 1920–34; Bos. (12) NL, 1935

Most runs batted in, season
190 Lewis R. (Hack) Wilson, Chi. NL, 155 games, 1930

Most runs batted in, game
12 James L. Bottomley, St. L. NL, Sept. 16, 1924

Most runs batted in, inning
7 Edward Cartwright, St. L. AA, Sept. 23, 1890

Most base hits
4,191 Tyrus R. Cobb, Det. AL, 1905–26; Phil. AL, 1927–28; 24 years

Most base hits, season
257 George H. Sisler, St. L. AL, 154 games, 1920

GREATEST BATTER of all time: Ty Cobb (Detroit AL) had highest lifetime batting average (.367), made most base hits (4,191) and scored most runs (2,244), as well as stealing the most bases (892).

**LONGEST HIT
IN MAJORS:**
Mickey Mantle (New
York AL) hit the
longest measured home
run (565 feet) in 1953.

Individual Batting Records (continued)

Most base hits, consecutive, game
7   Wilbert Robinson, Balt. NL, June 10, 1892, 1st game (7-ab), 6-1b, 1-2b
    Cesar Gutierrez, Det. AL, June 21, 1970, 2nd game (7-ab) 6-1b, 1-2b (extra-inning game)

Most hits in succession
12   M. Frank (Pinky) Higgins, Bos. AL, June 19–21 (4 games), 1938; Walter Dropo, Det. AL, July 14, July 15, 2 games, 1952

Most consecutive games batted safely, season
56   Joseph P. DiMaggio, N.Y. AL (91 hits—16-2b, 4-3b, 15 hr), May 15 to July 16, 1941

Most long hits, season
119   George H. (Babe) Ruth, N.Y. AL (44-2b, 16-3b, 59 hr), 152 games, 1921

Most total bases, lifetime
6,134   Stanley F. Musial, St. L. NL, 1941–44, 1946–63

Most total bases, season
457   George H. (Babe) Ruth, N.Y. AL, 152 g. (85 on 1b, 88 on 2b, 48 on 3b, 236 on hr), 1921

Most total bases, game
18   Joseph W. Adcock, Milw. NL (1-2b, 4-hr), July 31, 1954

Sluggers' percentage
The percentage is obtained by dividing the "times at bat" into total bases.
Highest slugging percentage, lifetime
.690   George H. (Babe) Ruth, Bos.-N.Y. AL, 1914–34; Bos. NL 1935

Triple-Crown winners
(Most times leading league in batting, runs batted in and home runs.)
2   Rogers Hornsby, St. L. NL, 1922 1925
    Theodore S. Williams, Bos. AL, 1942, 1947

Most Valuable Player, as voted by Baseball Writers Association
3 times James E. Foxx, Phil. AL, 1932, 33, 38
    Joseph P. DiMaggio, N.Y. AL, 1939, 41, 47
    Stanley F. Musial, St. L. NL, 1943, 46, 48
    Lawrence P. (Yogi) Berra, N.Y. AL, 1951, 54, 55
    Roy Campanella, Bklyn. NL, 1951, 53, 55
    Mickey C. Mantle, N.Y. AL, 1956, 57, 62

Most one-base hits (singles), season
199   William H. Keeler, Balt. NL, 128 games, 1897

Most two-base hits, season
67   Earl W. Webb, Bos. AL, 151 games, 1931

Most three-base hits, season
36   J. Owen Wilson, Pitts. NL, 152 games, 1912

LONGEST HITTING STREAK: Joe Di Maggio (New York AL) hit safely in 56 consecutive games in 1941. Included were 15 homers.

HOME RUN KING: Babe Ruth (New York AL) hit 714 round-trippers in his lifetime, 60 in one 154-game season in 1927.

IRON MAN: Lou Gehrig (New York AL) played in 2,130 consecutive games.

Individual Batting Records (continued)

Most home runs, lifetime
714 George H. (Babe) Ruth, Bos. AL, 1915 (4), 1916 (3), 1917 (2), 1918 (11), 1919 (29); N.Y. AL, 1920 (54), 1921 (59), 1922 (35), 1923 (41), 1924 (46), 1925 (25), 1926 (47), 1927 (60), 1928 (54), 1929 (46), 1930 (49), 1931 (46), 1932 (41), 1933 (34), 1934 (22); Bos. NL 1935 (6)

Most home runs, season (154-game schedule)
60 George H. (Babe) Ruth, N.Y. AL (28 home, 32 away), 151 gs, 1927

Most home runs, season (162-game schedule)
61 Roger E. Maris, N.Y. AL (30 home, 31 away), 161 gs. 1961

Most home runs, one month
18 Rudolph York, Det. AL, Aug. 1937

Most consecutive games hitting home runs
8-R Dale Long, Pitt. NL, May 19–28, 1956

Most home runs, one double header
5 Stanley F. Musial, St. L. NL, 1st game (3), 2nd game (2), May 2, 1954

Most home runs bases filled, lifetime
23 Henry Louis Gehrig, N.Y. AL 1927–1938

Most home runs with bases filled, season
5 Ernest Banks, Chi. NL, May 11, 19, July 17 (1st game), Aug. 2, Sept. 19, 1955
James E. Gentile, Balt. AL, May 9 (2), July 2, 7, Sept. 22, 1961

Most home runs, with bases filled, same game
2 Anthony M. Lazzeri, N.Y. AL, May 24, 1936
James R. Tabor, Bos. AL (2nd game), July 4, 1939
Rudolph York, Bos. AL, July 27, 1946
James E. Gentile, Balt. AL, May 9, 1961 (consecutive at-bats)
Tony L. Cloninger, Atl. NL, July 3, 1966
James T. Northrup, Det. AL, June 24, 1968 (consecutive at-bats)
Frank Robinson, Balt. AL, June 26, 1970 (consecutive at-bats)

Most bases on balls, game
6 Walter Wilmot, Chi. NL, Aug. 22, 1891
James E. Foxx, Bos. AL, June 16, 1938

Most bases on balls, season
170 George H. (Babe) Ruth, N.Y. AL, 152 games, 1923

Most consecutive pinch hits, lifetime
9 David E. Philley, Phil. NL, Sept. 9, 11, 12, 13, 19, 20, 27, 28, 1958; Apr. 16, 1959

CONSECUTIVE GRAND SLAMS: Jim Northrup (Detroit AL) in 1968 tied the record set by Jim Gentile (Baltimore AL) when he hit homers with bases loaded in two consecutive times at bat in consecutive innings. In 1970, Frank Robinson (Baltimore AL) performed the same feat. STRIKEOUT KING: Sandy Koufax (Los Angeles NL), youngest player ever to be elected to the Baseball Hall of Fame, holds the record of 382 strikeouts in a season and 31 strikeouts in two consecutive games.

Base Running

Most stolen bases, lifetime
892   Tyrus R. Cobb. Det. AL, 1905–26; Phil. AL, 1927–28

Most stolen bases, season since 1900
104   Maurice M. Wills, L.A. NL, 165 games, 1962

Most stolen bases, game
7   George F. (Piano Legs) Gore, Chi. NL, June 25, 1881
William R. (Sliding Billy) Hamilton, Phil. NL, 2nd game, 8 inn., Aug. 31, 1894

Most times stealing home, game
2   by 8 players

Most times stealing home, lifetime
32   Tyrus R. Cobb, Det.-Phil. AL, 1905–28

Fewest times caught stealing, season (50+ attempts)
2   Max Carey, Pitt. NL, 1922 (53 atts.)

Pitching

Most games, lifetime
1,054   J. Hoyt Wilhelm, N.Y.-St. L.-Atl.-Chi.-L.A. (432) NL, 1952–57, 69–71; Clev.-Balt.-Chi.-Cal. (622) AL, 1957–69

Most complete games, lifetime
751   Denton T. (Cy) Young, Clev.-St. L.-Bos. NL (428); Bos.-Clev. AL (323), 1890–1911

Most complete games, season
74   William H. White, Cin. NL, 1879

Most innings pitched, game
26   Leon J. Cadore, Bklyn. NL, May 1, 1920
Joseph Oeschger, Bos. NL, May 1, 1920

Lowest earned run average, league, lifetime
2.50   J. Hoyt Wilhelm, N.Y.-St. L.-Atl.-Chi.-L.A. NL, 1952–57, 69–71; Clev.-Balt.-Chi.-Cal. AL, 1957–69

Lowest earned run average, season
0.90   Ferdinand M. Schupp, N.Y. NL, 1916 (140 inn)
1.01   Hubert B. (Dutch) Leonard, Bos. AL, 1914 (222 inn)
1.12   Robert Gibson, St. L. NL, 1968 (305 inn)

Most games won, lifetime
511   Denton T. (Cy) Young, Clev. NL (239) 1890–98; St. L. NL (1899–1900; Bos. AL (193) 1901–08; Clev. AL (29) 1909–11; Bos. NL (4) 1911

Most games won, season
60   Charles Radbourne, Providence NL, 1884

Most consecutive games won, lifetime
24   Carl O. Hubbell, N.Y. NL 1936 (16); 1937 (8)

Most shutout games, season
16   George W. Bradley, St. L. NL, 1876
Grover C. Alexander, Phil. NL, 1916

PITCHER WITH LOWEST EARNED RUN AVERAGE: Hoyt Wilhelm (left), knuckleball pitcher for 9 teams in both leagues, has a lifetime ERA of 2.50. He also has played in the most games (1,054) through 1971. **PERFECT GAME PITCHER:** Jim Hunter (right) (Oakland AL), is the last one to have performed this feat (1968).

Pitching Records (continued)

Most shutout games, lifetime
113   Walter P. Johnson, Wash. AL, 21 years, 1907–27

Most consecutive shutout games, season
6   Donald S. Drysdale, L.A. NL, May 14, 18, 22, 26, 31, June 4, 1968

Most consecutive shutout innings
58   Donald S. Drysdale, L.A. NL, May 14–June 8, 1968

Most strikeouts, lifetime
3,497   Walter P. Johnson, Wash. AL 1907–27

Most strikeouts, season
505   Matthew Kilroy, Balt. AA, 1886 (Distance 50 ft)
382   Sanford Koufax, L.A. NL 1965 (Distance 60 ft 6 in.)

Most strikeouts, game (9 inn) since 1900:
19   Steven N. Carlton, St. L. NL vs N.Y., Sept. 15, 1969 (lost)
G. Thomas Seaver, N.Y. NL vs S.D., Apr. 22, 1970

Most strikeouts, extra-inning game
21   Thomas E. Cheney, Wash. AL vs Balt. (16 inns), Sept. 12, 1962 (night)

Special mention
1959   Harvey Haddix, Jr., Pitt. vs Milw. NL, May 26, pitched 12 "perfect" innings, allowed hit in 13th and lost

Most no-hit games, lifetime
4   Sanford Koufax, L.A. NL, 1962–63–64–65

Perfect game—9 innings
1880   John Lee Richmond, Worcester vs Clev. NL, June 12 1–0
John M. Ward, Prov. vs Buff. NL, June 17 AM...... 5–0
1904   Denton T. (Cy) Young, Bos. vs Phil. AL, May 5 ... 3–0
1908   Adrian C. Joss, Clev. vs Chi. AL, Oct. 2..................... 1–0
†1917   Ernest G. Shore, Bos. vs Wash. AL, June 23 (1st g.) 4–0
1922   C. C. Robertson, Chi. vs Det. AL, April 30............ 2–0
*1956   Donald J. Larsen, N.Y. AL vs Bklyn. NL, Oct. 8...... 2–0
1964   James P. Bunning, Phil. NL vs N.Y., June 21 (1st g.) 6–0
1965   Sanford Koufax, L.A. NL vs Chi., Sept. 9.............. 1–0
1968   James A. Hunter, Oak. AL vs Minn., May 8............ 4–0

†Starting pitcher, "Babe" Ruth, was banished from game by Umpire Owens after giving first batter, Morgan, a base on balls. Shore relieved and while he pitched to second batter, Morgan was caught stealing. Shore then retired next 26 batters to complete "perfect" game.
*World Series game.

Club Batting

Highest percentage, season
.343 Phil. NL, 132 games, 1894
.319 N.Y. NL, 154 games, 1930

Most runs, one club, game
36 Chi. NL (36) vs Louisville (7),
June 29, 1897

Most runs, one club, inning
18 Chi. NL, 7th inning, Sept. 6, 1883

Most runs, both clubs, inning
19 Wash. AA (14), Balt. (5), 1st inn.,
June 17, 1891

Most hits, one club, 9-inning game
36 Phil. NL, Aug. 17, 1894

Most hits, one club, inning
18 Chi. NL, 7th inning, Sept. 6, 1883

Fewest hits, both clubs, game
1 Chi. NL (0) vs L.A. (1), Sept. 9,
1965

Most home runs, one club season (154-
game schedule)
221 N.Y. NL, 155 games, 1947
Cin. NL, 155 games, 1956

Most home runs, one club, season (162-
game schedule)
240 N.Y. AL, 163 games, 1961

Fewest home runs (135 or more games),
one club, season
3 Chi. AL, 156 games, 1908

Club Fielding

Highest percentage, one club, season
.985 Balt. AL, 1964

Fewest errors, season
95 Balt. AL, 163 games, 1964

Most double plays, club, season
217 Phil. AL, 154 games, 1949

Most double plays, club, game
7 N.Y. AL, Aug. 14, 1942
Houst. NL, May 4, 1969

Most stolen bases (1900 to date), one
club, season
347 N.Y. NL, 154 games, 1911

Most stolen bases, one club, inning
8 Wash. AL, 1st inning, July 19,
1915
Phil. NL, 9th inning, 1st g., July
7, 1919

General Club Records

Shortest and longest game by time
51 minutes N.Y. NL (6), Phil. (1), 1st
g., Sept. 28, 1919
7.23 S.F. NL (8) at N.Y. (6) 23 inn.,
2nd g., May 31, 1964

Longest 9-inning game
4:18 S.F. NL (7) at L.A. (8), Oct. 2,
1962

Fewest times shutout, season
0 Bos. NL, 1894 (132 g.)
Phil. NL, 1894 (127 g.)
N.Y. AL, 1932 (155 g.)

Most consecutive innings shutting out
opponents
56 Pitt. NL, June 1–9, 1903

Highest percentage games won, season
.798 Chi. NL (won 67, lost 17), 1880
.763 Chi. NL (won 116, lost 36), 1906
.721 Clev. AL (won 111, lost 43), 1954

Most games won, season (154-game
schedule)
116 Chi. NL, 1906

Most consecutive games won, season
26 N.Y. NL, Sept. 7 (1st g.) to Sept.
30 (1 tie), 1916

Most pitchers used in a game, 9 innings,
one club
9 St. L. AL vs Chi., Oct. 2, 1949

Managers' consecutive championship
records
5 years Charles D. (Casey) Stengel,
N.Y. AL, 1949–50–51–52–53

World Series Records

Most series played
14 Lawrence P. (Yogi) Berra, N.Y.,
AL, 1947, 49–53, 55–58, 60–63
12 Mickey C. Mantle, N.Y. AL,
1951–53, 55–58, 60–64

World Series Records

Highest batting percentage (20 g. min.),
total series
.391 Louis C. Brock, St. L. NL, 1964,
67–68 (g-21, ab-87, h-34)

Highest batting percentage, 4 or more
games, one series
.625 4-game series, George H. (Babe)
Ruth, N.Y. AL, 1928

Most runs, total series
42 Mickey C. Mantle, N.Y. AL,
1951–53, 55–58, 60–64

Most runs, one series
9 George H. (Babe) Ruth, N.Y.
AL, 1928
Henry Louis Gehrig, N.Y. AL,
1932

Most runs batted in, total series
40 Mickey C. Mantle, N.Y., AL,
1951–53, 55–58, 60–64

Most runs batted in, game
6 Robert C. Richardson, N.Y. AL
(4) 1st inn., (2) 4th inn., Oct. 8,
1960

Most runs batted in, consecutive times at
bat
7 James L. (Dusty) Rhodes, N.Y.
NL, first 4 times at bat, 1954

Most base hits, total series
71 Lawrence P. (Yogi) Berra, N.Y. AL, 1947, 49–53, 55–58, 60–61

Most home runs, total series
18 Mickey C. Mantle, N.Y. AL, 1952 (2), 53 (2), 55, 56 (3), 57, 58 (2), 60 (3), 63, 64 (3).

Most home runs, 4-game series
4 Henry Louis Gehrig, N.Y. AL, 1928

Most home runs, game
3 George H. (Babe) Ruth, N.Y. AL, Oct. 6, 1926; Oct. 9, 1928

Pitchers' Records

Pitching in most series
11 Edward C. (Whitey) Ford, N.Y. AL, 1950, 53, 55–58, 60–64

Most victories, total series
10 Edward C. (Whitey) Ford, N.Y. AL, 1950 (1), 55 (2), 56 (1), 57 (1), 60 (2), 61 (2), 62 (1)

All victories, no defeats
6 Vernon L. (Lefty) Gomez, N.Y. AL, 1932 (1), 36 (2), 37 (2), 38 (1)

Most games won, one series
3 games in 5-game series Christy Mathewson, N.Y. NL, 1905
J. W. Coombs, Phil. AL, 1910
Many others won 3 games in 6-, 7-, and 8-game series

Most shutout games, total series
4 Christy Mathewson, N.Y. NL, 1905 (3), 1913

Most shutout games, one series
3 Christy Mathewson, N.Y. NL, 1905

Most strikeouts, one pitcher, total series
94 Edward C. (Whitey) Ford, N.Y. AL, 1950, 53, 55–58, 60–64

Most strikeouts, one series
23 in 4 games Sanford Koufax, L.A. NL, 1963
18 in 5 games Christy Mathewson, N.Y. NL, 1905
20 in 6 games C. A. (Chief) Bender, Phil. AL, 1911
35 in 7 games Robert Gibson, St. L. NL, 1968
28 in 8 games W. H. Dinneen, Bos. AL, 1903

Most strikeouts, one pitcher, game
17 Robert Gibson, St. L. NL, Oct. 2, 1968

World Series Winners

Most Series Won
20 New York AL, 1923, 1927, 1928, 1932, 1936, 1937, 1938, 1939, 1941, 1943, 1947, 1949, 1950, 1951, 1952, 1953, 1956, 1958, 1961, 1962

Highest attendance
420,784 L.A. NL, World Champions vs Chi. AL, 4–2, 1959

Baseball records from "The Book of Baseball Records" by Seymour Siwoff.

Earliest Games. The earliest game on record under the Cartwright rules was on June 19, 1846, in Hoboken, N.J., where the "New York Nine" defeated the Knickerbockers 23 to 1 in 4 innings. The earliest all-professional team was the Cincinnati Red Stockings in 1869.

Player Earnings. The greatest earnings as a baseball player is $1,091,477 amassed by Babe Ruth between 1914 and 1938.

Youngest Player

The youngest major league player of all time was the Cincinnati pitcher, Joe Nuxhall, who started his career in June, 1944, aged 15 years 10 months 11 days.

Highest Catch

Joe Sprinz (Cleveland AL) caught a baseball dropped from an airship at 800 feet in July, 1931. The force of catching the ball broke his jaw.

Basketball

Origins. *Ollamalitzli* was a 16th-century Aztec precursor of basketball played in Mexico. If the solid rubber ball was put through a fixed stone ring placed high on one side of the stadium, the player was entitled to the clothing of all the spectators. The captain of the losing team often lost his head (by execution).

Modern basketball was devised by the Canadian-born Dr. James A. Naismith (1861–1939) at the Training School of the International Y.M.C.A. College at Springfield, Massachusetts, in December, 1891, and first played on January 20, 1892. The first public contest was on March 11, 1892. The game is now a global activity.

BOXER CANNOT OUTREACH BASKETBALL PLAYER: Cassius Clay (who calls himself Muhammad Ali), dethroned heavyweight champion, is dwarfed by Wilt Chamberlain, who is 7 feet 1 inch tall.

WORLD'S TALLEST
BASKETBALL PLAYER:
At 7 feet 7.3 inches, the
Russian Vasiliy Akhtayev
played for Kazakhstan in
1956.

Greatest Attendances. The Harlem Globetrotters played an exhibition to 75,000 in the Olympic Stadium, West Berlin, Germany, in 1951. The largest indoor basketball crowd was at the Astrodrome, Houston, Texas, where 52,693 watched a game on January 20, 1968.

The Harlem Globetrotters set unapproached attendance records in their silver jubilee season of 1951–52. They won 333 exhibitions and lost 8 before over 3,000,000 spectators and traveled over 75,000 miles. The team was founded by Abraham M. Saperstein (1903–66) of Chicago, and their first game was played at Hinckley, Illinois, on January 7, 1927. In the 39 seasons to 1965, they won 8,434 "games" and lost 322. They have traveled almost 5,000,000 miles, visited 87 countries on six continents, and have been seen by an estimated 53,000,000 people.

World Olympic Champions. The U.S. has won the Olympic title since its inception at Berlin in 1936 7 times with 54 successive victories, and also the 1954 world title (instituted 1951). Brazil won the world title in 1959 and 1963.

Tallest Players. The tallest player of all time was Vasiliy Akhtayev (born 1935) of the U.S.S.R., who played for Kazakhstan in 1956, when measuring 7 feet 7.3 inches. The tallest woman player is Ulyana Semyonova (b. 1950), who plays for T.T.T. Riga, Latvia, and stands 6 feet 9½ inches. The tallest U.S. player is Ferdinand Lewis Alcindor (born April 16, 1947), now called Kareem Abdul-Jabbar, who stands 7 feet 2 inches in height.

Highest Scoring. Probably the most points scored by a college basketball team in a single game of regulation length was 207 by Bliss College (Columbus, Ohio) vs. Oberlin College of Commerce (88) on March 5, 1966. Playing for Coach J. J. Redman, two forwards scored 183 of the Bliss points—Ron Porter (96) and Jim Marshall (87).

Most Accurate Shooting. The greatest goal-shooting demonstration was made by an amateur, Ted St. Martin of Riverdale, California, who sank 200 baskets in a row at the local high school gym in a demonstration in mid-1972. His average of 90.45 per cent accuracy in shooting from the foul line in a 24-hour demonstration period is also probably a record.

N.B.A. RECORDS

The National Basketball Association's Championship series was established in 1947. Prior to 1949, when it joined with the National Basketball League, the professional circuit was known as the Basketball Association of America.

Note: The records below do not include play-off games with regular season marks unless specifically mentioned.

Games

Most consecutive games (not including play-off games), is 844 by Johnny Kerr (Philadelphia and Baltimore) between October 31, 1954 and November 4, 1965. Most minutes played in a season is 3,882 by Wilt Chamberlain (Philadelphia) in 1961–62. The Los Angeles Lakers set a record in winning 69 games against 13 losses in 1971–72. San Diego Rockets set a record by losing 67 games in 1967–68, and the Cleveland Cavaliers lost 67 also in 1970–71.

The most consecutive games played with no disqualification (963) on fouls is by Wilt Chamberlain between October 24, 1959 and mid-1972.

Longest Winning Streak

The Los Angeles Lakers won 33 consecutive games between October 31, 1971 and January 9, 1972, before the champion Milwaukee Bucks defeated them in Milwaukee, 120–104.

Most Points

The most points scored by an individual in one game is 100 by Wilt Chamberlain (Philadelphia) on March 2, 1962. In this game, Chamberlain made 36 field goals in a record 63 attempts, and scored a record 28 free throws. Chamberlain also set the record of points for a season with 4,029 in 1961–62, and 50.4 for the highest average scoring record. The most consecutive points without missing is 32 by Larry Costello (Syracuse) in December, 1961. By 1971, Wilt Chamberlain was all-time top scorer, with 29,122 points in 12 seasons.

The most points scored by a team in one game is 173 by Boston in February, 1959. Philadelphia scored the most points in a season, 10,143 in 1966–67. The highest scoring average in a season is 125.4 by Philadelphia in 1961–62. The highest score by two teams in one game is 316 by Philadelphia (169) and New York (147) in March, 1962, and tied in 1970 by Cincinnati (165) and San Diego (151).

Assists

Bob Cousy (Boston) made a record 28 assists in one game in February, 1959. Guy Rodgers (Chicago) made the most assists in a

MOST EXPENSIVE PLAYER: Pete Maravich signed a five-year contract with the Atlanta Hawks for approximately $1,500,000 after graduating from L.S.U. in 1970.

MOST ASSISTS IN ONE GAME: Bob Cousy, star of the Boston Celtics, made a record 28 assists in 1959.

REBOUND RECORD-HOLDER: Wilt the Stilt Chamberlain, who has played with various teams, is probably the greatest basketball player of all time. He made 55 rebounds in one game, 2,149 in a season. He also set records of 100 points in a game, 4,029 points in a season, most field goals (36 in a game, 18 in succession, 1,597 in a season), most free throws, and other records.

season, with 908 in 1966–67. The highest assist average for one year is 11.5 per game by Oscar Robertson in 1964–65.

The most assists by a team in one game is 51 by Sheboygan in March, 1950. The season record is 2,249 by Milwaukee in 1970–71.

Rebounds

Wilt Chamberlain (Philadelphia) made a record 55 rebounds in one game in November, 1960. The most rebounds in a season is 2,149 by Chamberlain in 1960–61.

The most rebounds by a team in one game is 112 by Philadelphia in November, 1959, tied by Boston in 1960. Boston made the most in a season (6,131) in 1960–61.

Field Goals

Wilt Chamberlain (Philadelphia) made the most field goals (36) in one game in March, 1962, and in November, 1963 (for San Francisco) shot 18 in succession.

The most in a season is 1,597 by Wilt Chamberlain in 1961–62; during the 1966–67 season Chamberlain (for San Francisco) set a record (683) for the highest field goal percentage, with 1,463 field goals made in 2,770 attempts.

Boston made the most field goals in one game (72) in February, 1959. The season record is 3,972 by Milwaukee in 1970–71.

The longest field goal on record is 84 feet 11 inches by George Linn, aged 20, of Alabama against North Carolina at Tuscaloosa, Alabama, in January, 1955.

Fouls

The most personal fouls in one season is 345 by Bailey Howell (Baltimore) in 1964–65.

Free Throws

The most free throws made by an individual in one game is 28 by Wilt Chamberlain on March 2, 1962, and the most scored in a season is 840 by Jerry West (Los Angeles) in 1965–66. The most consecutive foul shots made is 56 by Bill Sharman (Boston) in the 1959 play-offs.

Syracuse made the most free throws in one game, 59, in November, 1949. In 1960–61, Detroit set the season record at 2,408.

Most Valuable Player

Wilt Chamberlain was transferred from the San Francisco Warriors to the Philadelphia '76ers in exchange for three players and about $300,000 in 1965, and then he was traded to Los Angeles in 1968 for three players.

Most Expensive Player

In 1970, Pete Maravich of Louisiana State University signed a five-year contract with the Atlanta Hawks of the N.B.A. for a figure estimated at approximately $1,500,000, which may well be the biggest known contract in professional sports. (See photo, page 486.)

Bicycling

Earliest Race. The earliest recorded bicycle race was a velocipede race over two kilometers (1.24 miles) at the Parc de St. Cloud, Paris, on May 31, 1868 won by James Moore (G.B.).

Slow Cycling. Slow cycling records came to a virtual end in 1965 when Tsugunobu Mitsuishi, aged 39, of Tokyo, Japan, stayed stationary for 5 hours 25 minutes.

Highest Speed. The highest speed ever achieved on a bicycle is 127.243 m.p.h. by Jose Meiffret (born April, 1913), of France, using a 275-inch gear behind a windshield on a racing car at Freiburg, West Germany, on July 19, 1962. Antonio Maspes (Italy) recorded an unofficial unpaced 10.6 sec. for 200 meters (42.21 m.p.h.) at Milan on August 28, 1962.

The greatest distance ever covered in one hour is 76 miles 604 yards by Leon Vanderstuyft (Belgium) on the Montlhéry Motor Circuit, France, on September 30, 1928. This was achieved from a standing start paced by a motorcycle. The 24-hour record behind pace is 860 miles 367 yards by Hubert Opperman in Australia in 1932.

Most Olympic Titles. Cycling has been on the Olympic program since the revival of the Games in 1896. The greatest number of gold medals ever won is four by Marcus Hurley (U.S.) over the $\frac{1}{4}$, $\frac{1}{3}$, $\frac{1}{2}$ and 1 mile in 1904.

WINNER OF MOST TOUR DE FRANCE VICTORIES (5): Jacques Anquetil
of France winning for the fifth time in 1964 in the 2,861-mile race.

Tour de France

The greatest number of wins in the Tour de France (inaugurated
1903) is five by Jacques Anquetil (born Janaury 8, 1934) of France,
who won in 1957, 1961, 1962, 1963, and 1964. The closest race ever
was that of 1968 when after 2,898.7 miles over 25 days (June 27–
July 21) Jan Jannssen (Netherlands) (born 1940) beat Herman van
Springel (Belgium) in Paris by 38 seconds. The longest course was
3,569 miles on June 20–July 18, 1926.

World Titles

The only three cyclists to have won 7 world titles in any of the
world championship events are Leon Meredith (G.B.) who won the
Amateur 100-kilometer paced event in 1904–05–07–09–11–13;
Jeff Scherens (Belgium) and Antonio Maspes (Italy) who won the
Professional sprint title in 1932–33–34–35–36–37 and 1947 and in
1955–56–59–60–62–64–65.

One Hour and 24 Hour Records

The greatest distance covered in 60 minutes unpaced is 30 miles
214 yards by Ole Ritter (Denmark) at Mexico City, Mexico, on
October 10, 1968. The 24-hour record on the road is 507.00 miles
by Roy Cromock in Cheshire, England, on July 26–27, 1969.

Billiards

Earliest Mention. The earliest recorded mention of billiards was in a poem by Clément Marot (1496–1544) of France, and it was mentioned in England in 1591 by Edmund Spenser (*c.* 1552–1599). Rubber cushions were introduced in 1835 and slate beds in 1836.

Highest Breaks. Tom Reece (England) made an unfinished break of 499,135, including 249,152 cradle cannons (2 points each), in 85 hours 49 minutes against Joe Chapman at Burroughes' Hall, Soho Square, London, between June 3 and July 6, 1907. This was not recognized because press and public were not continuously present. The highest certified break made by the anchor cannon is 42,746 by W. Cook (England) from May 29 to June 7, 1907. The official world record under the then baulk line rule is 1,784 by Joe Davis (born April 15, 1901), in the United Kingdom Championship on May 29, 1936. Walter Lindrum (Australia) made an official break of 4,137 in 2 hours 55 minutes against Joe Davis at Thurston's, London, on January 19–20, 1932, before the baulk-line rule was in force. The amateur record is 702 by Robert Marshall versus Tom Cleary in the 1953 Australian Amateur Championship at Brisbane. Davis has an unofficial personal best of 2,502 (mostly pendulum cannons) in a match against Tom Newman in Manchester, England, in 1930.

Fastest Century. Walter Lindrum (1898–1960) of Australia made an unofficial 100 break in 27.5 seconds in Australia on October 10, 1952. His official record is 100 in 46.0 seconds, set in Sydney, 1941.

Most World Titles. The greatest number of world championship titles (instituted 1870) won by one player is eight by John Roberts, Jr. (England) in 1870 (twice), 1871, 1875 (twice), 1877 and 1885 (twice). Willie Hoppe (U.S.) won 51 "world" titles in the U.S. variants of the game between 1906 and 1952.

Most Amateur Titles. The record for world amateur titles is four by Robert Marshall (Australia) in 1936–38–51–62.

Bobsledding

Origins. The oldest known sled is dated *c.* 6500 B.C. and came from Heinola, southern Finland. The word toboggan comes from the Micmac American Indian word *tobaakan*. The oldest bobsledding club in the world is at St. Moritz, Switzerland, home of the Cresta Run, founded in 1887. Modern world championships were inaugurated in 1924. Four-man bobs were included in the first Winter Olympic Games at Chamonix, France, in 1924 and two-man boblets from the third Games at Lake Placid, New York, in 1932.

Cresta Run. The skeleton one-man toboggan dates, in its present form, from 1892. On the 1,325-yard-long Cresta Run at St. Moritz, Switzerland, dating from 1884, speeds of up to 83.8 m.p.h. were reached by Fl. Lt. (now Sqn. Ldr.) Colin Mitchell (Great Britain) in February, 1959. The record from the Junction (2,868 feet) is 43.59 seconds by Nino Bibbia (born September 9, 1924), of Italy, in 1965. The record from Top (3,981 feet) is 54.67 seconds by Bibbia on February 13, 1965. The greatest number of wins in the Cresta Run Grand National is seven by Bibbia in 1960–61–62–63–64–66–68. The greatest number of wins in the Cresta Run Curzon Cup (inst. 1910) is eight by Bibbia in 1950–57–58–60–62–63–64–69 who therefore won the Double in 1960–62–63–64.

Olympic and World Titles. The Olympic four-man bob has been won four times by Switzerland (1924–36–56–72). The U.S. (1932, 1936), Italy (1956, 1968) and West Germany (1952 and 1972) have won the Olympic boblet event twice.

The world four-man bob has been won nine times by Switzerland (1924–36–39–47–54–55–56–57–71). Italy won the two-man title 13 times (1954–56–57–58–59–60–61–62–63–66–68–69–71). Eugenio Monti (Italy) has been a member of 11 world championship crews.

Lugeing

In lugeing the rider adopts a sitting, as opposed to a prone position. It was largely developed by British tourists at Klosters, Switzerland, from 1883. The first European championships were at Reichenberg (now East) Germany, in 1914 and the first world championships at Oslo, Norway, in 1953. The International Luge

Federation was formed in 1957. Lugeing attracts more than 15,000 competitors in Austria.

Most World Titles. The most successful rider in the world championships is Thomas Köhler (East Germany), who won the single-seater title in 1962, 1966 and 1967, and shared in the two-seater title in 1967 and 1968 (Olympics). Miss Otrum Enderlein (East Germany) has won 3 times (1965–66–67).

Highest Speed. The fastest luge run is at Krynica, Poland, where speeds of more than 80 m.p.h. have been recorded.

Bowling

Origins. Bowling can be traced to articles found in the tomb of an Egyptian child of 5200 B.C. where there were nine pieces of stone to be set up as pins at which a stone "ball" was rolled. The ball first had to roll through an archway made of three pieces of marble. There is also resemblance to a Polynesian game called *ula maika* which utilized pins and balls of stone. The stones were rolled a distance of 60 feet. In the Italian Alps about 2,000 years ago, the underhand tossing of stones at an object is believed the beginnings of *bocci*, a game still widely played in Italy and similar to bowling. Bowling at pins probably originated in ancient Germany as a religious ceremony. Martin Luther is credited with the statement that nine was the ideal number of pins. In the British Isles, lawn bowls was preferred to bowling at pins. In the 16th century, bowling at pins was the national sport in Scotland. How bowling at pins came to the United States is a matter of controversy. Early British settlers probably brought lawn bowls and set up what is known as Bowling Green at the tip of Manhattan Island in New York but perhaps the Dutch under Henry Hudson were the ones to be credited. Some historians say that in Connecticut the tenth pin was added to evade a legal ban against the nine-pin game in 1845 but others say that ten pins was played in New York City before this and point to Washington Irving's "Rip Van Winkle" written about 1818 as evidence.

Lanes. In the U.S. there are 8,818 bowling establishments with 139,023 lanes in 1972 and about 40,000,000 bowlers. The world's largest bowling hall is the Tokyo World Lanes Bowling Center in Tokyo, Japan, with 252 lanes.

Organizations. The American Bowling Congress (ABC) comprises 4,000,000 men who bowl in leagues and tournaments. The Woman's International Bowling Congress (WIBC) has a membership of 3,000,000. An estimated 40,000,000 men, women and children bowl in either leagues or on a recreational basis in the U.S.

Highest Game. The greatest altitude at which a game has taken place is 25,000 feet, when Dick Weber played Sylvia Wene in a Boeing 707 "Starstream Astrojet" freighter of American Airlines on January 7, 1964.

League Scores

Highest Men's. The highest individual score for three games is 886 by Allie Brandt of Lockport, New York, in 1939. Maximum possible is 900 (three perfect games). Highest team score is 3,858 by Budweisers of St. Louis in 1958.

Highest Women's. The highest individual score for three games is 818 by Bev Ortner, Galva, Iowa in 1968. Highest team score is 3,379 by Freeway Washer of Cleveland in 1960. (Highest in WIBC tournament play is 737 by D. D. Jacobson in 1972.)

Consecutive Strikes. The record for consecutive strikes in sanctioned match play is 29 by Frank Caruna at Buffalo, New York, on March 5, 1924, and 29 by Max Stein at Los Angeles, on October 8, 1939.

Most Perfect Scores. The highest number of sanctioned 300 games is 24 (to 1972) by Elvin Mesger of Sullivan, Missouri. The maximum 900 for a three-game series has been recorded three times in unsanctioned games—by Leo Bentley at Lorain, Ohio, on March 26, 1931; by Joe Sargent at Rochester, New York, in 1934; and by Jim Murgie in Philadelphia, on February 4, 1937.

FIRST TEAM EVENT PERFECT GAME: Les Schissler of Denver claps his hands as his 12th ball scatters the pins for the only 300 game in the team event in the 67-year history of the American Bowling Congress Tournament, at Miami Beach, Florida, in 1967.

ABC Tournament Scores

Highest Individual. Highest three-game series in singles is 775 by Lee Jouglard of Detroit in 1951. Best three-game total in any ABC event is 792 by Jack Winters of Philadelphia in doubles in 1962. Winters also holds the record of 2,147 (679–792–676) for a nine-game All-Events total. Jim Stefanich of Joliet, Illinois, has won the most championships with 6 (team in 1963 and 1968; doubles in 1966 and 1969; singles in 1969; All-Events in 1968). This record was tied by Bill Lillard of Houston, Texas, with 6 (team in 1955, 1956, 1962 and 1971; doubles in 1956 and all-events in 1956).

Highest Doubles. The ABC record of 544 was set in 1946 by Joseph Gworek (279) and Henry Kmidowski (265) of Buffalo. The record score in a doubles series is 1,453, set in 1952 by John Klares (755) and Steve Nagy (698) of Cleveland.

Perfect Scores. Les Schissler of Denver scored 300 in the team event in 1967, the only one in that event. In all, there have been only twenty-three 300 games in the ABC tournament. (See photo, previous page.)

There have been 14 perfect games in singles, eight in doubles, and only one in team play.

Best Finishes in One Tournament. Les Schissler of Denver won the singles, All-Events, and was on the winning team in 1966 to tie Ed Lubanski of Detroit and Bill Lillard of Dallas as the only man to win three ABC crowns in one year. The best four finishes in one ABC tournament were third in singles, second in doubles, third in team and first in all events by Bob Strampe, Detroit, in 1967, and first in singles, third in team and doubles and second in All-Events by Paul Kulbaga, Cleveland, in 1960.

Attendance. Largest attendance on one day for an ABC tournament was 5,257 in Milwaukee in 1952. Total attendance record was also set at that tournament with 147,504 in 85 days.

Prize Winnings

Largest individual prize winner in an ABC tournament was Tom Hennessey of St. Louis, with $4,000 in 1965. Highest prize fund in one tournament was $756,721 in Detroit in 1971.

Youngest and Oldest Winners. The youngest champion was Harold Allen of Detroit who was a 1915 doubles winner at the age of 18. The oldest champion was E.D. (Sarge) Easter of Detroit, who, at the age of 67, was a winner in the 1950 team event. The oldest doubles team in ABC competition totaled 165 years in 1955: Jerry Ameling (83) and Joseph Lehnbeutter (82), both from St. Louis.

Strikes and Spares in a Row

In the greatest finish to win an ABC title, Ed Shay set a record of 12 strikes in a row in 1958, when he scored a perfect game for a total of 733 in the series.

The most spares in a row is 23, a record set by Lt. Hazen Sweet of Battle Creek, Michigan, in 1950.

World Championships

The Federation Internationale des Quilleurs world championships were instituted in 1954. The highest pinfall in the individual men's event is 5,963 for 28 games by Ed Luther (U.S.) at Milwaukee, Wisconsin, in 1971.

Marathon

Bill Halstead (U.S.) bowled 1,201 games (knocked down 165,959 pins) scoring 1,948 strikes, lifted 145.9 tons and walked 127.2 miles in 151 hours 25 minutes at Tampa, Florida, November 27 to December 3, 1966.

Boxing

Earliest References. The origins of fist-fighting belong to Greek mythology. The earliest prize-ring code of rules was formulated in England on August 10, 1743, by the champion pugilist Jack Broughton (1704–89), who reigned from 1729 to 1750. Boxing, which had in 1867 come under the Queensberry Rules, was not established as a legal sport in Britain until after the ruling of Mr. Justice Grantham on April 24, 1901, following the death of Billy Smith at Covent Garden, London.

Longest Fight. The longest recorded fight with gloves was between Andy Bowen and Jack Burke in New Orleans, on April 6–7, 1893. The fight lasted 110 rounds and 7 hours 19 minutes from 9:15 p.m. to 4:34 a.m., but was declared a no contest when both men were unable to continue. The longest recorded bare knuckle fight was one of 6 hours 15 minutes between James Kelly and Jonathan Smith at Melbourne, Australia, on October 19, 1856. The greatest recorded number of rounds is 278 in 4 hours 30 minutes, when Jack Jones beat Patsy Tunney in Cheshire, England, in 1825.

Shortest Fight. There is a distinction between the quickest knockout and the shortest fight. A knockout in 10½ seconds (including a 10-second count) occurred on September 29, 1946, when Al Couture struck Ralph Walton while the latter was adjusting a gum shield in his corner at Lewiston, Maine. If the time was accurately taken it is clear that Couture must have been more than half-way across the ring from his own corner at the opening bell.

The shortest fight on record appears to be one at Palmerston, New Zealand, on July 8, 1952, when Ross Cleverley floored D. Emerson with the first punch and the referee stopped the contest with a count 7 seconds from the bell.

Teddy Barker (U.K.) scored a technical knockout over Bob Roberts (Nigeria) at the first blow in a welterweight fight at Maesteg, Glamorganshire, Wales, on September 2, 1957. The referee stopped the fight without a count. (See photo.)

The shortest world heavyweight title fight occurred when Tommy Burns (1881–1955) (*né* Noah Brusso) of Canada knocked out Jem Roche in 1 minute 28 seconds in Dublin, Ireland, on March 17, 1908. The duration of the Clay vs. Liston fight at Lewiston, Maine, on May 25, 1965, was 1 minute 57 seconds (including the count) as timed from the video tape recordings despite a ringside announcement giving a time of 1 minute. The shortest world title fight was when Al McCoy knocked out George Chip in 45 seconds for the middleweight crown in New York on April 6, 1914.

Tallest and Heaviest. The tallest and heaviest boxer to fight professionally was Gogea Mitu (born 1914) of Rumania in 1935. He was 7 feet 4 inches and weighed 327 lbs. John Rankin, who won a fight in New Orleans, in November, 1967, was reputedly also 7 feet 4 inches.

World Heavyweight Champions

Longest and Shortest Reigns. The longest reign of any world heavyweight champion is 11 years 8 months and 9 days by Joe Louis (born Joseph Louis Barrow, at Lexington, Alabama, May 13, 1914), from June 22, 1937, when he knocked out James J. Braddock in the

ONE-BLOW FIGHT was won by technical K.O. in the first seconds in 1957 by Teddy Barker (U.K.), shown here in another bout. The referee stopped the fight without a count.

RETIRED
UNDEFEATED
HEAVYWEIGHT
CHAMPION: Rocky
Marciano (left) was also
the wealthiest boxer
from ring earnings.

8th round at Chicago until announcing his retirement on March 1, 1949. During his reign Louis made a record 25 defenses of his title. The shortest reign was by Primo Carnera (Italy) for 350 days from June 29, 1933 to June 14, 1934. However, if the disputed title claim of Marvin Hart is allowed, his reign from July 3, 1905, to February 23, 1906, was only 235 days.

Heaviest and Lightest. The heaviest world champion was Primo Carnera (Italy) (1906–67), the "Ambling Alp," who won the title from Jack Sharkey in 6 rounds in New York City, on June 29, 1933. He scaled 267 lbs., had the longest reach at $85\frac{1}{2}$ inches (fingertip to fingertip) and also the largest fists with a $14\frac{3}{4}$-inch circumference. The lightest champion was Robert Prometheus Fitzsimmons (1862–1917), who was born at Helston, Cornwall, England, and, at a weight of 167 lbs., won the title by knocking out James J. Corbett in 14 rounds at Carson City, Nevada, on March 17, 1897.

The greatest differential in a world title fight was 86 lbs. between Carnera (270 lbs.) and Tommy Loughran (184 lbs.) of the U.S., when the former won on points at Miami, Florida, on March 1, 1934.

Tallest and Shortest. The tallest world champion was the 6-feet-5.4-inch-tall Carnera, who was measured by Dr. Dudley Allen Sargent at the Hemingway Gymnasium of Harvard. Jess Willard was 6 feet $5\frac{1}{4}$ inches, not 6 feet $6\frac{1}{4}$ inches, according to strict bare foot measurement. The shortest was Tommy Burn (1881–1955) of Canada, world champion from February 23, 1906, to December 26, 1908, who stood 5 feet 7 inches.

Oldest and Youngest. The oldest man to win the heavyweight crown was Jersey Joe Walcott (born Arnold Raymond Cream,

CHAMPION BARE KNUCKLE FIGHT: $22,500 was the largest purse in the pre-glove era. This scene from Port Elizabeth, South Africa, occurred in a 27-round fight between Jack Cooper and Wolf Bendoff on July 29, 1889.

January 31, 1914, at Merchantville, New Jersey), who knocked out Ezzard Charles on July 18, 1951, in Pittsburgh, when aged 37 years 5 months 18 days. The youngest age at which the world title has been won is 21 years 331 days by Floyd Patterson (born Brooklyn, N.Y., January 4, 1935). After the retirement of Rocky Marciano, Patterson won the vacant title by beating Archie Moore in 5 rounds in Chicago, on November 30, 1956. He is also the only man ever to regain the heavyweight championship. He lost to Ingemar Johansson (Sweden) on June 26, 1959, but defeated him in a rematch on June 20, 1960, at the Polo Grounds, New York City.

Undefeated. Only James Joseph (Gene) Tunney (1926–28) and Rocky Marciano (1952–56) *finally* retired as undefeated champions. It may also be argued that James J. Jeffries (1899–1904) was never formally relieved of his title. Joe Louis made a comeback on September 27, 1950, to be defeated by Ezzard Charles in 15 rounds in New York City. (See photo, page 497.)

Cassius Marcellus Clay 7th (later Muhammad Ali Haj) (born Louisville, Kentucky, January 17, 1942) was undefeated in 29 fights during a professional career of 6 years and 5 months when stripped of his heavyweight title on March 22, 1967, for refusing to be inducted into the U.S. Army. On March 8, 1971, he fought and lost against Joe Frazier (b. South Carolina, February, 1944) at Madison Square Garden, New York City. (See photo.)

Earliest Title Fight. The first world heavyweight title fight, with gloves and 3-minute rounds, was between John L. Sullivan (1858–1918) and "Gentleman" James J. Corbett (1866–1933) in New Orleans, on September 7, 1892. Corbett won in 21 rounds.

UNDEFEATED IN 29 FIGHTS: Muhammad Ali Haj (born Cassius Clay), on the canvas, finally lost to Joe Frazier in 1971.

World Champions (any weight)

Longest and Shortest Reign. Joe Louis's heavyweight duration record stands for all divisions. The shortest reign has been 55 days by the French featherweight Eugène Criqui from June 2 to July 26, 1923. The disputed flyweight champion Emile Pladner (France) reigned only 47 days from March 2, to April 18, 1929, as did the disputed featherweight champion Dave Sullivan from September 26, to November 11, 1898.

Youngest and Oldest. The youngest at which any world championship has been claimed is 19 years 6 days by Pedlar Palmer (born November 19, 1876), who won the bantamweight title in London on November 26, 1895. Willie Pep (born William Papaleo, November 22, 1922), of the U.S., won the featherweight crown in New York on his 20th birthday, November 22, 1942. After Young Corbett III knocked out Terry McGovern (1880–1918) in two rounds at Hartford, Connecticut, on November 28, 1901, neither was able to get his weight down to 126 lbs., and the title was claimed by Abe Attell, when aged only 17 years 251 days. The oldest world champion was Archie Moore (U.S.), who was recognized as a light-heavyweight champion up to early 1962, when he was believed to be between 45 and 48 (born December 13, either 1913 or 1916). Bob Fitzsimmons (1872–1917) had the longest career of any official world titleholder with over 32 years from 1882 to 1914. He was an amateur from 1880 to 1882.

Longest Fight. The longest world title fight (under Queensberry Rules) was between the lightweights Joe Gans (1874–1910), of the U.S., and Oscar "Battling" Nelson (1882–1954), the "Durable Dane," at Goldfield, Nevada, on September 3, 1906. It was terminated in the 42nd round when Gans was declared the winner on a foul.

Most Recaptures. The only boxer to win a world title five times is Sugar Ray Robinson (b. Walker Smith, May 3, 1920) of the U.S., who beat Carmen Basilio (U.S.) in the Chicago Stadium on March 25, 1958, to regain the world middleweight title for the fourth time. The other title wins were over Jake LaMotta (U.S.) in Chicago on February 14, 1951, Randy Turpin (U.K.) in New York on September 12, 1951, Carl "Bobo" Olson (U.S.) in Chicago on December 9, 1955, and Gene Fullmer (U.S.) in Chicago on May 1, 1957. The record number of title bouts in a career is 33 or 34 (at bantam and featherweight) by George Dixon (1870–1909), *alias* Little Chocolate, of the U.S., between 1890 and 1901.

Most Titles Simultaneously. The only man to hold world titles at three weights simultaneously was Henry ("Homicide Hank") Armstrong (born December 22, 1912), now the Rev. Harry Jackson, of the U.S., at featherweight, lightweight and welterweight from August to December, 1938.

Greatest "Tonnage." The greatest "tonnage" recorded in any fight is 601 lbs. when Ewart Potgieter (South Africa) at 335 lbs. knocked out Bruce Olson (U.S.) at 266 lbs. at Portland, Oregon, on March 2, 1957. The greatest "tonnage" in a world title fight was

RECAPTURED TITLE CHAMPIONSHIP FOUR TIMES: Sugar Ray Robinson (left) of the U.S. wore the world middleweight crown a total of five times between 1951 and 1958.

488¾ lbs. when Carnera (259¼ lbs.) fought Paulino Uzcudum (229½ lbs.) of Spain in Rome, Italy, on October 22, 1933.

Most Knockdowns in Title Fights. Vic Toweel (South Africa) knocked down Danny O'Sullivan of London 14 times in 10 rounds in their world bantamweight fight at Johannesburg, on December 2, 1950, before the latter retired.

All Fights

Largest Purse. The greatest purse has been $2,500,000 each guaranteed to Joe Frazier and Muhammad Ali for their 15-round fight at Madison Square Garden, New York City, on March 8, 1971.

Highest Attendances. The greatest paid attendance at any boxing fight has been 120,757 (with a ringside price of $27.50) for the Tunney vs. Dempsey world heavyweight title fight at the Sesquicentennial Stadium, Philadelphia, on September 23, 1926. The indoor record is 37,321 at the Clay vs. Terrell fight in the Astrodome, Houston, Texas, on February 6, 1967. The highest non-paying attendance is 135,132 at the Tony Zale vs. Billy Prior fight at Juneau Park, Milwaukee, Wisconsin, on August 18, 1941.

Lowest. The smallest attendance at a world heavyweight title fight was 2,434 at the Clay vs. Liston fight on May 25, 1965.

Greatest Receipts. The greatest total receipts from any boxing fight have been those from the Frazier-Ali fight in Madison Square Garden, New York City, on March 8, 1971. The gate was $1,352,951 (20,455 paid attendance) but the total gross, including T.V. closed circuit transmissions and all other rights have been estimated at more than $20,000,000. The highest *gate* receipts were those for the Tunney-Dempsey fight of 1927 (see above) when 104,943 paid $2,658,660 with a ringside price of $40.

Highest Earnings in Career. The largest known fortune ever made in a fighting career is an estimated $8,000,000 amassed by Cassius Clay (Muhammad Ali). This sum includes $2,500,000 guaranteed to him from his losing fight with Joe Frazier on March 8, 1971 but not subsequent contests.

Including earnings for refereeing and promoting, Jack Dempsey has grossed over $10,000,000 to 1967.

Most Knockdowns. The greatest recorded number of knock-downs in a non-title fight is 47. This occurred in the fight between Oscar "Battling" Nelson (down 5 times) and Christy Williams (42) at Hot Springs, South Dakota, on December 26, 1902.

Most Knockouts. The greatest number of knockouts in a career is 136 by Archie Moore (born Archibald Lee Wright, December 13, 1913 or 1916), of the U.S. The record for consecutive K.O.'s is 44, set by Lamar Clark of Utah at Las Vegas, Nevada, on January 11, 1960. He knocked out 6 in one night (5 in the first round) in Bingham, Utah, on December 1, 1958.

Most Fights. The greatest recorded number of fights in a career is 1,309 by Abraham Hollandersky, *alias* Abe the Newsboy (U.S.), in the fourteen years from 1905 to 1918. He filled in the time with 387 wrestling bouts (1905–16).

Most Fights Without Loss. Hal Bagwell of Gloucester, England, was undefeated in 183 consecutive fights, of which only 5 were draws, between August 10, 1938, and November 29, 1948.

Greatest Weight Difference. The greatest weight difference recorded in a major bout is 140 lbs., between Bob Fitzsimmons (172 lbs.) and Ed Dunkhorst (312 lbs.) at Brooklyn, New York City, on April 30, 1900. Fitzsimmons won in two rounds.

Longest Career. The heavyweight Jem Mace, known as "the gypsy" (born at Norwich, England, April 8, 1831), had a career lasting 35 years from 1855 to 1890, but there were several years in which he had only one fight. He died, aged 78, in Jarrow on November 30, 1910. Walter Edgerton, the "Kentucky Rosebud," knocked out John Henry Johnson, aged 45, in 4 rounds at the Broadway A.C., New York City, on February 4, 1916, when aged 63.

Most Olympic Gold Medals. The only amateur boxer ever to win three Olympic gold medals is the southpaw László Papp (born 1926 in Hungary), who took the middleweight (1948) and the light-middleweight titles (1952 and 1956). The only man to win two titles in one meeting was O. L. Kirk (U.S.), who took both the bantam and featherweight titles at St. Louis, Missouri, in 1904.

Bridge (Contract)

Earliest References. Bridge (a corruption of Biritch) is of Levantine origin, having been played in Greece in the early 1880's. The game was known in London in 1886 under the title of "Biritch or Russian Whist."

Auction bridge (highest bidder names trump) was introduced in 1904, but was swamped by contract bridge, which was devised by Harold S. Vanderbilt (U.S.) on a Caribbean voyage in November, 1925. The new version became a world-wide craze after the U.S. vs. Great Britain challenge match between Ely Culbertson (born in Rumania, 1891) and Lt.-Col. Walter Buller at Almack's Club, London, on September 15, 1930. The U.S. won the 54-hand match by 4,845 points.

World Titles. The World Championship (Bermuda Bowl) has been won most often by Italy (1957–58–59, 1961–62–63, 1965–66–67–69), whose team also won the Olympiad in 1964 and 1968. Three of the Italian players, Massimo D'Alelio, Giorgio Belladonna and Pietro Forquet, were on 11 of these winning teams.

Highest Possible Scores (excluding penalties for rules infractions)

Opponents bid 7 of any suit or no trump, doubled and redoubled and vulnerable. Opponents make no trick.		Bid 1 no trump, doubled and redoubled, vulnerable	
		Below Line 1st trick (40×4)	160
Above Line 1st undertrick	400	*Above Line* 6 overtricks (400×6)	2,400
12 subsequent under-		2nd game of 2-Game	
tricks at 600 each	7,200	Rubber	*350
All Honors	150	All Honors (4 aces)	150
		Bonus for making redoubled	
		contract	50
	7,750	(Highest Possible Positive Score)	3,110

* In practice, the full bonus of 700 points is awarded after the completion of the second game, rather than 350 after each game.

Perfect Deals. The mathematical odds against dealing 13 cards of one suit are 158,753,389,899 to 1, while the odds against receiving a "perfect deal" consisting of all 13 spades are 635,013,559,596 to 1. The odds against each of the 4 players receiving a complete suit are 2,235,197,406,895,366,368,301,559,999 to 1. Instances of this are reported frequently but the chances of it happening genuinely are extraordinarily remote—in fact if all the people in the world were grouped in bridge fours, and each four were dealt 120 hands a day, it would require 2×10^{12} years before one "perfect" deal could be expected to recur.

In view of the fact that there should be 31,201,794 deals with two perfect hands for each deal with four perfect hands, and that reports of the latter far outnumber the former, it can be safely assumed that reported occurrences of perfect deals are, almost without exception, phony.

A recent claim of a perfect deal was in a women's bridge game at the Cocoa-Rockledge Country Club in Cocoa, Florida, reported by the Associated Press in February, 1970. Upon investigation it turned out that the deck had been separated into suits just prior to shuffling and cutting.

Longest Session. The longest recorded session is one of 176¾ hours by David Shapira, Michael Robertson, Richard Melville and Brian Moffett in Belmont Hall, Dundee University, Scotland, April 18–24, 1971.

Most Master Points. The player with the highest lifetime total of master points is Barry Crane, a Hollywood television producer, with 11,357 points by May, 1970. The most points scored in tournaments in one year is 1,434 by Paul Soloway of Los Angeles in 1969.

HIGHEST-PAID BULLFIGHTER: El Cordobés became a multi-millionaire in 1966. In 1970 alone he received $1,800,000 for 121 ring battles.

Bull Fighting

The first renowned professional bull fighter was Francisco Romero of Ronda, Andalusia, Spain, who fought in about 1700. The earliest treatise was *Tauromaquia o Arte torear* by José Delgado y Galvez. Spain now has some 190 active matadors. Since 1700, 42 major matadors have died in the ring.

Largest Stadiums and Gate. The world's largest bull-fighting ring is the Plaza, Mexico City, with a capacity of 48,000. The largest of Spain's 312 bullrings is the Plaza Monumental, Madrid, with a capacity of 23,663. The record gate has been $75,000, taken at the Tijuana Plaza Monumental, Mexico, on May 13, 1962.

Most Successful Matadors. The most successful matador measured by bulls killed was Lagartijo (1841–1900), born Rafael Molina, whose lifetime total was 4,867.

The longest career of any 20th century *espada* was that of Juan Belmonte (1892–1962) of Spain, who survived 29 seasons from 1909 to 1937 killing 3,000 bulls and being gored 50 times. In 1919, he killed 200 bulls in 109 *corridas*. In 1884, Romano set a record by killing 18 bulls in a day in Seville, and in 1949 El Litri (Miguel Báes) set a Spanish record with 114 *novilladas* in a season.

Highest Paid Matadors. The highest paid bull fighter in history is El Cordobés (born Manolo Benitez Pérez, probably on

May 4, 1936, in Cordoba, Spain), who became a multi-millionaire in 1966, during which year he fought 111 *corridas* up to October 4, receiving over $15,000 for each half-hour in the ring. On May 19, 1968, he received $25,000 for a *corrida* in Madrid and in 1970 an estimated $1,800,000 for 121 fights.

Canoeing

Origins. The acknowledged pioneer of canoeing as a sport was John Macgregor, a British barrister, in 1865. The Canoe Club was formed on July 26, 1866.

Most Olympic Gold Medals. Gert Fredriksson of Sweden won the 1,000-meter Kayak singles in 1948, 1952 and 1956, the 10,000-meter Kayak singles in 1948 and 1956, and the 1,000-meter Kayak doubles in 1960. With 6 Olympic titles and 3 others (1,000-meter K.1 in 1950 and 1954, and 500-meter K.1 in 1954) his total of world titles is 9.

The Olympic 1,000-meter record of 3 minutes 14.38 seconds represents an average speed of 11.51 m.p.h. and a rate of 125 strokes per minute.

Longest Journey

The longest canoe journey in history was one of 6,000 miles from New York City to Nome, Alaska, by Geoffrey W. Pope and Sheldon Taylor, both 24, from April 25, 1936 arriving on August 11, 1937. The journey was made entirely on the North American river system by paddle and portage.

Eskimo Rolls. The record for Eskimo rolls is 511 in 30 minutes by Mark Hewitt in the Swan River, West Australia, on April 12, 1972.

Transatlantic. In 1928 E. Romer (Germany) crossed the North Atlantic from Lisbon to the West Indies in a 19½-foot canvas sailing Kayak named *Deutsches Sport* in 58 days.

Downstream Canoeing

River	*Miles*	*Canoers*	*Location*	*Duration*
Rhine	820	Sgt. Charles Kavanagh	Chur, Switzerland to Willemstadt, Neths. in 1961	17½ days
Murray	1,300	Philip Davis and Robert S. Lodge	Albury, N.S.W. to Murray Bridge in 1970–71	36 days
Amazon	3,900	Stephan Z. Bezak (U.S.)	Atalaya to Estuary, June 21, 1970	
Nile (Egypt)	4,000	John Goddard (U.S.), Jean Laporte and André Davy (France)	Kagera to the Delta in 1954	9 months

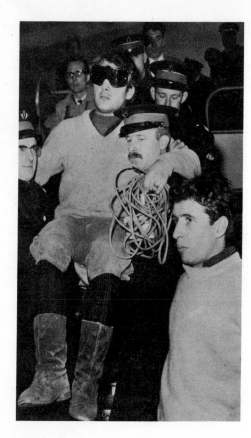

463 DAYS IN A CAVE:
This young Yugoslav,
Milutin Veljkovic, set the
endurance record.

Cave Exploration *(Spelunking)*

PROGRESSIVE CAVING DEPTH RECORDS

feet	Cave	Cavers * Leader	Date
210	Lamb Lair, Somerset, England	John Beaumont (explored)	c. 1676
454	Macocha, Moravia	Nagel	May, 1748
742	Grotta di Padriciano, Trieste, Italy	Antonio Lindner, Svetina	1839
1,079	Grotta di Trebiciano, Trieste	Antonio Lindner	April 6, 1841
1,293	Nidlenloch, Switzerland	—	1909
1,433	Geldloch, Austria	—	1923
1,476	Abisso Bertarelli, Yugoslavia	R. Battelini, G. Cesca	Aug. 24, 1925
1,491	Spluga della Preta, Venice, Italy	*L. de Battisti	Sept. 18, 1927
1,775	Antro di Corchia, Tuscany, Italy	E. Fiorentino Club	1934
1,980	Trou de Glaz, Isère, France	F. Petzl, C. Petit-Didier	May 4, 1947
2,389	Gouffre de la Pierre St. Martin, Básses-Pyrénées, France	*Georges Lépineux	Aug. 15, 1953
2,428	Gouffre Berger, Isère, France	J. Cadoux, G. Garby	Sept. 11, 1954
2,963	Gouffre Berger, Isère, France	*F. Petzl and 6 men	Sept. 25, 1954
3,230	Gouffre Berger, Isère, France	L. Potié, G. Garby et al.	July 29, 1955
>3,600	Gouffre Berger, Isère, France	Jean Cadoux and 2 others	Aug. 11, 1956
>3,600	Gouffre Berger, Isère, France	*Frank Saltè and 7 others	Aug. 23, 1962
>3,700	Gouffre Berger, Isère, France	Kenneth Pearce	Aug. 4, 1963
3,799	Gouffre de la Pierre Saint Martin	French team	Aug., 1966
3,872	Gouffre de la Pierre Saint Martin	C. Queffelec and 10 others	Aug., 1968
4,300	Gouffre de la Pierre Saint Martin	Ass. de Rech. Spéléo Internationale	Nov. 8–11, 1969

Duration. The endurance record for staying in a cave is 463 days by Milutin Veljkovic in the Samar Cavern, Kopajkosari, Yugoslavia from June 24, 1969 to September 30, 1970.

World's Deepest Caves

According to the latest available revised measurements, the deepest caves in the world are:

Feet	Cave	Location
4,300	Gouffre de la Pierre Saint Martin (1966)	Básses-Pyrénées, France/ Spain
3,750	Gouffre Berger	Sornin Plateau, Vercors, France
3,051	Réseau Trombe	Pyrénées, Haute-Garonne, France
2,906	Spluga della Preta	Lessinische Alps, Italy
2,641	Antro di Corchia	Apuanian Alps, Italy
2,573	Grotta del Monte Cucco	Perugia, Italy

Note: The Provetina Cave, Greece, has the world's longest vertical pitch of 1,298 feet. The highest known cave entrance in the world is that of the Rakhiot Cave, Nanga Parbat, Kashmir, at 21,860 feet.

Chess

Origins. The name chess is derived from the Persian word *shah*. It is a descendant of the game *Chaturanga*. The earliest reference is from the Middle Persian Karnamak (*c.* 590–628). It reached Britain in *c.* 1255. The *Fédération Internationale des Echecs* was established in 1924. There were an estimated 7,000,000 registered players in the U.S.S.R. in 1972.

World Champions. François André Danican, *alias* Philidor (1726–95), of France claimed the title of "world champion" from 1747 until his death. World champions have been generally recognized since 1843. The longest tenure has been 27 years by Dr. Emanuel Lasker (1868–1941) of Germany, from 1894 to 1921. The youngest was Paul Charles Morphy (1837–84) of New Orleans, who won the title in 1858, when aged 21, and held it until 1862.

The women's world championship was won three times by Yeliza-veta Bykova (U.S.S.R.) in 1953, 1958, and 1960. (See photo, next page.)

The world team championship (instituted 1927) has been won most often by the U.S.S.R.—11 times consecutively since 1952.

Longest Games. The most protracted chess game on record was one drawn on the 191st move between H. Pilnik (Argentina) and Moshe Czerniak (Israel) at Mar del Plata, Argentina, in April, 1950. The total playing time was 20 hours. A game of 21½ hours, but drawn on the 171st move (average over 7½ minutes per move), was played between Makagonov and Chekover at Baku, U.S.S.R., in 1945. A game of 221 moves between Kenneth Rogoff (U.S.) and Arthur Williams (U.K.) was played in Stockholm, Sweden, in August, 1969, but required only 4 hours 25 mins.

THREE TIMES WOMEN'S WORLD CHESS CHAMPION: Yelizaveta Bykova (U.S.S.R.) at the right.

Marathon. The longest recorded session is one of 101 hours between John P. Cameron and Jon Stevens at Ipswich, Suffolk, England, March 21–25, 1970.

The longest game at "lightning chess" (*i.e.* all moves completed by a player in five minutes) is 50 hours 2 minutes by Michael Dales and Martin Clark of Cordeaux High School, Lincolnshire, England, July 21–23, 1970.

Lawrence Grant and Dr. Munro MacLennan, are still playing a match begun at Aberdeen University, Scotland, on November 24, 1926. They make one move each time they correspond—most often by an annual Christmas card.

Shortest Game. The shortest recorded game between masters was one of four moves when Lazard (Black) beat Gibaud in a Paris chess café in 1924. The moves were: 1. P–Q4, N–KB3; 2. N–Q2, P–K4; 3. PxP, N–N5; 4. P–KR3, N–K6. White then resigned because if he played 5. PxN there would have followed Q–KR5 check and the loss of his Queen for a Knight by any other move.

Most Opponents. Records by chessmasters for numbers of opponents tackled simultaneously depend very much on whether or not the opponents are replaced as defeated, are in relays, or whether they are taken on in a simultaneous start. The greatest number tackled on a replacement basis is 400 (379 defeated) by the Swedish master Gideon Ståhlberg (died May 26, 1967), in 36 hours of play in Buenos Aires, Argentina, in 1940. Georges Koltanowski (Belgium, now of U.S.) tackled 56 opponents "blindfold" and won 50, drew 6, lost 0 in 9¾ hours at the Fairmont Hotel, San Francisco, on December 13, 1960.

Curling

Origins. An early form of the sport is believed to have originated in the Netherlands about 450 years ago. The first club was formed at Kilsyth, near Glasgow, in 1510. Organized administration began in 1838 with the formation of the Royal Caledonian Curling Club, the international legislative body based in Edinburgh. The first indoor ice rink to introduce curling was at Southport, England, in 1879.

The U.S. won the first Gordon International Medal series of matches, between Canada and the U.S., at Montreal in 1884. The first Strathcona Cup match between Canada and Scotland was won by Canada in 1903. Although demonstrated at the Winter Olympics of 1924, 1932 and 1964, curling is not yet included in the official Olympic program.

Most Titles. The most Strathcona Cup wins is seven by Canada (1903–09–12–23–38–57–65) against Scotland. The record for international team matches for the Scotch Cup and Silver Broom (instituted 1959) is ten wins by Canada, in 1959–60–61–62–63–64–66–68–69–70.

The world individual championship has been won five times by William Young (Falkirk, Scotland), in 1951, 1953–54, 1958 and 1960.

Marathon. The longest recorded curling match is one of 32 hours 6 minutes by two rinks (4 players=1 rink) from Newton Stewart & District Round Table, Kirkcudbrightshire, Scotland, May 2–3, 1971.

CURLING CHAMPION:
William Young of Scotland, the only man who has won the world individual title five times.

HIGHEST EQUESTRIAN JUMP: Captain Morales leaped 8 feet 1¼ inches on "Huaso" at Santiago, Chile, in 1949.

Equestrian Sports

Origin. Evidence of horse riding dates from an Anatolian statuette dated *c.* 1400 B.C. Pignatelli's academy of horsemanship at Naples dates from the sixteenth century. The earliest show jumping was in Paris in 1886. Equestrian events have been included in the Olympic Games since 1912.

Most Olympic Medals. The greatest number of Olympic gold medals by a horseman is four by three horsemen:—Lt. C. Ferdinand Pahud de Mortanges (Netherlands), who won the individual three-day event in 1928 and 1932 and was on the winning team in 1924 and 1928, by Major (later Col.) Henri St. Cyr (Sweden), who won the individual Grand Prix de dressage event in 1952 and 1956 and who was also on the winning team, and by Hans Winkler (Germany), who won the Grand Prix Jumping in 1956 and was on the winning team of 1956, 1960 and 1964. The most team wins in the Prix de Nations is four by Germany in 1936, 1956, 1960 and 1964.

The lowest score obtained by a winner was no faults, by F. Ventura (Czechoslovakia) in 1928 and by Pierre Jonqueres d'Oriola (France), the only two-time winner (1952 and 1964), in 1952.

Jumping Records. The official *Fédération Equestre Internationale* high jump record is 8 feet 1¼ inches by *Huasó*, ridden by Capt. A. Larraguibel Morales (Chile) at Santiago, Chile, on February 5, 1949, and 27 feet 2¾ inches for long jump over water by *Amado Mio* ridden by Col. Lopez del Hierro (Spain), at Barcelona, Spain, on November 12, 1951. *Heatherbloom*, ridden by Dick Donnelly was reputed to have covered 37 feet in clearing an 8-foot-3-inch *puissance* jump at Richmond, Virginia, in 1903. *Solid Gold* cleared 36 feet in August, 1936. *Jerry M* allegedly cleared 40 feet over water at Aintree, Liverpool, England, in 1912.

At Cairns, Queensland, *Golden Meade* ridden by Jack Martin cleared an unofficially measured 8 feet 6 inches on July 25, 1946. *Ben Holt* was credited with clearing 9 feet 6 inches at the 1938 Royal Horse Show, Sydney, Australia. The Australian record however is 8 feet 4 inches by C. Russell on *Flyaway* in 1939 and A. L. Payne on *Golden Meade* in 1946. The world's unofficial best for a woman is 7 feet 5½ inches by Miss B. Perry (Australia) at Cairns, Queensland, Australia, in 1940.

The greatest recorded height reached bareback is 6 feet 7 inches by *Silver Wood* at Heidelberg, Victoria, Australia, on December 10, 1938.

Marathon. The longest continuous period spent in the saddle is 38 hours by Joseph Roberts of the Leicester School of Equitation, England, in the Wimbledon Common-Putney Heath area, Greater London, on May 15–17, 1968.

CHAMPION FENCER: Christian d'Oriola of France (right) won most men's titles with the foil.

Fencing

Origins. Fencing was practiced as a sport in Egypt as early as the 12th century B.C. The first governing body for fencing in Britain was the Corporation of Masters of Defence founded by Henry VIII before 1540 and fencing was practiced as sport, notably in prize fights, since that time. The foil was the practice weapon for the short court sword from the 17th century. The épée was established in the mid-19th century and the light saber was introduced by the Italians in the late 19th century.

Most Olympic Titles. The greatest number of individual Olympic gold medals won is three by Nedo Nadi (Italy) in 1912 and 1920 (2) and Ramon Fonst (Cuba) in 1900 and 1904 (2). Nadi also won three team gold medals in 1920 making an unprecedented total of five gold medals at one Olympic meet. Italy has won the épée team title six times. France has won the foil team title five times. Hungary has won 9 out of 12 saber team titles. Aladár Gerevich (Hungary) was on the winning saber team in 1932, 1936, 1948, 1952, 1956 and 1960.

Most World Titles. The greatest number of individual world titles won is four by Christian d'Oriola (France) with the foil in 1947–49–53–54. He also won the Olympic titles in 1952 and 1956. (See photo, previous page.)

Ellen Müller-Priess (Austria) won the women's foil in 1947 and 1949 and shared it in 1950. She also won the Olympic title in 1932.

Italy won the men's foil team 13 times; Hungary the ladies' foil teams 11 times; Italy the épée teams 10 times and Hungary the saber teams 13 times.

Field Hockey

Origin. A representation of two hockey players apparently in an orthodox "bully" position was found in Tomb No. 16 at Beni Hasan, United Arab Republic (formerly Egypt) and has been dated to *c.* 2000 B.C. There is a reference to the game in Lincolnshire, England, in 1277. The oldest club is Blackheath, Kent, England, founded in 1861. The first country to form a national association was England (The Hockey Association) in 1886.

Earliest International. The first international match was the Wales *vs.* Ireland match on January 26, 1895. Ireland won 3–0.

Highest International Score. The highest score in international field hockey was when India defeated the U.S. 24–1 at Los Angeles, in the 1932 Olympic Games. The Indians were Olympic Champions from the re-inception of Olympic hockey in 1928 until 1960, when Pakistan beat them 1–0 at Rome. They had their seventh win in 1964. Four Indians have won 3 Olympic gold medals—Dhyan Chand and R. J. Allen (1928, 1932, 1936), Randhir Gentle (1948, 1952, 1956), and Leslie Claudius (1948, 1952 and 1956).

The highest score in a women's international match occurred when England defeated France 23–0 at Merton, Surrey, on February 3, 1923.

Longest Game. The longest international game on record was one of 145 minutes (into the sixth period of extra time), when Netherlands beat Spain 1–0 in the Olympic tournament at Mexico City on October 25, 1968.

Attendance. The highest attendance at a women's hockey match was 65,000 for the match between England and Wales at the Empire Stadium, Wembley, Greater London, on March 8, 1969.

Fishing

Largest Catches. The largest fish ever caught on a rod is an officially ratified man-eating great white shark (*Carcharodon carcharias*) weighing 2,664 lbs., and measuring 16 feet 10 inches long, caught by Alf Dean at Denial Bay, near Ceduna, South Australia, on April 21, 1959. Capt. Frank Mundus (U.S.) harpooned and landed a 17-foot-long 4,500-lb. white shark, after a 5-hour battle, off Montauk Point, Long Island, New York, in 1964.

The largest fish ever taken underwater was an 804-lb. giant black grouper or Jewfish by Don Pinder of the Miami Triton Club, Florida, in 1955.

The largest marine animal ever killed by hand harpoon was a blue whale 97 feet in length, killed by Archer Davidson in Twofold Bay, New South Wales, Australia, in 1910. Its tail flukes measured 20 feet across and its jaw bone 23 feet 4 inches. To date this has provided the ultimate in "fishing stories."

THE ULTIMATE IN ANGLING: Alf Dean (Australia) with his record 2,664-lb. white shark.

Fishing

(Sea fish records taken by tackle as ratified by the International Game Fish Association to June 30, 1967. Fresh-water fish are marked *)

Species	Weight in lbs.	oz.	Name of Angler	Location	Date
Amberjack	149	0	Peter Simons	Bermuda	June 21, 1964
Barracuda	103	4	C. E. Benet	West End, Bahamas	Aug. 11, 1932
Bass (Californian Black Sea)	563	8	James D. McAdam	Anacapa Island, California	Aug. 20, 1968
Bass (Giant Sea)	680	0	Lynn Joyner	Fernandina Beach, Florida	May 20, 1961
*Carp†	55	5	Frank J. Ledwein	Clearwater Lake, Minnesota	July 10, 1952
Cod	98	12	Alphonse J. Bielevich	Isle of Shoals, Massachusetts	June 8, 1969
Marlin (Black)	1,560	0	Alfred C. Glassell, Jr.	Cabo Blanco, Peru	Aug. 4, 1953
Marlin (Blue)	845	0	Elliot J. Fishman	St. Thomas, Virgin Is.	July 4, 1968
Marlin (Pacific Blue)	1,153	0	Greg D. Perez	Ritidian Point, Guam	Aug. 21, 1969
Marlin (Striped)	465	0	James Black	Mayor Island, New Zealand	Feb. 27, 1948
Marlin (White)	161	0	L. F. Hooper	Miami Beach, Florida	Mar. 20, 1938
*Pike (Northern)	46	2	Peter Dubuc	Sacandaga Reservoir, New York	Sept. 15, 1940
Sailfish (Atlantic)	141	1	Tony Burnand	Ivory Coast, Africa	Jan. 26, 1961
Sailfish (Pacific)	221	0	C. W. Stewart	Santa Cruz I., Galapagos Is.	Feb. 12, 1947
*Salmon (Chinook)§	92	0	H. Wichmann	Skeena River, B.C., Canada	July 19, 1959
Sawfish	890	8	Jack Wagner	Fort Amador, Canal Zone	May 26, 1960
Shark (Blue)	410	0	Richard C. Webster	Rockport, Massachusetts	Sept. 1, 1960
**Shark (Mako)	1061	0	Martha C. Webster	Rockport, Massachusetts	Aug. 17, 1967
Shark (White or Man-Eating)	2,664	0	James B. Penwarden	Mayor Island, New Zealand	Feb. 17, 1970
Shark (Porbeagle)	430	0	Alfred Dean (See photo)	Aduna, South Australia	Apr. 21, 1959
Shark (Thresher)	922	0	Desmond Bougourd	South of Jersey, England	June 29, 1959
Shark (Tiger)	1,780	0	W. W. Dowding	Bay of Islands, New Zealand	Mar. 21, 1937
*Sturgeon (White)	360	0	Walter Maxwell	Cherry Grove, South Carolina	June 14, 1964
Swordfish	1,182	0	Willard Cravens	Snake River, Idaho	Apr. 24, 1956
Tarpon	283	0	L. E. Marron	Iquique, Chile	May 7, 1953
*Trout (Lake)‖	63	2	M. Salazar	Lago de Maracaibo, Venezuela	Mar. 19, 1956
Tuna (Allison or Yellowfin)	296	0	Hubert Hammers	Lake Superior	May 25, 1952
Tuna (Atlantic Big-eyed)	295	0	Edward C. Malnar	San Benedicts Is., Mexico	Mar. 7, 1971
Tuna (Pacific Big-eyed)	435	0	Dr. Arsenio Cordeiro	San Miguel, Azores	July 8, 1960
Tuna (Bluefin)	1,065	0	Dr. Russel V. A. Lee	Cabo Blanco, Peru	April 17, 1957
Wahoo	149	0	Robert Glen Gibson	Cape Breton, Nova Scotia	Nov. 19, 1970
			John Pirovano	Cat Cay, Bahamas	June 15, 1962

† A carp weighing 83 lbs. 8 oz. was taken (not by rod) near Pretoria, South Africa. § A salmon weighing 126 lbs. 8 oz. was taken (not by rod) near Petersburg, Alaska. ‖ A 102-lb. trout was taken from Lake Athabasca, northern Saskatchewan, Canada, on August 8, 1961. **A 1,295-lb. specimen was taken by two anglers off Natal, South Africa, on March 17, 1939, and a 1,500-lb. specimen harpooned inside Durban Harbour, South Africa, in 1933.

Smallest Catch. The smallest full-grown fish ever caught is the *Schindleria praematurus*, weighing 1/14,000th of an ounce found near Samoa, in the central Pacific.

The smallest mature shark is the rare *Squalidus laticaudus*, found off the Philippines, which measures only 6 inches in length.

Surf Casting. The longest surf casting distance ever reported is one of 1,000 feet achieved on a beach in South Africa. The official world record under I.C.F. (International Casting Federation) rules is 528 feet 2½ inches by Walter Kummerov (West Germany).

Longest Fight. The longest recorded fight with a fish is 32 hours 5 minutes by Donal Heatley (b. 1938) (New Zealand) with a black marlin (estimated length 20 feet and weight 1,500 lbs.) off Mayor Island off Tauranga, New Zealand, January 21–22, 1968. It towed the 12-foot launch 50 miles before breaking the line.

Football

Origins. The origin of modern football stems from the "Boston Game" as played at Harvard. Harvard declined to participate in the inaugural meeting of the Intercollegiate Football Association in New York City in October, 1873, on the grounds that the proposed rules were based on the non-handling "Association" code of English football. Instead, Harvard accepted a proposal from McGill University of Montreal, Canada, who played the more closely akin English Rugby Football. The first football match under the Harvard Rules was thus played against McGill at Cambridge, Mass., in May, 1874. In November, 1876, a New Intercollegiate Football Association, based on modern football, was inaugurated at Springfield, Mass., with a pioneer membership of five colleges.

Professional football dates from the Latrobe, Pa. *vs.* Jeannette, Pa., match at Latrobe, in August, 1895. The National Football League was founded in Canton, Ohio, in 1920, although it did not adopt its present name until 1922. The year 1969 was the final year in which professional football was divided into separate National and American Leagues, for record purposes.

All-America Selections

The earliest All-America selections were made in 1889 by Caspar Whitney of *The Week's Sport* and later of *Harper's Weekly*.

College Series Records

The oldest collegiate series is that between Princeton and Rutgers dating from 1869, or 7 years before the passing of the Springfield rules. The most regularly contested series is between Lafayette and Lehigh, who have met 107 times between 1884 and the end of 1971.

Longest Streaks

The longest winning streak is 47 straight by Oklahoma. The longest unbeaten streak is 63 games (59 won, 4 tied) by Washington from 1907 to 1917.

COLLEGIATE ALL-TIME RECORDS

Points

Most in a Season ....243...Mayes McClain (Haskell) 1926
Most in a Game ....100...Leo Schlick (St. Viator)....................1916
Most in a Career ....465...Willie Heston (Michigan) 1901–4

Touchdowns

Most in a Game ....12...Leo Schlick (St. Viator)....................1916
Most in a Season ....30...John Imlay (Missouri Mines)..............1914

Field Goals

Most in a Game ....17...Forest Peters (Montana Freshmen)......1924
(Varsity) ....7...Edward C. Robertson (Purdue)............1900
Most in a Season ....18...Bob Jacobs (Wyoming).....................1969
Most in a Career ....37...Bob Jacobs (Wyoming).................1968–70

Points After Touchdown

Most in a Season ....64...Ivan Grove (Henry Kendall)..............1919

ALL-TIME INDIVIDUAL COLLEGIATE SEASON RECORDS*

Total Offense .... 3,343 yds....Bill Anderson (Tulsa)...............1965
Most Rushing and Passing Plays...........580...Bill Anderson (Tulsa)...............1965
Most Times Carried..........................358...Steve Owens (Oklahoma) 1969
Yards Gained Rushing...............1,881 yds....Ed Marinaro (Cornell)...........1971
Highest Average Gain per Rush ...11.51 yds....Glen Davis (Army).................1945
Most Passes Completed ....296...Bill Anderson (Tulsa)...............1965
Most Touchdown Passes ....39...Dennis Shaw (San Diego St.)......1969
Highest Completed Percentage.........68.7%...Jerry Rhome (Tulsa) 1964
Most Yards Gained Passing.........3,464 yds....Bill Anderson (Tulsa)...............1965
Most Passes Caught ....134...Howard Twilley (Tulsa)...........1965
Most Yards Gained on Catches...1,779 yds....Howard Twilley (Tulsa)...........1965
Most Touchdown Passes Caught............18...Tom Reynolds (San Diego St.)...1969
Most Passes Intercepted by...................14...Al Worley (Washington)........1968
Longest Field Goal (placed)............65 yds....John T. Haxall (Princeton)........1882
(drop kick).............. 63 yds....Mark Payne (Dakota Wesleyan)..1915
Longest Punt (in air).................... 89 yds....Albert Braga (San Francisco)......1937
Longest Run from Scrimmage.........115 yds....Wyllys Terry (Yale)...............1884
Longest Kickoff Return..............110 yds....Robert Hill (Army).................1907
Longest Punt Return ....110 yds....Oscar Morgan (Trinity)...........1904
110 yds....Ben Boynton (Williams)...........1920
Longest Scoring Pass (main)...........67 yds....John   Woerner   to   Maynard
in air   Schultz (Oregon State).........1935

* Major colleges only.

Longest Service Coach

The longest service head coach was Amos Alonzo Stagg, who served Springfield in 1890–91, Chicago from 1892 to 1932 and College of Pacific from 1933 to 1946, making a total of 57 years.

All-Star Games

The reigning N.F.L. Champions first met an All-Star College selection in the annual August series in Chicago in 1934. The highest scoring match was that of 1940 in which Green Bay beat the All-Stars 45–28. The biggest professional win was in 1949 when Philadelphia won 38–0, and the biggest All-Stars win was in 1943 when Washington was defeated 27–7.

Service

Most Seasons, Active Player
22 George Blanda, Chi. Bears 1949–58; Balt. 1950; AFL: Hou. 1960–66; Oak. 1967–71

Most Games Played, Lifetime
280 George Blanda, Chi. Bears 1949–58; Balt. 1950; AFL: Hou. 1960–66; Oak. 1967–71

Most Consecutive Games Played, Lifetime
182 Jim Ringo, Green Bay (126) 1953–63; Phil. (56) 1964–67

Most Seasons, Head Coach
40 George Halas, Chi. Bears 1920–29, 33–42, 46–55, 58–67

Scoring

Most Seasons Leading League
5 Don Hutson, Green Bay 1940–44
Gino Cappelletti, Bos. 1961, 63–66 (AFL)

Most Points, Lifetime
1647 George Blanda, Chi. Bears 1949–58; Balt. 1950; AFL: Hou. 1960–66; Oak. 1967–71 (9-td, 780-pat, 271-fg)

Most Points, Season
176 Paul Hornung, Green Bay 1960 (15-td, 41-pat, 15-fg)

Most Points, Rookie, Season
132 Gale Sayers, Chi. 1965 (22-td)

Most Points, Game
40 Ernie Nevers, Chi. Cards vs Chi. Bears, Nov. 28, 1929 (6-td, 4-pat)

Most Points, One Quarter
29 Don Hutson, Green Bay vs Det., Oct. 7, 1945 (4-td, 5-pat) 2nd Quarter

Touchdowns

Most Seasons Leading League
8 Don Hutson, Green Bay, 1935–38, 41–44

Most Touchdowns, Lifetime
126 Jim Brown, Cleve. 1957–65 (106-r, 20-p)

Most Touchdowns, Season
22 Gale Sayers, Chi. 1965 (14-r, 6-p, 1-prb, 1-krb)

Most Touchdowns, Rookie Season
22 Gale Sayers, Chi. 1965 (14-r, 6-p, 1-prb, 1-krb)

Most Touchdowns, Game
6 Ernie Nevers, Chi. Cards vs Chi. Bears, Nov. 28, 1929 (6-r)
William (Dub) Jones, Cleve. vs Chi. Bears, Nov. 25, 1951 (4-r, 2-p)
Gale Sayers, Chi. vs S. F., Dec. 12, 1965 (4-r, 1-p, 1-prb)

Most Consecutive Games Scoring Touchdowns
18 Lenny Moore, Balt. 1963–65

Points after Touchdown

Most Seasons Leading League
6 George Blanda, Chi. Bears 1956; AFL: Hou. 1961–62; Oak. 1967–71

Most Points After Touchdown, Lifetime
780 George Blanda, Chi. Bears 1949–58; Balt. 1950; AFL: Hou. 1960–66; Oak. 1967–69

Most Points After Touchdown, Season
64 George Blanda, Hou. 1961 (AFL)

Most Points After Touchdown, Game
9 Marlin (Pat) Harder, Chi. Cards vs N. Y., Oct. 17, 1948
Bob Waterfield, L. A. vs Balt., Oct. 22, 1950
Charlie Gogolak, Wash. vs N. Y., Nov. 27, 1966

Most Consecutive Points After Touchdown
234 Tommy Davis, S. F. 1959–65

Most Points After Touchdown (no misses), Season
56 Danny Villanueva, Dall. 1966

Most Points After Touchdown (no misses), Game
9 Marlin (Pat) Harder, Chi. Cards vs N. Y., Oct. 17, 1948
Bob Waterfield, L. A. vs Balt., Oct. 22, 1950

ENDURANCE RECORDS as well as passing and field goals records were set in 1971 by George Blanda (Oakland) who was still starring as a quarterback at the age of 44.

Field Goals

Most Seasons Leading League
5   Lou Groza, Cleve., 1950, 52–54, 57

Most Field Goals, Lifetime
271   George Blanda, Chi. Bears 1949–58; Balt. 1950; AFL: Hou. 1960–66; Oak. 1967–71

Most Field Goals, Season
34   Jim Turner, N.Y. 1968 (AFL)

Most Field Goals, Game
7   Jim Bakken, St. L. vs Pitt., Sept. 24, 1967

Most Consecutive Games, Field Goals
31   Fred Cox, Minn. 1968–70

Most Consecutive Field Goals
16   Jan Stenerud, K.C. 1969 (AFL)

Longest Field Goal
63 yds. Tom Dempsey, New Orl. vs Det. Nov. 8, 1970 (see photo)

Rushing

Most Seasons Leading League
8   Jim Brown, Cleve. 1957–61, 63–65

Most Yards Gained, Lifetime
12,312   Jim Brown, Cleve., 1957–65

Most Yards Gained, Season
1,863   Jim Brown, Cleve., 1963

Most Yards Gained, Game
247   Willie Ellison, L.A. vs N.O., Dec. 5, 1971

Longest Run from Scrimmage
97 yards Andy Uram, Green Bay vs Chi. Cards, Oct. 8, 1939 (td)
Bob Gage, Pitt. vs Chi. Bears, Dec. 4, 1949 (td)

Highest Average Gain, Lifetime (700 att.)
5.22   Jim Brown, Cleve. 1957–65 (2,359–12,312)

Highest Average Gain, Season (100 att.)
9.9   Beattie Feathers, Chi. Bears, 1934 (101–1004)

Highest Average Gain, Game (10 att.)
17.1   Marion Morley, Cleve. vs Pitt., Oct. 29, 1950 (11–188)

Most Touchdowns Rushing, Lifetime
106   Jim Brown, Cleve., 1957–65

Most Touchdowns Rushing, Season
19   Jim Taylor, Green Bay, 1962

Most Touchdowns Rushing, Game
6   Ernie Nevers, Chi. Cards vs Chi. Bears, Nov. 28, 1929

Passing

Most Seasons Leading League
6   Sammy Baugh, Wash., 1937, 40, 43, 45, 47, 49

Most Passes Attempted, Lifetime
4,953   John Unitas, Balt. 1956–71 (2,708 completions)

Most Passes Attempted, Season
508   C. A. (Sonny) Jurgensen, Wash., 1967 (288 completions)

Most Passes Attempted, Game
68   George Blanda, Hou. vs Buff., Nov. 1, 1964 (AFL) (37 completions)

Most Passes Completed, Lifetime
2,708   John Unitas, Balt. 1956–71 (4,953 attempts)

Most Passes Completed, Season
288   C. A. (Sonny) Jurgensen, Wash., 1967 (508 attempts)

Most Passes Completed, Game
37   George Blanda, Hou. vs Buff., Nov. 1, 1964 (AFL) (68 attempts)

Most Consecutive Passes Completed
15   Len Dawson, K.C. vs Hou., Sept. 9, 1967 (AFL)

Passing Efficiency, Lifetime (1,000 att.)
57.4   Bart Starr, Green Bay, 1956–71 (3,149–1,808)

Passing Efficiency, Season (100 att.)
70.3   Sammy Baugh, Wash., 1945 (182–128)

Passing Efficiency, Game (20 att.)
85.7   Sammy Baugh, Wash. vs Pitt., Oct. 14, 1945 (21–18)

Most Yards Gained Passing, Lifetime
38,657   John Unitas, Balt. 1956–71

Most Yards Gained Passing, Season
4,007   Joe Namath, N. Y. 1967 (AFL)

Most Yards Gained Passing, Game
554   Norm Van Brocklin, L. A. vs N. Y. Yanks, Sept. 28, 1951 (41–27)

Longest Pass Completion (all TDs)
99   Frank Filchock (to Farkas), Wash. vs Pitt., Oct. 15, 1939
George Izo (to Mitchell), Wash. vs Cleve., Sept. 15, 1963
Karl Sweetan (to Studstill), Det. vs Balt., Oct. 16, 1966
C. A. Jurgensen (to Allen), Wash. vs Chi., Sept. 15, 1968

Shortest Pass Completion for Touchdown
2″   Eddie LeBaron (to Bielski), Dall. vs Wash., Oct. 9, 1960

Most Touchdown Passes, Lifetime
283   John Unitas, Balt. 1956–71

Most Touchdown Passes, Season
36   George Blanda, Hou. 1961 (AFL)
Y. A. Tittle, N. Y. 1963

Most Touchdown Passes, Game
7   Sid Luckman, Chi. Bears vs N. Y. Nov. 14, 1943
Adrian Burk, Phil. vs Wash., Oct. 17, 1954
George Blanda, Hou. vs N. Y., Nov. 19, 1961 (AFL)
Y. A. Tittle, N. Y. vs Wash., Oct. 28, 1962
Joe Kapp, Minn. vs Balt., Sept. 28, 1969

**MOST EFFICIENT
PASSER:** Sammy
Baugh (Wash.) had an
85.7 per cent record in
one game with 20
attempts and 70.3
percentage for the
season in 1945. Baugh
also holds punting records.

**THREW MOST
TOUCHDOWN
PASSES** (one game):
Sid Luckman (Chi.)
shares record of 7 with
George Blanda and others.

HIGHEST SCORER: Don Hutson (Green Bay)
made 4 touchdowns and 5 points after to set a
record of 29 points in one quarter in 1945.

LONGEST FIELD GOAL in NFL competition (63 yards) was kicked by a man with only half a foot—Tom Dempsey of the New Orleans Saints, who wears a special shoe over his wooden foot, and has only a stump of a right arm. His record kick beat the Detroit Lions, 19-17, on the last play of the game on November 8, 1970.

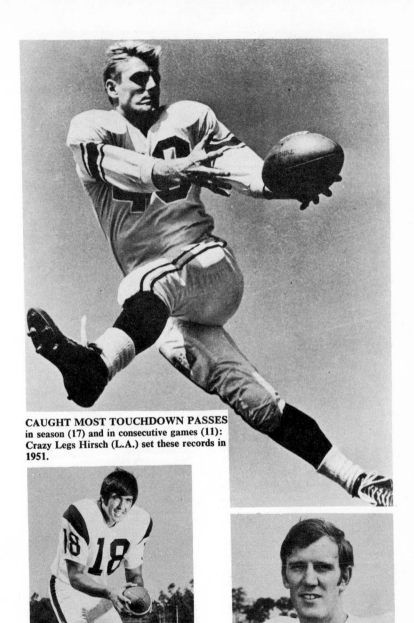

CAUGHT MOST TOUCHDOWN PASSES in season (17) and in consecutive games (11): Crazy Legs Hirsch (L.A.) set these records in 1951.

SNATCHED 4 OF HIS OWN FUMBLES (one game in 1969): Roman Gabriel (L.A.).

LONGEST PUNTER: Steve O'Neal (N.Y. Jets) kicked 98 yards in the AFL in 1969.

N.F.L. Records (continued)

Passing

Most Consecutive Games, Touchdown Passes
47 John Unitas, Balt., 1956–60

Passes Had Intercepted

Fewest Passes Intercepted, Season (100 att.)
1 Bill Nelsen, Pitt., 1966 (112 attempts)

Most Consecutive Passes Attempted, None Intercepted
294 Bryan (Bart) Starr, Green Bay, 1964–65

Most Passes Intercepted, Game
8 Jim Hardy, Chi. Cards vs Phil., Sept. 24, 1950 (39 attempts)

Lowest Percentage Passes Intercepted, Lifetime (1,000 att.)
3.24 Roman Gabriel, L. A. 1962–71

Lowest Percentage Passes Intercepted, Season (100 att.)
0.89 Bill Nelsen, Pitt., 1966 (1–112)

Pass Receptions

Most Seasons Leading League
8 Don Hutson, Green Bay. 1936–37, 39, 41–45

Most Pass Receptions, Lifetime
631 Raymond Berry, Balt., 1955–67

Most Pass Receptions, Season
101 Charley Hennigan, Hou. 1964 (AFL)

Most Pass Receptions, Game
18 Tom Fears, L. A. vs Green Bay, Dec. 3, 1950 (189 yds.)

Most Consecutive Games, Pass Receptions
96 Lance Alworth, San Diego 1962–69 (AFL)

Longest Pass Reception (all TDs)
99 Andy Farkas (Filchock), Wash. vs Pitt., Oct. 15, 1939
Bobby Mitchell (Izo), Wash. vs Cleve., Sept. 15, 1963
Pat Studstill (Sweetan), Det. vs Balt., Oct. 16, 1966
Gerry Allen (Jurgensen), Wash. vs Chi., Sept. 15, 1968

Shortest Pass Reception for Touchdown
2″ Dick Bielski (LeBaron), Dall. vs Wash., Oct. 9, 1960

Touchdowns Receiving

Most Touchdown Passes, Lifetime
100 Don Hutson, Green Bay, 1935–45

Most Touchdown Passes, Season
17 Don Hutson, Green Bay, 1942
Elroy (Crazy Legs) Hirsch, L. A., 1951
Bill Groman, Hou. 1961 (AFL)

Most Touchdown Passes, Game
5 Bob Shaw, Chi. Cards vs Balt., Oct. 2, 1950

MOST CONSECUTIVE GAMES (96) WITH PASS RECEPTIONS was the record set in 1969 in the AFL by Lance Alworth of the San Diego Chargers.

Most Consecutive Games, Touchdown Passes
11 Elroy (Crazy Legs) Hirsch, L.A., 1950–51
Gilbert (Buddy) Dial, Pitt.,9– 195 60

Pass Interceptions

Most Interceptions by, Lifetime
79 Emlen Tunnell, N. Y. (74), 1948–58; Green Bay (5), 1959–61

Most Interceptions by, Season
14 Richard (Night Train) Lane, L. A., 1952

Most Interceptions by, Game
4 By many players

Interception Yardage

Most Yards Gained, Lifetime
1,282 Emlen Tunnell, N. Y., 1948–58; Green Bay, 1959–61

Most Yards Gained, Season
349 Charley McNeil, San Diego 1961 (AFL)

Most Yards Gained, Game
177 Charley McNeil, San Diego vs Hou., Sept. 24, 1961 (AFL)

Longest Gain (all TDs)
102 Bob Smith, Det. vs Chi. Bears, Nov. 24, 1949
Erich Barnes, N. Y. vs Dall., Oct. 22, 1961

Touchdowns on Interceptions

Most Touchdowns, Lifetime
9 Ken Houston, Hou. 1967–71

Most Touchdowns, Season
4 Ken Houston, Hou. 1971

Punting

Most Seasons Leading League
 4 Sammy Baugh, Wash., 1940–43

Most Punts, Lifetime
 821 Bobby Joe Green, Pitt. 1960–61;
   Chi. 62–71

Most Punts, Season
 105 Bob Scarpitto, Den. 1967 (AFL)

Most Punts, Game
 14 Sammy Baugh, Wash. vs Phil.,
   Nov. 5, 1939
   John Kinscherf, N. Y. vs Det.,
   Nov. 7, 1943
   George Taliaferro, N. Y. Yanks
   vs L. A., Sept. 28, 1951

Longest Punt
 98 yards Steve O'Neal, N. Y. vs
   Den., Sept. 21, 1969 (AFL)

Average Yardage Punting

Highest Punting Average, Lifetime (300
 punts)
44.93 yards Sammy Baugh, Wash.,
 1937–52 (338)

Highest Punting Average, Season (20
 punts)
 51.3 yards Sammy Baugh, Wash.,
 1940 (35)

Highest Punting Average, Game (4
 punts)
 59.4 yards Sammy Baugh, Wash. vs
 Det., Oct. 27, 1940 (5)

Kickoffs

Yardage Returning Kickoffs

Most Yards Gained, Lifetime
5,538 Abe Woodson, S. F. (4,873),
 1958–64; St. L. (665), 1965–66

Most Yards Gained, Season
1,317 Bobby Jancik, Hou. 1963 (AFL)

Most Yards Gained, Game
 294 Wally Triplett, Det. vs L. A.,
   Oct. 29, 1950 (4)

Longest Kickoff Return for Touchdown
 106 Al Carmichael, Green Bay vs.
   Chi. Bears, Oct. 7, 1956
   Noland Smith, K.C. vs Den.,
   Dec. 17, 1967 (AFL)

Average Yardage Returning Kickoffs

Highest Average, Lifetime (75 returns)
 30.6 Gale Sayers, Chi. 1965–71

Highest Average, Season (15 returns)
 41.1 Travis Williams, Green Bay, 1967
   (18)

Highest Average, Game (3 returns)
 73.5 Wally Triplett, Det. vs L. A.,
   Oct. 29, 1950 (4-294)

Touchdowns Returning Kickoffs

Most Touchdowns, Lifetime
 6 Ollie Matson, Chi. Cards, 1952
   (2), 54, 56, 58 (2)
   Gale Sayers, Chi., 1965, 66 (2),
   67 (3)
   Travis Williams, G.B. 1967 (4),
   69, 71

Most Touchdowns, Season
 4 Travis Williams, Green Bay, 1967
   Cecil Turner, Chi. 1970

Most Touchdowns, Game
 2 Thomas (Tim) Brown, Phil. vs
   Dall., Nov. 6, 1966
   Travis Williams, Green Bay vs
   Cleve., Nov. 12, 1967

Fumbles

Most Fumbles, Lifetime
 89 John Unitas, Balt. 1956–71

Most Fumbles, Season
 16 Don Meredith, Dall., 1964

Most Fumbles, Game
 7 Len Dawson, K.C. vs San Diego,
   Nov. 15, 1964 (AFL)

Most Own Fumbles Recovered, Lifetime
 38 Jack Kemp, Pitt. 1957; AFL:
   L. A./San Diego 1960–62; Buff.
   1962–67, 69

Most Own Fumbles Recovered, Season
 8 Paul Christman, Chi. Cards, 1945
   Bill Butler, Minn., 1963

Most Own Fumbles Recovered, Game
 4 Otto Graham, Cleve. vs N. Y.,
   Oct. 25, 1953
   Sam Etcheverry, St. L. vs N. Y.,
   Sept. 17, 1961
   Roman Gabriel, L. A. vs S. F.,
   Oct. 12, 1969

Most Opponents' Fumbles Recovered,
 Lifetime
 22 Andy Robustelli, L. A. (13),
   1951–55; N. Y. (9), 1956–64
   Joe Fortunato, Chi. 1955–66

Most Opponents' Fumbles Recovered,
 Season
 9 Don Hultz, Minn., 1963

Most Opponents' Fumbles Recovered,
 Game
 3 Corwin Clatt, Chi. Cards vs Det.,
   Nov. 6, 1949
   Vic Sears, Phil. vs Green Bay,
   Nov. 2, 1952
   Ed Beatty, S. F. vs L. A., Oct. 7,
   1956

Longest Fumble Run
 98 George Halas, Chi. Bears vs
   Marion, Nov. 4, 1923 (TD)

Miscellaneous

Most Drop Kick Field Goals, Game
 4 John (Paddy) Driscoll, Chi. Cards
   vs Columbus, Oct. 11, 1925 (23,
   18, 50, 35 yards)
   Elbert Bloodgood, Kansas City
   vs Duluth, Dec. 12, 1926 (35, 32,
   20, 25 yards)

Longest Drop Kick Field Goal
 50 Wilbur (Pete) Henry, Canton vs
   Toledo, Nov. 13, 1922
   John (Paddy) Driscoll, Chi. Cards
   vs Milwaukee, Sept. 28, 1924;
   vs Columbus, Oct. 11, 1925

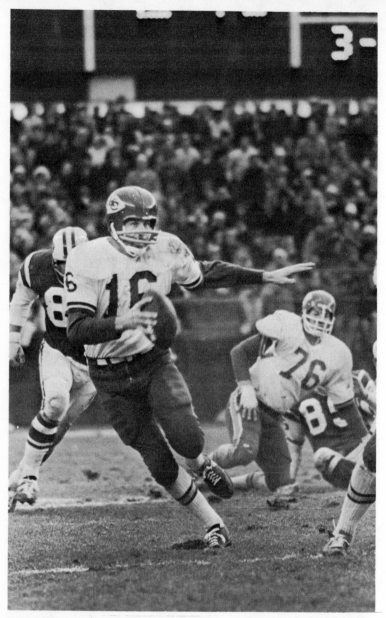

MOST SUCCESSFUL FORWARD PASSER: Len Dawson of the Kansas City Chiefs (AFL) completed 15 consecutive passes to set a world record in a game against Houston in September, 1967.

N.F.L. Records (continued)

Most Yards Returned Missed Field Goal
101 Al Nelson, Phil. vs Dall., Sept. 26, 1971 (TD)

Passer Catching Own Pass
John Unitas, Balt. vs Det., Nov. 18, 1956 (1 yard gain)
Y. A. Tittle, S. F. vs L. A., Oct. 4, 1959 (4 yard gain)
Milt Plum, Cleve. vs Chi. Cards, Oct. 18, 1959 (20 yard gain)
Bill Nelsen, Pitt. vs Dall., Oct. 31, 1965 (− 5 yards)

SEASON RECORDS—OFFENSE

Most Seasons League Champion
11 Green Bay, 1929–31, 36, 39, 44, 61–62, 65–67

Most Consecutive Games Without Defeat (Regular Season)
24 Canton, 1922–23 (Won–21, Tied–3)
Chicago Bears, 1941–43 (Won–23, Tied–1)

Most Consecutive Victories (All Games
18 Chicago Bears (1933–34; 1941–42)

Most Consecutive Victories (Regular Season)
17 Chicago Bears, 1933–34

Most Consecutive Shutout Games Won
7 Detroit, 1934

Scoring

Most Seasons Leading League
9 Chicago Bears, 1934–35, 39, 41–43. 46–47, 56

Most Points, Season
513 Houston 1961 (AFL)

Most Points, Game
72 Washington vs N. Y., Nov. 27, 1966

Most Touchdowns, Season
66 Houston, 1961 (AFL)

Most Touchdowns, Game
10 Philadelphia vs Cin., Nov. 6, 1934
Los Angeles vs Balt., Oct. 22, 1950
Washington vs N. Y., Nov. 27, 1966

Most Touchdowns, Both Teams, Game
16 Washington (10) vs N. Y. (6), Nov. 27, 1966

Most Points After Touchdown, Season
65 Houston, 1961 (AFL)
59 Los Angeles, 1950

Most Points After Touchdown, Game
10 Los Angeles vs Balt., Oct. 22, 1950

Most Points After Touchdown, Both Teams, Game
14 Chicago Cards (9) vs N. Y. (5), Oct. 17, 1948
Houston (7) vs Oakland (7), Dec. 22, 1963 (AFL)
Washington (9) vs N. Y. (5), Nov. 27, 1966

Most Field Goals Attempted, Season
49 Los Angeles, 1966
Washington, 1971

Most Field Goals Attempted, Game
9 St. Louis vs Pitt., Sept. 24, 1967

Most Field Goals Attempted, Both Teams, Game
11 St. Louis (6) vs Pitt. (5), Nov. 13, 1966

Most Field Goals, Season
34 New York, 1968 (AFL)

Most Field Goals, Game
7 St. Louis vs Pitt., Sept. 24, 1967

Most Field Goals, Both Teams, Game
8 Cleveland (4) vs St. L. (4), Sept. 20, 1964
Chicago (5) vs Phil. (3), Oct. 20, 1968

Most Consecutive Games Scoring Field Goals
31 Minnesota, 1968–70

First Downs

Most Seasons Leading League
7 Chicago Bears, 1935, 41, 43, 45, 48–49, 55

Most First Downs, Season
297 Dallas, 1968

Most First Downs, Game
38 Los Angeles vs N. Y., Nov. 13, 1966

Most First Downs, Both Teams, Game
58 Los Angeles (30) vs Chi. Bears (28), Oct. 24, 1954

Most First Downs, Rushing, Season
145 Green Bay, 1962

Most First Downs, Rushing, Game
25 Philadelphia vs Wash., Dec. 2, 1951

Most First Downs, Passing, Season
186 Houston, 1964 (AFL)
Oakland, 1964 (AFL)

Most First Downs, Passing, Game
24 Houston vs Buffalo, Nov. 1, 1964 (AFL)
Minnesota vs Baltimore, Sept. 28, 1969

Net Yards Gained (Rushes and Passes)

Most Seasons Leading League
12 Chicago Bears, 1932, 34–35, 39, 41–44, 47, 49, 55–56

Most Yards Gained, Season
6,288 Houston, 1961 (AFL)

Most Yards Gained, Game
735 Los Angeles vs N. Y. Yanks, Sept. 28, 1951 (181-r, 554-p)

Most Yards Gained, Both Teams, Game
1,133 Los Angeles (636) vs N. Y. Yanks (497), Nov. 19, 1950

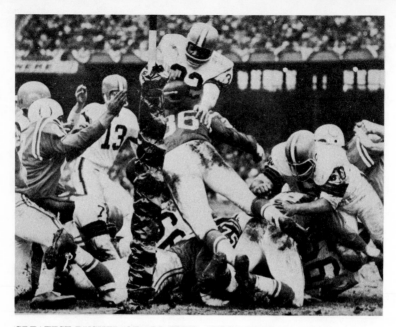

GREATEST RUSHER OF ALL TIME: Jim Brown (Cleve.) holds the record of 12,312 yards gained in a lifetime and 1,863 in a season, 1963. Here he is running against the Baltimore Colts in the 1964 championship game.

N.F.L. Team Records (continued)

Rushing

Most Seasons Leading League
11   Chicago Bears, 1932, 34–35, 39–42, 51, 55–56, 68

Most Rushing Attempts, Season
632   Philadelphia, 1949

Most Rushing Attempts, Game
72   Chicago Bears vs Brk., Oct. 20, 1935

Most Rushing Attempts, Both Teams, Game
108   Chicago Cards (70) vs Green Bay (38), Dec. 5, 1948

Most Yards Gained Rushing, Season
2,885 Detroit, 1936

Most Yards Gained Rushing, Game
426   Detroit vs Pitt., Nov. 4, 1934

Most Yards Gained Rushing, Both Teams, Game
595   L. A. (371) vs N. Y. Yanks (224), Nov. 18, 1951

Highest Average Gain Rushing, Season
5.7 Cleveland, 1963

Most Touchdowns Rushing, Season
36   Green Bay, 1962

Most Touchdowns Rushing, Game
6   By many teams. Last: N. Y. vs Boston, Oct. 27, 1968 (AFL)

Most Touchdowns Rushing, Both Teams, Game
8   Los Angeles (6) vs N. Y. Yanks (2), Nov. 18, 1951
Cleveland (6) vs L. A. (2), Nov. 24, 1957

Passing

Most Seasons Leading League
9   Washington, 1937, 39–40, 42–45, 47, 67

Most Passes Attempted, Season
592   Houston, 1964 (AFL)

Most Passes Attempted, Game
68   Houston vs Buffalo, Nov. 1, 1964 (AFL) (37 comp.)

Most Passes Attempted, Both Teams, Game
98   Minn. (56) vs Balt. (42), Sept. 28, 1969

Most Passes Completed, Season
301   Washington, 1967 (527-att.)

Most Passes Completed, Game
37   Houston vs Buffalo, Nov. 1, 1964 (AFL) (68 att.)

N.F.L. Team Records (continued)

Most Passes Completed, Both Teams, Game
56   Minn. (36) vs Balt. (20), Sept. 28, 1969

Most Yards Gained Passing, Season
4,392 Houston, 1961 (AFL)

Most Yards Gained Passing, Game
554   Los Angeles vs N. Y. Yanks, Sept. 28, 1951

Most Yards Gained Passing, Both Teams, Game
851   New York (505) vs Wash. (346), Oct. 28, 1962

Most Seasons Leading League (Completion Pct.)
9   Washington, 1937, 39–40, 42–45, 47–48

Most Touchdowns Passing, Season
48   Houston, 1961 (AFL)

Most Touchdowns Passing, Game
7   Chicago Bears vs N. Y., Nov. 14, 1943
Philadelphia vs. Wash., Oct. 17, 1954
Houston vs N. Y., Nov. 19, 1961 and Oct. 14, 1962 (AFL)
New York vs Wash., Oct. 28, 1962
Minnesota vs Balt., Sept. 28, 1969

Most Touchdowns Passing, Both Teams, Game
12   New Orleans (6) vs St. Louis (6), Nov. 2, 1969

Most Passes Had Intercepted, Season
48   Houston, 1962 (AFL)

Fewest Passes Had Intercepted, Season
5   Cleveland, 1960 (264-att.)
Green Bay, 1966 (318-att.)

Most Passes Had Intercepted, Game
9   Detroit vs Green Bay, Oct. 24, 1943
Pittsburgh vs Phil., Dec. 12, 1965

Punting

Most Seasons, Leading League (Avg. Distance)
6   Washington, 1940–43, 45, 58

Highest Punting Average, Season
47.6 Detroit, 1961

Punt Returns

Most Seasons, Leading League
8   Detroit, 1943–45, 51–52, 62, 66, 69

Most Yards Gained Punt Returns, Season
781   Chicago Bears, 1948

Most Yards Gained Punt Returns, Game
231   Detroit vs S. F., Oct. 6, 1963

Highest Average Punt Returns, Season
20.2 Chicago Bears, 1941

Most Touchdowns Punt Returns, Season
5   Chicago Cards, 1959

Most Touchdowns Punt Returns, Game
2   Detroit vs L. A., Oct. 14; vs Green Bay, Nov. 22, 1951
Chicago Cards vs Pitt., Nov. 1; vs N. Y., Nov. 22, 1959
New York vs Den., Sept. 24, 1961 (AFL)

Kickoff Returns

Most Seasons Leading League
5   New York, 1944, 46, 49, 51, 53

Most Yards Gained Kickoff Returns, Season
1,824 Houston, 1963 (AFL)

Most Yards Gained Kickoff Returns, Game
362   Detroit vs L. A., Oct. 29, 1950

Most Yards Gained Kickoff Returns, Both Teams, Game
560   Detroit (362) vs L. A. (198), Oct. 29, 1950

Highest Average Kickoff Returns, Season
28.9 Pittsburgh, 1952

Most Touchdowns Kickoff Returns, Season
4   Green Bay, 1967
Chicago, 1970

Most Touchdowns Kickoff Returns, Game
2   Chicago Bears vs Green Bay, Nov. 9, 1952
Philadelphia vs Dall., Nov. 6, 1966
Green Bay vs Cleve., Nov. 12, 1967

Fumbles

Most Fumbles, Season
56   Chicago Bears, 1938

Fewest Fumbles, Season
8   Cleveland, 1959

Most Fumbles, Game
10   Phil/Pitts vs N. Y., Oct. 9, 1943
Detroit vs Minn., Nov. 12, 1967
Kansas City vs Hou., Oct. 12, 1969 (AFL)

Most Fumbles, Both Teams, Game
14   Chicago Bears (7) vs Cleve. (7), Nov. 24, 1940
St. Louis (8) vs N. Y. (6), Sept. 17, 1961
Kansas City (10) vs Hou. (4), Oct. 12, 1969 (AFL)

Most Opponents' Fumbles Recovered, Season
31   Minnesota, 1963 (50 fumbles)

Most Opponents' Fumbles Recovered, Game
7   Buffalo vs Cinci., Nov. 30, 1969 (AFL)

Most Own Fumbles Recovered, Season
27   Philadelphia, 1946 (54 fumbles)
Minnesota, 1963 (45 fumbles)

Most Fumbles (Opponents' and Own) Recovered, Season
58   Minnesota, 1963 (95 fumbles)

N.F.L. Team Records (continued)

Most Fumbles (Opponents' and Own),
Recovered, Game
  10 Denver vs Buff., Dec. 13, 1964
      (AFL)

Penalties

Most Seasons Leading League, Fewest
Penalties
  9 Pittsburgh, 1946–47, 50–52, 54,
     63, 65, 68

Fewest Penalties, Season
  19 Detroit, 1937 (139 yards)

Most Penalties, Game
  22 Brooklyn vs Green Bay, Sept. 17,
     1944 (170 yards)
     Chicago Bears vs Phil., Nov. 26,
     1944 (170 yards)

Fewest Penalties, Game
  0 By many teams.

Fewest Penalties, Both Teams, Game
  0 Brooklyn vs Pitt., Oct. 28, 1934;
     vs Bos., Sept. 28, 1936
     Cleveland Rams vs Chi. Bears,
     Oct. 9, 1938
     Pittsburgh vs Phil., Nov. 10, 1940

Most Yards Penalized, Season
1,274 Oakland, 1969 (AFL)

Fewest Yards Penalized, Season
  139 Detroit, 1937 (19 pen.)

Most Yards Penalized, Game
  209 Cleveland vs Chi. Bears, Nov. 25,
     1951 (21 pen.)

DEFENSE

Fewest Points Allowed, Season
  20 New York, 1927

Fewest Touchdowns Allowed, Season
  3 New York, 1927

Fewest First Downs Allowed, Season
  86 Philadelphia, 1944

Fewest First Downs Allowed, Rushing,
Season
  35 Chicago Bears, 1942

Fewest First Downs Allowed, Passing,
Season
  33 Chicago Bears, 1943

Fewest Yards Allowed, Season
1,578 Chicago Cards, 1934

Fewest Yards Allowed Rushing, Season
  519 Chicago Bears, 1942

Fewest Touchdowns Allowed, Rushing,
Season
  1 New York Giants, 1927

Fewest Yards Allowed Passing, Season
  625 Chicago Cards, 1934

Most Opponents Tackled Attempting
Passes, Season
  67 Oakland, 1967 (AFL)

Fewest Touchdowns, Allowed Passing,
Season
  2 New York Giants, 1927

Most Seasons Leading League, Interceptions Made
  8 New York, 1937–39, 44, 48, 51,
     54, 61
     Green Bay, 1940, 42–43, 47, 55,
     57, 62, 65

Most Pass Interceptions Made, Season
  49 San Diego, 1961 (AFL)

Most Yards Gained, Interceptions,
Season
  929 San Diego, 1961 (AFL)

Most Yards Gained, Interceptions,
Game
  314 Los Angeles vs S. F., Oct. 18,
     1964

Most Touchdowns, Interception Returns, Season
  9 San Diego, 1961 (AFL)

Fewest Yards Allowed Punt Returns,
Season
  22 Green Bay, 1967

Fewest Yards Allowed Kickoff Returns,
Season
  293 Brooklyn, 1944

Most Touchdowns, Interception Returns, Game
  3 Baltimore vs Green Bay, Nov. 5,
     1950
     Cleveland vs Chi., Dec. 11, 1960
     Philadelphia vs Pitt., Dec. 12,
     1965
     Baltimore vs Pitt., Sept. 29, 1968
     Buffalo vs N. Y., Sept. 29, 1968
     (AFL)
     Houston vs S.D., Dec. 19, 1971

Football records compiled by
Elias Sports Bureau

Gliding

The earliest man-carrying glider was designed by Sir George Cayley (1773–1857) and carried his coachman (possibly John Appleby) about 500 yards across a valley near Brompton Hall, Yorkshire, England, in the summer of 1853. Gliders now attain speeds of 145 m.p.h. and the Jastrzab acrobatic sailplane is designed to withstand vertical dives at up to 280 m.p.h.

WORLD RECORDS

DISTANCE

Single seaters	907.7 miles	Hans-Werner Grosse (W. Germany) in an ASW-12 on April 25, 1972.

DECLARED GOAL FLIGHT

	653.1 miles	Klaus Tesch (W. Germany) in an LS-1, on April 25, 1972, from Hamburg to Nantes, France.

ABSOLUTE ALTITUDE

	46,266 feet	Paul F. Bikle, Jr. (U.S.) in a Schweizer SGS-1-23E over Mojave, Calif. (released at 3,963 feet) on Feb. 25, 1961 (also record altitude gain—42,303 feet).

GOAL AND RETURN

	569 miles	Karl Striedeck (U.S.) in an ASW-1S on November 7, 1971.

SPEED OVER TRIANGULAR COURSE

100 km.	96.34 m.p.h.	Walter Neubert (W. Germany) in a Kestrel 22m over U.S. on July 5, 1970.
300 km.	94.16 m.p.h.	Walter Neubert (W. Germany) in a Kestrel 604 over Kenya on March 3, 1972.
500 km.	85.25 m.p.h.	M. Jackson (South Africa) in a BJ-3 in South Africa on December 28, 1967

Golf

Origins. The earliest mention of golf occurs in a prohibiting law passed by the Scottish Parliament in March, 1457, under which "golfe be utterly cryed downe." The Romans had a cognate game called *paganica*, which may have been carried to Britain before 400 A.D. In February, 1962, the Soviet newspaper *Izvestiya* claimed that the game was of 15th-century Danish origin. Gutta percha balls succeeded feather balls in 1848, and were in turn succeeded in 1902 by rubber-cored balls, invented in 1899 by Haskell (U.S.). Steel shafts were authorized in 1929.

Clubs

Oldest. The oldest club of which there is written evidence is the Gentleman Golfers (now the Honourable Company of Edinburgh Golfers) formed in March, 1744—10 years prior to the institution of the Royal and Ancient Club at St. Andrews, Fife, Scotland. The oldest existing club in North America is the Royal Montreal Club (1873) and the oldest in the U.S. is St. Andrews, Westchester County, New York (1888).

Largest. The only club in the world with 15 courses is the Eldorado Golf Club in California. The club with the highest membership in the world is the Wanderer's Club, Johannesburg, South Africa, with 9,120 members, of whom 850 are golfers.

Courses

Highest. The highest golf course in the world is the Tuctu Golf Club in Morococha, Peru, which is 14,335 feet above sea level at its lowest point. Golf has, however, been played in Tibet at an altitude of over 16,000 feet.

Lowest. The lowest golf course in the world was that of the Sodom and Gomorrah Golfing Society at Kallia, on the northeastern shores of the Dead Sea, 1,250 feet below sea level. The clubhouse was burnt down in 1948 and the course is now no longer in use.

Longest Hole. The longest hole in the world is the 17th hole (par 6) of 745 yards at the Black Mountain Golf Club, North Carolina. It was opened in 1964. In August, 1927, the 6th hole at Prescott Country Club in Arkansas, measured 838 yards.

Largest Green. Probably the largest green in the world is the 5th green at Runaway Brook G.C., Bolton, Massachusetts, with an area greater than 28,000 square feet.

Biggest Bunker. The world's biggest trap is Hell's Half Acre on the 7th hole of the Pine Valley course, New Jersey, built in 1912 and generally regarded as the world's most trying course.

Lowest Scores

9 holes and 18 holes—Men. The lowest recorded score on any 18-hole course with a par of 70 or more is 55 first achieved by A. E. Smith, the English professional, at Woolacombe on January 1, 1936. The course measured 4,248 yards. The detail was 4, 2, 3, 4, 2, 4, 3, 4, 3 = 29 out, and 2, 3, 3, 3, 3, 2, 5, 4, 1 = 26 in.

Homero Blancas also scored 55 (27 + 28) on a course of 5,002 yards (par 70) at the Premier Golf Course, Longview, Texas, on August 19, 1962.

Nine holes in 25 (4, 3, 3, 2, 3, 3, 1, 4, 2) was recorded by A. J. "Bill" Burke in a round of 57 (32 + 25) on the 6,389-yard par 71 Normandie course in St. Louis on May 20, 1970.

The lowest recorded score on a long course (over 6,000 yards) is 58 by Harry Weetman (born October 25, 1920), the British Ryder Cup golfer, for the 6,171-yard Croham Hurst Course, Croydon, England, on January 30, 1956.

The United States P.G.A. tournament record for 18 holes is 60 by Al Brosch (30 + 30) in the Texas Open on February 10, 1951; William Nary in the El Paso Open, Texas, on February 9, 1952; Ted Kroll (born August, 1919) in the Texas Open on February 20, 1954; Wally Ulrich in the Virginia Beach Open on June 11, 1954; Tommy Bolt (born March, 1918) in the Insurance City Open on June 25, 1954; and Samuel Jackson Snead (born May 27, 1912) in the Dallas Open, in September, 1957. Souchak (see below) has also scored a 60. Snead had 59 in the Greenbrier Open (now called the Sam Snead Festival), a non-P.G.A. tournament, at White Sulphur Springs, West Virginia, on May 16, 1959.

36 holes. The record for 36 holes is 122 (59 + 63) by Sam Snead in the 1959 Greenbrier Open (now called the Sam Snead Festival) (non-P.G.A.) (see above) May 16–17, 1959. Horton Smith (see below) scored 121 (63 + 58) on a short course on December 21, 1928.

LOWEST SCORERS: Mickey Wright (left) holds the women's record for 18 holes with a 62 scored in 1964. Arnold Palmer (right) scored 276 for the 72-hole British Open to set a record in 1962.

72 holes. The lowest recorded score on a first-class course is 257 (27 under par) by Mike Souchak (born May, 1927) in the Texas Open at San Antonio in February, 1955, made up of 60 (33 out and 27 in), 68, 64, 65 (average 64.25 per round). The late Horton Smith (born 1908), a U.S. Masters Champion, scored 245 (63, 58, 61 and 63) for 72 holes on the 4,700-yard course (par 64) at Catalina Country Club, California, to win the Catalina Open on December 21–23, 1928.

The lowest 72 holes in a national championship is 262 by Percy Alliss (born January 8, 1897) of Britain, with 67, 66, 66 and 63 in the Italian Open Championship at San Remo in 1935, and by Liang Huan Lu (Taiwan) in the 1971 French Open at Biarritz.

Women. The lowest recorded score on an 18-hole course for a woman is 62 (30+32) by Mary (Mickey) Kathryn Wright (born May, 1935), of Dallas, on the Hogan Park Course (6,286 yards) at Midland, Texas, in November, 1964.

Highest Round Score. It is recorded that Chevalier von Cittern went round 18 holes at Biarritz, France, in 1888 in 316 holes—an average of more than 17 shots per hole.

Highest Single-Hole Scores. The highest score for a single hole in a tournament (the British Open) is 21 by a player in the inaugural meeting at Prestwick in 1860. Double figures have been recorded on the card of the winner only once, when Willie Fernie (1851–1924) scored a 10 at Musselburgh, Midlothian, Scotland, in 1883. Ray Ainsley of Ojai, California, took 19 strokes for the par-4 16th hole during the second round of the U.S. Open at Cherry Hills Country Club, Denver, Colorado, on June 10, 1938. Most of the strokes were used in trying to extricate the ball from a brook. Hans Merrell of Mogadore, Ohio, took 19 strokes on the par-3 16th (222 yards) during

FASTEST GOLF ROUND: It took only 14 minutes 02.2 seconds for 45 members of the Dungannon Golf Club in Ireland to play a round including holing out on 18 greens in 1971. Here spectators watch one of the golfers.

the third round of the Bing Crosby National Tournament at Cypress point Club, Del Monte, California, on January 17, 1959.

Most Shots—Women. A woman player in the qualifying round of the Shawnee Invitational for Ladies at Shawnee-on-Delaware, Pennsylvania, in *c.* 1912, took 166 strokes for the 130-yard 16th hole. Her tee shot went into the Binniekill River and the ball floated. She put out in a boat with her exemplary, but statistically minded, husband at the oars. She eventually beached the ball 1½ miles downstream, but was not yet out of the wood. She had to play through one on the home stretch.

Fastest and Slowest Rounds

With such variations in the lengths of courses, speed records, even for rounds under par, are of little comparative value.

On June 25, 1971, a golf ball was propelled from the first tee to the eighteenth green (and 18 times holed out) by 45 members of the Dungannon Golf Club (5,818 yards), County Tyrone, Northern Ireland, in 14 minutes 02.2 seconds.

The slowest tournament round was one of 5 hours 15 minutes by Sam Snead and Ben W. Hogan (born August 13, 1912) of the U.S. *vs.* Stan Leonard and Al Balding (born April, 1924) of Canada in the Canada Cup contest on the West Course, at Wentworth, Surrey, England, in 1956. This was a 4-ball medal round, everything holed out.

Most Rounds in a Day

The greatest number of rounds played in 24 hours is 22 rounds plus 5 holes (401 holes) by Ian Colston, 35 at Bendigo G.C., Victoria, Australia (6,061 yards) on November 27–28, 1971.

Edward A. Ferguson of Detroit played 828 holes (46 rounds) in 158 hours August 25 to September 1, 1930. He walked 327½ miles.

Longest Drive

In long-driving contests 330 yards is rarely surpassed at sea level. The United States P.G.A. record is 341 yards by Jack William Nicklaus (born Columbus, Ohio, January 21, 1940), weighing 206 lbs., in July, 1963.

The world record is 392 yards by an amateur member of the Irish P.G.A., Tommie Campbell, made at Dun Laoghaire, Co. Dublin, in July, 1964.

However, under freak conditions of wind, slope, parched or frozen surfaces, or ricochet from a stone or wall, much greater distances are achieved. The greatest recorded drive is one of 445 yards by E. C. Bliss (1863–1917), a 12-handicap player, at the 9th hole of the Old Course, Herne Bay, Kent, England, in August, 1913. Bliss, 6 feet tall and more than 182 lbs., drove to the back of the green on the left-handed dog-leg. The drive was measured by a government surveyor, Capt. Lloyd, who also measured the decline from tee to resting place as 57 feet.

Other freak drives include the driving of the 483-yard 13th hole at Westward Ho!, Devon, England, by F. Lemarchand, backed by a gale; and to the edge of the 465-yard downhill 9th on the East Devon Course, Budleigh, Salterton, Devon, England, by T. H. V. Haydon in September, 1934. Neither drive was accurately measured.

Perhaps the longest recorded drive on level ground was one of an estimated 430 yards by Craig Ralph Wood (1901–68) (U.S.) on the 530-yard 5th hole at the Old Course, St. Andrews, Fife, Scotland, in the Open Championship in June, 1933. The ground was parched and there was a strong following wind.

A drive of 2,640 yards (1½ miles) across ice was achieved by an Australian meteorologist named Nilstied at Mawson Base, Antarctica, in 1962. On the moon, the energy expended on a mundane 300-yard drive would achieve, craters permitting, a distance of a mile.

Longest Hitter. The golfer regarded as the longest consistent hitter the game has ever known is the 6-foot-5-inch tall, 230-lb. George Bayer (U.S.), the 1957 Canadian Open Champion. His longest measured drive was one of 420 yards at the fourth in the Las Vegas Invitational in 1953. It was measured as a precaution against litigation since the ball struck a spectator. Bayer also drove a ball pin high on a 426-yard hole in Tucson, Arizona. Radar measurements show that an 87-m.p.h. impact velocity for a golf ball falls to 46 m.p.h. in 3.0 seconds.

LONG DRIVE: In an exhibition, Tony Jacklin, British Open and U.S. Open champion in 1969 and 1970 respectively, in an attempt to drive a golf ball across the River Thames from the roof of the Savoy Hotel, London, 125 feet above street level, drove it 353 yards, but it fell short of the opposite bank.

Most Tournament Wins

The record for winning tournaments in a single season is 19 (out of 31) by Byron Nelson (born February 4, 1912), of Fort Worth, Texas, in 1945. Of these 11 were consecutive, including the U.S. Open, P.G.A., Canadian P.G.A. and Canadian Open, from March 16 to August 15. He was a money prize winner in 113 consecutive tournaments.

Most Titles

U.S. Open	W. Anderson	4	1901–03–04–05
	Robert Tyre Jones, Jr.	4	1923–26–29–30
	Ben W. Hogan	4	1948–50–51–53
U.S. Amateur	R. T. Jones, Jr. (1902–71)	5	1924–25–27–28–30
British Open	Harry Vardon (1870–1937)	6	1896–98–99, 1903, 1911–14
British Amateur	John Ball (1861–1940)	8	1888–90–92–94–99, 1907–10, 1912
P.G.A. Championship (U.S.)	Walter C. Hagen	5	1921–24–25–26–27
Masters Championship (U.S.)	Arnold D. Palmer	4	1958–60–62–64
U.S. Women's Open	Miss Elizabeth (Betsy) Earle Rawls	4	1951–53–57–60
	Miss "Mickey" Wright	4	1958–59–61–64
U.S. Women's Amateur	Mrs. Glenna Vare (*née* Collett)	6	1922–25–28–29–30–35

Jack Nicklaus (U.S.) is the only golfer who has won the British and U.S. Opens, the Masters and the P.G.A. crowns at least twice.

GOLF CHAMPIONS: Jack Nicklaus (left) is the only golfer who has won the British and U.S. Opens, the Masters and the P.G.A. tournaments twice each. The late Bobby Jones (right) won the U.S. Open 4 times and the U.S. Amateur title 5 times. He never turned professional, but he won 13 major titles in all.

The Open (British)

The Open Championship was inaugurated in 1860 at Prestwick, Ayrshire, Scotland. The lowest score for 9 holes is 29 by Tom Haliburton (Wentworth) and Peter W. Thomson (Australia), in the first round at the Open on the Royal Lytham and St. Anne's course at Lytham St. Anne's, Lancashire, England, on July 10, 1963.

The lowest scoring round is 63 (all in qualifying rounds) by Frank Jowle (born May 14, 1912) at the New Course, St. Andrews, Scotland (6,526 yards), on July 4, 1955, by Peter W. Thomson (born August 23, 1929), of Australia at Royal Lytham and St. Anne's, England (6,635 yards) on June 30, 1958, and Maurice Bembridge (Little Aston) at Delamere Forest, Cheshire, England, on July 7, 1967. The lowest 72-hole aggregate is 276 (71, 69, 67, 69) by Arnold Daniel Palmer (born September 10, 1929) of Latrobe, Pennsylvania, at Troon, Ayrshire, Scotland, ending on July 13, 1962. (See photo, page 531.)

U.S. Open

This championship was inaugurated in 1894. The lowest 72-hole aggregate is 275 (71, 67, 72 and 65) by Jack Nicklaus on the Lower Course (7,015 yards) at Baltusrol Golf Club, Springfield, New Jersey, on June 15–18, 1967, and by Lee Trevino (born Texas, 1940) at Oak Hill G.C., Rochester, New York, on June 13–16, 1968. The lowest score for 18 holes is 64, achieved three times: by Lee Mackey, Jr., at Merion Country Club in Ardmore, Pennsylvania, on June 8, 1950; by Tommy Jacobs on the 7,053-yard course at the Congressional Country Club, Washington, D.C. on June 19, 1964; and by Rives McBee at Olympic Country Club in San Francisco, on June 17, 1966.

U.S. Masters

The lowest score in the U.S. Masters (instituted at Augusta, Georgia, in 1934) was 271 by Jack Nicklaus in 1965. The lowest rounds have been 64 by Lloyd Mangrum (1st round, 1940) and Jack Nicklaus (3rd round, 1965).

U.S. Amateur

This championship was inaugurated in 1893. The lowest score for 9 holes is 30 by Francis D. Ouimet (1893–1967) in 1932.

British Amateur

The lowest score for nine holes in the British Amateur Championship (inaugurated in 1885) is 29 by Richard Davol Chapman (born March 23, 1911) of the U.S. at Sandwich in 1948. Michael Francis Bonallack (b. 1935) shot a 61 (32–29) at Ganton, Yorkshire, on July 27, 1968, in the 1st round.

Highest Prize

The greatest first place prize money was $60,000 (total purse $300,000) in the Dow Jones Open Invitational first played at Upper Montclair Country Club, Clifton, New Jersey, August 27–30, 1970. A prize of £25,000 (then $60,000) was also given for first place in the John Player Classic in England, September 6–8, 1970.

HIGHEST EARNINGS by a woman in a career were won by Kathy Whitworth (left) with $332,117. Highest in a season was Carol Mann (right) with $49,152 in 1969.

Highest Earnings

The greatest amount ever won in official golf prizes is $1,477,200 by Jack Nicklaus to March 6, 1972. His record for a season is $244,490.50 for 1971.

The highest career earnings by a woman is $332,117 by Kathy Whitworth through January 15, 1972. Miss Whitworth won 54 tournaments of the Ladies' P.G.A. The season record for women (all tournaments) is $49,152 (official earnings) by Carol Mann in 1969. She had 13 rounds in the 60's.

Youngest and Oldest Champions. The youngest winner of the British Open was Tom Morris, Jr. (born 1850, died December 25, 1875) at Prestwick, Ayrshire, Scotland, in 1868. The youngest winner of the British Amateur title was John Charles Beharrel (born May 2, 1938) at Troon, Ayrshire, Scotland, on June 2, 1956, aged 18 years 1 month. The oldest winner of the British Amateur was the Hon. Michael Scott at Hoylake, Cheshire, England, in 1933, when 54. The oldest British Open Champion was "Old Tom"

Morris (b. 1821) who was aged 46 when he won in 1867. The oldest U.S. Amateur Champion was Jack Westland (born 1905) at Seattle, Washington, in 1952.

Holes-in-One

Longest. The longest hole ever holed in one shot is the 10th hole (444 yards) at Miracle Hills Golf Club, Omaha, Nebraska. Robert Mitera achieved a hole-in-one there on October 7, 1965. Mitera, aged 21 and 5 feet 6 inches tall, weighed 165 lbs. A two-handicap player, he normally drove 245 yards. A 50-m.p.h. gust carried his shot over a 290-yard drop-off. The group in front testified to the remaining 154 yards.

The women's record is 393 yards by Marie Robie of Wollaston, Massachusetts, on the first hole at the Furnace Brook Golf Club, Wollaston, Massachusetts, on September 4, 1949.

Most. The greatest number of holes-in-one in a career is 37 by Art Wall, Jr. (born November, 1923), between 1936 and 1967. The record total number of "aces" recorded in the U.S. in a year was 18,319 (indicating more than 100 on some days) in 1969. Dr. Joseph O. Boydstone scored holes-in-one at the 3rd, 4th and 9th holes on the Bakersfield Public Golf Course, California, on October 10, 1961. The holes measured 210, 132 and 135 yards.

Consecutive. There is no recorded instance of a golfer performing three consecutive holes-in-one, but there are at least 13 cases of "aces" being achieved in two consecutive holes of which the greatest was Norman L. Manley's unique "double albatross" on two par 4 holes (330-yard 7th and 290-yard 8th) on the Del Valle Country Club course, Saugus, California, on September 2, 1964.

Two consecutive aces were scored back-to-back on the same hole by a father and son playing together in a unique performance on June 16, 1972, at Glen Eagles White Course in Lemont, Illinois. The hole was the 165-yard seventh, and the father, Charles Calozzo, teed off first, using a 5-wood. Then his son, Phil, using a 4-iron duplicated the feat.

Youngest and Oldest. The youngest golfer recorded to have shot a hole-in-one was Tommy Moore (6 years 36 days) of Hagerstown, Maryland, on the 145-yard 4th at the Woodbrier Golf Course, Martinsville, West Virginia, on March 8, 1968. The oldest golfer to have performed the feat was Walter Fast, aged 92 years 199 days, at Madison Golf Club, Peoria, Illinois, on June 25, 1971.

Throwing the Golf Ball

The lowest recorded score for throwing a golf ball around 18 holes (over 6,000 yards) is 93 by A. L. Gastin on the 6,220-yard University of Missouri course, Columbia, Missouri, on October 5, 1971.

Shooting Your Age

The record for scoring one's age in years over an 18-hole round is held by Weller Noble, who between 1955 (scoring 64 when aged 64) and December 31, 1971, has amassed 644 "age scores" on the

Claremont Country Club, Oakland, California (par 68) of 5,735 yards. The course is provenly harder than many of 6,000 yards or more on which to produce low scores.

The oldest player to score under his age is C. Arthur Thompson (born 1869) of Victoria, British Columbia, Canada, who scored 96 on the Uplands course of 6,215 yards on October 3, 1966. He was still in action, aged 101, in 1971.

World Cup (formerly Canada Cup)

The Canada Cup (instituted 1953) has been won most often by the U.S. with eleven victories in 1955–56, 1960–61–62–63–64–66–67–69–71. The only man to have been on six winning teams has been Arnold Palmer (1960 to 1967). The only man to take the individual title three times is Jack Nicklaus (U.S.) in 1963–64–71. The lowest aggregate score for 144 holes is 545 by Australia (Bruce Devlin and David Graham) at San Isidro, Buenos Aires, Argentina, on November 12–15, 1970, and the lowest score by an individual winner was 269 by Roberto de Vicenzo, 47, on the same occasion.

HIS SCORE LOWER THAN HIS AGE: C. Arthur Thompson of Victoria, B.C., Canada, is the oldest golfer to do this—he shot 96 at age 97 in 1966.

Greyhound Racing

Earliest Meeting. Modern greyhound racing originated with the perfecting of the mechanical hare by Oliver P. Smith at Emeryville, California, in 1919.

Fastest Dog. The highest speed at which any greyhound has been timed is 41.72 m.p.h. (410 yards in 20.1 secs.) by *The Shoe* for a track record at Richmond, New South Wales, Australia.

Gymnastics

Earliest References. Gymnastics were widely practiced in Greece during the period of the ancient Olympic Games (776 B.C. to 393 A.D.), but they were not revived until *c.* 1780.

World Championships. The greatest number of individual titles won by a man in the World Championships is 10 by Boris Shakhlin (U.S.S.R.) between 1954 and 1964. He was also on three winning teams. The women's record is 10 individual wins and 5 team titles by Larissa Semyonovna Latynina (born 1935, retired 1966) of the U.S.S.R., between 1956 and 1964.

Olympic Games. Italy has won most Olympic team titles with four victories in 1912, 1920, 1924 and 1932.

GYMNASTIC TITLE HOLDERS: Vera Caslavska-Odlozil (left), Czech gymnast, has been the most successful woman in Olympic Games competition with seven individual gold medals and a share of team silver medals. The late Lillian Leitzel (U.S.) (right) set the women's record for one-handed chin-ups with 27 in 1918.

WORLD CHAMPION TEN TIMES: Laressa Latynina (U.S.S.R.), who retired in 1966, also shared in 5 team titles.

The only man to win six gold medals is Boris Shakhlin (U.S.S.R.), with one in 1956, four (two shared) in 1960 and one in 1964.

The most successful woman has been Vera Caslavska-Odlozil (Czechoslovakia), with seven individual gold medals, three in 1964 and four (one shared) in 1968. She also won a team silver medal in 1960, 1964 and 1968, and an individual silver medal in 1968.

Chinning the Bar. The record for 2-arm chins from a dead hang position is 106 by William D. Reed (University of Pennsylvania) on June 23, 1969. The women's record for one-handed chin-ups is 27 in Hermann's Gym, Philadelphia, in 1918, by Lillian Leitzel (Mrs. Alfredo Codona) (U.S.), who was killed in Copenhagen, Denmark, on February 12, 1931. Her total would be unmatched by any male, but it is doubtful if they were achieved from a "dead hang" position. It is believed that only one person in 100,000 can chin a bar one-handed. Francis Lewis (born 1896) of Beatrice, Nebraska, in May, 1914, achieved 7 consecutive chins using only the middle finger of his left hand. His bodyweight was 158 lbs.

Rope Climbing. The U.S. Amateur Athletic Union records are tantamount to world records: 20 feet (hands alone) 2.8 secs., Don Perry, at Champaign, Illinois, on April 3, 1954; 25 feet (hands alone), 4.7 secs., Garvin S. Smith at Los Angeles, on April 19, 1947.

Push-ups. The great recorded number of consecutive push-ups is 6,006 in 3 hours 54 minutes by Chick Linster, aged 16, of Wilmette, Illinois, on October 5, 1965. Masura Noma of Mihara, Japan, did 1,227 push-ups in 37 minutes in January, 1968. Jim Slegh of Long Beach, California, did 72 one-arm push-ups on October 9, 1939.

Sit-ups. The greatest recorded number of consecutive sit-ups on a hard surface without feet pinned is 15,512 in 12 hours 24 minutes by Jonathan C. Mote (b. 1955) on April 9, 1972 at Hamilton Southeastern High School, Noblesville, Indiana.

Greatest Tumbler. The greatest tumbler of all time is Dick Browning (U.S.) who made a backward somersault over a 7-foot-6-inch bar at Santa Barbara, California, in April, 1954. In his unique repertoire was a "round-off," backward handspring, backward somersault with half-twist, walk-out, tinsica tigna round-off, backward handspring, double backward somersault.

Hand-to-Hand Balancing. The longest horizontal dive achieved in any hand-to-hand balancing act is 22 feet by Harry Berry (top mounter) and the late Nelson Soule (understander) of the Bell-Thazer Brothers from Kentucky, who played at state fairs and in vaudeville from 1912 to 1918. Berry used a 10-foot tower and trampoline for impetus.

Largest Gymnasium. The world's largest gymnasium is Yale University's Payne Whitney Gymnasium at New Haven, Connecticut, completed in 1932 and valued at $18,000,000. The building, known as the "Cathedral of Muscle," has nine stories with wings of five stories each. It is equipped with 4 basketball courts, 3 rowing tanks, 28 squash courts, 12 handball courts, a roof jogging track and a 25-yard by 42-foot swimming pool on the first floor and a 55-yard long pool on the third floor.

Handball (Court)

Origin. Handball is a game of ancient Celtic origin. In the early 19th century only a front wall was used, but later side and back walls were added. The court is now standardized 60 feet by 30 feet in Ireland and Australia, and 40 feet by 20 feet in Canada, Mexico and the U.S. The game is played with both a hard and soft ball.

The earliest international contest was in New York City in 1887, between the champion of the U.S. and Ireland. In 1970, there were 41 countries affiliated with the International Handball Federation and an estimated 5,000,000 participants.

Championship. World championships were inaugurated in New York in October, 1964, with competitors from Australia, Canada, Ireland, Mexico and the U.S. The individual winner was James Jacobs (U.S.), and the U.S. beat Canada for the team title.

In November, 1967, Canada and the U.S. shared the team title and in October, 1970, it was won by Ireland.

Most Titles. The most successful player in the U.S.H.A. National Four-Wall Championships has been James Jacobs (U.S.), who won 6 singles titles (1955–56–57–60–64–65) and shared in 6 doubles titles (1960–62–63–65–67–68).

Handball (Field)

Origins. Field handball was first played *c.* 1895. It was introduced into the Olympic Games at Berlin in 1936 as an 11-a-side outdoor game. The standard size of team for the indoor version has been 7 since 1952 and will be so at the Munich Olympic Games.

Championships. Germany won the Olympic title in 1936. The earliest international match was on March 8, 1935 when Sweden defeated Denmark.

Harness Racing

RECORDS AGAINST TIME
TROTTING

World (mile track)	1:54.8	Neville Pride (U.S.)	Sept. 10, 1969
Australia	2:01.8	Gramel, Harold Park, Sydney	1964
New Zealand	2:02.4	Control, Addington, Christchurch	1964

PACING

World (mile track)	1:52.0	Steady Star, Lexington, Ky.	1971
Australia	1:57.3	Halwes, Harold Park, Sydney	1968
New Zealand	1:56.2	Cardigan Bay, Wellington	1963

Highest Price. The highest price paid for a trotter is $3,000,000 for *Nevele Pride* by the Stoner Creek Stud of Lexington, Kentucky, from Louis Resnick and Nevele Acres in 1969. The highest for a pacer is $2,000,000 for *Bret Hanover* in 1966.

Greatest Winnings. The greatest amount won by a trotting horse is $1,300,855 by *Une de Mai* to August 31, 1971. The record for a pacing horse is $1,001,498 by *Rum Customer*, which was retired to stud in January, 1972.

Most Successful Driver
The most successful sulky driver has been Herve Filion (Canada) who reached a record of 3,477 wins in December, 1971.

HOCKEY originated in
Holland in the 17th century,
as this picture proves.

Hockey

Origins. There is pictorial evidence of hockey being played on ice
in the Netherlands as early as 1600. The modern game probably
originated in 1860 at Kingston, Ontario, Canada, but Montreal
and Halifax also lay claims as the originators.

Olympic Games. Canada has won the Olympic title six times
(1920–24–28–32–48–52) and the world title 19 times, the last being
at Geneva in 1961. The longest Olympic career is that of Richard
Torriani (Switzerland) from 1928 to 1948. The most gold medals
won by any player is three; this was achieved by four U.S.S.R.
players in the 1964–68–72 Games—Vitaliy Davidov, Aleksandr
Ragulin, Anatoliy Firssov and Viktor Kuzkin.

Stanley Cup. This cup presented by the Governor-General Lord
Stanley (original cost $48.67), became emblematic of world pro-
fessional team supremacy several years after the first contest at
Montreal in 1893. It has been won most often by the Montreal
Canadiens, with 17 wins in 1916, 1924, 1930, 1931, 1944, 1946,
1953, 1956 (winning a record 45 games), 1957, 1958, 1959, 1960,
1965, 1966, 1968, 1969 and 1971.

Longest Match. The longest match was 2 hours 56 minutes 30
seconds when the Detroit Red Wings eventually beat the Montreal
Maroons 1–0 in the sixth period of overtime at the Forum, Montreal,
at 2:25 a.m. on March 25, 1936.

Most Goals. Ottawa defeated Dawson City 23–2 at Ottawa on
January 16, 1905.

Most N.H.L. goals in a season: Phil Esposito (Boston Bruins)
scored 76 goals in 1970–71. The most points in a season is 152
(76 goals and 76 assists) by Esposito in the same season. The career

record for goals is 786 by Gordie Howe (b. 1928) (Detroit Red Wings) in his 25 seasons to 1970–71. He has also collected 500 stitches in his face.

Fastest Scoring. Toronto scored 8 goals against the New York Americans in 4 minutes 52 seconds on March 19, 1938. Bill Mosienko (Chicago) scored three goals in 21 seconds against New York Rangers on March 23, 1952.

Fastest Player. The highest speed measured for any player is 29.7 m.p.h. for Bobby Hull (Chicago Black Hawks). The highest puck speed is also attributed to Hull, whose left-handed slap shot has been measured at 118.3 m.p.h.

Horse Racing

Origins. Stone and bone carvings prove that horse racing is a sport at least thirty centuries old. The 23rd ancient Olympic Games of 624 B.C. featured horse racing. The earliest horse race recorded in England was one held in *c.* 210 A.D. at Netherby, Yorkshire, among Arabians brought to Britain by Lucius Septimius Severus (146–211 A.D.), Emperor of Rome. The oldest race still being run annually is the Lanark Silver Bell, instituted in Scotland by William Lion (1165–1214). Organized horse racing began in New York State at least as early as March, 1668.

Racecourses. The world's largest racecourse is the Newmarket course in England (founded 1636), on which the Beacon Course, the longest of the 19 courses, is 4 miles 397 yards long and the Rowley Mile is 167 feet wide. The border between Suffolk and Cambridgeshire runs through the Newmarket course. The world's largest racecourse grandstand was opened in 1968 at Belmont Park, Long Island, N.Y., at a cost of $30,700,000. It is 110 feet tall, 440 yards long and contains 908 mutuel windows. The greatest seating capacity at any racetrack is 40,000 at the Atlantic City Audit, New Jersey. The world's smallest is the Lobong racecourse, Darjeeling, West Bengal, India (altitude 7,000 feet), where the complete lap is 481 yards. It was laid out *c.* 1885 and used as a parade ground.

Longest Race

The longest recorded horse race was one of 1,200 miles in Portugal, won by a horse *Emir*, bred from Egyptian-bred Blunt Arab stock. The holder of the world's record for long distance racing and speed is *Champion Crabbet*, who covered 300 miles in 52 hours 33 minutes, carrying 245 lbs., in 1920.

In 1831, Squire George Osbaldeston (1787–1866), M.P. of East Retford, England, covered 200 miles in 8 hours 42 minutes at Newmarket, using 50 mounts, so averaging 22.99 m.p.h. In 1967, G. Steecher covered 100 miles on a single horse in 11 hours 4 minutes in Victoria, Australia.

Most Valuable Horse

The highest price ever paid for a stallion is $4,800,000, paid after the 1967 season by a syndicate for *Buckpasser*. The syndicate comprises 32 shares of $150,000 each, of which 16 were taken by Ogden Phipps.

UNBEATEN HORSE: The Hungarian mare foaled in 1874, "Kincsem," was the only horse to remain unbeaten in all her 54 races.

Victories. The horse with the best recorded win-loss record was *Kincsem*, a Hungarian mare foaled in 1874, who was unbeaten in 54 races (1877–1880), including the English Goodwood Cup of 1878.

Tallest. The tallest horse ever to race is *Fort d'Or*, owned by Lady Elizabeth (Eliza) Nugent (*née* Guinness) of Berkshire, England, which stands 18 hands 2 inches.

Jockeys. The most successful jockey has been Willie Shoemaker (b. weighing 2½ lbs. on August 19, 1931) now weighing 98 lbs. after 23 years in the saddle, beating Johnny Longden's lifetime record of 6,032 winners on September 7, 1970. Shoemaker, known as the Ice Man, stands 4 feet 11½ inches. On his 40th birthday he rode his 6,223rd winner which have since the first (on March 19, 1949) won $46,000,000. His 485 wins (from 1,683 mounts) in 1953 constitutes the record number of wins in any year.

The greatest amount ever won by any jockey in a year is $3,088,888 by Braulio Baeza (born Panama) in the U.S. in 1967, when he had 256 wins from 1,064 mounts.

The oldest jockey was Levi Barlingame (U.S.), who rode his last race at Stafford, Kansas, in 1932, aged 80. The youngest jockey was Frank Wootton (English Champion jockey 1909–12), who rode his first winner in South Africa aged 9 years 10 months. The lightest recorded jockey was Kitchener (died 1872), who won the Chester Cup in England on *Red Deer* in 1844 at 49 lbs. He was said to have weighed only 40 lbs. in 1840.

Trainers. The greatest amount ever won by a trainer in one year is $2,456,250, by Eddie Neloy in 1966, when his horses won 93 races.

TALLEST HORSE: "Fort d'Or," owned by Lady Elizabeth Nugent of Ireland, stands 18 hands 2 inches.

Horses

Speed Records

Distance	Time	m.p.h.	Name	Course	Date
¼ mile	20.8s.	43.26	*Big Racket* (U.S.)	Lomas de Sotelo, Mex. Feb. 5, 1945	
½ mile (stra.)	45.0s.	40.00	*Gloaming* (N.Z.)	Wellington, N.Z.	Jan. 12, 1921
½ mile	45.0s.	40.00	*Beau Madison* (U.S.)	Phoenix, Arizona	Mar. 30, 1957
	45.0s.	40.00	*Another Nell* (U.S.)	Cicero, Ill.	May 8, 1967
⅝ mile	53.6s.	41.98	*Indigenous* (G.B.)	Epsom, England	June 2, 1960
¾ mile	1m. 07.4s.	40.06	*Zip Pocket* (U.S.)	Phoenix, Arizona	Dec. 6, 1966
	1m. 07.4s.	40.06	*Vale of Tears* (U.S.)	Ab Sar Ben, Omaha, Nebr. June 7, 1969	
	1m. 06.2s.	40.78	*Broken Tindril* (G.B.)	*Brighton, England	Aug. 6, 1929
Mile	1m. 31.8s.	39.21	*Soueida* (G.B.)	*Brighton, England	Sept. 19, 1963
	1m. 31.8s.	39.21	*Loose Cover* (G.B.)	*Brighton, England	June 9, 1966
	1m. 32.2s.	39.04	*Dr. Fager* (U.S.)	Arlington, Ill.	Aug. 24, 1968
1½ miles	2m. 23.0s.	37.76	*Fiddle Isle* (U.S.)	Arcadia, Calif.	Mar. 21, 1970
2 miles	3m. 15.0s.	36.93	*Polazel* (G.B.)	Salisbury, England	July 8, 1924
3 miles	5m. 15.0s.	34.29	*Farragut* (Mex.)	Agua Caliente, Mex.	Mar. 9, 1941

* Course downhill for 2/3rd of a mile.

Dead Heats

There is no recorded case in turf history of a quintuple dead heat. The nearest approach was in the Astley Stakes, at Lewes, England, in August, 1880, when *Mazurka*, *Wandering Nun* and *Scobell* triple dead-heated for first place, just ahead of *Cumberland* and *Thora*, who dead-heated for fourth place. Each of the five jockeys thought he had won. The only two known examples of a quadruple dead heat were between *The Defaulter*, *Squire of Malton*, *Reindeer* and *Pulcherrima* in the Omnibus Stakes at The Hoo, England, on April 26, 1851, and between *Overreach*, *Lady Go-Lightly*, *Gamester* and *The Unexpected* at the Houghton Meeting at Newmarket, England, on October 22, 1855.

Greatest Winnings. The greatest amount ever won by a horse is $1,977,896 by *Kelso* (foaled in 1957) in the U.S., between 1959 and his retirement on March 10, 1966. In 63 races he won 39, came in second in 12 and third in 2. (See photo.)

The most successful horse of all time was *Buckpasser*, whose career winnings were $1,462,014 in 1965–66–67. He won 25 races out of 31. The most won by a mare is $783,674 by *Cicada*. In 42 races she won 23, came second in 8 and third in 6. The most won in a year is $817,941 by *Damascus* in 1967. His total reached $1,176,781 by December, 1968.

Largest Prizes. The richest race ever held was the All-American Futurity, a race for quarter-horses over 400 yards at Ruidoso Downs, New Mexico, on September 6, 1971. The prizes totaled $753,910.

Laico Bird, the 1967 winner of the All-American Futurity in 20.11 seconds received $228,300. The largest single prize ever paid was 1,094,126 francs, plus 78 per cent of the entry fees, making 1,480,000 francs ($299,600) to the owner of *Prince Royal II*, winner of the 43rd Prix de l'Arc de Triomphe at Longchamp, Pairs, on October 4, 1964.

Shortest Odds

The shortest odds ever quoted for any racehorse are 10,000 to 1 on for *Dragon Blood*, ridden by Lester Piggott (G.B.) in the Premio Naviglio in Milan, Italy, on June 1, 1967. He won. Odds of 100 to 1 on were quoted for the American horse *Man o' War* (foaled March 29, 1917, died November 1, 1947) on three separate occasions in 1920. In 21 starts in 1919–20 he had 20 wins and one second (on August 13, 1919 in the Sanford Memorial Stakes).

GREATEST MONEY-WINNING HORSE: Kelso, who retired in 1966, won almost $2,000,000 in prizes. In 63 races, he won 39 and placed second in 12 of them.

Pari-Mutuel Record

The U.S. pari-mutuel record pay-off is $941.75 to $1 on *Wishing Ring* at Latonia track, Kentucky, in 1912.

Biggest Win

The Hon. Raymond Guest (born 1908), U.S. Ambassador to Ireland, won £62,500 ($150,000) from William Hill on May 29, 1968, when his Derby winner *Sir Ivor* won £500 ($1,200) each way at 100–1 in September, 1967. Larger sums have reputedly been won but essential details are lacking.

FASTEST WOMAN SKATER: Rimma Zhukova (U.S.S.R.) (right) set the record for 5,000 meters, and has held it since 1953.

Ice Skating

Origins. The earliest reference to ice skating is that of a Danish writer dated 1134. The earliest English account of 1180 refers to skates made of bone. Metal blades date from probably *c.* 1600. The earliest skating club was the Edinburgh Skating Club, Scotland, formed in 1742. The earliest artificial ice rink in the world was the "Glaciarium," built in Chelsea, London, in 1876.

Longest Race. The longest race regularly held is the "Elfstedentocht" ("Tour of the Eleven Towns") in the Netherlands. It covers 200 kilometers (124 miles 483 yards) and the fastest time is 7 hours 35 minutes by Jeen van den Berg (born January 8, 1928) on February 3, 1954.

Largest Rink. The world's largest artificial ice rink is the Tokyo Ice Rink, completed in 1960, which has an ice area of 43,000 sq. ft. (or 0.99 of an acre). The largest artificial outdoor rink is the Fujikyu Highland Promenade Rink, Japan, opened at a cost of $938,000 in 1967 with an area of 165,750 square feet (3.8 acres).

Longest Marathon. The longest recorded skating marathon is one of 313.5 miles (50 hours 26 mins.) by Mark Koch at Greenville Community Rink, Penn., ending February 14, 1971.

OLYMPIC CHAMPION: Lidia Skoblikova (U.S.S.R.) earned 6 gold medals in speed skating, the most anyone has won.

Most Titles

World. The greatest number of world speed skating titles (instituted 1893) won by any skater is five by Oscar Mathisen (Norway) in 1908–09 and 1912–14, and Clas Thunberg (born April 5, 1893) of Finland, in 1923, 1925, 1928–29 and 1931. The most titles won by a woman is four by Mrs. Inga Voronina, *née* Artomonova (1936–66) of Moscow, U.S.S.R., in 1957, 1958, 1962 and 1965.

Olympic. The most Olympic gold medals won in speed skating is six by Lidia Skoblikova (born March 8, 1939), of Chelyaminsk, U.S.S.R., in 1960 (2) and 1964 (4).

WORLD SPEED SKATING RECORDS

Distance	mins. secs.	Name and Nationality	Place	Date
Men				
500 meters	38.00*†	Leo Linkovesi (Finland)	Davos, Switz.	Jan. 8, 1972
1,000 meters	1 18.80	Ard Schenk (Neth.)	Inzell, West Ger.	Feb. 22, 1971
1,500 meters	1 58.70	Ard Schenk (Neth.)	Davos, Switz.	Feb. 15, 1971
3,000 meters	4 12.00	Ard Schenk (Neth.)	Davos, Switz.	Feb. 15, 1971
5,000 meters	7 12.00	Ard Schenk (Neth.)	Inzell, West Ger.	Mar. 13, 1971
10,000 meters	14 55.96	Ard Schenk (Neth.)	Inzell, West Ger.	Mar. 14, 1971
Women				
500 meters	42.50	Anne Henning (U.S.)	Davos, Switz.	Jan. 7, 1972
1,000 meters	1 27.38	Anne Henning (U.S.)	Davos, Switz.	Jan. 8, 1972
1,500 meters	2 17.82	Nina Statkevich (U.S.S.R.)	Medeo, U.S.S.R.	Jan. 17, 1970
3,000 meters	4 50.30	Ans Schut (Neth.)	Inzell, West Ger.	Feb. 23, 1969
5,000 meters	9 01.60	Rimma Zhukova (U.S.S.R.)	Medeo, U.S.S.R.	Jan. 24, 1953

* Subject to ratification by the International Skating Union.
† This represents a speed of 29.43 m.p.h.

Figure Skating

World. The greatest number of men's figure skating titles (instituted 1896) is ten by Ulrich Salchow (born August 7, 1877), of Sweden, in 1901–05 and 1907–11. The women's record (instituted 1906) is ten titles by Sonja Henie (1912–69), of Norway, between 1927 and 1936.

Olympic. The most Olympic gold medals won by a figure skater is three by Gilles Grafström (born June 7, 1893), of Sweden, in 1920, 1924, and 1928 (also silver medal in 1932); and by Sonja Henie (see above) in 1928, 1932 and 1936.

Ice Yachting

Origin. The sport originated in the Netherlands (earliest patent is dated 1600). The earliest authentic record is Dutch, dating from 1768. The largest ice yacht built was *Icicle*, built for Commodore John E. Roosevelt for racing on the Hudson River, New York *c.* 1870. It was 68 feet 11 inches long and carried 1,070 square feet of canvas.

Highest Speed. The highest speed officially recorded is 143 m.p.h. by John D. Buckstaff in a Class A stern-steerer on Lake Winnebago, Wisconsin, in 1938. Such a speed is possible in a wind of 72 m.p.h.

Incidentally, in 1956, Richard Millet Denning reached 57.69 m.p.h. on his sand yacht *Coronation Year* Mk II at Lytham St. Anne's, Lancashire, England.

Jai-Alai *(Pelota)*

The game, which originated in Italy as *longue paume* and was introduced into the Basque country between Spain and France

WORLD'S FASTEST GAME: When the ball is in play in jai-alai, it can reach a speed of 160 m.p.h.

in the 13th century, is said to be the fastest of all ball games with speeds of up to 160 m.p.h. Gloves were introduced *c.* 1840 and the *chisterak* (basket-like glove) was invented *c.* 1860 by Gantchiki Dithurbide of Sainte Pée. The long *chistera* was invented by Melchior Curuchage of Buenos Aires, Argentina, in 1888. Games are played in a *fronton* (playing court) with both leather and rubber balls. The sport is governed by the International Federation of Basque Pelote.

The world's largest *fronton* was built for $4,500,000 in Miami, Florida.

Judo

Origin. Judo is a modern combat sport which developed out of an amalgam of several old Japanese fighting arts, the most popular of which was *ju-jitsu* (*jiu jitsu*), which is thought to be of pre-Christian Chinese origin. Judo has been greatly developed by the Japanese since 1882, when it was first devised by *Shihan* Dr. Jigoro Kano. World championships were inaugurated in 1956.

Highest Grade. The efficiency grades in Judo are divided into pupil (*kyu*) and master (*dan*) grades. The highest awarded is the extremely rare red belt *Judan* (10th *dan*), given only to seven men. The Judo protocol provides for a *Juichidan* (11th *dan*), who also would wear a red belt, and even a *Junidan* (12th *dan*), who would wear a white belt twice as wide as an ordinary belt, but these have never been bestowed.

Heaviest Champion. The heaviest world champion was Antonius (Anton) J. Geesink (born April 6, 1934), of the Netherlands, who won the 1964 Olympic open title in Tokyo at a weight of 238 lbs. He was 266 lbs. in 1965 and stands 6 feet 6 inches tall.

Marathon. The longest recorded Judo marathon is one of 13 hours by 6 members of the Docamanaka Judo Club, at Plumstead, London, England, on July 3, 1971.

Karate

Origins. Originally *karate* (empty hand) is known to have been developed by the unarmed populace as a method of attack on, and defense against, armed oppressors in Okinawa, in the Ryukyu Islands, in the 17th century. It is accepted that it may have been of Chinese origin. It was introduced into Japan in 1916.

The four major schools of *Karate* in Japan are *Shotokan*, *Wado-ryu*, *Goju-ryu*, and *Shito-ryu*. Military *Karate* for killing, as used by Korean troops, is *tae kwan do*.

Top Exponents. The only winner of two All-Japanese titles has been Hirokazu Kanazawa (6th *dan*) in 1957 and 1958. He won his first title with a broken arm. The highest *dans* among *karatekas* are Masatoshi Nakayama (born 1912), an 8th *dan* of the *Shotokan* school, and Yamaguchi Gogen (born 1907) a 10th *dan* of the *Goju-ryu karate do.*

HIGHEST RANKING IN KARATE: Masatoshi Nakayama (right) an 8th "dan" contests with Hirokazu Kanazawa, the only winner of two All-Japanese titles.

Greatest Force. The force needed to break a brick with a hand muscle is normally 130–140 lbs. The highest measured impact is 196 lbs.

Brick Breaking. The greatest feat of brick breaking was performed in Seattle, Washington, on September 18–20, 1971, by Bill Corbett who broke 3,500 bricks with his hand in 13 hours—sustained a rate of 269 per hour. He cracked his left wrist and raised $130.13 for charity.

Lacrosse

Origin. The game is of American Indian origin, derived from the inter-tribal game *baggataway*, and was played by Iroquois Indians in lower Ontario, Canada and upper New York State, before 1492. The game was included in the Olympic Games of 1908.

Longest Throw. The longest recorded throw is 162.86 yards, by Barney Quin of Ottawa, Canada, on September 10, 1892.

Highest Score. The highest score in any international match was Australia's 19–3 win over England at Manchester in May, 1972.

World Championship. The first World Tournament was held at Toronto, Canada, in 1967 and the U.S. won.

Motorcycling

Earliest Races. The first motorcycle race was one from Paris to Dieppe, France, in 1897. The oldest motorcycle races in the world are the Auto-Cycle Union Tourist Trophy (T.T.) series, first held on the 15¾-mile "Peel" ("St. John's") course on the Isle of Man in 1907, and still run on the island, on the "Mountain" circuit (37.73 miles) and, until 1959, on the Clypse circuit of 10.79 miles.

Longest Circuits. The 37.73-mile "Mountain" circuit, over which the two main T.T. races have been run since 1911, is the longest used for any motorcycle race, and has 264 curves and corners.

Fastest Circuit. The highest average lap speed attained on any closed circuit is 182 m.p.h. by a Kawasaki racer powered by a 748-c.c. 3-cylinder 2-stroke engine on a banked circuit in Tokyo, Japan, in December, 1971.

The fastest road circuit is the Francorchamps circuit near Spa, Belgium. It is 14.10 kilometers (8 miles 1,340 yards) in length and was lapped in 4 minutes 1.4 seconds (average speed of 130.658 m.p.h.) by Giacomo Agostini (born Lovere, Italy, June 16, 1942) on a 500-c.c. 3-cylinder M.V.-Agusta on lap 7 of the 500-c.c. Belgian Grand Prix on July 6, 1969.

Fastest Race. The fastest race in the world was held at Grenzlandring, Germany, in 1939. It was won by Georg Meier (b. Germany, 1910) at an average speed of 134 m.p.h. on a supercharged 500-c.c. flat-twin B.M.W.

The fastest road race is the 500-c.c. Belgian Grand Prix held on the Francorchamps circuit (8 miles 1,340 yards) near Spa, Belgium. The record for this 13-lap (113.898 miles) race is 54 minutes 18.1 seconds (average speed 125.850 m.p.h.) by Giacomo Agostini, on a 500-c.c. 3-cylinder M.V.-Agusta, on July 6, 1969.

Longest Race. The longest race is the 24-hour Bol d'Or at Montlhéry, Paris, France (3 miles 1,610 yards lap). The greatest distance ever covered is 1,835.95 miles (average speed 76.498 m.p.h.) by Thomas Dickie and Paul Anthony Smart on a 741-c.c. three-cylinder Triumph Trident on September 12–13, 1970.

World Championships. Most world championship titles (instituted by the Fédération Internationale Motorcycliste in 1949) won are 10 by Giacomo Agostini (Italy) in the 350-c.c. 1968, 69, 70, 71, and in the 500-c.c. 1966, 67, 68, 69, 70, 71. Giacomo Agostini is the only man to win two world championships in four consecutive years (350- and 500-c.c. titles in 1968–69–70–71). Agostini won 92 races in the world championship series between 1965 and June 9, 1972, including a record 19 in 1970, also achieved by Mike Hailwood in 1966.

Most Successful Machines. Italian M.V.-Agusta motorcycles won 34 World Championships between 1952 and 1971 and 237 World Championship races between 1952 and 1971. Japanese Honda machines won 29 World Championship races and five World Championships in 1966.

Most Successful Riders. The record number of victories in the Isle of Man T.T. races is 12 by Stanley Michael Bailey Hailwood (b. Oxford, England, April 2, 1940) now of Durban, South Africa, between 1961 and 1967. The first man to win three consecutive T.T. titles in two events was James A. Redman (Rhodesia) (b. Hampstead, London, England, November 8, 1931). He won the 250-c.c. and 350-c.c. events in 1963–64–65. Mike Hailwood is the only man to win three events in one year, in 1961 and 1967.

Speed Records. The official world speed record (average speed for two runs over a one-kilometer course) is 224.569 m.p.h. by Bill A. Johnson, aged 38, of Garden Grove, California, riding an unsupercharged Triumph Bonneville T120 "Streamliner," with a 667.25-c.c. parallel twin-cyclinder engine running on methanol and nitro-methane and developing 75 to 80 b.h.p., at Bonneville Salt Flats, Utah, on September 5, 1962. His machine was 17 feet long and weighed 400 lbs. His first run was at 227.169 m.p.h., lasting 9.847 seconds.

Calvin G. Rayborn (born San Diego, February 20, 1940) recorded higher speeds over the measured mile, without F.I.M. observers, at Bonneville on October 16, 1970, riding his 10-foot-3-inch-long 1,480-c.c. V-twin Harley Davidson streamlined running on methanol and nitro-methane. On the first run he covered the mile in 13.494 seconds (266.785 m.p.h.). On the second run his time was 13.626 seconds (264.201 m.p.h.). The average time for the two runs was 13.560 seconds (average speed 265.487 m.p.h.).

Jon S. McKibben, 33, of Costa Mesa, California, covered a measured mile one-way at Bonneville in 12.5625 seconds (286.567 m.p.h.) in November, 1971, riding his 21-foot-6-inch-long Reaction Dynamics *Honda Hawk* streamliner, powered by two turbocharged 736-c.c. in-line 4-cylinder Honda engines developing 140 b.h.p. each, running on methanol.

The official land speed record (see under *Auto Racing*) can be set only by 4-wheeled vehicles, so the F.I.M. recognizes 3-wheeled jet-powered vehicles as Class D motorcycles. The highest speed in a 3-wheeler was recorded by Norman Craig Breedlove (born 1937) of Los Angeles at Bonneville Salt Flats, on October 15, 1964. He drove the 8,500 lb. *Spirit of America*, measuring 39 feet 6 inches and powered by a General Electric J47–15 jet engine which could develop 5,700-lb. static thrust at sea level. In his first run, at 8:11 a.m. (local time), he covered the flying kilometer in 4.306 seconds (average speed 519.493 m.p.h.) and the mile in 7.013 seconds (513.332 m.p.h.). The second run, at 8:37 a.m., his times were 4.178 seconds for the kilometer (535.408 m.p.h.) and 6.668 seconds for the mile (539.892 m.p.h.); so the intervening distance (666 yards 1 foot 1.9 inches) was covered in 2.490 seconds average speed 547.415 m.p.h.). The average of the two runs were 4.242 seconds for the kilometer (527.331 m.p.h.) and 6.8405 seconds for the mile (526.277 m.p.h.).

The world record average speed for two runs over one kilometer (1,093.6 yards) from a standing start is 118.91 m.p.h. by Duncan Hocking (G.B.) on his supercharged 650-c.c. twin-cylinder Triumph running on methanol and nitromethane at Elvington Airfield, Yorkshire, England, on September 25, 1971. The faster run was made in 18.80 seconds.

The world record for two runs over 440 yards from a standing start is 92.879 m.p.h. (9.69 seconds) by Dave Lecoq on the supercharged 1,287-c.c. Drag-Waye powered by a flat four Volkeswagen engine, at Elvington Airfield, Yorkshire, England, on September 27, 1970. The faster run was made in 9.60 seconds. On the same day, he averaged 19.02 seconds (117.610 m.p.h.), but failed to better the previous record by the necessary one per cent margin.

The fastest time for a single run over 440 yards from a standing start is 8.68 seconds by E. J. Potter of Ithaca, Michigan, on his 5,359-c.c. Chevrolet Corvette V8 Special at Castlereagh Airstrip near Sydney, Australia, on January 26, 1970.

Mountaineering

Origins. Although bronze-age artifacts have been found on the summit of the Riffelhorn, Switzerland, mountaineering, as a sport, has a continuous history dating back only to 1854. Isolated instances of climbing for its own sake exist back to the fourteenth century. The Atacamenans built sacrificial platforms near the summit of Llullaillaco in South America (22,058 feet) in late pre-Columbian times, *c*. 1490.

Mount Everest. Mount Everest (29,028 feet) was first climbed at 11:30 a.m. on May 29, 1953, when the summit was reached by Edmund Percival Hillary (born July 20, 1919), of New Zealand, and the Sherpa, Tenzing Norkhay (born, as Namgyal Wangdi, in Nepal in 1914, formerly called Tenzing Khumjung Bhutia). The successful expedition was led by Col. (later Brigadier Lord) Henry Cecil John Hunt (born June 22, 1910). (See pages 411, 413 also.)

Subsequent ascents of Mount Everest are as follows:

Climbers	Date
Ernst Schmidt, Jürg Marmet	May 23, 1956
Hans Rudolf von Gunten, Adolf Reist	May 24, 1956
*Wang Fu-chou, Chu Yin-hua, Konbu	May 25, 1960
James Warren Whittaker, Sherpa Nawang Gombu	May 1, 1963
Barry C. Bishop, Luther G. Jerstad	May 22, 1963
Dr. William F. Unsoeld, Dr. Thomas F. Hornbein	May 22, 1963
Capt. A. S. Cheema, Sherpa Nawang Gombu	May 20, 1965
Sonam Gyaltso, Sonam Wangyal	May 22, 1965
C. P. Vohra, Sherpa Ang Kami	May 24, 1965
Capt. H. P. S. Ahluwalia, H. C. S. Rawat, Phu Dorji	May 29, 1965
Nomi Uemura, Tero Matsuura (Japan)	May 11, 1970
Katsutoshi Hirabayashi and Sherpa, Chotari	May 12, 1970

* Not internationally accepted.

Greatest Fall. The greatest recorded fall survived by a mountaineer was when Christopher Timms (Christchurch University, N.Z.) slid 7,500 feet down an ice face into a crevasse on Mt. Elie de Beaumont (10,200 ft.), New Zealand, on December 7, 1966. His companion was killed, but he survived with concussions, bruises and a hand injury.

OLYMPIC GOLD MEDAL: Highest award given in the Games. Only once has it been awarded eight times to an individual—Ray Ewry (U.S.) track star, 1900-08.

Olympic Games

Origins. The earliest celebration of the ancient Olympic Games of which there is a certain record is that of July, 776 B.C. (when Koroibos, a cook from Elis, won a foot race), though their origin probably dates from *c.* 1370 B.C. The ancient Games were terminated by an order issued in Milan in 393 A.D. by Theodosius I, "the Great" (*c.* 346–395), Emperor of Rome. At the instigation of Pierre de Fredi, Baron de Coubertin (1863–1937), the Olympic Games of the modern era were inaugurated in Athens on April 6, 1896.

Celebrations have been allocated as follows:—

I	Athens	April 6-15, 1896	XI	Berlin	Aug. 1-16, 1936
II	Paris	July 2-22, 1900	XII	*Tokyo then	
III	St. Louis	Aug. 29-Sept. 7, 1904		Helsinki	1940
†	Athens	Apr. 22-May 2, 1906	XIII	*London	1944
IV	London	July 13-25, 1908	XIV	London	July 29-Aug. 14, 1948
V	Stockholm	July 6-15, 1912	XV	Helsinki	July 19-Aug. 3, 1952
VI	*Berlin	1916	XVI	Melbourne	Nov. 22-Dec. 8, 1956
VII	Antwerp	Aug. 14-29, 1920	XVII	Rome	Aug. 25-Sept. 11, 1960
VIII	Paris	July 5-27, 1924	XVIII	Tokyo	Oct. 10-24, 1964
IX	Amsterdam	July 28-Aug. 12, 1928	XIX	Mexico City	Oct. 12-27, 1968
			XX	Munich	Aug. 26-Sept. 11, 1972
X	Los Angeles	July 30-Aug. 14, 1932	XXI	Montreal	July 18–Aug. 1, 1976

* Cancelled due to World Wars.
† Intercalated Celebration.

Most Olympic Titles. The greatest number of victories resulting in Olympic gold medals is nine by Mark Spitz (U.S.) who won 2 relay golds at Mexico in 1968 and 7 more (4 individual and 3 relay) at Munich in 1972. The later figure is an absolute Olympic record for one celebration at any sport. Spitz's equals the runner Paavo Nurmi's (Finland) absolute Olympic career record of 9 golds.

Most Gold Medals

In the ancient Olympic Games, victors were given a chaplet (head garland) of olive leaves. Milo (Milon of Kroton) won 6 titles at *palaisma* (wrestling), 540–516 B.C.

Individual. The most individual gold medals won by a male competitor is eight by Ray Ewry (U.S.) (see *Track*). The female record is seven by Vera Caslavska-Odlozil, of Czechoslovakia (see *Gymnastics*).

Oldest and Youngest Competitors. The oldest recorded competitor was Oscar G. Swahn (Sweden), who won a silver medal for shooting running deer in 1920, when aged 73. The youngest woman to win gold medals is Marjorie Gestring (U.S.) (b. November 18, 1922, now Mrs. Bowman) aged 13 years 9 months, in the 1936 women's springboard event. Bernard Malivoire, aged 12, coxed the winning French coxed pairs in 1952.

Longest Span. The longest competitive span of any Olympic competitor is 40 years by Dr. Ivan Osiier (Denmark), who competed as a fencer in 1908, 1912 (silver medal), 1920, 1924, 1928, 1932 and 1948, totaling seven celebrations. He refused to compete in the 1936 Games on the grounds that they were Nazi-dominated. The longest span for a woman is 24 years (1932–56) by the Austrian fencer Ellen Müller-Preiss.

The Winter Olympics were inaugurated in 1924 and have been allocated as follows:—

I	Chamonix, France	Jan. 25–Feb. 4, 1924
II	St. Moritz, Switzerland	Feb. 11–19, 1928
III	Lake Placid, New York	Feb. 4–13, 1932
IV	Garmisch-Partenkirchen, Germany	Feb. 6–16, 1936
V	St. Moritz, Switzerland	Jan. 30–Feb. 8, 1948
VI	Oslo, Norway	Feb. 14–25, 1952
VII	Cortina d'Ampezzo, Italy	Jan. 26–Feb. 5, 1956
VIII	Squaw Valley, California	Feb. 18–28, 1960
IX	Innsbruck, Austria	Jan. 29–Feb. 9, 1964
X	Grenoble and Chamonix, France	Feb. 6–18, 1968
XI	Sapporo, Japan	Feb. 3–13, 1972
XII	Denver, Colorado	Feb. 20–29, 1976

Largest Crowd. The largest crowd at any Olympic site was 150,000 at the 1952 ski-jumping at the Holmenkollen, outside Oslo, Norway. Estimates of the number of spectators of the marathon race through Tokyo, Japan, on October 21, 1964, have ranged from 500,000 to 1,500,000.

Pentathlon, Modern

The Modern Pentathlon (Riding, Fencing, Shooting, Swimming and Running) was inaugurated into the Olympic Games at Stockholm in 1912.

Most World Titles. The record number of world titles won is 5 by András Balczo (Hungary) in 1963, 1965, 1966, 1967 and 1969.

Point scores in riding, fencing, cross country and hence overall scores have no comparative value between one competition and another. In shooting and swimming (300 meters) where measurements are absolute the point scores are of record significance.

Shooting	1,066	P. Macken (Australia) and		
		R. Phelps (U.K.)	Leipzig	Sept. 20, 1965
	1,066	I. Mona (Hungary)	Jönköping	Sept. 11, 1967
Swimming	1,240	C. Richards (U.S.)	Warrendorf	Aug. 4, 1970

Pigeon Racing

Earliest References. Pigeon Racing was the natural development of the use of homing pigeons for the carrying of messages—a quality utilized in the ancient Olympic Games (776 B.C.–393 A.D.) The sport originated in Belgium. The earliest major long-distance race was from Crystal Palace, South London, England, in 1871.

Longest Flights. The greatest recorded homing flight by a pigeon was made by one owned by the 1st Duke of Wellington (1769–1852). Released from a sailing ship off the Ichabo Islands, West Africa, on April 8, it dropped dead a mile from its loft at Nine Elms, London, England, on June 1, 1845, 55 days later, having flown an airline route of 5,400 miles, but an actual distance of possibly 7,000 miles to avoid the Sahara Desert.

Highest Speeds. In level flight in windless condition it is very doubtful if any pigeon can exceed 60 m.p.h. The highest race speed is one of 3,229 yards (110.07 m.p.h.) in East Anglia, England, on May 8, 1965, which was strongly wind assisted. The world's longest reputed distance in 24 hours is 803 miles (velocity 1,525 yards per minute) by E. S. Peterson's winner of the 1941 San Antonio (Texas) Racing Club event.

Polo

Earliest Games. There is a record of polo having been played in Iran (Persia) in *c.* 525 B.C., although the name is derived from the Tibetan word *pula*. Stone goalposts (probably 12th century), 8 yards wide and 300 yards apart, still stand at Isfahan, Iran. The earliest club was the Kachar Club (founded in 1859) in Assam, India. The game was introduced into England from India in 1869 by the 10th Hussars at Aldershot, Hampshire, and the earliest match was one between the 9th Lancers and the 10th Hussars on Hounslow Heath, west of London, in July, 1871. The earliest international match between England and the U.S. was in 1886.

Playing Field. The game is played on the largest field of any ball game in the world. The ground measures 300 yards long by 160 yards wide with side boards or, as in India, 200 yards wide without boards.

Highest Handicap. The highest handicap based on eight 7½-minute "chukkas" is 10 goals, introduced in the United Kingdom and in Argentina in 1910. The most recent addition to the select ranks of the 32 players ever to have received 10-goal handicaps are H. Heguy, F. Dorignal and G. Dorignal, all of Argentina.

Highest Score. The highest aggregate number of goals scored in an international match is 30, when Argentina beat the U.S. 21–9 at Meadow Brook, Long Island, New York, in September, 1936.

Most Internationals. Thomas Hitchcock, Jr. (1900–44) played five times for the U.S. vs. England (1921–24–27–30–39) and twice vs. Argentina (1928–36).

Most Expensive Pony. The highest price ever paid for a polo pony was $22,000, paid by Stephen Sanford for Lewis Lacey's *Jupiter* after the 1928 U.S. vs. Argentina international.

Largest Trophy. Polo claims the world's largest sporting trophy —the Bangalore Limited Handicap Polo Tournament Trophy. This massive cup standing on its plinth is 6 feet tall and was presented in 1936 by the Indian Raja of Kolanke.

Powerboat Racing

Origins. The earliest application of the gasoline engine to a boat was Gottlieb Daimler's experimental powerboat on the Seine River, Paris, in 1887. The sport was given impetus by the presentation of a championship cup by Sir Alfred Harmsworth of England in 1903, which was also the year of the first offshore race from Calais to Dover.

Harmsworth Cup. Of the 25 contests from 1903 to 1961, the U.S. has won 16, the United Kingdom 5, Canada 3 and France 1.

The greatest number of wins has been achieved by Garfield A. Wood (U.S.) with 8 (1920–21, 1926, 1928–29–30, 1932–33). The only boat to win three times is *Miss Supertest III*, owned by James G. Thompson (Canada), in 1959–60–61. This boat also achieved the record speed of 115.972 m.p.h. at Picton, Ontario, Canada, in 1960.

Gold Cup. The Gold Cup (instituted 1903) has been four times won by Garfield A. Wood (U.S.) (1917, 1919–20–21) and by Bill Muncey (1956–57, 1961–62). The record speed attained is 120.356 m.p.h. by the Rolls-Royce engined *Miss Exide*, owned by Milo Stoen, and driven by Bill Brow at Seattle, Washington, on August 4, 1965.

Highest Off-shore Speed. The highest race speed attained is 74.32 m.p.h. by Don Aronow (U.S.) in his 32-foot *The Cigarette*, powered by two 475-h.p. Mercruiser engines over 214 miles at Viarreggio, Italy, on July 20, 1969.

Longest Race. The longest offshore race is the *Daily Telegraph and B.P.* Round Britain Race inaugurated in 1969 in 10 stages aggregating 1,403 miles.

Rodeo

Origins. Rodeo came into being with the early days of the North American cattle industry. The earliest references to the sport are from Sante Fe, New Mexico, in 1847. Steer wrestling began with Bill Pickett (Oklahoma) in 1903. The other events are calf roping, bull riding, saddle and bareback bronc riding.

The largest rodeo in the world is the Calgary Exhibition and Stampede at Calgary, Alberta, Canada. The record attendance has been 853,620 for 1969 (10 days). The record for one day is 127,043 in 1967.

Most World Titles. The record number of all-round titles is five by Jim Shoulders (U.S.), in 1949 and 1956–57–58–59 and Larry Mahan (1966–67–68–69–70). The record figure for prize money in a single season is $57,726 in the three riding events by Larry Mahan, aged 25, of Brooks, Oregon, in 1969. (See photo, page 563.)

Champion Bull. The top bucking bull is V-61, an 1,800-lb. Brahma owned by the Henry Knight Rodeo Company of Fowler, Colorado. He was never ridden in 9 years until John Quintana, 23, of Milwaukie, Oregon, succeeded in June, 1971, so scoring 94 points—an absolute rodeo record.

Champion Bronc. The greatest bucking bronco of all time was *Midnight*, owned by Verne Elliott of Platteville, Colorado. In seven years (1923–30) he was ridden by only four riders once each, and of these only Frank Studnick (at Pendleton, Oregon, in 1929) was not subsequently thrown because he did not mount him again.

CHAMPION BUCKING STEER: This crossbreed of a Brahma and a Hereford, named "Aught" (now dead), unseated 476 of his 482 mounts in under 8 seconds. He loved children.

LARGEST RODEO: This is the stampede event at the Calgary Exhibition in Canada, which has set attendance records for rodeos for a number of years.

Time Records. Records for timed events, such as calf roping and steer wrestling, are meaningless, because of the widely varying conditions due to the size of arenas and amount of start given the stock. The fastest time recently recorded for roping a calf is 7.5 seconds by Junior Garrison of Marlow, Oklahoma, at Evergreen, Colorado, in 1967, and the fastest time for overcoming a steer is, 2.4 seconds by James Bynum of Waxahachie, Texas, at Marietta, Oklahoma, in 1955.

The standard required time to stay on in bareback events is 8 seconds and in saddle bronc riding 10 seconds. In the now obsolete ride-to-a-finish events, rodeo riders have been recorded to have survived 90 minutes or more, until the mount had not a buck left in it.

PRIZE MONEY WINNER:
Larry Mahan won $57,726 in one
season in 3 riding events in 1969.

Roller Skating

Origin. The first roller skate was devised by Joseph Merlin of
Huy, Belgium, in 1760. Several "improved" versions appeared
during the next century, but a really satisfactory roller skate did not
materialize before 1866, when James L. Plimpton of New York
City produced the present four-wheeled type, patented it, and
opened the first public rink in the world at Newport, Rhode Island,
that year. The great boom periods were 1870–75, 1908–12 and
1948–54, each originating in the U.S.

Largest Rink. The largest indoor rink ever to operate was
located in the Grand Hall, Olympia, London, England. It had an
actual skating area of 68,000 square feet. It first opened in 1890,
for one season, then again from 1909 to 1912.

Roller Hockey. Roller hockey was first introduced in England
as Rink Polo, at the old Lava rink, Denmark Hill, London, in the
late 1870's. The Amateur Rink Hockey Association was formed in
1905, and in 1913 became the National Rink Hockey (now Roller
Hockey) Association. Britain was undefeated in all international
championships from 1925 to 1939. Portugal won 11 titles from 1947
to 1971.

Speed Records. The fastest speed (official world's record) is
25.78 m.p.h. by Giuseppe Cantarella (Italy) who recorded 34.9
seconds for 440 yards on a road at Catania, Italy, on September 28,
1963. The mile record on a rink is 2 minutes 25.1 seconds by Johnny
Ferriti (Italy). The greatest distance skated in one hour on a rink
by a woman is 20 miles 1,355 yards by C. Patricia Barnett (U.K.) at
Brixton, London, on June 24, 1962. The men's record on a closed
road circuit is 22 miles 465.9 yards p.h. by Alberto Civolani (Italy)
at Bologna, Italy on October 15, 1967.

Marathon Record. The longest recorded continuous roller skating marathon was performed by Professor Eckard with 108 hours at Rockhampton, Queensland, Australia, in 1913. The longest reported skate was by Clinton Shaw from Victoria, British Columbia, to St. John's, Newfoundland (4,900 miles) on the Trans-Canadian Highway *via* Montreal from April 1 to November 11, 1967.

Rowing

Oldest Race. The earliest established sculling race is the Doggett's Coat and Badge, first rowed on August 1, 1716, on a 5-mile course from London Bridge to Chelsea. It is still being rowed every year over the same course, under the administration of the Fishmongers' Company. The first English regatta probably took place on the Thames by the Ranelagh Gardens, near Putney, London, in 1775. Boating began at Eton, England, in 1793. The oldest club, the Leander Club, was formed in *c.* 1818.

Henley Royal Regatta. The annual regatta at Henley-on-Thames, Oxfordshire, England, was inaugurated on March 26, 1839.

Since 1839 the course, except in 1923, has been about 1 mile 550 yards, varying slightly according to the length of boat. In 1967, the shorter craft were "drawn up" so all bows start level. Prior to 1922, there were two slight angles. Classic Records (year in brackets indicates the date instituted):

			mins. secs.	
Grand Challenge (1839)	8 oars	Ratzeburger Ruderclub (W. Germany)	6:16	July 3, 1965
Thames Challenge Cup (1868)	8 oars	Isis, U.K.	6:35	July 3, 1965
Princess Elizabeth Cup (1946)	8 oars	Emanuel School, U.K.	6:44	July 1, 1965
		Tabor Academy, U.S. (twice)	6:44	July 3, 1965
Stewards' Challenge (1841)	4 oars	Quintin, U.K.	6:55	July 3, 1965
Visitors' Challenge (1847)	4 oars	St. Edmund Hall, Oxford	7:13	July 3, 1965
Wyfold Challenge (1855)	4 oars	Derby R.C., U.K.	7:06	July 3, 1965
Prince Philip Cup (1963)	4 oars	Leander, U.S.	7:03	July 3, 1965
Silver Goblets (1895)	Pair oar	Peter Gorny and Gunther Bergau (ASK Vorwaerts Rostock, East Germany)	7:35	July 1, 1965
Double Sculls (1939)	Sculls	Melch Buergin and Martin Studach (Grasshopper Club, Zürich)	7:01	July 3, 1965
Diamond Challenge (1844)	Sculls	Donald M. Spero (New York A.C., U.S.)	7:42	July 3, 1965

Olympic Games. Since 1900 there have been 100 Olympic finals, of which the U.S. has won 27, Germany 19 and the United Kingdom 14. Three oarsmen have won 3 gold medals: John B. Kelly (U.S.), father of Princess Grace of Monaco, in the sculls (1920) and double sculls (1920 and 1924); Paul V. Costello (U.S.) in the double sculls (1920, 1924 and 1928), and Jack Beresford (G.B.) in the sculls (1924), coxless fours (1932) and double sculls (1936).

TRIPLE WINNER OF OLYMPIC GOLD MEDAL: Jack Beresford of Great Britain is one of only three men who have won three rowing events—in 1924, 1932, and 1936.

Sculling. The record number of wins in the Wingfield Sculls (instituted 1830) is seven by Jack Beresford, Jr., from 1920 to 1926. The record number of world professional sculling titles (instituted 1831) won is seven by W. Beach (Australia) between 1884 and 1887. Stuart A. Mackenzie (Great Britain and Australia) performed the unique feat of winning the Diamond Sculls at Henley for the sixth consecutive occasion on July 7, 1962. In 1960 and 1962 he was in Leander colors.

Highest Rate. The highest rate of stroking recorded in international competition is 56 by the Japanese Olympic eight at Henley, England, in 1936.

Highest Speed. Speeds in tidal or flowing water are of no comparative value. The highest recorded speed for 2,000 meters by an eight in the World Championships is 5 mins. 43.61 secs. (13.02 m.p.h.) by Norway, in Ontario, Canada, on September 4, 1970, and in the Olympic Games 5 mins. 54.02 secs. (12.64 m.p.h.) by Germany at Toda, Japan, in 1964.

BLOCK SHOT
CHAMPION: Tom Frye
missed only 6 blocks out of
100,010 in 1959.

Shooting

Olympic Games. The record number of gold medals won is five by Morris Fisher (U.S.) with three in 1920 and two in 1924.

Record Heads. The world's finest head is the 23-pointer stag head in the Maritzburg collection, Germany. The outside span is 75½ inches, the length 47½ inches and the weight 41½ lbs. The greatest number of points is probably 33 (plus 29) on the stag shot in 1696 by Frederick III (1657–1713), the Elector of Brandenburg, later King Frederick I of Prussia.

Largest Shoulder Guns. The largest bore shoulder guns made were 2 bores. Less than a dozen of these were made by two English wildfowl gunmakers in *c.* 1885. Normally the largest guns made are double-barrelled 4 bore weighing up to 26 lbs. which can be handled only by men of exceptional physique. Larger smooth-bore guns have been made, but these are for use as punt-guns.

Highest Muzzle Velocity. The highest muzzle velocity of any rifle bullet is 7,100 feet per second (4,840 m.p.h.) by a 1937 .30 caliber M 1903 Standard U.S. Army Ordnance Department rifle.

Block Tossing. Using a pair of auto-loading Remington Nylon 66 .22 caliber guns, Tom Frye (U.S.) tossed 100,010 blocks (2¾-inch pine cubes) and hit 100,004—his longest run was 32,860—on October 5–17, 1959.

Clay Pigeon Shooting. The record number of clay birds shot in an hour is 1,308 by Joseph Nother (formerly Wheater) (born 1918) of Kingston-upon-Hull, Yorkshire, England, at Bedford on September 21, 1957. Using 5 guns and 7 loaders, he shot 1,000 in 42 minutes 22.5 seconds.

		Possible Score		
Free Pistol	50 m. 6 × 10 shot series	600—	572	G. J. Kosych (U.S.S.R.) Pilsen, 1969
Free Rifle	300 m. 3 × 40 shot series	1,200—1,157		G. L. Anderson (U.S.) Mexico City, 1968
Small Bore Rifle	50 m. 3 × 40 shot series	1,200—1,164		L. W. Wigger, Jr. (U.S.) Tokyo, 1964
		1,200—1,164		G. L. Anderson (U.S.) Johannesburg, 1969
Small Bore Rifle	50m. 60 shots prone	600—	599	N. Rotaru (Rumania) Moscow, 1972
Center-Fire Pistol	25 m. 60 shots	600—	597	T. D. Smith (U.S.) Sao Paulo, 1963
Rapid-Fire Pistol	25 m. silhouettes 60 shots	600—	598	G. Liverzani (Italy) Phoenix, Ariz. 1970
Running Target	50 m. 40 shots		171	M. Nordfors (Sweden) Pistoia, Italy, 1967
Trap	300 birds	300—	297	K. Jones (U.S.) Wiesbaden. 1966
Skeet	200 birds	200—	200	N. Durnev (U.S.S.R.) (see photo) Cairo, 1962
		200—	200	E. Petrov (U.S.S.R.) Phoenix, Ariz., 1970

Biggest Bag. The largest animal ever shot by any big game hunter was a bull African elephant (*Loxodonta africana*) shot by J. J. Fénykövi (Hungary), 48 miles north-northwest of Macusso, Angola, on November 13, 1955. It required 16 heavy caliber bullets from a 0.416 Rigby and weighed an estimated 24,000 lbs., standing 13 feet 2 inches at the shoulders. In November, 1965, Simon Fletcher, 28, a

SKEET SHOOTING CHAMPION: Nikolai Durnev (U.S.S.R.), who hit 200 in 200 shots.

Kenyan farmer, claims to have killed two elephants with one 0.458 bullet.

The greatest recorded lifetime bag is 556,000 birds, including 241,000 pheasants, by the 2nd Marquess of Ripon (1867–1923) of England. He himself dropped dead on a grouse moor after shooting his 52nd bird on the morning of September 22, 1923.

Shooting Bench-rest 1,000-yard Shooting. Smallest group 7$\frac{11}{16}$ths inches by Mary Louise DeVito on October 11, 1970 (7 mm-300 Wetherby); 10-shot possibles (score 5×10) Clifford Hocker, June 8, 1969 (300 Winchester Magnum) and Frank Weber, October 25, 1970 (6.5 × 300 Wetherby). All records at Pennsylvania 1,000-yard Benchrest Club Inc.

Revolver Shooting. The greatest rapid fire feat was that of Ed McGivern (U.S.), who twice fired from 15 feet 5 shots which could be covered by a silver half dollar piece in 0.45 of a second at the Lead Club Range, South Dakota, on August 20, 1932.

Quickest Draw. The super-star of fast drawing and winner of the annual "World's Fastest Gun" award from 1960–1971 is Bob Munden (b. Kansas City, Missouri, February 8, 1942). His records include Walk and Draw Level Blanks in 21/100ths sec. and Standing Reaction Blanks (4-inch balloons at 8 feet) in 20/100ths sec. both at Las Vegas, Nevada on August 9, 1966 and Self Start Blanks in 2/100ths sec. at Baldwin Park, California on August 17, 1968.

Skiing

Origins. The earliest dated skis found in Fenno-Scandian bogs have been dated to *c.* 2500 B.C. A rock carving of a skier at Rodoy, northern Norway, dates from 2000 B.C. The earliest recorded isolated military competition was in Oslo, Norway, in 1767, though it did not grow into a sport until 1843 at Tromso. Skiing was known in California by 1856, having been introduced by "Snowshoe" Thompson from Norway. The Kiandra Snow Shoe Club (founded 1878), in Australia, claims to be world's oldest. Skiing was not introduced into the Alps until 1883, though there is some evidence of earlier use in the Carniola district. The first Slalom event was run at Mürren, Switzerland, on January 21, 1922. The Winter Olympics were inaugurated in 1924.

Highest Speed. The highest speed claimed for any skier is 109.14 m.p.h. by Ralph Miller (U.S.) on the 62-degree slopes of the Garganta *Schuss* at Portillo, Chile, on August 25, 1955. Since the timing was only manual by two timekeepers standing half a kilometer back from a marked 50-meter section of *piste*, this claim cannot be regarded as reliable.

The highest speed recorded in Europe is 108.589 m.p.h. over a flying 100 meters by Luigi de Marco (Italy) on a 62.8 degree gradient on the Rosa plateau above Cervinia, Italy, on July 18, 1964.

The average race speeds by the 1968 Olympic downhill champion

BROUGHT SKIING TO AMERICA FROM NORWAY: "Snowshoe" Thompson introduced the sport to California in 1856.

on the Chamrousse course, Grenoble, France, were Jean-Claude Killy (France) (53.93 m.p.h.) and Olga Pall (Austria) (47.90 m.p.h.).

LEADING RACER: Jean-Claude Killy (France), before turning professional, won the Olympic downhill at 53.93 m.p.h. in 1968 and the World Cup twice.

LONGEST SKI JUMPER: Manfred Wolf (East Germany) holds the record at 165 meters (541.3 feet).

Duration. The longest non-stop overland skiing marathon was one that lasted 48 hours by Onni Savi, aged 35, of Padasjoki, Finland, who covered 305.9 kilometers (190.1 miles) between noon on April 19 and noon on April 21, 1966.

Most World Titles. The World Alpine Championships were inaugurated at Mürren, Switzerland, in 1931. The greatest number of titles won is 12 by Christel Cranz (born July 1, 1914), of Germany, with four Slalom (1934–37–38–39), three Downhill (1935–37–39) and five Combined (1934–35–37–38–39). She also won the gold medal for the Combined in the 1936 Olympics. The most titles won by a man is seven by Anton ("Toni") Sailer (born November 17, 1935), of Austria, who won all four in 1956 (Giant Slalom, Slalom, Downhill and the non-Olympic Alpine Combination) and the Downhill, Giant Slalom and Combined in 1958.

In the Nordic events Johan Gröttumsbraaten (born February 24, 1899), of Norway, won six titles (two at 18 kilometers and four Combined) in 1931–32. The record for a jumper is five by Birger Ruud (born August 23, 1911), of Norway, in 1931–32 and 1935–36–37.

The World Cup, instituted in 1967, has been twice won by Jean-Claude Killy (France) (born August 30, 1943) in 1967 and 1968; Karl Schranz (Austria) in 1969 and 1970 and Gustav Thöni (Italy) in 1971 and 1972. The women's cup has been won twice by Nancy Greene (Canada) 1967 and 1968), and by Annemarie Proell (Austria) in 1971 and 1972.

Most Olympic Victories. The most Olympic gold medals won by an individual for skiing is four (including one for a relay) by Sixten Jernberg (born February 6, 1929), of Sweden, in 1956–60–64. In addition, Jernberg has won three silver and two bronze medals. The only women to win three gold medals are Klavdiya Boyarskikh and Galina Koulakova both of U.S.S.R., who won the 5 kilometers and 10 kilometers, and were members of the winning 3 × 5 kilometers relay team, at Innsbruck, Austria, and Sapporo, Japan in 1964 and 1972 respectively.

Longest Jump. The longest ski jump ever recorded is one of

165 meters (541.3 feet) by Manfred Wolf (East Germany) at Planica, Yugoslavia, on March 23, 1969.

Greatest Race. The world's greatest Nordic ski race is the "Vasa Lopp," which commemorates an event of 1521 when Gustavus Vasa (1496–1560), later King of Sweden, skied 85 kilometers (52.8 miles) from Mora to Sälen, Sweden. The re-enactment of this journey in reverse direction is now an annual event, with 9,397 starters on March 4, 1970. The record time is 4 hours 39 minutes 49 seconds by Janne Stefansson on March 3, 1968.

Longest Run. The longest all-downhill ski run in the world is the Weissfluhjoch-Küblis Parsenn course (9 miles long), near Davos, Switzerland. The run from the Aiguille du Midi top of the Chamonix lift (vertical lift 8,176 feet) across the Vallée Blanche is 13 miles.

Longest Lift. The longest chair lift in the world is the Alpine Way to Kosciusko Châlet lift above Thredbo, near the Snowy Mountains, New South Wales, Australia. It takes from 45 to 75 minutes to ascend the 3.5 miles, according to the weather. The highest is at Chactaltaya, Bolivia, rising to 16,500 feet.

Skijoring. The record speed reached in aircraft skijoring (being towed by an aircraft) is 109.23 m.p.h. by Reto Pitsch on the Silsersee, St. Moritz, Switzerland, in 1956.

Ski-bob. The ski-bob was invented by a Mr. Stevens of Hartford, Connecticut, and patented (No. 47334) on April 19, 1892, as a "bicycle with ski-runners." The Fédération Internationale de Skibob was founded on January 14, 1961, in Innsbruck, Austria.

MOST TITLED SKIER: (Left) Toni Sailer (Austria) has won 7 world alpine titles, including all four in 1956, more than any other man. WOMEN'S OLYMPIC CHAMPION: (Right) Klavdiya Boyarskikh (U.S.S.R.) is the only woman to win 3 gold medals for skiing.

The highest speed attained is 103.4 m.p.h. by Erich Brenter (Austria) at Cervinia, Italy, in 1964.

Highest Altitude. Yuichiro Miura (Japan) skied 1.6 miles down Mt. Everest starting from 26,200 feet. In a run from a height of 24,418 feet he reached speeds of 93.6 m.p.h. on May 6, 1970.

Snowmobiling

Ky Michaelson, in the snowmobile *Sonic Challenger*, was timed at 114.5 m.p.h. over 440 yards at Mallet's Bay, Vermont, on February 15, 1970.

Soccer

Origins. A game with some similarities termed *Tsu-chin* was played in China in the 3rd and 4th centuries B.C. The earliest clear representation of the game is in a print from Edinburgh, Scotland, dated 1672–73. The game became standardized with the formation of the Football Association in England on October 26, 1863. A 26-a-side game, however, existed in Florence, Italy, as early as 1530, for which rules were codified in *Discorsa Calcio* in 1580. The world's oldest club was Sheffield F.C. of England, formed on October 24, 1857. Eleven for a side was standardized in 1870.

Highest Scores

Teams. The highest score recorded in any first-class match is 36. This occurred in the Scottish Cup match between Arbroath and Bon Accord on September 5, 1885, when Arbroath won 36–0 on their home ground. The goals were not fitted then with nets.

The highest goal margin recorded in any international match is 17. This occurred in the England vs. Australia match at Sydney on June 30, 1951, when England won 17–0.

Individuals. The most goals scored by one player in a first-class match is 16 by Stains for Racing Club de Lens vs. Aubry-Asturies, in Lens, France, on December 13, 1942.

Edson Arantes do Nascimento, *alias* Pelé (born June 28, 1940), of Santos, Brazil, scored 1,000 goals from 1957 to November 19, 1969. The 1,000th goal came for Pelé with a penalty for his club, Santos, in the Maracaña Stadium, Rio de Janeiro, when he was playing in his 909th first-class match. His final score was 1,026 goals.

Fastest Goals

The fastest goal on record was one variously claimed to be from 13 to 4 seconds after the kick-off by Jim Fryatt of Bradford in a Fourth Division match against Tranmere Rovers at Park Avenue, Bradford, England, on April 25, 1964.

The record for an international match is 3 goals in 3½ minutes by Willie Hall (Tottenham Hotspur) for England against Ireland on November 16, 1938, at Old Trafford, Manchester, England.

BIGGEST SCORER: Geoffrey Hurst (left, above) scored 3 goals for England in a World Cup final in 1966. HIGHEST CAREER SCORE: Pelé (right) of Brazil scored his 1,000th goal for his club, Santos, in 1969 in his 909th first-class match. A national hero, he led Brazil to their unique third World Cup in 1970.

Most Appearances

The greatest total of full international appearances is 110 by Pelé (see above) who played his 106th international for Brazil in their unique third victorious World Cup final on June 21, 1970. He scored 95 goals (12 of them in his 3 World Cup competitions) in these matches and retired on July 18, 1971.

Longest Match

The world duration record for a first class match was set in the Western Hemisphere club championship in Santos, Brazil, on August 2–3, 1962, when Santos drew 3–3 with Penarol F.C. of Montevideo, Uruguay. The game lasted 3½ hours, from 9:30 p.m. to 1 a.m.

Transfer Fees

The world's highest reported transfer fee is £400,000 ($1,120,000) for the Varese centerforward Pietro Anastasi, signed by Juventus on May 18, 1968.

Signing Fee. On May 26, 1961, Luis Suarez, the Barcelona inside-forward was transferred to Internazionale (Milan) for $405,200, of which Suarez himself received a record $165,200.

Crowds and Gates

The greatest recorded crowd at any football match was 199,854 for the Brazil vs. Uruguay World Cup final in Rio de Janeiro, Brazil, on July 16, 1950. The receipts were 6,000,000 cruzeiros (then $350,000).

Receipts

The greatest receipts at any match were £204,805 ($573,454) from an attendance of 93,000 at the World Cup final between England and West Germany at the Empire Stadium, Wembley, Greater London, on July 30, 1966.

World Cup

The *Fédération Internationale de Football* (F.I.F.A.) was founded in Paris on May 21, 1904, and instituted the World Cup Competition in 1930, two years after the four British Isles' associations had resigned. The record attendance was for the 1966 competition, which totaled 5,549,521.

The only country to win three times has been Brazil (1958–1962–1970).

The record goal scorer has been Just Fontaine (France) with 13 goals in 6 games in the 1958 competition. Eusebio Silva Ferrera (Portugal) scored 9 goals in 1966. The most goals scored in a final is 3 by Geoffrey Hurst (West Ham United) for England vs. West Germany on July 30, 1966.

Antonian Carbajal (b. 1929) played for Mexico in goal in the competitions of 1950–54–58–62 and 1966.

Soccer (Amateur)

Most Olympic Wins. The only countries to have won the Olympic football title three times is Hungary in 1952, 1964 and 1968. The United Kingdom won in 1908 and 1912 and also the unofficial tournament of 1900. These contests have now virtually ceased to be amateur. The highest Olympic score is Denmark 17 vs. France "A" 1 in 1908.

Marathons. The longest recorded 11-a-side soccer marathon played without substitutes is 20 hours by the Bosbury Youth Club at Wellington Heath, Worcestershire, England, on July 3, 1971. The indoor 5-a-side record (no substitute) is 51 hours by Beaconsfield Youth Club, Buckinghamshire, England, on June 25–27, 1971.

Largest Crowd. The highest attendance at any amateur match is 100,000 at the English Football Association Amateur Cup Final between Pegasus and Bishop Auckland at Wembley, London, on April 21, 1951.

Heading. The highest recorded number of repetitions for heading a ball is 3,412 in 34 minutes 8 seconds by Colin Jones, aged 15, at Queensferry, near Chester, England, on March 8, 1961.

Least Successful Goalkeeper. The goalkeeper of the Victoria Boys' and Girls' Club Intermediate "B" team in the 1967–68 season in the Association for the Jewish Youth League Under 16 Division 2 in London, England, let through 252 goals in the 12 league matches, an average of better (or worse) than 21 per match.

Squash

(Note: "1971," for example, refers to the 1971–72 season.)

Earliest Champion. Although racquets with a soft ball was evolved in *c.* 1850 at Harrow School (England), there was no recognized champion of any country until J. A. Miskey of Philadelphia won the American Amateur Singles Championship in 1906.

World Title. The inaugural international (world) championships were staged in Australia in August, 1967, when Australia won the team title in Sydney, and Geoffrey B. Hunt (Victoria) took the individual title, both titles being retained in 1969 and 1971.

Most Victories

Open Championship. The most wins in the Open Championship (amateur or professional), held annually in Britain, is seven by Hashim Khan (Pakistan) in 1950–51–52–53–54–55 and 1957.

Amateur Championship. The most wins in the Amateur Championship is six by Abdel Fattah Amr Bey (Egypt, now the United Arab Republic), later appointed Ambassador in London, who won in 1931–32–33 and 1935–36–37.

Professional Championship. The most wins in the Professional Championship is five by J. St. G. Dear (Great Britain) in 1935–36–37–38 and 1949, and Hashim Khan (Pakistan) in 1950–51–52–53–54.

Longest Championship Match. The longest recorded championship match was one of two hours 13 minutes in the final of the Open Championship of the British Isles in Birmingham in December, 1969, when Jonah P. Barrington (Ireland) beat Geoffrey B. Hunt (Australia) 9–7, 3–9, 3–9, 9–4, 9–4, with the last game lasting 37 minutes.

Most Victories in the Women's Championship. The most wins in the Women's Squash Rackets Championship is 11 by Mrs. Heather McKay (*née* Blundell) of Australia, 1961 to 1971.

Marathon Record. The longest recorded squash singles marathon was one of 47 hours 1 minute by Ebbisham Sports Club, Epsom, England on April 7–9, 1972, with 60 second breaks between games and 5 minute rests each completed hour.

Surfing

Origins. The traditional Polynesian sport of surfing in a canoe (*ehorooe*) was first recorded by the British explorer, Captain James Cook (1728–79) on his third voyage to Tahiti in December, 1771. Surfing on a board (*Amo Amo iluna ka lau oka nalu*) was first described ("most perilous and extraordinary . . . altogether astonishing, and is scarcely to be credited") by Lt. (later Capt.) James King of the

Royal Navy in March, 1779, at Kealakekua Bay, Hawaii Island. A surfer was first depicted by this voyage's official artist John Webber. The sport was revived at Waikiki by 1900. Australia's first club, the Bondi Surf Bathers Lifesaving Club, was formed in February, 1906. Hollow boards came in in 1929 and the plastic foam type in 1956.

Highest Waves Ridden. Makaha Beach, Hawaii, provides reputedly the best consistently high waves for surfing, often reaching the rideable limit of 30–35 feet. The highest wave ever ridden was the *tsunami* of "perhaps 50 feet," which struck Minole, Hawaii, on April 3, 1868, and was ridden to save his life by a Hawaiian named Holua.

Longest Ride. About 4 to 6 times each year rideable surfing waves break in Matanchen Bay near San Blas, Nayarit, Mexico, which make rides of *c.* 5,700 feet possible.

WORLD'S LARGEST SWIMMING POOL: The Orthlieb Pool in Casablanca Morocco, is 1,575 feet long and 246 feet wide.

Swimming

Earliest References. It is recorded that inter-school swimming contests in Japan were ordered by Imperial edict of Emperor Go-Yoozei as early as 1603. Competitive swimming originated in Britain in St. George's Pier pool, Liverpool, opened in 1828.

Largest Pools. The largest swimming pool in the world is the salt-water Orthlieb Pool in Casablanca, Morocco. It is 480 meters (1,574.8 feet) long and 75 meters (246 feet) wide, an area of 8.9 acres.

The largest land-locked swimming pool with heated water is the Fleishhacker Pool on Sloat Boulevard, near Great Highway, San Francisco. It measures 1,000 feet by 150 feet (3.44 acres), is up to 14 feet deep, and contains 7,500,000 gallons of heated water.

The world's largest competition pool is at Osaka, Japan. It accommodates 25,000 spectators.

Most Difficult Dives. Those with the highest tariff (degree of difficulty 2.9) are the "1½ forward somersaults with triple twist," the "2½ forward somersaults with double twist," and the "1½ reverse with 2½ twists." Joaquín Capilla of Mexico has performed a 4½-somersault dive from a 10-meter board, but this is not on the international tariff.

Long Distance Swimming

A unique achievement in long distance swimming was established in 1966 by the cross-channel swimmer Mihir Sen of Calcutta, India. These were the Palk Strait from India to Ceylon (in 25 hours 36 minutes on April 5–6); the Straits of Gibraltar (Europe to Africa in 8 hours 1 minute on August 24); the Dardanelles (Gallipoli, Europe, to Sedulbahir, Asia Minor, in 13 hours 55 minutes on September 12) and the entire length of the Panama Canal in 34 hours 15 minutes on October 29–31. He had earlier swum the English Channel in 14 hours 45 minutes on September 27, 1958.

Treading Water

The duration record for treading water (vertical posture) is 18 hours by Mark T. Lowder, 16, of Albemarle, North Carolina, July 20–21, 1972, at Rock Creek Park.

Fastest Swimmer. Excluding relay stages with their anticipatory starts, the highest speed reached by a swimmer is 4.89 m.p.h. by Stephen Edward Clark (U.S.), who recorded 20.9 seconds for a heat of 50 yards in a 25-yard pool at Yale University, on March 26, 1964. Mark Spitz (U.S.), in setting the 100-meter record of 51.9 secs. in 1970, required an average of 4.31 m.p.h.

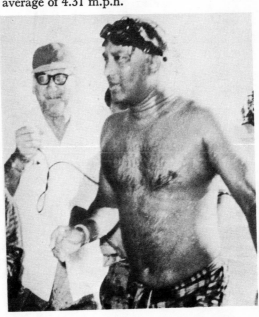

LONG DISTANCE SWIMMING RECORD HOLDER: Mihir Sen (India) has swum from India to Ceylon, and across the Dardanelles, Strait of Gibraltar, and the length of the Panama Canal.

SWIMMING—WORLD RECORDS—MEN

at distances recognized by the Federation Internationale de Natation Amateur. F.I.N.A. no longer recognizes any records made for non-metric distances. (A performance marked with an asterisk is the best improvement awaiting ratification.)*
Only performances set up in 50-meter pools are recognized as World Records.

Distance	Min. sec.	Name and Nationality	Place	Date
		FREE STYLE		
100 meters	51.2	Mark Spitz (U.S.)	Munich, West Germany	Sept. 3, 1972
200 meters	1:52.8	Mark Spitz (U.S.)	Munich, West Germany	Aug. 29, 1972
400 meters	4:00.1	Kurt Krumpholz (U.S.)	Chicago, Illinois	Aug. 4, 1972
800 meters	8:23.8	Brad Cooper (U.S.)	Sydney, Australia	Jan. 12, 1972
1,500 meters	15:52.6	Mike Jay Burton (U.S.)	Munich, West Germany	Sept. 4, 1972
4 × 100 Relay	3:26.4	U.S. National Team (David H. Edgar, John Murphy, Jerry Heidenreich, Mark Spitz)	Munich, West Germany	Aug. 28, 1972
4 × 200 Relay	7:35.8	U.S. National Team	Munich, West Germany	Aug. 31, 1972
		BREAST STROKE		
100 meters	1:04.9	Nobutaka Taguchi (Japan)	Munich, West Germany	Aug. 30, 1972
200 meters	2:21.6	John Hencken (U.S.)	Munich, West Germany	Sept. 2, 1972
		BUTTERFLY STROKE		
100 meters	54.3	Mark Spitz (U.S.)	Munich, West Germany	Aug. 31, 1972
200 meters	2:00.7	Mark Spitz (U.S.)	Munich, West Germany	Aug. 28, 1972
		BACK STROKE		
100 meters	56.3	Roland Mathes (East Germany)	Leipzig, East Germany	Apr. 9, 1972
100 meters	56.3*	Roland Mathes (East Germany)	Munich, West Germany	Sept. 4, 1972
200 meters	2:02.8	Roland Mathes (East Germany)	Leipzig, East Germany	July 10, 1972
200 meters	2:02.8	Roland Mathes (East Germany)	Munich, West Germany	Sept. 2, 1972
		INDIVIDUAL MEDLEY		
200 meters	2:07.2	Gunnar Larsson (Sweden)	Munich, West Germany	Sept. 3, 1972
400 meters	4:30.8	Gary Hall (U.S.)	Chicago, Illinois	Aug. 3, 1972
		MEDLEY RELAY		
4 × 100 meters	3:48.2	U.S. National Team (Back Stroke, Breast Stroke, Butterfly Stroke, Free Style) (Michael E. Stamm, Thomas E. Bruce, Mark Spitz, Jerry Heidenreich)	Munich, West Germany	Sept. 4, 1972

* Achieved in a Medley Relay.

MOST OLYMPIC TITLES: Dawn Fraser (Australia) (left, above) won 4 gold medals in 3 Games, while Mark Spitz (U.S.) (right) won 7 gold medals at one celebration at Munich in 1972.

Most World Records. Men: 32, Arne Borg (Sweden) (b. 1901), 1921–29. Women: 42, Ragnhild Hveger (Denmark) (b. December 10, 1920), 1936–42.

Most Olympic Titles. The greatest number of victories resulting in Olympic gold medals is nine by Mark Spitz (U.S.) who won 2 relay golds at Mexico in 1968 and 7 more (4 individual and 3 relay) at Munich in 1972. The later figure is an absolute Olympic record for one celebration at any sport. Spitz's equals the runner Paavo Nurmi's (Finland) absolute Olympic career record of 9 golds.

Dawn Fraser, M.B.E. (born Sydney, Australia, 1937), now Mrs. Gary Ware, won the 100-meter free-style in 1956, 1960 and 1964 and a fourth gold medal in the 4 × 100-meter free-style relay in 1956. Mrs. Patricia McCormick (U.S.) won four gold medals in the highboard and springboard diving contests in 1952 and 1956.

Ice Swimming

Wilhelm Simons (born 1899) of Berlin, Germany, swam 30 meters in 43.7 secs. in the Riessersee, near Garmisch-Partenkirchen, West Germany, on February 3, 1968. The ice had to be broken and the water temperature was 35.6°F.

Channel Swimming

Earliest Man. The first man to swim across the English Channel (without a life jacket) was the merchant navy captain Matthew Webb (1848–83) (G.B.), who swam breaststroke from Dover, England, to Cap Gris Nez, France, in 21 hours 45 minutes on August 24–25, 1875. Webb swam an estimated 38 miles to make the 21-mile crossing. Paul Boyton (U.S.) had swum from Cap Gris Nez to the South Foreland in his patent lifesaving suit in 23 hours 30 minutes on May 28–29, 1875. There is good evidence that Jean-Marie

SWIMMING—WORLD RECORDS—WOMEN

Distance	Min. sec.	Name and Nationality	Place	Date
		FREE STYLE		
100 meters	58.5	Shane Elizabeth Gould (Australia)	Sydney, Australia	Jan. 9, 1972
200 meters	2:03.6	Shane Elizabeth Gould (Australia)	Munich, West Germany	Sept. 1, 1972
400 meters	4:19.0	Shane Elizabeth Gould (Australia)	Munich, West Germany	Aug. 30, 1972
800 meters	8:53.7	Keena Rothhammer (U.S.)	Munich, West Germany	Sept. 3, 1972
1,500 meters	17:00.6	Shane Elizabeth Gould (Australia)	Sydney, Australia	Dec. 12, 1971
		FREE-STYLE RELAY		
4×100 meters	3:55.2	U.S. National Team (Sandra Neilson, Jennifer Jo Kemp, Jane Louise Barkman, Shirley Babashaff)	Munich, West Germany	Aug. 30, 1972
		BREAST STROKE		
100 meters	1:13.6	Catherine Carr (U.S.)	Munich, West Germany	Sept. 2, 1972
200 meters	2:38.5	Catie Ball (U.S.)	Los Angeles, California	Aug. 26, 1972
		BUTTERFLY STROKE		
100 meters	1:03.3	Mayumi Aoki (Japan)	Munich, West Germany	Sept. 1, 1972
200 meters	2:15.6	Karen Patricia Moe (U.S.)	Munich, West Germany	Sept. 4, 1972
		BACK STROKE		
100 meters	1:05.6	Karen Yvette Muir (South Africa)	Utrecht, Netherlands	July 6, 1969
200 meters	2:19.2	Melissa Belote (U.S.)	Munich, West Germany	Sept. 4, 1972
		INDIVIDUAL MEDLEY		
200 meters	2:23.1	Shane Elizabeth Gould (Australia)	Munich, West Germany	Aug. 28, 1972
400 meters	5:03.0	Gail Neal (Australia)	Munich, West Germany	Aug. 31, 1972
		MEDLEY RELAY		
4×100 meters	4:20.8	(Back Stroke, Breast Stroke, Butterfly Stroke, Free Style) U.S. National Team (Melissa Belote, Catherine Carr, Deena Diane Dearduff, Sandra Neilson)	Munich, West Germany	Sept. 3, 1972

SUPER-STAR: Shane Gould (Australia) (left) at age 15, broke every record in free style from 100 to 1,500 meters, between July, 1971 and January, 1972. DIVING CHAMPION: Pat McCormick (U.S.) shares the record for Olympic gold medals at 4, won in highboard and springboard in 1952 and 1956.

Saletti, a French soldier, escaped from a British prison hulk off Dover by swimming to Boulogne in July or August, 1815. The first crossing from France to England was made by Enrique Tiraboschi, a wealthy Italian living in Argentina, who crossed in 16 hours 33 minutes on August 11, 1923, to win a $5,000 prize.

Woman. The first woman to succeed was Gertrude Ederle (U.S.) who swam from Cap Gris Nez, France, to Dover, England, on August 6, 1926, in the then record time of 14 hours 39 minutes. The first woman to swim from England to France was Florence Chadwick of California, in 16 hours 19 minutes on September 11, 1951. She repeated this on September 4, 1953, and October 12, 1955.

Youngest. The youngest conqueror is Leonore Modell of Sacramento, California, who swam from Cap Gris Nez to near Dover in 15 hours 33 minutes on September 3, 1964, when aged 14 years 5 months.

Oldest. The oldest conqueror of the 21-mile crossing has been William E. (Ned) Barnie, who was 55 when he swam from France to England in 15 hours 1 minute on August 16, 1951.

Fastest. The fastest Channel swim took 9 hours 35 minutes, by Barry Watson, aged 25, of Bingley, Yorkshire, England, who left Cap Gris Nez, France, at 2 a.m. and arrived at St. Margaret's Bay, near Dover, at 11:35 a.m. on August 16, 1964. (See photograph, next page.)

FASTEST SWIMMER ACROSS THE ENGLISH CHANNEL: Barry Watson of England took only 9 hours 35 minutes to swim from Cap Gris Nez, France, to Dover in 1964.

The record for an England-France crossing is 9 hours 44 minutes by Lt. Richard Hart Davis, 26 (U.S. Army) of New Jersey on August 21, 1972.

The women's record in the reverse direction is 9 hours 59 minutes 57 secs. by Linda McGill, 21, of Sydney, Australia, who swam from France to England on September 29, 1967.

First Double Crossing. Antonio Abertondo (Argentina), aged 42, swam from England to France in 18 hours 50 minutes (8:35 a.m. on September 20 to 3:25 a.m. on September 21, 1961) and after about 4 minutes rest returned to England in 24 hours 16 minutes, landing at St. Margaret's Bay at 3:45 a.m. on September 22, 1961, to complete the first "double crossing" in 43 hours 10 minutes.

Fastest Double Crossing. The fastest double crossing, and only the second ever achieved, was one of 30 hours 3 minutes by Edward (Ted) Erikson, aged 37, a physiochemist from Chicago. He left St. Margaret's Bay, near Dover, at 8:20 p.m. on September 19, 1965, and landed at a beach about a mile west of Calais, after a swim of 14 hours 15 minutes. After a rest of about 10 minutes, he returned and landed at South Foreland Point, east of Dover, at 2:23 a.m. on September 21, 1965.

Most Conquests. Brojen Das (Pakistan) attempted a Channel crossing six times in 1958–61, succeeding on each occasion. Greta Andersen (U.S.) has also swum the Channel six times (1957–65).

Underwater. The first underwater cross-Channel swim was achieved by Fred Baldasare (U.S.), aged 38, who completed the distance from France to England with scuba in 18 hours 1 minute on July 11, 1962. Simon Paterson, aged 20, a frogman from Egham, Surrey, England, traveled underwater from France to England with an airhose attached to his pilot boat in 14 hours 50 minutes on July 28, 1962.

Table Tennis

Earliest Reference. The earliest evidence relating to a game resembling table tennis has been found in the catalogues of London sporting goods manufacturers in the 1880's. The old Ping Pong Association was formed there in 1902, but the game proved only a temporary craze until resuscitated in 1921.

Highest Speed. No conclusive measurements have been published, but Chuang Tse-tung (China) the world champion of 1961–63–65, has probably smashed at a speed of more than 60 m.p.h.

Youngest International. The youngest international (probably in any sport) was Joy Foster, aged 8, the 1958 Jamaican singles and mixed doubles champion.

Marathon Records. In the Swaythling Cup final match between Austria and Rumania in Prague, Czechoslovakia, in 1936, the play lasted for 25 or 26 hours, spread over three nights.

The longest recorded table tennis marathon with 4 players maintaining continuous singles is 500 hours (20 days 20 hours) by 8 players (all aged 16) (two sets of 4 players at separate tables) from

FASTEST SMASH IN TABLE TENNIS: The ball flies at more than 60 m.p.h. when smashed by Chuang Tse-tung of China.

Maryborough Boys' High School Interact Club, Queensland, Australia, November 30–December 21, 1970.

Most Wins in Table Tennis World Championships
(Instituted 1926–27)

Event	Name and Nationality	Times	Date
Men's Singles (St. Bride's Vase)	G. Viktor Barna (Hungary)	5	1930, 32, 33, 34, 35
Women's Singles (G. Geist Prize)	Angelica Rozeanu (Rumania)	6	1950, 51, 52, 53, 54, 55
Men's Doubles	G. Viktor Barna (Hungary) with two different partners	8	1929, 30, 31, 32, 33, 34, 35, 39
Women's Doubles	Maria Mednyanszky (Hungary) with three different partners	7	1928, 30, 31, 32, 33, 34, 35
Mixed Doubles (Men)	Ferenc Sido (Hungary) with two different partners	4	1949, 50, 52, 53
(Women)	M. Mednyanszky (Hungary) with three different partners	6	1927, 28, 30, 31, 33, 34

G. Viktor Barna gained a personal total of 15 world titles, while 18 have been won by Miss Mednyanszky

Event	Name and Nationality	Times	Date
Men's Team (Swaythling Cup)	Hungary	11	1927, 28, 29, 30, 31, 33, 34, 35, 38, 49, 52
Women's Team (Marcel Corbillon Cup)	Japan	8	1952, 1954, 1957, 1959, 1961, 1963, 1967 1971

Tennis

Origins. The modern game of lawn tennis is generally agreed to have evolved as an outdoor form of Royal Tennis, and to have first become organized with the court and equipment devised, and patented in February 1874, by Major Walter Clopton Wingfield, of England (1833–1912). This was introduced as "sphairistike," but the game soon became known as lawn tennis.

Oldest Courts. The oldest court for Royal Tennis is one built in Paris in 1496. The oldest of 16 surviving tennis courts in the British Isles is the Royal Tennis Court at Hampton Court Palace, which was built by order of King Henry VIII in 1529–30, and rebuilt by order of Charles II in 1660.

Greatest Domination. The earliest occasion upon which any player secured all four of the world's major titles was in 1935 when Frederick John Perry (U.K.) won the French title, having won Wimbledon (1934), the U.S. title (1933–34) and the Australian title (1934).

The first player to hold all four titles at the same time was J. Donald Budge (U.S.), who won the championships of Wimbledon (1937), the U.S. (1937), Australia (1938), and France (1938). He subsequently retained Wimbledon (1938) and the U.S. (1938). Rodney George Laver (Australia) repeated this grand slam in 1962 and in 1969 became the first to take all four of these now Open titles.

Two women players also have won all these four titles in the same tennis year. The first was Maureen Catherine Connolly (U.S.). She won the United States title in 1951, Wimbledon in 1952, retained the U.S. title in 1952, won the Australian in 1953, the French in 1953 and Wimbledon again in 1953. She won her third U.S. title in 1953, her second French title in 1954, and her third Wimbledon title in 1954. Miss Connolly (later Mrs. Norman

GRAND SLAM WINNERS: The only men to win all four major titles in the same year were Rod Laver (left) of Australia who performed the feat in 1962 and 1969, and Don Budge (right) of the U.S. who did it in 1937-38.

Brinker) was seriously injured in a riding accident shortly before the 1954 U.S. championships; she died in June, 1969, aged only 34.

The second woman to win the "grand slam" was Margaret Smith Court (Australia) in 1970. In the same year she earned $100,000 in prize money. (See photo.)

Greatest Crowd. The greatest crowd at a tennis match was 25.578 at the first day of the Davis Cup Challenge Round between

WOMAN GRAND SLAMMER: Margaret Smith Court (Australia) won $100,000 in 1970, while winning all four major tournaments.

Australia and the United States at White City, Sydney, Australia, on December 27, 1954.

Most Games

Singles. The greatest number of games ever played in a singles match is 126. Roger Taylor (U.K.) beat Wieslaw Gasiorek (Poland) 27–29, 31–29, 6–4 on an indoor court in Warsaw, Poland, on November 5, 1966, in a King's Cup tie. The match lasted 4 hours 35 minutes.

Doubles. The greatest number of games ever played in a doubles match is 147. Dick Leach and Dick Dell of the University of Michigan beat Tommy Mozur and Lenny Schloss 3–6, 49–47, 22–20 at Newport, Rhode Island, on August 18–19, 1967.

Longest Match. Mark Cox and Robert K. Wilson (G.B.) beat Charles M. Pasarell and Ron E. Holmberg (U.S.) 26–24, 17–19, 30–28 in a doubles match lasting 6 hours 23 minutes at the U.S. Indoor Championships at Salisbury, Maryland on February 16, 1968.

Fastest Service. The fastest service ever *measured* was one of 154 m.p.h. by Michael Sangster (U.K.) in June, 1963. Crossing the net the ball was traveling at 108 m.p.h. Some players consider the service of Robert Falkenberg (U.S.), the 1948 Wimbledon champion, as the fastest ever used.

Wimbledon Records

(The first Championship was in 1877. Professionals first played in 1968.) From 1971 the tie-break system was introduced, which effectually prevents sets proceeding beyond a 17th game, i.e. 9–8.

Most Appearances. Arthur W. Gore (1868–1928) of the U.K. made 36 appearances between 1888 and 1927, and was in 1909 at 41 years the oldest singles winner ever. In 1964, Jean Borotra (born August 13, 1898) of France made his 35th appearance since 1922.

Most Wins. Elizabeth Ryan (U.S.) won her first title in 1914 and her nineteenth in 1934 (12 women's doubles with 5 different partners and 7 mixed doubles with 5 different partners).

The greatest number of wins by a man at Wimbledon has been 15 by Hugh Lawrence Doherty (1875–1919) who won 5 singles (1902–3–4–5–6), 8 men's doubles (1897–8–9–1900–1 and 1903–4–5), partnered by his brother Reginald F. Doherty (1872–1911), and two mixed doubles (then unofficial) in 1901–2, partnered by Mrs. A. Sterry.

The greatest number of singles wins was eight by Mrs. F. S. Moody (*née* Helen Wills), now Mrs. Aiden Roark (U.S.), who won in 1927, 1928, 1929, 1930, 1932, 1933, 1935 and 1938.

The greatest number of singles wins by a man was seven by William C. Renshaw (G.B.), in 1881–2–3–4–5–6–9.

The greatest number of doubles wins by men was 8 by the brothers R. F. and H. L. Doherty (G.B.), as mentioned above.

The most wins in women's doubles were the 12 by Elizabeth Ryan (U.S.), mentioned above.

The greatest number of mixed doubles wins was 7 by Elizabeth Ryan (U.S.), as noted above. The men's record is four wins, shared

LONGEST WIMBLEDON MATCHES: Pancho Gonzalez (U.S.) (left) played 112 games in 5 hours 12 minutes in 1969, and finally beat Charles Pasarell (U.S.). Billie Jean King (U.S.) played 46 games against Margaret Smith Court in 1970, after playing in the longest doubles match in 1967.

by Elias Victor Seixas (U.S.) in 1953–54–55–56, and Kenneth N. Fletcher (Australia) in 1963–65–66–68.

Most Games—Singles. The most games in a singles match at Wimbledon was 112 when Ricardo Alonzo (Pancho) Gonzalez (U.S.) beat Charles M. Pasarell (U.S.) 22–24, 1–6, 16–14, 6–3, 11–9 in the first round on June 24–5, 1969. The match, which was interrupted by nightfall, lasted a total of 5 hours and 12 minutes.

Most Games—Doubles. The most games in a doubles match at Wimbledon was 98 when Eugene L. Scott (U.S.) and Nicola Pilic (Yugoslavia) beat G. Cliff Richey (U.S.) and Torben Ulrich (Denmark) by 19–21, 12–10, 6–4, 4–6, 9–7 in the first round of the men's doubles on June 22, 1966.

Most Games—Set. The most games in a set at Wimbledon was 62 when Pancho Segura (Ecuador) and Alex Almedo (Peru) beat Abe A. Segal and Gordon L. Forbes 32–30 in a second round match in 1968.

Most Games—Finals. The most games in a Wimbledon men's singles final was 58 when Jaroslav Drobny (then Egypt) beat Kenneth R. Rosewall (Australia) 13–11, 4–6, 6–2, 9–7 in 1954.

The most games in a Wimbledon ladies' singles final was 46 when Margaret Smith (Mrs. Barry M. Court) (Australia), 27, beat Billie Jean (Mrs. L. W.) King (U.S.) by 14–12, 11–9 on July 3, 1970, in a match lasting 2 hours 25 minutes. (See photo.)

The most games in a Wimbledon men's doubles final was 70 when John D. Newcombe and Anthony D. Roche (Australia) beat Kenneth R. Rosewall and Frederick S. Stolle (Australia) 3–6, 8–6, 5–7, 14–12, 6–3 in 1968.

The most games in a Wimbledon ladies' doubles final was 38, on two occasions. Mme. Simone Mathieu (France) and Elizabeth ("Bunny") Ryan (U.S.) beat Freda James (now Mrs. S. H. Hammersley) and Adeline Maud Yorke (now Mrs. D. E. C. Eyres) (both U.K.) by 6–2, 9–11, 6–4 in 1933, and Rosemary Casals and Mrs. Billie Jean King (U.S.) beat Maria Bueno (Brazil) and Nancy Richey (U.S.) 9–11, 6–4, 6–2 in 1967.

The most games in a Wimbledon mixed doubles final was 48 when Eric W. Sturgess and Mrs. Sheila Summers (South Africa) beat John E. Bromwich (Australia) and A. Louise Brough (U.S.) 9–7, 9–11, 7–5 in 1949.

Longest Match. The longest Wimbledon match was the 5 hours 12 minutes required by the Gonzalez vs. Pasarell match, mentioned above.

Youngest Champions. The youngest champion ever at Wimbledon was Charlotte Dod (1871–1960), who was 15 years 8 months old when she won in 1887.

The youngest male singles champion was Wilfred Baddeley (born January 11, 1872), who won the Wimbledon title in 1891 at the age of 19.

Richard Dennis Ralston (born July 27, 1942), of Bakersfield, California, was 25 days short of his 18th birthday when he won the men's doubles with Rafael H. Osuna (1938–69), of Mexico, in 1960.

Professional Tennis

Highest Prize Money. The highest prize money won in a year is $292,717 by Rod Laver (Australia) in 1971. The career total in 9 professional seasons was thus brought to a record $1,006,947. In 1971 Mrs. Billie Jean King (U.S.) won $117,000 (feminine record), which was more than any U.S. player that season.

Tennis Marathons

The longest recorded non-stop tennis game is one of 73 hours 25 minutes by Mel Baleson, 21, and Glen Grisillo, 29, both of South Africa, who played 1,224 games at the University of Nevada, Reno, Nevada, May 6–9, 1971.

Davis Cup

Most Victories. The greatest number of wins in the Davis Cup (instituted 1900) has been (inclusive of 1971) the United States with 23 over Australia's 22 wins.

Individual Performance. Nicola Pietrangeli (Italy) played 161 rubbers, 1954 to 1971, winning 117. He played 110 singles (winning 77) and 51 doubles (winning 40). He took part in 63 ties.

Greatest Number of Games. In a tie, the greatest number of games played was 281 in Perth, Australia, in 1960 when in the Inter-Zone final Italy beat the U.S. 3–2.

In a match, the greatest number of games played was 95 when at Edgbaston, Birmingham, England, in 1969 in the quarter-final of the European Zone, Wilhelm Bungert and Christian Kuhnke (Germany) beat Mark Cox and Peter Curtis (Great Britain) 10–8, 17–19, 13–11, 3–6, 6–2.

In a singles match the greatest number of games played was 86 when at Cleveland, Ohio, in the 1970 Challenge Round, Arthur Ashe (U.S.) beat Christian Kuhnke (W. Germany) 6–8, 10–12, 9–7, 13–11, 6–4.

Tiddleywinks

Accuracy. The lowest number of shots taken to pot 12 winks from 3 feet is 23, achieved by three Englishmen, the first in 1962, the others in 1963 and 1965.

Speed. The record for potting 24 winks from 18 inches is 21.8 seconds by Stephen Williams of Altrincham Grammar School, England, in May, 1966.

Marathon. Allen R. Astles of the University of Wales potted 10,000 winks in 3 hours 51 minutes 46 seconds in February, 1966. The most protracted game on record is one of 144 hours 2 minutes (with a team of six), by the 1st Helston Venture Scout Unit, Cornwall, England, on December 28, 1970 to January 3, 1971.

Track and Field

Earliest References. Track and field athletics date from the ancient Olympic Games. The earliest accurately known Olympiad dates from July 21 or 22, 776 B.C., at which celebration Coroebas won the foot race. The oldest surviving measurements are a long jump of 23 feet $1\frac{1}{2}$ inches by Chionis of Sparta in *c.* 656 B.C. and a discus throw of 100 cubits by Protesilaus.

Fastest Runner. Robert Lee Hayes (born December 20, 1942), of Jacksonville, Florida, was timed at 26.9 m.p.h. at the 75-yard mark of a 100-yard race in May, 1964. It has been estimated that between the 60- and the 75-yard marks at St. Louis, Missouri, on June 21, 1963, Hayes was running at 27.89 m.p.h. in his world record 9.1 sec. 100 yards. Wyomia Tyus (U.S.) was timed at 23.78 m.p.h. in Kiev, U.S.S.R., on July 31, 1965. (See photo, page 599.)

Earliest Landmarks. The first time 10 seconds ("even time") was bettered for 100 yards under championship conditions was when John Owen recorded $9\frac{4}{5}$ seconds in the A.A.U. Championships at Analostan Island, Washington, D.C., on October 11, 1890. The first recorded instance of 6 feet being cleared in the high jump was when Marshall Jones Brooks jumped 6 feet $0\frac{1}{8}$ inch at Marston, near Oxford, England, on March 17, 1876. The breaking of the "4 minute barrier" in the one mile was first achieved by Dr. Roger Gilbert Bannister (born Harrow, England, March 23, 1929), when he recorded 3 minutes 59.4 seconds on the Iffley Road track, Oxford, at 6:10 p.m. on May 6, 1954.

Longest Tug O'War. The longest recorded pull is one of 2 hours 41 minutes between "H" Company and "E" Company of the 2nd Battalion of the Sherwood Foresters (Derbyshire Regiment) at Jubbulpore, India, on August 12, 1889. "E" Company won.

WORLD RECORDS—MEN

The complete list of World Records for the 54 scheduled men's events (excluding the 6 walking records, see under Walking) passed by the International Amateur Athletic Federation as at January 1, 1972. Those marked with an asterisk are awaiting ratification.

RUNNING

Event	mins. secs.	Name and Nationality	Place	Date
100 yards	9.1	Robert Lee Hayes (U.S.)	St. Louis, Missouri	June 21, 1963
	9.1	Harry Winston Jerome (Canada)	Edmonton, Alberta, Canada	July 15, 1966
	9.1	James Ray Hines (U.S.)	Houston, Texas	May 13, 1967
	9.1	Charles Edward Greene (U.S.)	Provo, Utah	June 15, 1967
	9.1	John Wesley Carlos (U.S.)	Fresno, California	May 10, 1969
220 yards (straight)	19.5	Tommie C. Smith (U.S.)	San Jose, California	May 7, 1966
220 yards (turn)	20.0	Tommie C. Smith (U.S.)	Sacramento, California	June 11, 1966
440 yards	44.5	John Smith (U.S.)	Eugene, Oregon	June 26, 1971
880 yards	1:44.9	James Ronald Ryun (U.S.)	Terre Haute, Indiana	June 10, 1966
1 mile	3:51.1	James Ronald Ryun (U.S.)	Bakersfield, California	June 23, 1967
2 miles	8:17.8	Emile Puttemans (Belgium)	Edinburgh, Scotland	Aug. 21, 1971
3 miles	12:50.4	Ronald William Clarke (Australia)	Stockholm, Sweden	July 5, 1966
6 miles	26:47.0	Ronald William Clarke (Australia)	Oslo, Norway	July 14, 1965
10 miles	46:37.8	Jerome Drayton (Canada)	Toronto, Canada	Sept. 6, 1970
15 miles	1H 12:48.2	Ronald Hill (United Kingdom)	Bolton, Lancashire	July 21, 1965
100 meters	9.9	James Ray Hines (U.S.)	Sacramento, California	June 20, 1968
	9.9	Ronald Ray Smith (U.S.)	Sacramento, California	June 20, 1968
	9.9	Charles Edward Greene (U.S.)	Sacramento, California	June 20, 1968
	9.9	James Ray Hines (U.S.)	Mexico City, México	Oct. 14, 1968
	9.9*	Eddie Hart (U.S.)	Eugene, Oregon	July 1, 1972
	9.9*	Rey Robinson (U.S.)	Eugene, Oregon	July 1, 1972
200 meters (straight)	19.5	Tommie C. Smith (U.S.)	San Jose, California	May 7, 1966
200 meters (turn)	19.8	Tommie C. Smith (U.S.)	Mexico City, Mexico	Oct. 16, 1968
	19.8	Donald O'Riley Quarrie (Jamaica)	Cali, Colombia	Aug. 3, 1971
400 meters	43.8	Lee Edward Evans (U.S.)	Mexico City, Mexico	Oct. 18, 1968
800 meters	1:44.3	Peter George Snell (New Zealand)	Christchurch, New Zealand	Feb. 3, 1962
	1:44.3	Ralph D. Doubell (Australia)	Mexico City, Mexico	Oct. 15, 1968
	1:44.3	David Wottle (U.S.)	Eugene, Oregon	July 1, 1972
1,000 meters	2:16.2	Jürgen May (East Germany)	Erfurt, East Germany	July 20, 1965
	2:16.2	Franz-Josef Kemper (West Germany)	Hanover, West Germany	Sept. 21, 1966

FASTEST HUMANS EVER: Tommie Smith (U.S.) (top left) holds world records at 200 yards and 200 meters, both straight and with turn. James Ray Hines (U.S.) (top right) has twice run 100 meters at 9.9 seconds to share that record, and also shares the 100-yard record at 9.1 seconds. Lee Evans (U.S.) (lower left) is the champion at 400 meters. Ralph Doubell (Australia) (lower right) has shared with Peter Snell (N.Z.) the 800-meter record since 1968.

RUNNING (continued)

Event	mins. secs.	Name and Nationality	Place	Date
1,500 meters	3:33.1	James Ronald Ryun (U.S.)	Los Angeles, California	July 8, 1967
2,000 meters	4:56.2	Michel Jazy (France)	Saint-Maur les Fossés, France...	Oct. 12, 1966
3,000 meters	7:39.6	Kipchoge Keino (Kenya)	Hälsingborg, Sweden	Aug. 27, 1965
5,000 meters	13:16.6	Ronald William Clarke (Australia)	Stockholm, Sweden	July 5, 1966
10,000 meters	27:38.4	Lasse Viren (Finland)	Munich, West Germany	Sept. 3, 1972
20,000 meters	58:06.2	Gaston Roelants (Belgium)	Louvain, Belgium	Oct. 28, 1966
25,000 meters	1H15:22.6	Ronald Hill (United Kingdom)	Bolton, Lancashire, England	July 21, 1965
30,000 meters	1H31:30.4	James Noel Carroll Alder (United Kingdom)	Crystal Palace, London	Sept. 5, 1970
1 hour	12 miles 1,478 yards	Gaston Roelants (Belgium)	Louvain, Belgium	Oct. 28, 1966

HURDLING

Event	mins. secs.	Name and Nationality	Place	Date
120 yards (3' 6" hurdles)	13.0	Rodney Milburn (U.S.)	Eugene, Oregon	June 25, 1971
220 yards (2' 6") (straight)	21.9	Donald Augustus Styron (U.S.)	Baton Rouge, Louisiana	Apr. 2, 1960
440 yards (3' 0")	48.8	Ralph Mann (U.S.)	Des Moines, Iowa	June 20, 1970
110 meters (3' 6")	13.2	Karl Martin Lauer (West Germany)	Zürich, Switzerland	July 7, 1959
	13.2	Lee Quency Calhoun (U.S.)	Bern, Switzerland	Aug. 21, 1960
	13.2	Earl Ray McCullouch (U.S.)	Minneapolis, Minnesota	July 16, 1967
	13.2	Willie Davenport (U.S.)	Zürich, Switzerland	July 4, 1969
	13.2	Rodney Milburn Jr. (U.S.)	Munich, West Germany	Sept. 7, 1972
200 meters (2' 6") (straight)	21.9	Donald Augustus Styron (U.S.)	Baton Rouge, Louisiana	Apr. 2, 1960
200 meters (2' 6") (turn)	22.5	Karl Martin Lauer (West Germany)	Zürich, Switzerland	July 7, 1959
	22.5	Glenn Ashby Davis (U.S.)	Bern, Switzerland	Aug. 20, 1960
400 meters (3' 0")	47.8	John Akii-Bua (Uganda)	Munich, West Germany	Sept. 2, 1972
3,000 meters Steeplechase	8:22.0	Kerry O'Brien (Australia)	West Berlin, Germany	July 4, 1970

LONG DISTANCE CHAMPIONS: Ron Clarke (Australia) (top left) holds the records at 3 and 6 miles, and at 5,000 meters. Gaston Roelants (Belgium) (top right, #40) is the champion at 20,000 meters and ran a record 12 miles, 1,478 yards in the one-hour race. Jim Ryun (U.S.) (lower left) is the fastest miler ever, with a record at 3 minutes 51.1 seconds, and also holds records at 880 and 1,500 meters. HURDLING CHAMPION at 400 meters over 3-foot hurdles is John Akii-Bua (Uganda) who set the world record in the 1972 Olympics.

WORLD RECORDS—MEN (Continued)

FIELD EVENTS

Event	ft.	ins.	Name and Nationality	Place	Date
High Jump	7	6¼	Patrick Clifford Matzdorf (U.S.)	Berkeley, California	July 3, 1971
Pole Vault	18	5¾	Robert Lloyd Seagren (U.S.)	Eugene, Oregon	July 2, 1972
Long Jump	29	2½	Robert Beamon (U.S.)	Mexico City, Mexico	Oct. 18, 1968
Triple Jump	57	1	Pedro Duenos Perez (Cuba)	Cali, Colombia	Aug. 5, 1971
Shot Put	71	5½	James Randel Matson (U.S.)	College Station, Texas	Apr. 22, 1967
Discus Throw	224	5	L. Jay Silvester (U.S.)	Reno, Nevada	Sept. 18, 1968
	224	5	Rickard Bruch (Sweden)	Stockholm, Sweden	July 5, 1972
Hammer Throw	250	8	Walter Schmidt (West Germany)	Lahr, West Germany	Sept. 4, 1971
Javelin Throw	307	9	Janis Luis (U.S.S.R.)	Stockholm, Sweden	July 6, 1972

RELAYS

Event	mins. secs.	Team	Place	Date
4×110 yards (two turns)	38.6	University of Southern California, U.S. (Earl Ray McCullouch, Fred Kuller, Orenthal James Simpson, Lennox Miller (Jamaica))	Provo, Utah	June 17, 1967
4×220 yards and 4×220 meters	1:21.7	Texas Agricultural and Mechanical College (Donald Rogers, Rockie Woods, Marvin Mills, Curtis Mills)	Des Moines, Iowa	Apr. 24, 1970
4×440 yards	3:02.8	Trinidad and Tobago (Lennox Yearwood, Kent Bernard, Edwin Roberts, Wendell A. Mottley)	Kingston, Jamaica	Aug. 13, 1966
4×880 yards	7:11.6	Kenya (Naftali Bon, Hezekiah Nyamau, Thomas Saisi, Robert Ouko)	Crystal Palace, London	Sept. 5, 1970
4×1 mile	16:02.8	New Zealand (Kevin Ross, Anthony Polhill, Richard Tayler, Richard Quax)	Auckland, N.Z.	Feb. 3, 1972

GREATEST JUMP: Bob Beamon (U.S.) (top left) startled everyone when he exceeded the previous record long (broad) jump by 2 feet. No one has come close to his 29 feet 2½ inches, set in 1968. The SHOT PUT record which Randy Matson (U.S.) (top right) set in 1967 at 71 feet 5½ inches bettered his old mark by 10½ inches. The POLE VAULT record has been going up rapidly. Set by Bob Seagren (below) at 18 feet 5¾ inches it is more than 2 feet higher than in 1962.

WORLD RECORDS—MEN (Continued)

RELAYS (continued)

Event	mins. secs.	Team	Place	Date
4 × 100 meters	38.2	United States Olympic Team (Charles Edward Greene, Melvin Pender, Ronald Ray Smith, James Ray Hines)	Mexico City, Mexico ...	Oct. 20, 1968
4 × 400 meters	2:56.1	United States Olympic Team (Black, Taylor, Tinker, Hart) United States Olympic Team (Vincent Matthews, Ronald Freeman, G. Lawrence James, Lee Edward Evans)	Munich, West Germany Mexico City, Mexico ...	Sept. 10, 1972 Oct. 20, 1968
4 × 800 meters	7:08.6	West Germany "A" Team (Manfred Kinder, Walter Adams, Dieter Bogatzki, Franz-Josef Kemper)	Wiesbaden, West Germany	Aug. 13, 1966
4 × 1,500 meters	14:49.0	France "A" Team (Gérard Vervoort, Claude Nicolas, Michel Jazy, Jean Wadoux)	Saint-Maur, Paris, France	June 25, 1965

DECATHLON

8,454 points		Nikolay Avilov (U.S.S.R.)	Munich, West Germany	Sept. 7–8, 1972

THE MARATHON

There is no official Marathon record because of the varying severity of the courses. The best time over 26 miles 385 yards (standardized in 1924) in a championship race is 2 hours 09 minutes 28.0 seconds by Ronald Hill (United Kingdom) at Edinburgh, Scotland on July 25, 1970. The time of 2 hours 8 minutes 33.6 seconds (av. 12.24 m.p.h.) by Derek Clayton, the English-born Australian, at Antwerp, Belgium, on May 30, 1969 was incorrectly reported to have been run on a short course and is thus the fastest time on record.

The best time by a woman is 2 hours 46 minutes 30 seconds by Adrienne Beames (Australia), 28, at Werribee, Victoria, Australia, on August 31, 1971.

WORLD RECORDS—WOMEN

RUNNING

Event	mins. secs.	Name and Nationality	Place	Date
100 yards	10.0	Chi Cheng (Formosa)	Portland, Oregon	June 13, 1970
220 yards (turn)	22.6	Chi Cheng (Formosa)	Los Angeles, California	July 3, 1970
440 yards	52.4	Judith Florence Pollock (née Amoore) (Australia)	Perth, Western Australia	Feb. 27, 1965
880 yards	2:02.0	Dixie Isobel Willis (Australia)	Perth, Western Australia	Mar. 3, 1962
	2:02.0	Judith Florence Pollock (née Amoore) (Australia)	Stockholm, Sweden	July 5, 1967
	2:02.0	Madeline Jackson (née Manning) (U.S.)	Philadelphia	May 14, 1972

WORLD RECORDS—WOMEN (Continued)

RUNNING (continued)

Event	mins..secs.	Name and Nationality	Place	Date
1 mile	4:35.4	Ellen Tittel (West Germany)	Sittard, West Germany	Aug. 20, 1971
60 meters	7.2	Betty Cuthbert (Australia)	Sydney, N.S.W., Australia	Feb. 21, 1960
	7.2	Irina Robertovna Bochkaryova (née Turova) (U.S.S.R.)	Moscow, U.S.S.R.	Aug. 28, 1961
100 meters	11.0	Wyomia Tyus (U.S.)	Mexico City, Mexico	Oct. 15, 1968
	11.0	Chi Cheng (Formosa)	Vienna, Austria	July 18, 1970
	11.0	Renate Meissner (East Germany)	East Berlin, East Germany	Aug. 2, 1970
	11.0*	Renate Stecher (née Meissner) (East Germany)	East Berlin, East Germany	July 31, 1971
	11.0*	Renate Stecher (née Meissner) (East Germany)	Potsdam, East Germany	June 3, 1972
	11.0*	Ellen Stropahl (East Germany)	Potsdam, East Germany	June 15, 1972
	11.0*	Eva Gleskova (Czechoslovakia)	Budapest, Hungary	July 1, 1972
200 meters (turn)	22.4	Chi Cheng (Formosa)	Munich, West Germany	July 12, 1970
	22.4	Renate Stecher (East Germany)	Munich, West Germany	Sept. 7, 1972
400 meters†	51.0	Marilyn Neufville (Jamaica)	Edinburgh, Scotland	July 22, 1970
800 meters†	1:58.5	Hildegard Falck (West Germany)	Stuttgart, West Germany	July 11, 1971
1,500 meters	4:01.4	Ludmila Bragina (U.S.S.R.)	Munich, West Germany	Sept. 9, 1972

HURDLES

The I.A.A.F. scheduled world records for 100- and 200-meter hurdles were introduced on May 1, 1969. Inaugural ratifications have been made as follows:

100 meters	12.5*	Annelie Ehrhardt (East Germany)	Potsdam, East Germany	June 15, 1972
	12.5*	Pamela Ryan (née Kilborn) (Australia)	Warsaw, Poland	June 28, 1972
200 meters (2' 6")	25.7*	Pamela Kilborn (Australia)	Melbourne, Australia	Nov. 28, 1971

FIELD EVENTS

Event	ft.	ins.	Name and Nationality	Place	Date
High Jump	6	3¼	Ilona Gusenbauer (Austria)	Vienna, Austria	Sept. 4, 1971
	6	3¼	Ulrike Meyfarth (West Germany)	Munich, West Germany	Sept. 4, 1972
Long Jump	22	5¼	Heide Rosendahl (West Germany)	Turin, Italy	Sept. 3, 1970
Shot Putt	69	0	Nadyezda Chizhova (U.S.S.R.)	Munich, West Germany	Sept. 7, 1972
Discus Throw	215	5¾	Faina Melnik (U.S.S.R.)	Augsburg, West Germany	June 24, 1972
Javelin Throw	213	5	Ruth Fuchs (née Gamm) (East Germany)	Potsdam, East Germany	June 15, 1972

WORLD RECORDS—WOMEN (*Continued*)

PENTATHLON

Mary Elizabeth Peters (U.K.)........ Munich, West Germany   Sept. 2–3, 1972
(100 m. hurdles 13.3s.; Shot Put 53 ft. 1¼ in.; High Jump 5 ft. 11½ in.; Long Jump 19 ft. 7½ in.; 200 m. 24.1s.)

4,801 points

RELAYS

Event	mins. secs.	Team	Place	Date
4 × 110 yards	44.7	Tennessee State University (Diane Hughes, Debbie Wedgeworth, Mattline Render, Iris Davis)	Bakersfield, Calif.	July 9, 1971
4 × 220 yards	1:35.8*	Australia (Marian Hoffman, Jennifer Lamy, Raelene Boyle, Pamela Kilborn)	Brisbane, Australia	Nov. 9, 1969
4 × 440 yards	3:38.8	Atoms Track Club (U.S.) (M. McMillan, L. Reynolds, G. Fitzgerald, C. Toussaint)	Bakersfield, Calif.	July 10, 1971
4 × 100 meters	42.8	United States Olympic Team (Barbara Ferrell, Margaret Bayles (*née* Johnson), Mildrette Netter, Wyomia Tyus)	Mexico City, Mexico	Oct. 20, 1968
	42.8	West German Olympic Team	Munich, West Germany	Sept. 10, 1972
4 × 200 meters	1:33.8	United Kingdom National Team (Maureen Dorothy Tranter, Della P. James, Janet Mary Simpson, Valerie Peat (*née* Wild))	London, England	Aug. 24, 1968
4 × 400 meters	3:23.0	East German Olympic Team	Munich, West Germany	Sept. 10, 1972
4 × 800 meters	8:16.8	Germany (Ellen Tittel, Sylvia Schenk, Christa Merten, Hildegard Falck (*née* Janze))	Lübeck, Germany	July 31, 1971

FASTEST SPRINTERS: Wyomia Tyus (U.S.) (top left) was timed at 23.78 m.p.h. in Russia in 1965. She shares the 100-meter record at 11 seconds flat with Chi Cheng (Taiwan) (top right). The first and only girl to run 100 yards in 10 seconds flat, Chi Cheng also is the champion at 220 yards (with turn) and at 200 meters.

World Record Breakers

Oldest. The greatest age at which anyone has broken a standard world record is 35 years 255 days in the case of Dana Zátopkova, *née* Ingrova (born September 19, 1922), of Czechoslovakia, who broke the women's javelin record with 182 feet 10 inches at Prague, Czechoslovakia, on June 1, 1958.

On June 20, 1948, Mikko Hietanen (Finland) (born September 22, 1911) bettered his own world 30,000-meter record with 1 hour 40 minutes 46.4 secs. at Jyväskylä, Finland, when aged 36 years 272 days.

Youngest. Doreen Lumley (born September, 1921) of New Zealand, equaled the world's 100-yard-dash record for women with 11.0 seconds at Auckland, N.Z., on March 11, 1939, when aged only 17 years 6 months.

Shot Put with Both Hands. The greatest combined distance for putting the shot is 106 feet 10¼ inches (61 feet 0¾ inches with the right hand and 45 feet 9½ inches left hand) by William Parry O'Brien (born January 28, 1932), of the U.S., at Culver City, California, on August 17, 1962.

WORLD RECORD HOLDERS for women's high jump, Ulrike Meyfarth (West Germany) (left) 6 ft. 3½ in., and for shot putting, Nadyezhda Chizhova (U.S.S.R.) (right) 69 ft. 0 in. Both marks were achieved at the 1972 Olympics.

Most Records in a Day. The only athlete to have his name entered in the world records 6 times in one day was J. C. "Jesse" Owens (U.S.) who at Evanston, Illinois, on May 25, 1935, equalled the 100-yard running record with 9.4 secs. at 3:15 p.m.; long-jumped 26 feet 8¼ inches at 3:25 p.m.; ran 220 yards (straight away) in 20.3 secs. at 3:45 p.m., and 220 yards over low hurdles in 22.6 secs. at 4 p.m. The two 220-yard runs were also ratified as 200-meter world records.

Highest Jumper. There are several reported instances of high jumpers exceeding the official world record height of 7 feet 6¼ inches. The earliest of these came from unsubstantiated reports of Tutsi tribesmen in Central Africa clearing up to 8 feet 2½ inches, definitely however, from inclined take-offs. The greatest height cleared above an athlete's own head is 16⅞ inches, first achieved by Valeriy Brumel (born April 14, 1942), of the U.S.S.R., standing 6 feet 0⅞ inch tall, when clearing 7 feet 5¾ inches in Moscow, U.S.S.R., on July 21, 1963.

A greater differential of 17⅝ inches would have been achieved by Ni Chih-chin (also born on April 14, 1942), of China, standing 6 feet 0½ inch tall, when he cleared an unratifiable 7 feet 6⅛ inches in an exhibition at Changsha, China, on November 8, 1970.

The greatest height cleared by a woman above her own head is 6 inches by Miroslava Rezkova (Czechoslovakia), standing 5 feet

WOMEN'S LONG JUMP RECORD HOLDER: Heide Rosendahl (West Germany) jumped 22 feet 5¼ inches in Turin, Italy, in 1970.

6½ inches when she jumped 6 feet 0½ inches at Povozka Bystrica on July 20, 1969.

Standing High Jump. The best standing high jump is 5 feet 9¼ inches by Johan Christian Evandt (Norway) at Oslo, Norway, on March 4, 1962.

Three-Legged Race. The fastest recorded time for a 100-yard three-legged race is 11.0 seconds by Harry L. Hillman and Lawson Robertson at Brooklyn, New York City, on April 24, 1909.

Blind 100 Yards. The fastest time recorded for 100 yards by a blind man is 11.0 seconds by George Bull, aged 19, of Chippenham, Wiltshire, England, in a race at the Worcester College for the Blind, on October 26, 1954.

Pancake Race Record. The annual Housewives Pancake Race at Olney, Buckinghamshire, England, was first mentioned in 1445. The record for the winding 415-yard course is 63.0 seconds, set by Janet Bunker, aged 17, on February 7, 1967. The record for the counterpart race at Liberal, Kansas, is 59.1 seconds by Kathleen West, 19, on February 10, 1970.

Highest Race. The highest race regularly run is the Pike's Peak International Marathon (first held in 1955), covering 26.8 miles in

Colorado. The runners begin at the railroad depot in Manitou Springs (6,563 feet above sea level), go to the summit of Pike's Peak (14,110 feet) and return to Manitou Springs. The ascent of 7,547 feet covers 13 miles and the descent covers 13.8 miles. The best time for the race is 3 hours 53 minutes 57 seconds by John Ray Rose, aged 26, of Garden City, Kansas, on August 22, 1965. He completed the ascent in 2 hours 25 minutes.

Most Olympic Gold Medals. Ray C. Ewry (U.S.) won eight individual Olympic gold medals, three in 1900, three in 1904 and two in 1908. Paavo Johannes Nurmi (Finland) won six individual and three team race gold medals between 1920 and 1928.

The most wins by a woman is four by Francina E. Blankers-Koen (born April 26, 1918), of the Netherlands, in 1948 (100 and 200 meters, 80-meter hurdles, and the last stage in the 4 × 100-meter relay), and four by Betty Cuthbert (born April 20, 1938) of Australia in 1956 (100 meters, 200 meters and the last stage in the 4 × 100-meter relay) and 1964 (400 meters).

Most Medals. The most Olympic medals (of any metal) won by a man is 12 (9 gold and 3 silver) by Paavo Nurmi of Finland. The most won by a woman is seven by Shirley de la Hunty (*née* Strickland) of Australia between 1948 and 1956.

FIVE-TIME WORLD CHAMPION ON TRAMPOLINE: Judy Wills (left) even has a difficult maneuver named after her.

Trampolining

Origin. The sport of trampolining (from the Spanish word *trampolin*, a springboard) dates from 1936, when the prototype "T" model trampoline was developed by George Nissen (U.S.). Trampolines were used in show business at least as early as "The Walloons" of the period, 1910–12.

Most Difficult Maneuvers. The three most difficult maneuvers yet achieved are the triple twisting double back somersault, known as a Miller after the first trampolinist able to achieve it—Wayne Miller (U.S.) (born 1947), the women's Wills ($5\frac{1}{2}$ twisting back somersault) named after the five-time world champion, Judy Wills (U.S.) (born 1948) and the 4 consecutive triple somersaults uniquely performed, first in 1970, by Len Ranson (Australia).

Marathon Record. The longest recorded trampoline bouncing marathon is one of 505 hours, set by a team of 8 from the Ottawa Street Community Y.W.C.A. at Pro's Golf Centre, Stoney Creek, Ontario, Canada, June 22–July 13, 1971. Each person jumped 63 hours $7\frac{1}{2}$ minutes. The individual record is 44 hours 25 minutes by Gavin Jury of Richmond, New Zealand, October 24–26, 1970.

Most Titles. The only man to retain a world title (instituted 1964) have been Dave Jacobs (U.S.) the 1967–68 champion and Wayne Miller (U.S.), the 1966 and 1970 champion. Judy Wills won 5 women's titles (1964–65–66–67–68).

Volleyball

Origin. The game was invented as Minnonette in 1895 by William G. Morgan at the Y.M.C.A. gymnasium at Springfield, Massachusetts. The International Volleyball Association was formed in Paris in April, 1947. The ball travels at a speed of up to 70 m.p.h. when smashed over the net, which measures 7 feet 11.6 inches. In the women's game it is 7 feet 4.1 inches.

World Titles. World Championships were instituted in 1949. The U.S.S.R. has won six men's titles (1949, 1952, 1960, 1962, 1964 and 1968) in the eight meetings held. The U.S.S.R. won the women's championship in 1952, 1956, 1960, 1968 and 1970). The record crowd is 60,000 for the 1952 world title matches in Moscow, U.S.S.R.

Marathon. The longest recorded volleyball marathon is one of 125 hours by four sets of 6-a-side teams from the Four Grace Baptist Church Youth Club in Seattle, Washington, ending on July 31, 1971.

Walking

OFFICIAL WORLD RECORDS (Track Walking)
(As recognized by the International Amateur Athletic Federation)
(*Awaiting ratification)

Distance	hrs.	mins.	secs.	Name and Nationality	Date	Place
20,000 meters	1	25	19.4	Peter Frenkel and Hans-Georg Reimann (East Germany)	June 24, 1972	Erfurt
30,000 meters	2	14	45.6	Karl-Heinz Stadmuller (East Germany)	April 18, 1972	East Berlin
20 miles	2	31	33.0	Anatoliy S. Vedyakov (U.S.S.R.)	Aug. 23, 1958	Moscow
30 miles	3	56	12.6*	Peter Selzer (East Germany)	Oct. 2, 1971	Naumburg
50,000 meters	4	04	19.8	Peter Selzer (East Germany)	Oct. 3, 1971	Naumberg
2 hours	16 miles 992 yards			Peter Frenkel (East Germany)	Apr. 11, 1971	East Berlin

UNOFFICIAL WORLD BEST PERFORMANCES (Track Walking)
(Best valid performances over distances or times for which records are no longer recognized by the I.A.A.F.)

Distance	hrs.	mins.	secs.	Name and Nationality	Date	Place
5 miles		34	21.2	Kenneth Joseph Matthews (U.K.)	Sept. 28, 1960	London
10 miles	1	09	40.6	Kenneth Joseph Matthews (U.K.)	June 6, 1964	Walton-on-Thames
50,000 meters (road)	3	52	44.6	Bernd Kannenberg (West Germany)	1972	West Germany
1 hour	8 miles 1,294 yards			Grigoriy Panichkin (U.S.S.R.)	Nov. 1, 1959	Stalinabad
24 hours	133 miles 21 yards			Huw D. M. N. Neilson (U.K.)	Oct. 14–15, 1960	Walton-on-Thames

Road Walking. The record for walking across the U.S. from Los Angeles to New York is 53 days 12¼ hours by John Lees (England) between April 13 and June 6, 1972. The women's record for the 3,207-mile route is 86 days by Dr. Barbara Moore (*née*

Varvara Belayeva, b. in Kaluga, Russia, December 22, 1903), ending on July 6, 1960.

Walking on Crutches. David Ryder, 21, a polio victim from Essex, England, left Los Angeles on March 30 and arrived at New York City on August 14, 1970, after covering 2,960 miles on his crutches.

MOST CAPPED WATER POLOIST: Georgi Karparti (Hungary) (right) has 151, the greatest number of internationals.

Water Polo

Origins. Water polo was developed in England as "Water Soccer" in 1869 and was first included in the Olympic Games in Paris in 1900.

Olympic Victories. Hungary has won the Olympic tournament five times, in 1932, 1936, 1952, 1956 and 1964.

Most Caps. The greatest number of internationals is 151 by Georgi Karparti of Hungary to 1966. Karparti and Deszo Gyarmati both won 3 Olympic gold medals in 1952–56–64.

Water Skiing

Origins. The origins of water skiing lie in plank gliding or aquaplaning. A photograph exists of a "plank-riding" contest in a regatta won by a Mr. S. Storry at Scarborough, Yorkshire, England, on July 15, 1914. Competitors were towed on a *single* plank by a motor launch. The present-day sport of water skiing was pioneered by Ralph W. Samuelson on Lake Pepin, Minnesota, on two curved pine boards in the summer of 1922, though claims have been made for the birth of the sport on Lake Annecy (Haute Savoie), France, in 1920.

Jumps. The first recorded jump on water skis was by Ralph W. Samuelson, off a greased ramp in 1922. The longest official jump recorded is one of 169 feet by Wayne Grinditch, 17 (U.S.) at Callaway Gardens, Pine Mountain, Georgia in July, 1972. A minimum margin of 8 inches is required for sole possession of the world record.

The women's record is 111 feet by Barbara Clack (U.S.) at Callaway Gardens, Georgia set on July 11, 1971.

Buoys and Tricks. The world record for slalom is 38 buoys (6 passes through the course plus 2 buoys with a 75-foot rope shortened by 36 feet) by Mike Suyderhoud (U.S.) at Ruislip, England, on June 6, 1970, and by Robi Zucchi (Italy) at Canzo, Italy, on September 6, 1970. The highest recorded point score for tricks is 5,970 points by Ricky McCormick (U.S.) at the Martini International at Prince's, Bedfont, England in August, 1970.

Longest Run. The greatest distance traveled non-stop is 818.2 miles by Marvin G. Shackleford round McKellar Lake, Memphis, Tennessee, in 34 hours 15 minutes in September, 1960.

Highest Speed. The water skiing speed record is 125.69 m.p.h. recorded by Danny Churchill (U.S.) at the Oakland Marine Stadium, California, in 1971. Sally Younger, 17, set a feminine record of 105.14 m.p.h. at Perris, California in June, 1970. (See photo.)

Most Titles. World championships (instituted 1949) have been twice won by Alfredo Mendoza (U.S.) in 1953–55 and Mike Suyderhoud (U.S.) in 1967–69 and three times by Mrs. Willa McGuire (née Worthington) of the U.S., in 1949–50 and 1955.

FASTEST WOMAN WATER SKIER: Sally Younger, at the age of 17, sped 105.14 m.p.h. in June, 1970.

WATER SKI JUMPING:
Mike Suyderhoud (U.S.)
was the first man to surpass
160 feet.

Water Ski Kite Flying. The altitude record is 4,750 feet by Bill Moyes (Australia) on March 14, 1972. He was towed by a 435 h.p. Hamilton Jet Boat over Lake Ellesmere, New Zealand. The duration record is 15 hours 3 minutes by Bill Flewellyn (N.Z.) over Lake Bonney, South Australia in 1971.

Barefoot. The barefoot duration record is 67 minutes over about 36 miles by Stephen Z. Northrup (U.S.) in 1969. The backwards barefoot record is 33 minutes 19 seconds by Paul McManus (Australia) in 1969. A barefoot jump of 43 feet has been reported from Australia. The barefoot speed records are 87.46 m.p.h. by John Taylor (U.S.) on Lake Ming, California, on March 27, 1972, and for women 61 m.p.h. by Haidee Jones (Australia).

Weightlifting

Origins. Amateur weightlifting is of comparatively modern origin, and the first world championship was staged at the Café Monico, Piccadilly, London, on March 28, 1891. Prior to that time, weightlifting consisted of professional exhibitions in which some of the advertised poundages were open to doubt. The first 400-lb. clean and jerk is, however, attributed to Charles Rigoulet (1903–62), a French professional, with 402½ lbs. on February 1, 1929.

Greatest Lift. The greatest weight ever raised by a human being is 6,270 lbs. in a back lift (weight raised off trestles) by the 364-lb. Paul Anderson (U.S.) (b. 1933), the 1956 Olympic heavyweight

LIFTS MORE THAN THREE TONS: Paul Anderson of Toccoa, Georgia, who weighs 364 lbs., raised the greatest weight ever lifted by a human—6,270 lbs. in a back lift.

champion, at Toccoa, Georgia, on June 12, 1957. (The heaviest Rolls-Royce, the Phantom V, weighs 5,600 lbs.) The greatest by a woman is 3,564 lbs. with a hip and harness lift by Mrs. Josephine Blatt (*née* Schauer) (U.S.) (1869–1923) at the Bijou Theatre, Hoboken, New Jersey, on April 15, 1895.

The greatest overhead lift ever made by a woman, also professional, is 286 lbs. in a Continental jerk by Katie Sandwina, *née* Brummbach (Germany) (born January 21, 1884, died as Mrs. Max Heymann in New York City, in 1952) in *c.* 1911. This is equivalent to seven 40-pound office typewriters. She stood 6 feet 1 inch tall, weighed 220 lbs., and is reputed to have unofficially lifted 312½ lbs. and to have once shouldered a 1,200-lb. cannon.

Power Lifts. Paul Anderson as a professional has bench-pressed 627 lbs., achieved 1,200 lbs. in a squat, and dead-lifted 820 lbs. making a career aggregate of 2,647 lbs. The record (A.A.U.) for a single contest is an aggregate of 2,040 lbs. by Bob Weaver, set in 1967.

The highest official two-handed dead lift is 820 lbs. by Paul Anderson (U.S.). Hermann Görner performed a one-handed dead lift of 727½ lbs. in Leipzig on October 8, 1920. He once raised 24 men weighing 4,123 lbs. on a plank with the soles of his feet and also carried on his back a 1,444-lb. piano for a distance of 52 feet on June 3, 1921.

Peter B. Cortese (U.S.) achieved a one-arm dead lift of 22 lbs. over triple his body weight with 370 lbs. at York, Pennsylvania, on September 4, 1954.

It was reported that a hysterical 123-lb. woman, Mrs. Maxwell Rogers, lifted one end of a 3,600-lb. car which, after the collapse of a jack, had fallen on top of her son at Tampa, Florida, on April 24, 1960. She cracked some vertebrae.

Olympic Victories. The U.S.S.R. has won 18, the U.S. 14 and France 9 of the 68 titles at stake. The three most successful lifters in Olympic contests have been Louis Hostin (France) Light-

MIDDLEWEIGHT LIFTING CHAMPION: Viktor Kurentsov of the U.S.S.R.

heavy: silver 1928; gold 1932 and 1936. Tommy Kono (U.S.) Lightweight: gold 1952; light-heavy: gold 1956; middleweight: silver 1960. Yoshinobu Miyake (Japan) Bantam: silver 1960; featherweight: gold 1964; gold 1968.

WEIGHTLIFTING

(As supplied by Mr. Oscar State, General Secretary of the Fédération Internationale Halterophile)

Flyweight
(114½ lb.–52 kg.)

Press	265½	Adam Gnatov (U.S.S.R.)	U.S.S.R.	July 11, 1972
Snatch	231¼	Gyi Aung (Burma)	West Ger.	Aug. 27, 1972
Jerk	291	Adam Gnatov (U.S.S.R.)	U.S.S.R.	July 11, 1972
Total	754¾	Sandor Holczreiter (Hungary)	U.S.	Sept. 12, 1970

Bantamweight
(123¼ lb.–56 kg.)

Press	282	Rafael Belenkov (U.S.S.R.)	U.S.S.R.	April 12, 1972
Snatch	250	Koji Miki (Japan)	Japan	Nov. 15, 1968
Jerk	330½	Mohamed Nassiri (Iran)	Mexico	Oct. 13, 1968
Total	822	Imre Foldi (Hungary)	West Ger.	Aug. 28, 1972

Featherweight
(132¼ lb.–60 kg.)

Press	303½	Imre Földi (Hungary)	West Ger.	Mar. 4, 1972
Snatch	276½	Yoshinobu Miyake (Japan)	Japan	Oct. 28, 1969
Jerk	343¾	Dito Shanidze (U.S.S.R.)	Rumania	May 15, 1972
Total	887	Dito Shanidze (U.S.S.R.)	U.S.S.R.	Apr. 12, 1972
	887	Norair Nourikan (Bulgaria)	West Ger.	Aug. 29, 1972

Lightweight
(148¾ lb.–67.5 kg.)

Press	347	Mladen Kuchev (Bulgaria)	West Ger.	Aug. 30, 1972
Snatch	303	Waldemar Baszanowski (Poland)	Poland	Apr. 23, 1971
Jerk	391¼	Mukharbi Kirzhinov (U.S.S.R.)	West Ger.	Aug. 30, 1972
Total	1,013¾	Mukharbi Kirzhinov (U.S.S.R.)	West Ger.	Aug. 30, 1972

Middleweight
(165¼ lb.–75 kg.)

Press	367	Alexander Kolodkov (U.S.S.R.)	Sweden	Mar. 19, 1972
Snatch	321¾	Mohamed Trabulsi (Lebanon)	Jordan	June 30, 1972
Jerk	413¼	Viktor Kurentsov (U.S.S.R.)	Mexico	Oct. 16, 1968
Total	1,069	Yordan Bikov (Bulgaria)	West Ger.	Aug. 31, 1972

Light-heavyweight
(181¾ lb.–82.5 kg.)

Press	393½	Geradiz Ivanchenko (U.S.S.R.)	U.S.S.R.	May 18, 1972
Snatch	348½	Valeri Shariy (U.S.S.R.)	U.S.S.R.	July 13, 1972
Jerk	436½	Boris Pavlov (U.S.S.R.)	Sweden	Mar. 12, 1972
Total	1,162½	Valeri Shariy (U.S.S.R.)	U.S.S.R.	May 14, 1972

Middle-heavyweight
(198¼ lb.–90 kg.)

Press	436½	David Rigert (U.S.S.R.)	U.S.S.R.	July 13, 1972
Snatch	369¼	David Rigert (U.S.S.R.)	U.S.S.R.	July 13, 1972
Jerk	464	Vasili Kolotov (U.S.S.R.)	U.S.S.R.	July 13, 1972
Total	1,239¾	David Rigert (U.S.S.R.)	U.S.S.R.	July 13, 1972

Heavyweight
(242½ lb.–110 kg.)

Press	470½	Yuri Kozin (U.S.S.R.)	U.S.S.R.	July 14, 1972
Snatch	385¾	Yan Talts (U.S.S.R.)	U.S.S.R.	Apr. 14, 1972
Jerk	490½	Yan Talts (U.S.S.R.)	Rumania	May 20, 1972
Total	1,300¼	Valeriy Kakubovsky (U.S.S.R.)	U.S.S.R.	May 14, 1972

Super-heavyweight
(Above 242½ lb.–110 kg.)

Press	521¼	Vasili Alexeev (U.S.S.R.)	U.S.S.R.	Apr. 15, 1972
Snatch	396¾	Vasili Alexeev (U.S.S.R.)	U.S.S.R.	July 24, 1971
Jerk	523½	Vasili Alexeev (U.S.S.R.)	U.S.S.R.	Apr. 15, 1972
Total	1,421¾	Vasili Alexeev (U.S.S.R.)	U.S.S.R.	Apr. 15, 1972

SUPER-HEAVYWEIGHT CHAMPION: Vasiliy Alexeev (U.S.S.R.) holds the record in each category in his weight—press, snatch, jerk and total.

Wrestling

Earliest References. Wrestling holds and falls, depicted on the walls of the Egyptian tombs of Beni Hasan, prove that wrestling dates from 2000 B.C. or earlier. It was introduced into the ancient Olympic Games in the 18th Olympiad in *c.* 704 B.C. The Graeco-Roman style is of French origin and arose about 1860.

Sumo Wrestling. The sport's legendary origins in Japan were 2,000 years ago. The heaviest performer was probably Dewagatake, a wrestler of the 1920's who was 6 feet 5 inches tall and weighed up to 420 lbs. Weight is amassed by over-eating a high protein sea food stew called *chanko-rigori*. The tallest was probably Ozora, an early 19th century performer, who stood 7 feet 3 inches tall. The most successful wrestler has been Koki Naya (born 1940), alias Taiho ("Great Bird"), who won his 26th Emperor's Cup on September 10–24, 1967. He was the *Yokozuna* (Grand Champion) in 1967. The highest *dan* is Makuuchi. (See photos, next page.)

Most Olympic Titles. Two wrestlers have won three Olympic titles. They are:

Carl Westergran (Sweden)		Ivar Johansson (Sweden)	
Graeco-Roman Middleweight A	1920	Free-style Middleweight	1932
Graeco-Roman Middleweight B	1924	Graeco-Roman Welterweight	1932
Graeco-Roman Heavyweight	1932	Graeco-Roman Middleweight	1936

Best Record. Osamu Watanabe (Japan) won the free-style featherweight event in the 1964 Olympic Games. This was his 186th successive win and he has never been defeated. Aleksandr Medved (U.S.S.R.) uniquely won a seventh world title in Sofia, Bulgaria, on August 30, 1971.

SUMO WRESTLERS: Dewagatake (left) who weighed 420 lbs., and Taiho (right photo, with both feet planted), the current champion in Japan.

Longest Bout. The longest recorded bout was one of nearly 11 hours between Max Klein (Russia) and Alfred Asikainen (Finland) in the Graeco-Roman middleweight "A" event in the 1912 Olympic Games in Stockholm, Sweden.

Professional Wrestling. Modern professional wrestling dates from *c.* 1875 in the United States. Georges Karl Julius Hackenschmidt (1877–1968) made no submissions in the period 1898–1908. The highest paid professional wrestler ever is Antonino ("Tony") Rocca of Puerto Rico, with $180,000 in 1958. The heaviest wrestler was William J. Cobb of Macon, Georgia, who was billed in 1962 as the 802-lb. "Happy" Humphrey. What he lacked in mobility he possessed in suffocating powers. By July, 1965, he had reduced to a modest 232 lbs.

Yachting

Origin. Yachting dates from the £100 (now $250) stake race between King Charles II of England and his brother James, Duke of York, on the Thames River, on September 1, 1661, over 23 miles, from Greenwich to Gravesend. The earliest club is the Royal Cork Yacht Club (formerly the Cork Harbour Water Club), established in Ireland in 1720.

Most Successful. The most successful racing yacht in history was the British Royal Yacht *Britannia* (1893–1935), owned by King George V, which won 231 races in 625 starts.

Olympic Victories. The first sportsman ever to win individual gold medals in four successive Olympic Games has been Paul B. Elvström (Denmark) in the Firefly class in 1948 and the Finn class in 1952, 1956 and 1960. He has also won 8 other world titles in a total of 6 classes.

The lowest number of penalty points by the winner of any class in an Olympic regatta is 3 points [6 wins (1 disqualified) and 1 second in 7 starts] by *Superdocius* of the Flying Dutchman class (Lt. Rodney Pattison, British Royal Navy and Ian Macdonald-Smith, M.B.E.) at Acapulco, Mexico, in October, 1968.

America's Cup. The America's Cup races, open to challenge by any nation's yachts, began on August 8, 1870, with the unsuccessful attempt by J. Ashbury's *Cambria* (G.B.) to capture the trophy from the *Magic*, owned by F. Osgood (U.S.). Since then the Cup has been challenged by Great Britain in 15 contests, by Canada in two contests, and by Australia twice, but the United States holders have never been defeated. The closest race ever was the fourth race of the 1962 series, when the 12-meter sloop *Weatherly* beat her Australian challenger *Gretel* by about 3½ lengths (75 yards), a margin of only 26 seconds, on September 22, 1962. The fastest time ever recorded by a 12-meter boat for the triangular course of 24 miles is 2 hours 46 minutes 58 seconds by *Gretel* in 1962.

Little America's Cup. The catamaran counterpart to the America's Cup was instituted in 1961. The British club entry has won on each annual occasion to 1968 vs. the U.S. (1961–66 and 1968) and vs. Australia (1967). *Lady Hamilton* (G.B.) won in 1966–67–68.

Largest Yacht. The largest private yacht ever built was Mrs. Emily Roebling Cadwalader's *Savarona* of 4,600 gross tons, completed in Hamburg, Germany, in October, 1931, at a cost of $4,000,000. She (the yacht), with a 53-foot beam and measuring 407 feet 10 inches overall, was sold to the Turkish government in

OLYMPIC REGATTA WINNER with lowest number of penalty points was the "Superdocius" of the Flying Dutchman Class, 1968.

March, 1938. Operating expenses for a full crew of 107 men approached $500,000 per year.

The largest private sailing yacht ever built was the full-rigged 350-foot auxiliary barque *Sea Cloud* (formerly *Hussar*), owned by the oft-married Mrs. Marjorie Merriweather Post-Close-Hutton-Davies-May (born 1888), one-time wife of the U.S. Ambassador to the U.S.S.R. Her four masts carried 30 sails with the total canvas area of 36,000 square feet.

Largest Sail. The largest sail ever made was a parachute spinnaker with an area of 18,000 square feet (more than two-fifths of an acre) for Harold S. Vanderbilt's *Ranger* in 1937.

Highest Speed. A speed of 30 knots has been attained by *Lady Helmsman*, the 25-foot C-class catamaran built by Reg. White of Brightlingsea, Essex, England. The D-class catamaran *Beowulf V* (Steve Dashew) attained 27.56 knots (31.7 m.p.h.) inside Los Angeles Harbor in August, 1971.

Longest Race. The longest regularly contested yacht race is the biennial Los Angeles-Tahiti Trans Pacific event which is over 3,571 miles. The fastest time has been 8 days 13 hours 9 minutes by Eric Taberley's *Pen Duick IV* (France) in 1969.

LARGEST SAIL ever made was the parachute spinnaker on the "Ranger," Harold S. Vanderbilt's yacht in 1937.

PICTURE CREDITS

The editors and publisher wish to thank the following people and organizations for pictures which they supplied.

American Airlines; American Baseball League; American Basketball Association; American Bowling Congress; American Museum of Natural History, New York; Robert D. Archer, California; Argonne National Laboratories; Associated Newspapers Ltd., London; Associated Press Ltd.; Australian News and Information Bureau, New York.

Bell Howarth Ltd.; Bell Telephone Laboratories; Bernsen's International Press Service Ltd.; Bethlehem Steel; B.O.A.C.; B.O.A.C. British Transarctic Expedition; Boston Garden; The British Petroleum Company Ltd.; Business Men's Studio, Beaumont, Texas.

California State Library; Camera Press Ltd.; Cartier's, New York; Central Press Photos Ltd., London; Chesapeake Bay Bridge and Tunnel Commission; Christie, Manson and Woods, Ltd., London; Marty Clemens; George Craig; Crown Copyright; Cryer and Marchant Ltd.

Daily Express, London; Dell Publishing Company, New York; Department of Supply, Antarctic Division; Detroit Free Press; DeVere Helfrich; Alfred Dunhill Ltd.; A. Dupont.

Edinburgh University; Elvis Presley Fan Club; European, New York; Evening News, London.

Family Doctor; F.A.O.; Feyer-Wein; Ford Motor Company; Robert L. Foster; Fox Photos Ltd.; French Embassy, London; Marvin Frost.

General Electric Company; General Photographic Agency; Geodaetisk Institut, Copenhagen; Goodyear Aerospace Corporation; Goodyear News Bureau; Goodyear Tyre and Rubber Co. (G.B.) Ltd.; Gordon Gustar.

Bill Halkett; Harland and Wolff; Harvard University News Office; Charles E. Haskins; Her Majesty's Stationery Office, London; Holloman Air Force Base; Houston Sports Assoc. Inc.; F. Howell; Hsinsua Agency; J. L. Hudson Company, Detroit; Edwin G. Huffman; Hungarian News Agency; Huntsville Times (Photo by Dudley Campbell).

Imperial War Museum; Independent Newspapers Ltd., London. Japanese T.V. Channel Eight.

Kent and Sussex Courier; Keystone Press Agency; Keystone View Co.

E. D. Lacey; Ladies P.G.A.; Le Temps, Paris; Lincolnshire Standard; London Art Tech.

Metropolitan Museum of Art, New York; R. N. Misra; Mt. Everest Foundation; Mt. Wilson and Palomar Observatories.

National Archery Association; National Aeronautics and Space Administration; National Baseball Hall of Fame and Museum, Inc.; National Broadcasting Company; National Football League Properties, Inc.; National Geographic Society; New Country Artists Ltd.; New York Times; New York Zoological Society; New

Zealand Consulate, New York; New Zealand Herald and Weekly News; Norsk Photo; Norsk Telegram Kyras; North American Aviation Inc.; Northwest Newfoundland Club; Novosti Press Agency, Moscow.

Oklahoma Publishing Company; Ivan O'Riley.

Malcolm Pendrill Ltd.; Photo Reportage Ltd.; Photo Société Bertin; G. Pickett; Planet News; T. B. Pollard; Port of New York Authority; Pragopress, Prague; Press Association Photos, London; Professional Football, Office of the Commissioner; Pro Football Hall of Fame.

Radio Times Hulton Picture Library; Remington Arms; Richards Brothers Ltd.; Ringsport; Bernard Rouget; Royal Gardens, Kew.

Salzburg Landsverk ehrsamt; Schneider's Verkehsvere, Augsberg; Shell Photographic Service; Smithsonian Institution, Washington, D.C.; Sotheby's, London; A. G. Spaulding and Bros.; Sperryn's, London; Sport and General Press Agency Ltd., London; Squaw Valley Lodge; St. Louis Chamber of Commerce; Straits Times, Singapore; Milos Svobic.

The Thompson Organisation Ltd., London; Time; Triborough Bridge and Tunnel Authority; Twentieth Century Fox Productions.

United Nations, New York; United Pictorial Press; United Press International (U.K.); United Press International (U.S.); United States Air Force; United States Department of Interior, National Parks Service; United States Department of the Army; United States Forest Service; United States Information Service; United States Lawn Tennis Association; United States Navy; University Museum.

Fiona Vigers; Volkswagen of America, Inc.

Western Star; Charles Wherry; Wide World Photos; Wilson Sporting Goods Company; G. L. Wood; Hamilton Wright.

Zoological Society of London.

INDEX

g Force, highest withstood 45, 46
Galaxies, number, remotest, heaviest 141
Gallery, Art, 180
Games Manufacturer, largest 228
Garage, largest commercial, private 259
Gases, lightest, heaviest, highest and lowest melting and boiling points, commonest, rarest 150
Gasoline Consumption 308
Gas Pipeline, longest 335
Gas Tank, largest 290
Gastronomic Records 445–448
Gas Works, largest 334
Gecko, smallest reptile 73–74
Geese, highest-flying birds 71
Gems 156–161, most precious, largest, rarest, hardest, densest 156–157
General Merchandise, largest firm 228
Generator, power plants 330–331, largest 331, also see Power Producers
Gestation Periods, longest and shortest mammalian 54–55
Geyser, tallest 110
Gherkins, eating record 447
Ghosts, most durable 47
Giantesses, tallest 12–14
Giants, tallest 8–12
Giraffe, tallest animal 49
Glacier, longest 122–123
Glass, Stained 401, 402
Gliding, earliest, distance records, speed 529
Goby, smallest fish 80
Go-Go (dance) 428
Go-Kart, circumnavigation 472–473
Gold, largest nugget 161, 162, largest mines 291, largest reserves 380
Goldfish, oldest 81
Goldfish (Live), eating records 447
Gold Plate, highest price 241
Golf, earliest, oldest club, largest 529, highest course, lowest, longest hole, largest green, biggest bunker 530, lowest scores, highest scores, most shots one hole, fastest, slowest rounds 530–532, most rounds in day, longest drive, longest hitter 533, most tournament wins 535, British Open Tournament lowest scored, U.S. Open, U.S. Amateur, British Amateur, highest prize 536, highest earnings, youngest and oldest champions 537, holes-in-one—longest, most, consecutive, youngest and oldest golfer 538, throwing, shooting your age, World Cup 539
Gorge, largest, deepest, deepest submarine 124–125
Gorilla, largest primate 58
Grade, Steepest 314
Grain Elevator, largest 259
Grandparents, multiple great 26
Grand Prix Winners 471
Grapes, eating rcord 447
Grasshopper, largest 86
Gravedigging, burial alive 425, most 431

Greyhound Racing, earliest, fastest 540
Grocery Stores, chain, largest 228
Gross National Product (G.N.P.) 380
Guillotining, last public 371
Guitar, largest 202, playing 432
Gulf, largest 112
Guns, earliest 362, largest, greatest range, mortars, cannon, military engines 363; see also Pistols
Gusher, greatest 289, 290
Gymnastics, earliest, world championships 540, most Olympic wins 540–541, chinning, rope climbing, push-ups, sit-ups, tumbling, hand-to-hand balancing, largest gymnasium 542

Habitation, highest, northernmost, southernmost 257, northernmost permanently occupied 348
Hailstones, largest 129, worst disaster 458
Hair, longest 34; see also Beard, Moustache
Hairdressing, duration record 432
Halites, highest 118
Hamburger, largest 387, eating record 447
Handball, Court, origin, championships, most titles 543
Handball, Field, origins, championships 543
Handshaking 432
Handwriting, smallest 190
Hangar, largest world 258, aircraft, group 259
Hanging 372, 373, lynchings 374
Hardest Substance 153
Harmonium, marathon 202
Harness Racing, time records, highest price, greatest winnings 543
Hat, most expensive 242
Hearing, acuteness 40
Heart, longest stoppage 36, transplants 41
Hedge, tallest, tallest yew, tallest box 100
Helicopter, earliest, fastest, largest, highest 328
Herd, largest animal 54
Hibernation, longest mammalian 54
Hiccoughing, most persistent 37
High Diving 432, 433
Highway, see Roads
HiJack (Sky-Jack) 376
Hike, longest 432
Hitchhiking 432–433
Hockey, origins, most Olympic wins, Stanley Cup, longest match, most goals, fastest scoring, fastest player 544–545
Hockey, Field, see Field Hockey
Hoisting Tackle, largest 323
Honorary Degrees, most 431
Honors, Decorations and Awards 452–457
Hoop Rolling 433
Hop Field, largest 249
Horns, longest 62, longest prehistoric 92

Mammals, largest land 51, largest, heaviest, tallest, smallest, fastest 52, slowest, rarest, longest-lived, highest living 53, largest herd, longest and shortest gestation periods, largest litter, fastest breeder, heaviest brain, longest hibernation 54, smallest carnivores 55, largest feline, pinnipeds 56, bats 58, primates 58–60, rodents 60, tusks and horns 61–62, blood temperatures, most valuable furs, ambergris, marsupials 63, domesticated horses 64–65, dogs 65–66, cats 67–68, rabbits 68, extinct 90–92, earliest 95

Mandrill, largest monkey 59

Man (male), tallest 8–12, shortest 14–16, lightest 16–17, heaviest 17–18; see also **Humans**

Manufactured Articles 236–248

Manufacturing, see **Company**

Manuscript, highest price 190–191

Map, oldest 198

Marble, largest slab, 159, 161

March, longest 363, most rapid 364

Marine Disaster, worst 457

Marine Records; see **Diving** and **Swimming**

Marine Reptile, largest prehistoric 94

Marine Turbine, largest 331

Marquee, largest 287

Marriage, ages 350, longest engagement, greatest number, oldest bride and bridegroom, longest, most-married, largest mass ceremony 421–422

Marsupials, largest, smallest, rarest, longest jump 63–64

Maser 175

Mass Killings, see **Killing**

Masts, television and radio 267–268

Matchbox Labels, oldest, longest 243

Mathematics, human ability at 41–42

Meat, greatest eaters 385, eating record 447

Mechanical World 294–341

Medals, rarest British, U.S.S.R., U.S., most bemedalled person 452–453, 454

Medicine, see **Pills**

Melting Points, gases, highest and lowest 150; metals, highest and lowest 151

Memory, Human 41

Menu, longest 243

Merchandiser, largest 228

Mercury, smallest planet 136–137

Message in a Bottle 436

Metals, lightest, densest 150, lowest and highest melting and boiling points, expansion, highest ductility, tensile strength, rarest, commonest, most magnetic and non-magnetic, newest, purest 151–152

Meteorites, largest, largest crater, tektites 130–132

Meteoroids, meteor shower, meteorites 130–132

Meteorological Records, see **Weather**

Meteor Shower, greatest 130

Metropolitan Area, most populous 346

Microbes, protista, bacteria, viruses 96–97

Microscope, most powerful, smallest 172

Midget, shortest 14–15

Military and Defense 358–365

Military Awards, most clusters and gold medals 453, anti-submarine, U-boat, greatest reception 454, 455

Milk, drinking record 447

Milk Yields, lifetime, lactation 250, hand milking, goat 251

Millionaires, number U.S., multi-milionaire, 449–450

Millionairess, wealthiest, youngest, earliest, self-made 450

Millipedes, longest, shortest, most legs 87

Minaret, tallest 398

Mine, earliest, deepest, deepest terminal, largest gold, richest, largest iron, copper, silver, lead, zinc, salt, quarries, excavation, open pit 291–293

Mineral Water, largest firm 229

Miniature Portrait, most expensive 178

Mining, greatest depth, shaft sinking record 419, worst disaster 458

Mink, highest price 63, coat 241

Mint, largest 384

Miser, greatest 449, 450

Missiles, guided 142–146

Moats, largest 261

Mobile, largest, heaviest 180, 181

Modern Painting, most expensive 178

Model Aircraft, speed record 330

Model Railroad, record run 319

Molars, earliest 39

Mollusks, largest, largest octopus, most ancient shells, largest, smallest, rarest, longest-lived shell, largest snail, fastest snail 88–90, largest extinct shelled 96, earliest 95

Monarchs, see **Royalty**

Monetary and Finance 379–382

Monkey, largest and smallest 59

Monorail, highest speed 318

Monuments, tallest, tallest column, largest prehistoric 282–283, largest monumental brass 401–402

Moon 132–134, distance, closest approach, first direct hit, first photographic image, first soft landing, blue moon 132, largest and deepest crater, highest mountains, temperature extremes, moon rocks 133–134, first manned flight, first landing, longest mission, longest duration on, most expensive project 148, lunar conquest 405, 407

Moose, Alaskan, largest deer 61

Morbidity, highest 33

Morse Code, highest speed 436

Mortars, largest 363

Mosaic, largest 180–181

Mosque, largest 397

Mosses, smallest 103

Prison, longest sentences 373, escape 374, largest, smallest, most secure, penal camps, 378, 379
Prisoner, oldest 373
Prize, largest TV 214, Nobel 455, 456
Prize Winning 439–440
Professor, youngest, most durable 395–396
Profit, greatest net by company 223
Propeller, ship's largest 302, largest aircraft 326
Proper Motion, definition 130
Protein, highest consumption, lowest 385
Protista, largest, smallest, longest-lived, fastest-moving, fastest reproduction, densest 96–97
Protozoa, see Protista
Prunes, eating record 447
Psychiatrists and Psychologists 351, fastest 440
Publication, largest 191
Public Relations, largest company 230
Publishers, largest, fastest 196, largest enterprise 230
Pulsars 141
Pump Turbine, largest 333
Puzzles, crossword 198, jig-saw 242
Pygmy Marmoset, smallest monkey 59
Pyramid, largest, oldest 280–281

Quadruplets, heaviest 28
Quarries, deepest excavation, largest stone removed 293
Quasar 141, 143
Queen, see Royalty
Quietest (Place) 170
Quintuplets 28
Quiz, largest TV prize 214
Quoit Throwing 440

Rabbit, largest, oldest, most prolific 68–69
Race (human), tallest, shortest 16
Radar Installations, largest 338
Radio Broadcasting, most stations, most sets 212, origins, earliest patent, earliest broadcast, first transatlantic transmissions, longest broadcast 213, highest masts 267–268
Radio Telescope, largest 163, 164
Raft, longest voyage 402, longest survival 420
Railroad Disaster, worst 458
Railroads, bridge 271, earliest, fastest, electric, steam, fastest regular run, longest non-stop run, most powerful locomotive, steepest grade 313–314, progressive speed records, busiest railroad, widest gauge, longest straight length, longest electric line, highest altitude track, stations, freight trains, greatest load 315–316, longest electrified line, most expensive freight rate, subways 317, monorail, fastest tracked vehicle, model railway 318–319, worst disaster 458

Rainfall, most intense 127, greatest, lowest, greatest mean, longest drought 128
Rainy Days, most in year 128
Rallies (car), earliest, longest, smallest car 473
Range, greatest human voice 40
Ransom 375, 376
Rapids, fastest 120
Rat, Moon, largest insectivore 60, 61
Rat, Rice, rarest rodent 60
Ratting, dog 67, cat 68
Ravioli, eating 447
Reactor (atomic), largest 331
Real Estate, highest rent, most directorships; see also Land
Reception, greatest ticker-tape 454, 455
Recitation, fastest 42
Records (phonograph) oldest, earliest jazz 218, most successful artist 218, 219, most successful group, golden discs, earliest, most golden discs, youngest artist, most recorded song, biggest sellers, top selling "pop," most recordings, greatest monopoly of sales charts 219–220, long-playing records, best-seller, first classical, longest, fastest seller 221, advance sales, highest fee, longest title 222
Reef, longest 116
Reflecting Telescope, largest 163
Reflexes, fastest 47
Refracting Telescope, largest 163
Religion, 396–403, most prevailing, smallest number of followers, 396
Religious Buildings, largest temple, mosque, synagogue, cathedrals, churches, smallest, oldest, tallest spires, minaret, pagoda 396–399
Remoteness, greatest from land 112, 114, remotest visible body, farthest visible object 141, most remote town from sea 348
Reproductivity, human 25–30
Reptiles, largest and heaviest, smallest, fastest, largest lizard, oldest lizard 73–74, chelonians, largest, longest-lived, slowest moving 74–75, longest snakes, shortest, heaviest, oldest, fastest-moving, most venomous snake, longest fangs 75–77, snakes, largest extinct 94, earliest 95
Republic, smallest 343
Reserve, smallest nature 105
Reservoir, largest 276, largest reservoir project 277
Restaurant, largest chain 230
Retail Establishments 225–228, 231, 233
Rhinoceros, rarest placental mammal 53, largest prehistoric 91, 92, longest horns 62
Rhododendron, largest 99
Ribbon Worms 90
Riding in Armor, duration record 440
Riot, worst disaster 158

Twins, heaviest 18, 19, 29, Siamese 27, 30, lightest, oldest 29–30

Twist (dance), duration record 430

Typewriter, most traveled 445

Typhoid Carrier, most notorious 33

Typing, fastest, slowest, duration record 444–445

Ulcer, Duodenal, earliest 36

Underground Factory, largest 257

Underground Railroads, see Subway

Underwater, duration record 45, submergence 418

Union, Trade, largest, longest working week, labor disputes 384

Universe, 130–148, motion, farthest visible object, heaviest galaxy, quasars, "pulsars," remotest object 140–142

University, oldest, largest buildings, greatest enrollment, largest, richest 394–395, youngest professor, most durable professor 395–396

Vacuum, highest 169

Vase, most expensive 248

Vat, largest 287–288

Vehicle, most massive, longest 309, largest road haul, amphibious 310, 311, largest tires, tractor, longest skid marks 311, most per mile of road 389; see also Road Vehicles

Vein, largest human 35

Verbs, most and least regular 183

Vertebrates, earliest 95

Vessels, see Ships

Viaduct, longest, longest railroad 273

Village, highest, oldest 347; see also Town

Vine, largest 99

Violin, most valuable, smallest 203

Violinist, greatest earnings 206

Virus, largest, smallest, sub-viral agents 97

Viscosity, lowest 170

Visible Object, smallest 39

Visual Acuity, human 39, bird 72

Vocabulary, largest 183

Voice, human, highest, lowest, greatest range 39–40, loudest insect 85

Volcanoes, total number, greatest eruption, explosion, highest extinct, dormant and active, northernmost, southernmost, largest crater 108–109

Volleyball, origin, world titles, marathon 604

Voltages, highest carried 337

Vowels, most and least in a language 185

Voyage, slowest by sailing ship 302

Waist, smallest 31, 32

Walk in Space, first 147

Walking, endurance record, longest race, walking backwards 420, hike 432, tightrope 443–444, on hands 445, track walking world records, road walking, walking on crutches 604–605

Wall, longest 287

Walrus, largest, smallest, fastest, deepest 56, longest-lived, rarest 58

War, longest, shortest, bloodiest, most costly, bloodiest civil war 358, bloodiest battle, worst sieges, largest armed forces 359, greatest invasions, seaborne, airborne, greatest evacuation, defense 360–361, navies 361, armies 361–364, air forces 364–365; see also Military Awards

Warehouse, largest 259

Warship, fastest 295

Watches, oldest, most expensive, smallest 341

Water, fresh, consumption 388

Waterbeds 236

Waterfalls, highest, greatest, widest 120–122

Water Fleas, smallest crustacean 84

Water Polo, origins, Olympic victories, most caps 605

Water Skiing, origins, jumps, buoys and tricks, longest run, highest speed, most titles 605–606, water-ski kite flying, bare foot 607

Water Speed, record 409, 410

Waterspout, highest 127

Waterways, Inland, greatest length, longest navigable 394

Waterwheel, largest 286

Wave, highest, greatest tidal 113

Wealth, national 335, individual 448–452, richest ruler 448–449, richest private citizen 449, highest earnings 450–451, highest and lowest incomes 451

Weasel, smallest carnivore 55

Weather, shade and screen temperature tables, greatest temperature ranges, atmospheric temperatures, upper atmosphere, most equable temperature, deepest permafrost 126, humidity and discomfort, most intense rainfall, lightning, waterspouts, cloud extremes 127–128, weather records 128–129

Web, largest and smallest spider 83

Weed, worst 100

Weight, lightest and heaviest human 16–18, 19, gaining 20

Weightlifting, origins, greatest lift, power lifts, Olympic victories 607–610, world records 610

Well Water, deepest 290, progressive records 291

Index by Lillian D. Reiter

ABOUT THE AUTHORS

Ross (left) and NORRIS McWHIRTER are not only twins; they
have almost identical biographies. Born in London in 1925,
they were both educated at Trinity College, Oxford University, where they received M.A. degrees in Economics Law.
They both served in the Royal Navy. They were both members of the Oxford University track team. They were both
candidates for the Conservative Party in the 1964 General
Election. They both work for the B.B.C. as TV and radio
commentators and wrote a joint Sunday newspaper column
in the *Observer* for more than seven years.

They are both contributors to the *Encyclopaedia Britannica*
and are joint compilers and editors of the *Dunlop Illustrated
Encyclopedia of Facts*.

Norris McWhirter is married and has a son and a daughter.
His brother is married and has two sons.